Research Methods in Library and Information Science

RESEARCH METHODS IN LIBRARY AND INFORMATION SCIENCE

SEVENTH EDITION

Lynn Silipigni Connaway
and Marie L. Radford

Library and Information Science Text Series

LIBRARIES
UNLIMITED®

An Imprint of ABC-CLIO, LLC
Santa Barbara, California • Denver, Colorado

Library of Congress Cataloging-in-Publication Data

Names: Connaway, Lynn Silipigni, author. | Radford, Marie L., author.
Title: Research methods in library and information science /
   Lynn Silipigni Connaway and Marie L. Radford.
Description: Seventh edition. | Santa Barbara, California : Libraries
   Unlimited, [2021] | Series: Library and information science text series |
   Includes bibliographical references and indexes.
Identifiers: LCCN 2020056679 (print) | LCCN 2020056680 (ebook) |
   ISBN 9781440878718 (hardcover ; acid-free paper) |
   ISBN 9781440878572 (paperback ; acid-free paper) |
   ISBN 9781440878589 (ebook)
Subjects: LCSH: Library science—Research—Methodology. |
   Information science—Research—Methodology.
Classification: LCC Z669.7 .P68 2021 (print) | LCC Z669.7 (ebook) |
   DDC 020.72/1—dc23
LC record available at https://lccn.loc.gov/2020056679
LC ebook record available at https://lccn.loc.gov/2020056680

ISBN: 978-1-4408-7871-8 (hardcover)
        978-1-4408-7857-2 (paperback)
        978-1-4408-7858-9 (ebook)

25 24 23 22 21   1 2 3 4 5

This book is also available as an eBook.

Libraries Unlimited
An Imprint of ABC-CLIO, LLC

ABC-CLIO, LLC
147 Castilian Drive
Santa Barbara, California 93117
www.abc-clio.com

This book is printed on acid-free paper ∞

Manufactured in the United States of America

Contents

Illustrations

FIGURES

TABLES

Text Boxes

Preface

With tempestuous 2020 now in the rearview mirror, despite the difficulties posed by the COVID-19 pandemic and racial inequities, the research community continues to move forward. It is more critical than ever to conduct research addressing how libraries and the information community are able to provide welcoming places, deeper understanding of research problematics in the field, and credible information for all. These are areas where we, as members of an information profession and discipline, can make an impact within our communities and society.

We really are excited about the seventh edition of this research methods book. We owe a debt of gratitude to Ronald Powell for his vision as sole author for the first edition of this book, published in 1985, and subsequent updating of the second and third editions. He invited one of us, Lynn Silipigni Connaway, to be his coauthor beginning with the fourth edition in 2004. Ron and Lynn collaborated on the fourth and fifth editions. Ron announced that he was stepping down for revision of the sixth edition. Both the sixth edition and this seventh edition have been coauthored by us, Lynn Silipigni Connaway and Marie L. Radford.

Previous editions of this book have had a strong focus on quantitative methods. Our collaboration on two major grant projects beginning in 2005 (Radford and Connaway 2005–2008; Radford, Connaway, and Shah 2011–2014) has involved a mixed-method approach that involves a blend of qualitative and quantitative research. We have had positive experiences in our collaboration during the past fifteen years and have been very productive in contributing to both the scholarly and professional literature. Lynn's team at OCLC research has addressed how individuals engage with technology and get their information in an online environment in the digital visitors and residents (V&R) project (2020). This research is extremely relevant today in the limits placed on our in-person activities. We also have studied how public librarians have collaborated with other community agencies to address the opioid crisis (2020) another social issue that has continued to become more important in difficult socioeconomic times. We also are identifying the changes that have had to be made in libraries and how these changes are developing into a new model library (2020). Our partnership provides a balanced view of research that embraces the entire spectrum of methods available in library and information science (LIS). Additionally, we are excited to share our expertise and experiences in research design, data collection, analysis, the writing process, and dissemination of findings gained during our grant-funded collaborations and other research projects. We have designed this edition to feature more examples carefully selected from research conducted by the authors and other LIS scholars.

Approximately 40 to 45 percent of the content for this seventh edition is new. These changes include a reorganization of several chapters, including providing separate chapters on survey research and the questionnaire, now chapter 5, and sampling, now chapter 6, which previously were combined in one chapter. Additionally, the chapter on writing the research proposal was moved forward from the back of the book to become chapter 3 in recognition that the proposal is among the initial parts of research endeavors. Quite a few new sections were added to address timely scholarly areas, trends, issues, and methods. These include: critical methods, data management, and reuse; new modes for collaboration; ethics for research in the digital environment; data science; artificial intelligence and machine learning; visualization and display of quantitative data; visualization and display of qualitative data; new modes for data collection; critical approaches, digital ethnography; design thinking and research for innovation; social justice research in LIS; graphic presentation, visualization, and display of data; and presentations—in-person and virtual. Every chapter has been fully revised, including updates to the cited references, with an added emphasis on recent citations, expanded examples of research from diverse voices and from an international perspective, and enlarged sections on timely issues such as scholarly communication and technical methods such as data visualizations, design thinking, and computer-assisted software for both qualitative and quantitative data analysis. Also, we were grateful to receive very positive feedback on the new series of text boxes that were initiated in the sixth edition. We have updated these and greatly expanded the number and scope of the text boxes to include thirty-five contributions from a diverse group of thirty-three experts. Among our new text boxes are those devoted to indigenous research, scholarly communication, the scholarship of dialog, data reuse, constructivist grounded theory, digital ethnographic methods, data visualization, the mapping method, and sustainable development goals.

Specifically designed for LIS master's and doctoral students, LIS faculty, and professional librarians, this text provides a broad overview of the research process and explains both quantitative and qualitative research methods with an acknowledgement of the power of their integration for a mixed-method research design. It provides practical instruction and guidance to LIS scholars, professionals, and students who want and need to conduct research and publish their work. The inclusion of the principles, data collection techniques, and analyses of quantitative and qualitative methods, as well as the advantages and limitations of each method and updated examples and citations, provide a broad introduction to research design. The discussion of the scientific method, sampling, validity, reliability, and ethical concerns, along with experimental research design, ethnographic methods, critical approaches, user experience (UX), and usability testing offer a well-rounded overview of these research methods and design. Not only will LIS students, scholars, and professionals consult the text for instruction on conducting research using this array of methodological tools, but they also will use it for guidance in critically reading and evaluating research publications, proposals, and reports. This text cannot be all-inclusive but does provide an overview of the LIS research environment with references to more in-depth works on specific data collection and analysis methods.

The authors would like to thank those colleagues who shared their expertise in writing short essays and text boxes. We also are indebted to Diana Floegel, doctoral candidate, and Kaitlin Montague, doctoral student, who are both from Rutgers, The State University of New Jersey, for their assistance in the preparation of this revised edition, especially in wrangling our enormous numbers of citations and providing expertise in assembling bibliographies for the many new sections we added. Kaitlin Montague also created both the subject and author indexes for this book. We appreciate the efforts of Laureen Cantwell, head of access services and outreach at the Tomlinson Library, Colorado Mesa University in Grand Junction, and Kem Lang, library manager and corporate archivist at the OCLC library, for providing quick access to requested materials, which greatly helped us to stay on target for deadlines. Marie acknowledges the support and friendship of the members of her writing group who kept her on track for this book project, especially during the long months of the pandemic, Dr. Jeff Lane and Nicole Weber of Rutgers University, Dan Delmonico of the University of Michigan, and Jabari Evans of Northwestern University. We appreciated those LIS faculty who had used the sixth edition in their courses and who were generous in providing key suggestions that guided our revision and those who provided reviews and endorsements of the seventh edition. We also want to thank Jessica Gribble, Emma Bailey, and the staff at Libraries Unlimited, an imprint of ABC-CLIO, for their excellent editorial and production assistance and enthusiastic support of our writing efforts.

We are ever appreciative of our spouses, Jim and Gary, for their understanding of the extensive time required for our substantial revision of this book. Their unconditional love, good humor, and vocal encouragement, especially during stay-at-home and lockdown orders during the COVID-19 pandemic, helped greatly to make this book a reality.

REFERENCES

"Digital Visitors and Residents." 2020. OCLC. https://www.oclc.org/research/areas/user-studies/vandr.html.

"The New Model Library." 2020. OCLC. https://www.oclc.org/research/areas/library-enterprise/new-model-library.html.

"Public Libraries Respond to the Opioid Crisis with Their Communities." 2020. Web-Junction. https://www.webjunction.org/explore-topics/opioid-crisis.html.

Radford, Marie L., and Lynn Silipigni Connaway. 2005–2008. "Seeking Synchronicity: Evaluating Virtual Reference Services from User, Non-User, and Librarian Perspectives." Funded by the Institute for Museum and Library Services (IMLS), Rutgers University, and OCLC. https://www.oclc.org/research/areas/user-studies/synchronicity.html.

Radford, Marie L., Lynn Silipigni Connaway, and Chirag Shah. 2011–2014. "Cyber Synergy: Seeking Sustainability through Collaboration between Virtual Reference and Social Q&A Sites." Funded by the Institute of Museum and Library Services (IMLS): Rutgers University and OCLC. https://www.oclc.org/research/areas/user-studies/synergy.html.

1

Research and Librarianship

INTRODUCTION

Why is it important for masters of library and information science (MLIS) students and library professionals to learn about research? After all, what has research got to do with the practical skills and education needed to become a librarian, administrator, or manager? Why should I learn all about the tools and procedures of stuffy research that nobody cares about? You may well ask these questions, especially if you are just at the beginning of your career. Those contemplating advanced studies, such as a PhD, or those already working in academic libraries, will see the relevance immediately. But what about the rest of our readers?

There are many answers to these questions, as there are enormous benefits to the library and information science (LIS) field, to the practice of librarianship, and to you as an individual. These also are emphasized elsewhere in this text, but here are a few major reasons:

- "There is nothing so practical as a good theory," according to Kurt Lewin, the founder of modern social psychology who championed the use of theory. He believed that the creation of a theory that could be empirically confirmed was at the heart of science, research, and professional practice (Jaeger and Bertot 2013, 91).
- There is a growing trend for all types of libraries to prove their value to stakeholders through valid assessment and evaluation measures (see chapters 1 and 12). Therefore, MLIS students and practitioners must be well-versed in methods and analysis.
- To be able to be an educated consumer of research literature, one must be acquainted with, and able to judge, quality research.
- To be able to detect fake information and false claims, it is beneficial to become a critical consumer of research studies.

- Innovative LIS research that has not been previously enacted can both inform practice, as well as advance theoretical development.
- Even for those who may not think that a PhD is in their future, they may change their minds after becoming more involved in the research process, or after years in practice.

The above are enduring reasons to become knowledgeable about research. In the current moment, despite the social, economic, and public health challenges (including the COVID-19 pandemic and its aftermath) and their impact on our research practices, the basics have not changed. However, we do need to consider the utility of being open to adapt to new ways of doing things. We are in a "Zoom moment," in which we have been obliged to fully embrace techniques and tools for data collection and analysis that may have been around for quite a while (think Skype) but now are becoming ubiquitous (think Zoom). Reflecting on some of the broad impacts on research methods, it can be seen that some things have become much more difficult, some easier. For example, funding the cost of doing research (such as travel expenses) can be down, but experiencing technology glitches can be up. In-person interviews and focus groups have been impossible, but virtual ones have become more sophisticated, and most people have now experienced virtual encounters with loved ones and friends. Familiarity with the technology is a plus for researchers seeking to recruit participants. More on this topic will be found throughout this book. We start with some fundamental definitions.

Definition of Research

When put on the spot and asked to define "research," what would most people say? Many people in the LIS field may have naïve ideas or even misconceptions about the research process. Some of these misconceptions are grounded in the American system of undergraduate- and master's-level work, which regularly educates students to do a research paper, consisting of a literature review and discussion of a particular topic or issue. Usually, these assignments are on topics students may not be particularly interested in, although if given a personal choice of focus, and if the student has sound writing ability, sometimes compiling these reviews can become a joy rather than an onerous task. Views of what constitutes research are often shaped by students' early efforts to search for, read, and summarize scholarly articles; work these into a coherent paper; and carefully cite them correctly. Master's students delve more deeply into areas that are more relevant (and even exciting), but the term paper or research paper still is a standard assignment. Those educated in this system become accustomed to thinking of "search/synthesis" as being equal to "research." Search/synthesis does not equal research in the sense that is intended here.

Those holding a master's or doctoral degree in LIS, or in another subject area whose program's curriculum offers a research methods course, will have a different idea of what research is, a more nuanced idea. This book may be an assigned text for such a course, or perhaps is being used as a refresher or primer for LIS practitioners who have not taken a research course (or at least not recently). This book is designed to be a comprehensive overview about research, in the sense of deep study of a particular phenomenon, in our case, one that is related to the LIS field. It provides an overview of methods and theoretical foundations, as well as helpful resources for every stage of the research process. It also asserts that designing, conducting, and writing up research can be enjoyable and extremely satisfying, perhaps one of the most important and lasting contributions one can make as an LIS scholar and professional. Jaeger and Bertot wrote that much recent LIS scholarship has "examined various aspects of the difficulties faced by libraries driven by economic struggles and changing politics. While these are very practical real problems facing libraries, research in the field still can do a tremendous amount to help libraries navigate through the challenging waters in which they now find themselves" (Jaeger and Bertot 2013, 91). They advocated stronger connections between research and practice and assert that libraries "truly need all of the help research can provide in terms of demonstrating their value, creating more effective services, using resources effectively, improving community outreach, advocating for support, providing inclusive services to their communities, and myriad other ways" (Jaeger and Bertot 2013, 91). Of course, research takes interest, knowledge, time, and effort. However, it definitely is worth the struggle and also can provide opportunities for adventure, discovery, and surprise that lead many to the conclusion that research can be pleasurable (dare we say fun?).

Let's start with the basics, considering research in the general sense. *Merriam-Webster Online Dictionary* (2020) defined it as "studious inquiry or examination; especially: investigation or experimentation aimed at the discovery and interpretation of facts, revision of accepted theories or laws in the light of new facts, or practical applications of such new or revised theories or laws." Creswell (2011) defined research as "a process of steps used to collect and analyze information to increase our understanding of a topic or issue," and outlined three key steps, "1. Pose a question, 2. Collect data to answer the question, and 3. Present an answer to the question."

These general definitions suggest at least two major types of research, one of which is *basic research*. Also referred to as pure, theoretical, or scientific research, it primarily is interested in deriving new knowledge and is at most only indirectly involved with how that knowledge will be applied to specific, practical, or real problems. Or, as the American Association of University Professors stated, scientific research is "any activity designed to test a hypothesis, permit conclusions to be drawn, and thereby to develop or contribute to generalizable knowledge expressed in theories, principles, and statements of relationships" (Jarvis Thomson et al. 2006, 95). Basic research, particularly if quantitative in nature, usually is designed to produce new knowledge that is generalizable (meaning that the findings usually derived from a random and representative sample of cases have applicability to a larger population that the sample represents; more on this is found in chapter 6).

The second major type of research (and the type that this book is primarily highlighting) is usually known as *applied research*, and it encompasses a variety of specific research techniques, such as systems analysis and operations research. In contrast to pure or basic research, applied research emphasizes the solving of specific problems in real situations. Much of the library-related research has been applied research dealing with everything from evaluating e-collections, to assessment of reference services, to analyzing integrated library systems (ILS). A portion of recent LIS applied research has been characterized as community based and/or participatory research (see chapter 14 for additional information).

But in spite of the fact that basic and applied research have tended to be done in isolation from one another, they are not necessarily dichotomous. As Shera noted, "Research is no less 'pure' for leading to useful results, though it most certainly does not have to possess immediate applicability to qualify as research" (Shera 1964, 143). In other words, basic research often leads to practical applications, while applied research frequently acts as a foundation for subsequent theoretical or basic research. Stokes also dismissed this dichotomous notion of the relationship between basic and applied research. When discussing Pasteur's philosophy of research, Stokes described it as the integration of both basic research in his search for knowledge and applied research in his quest to solve practical problems (Stokes 1997).

In addition to the distinctions described above, research can be further divided by type of method, usually seen as a dichotomy between quantitative and qualitative approaches, although this book takes the perspective that it is more of a continuum than a dichotomy. Quantitative research methods "use measurements and statistics to transform empirical data into numbers and to develop mathematical models that quantify behavior" (Tracy 2013, 36). Qualitative research methods focus on observing events from the perspective of those involved and attempt to understand why individuals behave as they do. They involve "collection, analysis, and interpretation of interview, participant observation, and document data in order to understand and describe meanings, relationships and patterns" (Tracy 2013, 36). Qualitative methods take a more interpretive, naturalistic approach to the resolution of research problems, grounded in participant reports (Denzin and Lincoln 2011). Some research projects use a mixed methods approach (see Michelle Kazmer's text box 2.1 in chapter 2), including both quantitative and qualitative research methods to study and report behaviors and events. Mixed methods can complement one another and strengthen the research design by mitigating flaws or weaknesses that can be found in single-method designs (Miles, Huberman, and Saldaña 2020). The goal of this book is to provide you with a well-stocked toolbox of methods to choose from, so quantitative methods are discussed in depth in chapters 4–8, and chapters 9–11 describe qualitative methods, with mixed methods being featured in chapter 2 and historical research being covered in chapter 13.

Why is it important for LIS students, scholars, and professionals to become familiar with and well-versed in research methods? Here are a few reasons to contemplate:

Understanding LIS research literature can improve library practice, management, and professional decision making (Jaeger and Bertot 2013). The American Library Association (ALA) promoted the need for the dissemination of research findings for support of professional practice and published "recommendations related to the effective dissemination of research" (American Library Association 2001).

Increased research activity will lead to additional expansion and refinement of the profession's theoretical underpinnings. Kumasi, Charbonneau, and Walster analyzed how theory was used in LIS research and recommend that theoretical application and development become more robust in published research articles (Kumasi, Charbonneau, and Walster 2013).

Another benefit of having a reasonable mastery of basic research methods is that it should allow one to understand and critically evaluate the research reports of others. The more one knows and understands the research process, the better able one is to evaluate, question, and utilize the literature by acknowledging its limitations. Some librarians, particularly special and academic librarians, are expected to evaluate or screen research reports (i.e., serve as research intermediaries) for their clientele. Academic librarians serve on reappointment and tenure committees for colleagues and must be able to critically evaluate all types of research and publications.

For those librarians who serve researchers, another reason to cultivate a basic knowledge of research methods is the greater understanding of scholars' needs provided by this awareness. Only when the librarian knows the basic scholarly process can the researcher's needs be fully anticipated and met. Kennedy and Brancolini (2012, 431) point out, "Librarians in an academic setting are integrally involved with providing research services to faculty, students, and staff of higher education institutions." In addition, the librarian's status is likely to benefit from being knowledgeable about the researchers' techniques and from being able to discuss them intelligently with his or her clientele. According to Clark (1997, 145), "An understanding of research can help improve the way in which librarians support researchers and encourage the use of small-scale research projects to support their work."

Perhaps most important among the benefits one could expect to realize from a study of research methods is gaining the ability to conduct research. For many librarians, especially in academic settings, research activities are not only desirable but a necessity. A number of academic institutions expect their professional librarians to meet the same requirements for promotion and tenure as do their regular teaching faculty, and these usually include research and publishing. According to the Association of Research Libraries (ARL) ("Scholars & Scholarship" n.d.), "Research libraries partner in the creation of new research and scholarship while they also manage vast collections in print, special collections, media, and other formats." If these librarians, and others, are to conduct the kind of rigorous research that they and their profession need, a thorough understanding of basic research methods is absolutely essential.

Research also can be both personally and professionally satisfying and enjoyable: "Work is play when it's something you like" (Goldsmith 2009, 91). McKnight asserted: "There are so many rewards for publishing! First, of course, is your personal feeling of accomplishment. You include your publications, not your submissions, on your resume and in your tenure material. Colleagues will read your work and carry on the conversation with their responses in person, or in print, citing your work. You can find your citations in major bibliographic databases. No one ever has to know how many reincarnations your manuscript had before it was published. The process often takes more time than expected, but if the subject really interests you and your co-authors, you can enjoy the journey" (McKnight 2009, 115). Hahn and Jaeger (2013, 241) also listed additional personal rewards, including "gaining intellectual stimulation and fresh challenges—research is fun."

An awareness of research methods and design also should prove helpful for those preparing proposals to obtain financial support for their research activities (see also chapter 13). In addition, it has been pointed out that the study of research methods can improve one's ability to think critically and analytically—competencies associated with leadership. A library's involvement in research can even improve staff morale and enhance the library's status in its community.

Recently there has been much discussion about evidence-based research. This has been percolating in the K–12 and higher education literature for quite some time. Todd (2015) has been a leader in voicing the need for evidence-based practice and research in school libraries. Evidence-based decision making is another important focus within LIS, which requires collecting and analyzing relevant data to make informed decisions for services, policies, and so forth (Todd 2015). It "incorporates a decision-making framework based on the best available research evidence with professional knowing and experience to make professional decisions and take professional action, and to implement and continuously improve professional practice, as well as a framework for documenting evidence of outcomes" (Todd 2009, 88). Evidence-based research and practice has been also proliferating within the medical library community, which has a particular responsibility for supporting medical research and for making informed administrative decisions (Lauseng, Howard, and Johnson 2019), made more critical during the COVID-19 pandemic.

Evidence-based research and decision making is part of a larger movement that is overtaking libraries: the assessment imperative (see chapter 12 for additional information).

THE ASSESSMENT IMPERATIVE

Sassen and Wahl (2014) referred to library assessment concerns as "hot button issues at campuses across the country." Those concerned about the status of the LIS profession have commented on the need for more and better basic and applied research, which is seen as crucial for continued growth, especially in the current climate of budget tightening and the need for libraries to prove their worth. Connaway saw these realities as opportunities: "However, times of economic hardship can provide opportunity for libraries. Specifically, it can be an opportunity to assess current library services and systems and to develop new ones that better meet the needs of users and prospective users. In order to accomplish this, LIS professionals must know how to assess the value and use of these services and systems" (Connaway 2014, 1). The Association of College and Research Libraries (ACRL) report *Value of Academic*

Libraries (2011) stated: "Librarians are increasingly called upon to document and articulate the value of academic and research libraries and their contribution to institutional mission and goals." Assessment for academic libraries is seen as urgent and needing clear focus to be effective (Connaway 2018a; Connaway et al. 2017). This reality is not only true for academic libraries but also increasingly for all types of libraries, and has resulted in a strong push for all types of assessment activities that "document and articulate" value for stakeholders and funders beyond the usual statistics to track quality (Connaway 2014, 1).

Library assessment can be defined as the process of defining, selecting, designing, collecting, analyzing, interpreting, and using information to increase service/program effectiveness (Connaway and Radford 2013). Assessment activities answer questions like the following (Connaway and Radford 2013):

- What do users/stakeholders want and need?
- How can services/programs better meet needs?
- Is what we do working?
- Could we do better?
- What are problem areas?

Assessment can be formal or informal, and a research-driven approach is necessary to underpin a formal assessment process. For an assessment to be recognized as valid and rigorous, it must use accepted quantitative and qualitative methods and be data driven and evidence based. Anecdotal, informal assessment, relying on casual observation and traditional data collection measures (e.g., use of statistics and gate counts), used to be the norm but is no longer adequate to show value. Output measures quantify the work done (e.g., number of books/e-books circulated, number of articles downloaded, number of reference questions answered, and instruction or program attendance). However, by themselves, they do not holistically relate these factors to overall effectiveness. "Output measures suggest demand, performance efficiency, and customer satisfaction, but do not describe performance or identify the outcomes or benefits resulting from the use of library services and systems" (Connaway 2014, 1). See also Pung, Clarke, and Patten (2004). For example, a library can put on fifty programs in a year, but what is their quality? Are they on hot topics of interest to users? Input measures are counts and inventories of available resources (e.g., budget figures, numbers/types of items/volumes in collections, amount of space, counts and types of equipment, and numbers of staff). These can be measured against standards but are not sufficient for overall assessment. For example, a library can have a large collection of books and other media, but how old is the collection? What condition are the items in? How accessible are they to users?

One current trend that takes a different approach is to define and measure outcomes rather than inputs or outputs. These are defined as "the ways in which library users are changed as a result of their contact with the library's resources and programs" ("Task Force on Academic Library Outcomes Assessment Report" 2006). Field and Tran argue that in order for a library to articulate its public value, it must define "the outcomes it sets out to achieve" (Field and Tran 2018, 120).

An evolving assessment culture is driving all types of libraries to make a firm commitment to ongoing efforts to understand users and measure how well their needs are being met (Connaway 2014). Outcomes assessment centers on evaluating changes in service and resource use for clients. It uses a variety of methods to identify benchmarks, to discover best practices, and to corroborate conclusions. It is best done as a continuous process, which need not address every aspect of service/collections but can be focused on a small number of outcomes. Some examples of user-centered outcomes are the following (Connaway and Radford 2013):

- The user matches information need to information resources.
- The user can organize an effective search strategy.
- The user effectively searches the online catalog and retrieves relevant resources.
- The user can find appropriate resources.

Many academic libraries have included assessment activities as a major focus of their strategic plans and are seeking additional ways to measure impact and establish a clear connection between library activities and student/faculty success. One tool that enables a longitudinal comparison is LibQUAL+ and LibQUAL Lite (http://www.libqual.org); these are web-based survey tools from the ARL that seek to identify user needs and expectations, and reveal gaps in performance. According to the LibQUAL+ home page, more than fifty refereed journal articles have been published using these instruments, including McCaffrey (2019) and Sullo (2019).

An ongoing effort, assessment, when it is done correctly, takes dedicated human and budget resources. "Assessment takes time and effort to plan and a formal evaluation requires a financial investment from the organization. Formal assessment is data-driven and evidence-based and utilizes accepted research methods and data collection techniques. It is recognized as a rigorous, ongoing process" (Connaway 2014, 1). See also Connaway and Radford (2013). An understanding of the steps involved in the assessment process and plan is integral to its success (Connaway 2018a, 2018b). Making the commitment is a difficult challenge; it is clear that librarians are busy with day-to-day work, and some feel that assessment can become another burden. Assessment tools involve research methods that are described in this book, including quantitative and qualitative methods such as analytics, survey research, interviews, focus group interviews, and structured observations.

SCHOLARLY COMMUNICATION

Research in LIS is situated in the larger body of research in the social sciences and humanities. It is necessary here to include a recognition of the system of scholarly communication within which all research resides. Scholarly communication has been defined by the ACRL as "the system through which research and other scholarly writings are created, evaluated for quality, disseminated to the scholarly community and preserved for future use. The system includes both formal means of communication, such as publication in peer-reviewed journals, and informal channels . . ." ("Scholarly Communication Toolkit: Scholarly Communication Overview" n.d.). Scholarly communication covers the entire life cycle of scholarly research with the component parts of (a) research data collection and analysis, (b) authoring, (c) peer review, (d) publication, (e) discovery and dissemination, usually depicted as a circular process ("Scholarly Communication Toolkit: Scholarly Communication Overview" n.d.). It is important to note that this system is used by scholars "to develop ideas, exchange information, build and mine data, certify research, publish findings, disseminate results, and preserve outputs. This vast and changing system is central to the academic enterprise, which makes it central to the work of academic librarians" (Keener et al. 2015). Libraries have recently changed their approach to scholarly communication in that they have become more involved as information producers, rather than passive consumers (Keener et al. 2015).

The open access (OA) movement and the rapid rise of institutional repositories have had a direct impact on enlarging the scope of core mission, especially for academic libraries (Cullen and Chawner 2011). Within the OA movement, authors and publishers are being urged to assert more control over intellectual property rights, such as copyright. The COVID-19 pandemic has prompted innovation in OA practices. Tavernier writes in *College & Research Libraries News:* "In the wake of COVID-19, many publishers have tacitly agreed that open access is beneficial to scientific advancement and necessary to move science forward to combat disease. Publishers have committed to open access publication of scientific articles relating to the disease. Some are facilitating rapid and open peer review and fast-tracking the publishing of related research. Pulitzer Prize–winning journalist Michael Hiltzig refers to this convincing demonstration of the value of open access to scientific research as one of the most important positive disruptions caused by COVID-19" (Tavernier 2020, 226). Tavernier concludes by questioning whether "after COVID-19 subsides governments, scientists, and global institutions will find it acceptable for publishers to continue to put paywalls around research—decelerating scientific, scholarly, and social advancement. It becomes possible to question whether commercial publishers should govern, i.e., be the principal decision-makers about, and gatekeepers of, access to knowledge. Most importantly, it becomes possible to question what type of scholarly publishing system we (collectively as a society) want, and to design it accordingly" (Tavernier 2020, 229).

An alternative to paywalls and subscription databases that grants reproduction and reuse rights to others that goes beyond fair use has been made possible through the Creative Commons license ("Copyright & Intellectual Property" 2020; "Creative Commons" 2020). In the increasingly digital library and digital publishing environments, these rights have become more complex. Another complexity that has become controversial is revealed when one studies the traditional mechanisms of scholarly publication in contrast to the more recent business model, in which for-profit companies have asserted more gatekeeping, adding restrictions that constrain the use of scholarly information. Dillon asserted that there is a long-running "crisis" in scholarly communication characterized as having arisen from the "hypercompetitive academic environment and a ruthless academic winnowing and reward system" driven by large commercial publishers and library consortia (Dillon 2012, 609).

There is a rich body of research and white papers on scholarly communication, using a variety of methodological approaches, which has touched on topics such as:

- Trust in scholarly communication (Haider and Åström 2017).
- Library publishing services and how they facilitate scholarly communication (Park and Shim 2011).
- The role of libraries in scholarly identity work via social networking sites (Radford et al. 2020).
- Engaging LIS students in the economics of information and scholarly communication (Warren and Duckett 2010).
- Scholarly communication practices of librarians and archivists (Sugimoto et al. 2014).

Shorish and Hall (2019) provide an excellent overview of how the ACRL created a research agenda relating to scholarly communication. The ARL ("Scholars & Scholarship" n.d.) concludes that "a new openness in scholarly and research environments is transforming how knowledge is created, shared, and sustained. We contribute to this transformation by deeply engaging with scholarly communities and acting collectively to reduce friction between users and the information they seek and create." This is a lofty goal that is worth increased attention by researchers. See text box 1.1 for additional insight on research in scholarly communication.

Text Box 1.1: Scholarly Communication

C. Sean Burns

I study scholarly communication because it, and academic libraries, are topics I still think about at the end of the day. I think that how scholars communicate can yield philosophical and sociological insights about the nature of knowledge and about our institutions and cultures, but there are also quite interesting technical problems to study within this area.

I am also interested in scholarly communication because of its impact on the function of academic libraries, which I find to be among the most fascinating of things. Although many of my research projects do not explicitly reference academic libraries, I find that I constantly make mental references to them when undergoing these other projects. In a sense, I am driven to study all sorts of things with the constant long-term goal of building a more complete and holistic mental model of the academic library.

It is good to consider the content of one's analytical toolbox. Susan Haack (2007), a philosopher of science, wrote that doing science fundamentally means doing one's absolute hardest to get at the truth of a matter. In my view, that partly means having the appropriate analytical tools, qualitative, quantitative, and historical methods, in my toolbox and using them well.

My collaborations have helped me to check my assumptions and biases and have led to more robust research. In that vein, it is good to be thoughtful about with whom you collaborate and to be humble and open in that collaboration. One of my biggest challenges involved a project with someone outside our field, and it was a great challenge because of our different scientific backgrounds. However, we conducted important work together, and I am a far better researcher and person, hopefully, because of that work with this individual. I would encourage collaboration with others in different fields but understand that there may be vastly different assumptions involved.

Burns, C. Sean, and Charles W. Fox. (2017). Language and socioeconomics predict geographic variation in peer review outcomes at an ecology journal. *Scientometrics, 113*(2), 1113–1127. https://doi.org/10.1007/s11192-017-2517-5

Reference

Haack, Susan. 2007. *Defending Science—within Reason: Between Scientism and Cynicism.* Buffalo, NY: Prometheus Books.

RESEARCH DATA MANAGEMENT AND REUSE

Another aspect of scholarly communication is research data management (RDM), which "consists of a number of different activities and processes associated with the data lifecycle, involving the design and creation of data, storage, security, preservation, retrieval, sharing, and reuse, all taking into account technical capabilities, ethical considerations, legal issues, and governance frameworks" (Cox and Pinfield 2014, 300). This aspect of the research process has become more popular in the past decade. The emphasis on managing and sharing research data originated from the need to comply with the requirements of research funding agencies, that is, the Institute for Museum and Library Services (IMLS), National Institutes of Health (NIH), National Science Foundation (NSF), European Commission, Arts and Humanities Research Council (AHRC), Economic and Social Research Council (ESRC), Australian Research Council (ARC), and some publishers; the move toward open data from the scientific community; validation of findings and data integrity; increased dissemination and impact; ability for other researchers to reuse the data; and increased efficiency for the use of the data (Sanjeeva 2018). Borgman (2007) called on publishers, librarians, funding agencies, and researchers to work collaboratively to develop a scholarly infrastructure for the sharing of research data. She continued to call for infrastructures for the management and sharing of data to ensure that data are discoverable, described, and preserved for future use and provides case studies describing scholars' data practices (Borgman 2016; Radford et al. 2015).

The need for RDM has provided a new opportunity for academic librarians to be a part of the development of the policies and processes at an institutional level. However, as with all new opportunities, there are some challenges that must be addressed. Cox and Pinfield (2014) conducted a survey of eighty-one library staff in higher education and research institutions. In a qualitative study conducted with interviews of thirty-six US academic library professionals to learn how library staff were involved in RDM and if it was part of their strategic priorities, Faniel and Connaway (2018) identified factors that facilitate or constrain RDM activity for librarians. Both studies indicate that library staff often need to learn new skills and educate the academic community about what they can offer researchers. RDM was seen as an important and exciting new role by and for library staff that could position the library in a critical role within the academic community.

Auckland (2012) identified the potentially most significant gaps in skills for librarians for offering RDM service. She also provided roles in which librarians could fill to support researchers in managing data. These include:

- Identifying funding opportunities.
- Alerting researchers to content and embedding in research groups.
- Providing training and support in information management, that is, creating and storing bibliographic references.
- Advising researchers on how to identify preexisting data.
- Accessing, organizing, storing, analyzing, and reusing data.
- Identifying and promoting virtual networking opportunities within different disciplines.
- Analyzing and interpreting research data.
- Writing and disseminating findings.
- Interpreting copyright agreements and requirements.
- Preserving research data.
- Measuring the impact of the research.
- Introducing researchers to emerging technology.

ACRL has published two volumes that provide an excellent overview of RDM, the rationale for the development of data repositories, and a detailed overview of the steps required to curate a data set. Volume one (Johnston 2017a) provides the theories, frameworks, and research addressing RDM while volume two (Johnston 2017b) includes thirty case studies written by practicing subject librarians, archivists, data curators, RDM specialists, digital library staff, and institutional repository managers.

Research has focused on researchers in different disciplines and how they manage and preserve their data for other researchers to access and use (Faniel and Jacobsen 2010; Faniel, Kriesberg, and Yakel 2012; Faniel, Kriesberg, and Yakel 2016; Tenopir et al. 2020). Tenopir et al. (2020) provide an international overview of scientists' practices and perceptions of data management. One thousand seventy-two responses were received. The majority of the respondents were in the sciences, that is, physical sciences, life sciences, and computer science and engineering. Since the researchers collected quantitative data and there was a large sample size, the Pearson's chi-square was used to test the independence of the variables. More than three-quarters of the researchers stated they rely on colleagues to find data to answer their research questions or find the data themselves. About two-thirds of the respondents indicated they search for the data on their own and without the assistance of a data manager or librarian. This finding indicates a great opportunity for librarians to demonstrate their knowledge and skills for the management and reuse of research data. Faniel and Yakel have conducted data reuse studies with social scientists, archeologists, and zoologists using qualitative (Faniel, Frank, and Yakel 2019; Faniel and Yakel 2017), quantitative (Faniel, Kriesberg, and Yakel 2016; Tenopir et al. 2014, 2015), and mixed methods (Faniel and Yakel 2017). For more information on data management and reuse, see text box 1.2.

Text Box 1.2: Data Management and Reuse

Ixchel Faniel

When I decided to study data reuse within disciplinary communities, there were few studies examining research data management phenomena from the perspective of the people who would be reusing the data. It bothered me, because I thought the success of research data management hung on knowing more about data reuse needs and practices.

Both qualitative and quantitative methodologies have been invaluable in my early studies. Individual interviews yielded rich descriptions of data reuse needs and practices across multiple disciplines (Faniel, Frank, and Yakel 2019). Questionnaires were used to survey large groups of reusers and test statistical models, such as examining the precursors to data reuse satisfaction (Faniel, Kriesberg, and Yakel 2016).

My early days of studying data reuse turned into a research program that I love and one that evolves as I grow through new questions and new and lasting collaborations. My perspective also has broadened. I realized studying data reuse would be most effective when studied in light of other activities occurring during the data life cycle, such as data production, sharing, and curation (Yakel, Faniel, and Maiorana 2019). Consequently, the people and the practices I study have expanded. I have also incorporated different data collection techniques, such as focus group interviews, observations, email exchanges, project documents and databases, and repository data deposit forms.

My advice to beginning researchers. First, look to the literature to see what's been done in your area of interest. What questions have been asked? What questions have been adequately answered? What methods have been used? What were the results? Second, look beyond the journals in your discipline. I have drawn from multiple literatures, because other disciplines have studied similar phenomena and have more well-developed concepts that can be adapted. Third, consider working with other researchers and practicing professionals who bring different perspectives and subject-matter and methodological expertise. It's not just about sharing the workload; my collaborators have broadened my perspective, my knowledge, and the impact of my work.

References

Faniel, Ixchel M., Rebecca D. Frank, and Elizabeth Yakel. 2019. "Context from the Data Reuser's Point of View." *Journal of Documentation* 75(6): 1274–97. https://doi.org/10.1108/JD-08-2018-0133.

Faniel, Ixchel M., Adam Kriesberg, and Elizabeth Yakel. 2016. "Social Scientists' Satisfaction with Data Reuse." *Journal of the Association for Information Science and Technology* 67(6): 1404–16. https://doi.org/10.1002/asi.23480.
Yakel, Elizabeth, Ixchel M. Faniel, and Zachary J. Maiorana. 2019. "Virtuous and Vicious Circles in the Data Life-Cycle." *Information Research* 24(2). http://informationr.net/ir/24-2/paper821.html.

New Modes for Collaboration

As noted above, economics, social norms, and the COVID-19 pandemic have changed the way that we collect data, but also the way that we collaborate. Because of the pandemic, economics, and social norms, collaboration often cannot take place in the traditional face-to-face (FtF) mode with those you are in close geographical proximity to (including coworkers, colleagues, and classmates). The good news is that technical innovation has increasingly enabled teams of researchers in LIS to work effectively together regardless of their locations and time zones (Radford et al. 2015). Cloud computing and sites such as Box.com, Dropbox.com, Share Point, OneDrive, and GoogleDocs have brought document sharing and collaborative editing to a new level, although privacy remains a concern. Bibliographic citation platforms including Zotero (basic version free), RefWorks (proprietary), and others have enabled teams to build shared bibliographies.

It is obvious that since COVID-19, virtual collaboration has become ubiquitous and had been trending well before the pandemic. Alaiad and Yazan surveyed 1,372 business respondents from eighty countries and found that "85% worked on virtual teams" and that these teams were playing an "increasingly important role" (Alaiad, Alnsour, and Alsharo 2019, 211). According to Monzani, Ripoll, Pieró, and Van Dick (2014): "Virtual work has become an increasingly central practice for the organization of the 21st century. While effective virtual workgroups can create synergies that boost innovation and performance, ineffective workgroups become a great burden" (Monzani et al. 2014, 279). Rysavy and Michalak (2020) wrote about how one academic library shifted to remote teams and working from home overnight due to COVID-19 and discuss how online tools enhanced this experience, enabled effective communication, and empowered collaboration. Similarly, Weimann, Pollock, Scott, and Brown (2013) provide recommendations for avoiding problems and ensuring greater effectiveness for virtual research teams.

Bradley, Baur, Banford, and Postlethwaite (2013) found that the participation of "agreeable" members positively affects virtual team cohesion and communication. Monzani and colleagues (2014) warned that working virtually in teams over a long period of time, but infrequently participating in FtF meetings, can have a negative effect, including development of perceptions of "loafing." Yilmaz and Peña (2014) suggest that interpersonal communication dynamics can go wrong in virtual teams in instances when "in-groups" and "out-groups" form or when a teammate behaves negatively. They apply social identity models and social information processing theory in research with sixty-four participants, divided into teams of four via a live chat platform. According to Scott (2013, 301), "Team members separated by time, distance, and culture often struggle with issues of trust, conflict, and potentially divisive subgroups. With global virtual teams becoming increasingly common in organizations, it is important to understand how to minimize such interactional difficulties."

Cummings and Dennis (2018) argue that social media has forever altered the way that team members become acquainted. People now have the ability to view profiles, including via those enterprise social networking sites that companies in the information industry have developed. These initial virtual impressions leave lasting effects that can impact the ability of the team to be productive (Cummings and Dennis 2018). This assertion can carry over to the virtual research team environment, wherein collaborators from different universities or libraries may never have met. Decreased travel to conferences and scholarly meet-ups, prevented by COVID-19 precautions or travel bans, will certainly have continued impact on limiting FtF collaboration for some time to come.

Regardless of the mode of collaboration, be it video conferencing, phone call, or email, collaboration will enable you to accomplish more in the same amount of time.

Another form of collaboration that is becoming more popular is collaborative writing that involves two or more people coming together in person or virtually to write on independent projects. In formal mentoring programs, such as the Program for Early Career Excellence (PECE) at Rutgers University (2020), individuals, in this case, early career faculty in their first three years from underrepresented groups, are invited to pair up with mentors or with other mentees. The pairs agree to a schedule of collaborative writing such as 2 hours per week, or can be longer or more frequent, depending on the pair/group. Pre-COVID-19, people might meet in coffee shops or other public places; during the pandemic, the writing sessions would take place via Zoom, Skype, Teams, WebEx, or another video platform. Formats can be flexible, depending on those participating, but generally, these sessions start by each person setting a goal for the first segment (perhaps 45 minutes to an hour), briefly describing their goal, and appointing a time-keeper. After the first segment, the participants come together to report on their goal and to set a goal for the second segment. A 10-minute break can be taken during which participants decide what should be done (e.g., no writing for 10 minutes, including email, standing up and stretching). After the second writing session of 45 minutes or so, each person gives a second brief report and arrangements are made for the next session. The value in these sessions is that they provide a regular structure with accountability for participants, for an activity (writing) that can lack structure. It also provides an opportunity to set and to talk about short-term and long-term goals. These sessions also provide a respite from the onslaught of social media, email, and other distractions that can interrupt the flow of writing. Phones are turned off or set on airplane mode; email is ignored for the duration. This approach invites a period of intense focus on the project; the short bursts of writing can be extremely productive for this reason. Of course, writing retreats of longer duration can also take place, under the auspices of mentoring, writing, or doctoral programs. The next section discusses additional ways to leverage your time for greater research productivity.

Time Management

One of the most difficult obstacles to overcome for professional librarians, library students, and scholars alike is finding the time to think, do the research, and (most difficult of all) to write. In a study of practices of ARL member institutions, Smigielski, Laning, and Daniels (2014) found that one of the most important mechanisms to support publication and research for librarians is "protected time," which includes dedicated work time/release time and sabbaticals. They note: "Librarians report difficulties in finding time for research and writing or having to resort to doing this work on their personal time, given the institutional needs that pressure them" (Smigielski, Laning, and Daniels 2014, 267). Sassen and Wahl confirm this finding and also call for more research into administrative support for research, asserting that few studies have investigated this issue. They provide an overview of the research that has been done and find that formal and informal mentoring also is important for productivity (Sassen and Wahl 2014). Lee's book (2011), *Mentoring in the Library: Building for the Future*, provides an in-depth overview of recommended mentoring models and benefits.

To discover what access early career academic librarians had to research support mentoring, Ackerman, Hunter, and Wilkinson (2018) surveyed > 200 pretenure or recently tenured academic librarians. They found that this group needed support activities that targeted (a) research design and methods, (b) work practices and accountability, and (c) emotional elements. Respondents reported that they relied heavily on informal mentoring.

In a similar study with at a later career stage, Couture, Gerke, and Knievel (2020) conducted a survey of tenured academic librarians to investigate post-tenure mentoring. Findings indicate that few structured mentoring programs, including research efforts, are available for those post-tenure who are working toward promotion. They also found five factors that influence decisions on whether to seek promotion: financial, political, workload, work-life balance, and process/procedural.

It may be necessary for those interested in continuing a research agenda past tenure to seek out mentoring through professional organizations, such as the International Federation of Library Associations (IFLA), ACRL, Association for Information Science and Technology (ASIS&T), the Association for Library and Information Science Educators (ALISE), or the ALA, or to engage in informal mentoring by seeking advice from those who have been promoted above tenure rank. Another suggestion for academic librarians, if you are in an institution that has release time for research, is to spend some time finding out about the process and talk to people who have been successful in obtaining time (generally one day per week for a semester, or a block of time that is to be devoted to research activities). If there is a faculty committee that makes the decisions on applications, volunteer to be on the committee so you can gain a better idea of what makes for a successful application, to inform your future submissions. Cabanac and Hartley (2013) write that protecting personal time and work-life balance may be getting more difficult to achieve. In their study of *Journal of the Association for Information Science and Technology (JASIS&T)* authors and editors, they found a rising trend for writing and editing activity on the weekends, indicating an expansion of the five-day workweek for scholars. Sassen and Wahl agree: "Additionally, it may be time for university administrators to consider the applicability of research being done at their institutions on the impact of long work hours on workers, their families, their employers, and their communities with respect to their librarians and faculty" (Sassen and Wahl 2014, 280). Oud (2008) conducted a survey of librarians with three years of experience or fewer and found that time management and workload management were among the hardest things to learn in the academic setting.

There are numerous articles and books on strategies for managing time for librarians (Craver 2019; Gray 2017; Hough 2018; Rush 2020). Technology is a boon as well as a challenge for time management. One often-reported time trap for librarians and academics is email. Two suggestions for managing email are to (1) work on your top priority for 15 to 30 minutes before opening email and (2) checking email at specified times, rather than continually, and setting a time limit. One suggestion is to check email at 9:00 a.m. and 4:00 p.m. only. This allows you to be responsive to most email within the business day.

Technology also can offer some help with time management websites and mobile apps, which are becoming more abundant. Fourie and Fourie (2013) present a useful and extensive table of websites with addresses and descriptions, including task managers, to-do lists, task-tracking sites, collaboration aids, time management analytics tools, and brainstorming or idea generators. Time tracker apps are available such as Rescue Time (www.rescuetime.com), Time Doctor (www.timedoctor.com), Freedom (freedom.to), and Forest (forestapp.cc). These track the amount of time you spend on various tasks (such as social media sites, work, online shopping, video watching, etc.) to give you an accurate look of how you spend your time on your computer or mobile device. Plus, they are programmable to your needs and can give you notifications if you are spending too much time on these tasks. A good thing about time management efforts is that often just a bit of thought and small actions (such as finding a great app or taking a few minutes every day to prioritize work) can have a major impact. See text box 1.3 for additional time management tips for social media.

Text Box 1.3: Top Time Management Tips for Social Media

For some, social media has become a time sink. Here are some tips and tactics for managing your Facebook, Instagram, TikTok, Snapchat, Twitter, Pinterest, LinkedIn, and other proclivities (Aileron 2013):

- Get into a routine. Incorporate social media into your daily routine, such as checking your favorite site during your morning coffee. Having a routine will allow you to show up on sites consistently instead of spending 3 hours trying to catch up on what you missed and posting all at once.

- Use mobile apps. The next time you are waiting for a Zoom meeting to start or when waiting at the doctor's office, apps will allow you to check up on social media during time you otherwise would have lost.
- Set a time limit. It is easy to get distracted by social media, so set a time limit for yourself for when you have to get on and off. Dedicate a specific amount of time that works for you, but do not let it take over your life. Apps like Anti-social (anti-social.cc) can help.
- Use a time tracker. Commercial trackers such as Rescue Time (www.rescuetime.com), Time Doctor (www.timedoctor.com), or Workrave (www.workrave.org) track the amount of time you spend on various tasks—social media sites, work, online shopping, video watching, and so forth—giving you an accurate look at how you spend your time on your phone, computer, or mobile device. Plus, they are programmable to your needs and can send you notifications if you are spending too much time on these tasks.
- Let automated tools assist you. There are plenty of tools available to help you schedule posts on various social media sites ahead of time (such as Hootsuite.com or Buffer.com). Use these to post at high-traffic times when your post is more likely to be seen by others, rather than all at once.
- Know your strengths and what you enjoy the most (which are often the same). Then, spend about 60 percent or more of your allotted social media time on that activity instead of wasting time on several social media sites that do not quite click with you.
- Turn off notifications. Do not have your computer or phone ping every time you have a notification on a social media site. These notifications will interrupt you and decrease your overall productivity.
- Find the right blend. Do not just stick to one activity (although you can have a primary one). Instead, experiment a little and find a good blend of publishing, sharing, and interacting on a few different social media sites. Do not spread yourself too thin, but do not put all your eggs in one basket, either.
- Take a break. You do not always need to be on social media. Schedule periods of time when you are completely offline. Taking a step back can do wonders for your stress level.

Be aware of the benefits and drawbacks of using social media as a tool for establishing and maintaining your scholarly identity as a student, library professional, and/or scholar. Radford, Kitzie, Mikitish, Floegel, Radford, and Connaway interviewed librarians, doctoral students, and faculty to discover possible opportunities and pitfalls of using social media to establish and maintain your scholarly identity, plus to investigate the role that librarians might play in educating and assisting with using social media tools. Use of social media sites such as Academia.edu and ResearchGate were found to be confusing and time consuming, but also beneficial in promoting one's work and in establishing networks with like-minded researchers (Radford et al. 2020).

References

Aileron. 2013. "10 Social Media Time Management Tips for Small Business." *Forbes.* https://www.forbes.com/sites/aileron/2013/04/01/10-social-media-time-management-tips-for-small-business/#62ae86e62faa.

Radford, M. L., V. Kitzie, S. Mikitish, D. Floegel, G. P. Radford, and L. S. Connaway. 2020. "People are Reading Your Work," Scholarly Identity and Social Networking Sites. *Journal of Documentation* 76(6): 1233–1260. https://doi.org/10.1108/JD-04-2019-0074.

OVERVIEW OF PREVIOUS LIBRARY AND INFORMATION SCIENCE RESEARCH

Current Library and Information Science Research Environment

Undoubtedly there are many challenges and obstacles to overcome for those embarking on library research, and also for the larger world of higher education and social science academics. According to Connaway (2015, 2):

> These include reduced funding opportunities because of more restricted national, international, and federal research initiatives; difficulty of articulating the scholarly value of the research based on a theoretical framework; not making the connection between the implications of research results and findings to the practical profession of LIS; limited relationships with scholars and research in other disciplines; the communication of research and outputs to traditional dissemination channels such as scholarly and professional presentations and publications and limited utilization of blogs, social media, and webinars; and inconsistent quality of the research data collection methods and analysis.

These challenges are indeed numerous, and the COVID-19 pandemic has thrown additional obstacles in the way of researchers, as discussed at the beginning of this chapter. Historically, there has been a long list of grievances many have had with LIS research (Connaway and Powell 2010). It has been easier to find criticism than praise of library research. Decades ago, Zweizig called for improvements in research methodologies, especially as they relate to users of library services (1976). Busha and Harter (1980, 8) stated that "a large proportion of librarianship's research has been uneven in quality and demonstrably weak methodologically." Shaughnessy (1976) has been even more critical, contending that traditionally the field has permitted much of what is not actually research to be called research. Converse (1984, 236) identified shortcomings in the purpose of LIS research. He noted "a failure to ask the right questions and to establish a proper theoretical foundation for later research or application."

Julien, Pecoskie, and Reed conducted a content analysis of information behavior research in 2011 and found a gap between the quality and quantity of research published by practitioners and academic faculty. However, they also discovered signs of improvement, including "an increasingly interdisciplinarity reflected in the information behavior research literature. This suggests a maturing field and may encourage scholars in the area to expand their explorations of literature outside LIS for relevant work and theory" (Julien, Pecoskie, and Reed 2011, 19).

Research Methods in Library and Information Science

What are the most used methods in LIS? This chapter highlights the relatively recent record of trends in library research. Readers wishing to learn more about the history of library science research may want to consult Jackson's brief history of research in librarianship in the United States and Canada (1976) or Busha's review of the past status of library science research (1981). According to Shera, Ralph Beals (1964) once categorized library literature into the tripartite classification of "Glad Tidings," "Testimony," and "Research," and noted that there was little of the last. Goldhor (1972), in his text on library research, proclaimed that it features (1) a relatively small body of published research as defined in the narrow sense; (2) a larger amount of published and unpublished services studies, or applied research; (3) an even larger number of reports or descriptions of specific situations, or simply opinions; and (4) original data. Most library-related research prior to the 1980s has been characterized as applied in nature (Busha and Harter 1980). In the early 1990s Losee and Worley (1993, ix) stated: "There is a tendency among information professionals to write and publish in the 'How I done it good' genre, a genre that is very situation-specific."

Bao (2000) analyzed the articles published in *College & Research Libraries* (*C&RL*) and the *Journal of Academic Librarianship* (*JAL*) between 1990 and 1999. The majority of the refereed articles addressed collections, services, staffing, and the internet, indicating that some of the major research areas identified by the College Library Section of ACRL had not been studied by the authors included in the sample.

Similarly, Hildreth and Aytac examined 206 randomly selected articles in twenty-three LIS journals published between 2003 and 2005 using thirty-five factors, such as authorship, topic, type of research, and data collection method. They concluded that "there is little difference in the quality and organization" between the published reports of practitioner and academic research. Not surprisingly, "practitioners conduct more library-specific studies and academics conduct more use and user studies" (Hildreth and Aytac 2007, 254). The authors confirmed that qualitative research methods are being used but found that the numbers of such studies have "leveled off," and they express concern about library practitioners' limited use of qualitative research methods (Hildreth and Aytac 2007).

Hider and Pymm analyzed journals within and outside of librarianship published in 2005 to identify the strategies and data collection techniques used in research-related articles. They found that the survey was the most-used strategy (30.5 percent) for all journals examined, and "the leading technique was questionnaire/interview" (32.5 percent). Experimental design (20.8 percent) was the second most-used technique, and content analysis was "the only other specific technique with more than 10 percent" (Hider and Pymm 2008, 111). Historical research only was very low (1.2 percent) and showed a marked decline when compared with the results reported for 1975 and 1985 by Järvelin and Vakkari (1990) and Kumpulainen (1991). Thirty-two percent of all the journals reported no empirical research (these were discussions and theoretical papers), and there was no significant difference between the librarianship and nonlibrarianship journals. In the 1985 analysis, 55.9 percent of the articles reported no empirical research, which may indicate that discussion and theoretical papers were less likely to be published in 2005. Hider and Pymm (2008) reported that "qualitative approaches including case studies and ethnography are now well established." Bibliometrics still are "valuable tools of investigation," and "the largely quantitative technique of transaction log analysis has grown rapidly to become a major instrument." Approximately 26 percent of the articles in the librarianship journals used both quantitative and qualitative analyses, while 12.2 percent of the articles in the nonlibrarianship journals used both analyses (Hider and Pymm 2008, 111).

Julien, Pecoskie, and Reed reviewed 749 articles indexed in *Library Literature and Information Science Full-text* from 1999 to 2008 and discovered that for information behavior research, the questionnaire was the most-used method, followed by interviews, with nearly one-third using mixed methods. Questionnaires and interviews were dropping in overall numbers but still very popular (Julien, Pecoskie, and Reed 2011).

Chu studied 1,162 articles from top tier LIS publications, including *Journal of Documentation*, *JASIS&T*, and *Library & Information Research*, from 2001 to 2010, and concluded that researchers no longer are limited to traditional approaches. She concluded:

> The LIS field is maturing in terms of research method selection and application in that a greater number and wider variety of research methods are used in all the research publications this study examines. All the methods reported in the 1162 scholarly publications in a sense constitute a toolbox of research methods. Scholars are no longer limited to the research methods traditionally applied in LIS explorations (e.g., questionnaire and historical method). Researchers can instead choose research methods from this expanded toolbox according to their study objectives. (Chu 2015, 41)

Research by Luo and McKinney (2015) reviewed research methods in the *Journal of Academic Librarianship* and found that questionnaires were by far the first choice of those publishing in that journal, being the largest proportion of the research methods used (47.6 percent), followed by content analysis (27.2 percent), with semistructured interviews in third place (14 percent).

Greifeneder examined *JASIS&T*, *Information Research*, *Journal of Documentation*, and the *iConference Proceedings*, with years varying by journal, but all between 2012 and 2014. She discovered that the most-often-used methods were, in order of frequency, interviews, surveys, and content analysis. These results echoed those of Luo and McKinney. Interestingly, Greifeneder (2014) found that nearly half of the published studies used a combination of mixed methods or a minimum of two methods; however, there were no instances of combined qualitative and quantitative methods.

Using a bibliometric and text-mining analysis, Hodonu-Wusu and Lazarus analyzed a sample of 500 most-cited articles from 1980 through 2017. They found that between 1980 and 1997 there was a low number of LIS research publications, but 1998 to 2016 saw a systematic increase, with 2016 being the most prolific year for published articles (Wusu and Lazarus 2018).

One interesting content analysis study by Matusiak reviewed research methodology on the topic of visual literacy published from 2011 to 2017 in academic journals. She notes that "LIS literature recognizes the importance of visual competencies for 21st-century learners and provides useful guidelines for integrating visual literacy into library instruction sessions or embedding it into the curriculum" (Matusiak 2020, 174). She found that 33 percent adopted a quantitative approach, with surveys being the most popular method. Mixed methods as well as qualitative methods, although in the minority, reflected a larger scope of data collection and analysis approaches. One-third did not describe any research method.

RECOMMENDATIONS FOR FUTURE RESEARCH IN LIBRARY AND INFORMATION SCIENCE

As Busha noted, past weaknesses of library-related research can at least partially be explained by the fact that "research in librarianship is still relatively young. Clear conceptions of the goals, objectives, and methodologies of library science research are only now beginning to be solidly formulated" (1981, 2). Wiegand (1999, 2015) calls for the integration of a variety of scholarship and methodological approaches from outside of LIS to avoid continuation of a narrow perspective that has pervaded the field. However, if LIS is growing with the integration of methods from other disciplines, such as sociology, psychology, linguistics, statistics, computer science, communication, and history, who is going to be qualified to conduct the kinds of research needed, how will they be educated, and how will practitioners be equipped to read and utilize this research? Shera (1964, 200–201) provided at least one answer to these questions when he wrote, "Research is too important to be left to dilettantes and amateurs, and its pursuit should be reserved for those who are qualified for it by aptitude, education, and motivation." Education appears to be one key to solving the problem. Not only can education provide the basic skills needed for conducting research, but it can help to shape attitudes and increase motivation.

Logically, the major responsibility for imparting research skills to librarians and library scholars must belong to the LIS education programs. As Shera (1972, 200–201) pointed out, a specific part of the course of study for a graduate student in librarianship should be the acquiring of a "knowledge of the principles and methods of research as applied to the investigation of library problems, together with the ability to evaluate research results, especially research in librarianship." And as Muller (1967, 1129) wrote, "Students should learn to appreciate the contribution of research and be urged to rid themselves of the notion that research is something esoteric, remote, or impractical." Yet most students view LIS programs as primarily concerned with providing professional skills, not academic training (Converse 1984), and "too few practitioners have education in the research or knowledge creating process" (Robbins 1990, 127).

The track record of LIS programs regarding the teaching of research skills is not outstanding, although Wildemuth (2017, 4) states that "most information professionals receive formal education in research methods during their master's degree education." LIS curricula have been revised in recent years to have more emphasis on technical innovation, data science, and web-based searching. Research methods courses, although offered as electives, are seldom required. Students may not understand the need for taking a research methods course, particularly if they are not planning to work in academic libraries, or thinking about doctoral studies following the completion of their MLIS degree. Most current MLIS students have the short-term goal of getting a professional position in LIS. Matusiak and others (2020; Kennedy and Brancolini 2012) assert that library professionals use social science methods but feel that they have not been adequately educated in research methods.

In 2003 Hernon and Schwartz (2003) referred to this as a crisis that should not be allowed to continue, but four years later they still concluded that graduates of LIS programs "might emerge with little or no understanding of the research process and how to gather and interpret evidence related to accountability, effectiveness, efficiency, or continuous quality improvement in programs and services" (Hernon and Schwartz 2007, 161).

LIS programs do not have the sole responsibility for educating competent researchers. It also is the responsibility of professional associations and, in some cases, research organizations, to provide appropriate continuing education opportunities. If libraries and other employers expect librarians to equip themselves to do research, then they must be prepared to provide appropriate incentives, support, and rewards. For example, release time, special leaves, and sabbaticals can be arranged to allow more time for research. Administrative support can be provided through salary increases, in-house training, and financial and clerical support for research projects (Smigielski, Laning, and Daniels 2014). Relevant courses such as those in statistical analysis can be taken in departments outside the LIS program when desirable or necessary. Ultimately, of course, it is the responsibility of the would-be researcher to take advantage of continuing education and staff development programs and to commit to a substantial program of self-study.

A statement made by Goldhor (1972, 2) almost four decades ago still rings true: "Librarianship today is particularly in need of the generalized truths which scientific research is designed to uncover." The research problems will ultimately direct the methodologies employed, which justifies the sustained development of research theories and models as described by Glazier and Grover (2002) in their multidisciplinary framework for theory building. If we are to realize the professional growth needed by the field of LIS, "Our attention must increasingly be devoted to research which is more basic and less applied" (Shaughnessy 1976, 44–52). Hernon (2001, 88) further stated that "we must all raise our expectations and challenge the profession to value and use research."

Fortunately, there are promising signs. The professional associations continue to establish more units concerned with research. At the annual conferences of the ALA, a considerable number of programs and committee meetings deal directly with research and statistics. Both ACRL and the ALA Library Research Round Table (LRRT) have established research mentoring programs to help members with various aspects of the research process.

The creation and dissemination of research is central to the vision statement of ASIS&T ("About ASIS&T" n.d.), which includes the following statement: "Advancing knowledge about information, its creation, properties, and use; Providing analysis of ideas, practices, and technologies; Valuing theory, research, applications, and service; Nurturing new perspectives, interests, and ideas; Increasing public awareness of the information sciences and technologies and their benefits to society."

There have been seven national Library Research Seminars (LRS) sponsored by the ALA's LRRT since 1996. The seventh one took place in 2019 at the University of South Carolina. Each LRS received numerous proposals for papers representing a wide range of methodologies, including content analysis, historiography, path analysis, discourse analysis, transaction log analysis, protocol analysis, survey, modeling, mixed methods, and meta-analysis. The research topics were equally diverse and often interdisciplinary. These research seminars provided effective forums solely devoted to research ideas and methodologies.

It always is difficult to predict the future, but research in LIS most likely will continue to incorporate more multidisciplinary and qualitative methods (McClure and Bishop 1989). Using keyword clustering and analysis, Liu and Yang examined LIS publications in the Web of Science from 2008 to 2017 to discover trends in research topics in LIS. They found that "in the most recent decade the most popular research topics in the LIS journals are closely related to Social Media, Data, Web, Information Retrieval, Information Literacy, Students, Evaluation, Collaboration, Knowledge Management, User Studies, and Information Management" (Liu and Yang 2019, 283). Additionally, they suggested that these topics have three implications: "the library service transition to digital platform, the patron-centralization concept, and the emergence of data governance and librarianship" (Liu and Yang 2019, 283). Furthermore, in tier one journals, author-supplied "keywords relating to human-computer interaction field are also identified in the top 20, including Information Seeking and Information Behavior." The authors believe that user-driven design has emerged in the practice of librarianship and LIS. Liu and Yang (2019) assert that these topics will continue to be popular LIS research trends in the coming years.

Given the events of 2020 and into 2021, two additional vitally important strands of scholarship are already being pushed forward urgently. The first of these is research related to the COVID-19 pandemic, the impact on library services and collections, and the critical role of accurate health and wellness information. The second of these is research related to the societal upheaval brought on by George Floyd's murder at the hands of the Minneapolis police, the Black Lives Matter movement, and attention to scholarship in social justice; equality, inclusion, and diversity within LIS. Without a doubt, LIS scholars already are responding to these two cataclysmic events, and will continue to do so.

Jaeger and Bertot (2013, 92) envision the need for greater quantity of LIS research to inform library practice: "Research about practice with clear outcomes to help practice is the core to keeping library research vibrant and relevant."

In conclusion, there is evidence that the quality of LIS research is improving. Hopefully there also is increasing recognition "that the results of research in a broad spectrum of effort extending well beyond librarianship will, in large measure, determine the future directions of library services and the nature of the profession itself"—a statement that still resonates fifty years later (American Library Association 1970).

The limitations of earlier research are not the only reasons for calling for better-conducted research. A number of positive justifications can be made for more rigorous research and, in particular, basic research. Connaway (2015, 4) also sees the opportunity that these challenges present:

> These challenges create opportunities for us, opportunities for engagement and progress. Our research can influence practice by engaging users and potential users of library services and systems in user-centered research approaches to develop services and systems that integrate into their work flows and lifestyles. By building on theoretical frameworks and previous research, new models and theories will emerge. We, as researchers, also should concentrate on relationship building with LIS practicing professionals and researchers in addition to researchers in other disciplines and within other institutions. I believe the African proverb, 'If you want to go fast, go alone. If you want to go far, go together,' is quite appropriate. Through collaboration and cumulative research, the scholarly record of LIS research will continue to grow and mature.

SUMMARY

This chapter has provided an overview of what research is, including major definitions (basic and applied), introductory discussion of methods (qualitative, quantitative, and mixed), and the benefits of research. In addition, it includes a discussion of the assessment imperative that is having an impact on all types of libraries, resulting in an evolving assessment culture, with a focus on identifying and measuring user-centered outcomes. The scholarly communication process is defined and discussed, as is the topic of data management and reuse. Each of the last two topics also feature text boxes of voices from the field to further illustrate their qualities (see text box 1.1 and text box 1.2). An additional text box provided practical recommendations on tips for time management when using social media (see text box 1.3).

This chapter also presented an overview of previous LIS research, including its challenges and past research record. It provided a summary of the most utilized research methods over the past years, with surveys, interviews, content analysis, and historical methods being some of the most frequently used methods. This overview also called attention to the research divide between practitioners and academics, the focus on quantitative methods with limited use of qualitative research methods and mixed methods. Recommendations for future research were suggested with an emphasis on the importance of LIS education that prepares students in basic research methods. Professional associations also have a responsibility to help train future researchers. The chapter concludes with an acknowledgment of promising signs for future developments in research, including increased collaboration and incorporation of multidisciplinary and qualitative methods. It also acknowledges the impact of the COVID-19 pandemic and the increased attention to equity, inclusion, and diversity as well as social justice initiatives that are following George Floyd and Breonna Taylor's deaths.

REFERENCES

"About ASIS&T." n.d. Association for Information Science and Technology (ASIS&T). Accessed May 25, 2020. https://www.asist.org/about.

Ackerman, Erin, Jennifer Hunter, and Zara T. Wilkinson. 2018. "The Availability and Effectiveness of Research Supports for Early Career Academic Librarians." *The Journal of Academic Librarianship* 44(5): 553–68. https://doi.org/10.1016/j.acalib.2018.06.001.

Alaiad, Ahmad, Yazan Alnsour, and Mohammad Alsharo. 2019. "Virtual Teams: Thematic Taxonomy, Constructs Model, and Future Research Directions." *IEEE Transactions on Professional Communication* 62(3): 211–38. https://doi.org/10.1109/TPC.2019.2929370.

American Library Association. 1970. *Policy Statement on the Role of Research in the American Library Association.* Chicago: American Library Association.

American Library Association. 2001. "Dissemination of Research in LIS." Text. http://www.ala.org/aboutala/offices/ors/orscommittees/dissemination/dissemination.

Auckland, Mary. 2012. "Re-Skilling for Research: An Investigation into the Role and Skills of Subject and Liaison Librarians Required to Effectively Support the Evolving Information Needs of Researchers." Research Libraries UK. http://https://www.rluk.ac.uk/wp-content/uploads/2014/02/RLUK-Re-skilling.pdf.

Bao, Xue-Ming. 2000. "An Analysis of the Research Areas of the Articles Published in C&RL and JAL between 1990 and 1999." *College & Research Libraries* 61(6): 536–44. https://doi.org/10.5860/crl.61.6.536.

Borgman, Christine L. 2007. *Scholarship in the Digital Age: Information, Infrastructure, and the Internet.* Cambridge, MA: The MIT Press. https://mitpress.mit.edu/books/scholarship-digital-age.

Borgman, Christine L. 2016. *Big Data, Little Data, No Data.* Cambridge, MA: The MIT Press. https://mitpress.mit.edu/books/big-data-little-data-no-data.

Bradley, Bret H., John E. Baur, Christopher G. Banford, and Bennett E. Postlethwaite. 2013. "Team Players and Collective Performance: How Agreeableness Affects Team Performance Over Time." *Small Group Research* 44(6): 680–711. https://doi.org/10.1177/1046496413507609.

Busha, Charles A. 1981. "Library Science Research: The Path to Progress." In *A Library Science Research Reader and Bibliographic Guide*, edited by Charles A. Busha. Littleton, CO: Libraries Unlimited.

Busha, Charles H., and Stephen P. Harter. 1980. *Research Methods in Librarianship: Techniques and Interpretation.* Cambridge, MA: Academic Press.

Cabanac, Guillaume, and James Hartley. 2013. "Issues of Work–Life Balance among JASIST Authors and Editors." *Journal of the American Society for Information Science and Technology* 64(10): 2182–86. https://doi.org/10.1002/asi.22888.

Chu, Heting. 2015. "Research Methods in Library and Information Science: A Content Analysis." *Library & Information Science Research* 37(1): 36–41. https://doi.org/10.1016/j.lisr.2014.09.003.

Clark, John. 1997. "The Research Process: A Beginner's Guide." *Health Libraries Review* 14(3): 145–55. https://doi.org/10.1046/j.1365-2532.1997.08585.x.

Connaway, Lynn Silipigni. 2014. "Why Libraries? A Call for Use-Centered Assessment." *Textos Universitaris de Biblioteconomia | Documentacio* 32: 1.

Connaway, Lynn Silipigni. 2015. "Research Challenges: The Pathway to Engagement and Progress." Presented at the ILL International Seminar on LIS Education and Research: Challenges of LIS Research, Barcelona, Spain, June 4.

Connaway, Lynn Silipigni. 2018a. "Rust Never Sleeps—Not for Rockers, Not for Libraries." *OCLC Next* (blog). August 1. https://blog.oclc.org/next/rust-never-sleeps-not-for-rockers-not-for-libraries.

Connaway, Lynn Silipigni. 2018b. "Advice from the Trenches: You're Not Alone." *Hanging Together* (blog). August 10. https://hangingtogether.org/?p=6790.

Connaway, Lynn Silipigni, William Harvey, Vanessa Kitzie, and Stephanie Mikitish. 2017. *Academic Library Impact: Improving Practice and Essential Areas to Research.* Chicago: Association of College and Research Libraries.

Connaway, Lynn Silipigni, and Ronald R. Powell. 2010. *Basic Research Methods for Librarians.* 5th ed. Santa Barbara, CA: Libraries Unlimited.

Connaway, Lynn Silipigni, and Marie L. Radford. 2013. "Academic Library Assessment: Beyond the Basics." Raynor Memorial Libraries, Marquette University, July 18.

Converse, W. R. 1984. "Research: What We Need, and What We Get." *Canadian Library Journal* 41(5): 235–41.

"Copyright & Intellectual Property." 2020. Association of Research Libraries. https://www.arl.org/category/our-priorities/advocacy-public-policy/copyright-and-ip.

Couture, Juliann, Jennie Gerke, and Jennifer Knievel. 2020. "Getting into the Club: Existence and Availability of Mentoring for Tenured Librarians in Academic Libraries." *College & Research Libraries* 81(4): 676–700. https://doi.org/10.5860/crl.81.4.676.

Cox, Andrew M., and Stephen Pinfield. 2014. "Research Data Management and Libraries: Current Activities and Future Priorities." *Journal of Librarianship and Information Science* 46(4): 299–316. https://doi.org/10.1177/0961000613492542.

Craver, Kathleen W. 2019. *School Libraries in a Time of Change: How to Survive and Thrive.* Santa Barbara, CA: ABC-CLIO.

"Creative Commons." 2020. Creative Commons. https://creativecommons.org.

Creswell, John W. 2011. *Educational Research: Planning, Conducting, and Evaluating Quantitative and Qualitative Research.* 4th ed. London: Pearson.

Cullen, Rowena, and Brenda Chawner. 2011. "Institutional Repositories, Open Access, and Scholarly Communication: A Study of Conflicting Paradigms." *The Journal of Academic Librarianship* 37(6): 460–70. https://doi.org/10.1016/j.acalib.2011.07.002.

Cummings, Jeff, and Alan R. Dennis. 2018. "Virtual First Impressions Matter: The Effect of Enterprise Social Networking Sites on Impression Formation in Virtual Teams." *MIS Quarterly* 42(3): 697–718. https://doi.org/10.25300/MISQ/2018/13202.

Denzin, Norman K., and Yvonna S. Lincoln. 2011. *The Sage Handbook of Qualitative Research.* 4th ed. Thousand Oaks, CA: Sage.

Dillon, Dennis. 2012. "Hand Wringing in Paradise: Scholarly Communication and the Intimate Twinges of Conscience." *Journal of Library Administration* 52(6–7): 609–25. https://doi.org/10.1080/01930826.2012.707957.

Faniel, Ixchel, and Lynn Connaway. 2018. "Librarians' Perspectives on the Factors Influencing Research Data Management Programs." *College & Research Libraries* 79(1): 100–19. https://doi.org/10.5860/crl.79.1.100.

Faniel, Ixchel M., Rebecca D. Frank, and Elizabeth Yakel. 2019. "Context from the Data Reuser's Point of View." *Journal of Documentation* 75(6): 1274–97. https://doi.org/10.1108/JD-08-2018-0133.

Faniel, Ixchel M., and Trond E. Jacobsen. 2010. "Reusing Scientific Data: How Earthquake Engineering Researchers Assess the Reusability of Colleagues'

Data." *Computer Supported Cooperative Work (CSCW)* 19(3–4): 355–75. https://doi.org/10.1007/s10606-010-9117-8.

Faniel, Ixchel M., Adam Kriesberg, and Elizabeth Yakel. 2012. "Data Reuse and Sensemaking among Novice Social Scientists." *Proceedings of the American Society for Information Science and Technology* 49(1): 1–10. https://doi.org /10.1002/meet.14504901068.

Faniel, Ixchel M., Adam Kriesberg, and Elizabeth Yakel. 2016. "Social Scientists' Satisfaction with Data Reuse." *Journal of the Association for Information Science and Technology* 67(6): 1404–16. https://doi.org/10.1002/asi .23480.

Faniel, Ixchel M., and Elizabeth Yakel. 2017. "Practices Do Not Make Perfect." In *Curating Research Data: Practical Strategies for Digital Repository*, edited by Lisa R. Johnston, 23. Chicago: Association of College and Research Libraries; a division of the American Library Association. http://www.ala.org/acrl /sites/ala.org.acrl/files/content/publications/booksanddigitalresources /digital/9780838988596_crd_v1_OA.pdf.

Field, Nick, and Rosie Tran. 2018. "Reinventing the Public Value of Libraries." *Public Library Quarterly* 37(2): 113–26. https://doi.org/10.1080/01616846.2017 .1422174.

Fourie, Ina, and Herman Fourie. 2013. "Getting It Done on Time." Edited by Mu-Yen Chen. *Library Hi Tech* 31(2): 391–400. https://doi.org/10.1108/07378831 311329121.

Glazier, Jack D., and Robert Grover. 2002. "A Multidisciplinary Framework for Theory Building." *Library Trends* 50(3): 317–29.

Goldhor, Herbert. 1972. *An Introduction to Scientific Research in Librarianship.* Urbana, IL: University of Illinois, Graduate School of Library Science.

Goldsmith, Kenneth. 2009. *I'll Be Your Mirror: The Selected Andy Warhol Interviews.* New York: Carroll & Graf.

Gray, Jamie M. 2017. *Becoming a Powerhouse Librarian: How to Get Things Done Right the First Time.* New York: Rowman & Littlefield.

Greifeneder, Elke. 2014. "Trends in Information Behaviour Research." *Proceedings of ISIC: The Information Behaviour Conference* 19(4). https://curis.ku.dk/ws /files/137513587/Trends_in_information_behaviour_research.htm.

Hahn, Trudi Bellardo, and Paul T. Jaeger. 2013. "From Practice to Publication: A Path for Academic Library Professionals." *College & Research Libraries News* 74(5): 238–42. https://doi.org/10.5860/crln.74.5.8944.

Haider, Jutta, and Fredrik Åström. 2017. "Dimensions of Trust in Scholarly Communication: Problematizing Peer Review in the Aftermath of John Bohannon's 'Sting' in Science." *Journal of the Association for Information Science and Technology* 68(2): 450–67. https://doi.org/10.1002/asi.23669.

Hernon, Peter. 2001. "Editorial: Components of the Research Process: Where Do We Need to Focus Attention?" *The Journal of Academic Librarianship* 27: 88.

Hernon, Peter, and Candy Schwartz. 2003. "We Will Not Rest on Our Laurels!" *Library & Information Science Research* 25(2): 125–26. https://doi.org/10 .1016/S0740-8188(03)00002-1.

Hernon, Peter, and Candy Schwartz. 2007. "A Need for a Greater Commitment in the Profession to Research and Evaluation." *Library & Information Science Research* 29(2): 161–62. https://doi.org/10.1016/j.lisr.2007.04.005.

Hider, Philip, and Bob Pymm. 2008. "Empirical Research Methods Reported in High-Profile LIS Journal Literature." *Library & Information Science Research* 30(2): 108–14. https://doi.org/10.1016/j.lisr.2007.11.007.

Hildreth, Charles R., and Selenay Aytac. 2007. "Recent Library Practitioner Research: A Methodological Analysis and Critique." *Journal of Education for Library and Information Science* 48(3): 236–58.

Hough, Brenda. 2018. *Crash Course in Time Management for Library Staff.* Santa Barbara, CA: ABC-CLIO.

Jackson, Sidney L. 1976. "Environment: Research." In *A Century of Service: Librarianship in the United States and Canada,* edited by Sidney L. Jackson, Eleanor B. Herling, and E. J. Josey, 341–54. Chicago: American Library Association.

Jaeger, Paul T., and John Carlo Bertot. 2013. "Research and Practice, Research in Practice: *Library Quarterly* in the Twenty-First Century, Part 3." *The Library Quarterly* 83(2): 91–93. https://doi.org/10.1086/669553.

Järvelin, Kalervo, and Pertti Vakkari. 1990. "Content Analysis of Research Articles in Library and Information Science." *Library & Information Science Research* 12(4): 395–421.

Jarvis Thomson, Judith, Catherine Elgin, David A. Hyman, Philip E. Rubin, and Jonathan Knight. 2006. "Research on Human Subjects: Academic Freedom and the Institutional Review Board | AAUP." https://www.aaup.org/report/research-human-subjects-academic-freedom-and-institutional-review-board.

Johnston, Lisa R., ed. 2017a. *Curating Research Data: Practical Strategies for Your Digital Repository.* Vol. One. Chicago: Association of College and Research Libraries; a division of the American Library Association. http://www.ala.org/acrl/sites/ala.org.acrl/files/content/publications/booksanddigitalresources/digital/9780838988596_crd_v1_OA.pdf.

Johnston, Lisa R., ed. 2017b. *Curating Research Data: A Handbook of Current Practice.* Vol. Two. Chicago: Association of College and Research Libraries; a division of the American Library Association. http://www.ala.org/acrl/sites/ala.org.acrl/files/content/publications/booksanddigitalresources/digital/9780838988633_crd_v2_OA.pdf.

Julien, Heidi, Jen (J. L.) Pecoskie, and Kathleen Reed. 2011. "Trends in Information Behavior Research, 1999–2008: A Content Analysis." *Library & Information Science Research* 33(1): 19–24. https://doi.org/10.1016/j.lisr.2010.07.014.

Keener, Molly, Joy Kirchner, Sarah Shreeves, and Lee Van Orsdel. 2015. "10 Things You Should Know about . . . Scholarly Communication." *Copyright, Fair Use, Scholarly Communication, Etc.*, March. https://digitalcommons.unl.edu/scholcom/47.

Kennedy, Marie, and Kristine Brancolini. 2012. "Academic Librarian Research: A Survey of Attitudes, Involvement, and Perceived Capabilities." *College & Research Libraries*, September. https://digitalcommons.lmu.edu/librarian_pubs/36.

Kumasi, Kafi D., Deborah H. Charbonneau, and Dian Walster. 2013. "Theory Talk in the Library Science Scholarly Literature: An Exploratory Analysis." *Library & Information Science Research* 35(3): 175–80. https://doi.org/10.1016/j.lisr.2013.02.004.

Kumpulainen, Sisko. 1991. "Library and Information Science Research in 1975: Content Analysis of the Journal Articles." *Libri; København* 41(1): 59–76.

Lauseng, Deborah L., Carmen Howard, and Emily M. Johnson. 2019. "Professional Development in Evidence-Based Practice: Course Survey Results to Inform Administrative Decision Making." *Journal of the Medical Library Association: JMLA* 107(3): 394–402. https://doi.org/10.5195/jmla.2019.628.

Lee, Marta K. 2011. *Mentoring in the Library: Building for the Future.* Chicago: ALA Editions.

Liu, Guoying, and Le Yang. 2019. "Popular Research Topics in the Recent Journal Publications of Library and Information Science." *The Journal of Academic Librarianship* 45(3): 278–87. https://doi.org/10.1016/j.acalib.2019.04.001.

Losee, Robert M., and Karen A. Worley. 1993. *Research and Evaluation for Information Professionals.* 2nd ed. San Diego: Academic Press.

Luo, Lili, and Margaret McKinney. 2015. "JAL in the Past Decade: A Comprehensive Analysis of Academic Library Research." *The Journal of Academic Librarianship* 41(2): 123–29. https://doi.org/10.1016/j.acalib.2015.01.003.

Matusiak, Krystyna K. 2020. "Studying Visual Literacy: Research Methods and the Use of Visual Evidence." *IFLA Journal* 46(2): 172–81. https://doi.org/10.1177/0340035219886611.

Matusiak, Krystyna K., and Kawanna Bright. 2020. "Teaching Research Methods in Master's-Level LIS Programs: The United States Perspective." *Journal of Education for Library and Information Science* 61(3): 357–82. https://doi.org/10.3138/jelis.61.3.2020-0001.

McCaffrey, Ciara. 2019. "Transforming the University Library One Step at a Time: A Ten Year LibQUAL+Review: New Review of Academic Librarianship: Vol 25, No 1." *New Review of Academic Librarianship* 25(1): 59–75.

McClure, Charles R., and Ann Bishop. 1989. "The Status of Research in Library/Information Science: Guarded Optimism." *College & Research Libraries* 50(2): 127–43. https://doi.org/10.5860/crl_50_02_127.

McKnight, Michelynn. 2009. "Professional Publication: Yes, You Can!" *The Journal of Academic Librarianship* 35(2): 115–16. https://doi.org/10.1016/j.acalib.2009.01.001.

Miles, Matthew B., A. Michael Huberman, and Johnny Saldaña. 2020. *Qualitative Data Analysis: A Methods Sourcebook.* 4th ed. Thousand Oaks, CA: Sage. https://www.vitalsource.com/products/qualitative-data-analysis-matthew-b-miles-v9781506353081.

Monzani, Lucas, Pilar Ripoll, Jose María Peiró, and Rolf Van Dick. 2014. "Loafing in the Digital Age: The Role of Computer Mediated Communication in the Relation between Perceived Loafing and Group Affective Outcomes." *Computers in Human Behavior* 33 (April): 279–85. https://doi.org/10.1016/j.chb.2014.01.013.

Muller, Robert H. 1967. "The Research Mind in Library Education and Practice." *Library Journal* 92: 1129.

Oakleaf, Megan J. 2010. *The Value of Academic Libraries: A Comprehensive Research Review and Report.* Chicago: Association of College and Research Libraries, American Library Association.

Oud, Joanne. 2008. "Adjusting to the Workplace: Transitions Faced by New Academic Librarians." *College & Research Libraries* 69(3): 252–67. https://doi.org/10.5860/crl.69.3.252.

Park, Ji-Hong, and Jiyoung Shim. 2011. "Exploring How Library Publishing Services Facilitate Scholarly Communication." *Journal of Scholarly Publishing* 43(1): 76–89. https://doi.org/10.3138/jsp.43.1.76.

"Program for Early Career Excellence (PECE)." 2020. Office of the Executive Vice President for Academic Affairs. https://academicaffairs.rutgers.edu/program-early-career-excellence.

Pung, Caroline, Ann Clarke, and Laurie Patten. 2004. "Measuring the Economic Impact of the British Library." *New Review of Academic Librarianship* 10(1): 79–102. https://doi.org/10.1080/13614530412331296826.

Radford, Marie L., Lynn Silipigni Connaway, Gary Burnett, and Suzie Allard. 2015. "Virtual Windows: Research Collaborations across Culture, Space, and

Time." Panel presentation presented at the 2015 ALISE Conference, Chicago, January 27.

Radford, Marie L., Vanessa Kitzie, Stephanie Mikitish, Diana Floegel, Gary P. Radford, and Lynn Silipigni Connaway. 2020. "'People Are Reading Your Work,' Scholarly Identity and Social Networking Sites." *Journal of Documentation* (ahead-of-print). https://doi.org/10.1108/JD-04-2019-0074.

"Research | Definition of Research by Merriam-Webster Online Dictionary." 2020. Merriam-Webster. https://www.merriam-webster.com/dictionary/research.

Robbins, Jane B. 1990. "Research in Information Service Practice." *Library & Information Science Research* 12: 127.

Rush, Elizabeth Barrera. 2020. *The Efficient Library: Ten Simple Changes That Save Time and Improve Service.* Santa Barbara, CA: ABC-CLIO.

Rysavy, Monica D. T., and Russell Michalak. 2020. "Working from Home: How We Managed Our Team Remotely with Technology." *Journal of Library Administration* 60(5): 532–42.

Sanjeeva, Meghana. 2018. "Research Data Management: A New Role for Academic/Research Librarians." JM Patel College, Mumbai. https://www.research gate.net/publication/323604761_RESEARCH_DATA_MANAGEMENT_A _NEW_ROLE_FOR_ACADEMICRESEARCH_LIBRARIANS.

Sassen, Catherine, and Diane Wahl. 2014. "Fostering Research and Publication in Academic Libraries." *College & Research Libraries* 75(4): 458–91. https://doi .org/10.5860/crl.75.4.458.

"Scholarly Communication Toolkit: Scholarly Communication Overview." n.d. Accessed October 22, 2020. https://acrl.libguides.com/scholcomm/toolkit /home.

"Scholars & Scholarship." n.d. Association of Research Libraries. Accessed October 22, 2020. https://www.arl.org/category/our-priorities/scholars-scholarship.

Scott, Muriel E. 2013. "'Communicate through the Roof': A Case Study Analysis of the Communicative Rules and Resources of an Effective Global Virtual Team." *Communication Quarterly* 61(3): 301–18. https://doi.org/10.1080 /01463373.2013.776987.

Shaughnessy, Thomas W. 1976. "Library Research in the 70's: Problems and Prospects." *California Librarian* 37: 44–52.

Shera, Jesse Hauk. 1964. "Darwin, Bacon, and Research in Librarianship." *Library Trends* 13(1): 143.

Shera, Jesse Hauk. 1972. *The Foundations of Education for Librarianship.* New York: Becker & Hayes.

Shorish, Yasmeen, and Nathan Hall. 2019. "Creating the ACRL Research Agenda for Scholarly Communication: A Move towards More Equitable, Open Systems." *College & Research Libraries News* 80(8): 430–42. https://doi.org/10 .5860/crln.80.8.430.

Smigielski, Elizabeth M., Melissa A. Laning, and Caroline M. Daniels. 2014. "Funding, Time, and Mentoring: A Study of Research and Publication Support Practices of ARL Member Libraries." *Journal of Library Administration* 54(4): 261–76. https://doi.org/10.1080/01930826.2014.924309.

Stokes, Donald E. 1997. *Pasteur's Quadrant: Basic Science and Technological Innovation.* Washington, DC: Brookings Institution Press.

Sugimoto, Cassidy R., Andrew Tsou, Sara Naslund, Alexandra Hauser, Melissa Brandon, Danielle Winter, Cody Behles, and S. Craig Finlay. 2014. "Beyond Gatekeepers of Knowledge: Scholarly Communication Practices of Academic Librarians and Archivists at ARL Institutions." *College & Research Libraries* 75(2): 145–61. https://doi.org/10.5860/crl12-398.

Sullo, Elaine. 2019. "Seven Years of Noise Reduction Strategies in an Academic Library Improve Students' Perceptions of Quiet Space, Especially among Graduate Students." *Evidence Based Library and Information Practice* 14(4): 179–81. https://doi.org/10.18438/eblip29637.

"Task Force on Academic Library Outcomes Assessment Report." 2006. Text. Association of College & Research Libraries (ACRL). July 25. http://www.ala.org/acrl/publications/whitepapers/taskforceacademic.

Tavernier, Willa. 2020. "COVID-19 Demonstrates the Value of Open Access: What Happens next?" *College & Research Libraries News* 81(5): 226–30. https://doi.org/10.5860/crln.81.5.226.

Tenopir, Carol, Elizabeth D. Dalton, Suzie Allard, Mike Frame, Ivanka Pjesivac, Ben Birch, Danielle Pollock, and Kristina Dorsett. 2015. "Changes in Data Sharing and Data Reuse Practices and Perceptions among Scientists Worldwide." Edited by Peter van den Besselaar. *PLOS ONE* 10(8): e0134826. https://doi.org/10.1371/journal.pone.0134826.

Tenopir, Carol, Natalie M. Rice, Suzie Allard, Lynn Baird, Josh Borycz, Lisa Christian, Bruce Grant, Robert Olendorf, and Robert J. Sandusky. 2020. "Data Sharing, Management, Use, and Reuse: Practices and Perceptions of Scientists Worldwide." *PLOS ONE* 15 (March). https://doi.org/10.1371/journal.pone.0229003.

Tenopir, Carol, Robert J. Sandusky, Suzie Allard, and Ben Birch. 2014. "Research Data Management Services in Academic Research Libraries and Perceptions of Librarians." *Library & Information Science Research* 36(2): 84–90. https://doi.org/10.1016/j.lisr.2013.11.003.

Todd, Ross J. 2009. "School Librarianship and Evidence Based Practice: Progress, Perspectives, and Challenges." *Evidence Based Library and Information Practice* 4(2): 78–96. https://doi.org/10.18438/B8BS62.

Todd, Ross J. 2015. "Evidence-Based Practice and School Libraries: Interconnections of Evidence, Advocacy, and Actions." *Knowledge Quest* 43(3): 8–15.

Tracy, Sarah J. 2013. *Qualitative Research Methods: Collecting Evidence, Crafting Analysis, Communicating Impact.* Hoboken, NJ: Wiley-Blackwell.

"Value of Academic and Research Libraries." 2011. Text. Association of College & Research Libraries (ACRL). September 13. http://www.ala.org/acrl/issues/value.

Warren, Scott, and Kim Duckett. 2010. "'Why Does Google Scholar Sometimes Ask for Money?' Engaging Science Students in Scholarly Communication and the Economics of Information." *Journal of Library Administration* 50(4): 349–72. https://doi.org/10.1080/01930821003667021.

Weimann, Peter, Michael Pollock, Elsje Scott, and Irwin Brown. 2013. "Enhancing Team Performance through Tool Use: How Critical Technology-Related Issues Influence the Performance of Virtual Project Teams." *IEEE Transactions on Professional Communication* 56(4): 332–53. https://doi.org/10.1109/TPC.2013.2287571.

Wiegand, Wayne, comp. 1999. "Libraries in the U.S. Timeline." *American Libraries* 30(11).

Wiegand, Wayne A. 2015. "'Tunnel Vision and Blind Spots' Reconsidered: Part of Our Lives (2015) as a Test Case." *The Library Quarterly* 85(4): 347–70. https://doi.org/10.1086/682731.

Wildemuth, Barbara M. 2017. *Applications of Social Research Methods to Questions in Information and Library Science.* 2nd ed. Santa Barbara, CA: ABC-CLIO.

Wusu, Oluwaseyi H., and Nneka G. Lazarus. 2018. "Major Trends in LIS Research: A Bibliometric Analysis." *Library Philosophy and Practice*, 1–21.

Yilmaz, Gamze, and Jorge Peña. 2014. "The Influence of Social Categories and Interpersonal Behaviors on Future Intentions and Attitudes to Form Subgroups in Virtual Teams." *Communication Research* 41(3): 333–52. https://doi.org/10.1177/0093650212443696.

Zweizig, Douglas L. 1976. "With Our Eye on the User: Needed Research for Information and Referral in the Public Library." *Drexel Library Quarterly* 12: 48–58.

2

Developing the Research Study

According to Leedy and Ormrod (2019), "More time and expense are wasted by going off half-prepared—with only a vague set of ideas and procedures—than in any other way" (82).

PLANNING FOR RESEARCH: GETTING STARTED

The first question that a student or researcher may well ask is "Where do I begin?" What is the best way to get started? In 1899 the following words were stenciled over the Smithsonian Institution's south entrance transom by order of its secretary, Samuel P. Langley): "Knowledge Begins in Wonder" ("The Children's Room in the Smithsonian Institution Building Knowledge Begins in Wonder, Introduction," 2015). Langley realized his dream that the Smithsonian should be one of the first museums in the country to have a children's room, to stimulate and satisfy children's as well as adults' sense of wonder and curiosity. It is this wonder and curiosity of researchers that leads to scholarly inquiry. Leedy and Ormrod (2004) pointed out that "by asking questions, we strike the first spark igniting a chain reaction that leads to the research process. An inquisitive mind is the beginning of research" (85). Carlton Cuse reminded us that the creative process is dynamic and that one needs to be open to its evolution: "The creative process is not like a situation where you get struck by a single lightning bolt. You have ongoing discoveries, and there are ongoing creative revelations. Yes, it's really helpful to be marching toward a specific destination, but, along the way, you must allow yourself room for your ideas to blossom, take root, and grow" (Ryan 2010). In research, sometimes you can start out going in one direction, but end up someplace else entirely. It is not unusual for research directions and especially findings to be surprising, which can help to hold one's interest throughout the process. Let's take a deeper look into the totality of what is involved in the research journey.

Philosophical Underpinnings and Assumptions

Creswell and Poth (2016) remind us that "whether we are aware of it or not, we always bring certain beliefs and *philosophical assumptions* to our research. . . . The difficulties lie first in becoming aware of these assumptions and beliefs" since frequently "these philosophical assumptions inform our choice of theories that guide our research" (15). Our philosophical orientation is defined as a "worldview that underlies and informs methodology and methods" (Corbin and Strauss 2014, 22).

Research is as much about perspective as it is about method, if it is thought of as a way of thinking about and seeing social reality. Experts have identified four philosophical assumptions that people make when undertaking research, also known as epistemologies and ontologies. These assumptions include ontological, epistemological, axiological, and methodological (Creswell and Poth 2016). Let's take these one at a time.

Ontology is the study of the nature of being. It investigates how objects, concepts, and other entities are represented in our area of interest and what are the relationships among them. Ontology asks "what is the nature of reality?" (Creswell and Poth 2016, 20). In qualitative or critical approaches to research, for example, the idea of multiple realities can be embraced. Phenomenological research accepts that different individuals taking part in a study can view their experiences quite differently (Creswell and Poth 2016). In quantitative approaches, there may be a more scientific approach that rejects the idea of multiple reality in favor of discovering one scientific truth that can be discovered. Ontologies often are represented as hierarchical structuring of knowledge about things by subcategorizing them by essential, relevant, and/or cognitive qualities.

Epistemology is a branch of philosophy that centers on the nature and origin of knowledge. It asks the questions "how do we know what we know?" as well as "what counts as knowledge? How are knowledge claims justified? What is the relationship between the researcher and that being researched?" (Creswell and Poth 2016, 20). For qualitative researchers, an underpinning philosophy is to get as close an understanding of participants as possible. For example, the ethnographer must thus engage in real-life settings or enter the "field" to get a clear, 360-degree view of the scene being investigated. For quantitative researchers, knowledge is constructed more concretely through carefully constructed experiments, trials, and numerical data.

Axiological assumptions concern the underlying value structure of the research. They ask "what is the role of values?" (Creswell and Poth 2016, 20). In qualitative work, the subjective role of the researcher is acknowledged. This means that "inquirers admit the value-laden nature of the study and actively report their values and biases as well as the value-laden nature of information gathered from the field. We say that researchers 'position themselves' by identifying their 'positionality in relation to the context and setting of the research'"

(Creswell and Poth 2016, 21). In quantitative research, every effort is made to reduce or eliminate all bias and to control for possible confounding factors or variables.

Methodological assumptions are concerned with the procedures and practices of research, asking the questions "what is the process of research? What is the language of research?" (Creswell and Poth 2016, 21) As discussed below, here it is considered whether we will take an inductive (collecting data and deriving findings) or deductive (starting with a theoretical framework and top down) approach. In qualitative research, as will be discussed in chapter 9, an inductive frame is used, research questions or problematics are explored, and method can be flexible, depending on unfolding analysis. In quantitative research, as discussed in chapter 4, a deductive frame is used which involves hypothesis testing and carefully constructed methods that mostly follow established practice.

Paradigms That Shape Research Development

Paradigms are basic belief systems that are based on the four philosophical assumptions we have just discussed. From a scientific perspective, Kuhn (2012) put forth the idea of a paradigm and identified six ways of knowing: authority, religion, tradition, intuition, creativity, and science. Paradigms "represents a worldview that defines, for its holder, the nature of the 'world,' the individual's place in it, and the range of possible relationships to that world and its parts" (Guba and Lincoln 1993, 107). According to Bates (2005, 2), Kuhn considered a paradigm to be "the metatheory, the theory, the methodology, and the ethos, all combined of a discipline or specialty." For a longer discussion of metatheory, theories of knowledge, and basic domain assumptions of research in LIS, see discussion by Jack D. Glazier (2017).

Let's take a look at four major paradigms that shape social science research: positivist, postpositivist, interpretive, and critical.

Positivist assumptions have dominated social science research up until the 1980s (Lindlof and Taylor 2019). According to Guba, the positivist paradigm embraces the idea of realism, that there is a real world out there waiting and needing to be discovered. It is governed by natural laws and mechanisms that are fixed. Following from the idea of realism is objectivism that posits that since a real world exists, it must therefore be studied objectively with the researcher maintaining a distant and noninteracting position to exclude values and bias from tainting or influencing the research. Positivist approaches also take an experimental/manipulative stance in which questions and hypotheses are formulated in advance and then empirically tested under controlled conditions (Guba 1990).

The *postpositive paradigm* takes a different position. "Postpositivists do not believe in strict cause and effect but rather recognize that all cause and effect is a probability that may or may not occur. Postpositivism has the elements of being reductionistic, logical, empirical, cause-and-effect oriented and deterministic based on a priori theories" (Creswell and Poth 2016, 23). Researchers embracing postpositivist viewpoints "believe in multiple perspectives from participants rather than a single reality, and espouse rigorous methods of qualitative data collection and analysis. They use multiple levels of data analysis for rigor, employ computer programs to assist in their analysis, encourage the use of validity approaches, and write their qualitative studies in the form of scientific reports, with a structure resembling quantitative articles (e.g., problem, questions, data collection, results, conclusions)" (Creswell and Poth 2016, 23–24). Postpositivists believe that humans interact in patterned ways that can be identified and that reduction of bias in research is both attainable and desirable and may use mixed methods that include both qualitative and quantitative methods, regarding both of these as legitimate for conducting research (Lindlof and Taylor 2019).

The *interpretive/social constructivism paradigm* holds that realities are socially constructed by and between individuals in their expressive and interpretive experiences. These realities are multiple, simultaneous, and local, and thus research should focus on a deep understanding of human actions, motives, perceptions, and feelings. Truth is constructed within experience, and any truth claims are positional and partial with true knowledge discovered through prolonged immersion and extensive conversation/dialog in real-world social settings. Interpretive scholars take the stance that research is holistic and descriptive, establishing meaning in the totality of experience (Lindlof and Taylor 2019). The interpretive and constructivist worldview is found in phenomenological studies and in Charmaz's (2014) grounded theory approach.

The *postmodern paradigm* is focused on critiques that aim to change people's ways of thinking. "The basic concept is that knowledge claims must be set within the conditions of the world today and in the multiple perspectives of class, race, gender, and other group affiliations" (Creswell and Poth 2016, 26). Examples of postmodern thinking can be found in the work of Foucault, Derrida, Lyotard, Giroux, Friere, and others (Creswell and Poth 2016). These writers concern themselves with impacts on underrepresented or oppressed groups as a result of the presence of hierarchies, power structures, and institutional control.

The *critical paradigm* arises from the critical tradition of the modernist, Frankfurt school as seen in the work of Marx, Horkheimer, Adorno, Marcuse, Habermas, and others. It is concerned with problematics surrounding control and injustice from the evolution of industrial/corporate capitalism. Under this umbrella are usually grouped approaches that include feminist theory, postcolonialism studies, critical race theory, cultural studies, queer theory, and disability theories. Critical theorists view communication as always or already mediated by power relations and as socially and historically constructed (Lindlof and Taylor 2019).

These assumptions and paradigmatic frames, along with the methods that they shape and inform, will be further discussed in the chapters to follow. It is useful to consider these key (and sometimes subtle, as opposed to overt) underpinnings to scholarly investigation and keep them in mind, as they have a critical role to play in the initial and evolving plan that is made for any research project. Clearly, these assumptions also "often frame the more specific decisions you will make when designing a research study"

(Wildemuth 2017, 115). Below, more of the nitty-gritty of research design and practice are discussed.

A General Outline for Research

Given differences in subject disciplines and/or the types of data to be collected, researchers find it necessary to employ a variety of specific methodologies, as demonstrated in other chapters in this book, but it is important to note that mainstream quantitative and qualitative research generally follow fairly standard outlines and exhibit similar characteristics. In developing a research study, the LIS investigator typically begins with a question about something of interest, which can be a course assignment, thesis, or a new idea or project that can be part of a long-standing research agenda. For example, after preparing an annual report, a college librarian may notice a trend in the circulation, downloads, and gate-count statistics and wonder why library use seems to be declining, or better yet, increasing. A public librarian might attend an innovative workshop on library use of social media such as Instagram (perhaps spotlighting popular hashtags such as #Bookstagram or #LibrariesOfInstagram or #BookfaceFriday) at a regional conference and begin to wonder about social media trends, as well as the impact on community-building efforts in public libraries around the country (Springen 2019). As early as this point, and throughout the development of the research study, the investigator is likely to benefit from a thorough review of the literature to see what is known already about this particular question or area of interest. A secondary purpose for the literature review is to identify what gaps exist to uncover what has not yet been discovered. Finding a gap in the literature can result in an "aha" moment, when researchers figure out how they can make an important contribution to the LIS literature, as well as satisfy their own curiosity. Also, locating a gap in extant literature can be important when seeking to publish in journals or make presentations at conferences. Editors and conference organizers are eager to publish work that addresses an aspect of a significant problem that has not yet been explored or is being explored (perhaps even replicated) in a new context or using different methods.

Literature Review of Related Research

The review of related research, or literature review, is perhaps one of the most important initial steps in embarking on a new research project. It is worth noting that there is a misunderstanding about the timing of the literature review for the grounded theory approach (Glaser 1978; Glaser and Strauss 1967). Glaser and Strauss's text (1967) suggests that the literature review might distort data interpretation and should be delayed until analysis has been finished. This aligns with a more classical approach to grounded theory. Kathy Charmaz, a constructivist grounded theorist, asks, "When should you delve into the literature? How do you go about doing it? What do you need to cover? The place of the literature review in grounded theory research has long been both disputed and misunderstood" (Charmaz 2014, 306). She said that "now grounded theorists increasingly recognize that a lack of familiarity with relevant literatures is unlikely and untenable. . . . Researchers typically hold perspectives and possess knowledge in their fields before they decide on a research topic. Examining committees expect such expertise, funding agencies require it" (Charmaz 2014, 306). Charmaz (2014) advocates adopting the "theoretical agnosticism" stance of Henwood and Pidgeon (2003). "Consider treating extant concepts as problematic and then look for the extent to which their characteristics are lived and understood, not as given in textbooks" (Charmaz 2014, 306).

Charmaz's questions regarding what to cover and how to go about doing a literature review are important for any project, including master's and doctoral coursework. A sound literature review identifies, cites, and provides a brief overview of related research studies. The literature review describes the foundation on which the proposed study will be built by discussing published scholarship done by others, evaluating their methodologies and findings, and stating how the proposed research will differ. It is not just a string of citations, but rather is a presentation of an argument that builds to the gap identification and the rationale for the problem statement for the study that is being undertaken. Nonresearch reports, blog posts, and opinion pieces should generally be excluded from consideration, unless they are particularly insightful or represent all that has been written on the problem, which may be the case for leading-edge issues. In a thorough research review, it is desirable, if not essential, that related research in other fields be cited as well. The LIS research environment of the past has not had a strong relationship with other disciplines and has often lacked connection with previous research, outside of and also within its domain (Connaway 2015). Ignoring what has been discovered or theorized outside of LIS can be lead to "blind spots and tunnel vision," according to Wiegand (2015). In some cases, the research done in other fields may be all that exists of any real importance.

It is important to set boundaries, since the literature review cannot cover everything. Identify the major areas of research to cover. Some find it useful to draw a Venn diagram of topics to include. This diagram also can help to identify topics that will not be included. After all, time is not unlimited, although surveying the literature can be seen as a lengthy and iterative process, especially for long-term projects, such as theses or dissertations. The literature review should thus be selective and should group the cited studies in a logical fashion that essentially allows the researcher to demonstrate expertise and establish credibility on the topic for anyone who will read or review this work (especially for dissertation work, publication, or presentation). It should be an easy task for the reader to see the connections among cited studies and to quickly grasp the important benchmark works and authors that the proposed study will build on.

Also usually included in the literature review is a section that establishes the theoretical or conceptual framework for the subsequent research project, particularly the development of the hypothesis (for quantitative work), research questions (for qualitative work), or problem statement (for critical methods). This review also helps to identify the best approach to seeking a solution to the problem. It answers these questions: What is already known? What methods have been used in prior work? What are the strengths and weaknesses of this scholarship? Before continuing with the development of the research study, it is essential to perform this thorough scan of the scholarly landscape.

One way to begin this process is to delve into indexes and publications that identify in-progress and completed research in LIS. A selective list follows:

Information Research Watch International (Published by Cambridge Scientific Abstracts London, 2000–). Published bimonthly in electronic format, this journal is intended for those who need to keep abreast of research and development work in international librarianship, information science, archives, documentation, and the information aspects of other fields. Each entry provides an overview of a research project and information about personnel, duration, funding, and references.

Inspec (Boston: EBSCO, Created by the UK Institution of Engineering and Technology, 1969–). An international bibliographic database that contains over 18 million records abstracts and indexing for nearly 5,000 journals, over 2,500 conference proceedings, patents, reports, and videos and other literature. Its audience includes librarians and information scientists.

The Library and Book Trade Almanac (formerly the *Bowker Annual*) (New Jersey: Information Today, 1956–). Annual. It includes a yearly report from the ALA Office for Research and Statistics, and also summarizes important grant projects and features a list of "Awards and Grants That Honor and Support Excellent Research" for the current year. It lists award winners from professional LIS organizations, including the Association for Library and Information Science Education (ALISE).

Library and Information Research (formerly *Library and Information Research News*) (London: CILIP, 1970s–). A quarterly publication from CILIP, the British counterpart to ALA, that includes refereed and nonrefereed papers, news, and book reviews, available at https://lirgjournal.org.uk/index.php/lir.

Library and Information Science Abstracts (LISA) (San Diego: ProQuest, 1969–). An international abstracting and indexing tool designed for library professionals and other information specialists. Covers 1969 to present and is updated every two weeks.

Library, Information Science, & Technology Abstracts (LISTA) (London: Library Association, 1969–). This basic and general service is updated regularly and provided free by EBSCO via http://www.libraryresearch.com. It has some links to full text but primarily contains citations and abstracts.

Library Literature & Information Science Full Text (formerly *Library Literature*) (Boston: EBSCO, 1934–). Updated daily this index cites journal articles, books, and other published research studies, with coverage from 1984 to present, full text from 1997, differs by publication.

New Review of Information Networking (formerly *New Review of Information and Library Research*) (London: Taylor & Francis, 1995). A biannual publication that covers topics such as the behavior of the network user, the roles of networks in teaching and learning, implications of networks for library services, and the development of information strategies, available at https://www.tandfonline.com/loi/rinn20.

ProQuest Dissertations & Theses Global (formerly *Dissertation Abstracts International*) (San Diego: ProQuest, 1938–). This database is continually updated, covering dissertations and master's theses, internationally from 1637, US from 1861 to present, full text from 1997. It is available only in electronic format, with over 4 million titles and over 2 million in full text. Dissertations and theses are useful for researchers, as they provide excellent examples of exhaustive literature reviews, sound problem statements, and hypotheses or research questions.

Social Science Research Network (SSRN, http://www.ssrn.com) (Amsterdam: Elsevier) encourages the early distribution of research results by publishing submitted abstracts and the dissemination of scholarly papers. According to their website, SSRN contains 950,000+ research papers from ~500,000 researchers in more than fifty disciplines. You can subscribe to their newsletter for free.

Professional associations also are sources of information about in-progress and/or recently completed research. The American Library Association (ALA) Library Research Round Table (LRRT, http://www.ala.org/lrrt) has a strong research focus. Yearly membership is free for graduate students who are student members of ALA. Its objectives are to extend and improve library research; to offer programs aimed at describing, criticizing, and disseminating library research findings; and to educate ALA members about research techniques and their usefulness in obtaining information with which to reach administrative decisions and solve problems. LRRT has a virtual mentoring program that matches mentees with mentors based on research interests (http://www.ala.org/rt/lrrt /membershipprogram). Those interested in library history might wish to join the Library History Round Table (LHRT). According to its website, the LHRT's mission is "to facilitate communication among scholars and students of library history, to be active in issues, such as preservation, that concern library historians" (ala.org /ala/lhrt/lhrthome.htm). ALA's Office for Research and Statistics (ORS, https:// www.ala.org/ala/ors/researchstatistics.htm) also serves as a vital source of information about current research in progress. According to its website:

> The mission of the Office for Research and Statistics (ORS) is to provide leadership and expert advice to ALA staff, members and public on all matters related to research and statistics about libraries, librarians, and other library staff, represent the Association to Federal agencies on these issues; and initiate projects needed to expand the knowledge base of the field through research and the collection of useful statistics. ("Office for Research and Statistics" 2020)

ORS also offers Librarian and Research Knowledge Space (LARKS, http:// www.ala.org/research/larks), a site that curates research-related resources and information for LIS students, librarians, and researchers. By clicking the "Research Methods" button (http://www.ala.org/research/larks/research methods) one can find an excellent list of places to start learning about methods, including a list of wikis and open-access tools. LARKS also features a table of research methods with brief descriptions and examples (http://www .ala.org/research/larks/researchmethods). Additionally, there is a button for LIS students (http://ala.org/tools/research/larks/students) that provides links to Research Terminology, and a brief explanation of Philosophy of Research Approaches "(or a brief push to learn about the Pesky Paradigms of Positivism, Post-Positivism and Interpretivism)."

Many reports of completed research and research in progress are available on the web. The federally funded Institute for Museum and Library Services (IMLS) (http://imls.gov) funds numerous grant projects every year and provides information on completed and in-progress research. In addition, an online database, Federal Research in Progress (available via EBSCOhost), occasionally includes library-related research being performed under the sponsorship of US government agencies, such as the IMLS. All of its records include title, principal investigator, performing organization, and sponsoring organization.

In the course of the literature review, key articles will be unearthed, each of which should have a bibliography, which can be mined for citations to additional articles and papers to read (aka the pearl-growing technique) (Bates 1981). Once the investigator has tracked down all the important leads and read as much relevant literature as possible, given time constraints and attention span, attention must be given to curate these resources in an online citation manager, like Zotero or RefWorks, taking notes and identifying key quotes. When the researcher is ready, it is time to draft the literature review. One way to start is with a traditional outline, a plan for the major and minor sections of the literature review. Organizing by concepts is usually more effective than chronological order, although if providing historical context for a study is important, part of the review may be chronological. It is vital to make sure that you include the major authors and benchmark works, as well as the most current information on the topic. Writing the review may take several drafts and, as previously noted, should not just be a series of cites that seem to be randomly strung together. Rather, with the topic organization, similar articles can be further grouped by method, findings, or theoretical orientation. It is recommended that drafts be shared with colleagues to get feedback and constructive criticism so that additional insights and suggestions can be incorporated. It is frequently the case that the literature review can take a long time to perfect, so at some point it must be set aside to actually design and conduct the research itself. For more about the literature review, see chapter 3.

IDENTIFICATION OF THE PROBLEM

Usually in concert with the literature review, the researcher needs to identify/articulate the problem at hand. The research problem is essentially the topic to be investigated or what needs to be known. It is assumed that individuals plan a research study because they have identified some problem worthy of investigation. Returning to our academic librarian facing a downward trend in library use, they may have a hunch that library use is low because the majority of the students do not have adequate library skills. The actual problem facing the librarian may be lack of knowledge or experience using the library systems and services, which ultimately tend to be evidenced by low library use. The librarian also may conclude that they are actually confronted with several problems, or at least subproblems of the main problem. For example, the researcher may need to consider specific differences in library expertise or academic levels, such as undergraduate or graduate students.

"Formulating a research topic lies at the foundation stage of a research project that has a major impact and effect on the subsequent stages and outcomes of a research project," according to Ameen, Batool, and Naveed (2019). But given the primary importance of identifying a problem before conducting research, where and how are problems found? The answer to the first part of this question is that problems can be found in a variety of places, as discussed above and in chapter 1. In response to the second part of the question, a variety of approaches can be taken. For example, one important, if not essential, approach for identifying problems for research in a given field is to develop a thorough knowledge and understanding of that field. More specifically, the would-be researcher should be fully familiar with the known facts and accepted ideas in the field; be knowledgeable about previous, related research in the area; and be aware of gaps in knowledge in the field or in areas that have not been previously researched.

These objectives can be met, at least in part, by the broad literature review discussed above. Doctoral dissertations are particularly good sources of suggestions for further research. Another potentially useful activity can be checking new bibliographies, published literature reviews, curated websites, and other lists of related materials. Many journal articles include a section that outlines recommendations for future research, some specifically calling attention to a research agenda. For example, Barriage and Hicks (2020) propose this list of themes and ideas for future research on the role that mobile apps can play in information research that arose from their research that describes two recent studies that used mobile apps (specifically PixStori and EthOS) in exploring childrens' and young adults' information practices. They describe a research agenda and provide the below themes (bolding added) with bullets on ideas for future research:

Effects of mobile apps on data quality
- Comparison of data produced through mobile apps to other established methods of photo-elicitation
- Comparison of apps with use of image-based social networks for photo-elicitation studies

Co-production of knowledge
- Examination of the impact that researcher co-presence rather than co-location has on information studies
- Examination of the impact of apps on the use of manual diary and check-in research methods

Scope of information research
- Integration of sound into information research
- Examination of the role that apps can play in extending health information research

Mobility and information practice
- Integration of mobility into information research
- Examination of apps as material, boundary objects.

Certainly, the value of research agendas found in published articles can be seen in the above example.

Other techniques that can be used to identify research topics or problems include discovering previous research that you may disagree with and developing a study to test its findings, becoming involved in the design and development of research tools and techniques relevant to some area of interest, and attempting to deal with actual problems in real work situations. Networking to share ideas and information with colleagues can be a very productive activity as well. Perhaps there is research already under way in nearby libraries, universities, or professional organizations that is of interest. Volunteering to be a collaborator with an admired colleague or faculty member or to serve on a research-related committee is a great way to be gently introduced to research and to perhaps discover a mentor. Following researchers that you admire on social networking sites, such as Twitter or one of the academic social networking platforms such as Orchid or ResearchGate, also can help to keep you abreast of trending topics and recent research (Radford et al. 2020). Radford, Kitzie, Mikitish, Floegel, Radford, and Connaway found that the most frequently used site by academic librarians for networking and other scholarly identity work was Twitter.

Perhaps the two best means of identifying research topics or problems are being curious about items of interest and being an active critical reader and thinker. Being alert to opportunities suggested by library innovations, or by current national or global events, is also one way to identify viable topics. For example, one of the authors became curious about the impact of the COVID-19 pandemic on the use of virtual reference services (VRS) while physical libraries were shut down. She and two of her doctoral students, one of which is in charge of VRS at Rutgers University, decided to seize the moment to do two longitudinal surveys and twenty-eight interviews to find out (Radford, Costello, and Montague 2020). Research problems abound, and one needs to recognize them and then decide to take them seriously as being worthy of study. By being an inquisitive, critical observer, engaged in active wondering, research problems will present themselves.

Characteristics of a Problem Suitable for Research

Exactly what makes a problem worthy of your time, energy, blood, sweat, and tears? A suitable problem should exhibit several characteristics. First, it should represent conceptual thinking, inquiry, and insight—not merely activity. For example, simply collecting data and making comparisons are not activities representative of true research problems. Merely stating what your library does about such and such a problem is considered an informal case study, not true research, even though some LIS journals publish these "how I run my library good" pieces. Questions that arise by studying a subject field and reading earlier research are more likely to be indicative of those leading to conceptually developed research problems. For more practical applications, one could first do a literature search to see what other libraries have done about a particular problem and make a choice to conduct research, perhaps of the applied, assessment, or evaluation variety (see chapter 14 for more on this topic and about evidence-based research). For quantitative research, the variables related to the problem should represent some sort of meaningful relationship. The study of miscellaneous, unrelated facts is not likely to be true research, though it may lead to true research. For example, a tabulation of library circulation statistics or article downloads is nothing more than a series of calculations, which at best may provide the basis for a thorough categorization of such statistics. On the other hand, if the access services librarian wonders about the nature of the relationship between certain circulation statistics (such as downloads from online journals) and certain user characteristics (such as undergraduate vs. graduate status or academic major), they may in effect be conducting exploratory research and be well on the way to identifying a problem for more formal research.

Inherent in a problem representing some kind of relationship between two or more variables is consideration of the cause of the relationship. If evidence suggests, for example, a relationship between the level of college library online resource use and the academic level of student users, why does such a relationship exist? Why does a higher academic level seem to "cause" greater use of the online journal collections and indexes? Again, what is the nature of the relationship, and does the research problem incorporate this concern? Or, if there is not a causal relationship between the variables, how are they related, if at all? To answer this, the problem must reflect some interpretation of the relationship. For example, perhaps the variables are not related directly but indirectly, through the influence of yet another variable or variables, such as curriculum or student major (e.g., science, humanities, social science). Only a problem represented by a conceptual, insightful development and statement will lead to this kind of understanding.

Researchers should address several more practical considerations before settling on a specific problem. Among these is their interest in the problem. Does it represent a topic that they are likely to enjoy researching after several months, if not years, of study? This is a question that is particularly important for doctoral students to ask themselves.

Does the problem represent an area of research that is reasonably original? Does anyone have a prior claim to the area? Again, this is of particular concern to doctoral students. However, a problem does not have to be entirely new and not previously researched in order to be worthy of investigation. Some of the most important research builds on and improves or refines previous research. The degree of originality desired will depend, in part, on the purpose of the research.

More important is the question of whether the research will contribute to the knowledge of the field and ultimately have some impact, or, is it the case that the problem represents a trivial question of no real importance? The problem also should point to research that is manageable; after all, one of the goals of a research project is to complete it! Real constraints, such as time and available fiscal resources, can make it difficult or impossible to conduct perfectly designed research. Privacy or other ethical issues can be of deep concern. It may be great to want to find out if "emotional contagion" is possible for people's friends or their friend's friends on Facebook, but informed consent may be difficult (or impossible) to obtain (Kramer, Guillory, and Hancock 2014). (More on ethical concerns can be found in chapter 4). The researcher typically is in the position of having to compromise what is ideal and what is practical or doable. This is particularly true of research that is relatively applied in nature. A library study to investigate information practices of young adults that involves conducting virtual or in-person focus group interviews with teens, for example, may find that ethical concerns, as well as recruitment realities, require some fiscal resources for providing compensation and/or incentives such as pizza (always a hit with hungry teens at lunch or after school) or a gift card for a virtual group. Now you can also use your mobile phone, tablet, or video conferencing apps such as Zoom, Teams, or WebEx. Perhaps a room rental fee must be negotiated as well for an on-ground focus group interview. Where will the researcher obtain needed audio recording equipment? Will funds be needed to use an online transcription service or hire a transcriber if needed? All of these considerations need to be accommodated to ascertain whether a problem is suitable in a given situation.

Statement of the Problem

Having identified a suitable problem for research, the next logical step is to write a statement of it. It may take some time (and many drafts!) to reach a problem statement that is clear, specific, and compelling. Perhaps it goes without saying, but the problem should be written in complete, grammatical sentences, not in phrases or bullet points. For example, the problem statement "library instruction and library use" would be better expressed as: "The problem to be resolved is whether providing undergraduate students with library instruction will have some effect on their use of the library." Since this statement should guide all of the research that follows, it should be written as clearly as possible and be articulated in specific, straightforward, unambiguous terms; vague terms and clichés are to be avoided. It is a good idea to edit the problem statement as initially written at least once, but perhaps several times, to eliminate needless or ambiguous words and to increase its precision and clarity.

In addition, the problem statement should be realistic, not so broad in scope that it will be unmanageable. For example, the problem statement just given was "whether providing undergraduate students with library instruction will have some effect on their use of the library." While this was seen as an improvement on the preceding phrase, in light of our criteria for a suitable statement, it still needs work. Though it seems reasonably clear, it should be more precise or specific and thereby more manageable. An improved problem statement might be: "The problem to be resolved by this study is whether the frequency of library use of first-year undergraduate students given course-integrated information literacy instruction (ILI) is different from the frequency of library use of first-year students not given course-integrated ILI."

According to Badke (2019, 55), "The field of information literacy has produced hundreds of studies demonstrating that the average university student, even in upper levels of study, has difficulty formulating a research problem statement. . . ." Clear problem statements may be difficult to find even in published research, as Hernon and Metoyer-Duran (1993, 71) stated, "Many studies published in LIS do not contain a problem statement or confuse such a statement with a statement of purpose." The issue of absent or incomplete problem statements was mentioned again by Hernon and Schwartz (2007, 308). Based on lectures by David Clark, they suggested writing three short sentences: "(1) the lead-in, (2) a statement about originality, and (3) a justification" (Hernon and Schwartz 2007). The *problem* is what the research is about, and the *purpose* is why the research is to be conducted. For example, one might conduct research on the relationship between certain teaching methods and the effectiveness of ILI (the problem) in order to increase the success of future ILI programs (the purpose).

Identifying Subproblems

Virtually all problems contain components or subproblems, which should be appropriate for study, to aid greater understanding even if finding a solution is not a goal or possible. Subproblems can facilitate resolving a large problem piecemeal, as they are often more manageable or researchable than the general problem and can be investigated separately. They should be amenable to some realistic research method and suggest adequate data with which to resolve the problem. In addition, the subproblems should, when combined, equal the whole of the main problem. On the other hand, the subproblems should not add up to more than the totality of the main problem. If they do, it is likely that the main problem actually represents more than one problem. While rules of thumb should be used with caution, most well-defined research problems can be broken down into between two and six subproblems. More than that may suggest that the main problem was too broadly or vaguely conceived.

Identifying subproblems is generally a relatively straightforward process involving two basic, related steps. The researcher should (1) break the main problem down into its components, and (2) identify the words that indicate a need for the collection and interpretation of data. In order to illustrate this process, it is necessary to return to the last formulation of the problem. It was as follows:

> The problem to be resolved by this study is whether the frequency of library use of first-year undergraduate students given course-integrated information literacy instruction is different from the frequency of library use of first-year undergraduate students not given course-integrated information literacy instruction.

In analyzing this problem statement, one can see that there are three components that will require investigation before the main problem can be resolved. These three subproblems can be written as follows:

- What is the frequency of library use of the first-year undergraduate students who did receive course-integrated ILI?
- What is the frequency of library use of the first-year undergraduate students who did *not* receive course-integrated ILI?
- What is the difference in the frequency of library use between the two groups of undergraduate students?

As is commonly done, these subproblems have been posed as questions. Again, they are questions that must be answered before the main, more complex problem can be resolved. In many studies, the researcher will attempt to do no more than answer one or two subproblems or research questions; additional studies may be necessary to deal with the entire problem.

Having identified and stated a satisfactory research problem, the investigator's attention should next turn to providing further guidance for the study. For example, the researcher should indicate precisely the limitations of the problem, which in turn help to limit the goals of the study. Some limitations implicit in the problem statement given above include the fact that it is concerned with the frequency of library use, not quality. It is concerned with course-integrated ILI as opposed to the many other types of instruction (e.g., one-on-one, point-of-use, live chat VRS sessions) that could have been considered.

The researcher also should contemplate providing both conceptual and operational definitions for important terms related to the study, particularly if they are used in an unusual sense or can be interpreted in more than one way. One source for finding conceptual definitions for LIS terms is ODLIS: Online Dictionary for Library and Information Science. This procedure is covered in more detail later in the chapter, but generally speaking, this step is necessary to indicate how certain terms are to be used by the researcher in relation to the study and its theoretical approach.

Further delineation of the problem can be achieved by stating assumptions, or what the researcher takes for granted. Returning to our problem on library instruction, the researcher appears to be assuming, for example, that those persons teaching the ILI can, in fact, teach well. The quality of their teaching is not something that will be tested in the study. The research also may be assuming that the student is paying attention to the instruction, rather than checking Instagram, daydreaming, or falling asleep from a late night's celebration of a friend's birthday. If the instruction is being delivered virtually, there are even more possible distractions and/or variables, including technical problems, whether the students are using their phones, laptops, or tablets, and the quality of their wi-fi connectivity.

Also, when feasible the researcher should develop one or more hypotheses or research questions to further limit the problem and project. Development of the hypothesis, as well as identification of the basic assumptions, are treated in greater depth elsewhere in the text (see chapter 4). Having identified and refined the specific research problem, the researcher should then attempt to place the problem in its broader theoretical framework.

THE ROLE OF THEORY IN THE DESIGN OF RESEARCH

Definition of Theory

This section will define theory, discuss why it is useful for LIS research, and explain how to discover a theoretical framework for your research project. Starting with the big picture, the idea of metatheory (or theory about theory) can be considered briefly and follows from the discussion above about philo-sophical assumptions and overarching paradigms. Every field has metatheory, whether recognized as such or not: "Metatheory can be seen as the philosophy behind the theory, the fundamental set of ideas about how phenomena of interest in a particular field should be thought about and researched" (Bates 2005, 2). Bates (2005) identified thirteen LIS metatheories that guide and inform theoretical development:

1. Historical
2. Constructivist
3. Constructionist/discourse—analytic
4. Philosophical—analytic
5. Critical
6. Enthnographic
7. Sociocognitive
8. Cognitive
9. Bibliometric
10. Physical—info transfer
11. Engineering
12. User-centered design
13. Evolutionary

Closely related to metatheory is the idea of paradigm, as presented by Kuhn (2012) in the field of science, as discussed above.

Theory is generally defined as: "A plausible or scientifically acceptable general principle or body of principles offered to explain phenomena" ("Theory | Definition of Theory by Merriam-Webster" 2020). Or, as "A systematic explanation for observations that relate to a particular aspect of life" (Babbie 2021, 42). Theory also has been defined as establishing interrelationships among a set or sets of variables on the basis of the rules of logic. Glazier and Grover (2002, 319) said: "Theories may be described as generalizations that seek to explain relationships among phenomena." McGrath (2002, 310) defined theory as "an explanation for a quantifiable phenomenon." It also can be thought of as a unified explanation for discrete observations, noting that "a unified theory is simply one that reconciles or incorporates other theories" (McGrath 2002, 310). However, the idea of a unified theory for any discipline seems quite elusive in the social sciences.

Some scholars believe that the role of theory in the design of a research study is maligned, ignored, or misunderstood in much of the LIS literature. McKechnie and Pettigrew (2002) did a content analysis of 1,160 LIS articles published between 1993 and 1998 and found that 34.2 percent of the articles incorporated theory in the title, abstract, or text. They found that LIS research is largely atheoretical, lacking in any theoretical grounding. They also found that LIS scholars do not share a single perspective about what theory comprises or how it should be used in research.

Similarly, Kim and Jeong, conducted "a content analysis of 1661 articles in four LIS journals from 1984–2003" (2006, 548) to identify the number and quality of articles that have contributed to the development or use of theory.

Forty-one percent of the articles were identified as contributing to or using theory. The majority of these articles addressed the topics of information seeking, use, and retrieval.

Chu (2015) identified theoretical approaches in LIS through quantitative and qualitative analysis of 1,162 research articles from three major journals published from 2001 to 2010. Findings indicate that a broader variety of research methods have been used than previous research determined. Chu's content analysis revealed that the top three methods used were content analysis, experiment, and theoretical approach, although previous work had found that questionnaire survey and historical method were the top two. Chu found that the theoretical approach was used in *Journal of Documentation* articles (38 percent), *Library and Information Science Research* (15 percent), and *Journal of the American Society for Information Science & Technology* (12 percent). When compared to Powell's work (1999) analyzing journal articles from 1950 to 1975, which had found far fewer articles using the theoretical approach, Chu's analysis indicates that the use of theoretical frameworks in LIS is rising.

Additionally, Kumasi, Charbonneau, and Walster (2013) reviewed the use of theory in seven prominent LIS research journals from 2000 to 2011. Using analytic induction to identify categories, they found that treatment of theory fell into three types: minimal (theory dropping or positioning), moderate (theory diversification or conversion), and major (theory application, generation, or testing). They note that authors need to "make their theoretical decisions and influences more explicit to readers in their discussions of theory" (Kumasi, Charbonneau, and Walster 2013, 180). Unfortunately, although these authors provided examples of research from the different types, they did not state percentages, so it is not possible to compare the findings to those of Kim and Jeong (2006).

Consider how one might discover a suitable theory or framework for a developing research study. The literature review may have suggested a theoretical framework that others have applied to a particular problem, or the researcher already may know of a theory they believe would fit the problem. A concise theoretical overview compiled by Fisher, Erdelez, and McKechnie (2005) is an excellent resource for those wishing to learn more about theories relating to information behavior. For interdisciplinary work, frequently there are discipline-specific guides to theory that can be very useful. For example, Littlejohn (2016) has compiled an excellent book that overviews human communication theory. According to Littlejohn (2016, 7), theories are usually viewed as encompassing four dimensions: "(1) *philosophical* assumptions, or basic beliefs that underlie the theory; (2) *concepts*, or building blocks of the theory; (3) *explanations*, or dynamic connections made by the theory; and (4) *principles* or guidelines for action." He states that "most scholars believe that a theory worthy of the name must have at least the first three dimensions, assumptions, concepts, and explanations" and that the "inclusion of principles is somewhat controversial" (Littlejohn 2016, 7).

One contribution of research that applies existing theory from outside of LIS would be to expand the theory. Radford and colleagues (Connaway and Radford 2020; Radford 1996, 2001, 2006; Radford and Radford 2016) have published two books and several articles on applying communication theory to library contexts, especially in the area of reference services. Radford and Connaway (Radford and Connaway n.d.; Radford and Connaway 2009; Radford and Radford 2016) have developed a model for synchronous reference encounters, also based on communication theory (see figure 2.1). As another example, perhaps a sociological theory had been used to explore politeness

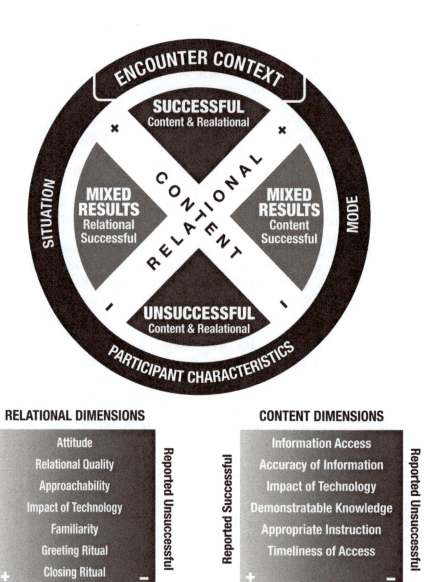

Figure 2.1. Content/Relational Model of Success in Reference Encounters
Source: Created by Marie L. Radford and Lynn Silipigni Connaway. Copyright 2015 Marie L. Radford and OCLC.

rituals in face-to-face (FtF) contexts, but not for VRS. This was the case for the face-work framework of Erving Goffman that was applied to VRS transcripts after having first been applied in FtF settings (Radford et al. 2011).

It is more common to adopt or adapt existing theory either within or outside of LIS than to create new theory for LIS researchers, but it is recommended here that no matter where the theory originates, grounding investigations in theory is superior to doing atheoretical work that can reduce impact. Published examples of theory building include works by Mellon and Poole. Based on data gathered from diaries and essays, Mellon (1986) constructed a grounded theory (a unique theory based on the event or situation studied) of library anxiety. Poole (1985), after analyzing ninety-seven studies published in the *Annual Review of Information Science and Technology,* constructed three theoretical statements on the behavior of scientists and engineers in formal information systems. For those who are unable to find any existing theory that relates to their topic of inquiry, they may be interested in creating new LIS theory, and the grounded theory approach is covered in chapter 10. Atheoretical work is often found in LIS publications, for example, when surveys are constructed for specific library purposes (perhaps to assess user satisfaction with a particular program or service). These can be useful for measuring success in one particular setting, but do not have wider applicability or impact in the field. More about survey research is found in chapter 5.

Keeping in mind the main problem, any subproblems, and the relevant theory, the researcher should consider developing one or more hypotheses or research questions to guide the future investigation or study. In this case, a librarian may wish to hypothesize that library or literacy instruction has a positive effect on library use. This hypothesis may be based on obvious assumptions, such as "ILI will in fact be reasonably effective at teaching certain information literacy skills," or "students will be able to transfer skills learned as a result of an instructional program to actual use of library resources and services." An example of a research question might be: "What is the effect of ILI on the amount of use of library resources and services for first-year undergraduate students?" Or "Does ILI increase the use of library resources and services for first-year undergraduate students?"

Throughout this process, but perhaps particularly at this point, when research questions or hypotheses have been developed, the researcher will need to design a plan for investigating the problem. It is necessary to decide what methodology and data collection techniques to use in the investigation. One part of this decision is to figure out what type of method would work best with the particular problem that has been identified. Additionally, thought is needed to consider their research skills and prior experience, availability of collaborators or mentors, if needed, and their particular strengths. Also, again, consider the goal of the research. Is it for an internal report that is due in thirty days? If so, a simple, even perhaps "quick and dirty" online user survey could be done using Qualtrics or Survey Monkey. (See chapter 5 for more on online survey software.) Is it for publication or presentation, or for a master's thesis or dissertation? If so, a more complex, valid, and reliable method must be undertaken.

If a quantitative method is selected, such as conducting an experiment during which a particular type of ILI would be given, and after which the students' information literacy skills would be evaluated through a posttest, there will be many decisions to make. Who will be the test group? Will there be a control group? What will be the focus of the ILI? How many students/classes will be included? Which classes would be best: basic English? science? social science? At what point in the semester should the experiment be done? What software is needed for analysis?

Alternatively, the decision could be made to conduct a survey in which undergraduate students would be asked about their use of library resources and services and/or their information literacy skills. This choice also has many of the same decision points: who, when, how many, what majors, what level, what software?

To address the hypothesis, or to answer research questions, the researcher must be thoughtful about what information (data) is needed to solve the problem. What will the desired results look like? How much data should be collected and what type? How will analysis be conducted? For quantitative methods, the data will need to be analyzed with regard to their significance. Data collected during the ILI study could include scores on tests, Likert-type scales (the survey-type questions that have participants rate seven-point or five-point statements by selecting a range of answers from strongly agree, to neutral, to strongly disagree) that measure attitudes toward library resources and services, and self-perceptions of information literacy skills (Miles, Huberman, and Saldaña 2020).

At all times, the researcher should keep in mind that this process is generally recursive and circular in nature. The analysis and interpretation of the results may well lead to new questions or fail to answer the original questions, thereby restarting the research process. Data analysis can result in new theoretical insights, which may involve a return to another tack for the literature review. Leedy, Ormrod, and Johnson (2019, 3) developed a diagram, reproduced here as figure 2.2, which helps to illustrate the circular nature of research. As they state, "Every researcher soon learns that genuine research yields as many problems as it resolves. Such is the nature of the acquisition of knowledge" (Leedy, Ormrod, and Johnson 2019, 8).

This happened for this book's authors, who found a theoretical match during data collection and analysis that had not been anticipated at the start of a large grant-supported project. This unexpected (and important) discovery led back to the literature, this time to explore the theoretical framework of communities of practice with relationship to VRS (Radford et al. 2017). Also, another example can be found in the authors' previous grant-funded project, the results of which were published as "Seeking Synchronicity: Evaluating Virtual Reference Services from User, Non-User, and Librarian Perspectives" (Connaway and Radford 2020). In this case, early in the data collection phase, more focus group interviews were added in response to interesting results found for the first focus group interview with the young millennial group of participants, who were teenagers at the time. Because of this change, three focus groups were conducted with this participant group instead of one. Compelling evidence found that their information-seeking and communication

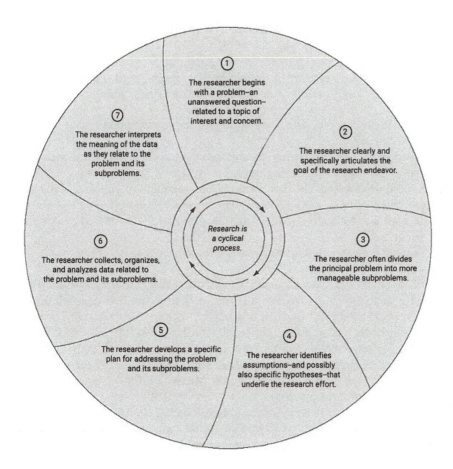

Figure 2.2. The Research Cycle
Source: Leedy, P., J. Ormrod, and L. Johnson. 2019. *Practical Research: Planning and Design*, 12th ed. Reprinted by permission of Pearson Education Inc.

behaviors were radically different from the older adults in this project, and their attitudes toward librarians and libraries could be further explored in subsequent phases of the grant, including intense analysis of virtual reference transcripts (Radford and Connaway 2007).

Theory helps to produce an economy of research effort. It can be used to identify the most important and/or manageable propositions for testing, define and limit the area of research, and relate the research to other relevant studies. "In the most general terms, scientific theory deals with logic, data collection with observation, and data analysis with patterns in what is observed and, where appropriate, the comparison of what is logically expected with what is actually observed" (Babbie 2021, 8). In short, the main value of theory in research derives from its ability to "summarize existing knowledge, to provide an explanation for observed events and relationships, and to predict the occurrence of as yet unobserved events and relationships on the basis of the explanatory principles embodied in the theory" (Babbie 2016, G12).

Research Design

The goal of the design process is to figure out what is needed to answer a particular question, explore a problematic, or test a particular hypothesis. Maxwell (2013) suggests five components of the design process:

- Establishing goals: Why is this study being undertaken and why is it worthwhile?
- Developing the conceptual framework: What is already known? What previous research and theory can inform this study?
- Articulating research questions: What specifically will the study help to understand?
- Selecting methods: What will be done to answer the research questions?
- Testing validity: How might results be wrong?

Maxwell believes that you should start with goals that consider the end product from the very start. What do you envision as the desired outcome? Research projects do not exist in a vacuum; rather, they are usually part of a research agenda, an ongoing series of smaller investigations that generally focus on a larger goal (or broader problematic) and may wind up constituting a brief period of time, or may evolve over time to become the life's work of the researcher. Consider your research goals. Maxwell (2013) suggests three: personal, intellectual, and practical.

According to Miles, Huberman, and Saldaña (2020, 15), "conceptual frameworks also are referred to as theoretical frameworks; they "can be simple or elaborate, descriptive or casual, commonsensical or theory driven." The conceptual framework articulates an "argument about why the topic one wishes to study matters, and why the means proposed to study it are appropriate and rigorous" (Ravitch and Riggan 2012). For more on conceptual frameworks, see chapter 9.

Above we have discussed establishing goals and formulating the problem statement, and chapter 9 covers developing the research questions. Selecting methods will be covered in the following chapters, as it involves learning about the various data collection and analysis tools and deciding which type of method would be best. Will you be testing a hypothesis (quantitative), addressing research questions or investigating problematics (qualitative), or taking a critical approach to analysis? Or will you be embarking on a mixed-methods design that combines one or more approaches as is discussed below in this chapter?

Another way to look at this is to think about the underlying logic for the research. Theories originate from induction (i.e., reasoning from the particular to the general, e.g., grounded theory) (Charmaz 2014) or deduction (i.e., reasoning from the general to the particular, usually by testing them against specific observations). Historically, research to uncover new knowledge has used two types of logic: deductive (usually underlying quantitative inquiry) or inductive (usually qualitative). Aristotle (1989) is credited as the first person to study formal logic (which he called analytics). Deductive or systematic logic is characterized by use of the syllogism. A syllogism starts with a basic premise, which then is logically applied to a particular case; for example, "All people are mortal; Skyler Doe is a person; therefore, Skyler Doe is mortal." The truth of the conclusion obviously depends on the truth of the basic premise, which in this example is "All people are mortal."

In contrast to the deductive method, inductive reasoning proceeds from particular instances to general principles, or from facts to theories. Using inductive logic, one might note that Skyler Doe is mortal and then observe a number of other people as well. One might next decide that all of the *observed* people were mortals and arrive at the conclusion that *all* people are mortal. The obvious limitation to this method is that it is virtually impossible to observe all of the instances supporting the inductive generalization. However, we do have the case of the black swan, in which all one needs to do is find one (just one) black swan (native to Australia) to disprove the long-held ancient belief (and false syllogism) that "all swans are white" (Crupi 2015.

Here's one more example that may help illustrate the distinction between deductive and inductive logic. Suppose one wishes to discover the possible relationship between the amount of ILI received by certain undergraduate college students and their subsequent academic performance. The deductive method usually involves development and testing of hypotheses (see chapter 4 for more about formulating hypotheses). Using this method, it could be hypothesized that ILI improves academic performance. One could then specify that ILI would be represented by the number of hours spent receiving ILI in an English literature course, and that academic performance would be represented by the final grade for the course. If one were to observe that, as the hours of instruction increase, grades improve, one could then conclude that the hypothesis is correct in describing the relationship that exists.

On the other hand, using inductive reasoning, a researcher could start with an observation that the students in a particular English literature class who had received ILI seemed to do quite well in the course. The researcher could then wonder if most ILI methods have a positive effect on the academic performance of college students and could proceed to make a variety of observations related to both ILI and academic performance. Next, the investigator would look for a pattern that best represents or summarizes these observations. In other words, one would attempt to generalize based on observations that ILI of all types tends to improve academic performance. As Babbie (2021) pointed out, with the deductive method one would have reasoned *toward* observations, whereas with the inductive method one would have reasoned *from* observations.

Thus, choosing a research design begins with delineating a problem, then deciding if you want to test a hypothesis taking a quantitative approach or understand research questions or problematics taking a qualitative or critical approach.

Differences in Quantitative and Qualitative Design

The chapters that follow present a toolbox of quantitative, qualitative, and critical research methods. These methods are sometimes seen as oppositional, especially when they are defined by method rather than by philosophical assumptions. In this text they are viewed as complementary. *Qualitative research* is a broad term for a wide range of naturalistic techniques concerned more with interpretation and meaning of phenomena, rather than statistical frequency or correlation. Note that apart from qualitative research, critical theory and critical methods are discussed briefly above in the section on the critical paradigm and fit into Bate's list of LIS metatheories. These methods will be discussed further in chapter 10.

The underlying ideology is that behavior can be explained only by the perspectives and highly subjective constructions of respondent(s) or participant(s), not by any objective truth. As noted above, inductive reasoning starts with observed data about a particular problem/phenomenon and moves toward developing a generalization that helps to understand or explain relationships.

Here is an example of a snippet of qualitative data, from an open-ended online survey question from the "Seeking Synchronicity" grant project (Connaway and Radford 2020). The respondent is a user of library services but has not used virtual (chat or email) reference services. When asked to describe an unsuccessful encounter with a librarian, the respondent, in the nineteen- to twenty-eight-year-old age group, gave this response:

> It was a while ago, but I asked the reference librarian where to find books relating to a certain topic I was studying in school at the time and she just kind of said "over there" and pointed. . . . She did not seem engaged or interested in truly helping me find the books and didn't really care that I never found them[.] I was w[a]ndering all over looking and she just sat there. . . . She did not seem interested in helping me, let alone exhaust all of her means for doing so. Ever since then, I usually avoid that person and go to the one who has helped me successfully.

As can be seen in this example, a rich description of an encounter from the participant's perspective is possible with qualitative methods. However, because this open-ended survey response is from one person's perspective, it cannot be used to generalize to others. It is one account. By placing it together with other accounts, observations, and interviews, the researcher can make an initial assessment of whether this account is part of a pattern or is an anomaly, only one person's reality. Here the interpretive, subjective nature of the underlying phenomenological traditions of qualitative research can be seen. This is covered in greater depth in chapters 9 through 12.

Quantitative methods are fundamentally different from, but not fundamentally opposed to, qualitative methods, and as discussed below, can be used in conjunction with or in combination with the latter. Quantitative methods are deductive in nature, generally use numerical data, and are seen as more structured and objective. The gold standard is to identify representative members of a population, choose a random sample, and perform statistical analyses that allow a generalized truth to be applied to the entire population. At the most basic level, quantitative methods use numbers to describe phenomena, rather than text. So, counts, averages, percentages, standard deviations, and levels of significance are typically seen to describe quantitative data, although sometimes they can be found in qualitative analysis. Quantitative methods are covered to a greater extent in chapters 4 through 8.

Mixed Methods

In considering method for a proposed investigation, it is important to consider whether it is desirable to approach the hypothesis or research questions from more than one way. According to Miles, Huberman, and Saldaña (2020, 35), "We have to face the fact that numbers and words are *both* needed if we are to understand the world. The question is not whether the two sorts of data and their associated methods can be linked during study design but it should be done, how it will be done, and for what purposes." There is a continuum of dimensions along which any particular research may be placed. It is possible to apply and blend different approaches, or mixed methods, at any or all stages throughout the research. Mixed methods involve using multiple methods of data collection, either qualitative (such as focus groups interviews plus observation) or quantitative (such as quantitative survey plus experiment) or a blend of both types (such as interviews plus experiment) (Bryman 2006). This approach has had many labels such as multimethods, multistrategy, mixed methodology, mixed models, mixed approaches, and mixed-methods research (MMR). Fidel analyzed 465 articles published in four LIS research journals. Five percent (twenty-two articles) used the MMR approach, "which integrates qualitative and quantitative methods in one study." Fidel also reported that the use of the MMR name or recognition of MMR "was absent from these articles and from the methodological literature in LIS" (Fidel 2008, 265).

Mixed methods can be beneficial in that they provide the opportunity for triangulation, a term coined by Webb et al. (1966), which evokes multiple data collection methods and/or multiple investigators, and/or multiple contexts/situations. Triangulation enhances explanations and, according to Lindlof and Taylor (2019), we can engage it in at least three ways: by comparing multiple sources of data, we can use multiple methods, or we can use multiple researchers. Miles, Huberman and Saldaña also add two more ways: theory and data type. They advise that "the aim is to pick triangulation sources that have different foci and different strengths, so that they can complement each other" (Miles, Huberman, and Saldaña 2020, 294). "Stripped to its basics, triangulation is supposed to support a finding by showing that at least three independent measures of it agree with it or, at least, do not contradict it" (Miles, Huberman, and Saldaña 2020, 294). Miles, Huberman, and Saldaña (2020) also pointed out that although designing and conducting a mixed-methods research project involves careful planning and more effort in execution, the benefits greatly outweigh the difficulties (including philosophical ones). They also noted that "much has been written about triangulation as a near-obligatory method of confirming findings" (Miles, Huberman, and Saldaña 2020, 293). There are a number of studies that argue the virtues of mixed methods as leading to greater understanding of the "why" questions and/or validation of results (Gooding 2013). "Especially when one is seeking to get in-depth, nuanced data, a combination of qualitative and quantitative methods (such as conducting a series of focus group interviews to inform survey development, or developing a survey that poses some open-ended questions in addition to five or seven point Likert scales) or a purely qualitative approach (such as observations, interviews, or discourse analysis) can provide rich results that do get to this critically important aspect of unveiling the 'Why of Data'" (Radford 2011, xi). One can expect triangulation to help with corroboration, which "enhances the trustworthiness of our analysis" (Miles, Huberman, and Saldaña 2020, 294). If triangulation results in inconsistent or conflicting findings, "this can push us to more closely examine the integrity of the data collection methods and even the data themselves. Inconsistent and conflicting findings force us to explain why they exist" (Miles, Huberman, and Saldaña 2020, 294).

One example of a mixed-methods study is by Ruddock and Hartley, who chose to investigate "How UK Academic Libraries Choose Metasearch Systems." Their project used qualitative and quantitative methods including: a literature review, semistructured interviews, and an online questionnaire (Ruddock and Hartley 2010). Another example is provided by Stokes and Urquhart who developed a qualitative interpretative categorization method for use in information behavior research that employs a mixed-methods design. They tried out their method in integrating interview data from nursing students along with quantitative findings. They concluded that their categorization method "offers a systematic approach to integrating qualitative data into a predominately quantitative mixed methods study" (Stokes and Urquhart 2013, n.p.).

The key issue when considering the research design using a blend of methods is to clarify what is being mixed and how it is being mixed; for example:

- Primary paradigm (positivist/rationalistic or interpretive/critical/naturalistic).
- Disciplinary tradition (social sciences, humanities, history, pure science).
- Type of investigation (exploratory or confirmatory).
- Types of methods and/or data collection instruments used.
- Type of data used (textual or numeric; structured or unstructured).
- Logic used (inductive or deductive).
- Method of analysis (interpretive, qualitative, or statistical, quantitative).
- Approach to explanation (variance theory or interpretivist theory). (Miles, Huberman, and Saldaña 2020)

There are many reasons for using mixed methods. Miles, Huberman, and Saldaña suggested that qualitative researchers think about the purposes of the research and expected audience. They suggested that the question of whether qualitative data are sufficient, or whether it would be strengthened and complemented by some type of quantitative or numerical evidence (Miles, Huberman, and Saldaña 2020). Another important reason for mixing methods has to do with avoiding bias that may not be readily apparent with only one method. For example, in a qualitative study, observation may suggest one interpretation, but interviews with participants may reveal that this initial interpretation is not correct. For example, Radford observed academic library reference desk encounters, one of which appeared to be a perfectly normal interaction. However, when interviewing the librarian, it was revealed that the student was cheating, doing a take-home exam for a friend, which the librarian concluded, based on her knowledge of the assignment in question and the information literacy session connected to it (Radford 1999). Without the interview, this observation would not have been sufficient to understand the encounter. Here are some further reasons for using mixed methods:

- *Triangulation*: convergence, corroboration, correspondence, or results from different methods.
- *Complementarity*: elaboration, enhancement, illustration, clarification of results from one method with those of another.
- *Development*: uses results from one method to help develop or inform another.
- *Initiation*: discovery of paradox and contradiction, new perspectives or frameworks, recasting of questions or interpretation of results from one method to another.
- *Expansion*: extends breadth and range of research by using different methods for different inquiry components. (Bazeley 2004)

To listen to an esteemed qualitative expert on this topic, there are two online videos that are recommended to provide explanations of mixed methods, "What is mixed methods research?" (Creswell 2013a) and: "Telling a complete story with qualitative and mixed methods research" (Creswell 2013b) both by John W. Creswell. Along with the information provided by the videos, and above, consider these key questions once the decision has been made to implement a mixed-methods design:

- Are the methods employed simultaneously or sequentially? If sequentially, which one first? Why?
- Which method, if any has priority? And why?
- What is the function of the decision to use mixed methods (e.g., triangulation, explanation, or exploration)?
- Are quantitative and qualitative data collected simultaneously or sequentially? Again, if sequentially, in what order? Why?
- How do the mixed methods impact on data analysis—analysis by method and analyzed sequentially, integrated analysis, cross-method analysis? (Bazeley 2004)

Taking the *Seeking Synchronicity: Evaluating Virtual Reference Services from User, Non-User, and Librarian Perspectives* grant project funded by IMLS, Rutgers, and OCLC as an example, the researchers (this book's authors) took a mixed-methods approach (Connaway and Radford 2020). They designed and carried out a three-year, four-phase study that began with a transcript analysis, simultaneously and sequentially accompanied by focus group interviews, individual interviews, and an online survey. This design enabled each of the four phases to build on one another, so that the transcript analysis and focus group interviews informed the development of the individual interviews, which then informed the construction of the questions for the online survey. In addition, through using triangulation, the findings from each phase supported those of the other phases. Focus group interview findings (with VRS librarians, users, and potential users) also were corroborated by individual interviews (with different VRS librarians, users, and potential users). This multimethod, multiphase project resulted in a number of major findings with both theoretical and practical applications (Connaway and Radford 2020).

As parting advice on mixed methods, Miles, Huberman and Saldaña (2020) have three suggestions: (1) to think about the purpose of your research and your research questions and to consider if qualitative and quantitative methods will be complementary; (2) for lone researchers doing your own individual study, will you have the bandwidth to manage a combination of methods and data, and will you have the technical support needed; if not, finding a mentor is advised; and finally (3) for those who will be in a research team setting, how specifically will labor be divided to avoid methodological disagreements about which type of data are most trusted. For more on mixed methods, see text boxes 2.1 and 2.2.

More will be covered on research design in regard to particular methods in the chapters to come. However, it cannot be overstated that it is necessary to have a well-thought-out design, or plan for the project, before starting. An excellent and highly recommended technique for "crash testing" the proposed study is to conduct a pilot study, although before the pilot study is discussed, it is necessary to say a word about testing/applying the theory.

Text Box 2.1: Mixed Methods

Michelle Kazmer

My career is a mixed method. I combined a degree in mechanical engineering (which I loved) with a degree in information science (which is my passion), where I've focused on qualitative methods. To answer the kinds of questions I'm drawn to, and to have a meaningful effect on people's lives, often requires mixed methods and also the thoughts and ideals offered by multiple scholars with different backgrounds. I know how to represent the world using mathematics, and I value knowledge gained quantitatively; I also believe that cocreating meaning and understanding with research participants is often best done qualitatively, and that the combination of these approaches is most powerful.

Mixed-methods research is often thought of as quantitative/qualitative, but other approaches are important to consider: design, participatory, radical action, etc. Do not think of mixed methods as "survey plus interview" (or worse, "survey with open-ended questions tacked onto the end"). Mixed methods should be deeply integrated from the genesis of a project, and not be conducted along parallel tracks that do not intersect. Mixing methods effectively means equal attention to all stages of the research process, from problem statement or hypothesis through analysis. Do not focus on the data collection methods to the detriment of the other phases. Rather than quantitative findings followed by a few attractive quotes from the qualitative data organized according to "themes," the findings from mixed methods should be iterative and mutually informing.

Very few people can do mixed-methods research alone, so embrace cooperative research. Each researcher needs to understand all the methods being used, but it's natural that each person will have more expertise in one area. Find research partners who have a deep and true appreciation for one another's contributions; mixed-methods research just to satisfy a funding agency is never as fulfilling or productive as it could be. Work closely together so that the overall research design does not privilege one method over another just for the sake of method, but so that the combined approach will answer the research questions and allow you to effect change in the world.

Further Reading

Glueckauf, Robert L., W. Shuford Davis, Floyd Willis, Dinesh Sharma, David J. Gustafson, Jocelyn Hayes, Mary Stutzman, et al. 2012. "Telephone-Based, Cognitive-Behavioral Therapy for African American Dementia Caregivers with Depression: Initial Findings." *Rehabilitation Psychology* 57(2): 124–39. doi:10.1037/a0028688.

Granikov, Vera, Quan Nha Hong, Emily Crist, and Pierre Pluye. 2020. "Mixed Methods Research in Library and Information Science: A Methodological Review." *Library & Information Science Research* 42(1): Article 101003. doi:10.1016/j.lisr.2020.101003.

Koh, Kyungwon, John T. Snead, and Kun Lu. 2019. "The Processes of Maker Learning and Information Behavior in a Technology-Rich High School Class. *Journal of the Association for Information Science & Technology* 70(12): 1395–1412. doi:10.1002/asi.24197.

Wells, Brittny A., Robert L. Glueckauf, Daniel Bernabe, Jr., Michelle M. Kazmer, Gabriel Schettini, Jane Springer, Dinesh Sharma, Hongdao Meng, Floyd B. Willis, and Nell Graff-Radford. 2017. "African American Dementia Caregiver Problem Inventory: Descriptive Analysis and Initial Psychometric Evaluation." *Rehabilitation Psychology* 62(1): 25–35. doi:10.1037/rep0000110.

Text Box 2.2: Geographic Information Systems

Wade Bishop and Lauren Mandel

A geographic information system (GIS) is any tool that stores, manipulates, analyzes, and visualizes geospatial data. Geospatial data generally consists of facts and/or evidence pertaining to events, activities, and things located on (or near) the surface of the earth. If one considers word processing software as central to processing, manipulating, and visualizing textual information, then a GIS is the equivalent processing system for geospatial data (Bishop and Grubesic 2016). GIS is widely used in science, social science, and the humanities, as a great deal of real-world phenomena may be mapped and spatially analyzed to gain deeper understanding—from assessing sea-level rise to tracking the spread of infectious disease, such as COVID-19, to charting the history of publishing with a spatial lens (Bishop, Mandel, and McClure 2011; Blaschke and Merschdorf 2014; MacDonald and Black 2000). A literature review demonstrates the volume of work in this area, 3,290 articles in all three *Web of Science* indices over the years 2003–2012 (Wei, Grubesic, and Bishop 2015). With the rise of Web 2.0 and more user-friendly graphical user interfaces, GIS is gaining both expert and novice users. GIS offers another suite of research methods for LIS to measure, analyze, and visualize library services and resources.

Use of GIS in LIS began with Christie Koontz's groundbreaking work on analyzing public libraries' service area populations, *Library Facility Siting and Location Handbook*

(1997). Koontz recognized the value of GIS to assess library services and resources just as other sectors inform decisions of where to place outlets and how to tailor services based on market research that includes geospatial variables. Her work used both quantitative (e.g., demographics, usage statistics) and qualitative (e.g., user interviews) methods.

The published LIS research utilizing GIS falls into two broad categories: analyzing service area populations (data from outside libraries) and facilities management (data from inside libraries) (Bishop and Mandel 2010; Mandel, Bishop, and Orehek 2020). Koontz's work continued in the analysis of library service populations informed by user demographics, including facility openings and closings (Koontz, Jue, and Bishop 2009). Beyond locations, public library attributes such as internet connectivity and access were analyzed (Bishop, Mandel, and McClure 2011). The relationship between library locations, distance, and patrons' visiting behavior has been explored (Park 2012). With more easily available geospatial data of US public libraries funded through the Institute of Museum and Library Services, Donnelly (2014) studied the geographic distribution of public libraries, noting areas that had high and low service and use. Work beyond the United States continues to expand, as demographic data combined with geospatial data were used in Slovenia to support community analysis and library service planning (Vidiček and Novljan 2010). Also, Hashmi (2019) used GIS to survey the geographical characteristics of communities to determine how well libraries in Islamabad, Pakistan, served their communities in education and political engagement.

LIS studies that utilize GIS to analyze and visualize activity within a library include two foci: analysis of collections and library space usage. The pioneer of GIS research inside the library was Jingfeng Xia. Xia used GIS to visualize use of study space (2005b), in-library use of books (2004a), book usage data in relation to the height of bookshelves (2004b), and geolocating books to facilitate user access (2005a). More recent work on collection management has used GIS to evaluate the efficiency of current layouts and practices such as purchasing and weeding in an effort to inform future design of facilities (Pournaghi 2017). Other work using GIS has focused on how patrons figure out where they are and how to get from point A to point B in the library (i.e., wayfinding). Wayfinding examples include Mandel (2010, 2013) and Luo (2018) collecting observational data about how patrons traveled from one place to another within a library, spatially analyzing their routes to inform design. The emergence of mobile apps has helped navigation in all aspects of life, even finding books (Aguilar-Moreno, Montoliú-Colás, and Torres-Sospedra 2016).

Maps afford the opportunity to see *where* phenomena occur in a way that tables and charts do not. A table can list the various routes patrons have taken in a library, but a map shows where those routes intersect, where people turn, where people look at signs, and so forth. A pie chart can show the demographic breakdown of a library's service population, but a map can show how far away from the library those people live in terms of walking distance, travel time on bus routes, etc. An integrated library system (ILS) can formulate a list of books on a certain topic with call numbers, but a GIS-enabled ILS can produce a map with directions for how to physically locate those books within the library.

Utilizing GIS as a data analysis and visualization tool may benefit many other avenues of LIS research. For example, recent work using patron demographics and drive-time analysis led to efficient routes that save time and reduce the environmental impact of bookmobiles (ArcGIS 2020). Libraries could use GIS to research past natural disasters to assist in planning for the response and recovery to future natural disasters and anthropogenic hazards. With the growth in geohumanities, libraries could also incorporate GIS into genealogical and historical research as many aspects of this research relate to places and place history. The power of GIS to support library research is almost limitless given the connection of places to many information needs.

References

Aguilar-Moreno, Estefanía, Raúl Montoliú-Colás, and Joaquín Torres-Sospedra. 2016. "Indoor Positioning Technologies for Academic Libraries: Towards the Smart Library." *El Profesional de la Informacion* 25(2). https://doi.org/10.3145/epi.2016.mar.17.

ArcGIS. 2020. "For Book Deliveries, Local Library Turns to GIS." *Esri* (blog). June 30. https://www.esri.com/about/newsroom/arcnews/for-book-deliveries-local-library-turns-to-gis.

Bishop, Bradley Wade, and Tony H. Grubesic. 2016. *Geographic Information: Organization, Access, and Use.* Springer Geography. Springer International Publishing. https://doi.org/10.1007/978-3-319-22789-4.

Bishop, Bradley Wade, and Lauren H. Mandel. 2010. "Utilizing Geographic Information Systems (GIS) in Library Research." *Library Hi Tech* 28(4): 536–47. https://doi.org/10.1108/07378831011096213.

Bishop, Bradley Wade, Lauren Mandel, and Charles McClure. 2011. "Geographic Information Systems (GIS) in Public Library Assessment." *Library and Information Science Research Electronic Journal* 21(1). https://digitalcommons.uri.edu/lsc_facpubs/2.

Blaschke, Thomas, and Helena Merschdorf. 2014. "Geographic Information Science as a Multidisciplinary and Multiparadigmatic Field." *Cartography and Geographic Information Science* 41(3): 196–213. https://doi.org/10.1080/15230406.2014.905755.

Donnelly, Francis, P. 2014. "The Geographic Distribution of United States Public Libraries: An Analysis of Locations and Service Areas." *Journal of Librarianship and Information Science* 46(2): 110–29.

Hashmi, Fakhar Abbas. 2019. "Political Discourse: Do Public Libraries Serve as a Fertile Ground?" *Library & Information Science Research* 41(3): 100965. https://doi.org/10.1016/j.lisr.2019.100965.

Koontz, Christie M. 1997. *Library Facility Siting and Location Handbook.* Westport, CT: Greenwood Press.

Koontz, Christie M., Dean K. Jue, and Bradley Wade Bishop. 2009. "Public Library Facility Closure: An Investigation of Reasons for Closure and Effects on Geographic Market Areas." *Library & Information Science Research* 31(2): 84–91. https://doi.org/10.1016/j.lisr.2008.12.002.

Luo, Jiebei. 2018. "Habitual Wayfinding in Academic Libraries: Evidence from a Liberal Arts College." *Library & Information Science Research* 40(3): 285–95. https://doi.org/10.1016/j.lisr.2018.09.011.

MacDonald, Bertrum H., and Fiona A. Black. 2000. "Using GIS for Spatial and Temporal Analyses in Print Culture Studies: Some Opportunities and Challenges." *Social Science History* 24(3): 505–36.

Mandel, Lauren H. 2010. "Toward an Understanding of Library Patron Wayfinding: Observing Patrons' Entry Routes in a Public Library." *Library & Information Science Research* 32(2): 116–30. https://doi.org/10.1016/j.lisr.2009.12.004.

Mandel, Lauren H. 2013. "Finding Their Way: How Public Library Users Wayfind." *Library & Information Science Research* 35(4): 264–71. https://doi.org/10.1016/j.lisr.2013.04.003.

Park, Sung Jae. 2012. "Measuring Public Library Accessibility: A Case Study Using GIS." *Library & Information Science Research* 34(1): 13–21. https://doi.org/10.1016/j.lisr.2011.07.007.

Pournaghi, Roya. 2017. "GIS as a Supporting Instrument for Making Decisions about the Library Sources Collection Management." *Collection Building* 36(1): 11–19. https://doi.org/10.1108/CB-06-2016-0014.

Vidiček, Matija, and Silva Novljan. 2010. "Usability of GIS Methodology at Library Service Planning: Some Examples." *Knjižnica. Revija Za Področje Bibliotekarstva in Informacijske Znanosti* 54(1–2). https://knjiznica.zbds-zveza.si/knjiznica/article/view/5978.

Wade Bishop, Bradley, and Lauren H. Mandel. 2010. "Utilizing Geographic Information Systems (GIS) in Library Research." *Library Hi Tech* 28(4): 536–47. https://doi.org/10.1108/07378831011096213.

Wei, Fangwu, Tony H. Grubesic, and Bradley Wade Bishop. 2015. "Exploring the GIS Knowledge Domain Using CiteSpace." *The Professional Geographer* 67(3): 374–84. https://doi.org/10.1080/00330124.2014.983588.

Xia, Jingfeng. 2004b. "Library Space Management: A GIS Proposal." *Library Hi Tech* 22(4): 375–82.

Xia, Jinfeng. 2005a. "Locating Library Items by GIS Technology." *Collection Management* 30(1): 63–72.

Testing or Applying the Theory

Having identified a suitable theory, the next requisite step is to test it or to apply it. The sections of this text that relate to quantitative methods are directly or indirectly concerned with testing procedures. The chapters on qualitative methods take an approach that applies or builds theory to problematics, to see if the theory can enhance our understanding. To foreground the quantitative sections, a brief indication of some of the implications of theory testing is provided. Also, a well-constructed, informative theory applied to a quantitative research design would provide specific hypotheses or statements of certain relationships by which the theory can be tested. One way to get started with theory testing or application is to conduct a pilot study.

The Pilot Study

Sometimes the most difficult part of the research project is getting started. Doing a trial run with a small number of participants can be a good way to jump-start a project without too much risk. This small exploratory trial run is known as a "pilot study." The pilot study is a critical step that tests whether the research design is realistic and doable. It can involve conducting a small version of the entire study or just testing a particular instrument (like a survey), procedure, or protocol (like focus group interview logistics and questions) (Persaud 2010). Inclusion of a pilot study is considered to be an expected part of the research design process (Fink 2003). According to the *Encyclopedia of Research Design*, pilot studies have been in use since the 1940s and are useful for qualitative and quantitative approaches: "The major objective of the pilot study is to discover problems prior to the main study so that the researcher can take corrective action to improve the research process, and thus the likelihood of success of the main study" (Persaud 2010, 1032). They also help to identify what might be some good features of a chosen research design, or what might be some potential problems, so troubleshooting can take place before a research disaster strikes. For example, the researcher may want to recruit a large number of survey respondents from a particular demographic group (e.g., teens or undergrads) that has used a particular library service (e.g., teen program or information literacy instruction). Embarking on a pilot study with a few respondents immediately can help the researcher ascertain whether she or he can find people with the desired experience and how difficult it will be to recruit them into the study (e.g., schedule a focus group interview and have them show up). This also gives the researcher a glimpse into how the final data will look and how analysis will take place.

Another major function of the pilot study is to improve the validity of instruments, such as questionnaires, according to van Teijlingen and Hundley (2001), who discussed both the importance of pilot studies and problems associated with them. One limitation of the pilot study for survey questionnaires that they noted is that "completing a pilot study successfully is not a guarantee of the success of the full-scale survey."

Although they do not guarantee success, pilot studies can be extremely useful and are highly recommended by the authors, who have used them on numerous occasions (Radford 1993, 1999). It is also important to present and publish pilot study results, as long as they are described clearly as exploratory and preliminary (van Teijlingen and Hundley 2001).

SUMMARY

This chapter has some key takeaways, which are briefly summarized here. It is argued that research is as much about perspective as it is about method, if it is thought of as a way of thinking about and seeing social reality. Experts have identified four philosophical assumptions that are discussed in the context of thinking of underpinnings for research design. These include ontological, epistemological, axiological, and methodological. Additionally, four major paradigms that shape social science research—positivist, postpositivist, interpretive, and critical—were reviewed.

The chapter provided guidelines and suggestions for how to get started with a research project. An important initial component is the literature review, and it is suggested that one maintain an interdisciplinary focus and cite from other fields, as appropriate. It also is important to identify gaps in knowledge within the field to address in the research study. Be a conceptual thinker, especially in relating identified problems to these larger gaps observed in the research, rather than simply developing a problem based on observation or anecdotal evidence. Think of relationships: What are the relationships between some of the phenomena being observed, and how do these relate to the larger research problem? The researcher should be strategic in identifying a problem or issue that will make a meaningful contribution to the field, not something that will have a local or smaller impact.

Before embarking on a new research project, make sure it is manageable, seeking to account for costs in both time and money, as well as ethical concerns. Do not confuse problem, purpose statement, and research questions; all are necessary when formulating a research problem, but these definitions, while not mutually exclusive, relate to one another. Research should be grounded in theory, either extant theoretical frames, or one that emerges from the data, if a grounded theory approach is taken. Most researchers will adopt or adapt existing theory, but some also will create new theory. A theoretical work generally does not make a contribution to the broader LIS field.

This chapter also puts forth the idea that the research process should be regarded as circular and iterative, rather than linear, and that researchers should be aware of the general domain assumptions that are brought to any research study, as these will color the design and subsequent findings. For quantitative work especially, one should seek to be as objective as possible within the given research domain of interest by being as aware and reflective as possible of recognized internal belief and value systems. This text also suggests that inductive and deductive research methods should not be viewed as oppositional, but rather as complementary. Mixed methods can be very useful in adding trustworthiness and validity through multiple sources, methods, or data types.

Finally, pilot studies are highly recommended, although not necessary. They have many functions, including trying out the method and identifying any problems in the research design.

REFERENCES

Ameen, Kanwal, Syeda Hina Batool, and Muhammad Asif Naveed. 2019. "Difficulties Novice LIS Researchers Face While Formulating a Research Topic." *Information Development* 35(4): 592–600. https://doi.org/10.1177/0266666918774875.

Aristotle. 1989. *Prior Analytics*. Translated by Robin Smith. Indianapolis: Hackett.

Babbie, Earl R. 2016. *The Practice of Social Research*. 14th ed. Belmont, CA: Cengage Learning.

Babbie, Earl R. 2021. *The Practice of Social Research*. 15th ed. Boston: Cengage Learning.

Badke, William E. 2019. "Ten Considerations for Inquiry-Based Learning." *Online Searcher (Medford, N.J.)* 43(1): 55–57.

Barriage, Sarah, and Alison Hicks. 2020. "Mobile Apps for Visual Research: Affordances and Challenges for Participant-Generated Photography." *Library & Information Science Research* 42(3): 101033. https://doi.org/10.1016/j.lisr.2020.101033.

Bates, Marcia J. 1981. "Search Techniques." *Annual Review of Information Science and Technology* 16: 139–69.

Bates, Marcia J. 2005. "An Introduction to Metatheories, Theorism, and Models." In *Theories of Information Behavior*, edited by Karen E. Fisher, Sandra Erdelez, and Lynne McKechnie, 2–24. Medford, NJ: Information Today.

Bazeley, Pat. 2004. "Issues in Mixing Qualitative and Quantitative Approaches to Research." In *Applying Qualitative Methods to Marketing Management Research*, edited by Renate Buber, Johannes Gadner, and Lyn Richards, 141–56. London: Palgrave Macmillan.

Bryman, Alan. 2006. "Integrating Quantitative and Qualitative Research: How Is It Done?" *Qualitative Research* 6(1): 97–113. https://doi.org/10.1177/1468794106058877.

Charmaz, Kathy. 2014. *Constructing Grounded Theory*. Thousand Oaks, CA: Sage.

"The Children's Room in the Smithsonian Institution Building Knowledge Begins in Wonder, Introduction." 2015. The Smithsonian Institution Preservation. https://www.si.edu/ahhp/childrensroomintroduction.

Chu, Heting. 2015. "Research Methods in Library and Information Science: A Content Analysis." *Library & Information Science Research* 37(1): 36–41. https:// doi.org/10.1016/j.lisr.2014.09.003.

Connaway, Lynn Silipigni. 2015. "Research Challenges: The Pathway to Engagement and Progress." Presented at the the ILL International Seminar on LIS Education and Research: Challenges of LIS Research, Barcelona, Spain, June 4.

Connaway, Lynn Silipigni, and Marie L. Radford. 2020. "Seeking Synchronicity: Revelations and Recommendations for Virtual Reference." OCLC. May 4. https:// www.oclc.org/content/research/publications/2011/synchronicity.html.

Corbin, Juliet, and Anselm Strauss. 2014. *Basics of Qualitative Research: Techniques and Procedures for Developing Grounded Theory.* 4th ed. Thousand Oaks, CA: Sage.

Creswell, John W. 2013a. *What Is Mixed Methods Research?* YouTube. https:// www.youtube.com/watch?v=1OaNiTlpyX8.

Creswell, John W. 2013b. *Telling a Complete Story with Qualitative and Mixed Methods Research.* YouTube. https://www.youtube.com/watch?v=l5e7kVzMIfs.

Creswell, John W., and Cheryl N. Poth. 2016. *Qualitative Inquiry and Research Design: Choosing among Five Approaches.* Thousand Oaks, CA: Sage.

Crupi, Vincenzo. 2015. "Inductive Logic." *Journal of Philosophical Logic* 44 (40th anniversary issue): 641–50.

Fidel, Raya. 2008. "Are We There Yet? Mixed Methods Research in Library and Information Science." *Library & Information Science Research* 30(4): 265–72. https://doi.org/10.1016/j.lisr.2008.04.001.

Fink, Arlene. 2003. *The Survey Handbook.* 2nd ed. Thousand Oaks, CA: Sage.

Fisher, Karen E., Sanda Erdelez, Lynne McKechnie, and American Society for Information Science and Technology. 2005. *Theories of Information Behavior.* Medford, NJ: Information Today.

Glaser, Barney G. 1978. *Theoretical Sensitivity: Advances in the Methodology of Grounded Theory.* Mill Valley, CA: The Sociology Press.

Glaser, Barney G., and Anselm L. Strauss. 1967. *The Discovery of Grounded Theory: Strategies for Qualitative Research.* Chicago: Aldine.

Glazier, Jack D. 2017. "Domain Assumptions of Research." In *Research Methods in Library and Information Science,* 6th ed., Lynn Silipigni Connaway and Marie L. Radford, 46–60. Santa Barbara, CA: Libraries Unlimited.

Glazier, Jack D., and Robert Grover. 2002. "A Multidisciplinary Framework for Theory Building." *Library Trends* 50(3): 317–29.

Gooding, Paul. 2013. "Mass Digitization and the Garbage Dump: The Conflicting Needs of Quantitative and Qualitative Methods." *Literary and Linguistic Computing* 28(3): 425–31. https://doi.org/10.1093/llc/fqs054.

Guba, Egon G. 1990. *The Paradigm Dialog.* Thousand Oaks, CA: Sage.

Guba, Egon G., and Yvonna S. Lincoln. 1993. "Competing Paradigms in Qualitative Research." In *Handbook of Qualitative Research,* Norman K. Denzin and Yvonna S. Lincoln, 105–17. Thousand Oaks, CA: Sage.

Henwood, Karen, and Nick Pidgeon. 2003. "Grounded Theory in Psychological Research." In *Qualitative Research in Psychology: Expanding Perspectives in Methodology,* 131–55. Washington, DC: American Psychological Association.

Hernon, Peter, and Cheryl Metoyer-Duran. 1993. "Problem Statements: An Exploratory Study of Their Function, Significance, and Form." *Library & Information Science Research* 15(1): 71–92.

Hernon, Peter, and Candy Schwartz. 2007. "What Is a Problem Statement?" *Library & Information Science Research* 3(29): 307–9. https://doi.org/10.1016/j.lisr.2007.06.001.

Kim, Sung-Jin, and Dong Y. Jeong. 2006. "An Analysis of the Development and Use of Theory in Library and Information Science Research Articles." *Library & Information Science Research* 28(4): 548–62. https://doi.org/10.1016/j.lisr.2006.03.018.

Kramer, A. D. I., J. E. Guillory, and J. T. Hancock. 2014. "Experimental Evidence of Massive-Scale Emotional Contagion through Social Networks." *Proceedings of the National Academy of Sciences* 111(24): 8788–90. https://doi.org/10.1073/pnas.1320040111.

Kuhn, Thomas S. 2012. *The Structure of Scientific Revolutions: 50th Anniversary Edition.* 4th ed. Chicago; London: University of Chicago Press.

Kumasi, Kafi D., Deborah H. Charbonneau, and Dian Walster. 2013. "Theory Talk in the Library Science Scholarly Literature: An Exploratory Analysis." *Library & Information Science Research* 35(3): 175–80. https://doi.org/10.1016/j.lisr.2013.02.004.

Leedy, Paul D., and Jeanne E. Ormrod. 2004. *Practical Research: Planning and Design.* 8th ed. Upper Saddle River, NJ: Prentice Hall.

Leedy, Paul, Jeanne E. Ormrod, and Laura R. Johnson. 2019. *Practical Research: Planning and Design,* 12th ed. Upper Saddle River, NJ: Prentice Hall. Lindlof, Thomas R., and Bryan C. Taylor. 2019. *Qualitative Communication Research Methods.* 4th ed. Los Angeles: Sage.

Littlejohn, Stephen W., Karen A. Foss, and John G. Oetzel. 2016. *Theories of Human Communication.* 11th ed. Long Grove, IL: Waveland Press.

Mandel, Lauren H., Bradley Wade Bishop, and Ashley Marie Orehek. 2020. "A New Decade of Uses for Geographic Information Systems (GIS) as a Tool to Research, Measure and Analyze Library Services." *Library Hi Tech* (ahead of print). https://doi-org.proxy.libraries.rutgers.edu/10.1108/LHT-03-2020-0052.

Maxwell, Joseph A. 2013. *Qualitative Research Design: An Interactive Approach.* Thousand Oaks, CA: Sage.

McGrath, William E. 2002. "Current Theory in Library and Information Science." *Current Theory in Library and Information Science* 50(3): 310.

McKechnie, Lynne, and Karen E. Pettigrew. 2002. "Surveying the Use of Theory in Library and Information Science Research: A Disciplinary Perspective." *Library Trends* 50(3): 406–17.

Mellon, Constance A. 1986. "Library Anxiety: A Grounded Theory and Its Development." *College & Research Libraries* 47(2): 160–65.

Miles, Matthew B., A. Michael Huberman, and Johnny Saldaña. 2020. *Qualitative Data Analysis: A Methods Sourcebook.* 4th ed. Thousand Oaks, CA: Sage. https://www.vitalsource.com/products/qualitative-data-analysis-matthew-b-miles-v9781506353081.

"Office for Research and Statistics." 2020. American Library Association Office for Research and Statistics. https://www.ala.org/ala/ors/researchstatistics.htm.

Persaud, Nadini. 2010. "The Pilot Study." In *Encyclopedia of Research Design,* edited by Neil J. Salkind, 1032–33. Thousand Oaks, CA: Sage.

Poole, Herbert. 1985. *Theories of the Middle Range.* New York: Ablex.

Powell, Ronald R. 1999. "Recent Trends in Research: A Methodological Essay." *Library & Information Science Research* 21(1): 91–119. https://doi.org/10.1016/S0740-8188(99)80007-3.

Radford, Marie L. 1993. "Relational Aspects of Reference Interactions: A Qualitative Investigation of the Perceptions of Users and Librarians in the Academic Library." Unpublished Doctoral Dissertation, New Brunswick, NJ: Rutgers, The State University of New Jersey.

Radford, Marie L. 1996. "Communication Theory Applied to the Reference Encounter: An Analysis of Critical Incidents." *The Library Quarterly: Information, Community, Policy* 66(2): 123–37.

Radford, Marie L. 1999. *The Reference Encounter: Interpersonal Communication in the Academic Library.* Chicago: American Library Association.

Radford, Marie L. 2001. "Encountering Users, Encountering Images: Communication Theory and the Library Context." *Journal of Education for Library and Information Science* 42(1): 27–41. https://doi.org/10.2307/40324035.

Radford, Marie L. 2006. "Encountering Virtual Users: A Qualitative Investigation of Interpersonal Communication in Chat Reference." *Journal of the American Society for Information Science and Technology* 57(8): 1046–59. https://doi.org/10.1002/asi.20374.

Radford, Marie L. 2011. "Foreword." In *Using Qualitative Methods in Action Research: How Librarians Can Get to the Why of Data,* edited by Douglass Cook and Leslie Farmer, xi–xii. Chicago: ACRL.

Radford, Marie L., and Lynn Silipigni Connaway. n.d. "Thriving on Theory: A New Model for Virtual Reference Encounters." *Proceedings of the 72nd ASIS&T Annual Meeting 2009:* 6–11.

Radford, Marie L., and Lynn Silipigni Connaway. 2007. "'Screenagers' and Live Chat Reference: Living up to the Promise." *Scan* 26(1): 31–39.

Radford, Marie L., and Lynn Silipigni Connaway. 2009. "Creating a New Theoretical Model for Reference Encounters in Synchronous Face-to-Face and Virtual Environments." Presented at the 2009 ALISE Conference, Denver, January 20.

Radford, Marie L., Lynn Silipigni Connaway, Stephanie Mikitish, Mark Alpert, Chirag Shah, and Nicole A. Cooke. 2017. "Shared Values, New Vision: Collaboration and Communities of Practice in Virtual Reference and SQA." *Journal of the Association for Information Science and Technology* 68(2): 438–49. https://doi.org/10.1002/asi.23668.

Radford, Marie L., Laura Costello, and Kaitlin Montague. 2020. "Chat Reference in the Time of COVID-19: Transforming Essential User Services." Proceedings of the ALISE Annual Conference.

Radford, Marie L., Vanessa Kitzie, Stephanie Mikitish, Diana Floegel, Gary P. Radford, and Lynn Silipigni Connaway. 2020. "'People Are Reading Your Work,' Scholarly Identity and Social Networking Sites." *Journal of Documentation* (ahead-of-print). https://doi.org/10.1108/JD-04-2019-0074.

Radford, Marie L., and Gary P. Radford. 2016. *Library Conversations: Reclaiming Interpersonal Communication Theory for Understanding Professional Encounters.* Chicago: ALA Neal-Schuman.

Radford, Marie L., Gary P. Radford, Lynn Silipigni Connaway, and Jocelyn A. DeAngelis. 2011. "On Virtual Face-Work: An Ethnography of Communication Approach to a Live Chat Reference Interaction." *The Library Quarterly* 81(4): 431–53. https://doi.org/10.1086/661654.

Ravitch, Sharon M., and Matthew Riggan. 2012. *Reason and Rigor: How Conceptual Frameworks Guide Research.* Thousand Oaks, CA: Sage.

Ruddock, Bethan, and Dick Hartley. 2010. "How UK Academic Libraries Choose Metasearch Systems." *Aslib Proceedings: New Information Perspectives* 62(1): 85–105. https://doi.org/10.1108/00012531011015226.

Ryan, Mike. 2010. "Damon Lindelof and Carlton Cuse on the End (?) of Lost." *Vulture,* May 11. https://www.vulture.com/2010/05/lost_showrunners_damon_lindelo.html.

Springen, Karen. 2019. "Librarians Harness Instagram." *PublishersWeekly.Com.* https://www.publishersweekly.com/pw/by-topic/childrens/childrens -industry-news/article/79540-library-stagrams.html.

Stokes, Peter, and Christine Urquhart. 2013. "Qualitative Interpretative Categorisation for Efficient Data Analysis in a Mixed Methods Information Behaviour Study." *Information Research* 18(1). http://informationr.net/ir/18-1 /paper555.html#.Xv4_2GpKgUQ.

Teijlingen, Edwin R. van, and Vanora Hundley. 2001. "The Importance of Pilot Studies." https://aura.abdn.ac.uk/handle/2164/157.

"Theory | Definition of Theory by Merriam-Webster." 2020. Merriam-Webster. https://www.merriam-webster.com/dictionary/theory.

Webb, Eugene J., Donald T. Campbell, Richard D. Schwartz, and Lee Sechrest. 1966. *Unobtrusive Measures: Non-Reactive Research in the Social Sciences.* Chicago: Rand McNally.

Wiegand, Wayne A. 2015. "'Tunnel Vision and Blind Spots' Reconsidered: Part of Our Lives (2015) as a Test Case." *The Library Quarterly* 85(4): 347–70. https://doi.org/10.1086/682731.

Wildemuth, Barbara M. 2017. *Applications of Social Research Methods to Questions in Information and Library Science.* 2nd ed. Santa Barbara, CA: ABC-CLIO.

3

Writing the Research Proposal

Begin with the end in mind (Covey 1990)! The researcher who has a clear idea of a completed project, even envisioning possible results, planning for visual display of the data and results (refer to chapters 8, 10, and 15) as well as choosing venues for presentation and publication, has a head start. There is no doubt that to achieve a high quality of research, it must be well planned, and a key step in the right direction is the preparation of a solid research proposal. A research proposal can be thought of as being like an architect's blueprint. One would not consider building a house without a detailed blueprint as a guide. During the course of a major research project, an individual is going to put forth a high-level intellectual effort and will invest a significant amount of time (perhaps years, as is the case for doctoral dissertations).

Initial investment of thought and energy in the development of the proposal can save time in the end by helping to reduce wasted effort and by providing a more efficient, problem-free study, because this preliminary effort compels the researcher to clarify the exact nature of the investigation. The proposal should clearly and as completely as possible detail the procedures that will be followed. This will enable the researcher to be better prepared to carry out all of the necessary, relevant steps. Whether one is a doctoral student or an experienced researcher, seeking input, feedback, and advice from mentors, advisers, and trusted colleagues is essential at this formative phase, as well as throughout the research project.

From the start, it is advisable to create a timeline that indicates the progress to be expected at various stages of the project. While the preliminary deadlines (or target dates, which sound less threatening) indicated by such a timetable will not always be met, the attempt to meet them should provide incentive and a degree of accountability. Proposals usually are necessary for applying for outside funding or grants for research projects and generally require the submission of a detailed timeline that is connected to the budget. This requirement demands that the researcher be able to project progress and expenditures for the duration of the funding, which can be one to three years.

It also assists in ensuring that the funds are spent at the expected pace (sometimes colorfully called the "burn rate"). Although even a multiyear grant award may be transferred at the beginning of the project, funding agencies require that the budgeted amount be dispersed in a regular and ongoing way, in accordance with the researcher's stated plan, not all at once at the beginning or in a rush at the end of the project.

The proposal also can provide the basis for identifying and discussing the strengths and weaknesses of the proposed project, help to uncover conceptual and theoretical errors, and point out weaknesses in selected designs and methods, so that these can be corrected at the outset. In addition, the research proposal is useful for announcing one's intentions and therein providing enough detail about the proposed project to prevent misinterpretations about research goals and techniques to be applied. Research proposals are required of doctoral students as an indication that the topic is worthy of investigation, that the methods and research plan are appropriate and realistic, and that the student is fully prepared to conduct the research properly. The dissertation proposal serves as a contract between the student and the adviser, so that everyone is on the same page, especially with regard to expectations for the completed dissertation (since every student does eventually want to get done!).

Starting with a strong and detailed proposal, be it for a funded project or for a dissertation, is an excellent foundation. Crafting a reasonable and realistic plan is especially important, because if (when?) the proposal is accepted (or the grant funded), the researcher actually will have to do the work and carry out the research plan!

ORGANIZATION AND CONTENT OF A TYPICAL PROPOSAL

The format of a research proposal will vary somewhat according to its purpose and the institutions involved, but the major components are generally the same and are presented below in the order in which they usually occur. (See also text box 3.1, Saracevic's "Content of a Proposal for a Research Project" in this chapter, for additional information about the components of a proposal.)

Title Page

Most sponsoring agencies specify the format for the title page and may provide a special form. Likewise, universities usually specify the format to be followed by doctoral students. Close attention should be paid to the instructions for the title page. Regardless of the format used, the title of the proposal should accurately reflect the contents and the scope of the suggested study. It also is a good idea to think about important keywords and include these in the title. A catchy title may be more important for a grant proposal (it may make it easier for grant reviewers to remember and discuss your proposal) than for a dissertation. Some sage advice for a dissertation title is to make it descriptive but to save the best title for the book!

Abstract

Most research proposals, with the possible exception of dissertation proposals, should provide a short summary or abstract of about two hundred words. The abstract should touch on every major component of the proposal except the budget, if there is one. Some readers only read the abstract, while others rely on it for a quick overview of the proposal. Some sponsoring agencies use the abstract to weed out unsuitable proposals and to disseminate information. Consequently, the writing of the abstract should be done with care. Pay attention to the required word length and keep within the limit. Although it appears early in the proposal, it may be the last thing that is composed, as it may change throughout the process of writing the proposal.

Table of Contents

A table of contents is not always deemed necessary, especially for brief proposals, but it is useful for presenting an overview of the organization of the proposal. In addition to outlining the major components of the proposal, it may provide lists of illustrations, tables, appendices, etc. For longer proposals, including the dissertation proposal, the table of contents is required and actually can come in handy as a finding tool, since there will be no index for reference.

Introduction and Statement of the Problem

An introduction not always is considered necessary, as it tends to duplicate information that follows. But an opening statement characterizing what is being proposed can help to introduce the subject to the reader. Some authors use introductions to outline the major components of the proposal. If included, it should be brief and avoid unnecessary redundancy.

The first section of the typical proposal, if there is not a separate problem section, also presents the problem to be studied and provides a brief historical background for the problem if appropriate. If the problem warrants being divided into subproblems, they are identified at this point. This section also should indicate the significance or importance of the proposed study or state why a solution is needed and identify anticipated benefits and their significance. "It is imperative to make the case for the project and to specifically state its importance to the knowledge base and research literature"; therefore, "the proposal should include a justification for the research" (Connaway 2005). A clear and compelling statement of significance is vital, as it answers the all-important question "so what?" What is the point of doing the research? For funders, the question is: "Why should this project be funded rather than other projects?" It is best if the proposal has a definitive answer to the "so what" question. Although it may be clear to the researcher, who is deeply invested in the problem at hand, the reader does not want to search for significance, or worse, have to guess at it.

To obtain the background provided in this section, and possibly elsewhere in the proposal, a variety of sources of information may be consulted. The following list includes some of the types of background information often needed for writing a research proposal, as well as examples of common sources of such information in LIS. Most of these sources are provided by US government agencies or American associations or institutions.

1. **Terminology:** *The ALA Glossary of Library and Information Science*, 4th ed., edited by Michael Levine-Clark and Toni M. Carter (2013); *Harrod's Librarian's Glossary and Reference Book*, 10th ed., edited and compiled by Ray Prytherch (Harrod 2005); *Dictionary of Information Science and Technology*, 2nd ed., edited by Mehdi Khosrow-Pour (IGI Global 2007) (Khosrow-Pour and IGI Global 2013), e-book (https://www.worldcat.org/title/dictionary-of -information-science-and-technology/oclc/1102541190&referer=brief _results); *Concise Dictionary of Library and Information Science*, 2nd ed., edited by Stella Keenan and Colin Johnston (Bowker-Saur, 2000); *Dictionary of Information and Library Management*, 2nd ed., edited by Janet Stephenson (A. & C. Black, 2007); *ODLIS: The Online Dictionary for Library and Information Science*, edited by Joan M. Reitz (Libraries Unlimited/ABC-CLIO), http:// www.abc-clio.com/ODLIS/odlis_m.aspx; and *Glossary of Library Terms* (University Library, University of Illinois at Urbana-Champaign), https:// guides.library.illinois.edu/c.php?g=347755&p=2344964.

2. **Brief background:** *Encyclopedia of Library and Information Science*, 3rd ed., edited by Marcia Bates and Mary Niles Maack, vols. 1–4 (CRC Press, 2011), also available online with the purchase of the print version; *Encyclopedia of Library and Information Science*, vols. 1–73 (Marcel Dekker, 1968–2003); and *Encyclopedia of Information Science and Technology*, 3rd ed., edited by Mehdi Khosrow-Pour, vols. 1–5 (Idea Group Reference, 2015).

3. **Trends:** *Library Trends* ("Library Trends | JHU Press" n.d.) is an excellent source for trending LIS research. The International Federation of Library Associations (IFLA) publishes a *Trend Report* (https://trends.ifla.org/). See also regular updates from the ACRL Research and Planning Review Committee, for example, for the annual "Top Trends in Academic Libraries," in *College & Research Libraries News* and the biennial environmental scan. Also, ACRL's Environmental Scan for 2019 is available (http://www.ala.org /acrl/sites/ala.org.acrl/files/content/publications/whitepapers /EnvironmentalScan2019.pdf).

4. **Statistics and related information:**
   (a) Agencies regularly gathering and publishing statistics about libraries or librarians:
      i) Association for Library and Information Science Education—*Library and Information Science Education Statistical Report*, 1980–, annual (http://www.alise.org/statistical-reports-2).
      ii) American Library Association (ALA). A number of units within ALA are concerned with collecting and reporting library-related statistics. The Office for Research and Statistics has issued several statistical reports, as well as a series of research monographs available online at http://www.ala.org/tools/topics/research. *The State of*

America's Libraries Report is published annually by ALA as a digital supplement to *American Libraries* (http://www.ala.org/news/state-americas-libraries-report-2020). The Association of College and Research Libraries regularly compiles and publishes *Academic Library Trends and Statistics* (http://www.ala.org/acrl/publications/trends).

iii) Association of Research Libraries—*ARL Statistics*, annual (published as the Gerould statistics from 1907 to 1908 through 1962–1963; *ARL Annual Salary Survey*, 1973—) (http://www.arlstatistics.org/home). Academic Library Statistics (ACRL Metrics) (http://www.ala.org/acrl/publications/trends).

iv) Information Today, Inc.—*American Library Directory*, 1923–, biennial (http://infotoday.stores.yahoo.net/american-library-directory-220132014.html); and *The Library and Book Trade Almanac*$_{TM}$ from 1956 to present (http://books.infotoday.com/directories/Library-and-Book-Trade-Almanac.shtml), 1956–.

v) National Center for Education Statistics (NCES) (https://nces.ed.gov), US Department of Education (http://www.ed.gov) periodically collects statistics from school, public, and academic libraries. The frequency and titles of the reports vary. The Institute of Museum and Library Services (IMLS) provides a data catalog for public and state library and other agencies' survey data (https://www.imls.gov/research-tools/data-collection) and publishes the Public Libraries Survey (PLS) (http://www.imls.gov/research-evaluation/data-collection/public-libraries-united-states-survey). The IPEDS (Integrated Postsecondary Education Data System) data are available online at https://nces.ed.gov/ipeds.

vi) Special Libraries Association—results of its salary survey are published every two years with annual updates (https://www.sla.org/shop/salary-survey).

vii) American Association of School Librarians—collects data on school libraries (http://www.ala.org/aasl/advocacy/research/slc).

(b) Other sources of statistics:

i) State library agencies—most state libraries collect statistics on public libraries. The Library Research Service (LRS) of the Colorado State Library gathers and reports statistics on Colorado and national public and school libraries. The LRS web page provides data, reports, and other resources (http://www.lrs.org/) that include information on research and statistics. The IMLS collects data on state library administrative agencies biannually (https://www.imls.gov/research-evaluation/data-collection/state-library-administrative-agency-survey) and publishes the results from the survey.

ii) Individual libraries—a few libraries collect data on a regional or national level. Annual reports of individual libraries can be useful also, but the lack of standardization presents some problems for analysis.

iii) Library research centers—the Center for Informatics Research in Science and Scholarship (CIRSS), formerly the Library Research

    Center (LRC), of the University of Illinois School of Information Sciences. Its web page (http://cirss.lis.illinois.edu) includes information about the center's current projects.

  (c) Sources for national data (this list is adapted from ALA LARKS: http://www.ala.org/research/larks/researchtools).

    i) US Census Bureau (http://www.census.gov).

    ii) Bureau of Labor Statistics (http://www.bls.gov and Public Data Application Programming Interface (API) http://www.bls.gov/developers).

    iii) US Department of Commerce Bureau of Economic Analysis (http://www.bea.gov).

    iv) Centers for Disease Control and Prevention (CDC) National Center for Health Statistics (http://www.cdc.gov/nchs).

    v) Cultural Policy and the Arts National Data Archive (CPANDA) (http://www.cpanda.org/cpanda/about).

5. **Directory-type information:** *American Library Directory* (http://www.americanlibrarydirectory.com); *The ALA Online Handbook of Organization* (http://www.ala.org/aboutala/governance/handbook); and the websites of some organizations that list their members.

6. **Bibliographical data:** See the indexes cited in the section "The Literature Review of Related Research" in this chapter.

7. **Other resources include:** ALA's *Library Technology Reports* (http://www.alatechsource.org/taxonomy/term/106); reports of the Council on Library and Information Resources (CLIR, http://www.clir.org/pubs/reports); ARL *SPEC Kits* (http://publications.arl.org/SPEC_Kits); and *CLIP Notes*, published by ACRL (http://www.ala.org/acrl/publications).

THE LITERATURE REVIEW OF RELATED RESEARCH

    What already is known about the research topic? What has been found out through scholarly investigation, and what are the gaps? What methods have been used to tackle similar problems? The literature review of related research is, in effect, an expansion of the historical background presented in the problem section. It cites and gives a brief overview of the related research studies that have been conducted. The literature review section of the proposal describes the foundation on which the proposed study will be built by considering the work done by others, evaluating their methods and results, and stating what gaps there are and how the proposed research will address these. The literature review should be selective (the final report often contains additional works or information) and should group the cited studies in a logical fashion, often crafting an argument to bolster the claim that the proposed research is necessary and significant.

    In this section the theoretical or conceptual framework is established for the subsequent stages, particularly the development of the hypothesis or research questions. As described in chapter 2, the literature review helps to suggest the best approach to seeking a solution to the problem. Before continuing with the research study, it is essential to know what has already been done.

In addition to describing the available literature, it also is expected that quotations will be used judiciously to bolster arguments and illustrate ideas. But when and how should quotes be used? Eco (2015, 263), writing about the dissertation thesis, noted that "many texts by other authors" will be quoted, including primary sources, and the secondary materials, also known as critical literature. He provided the following guidelines:

- "Quote the critical literature only when its authority corroborates or confirms your statements" (Eco 2015, 263). It seems logical, if the literature review is viewed as an argument, that the researcher looks for and cites authoritative support. It is not necessary to quote something if it does not add anything new or if it is obvious.
- "If you don't want readers to presume that you share the opinion of the quoted author, you must include your own critical remarks before or after the passage" (Eco 2015, 157). It is a mistake to string quotations together without inserting an interpretation or explanation of how each of them contributes to the literature or the argument. Bald quotations standing on their own invite misinterpretation, or confusion on the part of the reader.
- "Make sure that the author and the source . . . of your quote are clearly identifiable" (Eco 2015, 157). Eco's quote identifies another characteristic of a good proposal: it is correctly cited. Failure to cite correctly can result in inadvertent plagiarism.

Writing a solid literature review is not an easy task and involves a high level of thinking to both summarize and synthesize the available literature. For dissertation proposals, the literature review should be as comprehensive as possible, to make sure that the researcher is not inadvertently replicating research without knowing it. To replicate a study is not necessarily bad, especially if it is done in a different context (e.g., applying and extending a study on information literacy to online education). However, to not be aware of and cite a study one is about to replicate is a major gaff, which has the potential to be professionally damaging.

RESEARCH DESIGN

Following the literature review, the next section usually is devoted to a description of the proposed research methods (see chapter 2 for more on research design features). Almost always written for the specialist rather than the layperson, the research design component includes the following elements:

- **Goals and objectives:** Statements emphasizing the major purposes of the research method.
- **Hypothesis or research questions:** The major research hypothesis/ hypotheses (major, secondary, and/or alternative as appropriate) or research questions should be stated next. They naturally follow from

the gaps revealed in the literature review. As previously discussed, the researcher may have concluded that the development and testing of formal hypotheses is not feasible or desirable (as in the case of qualitative approaches). Thus, they may decide instead to pose one or more research questions to be answered.

- **Assumptions:** In quantitative studies, basic assumptions are usually given after the hypothesis statement. These are needed to help support the hypothesis and therefore logically occur at this point. They should directly relate to and build the case for the hypothesis, as opposed to the method.

- **Definitions:** For quantitative studies, the operational or working definitions for key terms, including those that are used in a unique way, logically follow the hypothesis and assumptions. There is some disagreement about how much detail should be provided here, rather than in the section describing the data collection instrument, but the operational definitions should at least tell what is to be observed and imply how. For example, an operational definition of library use may specify that external circulations are to be measured by analyzing circulation records. Many researchers prefer to incorporate the hypothesis, assumptions, and definitions in the problem section, but may repeat them here. For qualitative approaches, it often is common to see the definitions of key terms in the text as they appear and also included as an appendix at the end of the proposal.

- **Method:** This section of the proposal is where the researcher describes how the study will be organized and the situation in which the hypothesis will be tested or the research questions addressed. The techniques and tools that will be used to collect data should be explained in detail. For quantitative studies this includes a description of the kind of data that will be collected to test the hypothesis, including (a) the criteria for admissibility of data, (b) whether it will be limited to primary or secondary data, (c) the likely sources of these data, (d) sampling technique, and (e) the type(s) of data collection methods or tools (e.g., questionnaire) to be used to gather the data. If a pilot study and/or a pretest is to be conducted, it too should be described in detail. Similarly, qualitative approaches should describe the methods of data collection (e.g., individual interviews, focus group interviews), as well as how participants will be selected and recruited. If the project will have mixed methods or multiple phases, these each should be described, with a rationale given for the sequencing and other choices made. Large grant projects may have multiple distinct phases, each of which has a different method, and in which initial phases may be structured to inform latter phases. For example, the "Public Libraries Respond to the Opioid Crisis with Their Communities" (2020) IMLS-funded grant project included eight case studies. Each case study included a review of the libraries' policies, procedures, programming, services, and marketing and promotion of their offerings to the community addressing the opioid epidemic as well as the libraries' financials and the communities' demographics. The researchers visited each case study site for several days to identify programs and to conduct individual semistructured interviews with library staff, library board members, staff at community partner organizations, and members of the community.

- **Analysis:** This part of the proposal describes how the data will be analyzed and generally does not need to be very specific, although for dissertation proposals and some large grant proposals it will be necessary to provide more detail, so check these requirements as appropriate to clarify. In the case of quantitative methods, for example, the specific statistical tests, if any, to be employed in the analysis probably do not need to be itemized here. But at least the general kinds of analysis to be used (e.g., descriptive, bivariate, multivariate, inferential) should be specified along with the rationales for using them. "Dummy tables" may be provided at this point to illustrate how the data will be categorized and analyzed. For qualitative studies, the researcher should describe the process that will be used to analyze the data, including intercoder reliability (ICR) tests if appropriate. For both quantitative and qualitative approaches, it also is advisable to specify which computer statistical packages are to be used.

Institutional Resources

It is useful to describe relevant institutional resources that are available to support the proposed research project. Such a section is particularly advisable for grant proposals requesting external funding, and some may request or require a statement of institutional support. Items in this section may include computer facilities, library resources, incentives for study participants, travel, research personnel, technical assistance, and facilities.

Personnel

A section describing personnel who will be paid with project funds may be necessary only for grant proposals or for projects involving a relatively large number of people. Funding agencies often encourage or require collaboration. "Collaboration is an important aspect of any project and encourages researchers to address differences," which "often lead to significant new insight and innovation" (Connaway 2005, 263). A personnel section is rarely needed for individual research projects, such as dissertation research, though funding agencies often require the submission of a résumé for the principal investigator (PI). If a personnel section is included, it should provide relevant background information about the research staff, emphasizing their qualifications and what they will contribute to the project. Costs relating to personnel are covered next in the discussion of the budget.

Budget

Show me the money! If a researcher needs funds to carry out the research, creating a budget is imperative. Budget sections are required for requests for grant funding, but also are useful for dissertation research and studies being carried out that are institution-funded (such as a school library that wishes to measure the effect of creating a sustained silent reading program, public librarians who want to evaluate an adult education program, or an academic librarian conducting a study of space utilization prior to a renovation). Assistance in preparing budgets for grants can be found in books by Landau (2011), Staiens (2016), and Gerding and MacKellar (2017).

The budget has two main functions. First, it estimates, as realistically as possible, the costs of achieving the objectives of the proposed research. The budget thus helps the researcher to determine whether the proposed project is economically feasible. Second, the budget provides a means to monitor the project's financial activities throughout the research process, essentially to track how closely actual progress in achieving the objectives is being made relative to the proposed budget. The timeline ensures that the researcher does not run out of money before the project is finished, which can mean that it may have to be suspended without completion or be put on hold while additional funding is sought. Either way, this is best avoided by careful attention to the development of the budget (and keeping tabs on expenditures as they occur).

Before considering some of the specific items that should be included in a proposed budget, there are several general points or guidelines worth mentioning, keeping in mind that only grant proposals are likely to have a budget section. Regarding time and personnel, the most common approach to estimating these factors is to list the various stages of the project (such as developing the data collection tools and data analysis) and to calculate how much time and how many staff hours will be required for each. Such estimates usually are based on the researcher's experience and/or knowledge of similar studies, but it should be remembered that almost every operation takes longer than expected. It can be argued that the estimates should provide additional time for snags or problems, up to an additional 50 percent of the initial estimates.

Budgets are more likely to be underestimated than overestimated, because the researcher may not realize how much work actually is involved. Qualitative data analysis especially is labor intensive and requires extra time for careful coding of usually large amounts of text. In addition, it is not unheard of for passionate researchers to get carried away in "the thrill of the chase" with collecting data or following new leads and in the process collect too much data, including some that might turn out to be irrelevant (here the caution is for qualitative researchers to stick to the data that answer the research questions and save additional forays for future research). Also, the researcher can be highly motivated and anxious to receive approval of the budget and proposal and may be prone to underestimating for that reason. Researchers typically overestimate the amount of time that they can devote to the project and may have several grant projects (and other writing projects) under way simultaneously. So again, a realistic budget in comparison to what is described as the research design is critical. A certain amount of budget flexibility is desirable, and underestimating costs reduces that potential, so making a deliberately low estimate for the budget is a mistake. If the budget looks too large, reduce the amount of work proposed.

In order to decrease the likelihood of underestimating the budget, it is advisable to check the correctness of the figures at the last minute. For example, perhaps the researcher's university has just increased the percentage for facility and administrative (F&A) costs, commonly known as "indirect cost." Or perhaps it has changed the percentages in fringe benefits that accompany salary figures. Find out if any raise was recently granted to staff. This is especially important for multiyear budgets, since costs tend to rise each year. An incorrect number in year one can be multiplied as time passes and result in a salary or F&A budget shortfall. In addition, it is advisable to build in a hedge against inflation, or to increase the figures for subsequent years of a multiyear proposal by a reasonable percentage. Explanations of how the major budget figures were calculated should be provided.

Another rule of thumb worth noting is that the budget should be fitted to the research project, not vice versa. One should not decide how much money is available or is likely to be obtained, then design a study within those constraints. Instead, the researcher should design the study to investigate the problem, then determine how much such an investigation will cost. Perhaps the project can then be reduced, if necessary. Determining the budget before designing the study is comparable to selecting a methodology before identifying the problem to be studied. Also, the amount of time and personnel needed for the different stages of a research project will depend to some extent on the type of study being proposed. For example, an exploratory study typically requires a relatively greater amount of time for data analysis than does a more focused study in which the researcher has a better-defined notion of the big picture.

A typical budget usually will contain at least the following items:

- **Salaries and wages:** Personnel costs are determined essentially by translating the time and staffing into appropriate salaries and wages. Usually included here are fringe benefits, if paid, and the costs of any contractual services, such as a consultant's fee. These can be calculated in terms of percentages. If the principal investigator (PI) will devote one day per week to the project, this would translate to 20 percent of an annual salary.
- **Space:** Itemized here are the costs, if any, of providing space for the project. For example, the rental of an office for staff or rooms to conduct focus group interviews would be included here.
- **Equipment:** Equipment costs are included here, whether purchased or rented. Pay attention to whether or not equipment is eligible for funding. Some granting agencies restrict computer technology purchases, so the specific grant guidelines should be kept in mind. For example, do not ask for three tablet computers for data collection if the grant specifies no technology purchases. Software purchases and site licenses also may go in this category; check the grant guidelines. Licenses for software packages such as Statistical Product and Service Solutions (SPSS) or NVivo may be annual fees, so be sure to include these in each year of the budget.

- **Materials and supplies:** Provided here are the costs for consumable materials and items such as miscellaneous office supplies, paper, and printer ink.
- **Travel expenses:** Many grant funders expect that results will be disseminated through conference presentations, so a reasonable amount per trip can be estimated. For example, "travel to three national conferences @ $1,800 per trip" could be included. Also, if the researcher has to travel to conduct focus group or individual interviews or to meet with collaborators at other institutions, this should be included in the travel budget.
- **Support services:** Expenses related to the use of services and facilities such as computers and photocopiers are included here.
- **Miscellaneous expenses:** Additional costs related to telephone service, purchase of books, media, postage, and so forth are listed here.
- **Indirect costs:** These include F&A costs, also known as "indirect cost." These are costs that cannot directly be identified with a particular project, such as library services, utilities, accounting, maintenance, and secretarial support. These often are figured as a percentage of salaries and wages or of modified total costs. This figure usually is somewhere between 30 and 70 percent of direct costs. The exact percentage, and the basis for figuring it, usually is established or negotiated by the institution with which the researcher is affiliated and the funding agency.
- **Budget summary and justification:** If the budget is relatively long, it may be advisable to provide a summary, listing major items only. If a budget justification is required, this involves a sentence or two explaining each budget item and why it is necessary for the project.

A sample of a typical twenty-four-month budget is presented in table 3.1. In this example, the first column represents the item, the second the proposed contribution of the funding agency, and the third and fourth columns the support to be provided by the researchers' organizations. (Usually, the greater the proportion the parent organization is prepared to provide, the greater are the chances of obtaining outside funding.)

ANTICIPATED RESULTS

The next common section in the research proposal is an evaluation of expected project results, or the likely impact of the study. This information is particularly important for grant proposals, as the potential funding agency must be convinced of the value of the research project.

Indicators of Success

Some granting agents, including IMLS, require the articulation of the indicators of success for the project. These include national impact, current significance, strategic collaborations, and demonstrated expertise. This is the

Table 3.1.   Sample Twenty-Four-Month Budget for Grant

Item	Requested from Funding Agency	Partner Cost Share	Partner Cost Share
Personnel			
Co-principal investigators, 25% annual salary	$42,181.00	$61,845.00	$61,827.00
Fringe benefits rate: 30%	$5,284.42	$18,553.50	$13,698.30
Co-principal investigator, 12.5% annual salary			$75,926.00
Fringe benefits rate: 35.4%			$26,877.81
Software engineer, 10% annual salary		$14,884.00	$14,884.00
Fringe benefits rate: 30%		$4,465.20	$4,465.20
Research assistant/$15 hour	$74,230.00		
Fringe benefits rate: 15%	$7,850.00		
Tuition	$10,500.00		
Internal advisory board, 5% annual salary		$15,980.00	$15,980.00
Fringe benefits rate: 30%		$4,794.00	$4,794.00
Subtotal	*$140,045.42*	*$120,521.70*	*$218,452.31*
Consultant Fees			
Interview participants, 150/$30 each	$4,500.00		
Interview participants, 10/$50 each	$500.00		
Subtotal	*$5,000.00*	*$0.00*	*$0.00*
Hardware and Software			
Computer equipment	$2,300.00	$1,000.00	
Software	$2,600.00	$1,000.00	$1,000.00
Miscellaneous supplies	$680.00		
Subtotal	*$5,580.00*	*$2,000.00*	*$1,000.00*
Travel—Each trip estimated to cost $1,800	*$19,473.00*	*$3,600.00*	*$3,600.00*

(*continued*)

Table 3.1. (continued)

Item	Requested from Funding Agency	Partner Cost Share	Partner Cost Share
Indirect Costs			
15% for indirect costs on partner's expenses as a subcontractor	$9,500.00		
15% for indirect costs on partner's cost share		$18,764.00	
Subtotal	*$9,500.00*	*$18,764.00*	*$0.00*
Services			
Subaward to partner, first $25,000 accrues indirect	$25,000.00		
Subaward to partner, over $25,000 no indirect	$58,330.00		
Subtotal	*$83,330.00*	*$0.00*	*$0.00*
Totals	**$262,928.42**	**$144,885.70**	**$223,052.31**

description of how the researcher will measure the success of the project based on the four criteria.

Diversity Plan

IMLS requests a Diversity Plan, if it is applicable to the research, that describes how the project will engage underserved or diverse communities (see also chapter 14). IMLS provides some questions for consideration.

- How will the project strengthen the field's commitment to diversity, equity, and inclusion?
- How will you include a diversity of perspectives in the project?
- How are the relevant participants and communities involved in defining the challenges or opportunities and creating and implementing the project? ("National Leadership Grants for Libraries" n.d., 18)

Limitations of the Study

Typically, the last section of a research proposal points out the limitations of the project. While the researcher does not want to be negative at this point, it is important to note, in a few concise statements, the limitations imposed by the research method, setting, and so forth. All research has limitations, and in essence, the researcher is stating what these are, not denigrating the value of the study. For example, the results of a study with a small, nonrandom sample may not be generalizable to the population, and this could be included as a limitation.

Back Matter

Immediately following the text, the writer usually provides the list of cited references. If there are fewer than six, they often are inserted in the text; if more, a separate section is probably warranted. After the list of references, the writer may choose to provide a bibliography, which will list all the works consulted in writing the proposal and possibly other suggested readings. In a short proposal this usually is unnecessary.

If the author wishes to provide the reader with additional information that is not crucial to the text, then they may wish to include one or more appendixes. This should not be overdone, however, especially in grant proposals. If there is any doubt about the need to include some information in an appendix, then it probably is best to omit it. If not required, it is important to include an appendix with the timetable outlining the dates by which stages of the proposed project are to be completed. If not provided in a separate section, this information may be integrated throughout the text or even provided as a separate document.

The Dissertation Proposal: Further Guidance

Islam's book, *Social Research Methodology and New Techniques in Analysis, Interpretation, and Writing* (2018), includes chapters on designing qualitive, quantitative, and mixed-methods research doctoral proposals, with eight examples of doctoral proposals. The preceding description of the components of a proposal is further augmented in text box 3.1, which was created by Tefko Saracevic for doctoral students. It briefly summarizes the dissertation proposal and poses important questions that the proposal must address.

Text Box 3.1: Content of a Proposal for a Research Project

Tefko Saracevic

Every proposal for a thesis or any other research *must* have the following content:

1. Title
2. **Purpose:** Statement about the general *problem addressed*. This specifies the topic or area of work. It sets the stage for broadly identifying the area of research and the problems encountered in that area.
3. **Justification:** An explanation of the *significance* of this area of inquiry.

4. **Previous work:** A review of the most pertinent literature, works, or achievements related to the problem at hand. This can include a few general works and a few significant applications or research studies. This can be a sample of the relevant literature, stated as an indication of what will be extended.
5. **Theory or model:** Any theoretical background that will be used or may apply to the investigation of the problem in this study. Or if there is no applicable theory, any model(s) that may be applicable. This can be extracted from the literature and modified as necessary. It can also be said that this is the starting model, and it will be modified after the investigation; thus, development of a model can be one of the research objectives.
6. **Research objectives:** The specific issues addressed in the framework of this problem. This can be in terms of either questions (ending with a "?"), statements of specific issues, or hypotheses that will be tested. For each research question there will be also a methodology, and at the end of research, a set of findings or answers with discussion. Purpose is general. Objectives are specific and directly connected with what is planned to be done.
7. **Methodology:** Methods and procedures to be used for each research question. These methods may include a survey of literature on the basis of which models may be developed or extended; collection and synthesis of data; surveys of given populations or institutions; observation of practices or behaviors; experiments; etc. Social science, ethnographic, systems, historical, political science, and other methodologies can be used.
8. **Analysis:** Methods and procedures used in analysis and synthesis of gathered data. This may be subsumed under methodology in general.
9. **Expectation:** A projection of results or achievements as the results of the proposed research. This can be short and general.

Summary: This can be summarized in questions to be answered in each section:

1. What do you *call* this investigation?
2. What *problem* or area will you investigate in general?
3. Why is this problem *important* to investigate?
4. What was *previously done* in relation to this problem? What were some of the significant studies?
5. What theory or model is going to guide your research?
6. What will you *specifically* investigate or do in the framework of that problem? What are your specific research questions or hypotheses?
7. How will each research question be *addressed*?
8. How will the results be *analyzed*?
9. What are the *deliverables*? What can or will be gained by investigation of this problem?

Organization: It is not necessary to follow exactly this order, but it is important that *all* of these points be clearly and directly addressed. For instance, it is usual to have the problem statement in the introduction. This can be followed by research objectives, and then other points, rather than following the order above.

Starting: To start developing the proposal in your own mind and on paper, it is best first to state clearly the problem and research questions, and as necessary restate them as you go along. The process of developing a proposal is not linear but reiterative, with a lot of feedback loops. Start with concentrating on questions 2 and 6.

Extensions: This list may be modified for the organization and writing of papers presenting results of research or for papers critically reviewing works related to a research topic or an area of scholarly studies.

CHARACTERISTICS OF A GOOD PROPOSAL

As Leedy, Ormrod, and Johnson stated, "Good research requires that those who undertake it be able to think clearly, without confusion" (2019, 126). Therefore, it is essential that a research proposal be a straightforward document that includes only information that contributes to an understanding of the problem and its proposed solution. While it should be well written, its primary purpose is to communicate clearly, not to be a literary masterpiece. To that end, the language should be clear and precise and represent conventional prose. The proposal should be logically organized, and it should make ample use of headings and subheadings.

The general format should be attractive, conform to external mechanics of good form (such as margins and pagination), and be neat and free of typographical or grammatical errors. The proposal should represent a high level of scholarship, as evidenced by insight into the problem, imagination in the design of the study, adequate grasp of research and statistical tools, and display of a scientific attitude. Most funding agencies now accept or require electronic proposals and submissions, which may have strict conventions (e.g., for file names and formats), such as Grants.gov (http://www.grants .gov), which is used for federal granting agencies. Be aware of page length; if a grant stipulates ten pages maximum with certain margins and font size, it is important to adhere to these requirements or risk outright rejection of the proposal.

Features That Detract from a Proposal

Unfortunately, numerous features of a proposal may diminish its effectiveness. Poor writing that is sloppy, unedited, or poorly organized is an obvious flaw, so proofread all work carefully and seek input from advisers and other mentors. Such weaknesses are always to be avoided, but they are particularly crucial when applying for funding. Some of these deficiencies are obvious, though still surprisingly common. Babbie's advice is "to follow this procedure: Write, Read Strunk and White, Revise, Reread Strunk and White, Revise again" (2021, 511). The book *The Elements of Style* by Strunk and White (2019) is a small book with excellent tips for writing clearly and succinctly. Babbie (2021, 491–514) includes a chapter on reading and writing social research that is an excellent resource for writing papers, reports, and proposals. Leedy, Ormrod, and Johnson (2019, 372–97) include a chapter on planning and preparing a final research report that includes sage advice and a reading list that could be beneficial when writing a proposal or report.

Also, as noted previously, failure to completely and accurately cite all sources detracts from the proposal and may result in accidental plagiarism, which is to be strictly avoided. In these times of cut and paste from primary or secondary sources, it is critical that researchers consistently and diligently track all direct quotations and cite ideas from others. Be aware of the preferred citation style for dissertations and grant proposals and use the most current citation manual. There are many resources online to assist with citation formats, including the following:

- APA (American Psychological Association) Style (http://www.apastyle .org). Features tutorials, webinars, handouts, guides, and sample papers.
- The MLA (Modern Language Association) Style Center (https://style .mla.org). Includes FAQs and an interactive template to create bibliographies in MLA Style (https://style.mla.org/interactive-practice -template).
- *The Chicago Manual of Style Online* (https://www.chicagomanualofstyle .org/home.html). Provides video tutorials, a citation quick guide, Q&A, users forum, and librarian, teacher, and student resources.
- The Purdue Writing Lab (OWL) (https://owl.purdue.edu). Features vidcasts [sic] via YouTube, APA and MLA formatting and style guides.
- Cornell University Library, Citation Management (https://www.library .cornell.edu/research/citation). Includes APA, MLA, and Chicago citation styles and guides, and information about citation tools such as Zotero, Mendeley, and Endnote.

In addition, proposals sometimes fall short of conforming to the guidelines of the funding or approving agency or do not address the research area or interests of the agency. That is not to say that researchers should not be creative in identifying possible sources of funding, but that they must tailor the proposal according to guidelines and make sure their work fits into the topics supported by the call for submissions. Proposals also suffer if they are incomplete. It is not unusual for research proposals to lack a clear and explicit budget, for example. Some agencies provide a checklist of required components for the submission. If such a checklist is available, keep it close by and refer to it often in the course of the grant preparation. Use the list as a last final check before submitting the document. If anything major is missing, it is horrifying to discover this at the last minute. See "Improving the Grant Proposal" for additional tips for avoiding rejection of a grant proposal.

Many other characteristics may weaken a grant proposal, some as minor as the font size. As already noted, but worth repeating, it is essential that applicants adhere to the funding agency's description and guidelines for formatting specifications, such as font size, spacing, and page limits (Connaway 2005). It is essential, of course, that grant proposals meet the submission deadline, if there is one.

OBTAINING FUNDING FOR LIBRARY AND INFORMATION SCIENCE RESEARCH

When seeking external funding for a research project, there are a variety of resources to which the researcher can turn for guidance. If the proposal has been written in response to a request for proposal (RFP) from a specific funding agency or in response to a clear indication that a funding agency is interested

Table 3.2. Improving the Grant Proposal

The National Institutes of Health (NIH), a major provider of project grants to colleges and hospitals, approves less than half of the grant applications it receives. The NIH website, http://www.nih.gov, includes grant guidelines and funding opportunities. A presentation on grant writing from St. Louis University lists the top ten reasons, in order from the tenth to the top reason, why grant proposals fail, as outlined in an NIH-sponsored grantmanship meeting (Marcinkowski and Schuelke 2017). These reasons are listed below, along with advice. The NIH National Institute of Allergy and Infectious Diseases (NIAID) provides excellent advice on writing a research plan ("Write Your Research Plan | NIH: National Institute of Allergy and Infectious Diseases" n.d.).

10. Uncritical approach
    - Ensure that your project tackles an important and unique problem, that your hypothesis or research questions are well-focused and addressed by your specific aims, and that your methodology can help meet these aims. If reviewers feel you're fishing for data and not pursuing a logical progression of methods to answer specific questions, they will not be enthusiastic about your project.
    - The application should be like a story that describes the goal (question to answer) and how the applicant is going to meet it (the aims and approaches).
9. Lack of sufficient experimental detail
8. Unrealistically large amount of work
    To evaluate the complexity of a project, NIH researchers use the BEST system:
    - Budget—asking for too little is a sign that you do not understand the scope.
    - Effort—setting an insufficient level of effort shows you're not aware of how much work is involved.
    - Specific Aims—not having the appropriate number of aims could mean you do not grasp the complexity of your proposed research.
    - Time—requesting too few years for your grant indicates you think your research may take less time than your scope requires.
7. Absence of acceptable scientific rationale
    Ask yourself the following questions:
    - Does the project address an important problem or a critical barrier to progress in the field?
    - If the aims of the project are achieved, how will scientific knowledge, technical capability, and/or clinical practice be improved?
    - How will successful completion of the aims change the concepts, methods, technologies, treatments, services, or preventative interventions that drive this field?
6. Questionable reasoning in experimental approach
5. Uncertainty concerning future directions
    - Write an impact statement, which briefly summarizes the big picture of the project, as well as future implications.
    - Describe potential pitfalls and alternative approaches, and address future directions.

(continued)

Table 3.2.   (continued)

4. Lack of experience in essential methodology
   - Justify choice of methods and convince reviewers that you know your methods. If you do not, show that you've enlisted collaborators who can do what you propose.
3. Lack of knowledge of relevant published work
2. Diffuse, unfocused, or superficial research plan
   - Develop a hypothesis or research questions before embarking on data collection.
   - Maintain a key balance between an addressable scientific gap and the knowledge base needed to support the hypothesis or research questions.• Determine two to four aims that are addressed by the research project. Focus your aims by making each one an achievable objective with clear end points your peer reviewers can easily assess.
1. Lack of original ideas
   - Use sounding boards to pitch idea to others and determine whether the project is original and important.
   - Find out high-priority areas by either speaking with an NIH program officers or looking at council-approved concepts. However, the NIH cautions not to make high priority the basis for describing the significance of a research project.
   - Justify the significance of the data.

in proposals on a topic, seeking funds is relatively straightforward. The agency's website should have a listing of grant support staff, who should be contacted at an early stage and asked for whatever advice they are able to give as the proposal develops. In most cases, the agency also will provide material describing what it wants and appropriate application forms on its website. In some cases, an agency will refer you to previous projects it has funded and/or volunteer to critique drafts of the proposal. The amount of help an agency is willing to give varies widely. In any case, it is wise to be aware that assistance in developing a proposal is not a promise that the proposal will be funded. Agencies may deliberately encourage several people to prepare requests so that they can pick the one they judge will make the best use of available funds.

In lieu of a relatively firm commitment via RFP from a funding agency that promises to entertain grant proposals that mirror the researcher's needs, it falls on the researcher to identify likely sources of support. Individuals working in the same subject area are possible sources of suggestions for funding as well as informal and formal sources. Professional organizations also may be able to give useful advice. For example, ALA's Office for Research Statistics sponsors the Librarian and Researcher Knowledge Space (LARKS) website, which has an excellent section on grant resources that provides descriptions and URLs for grant-funding agencies and a selected bibliography for further reading (http://www.ala.org/research/larks/grants).

For those needing information about granting foundations and agencies and about specific grants, there are numerous standard works available, including *Catalog of Federal Domestic Assistance, Annual Register of Grant Support, The Foundation Directory, The Grants Register, Directory of Research Grants*, the daily *Federal Register,* the *Foundation Reporter*, and *Commerce Business Daily*. Other databases are the Sponsored Programs Information Network (SPIN) and *The Foundation Directory*. A subscription-based directory, *GrantForward* (https://www.grantforward.com/index), has a free trial option, but a subscription held by your institution or a personal membership is needed for ongoing use. Grants available from every US government agency are collected on the website (http://www.grants.gov). An ever-increasing amount of information about grants can be found online. Among other resources found there are documentation for grant applications; subject guides to funding agencies, often with links to their home pages; and various discussion lists. Gerding and MacKellar maintain a *Library Grants* blog that is frequently updated (http://librarygrants .blogspot.com). Various workshops and seminars on obtaining grants are regularly held in-person and online, and some master's programs include courses on grant writing, including those for LIS students.

General advice and information about grants and funded research in LIS can be found from Landau (2011), Staines (2016), and Gerding and MacKellar (2017), who have written comprehensive resources for libraries on obtaining funding and preparing grant proposals. Another useful resource is Maxwell's (2014) *The ALA Book of Library Grant Money.*

In considering and applying to potential funding agencies, it is critical to identify organizations that would appear to have an interest in, and something to be gained from, one's proposed research. On the other hand, it is possible to be imaginative in identifying such agencies and not restrict one's efforts to only the most obvious organizations. Experienced scientists identify tips for writing successful grant proposals in an online *Nature* article (Sohn 2019). After identifying possible research agencies, one should gather as much information as possible about the agencies' interests and what they have supported in the past. As noted previously, it usually is advisable to contact the potential grantors at an early date to inform them of one's intent to apply for support and to provide the agency with a brief, written description of the proposed research. Feedback gained at this stage can help to assess the interest of the organization, refine the project, and expedite consideration of the formal proposal to follow. Personal contact at this point can be especially beneficial. For additional excellent grant-getting advice, see the tips in text box 3.2 by Stephanie Harmon, program design and development manager at OCLC Research.

Text Box 3.2: Finding Funding: Tips for Developing Successful Grant Proposals

Stephanie Harmon

Get an early start. It takes time to assess needs and gather data to make a compelling case for a proposal. You will also need time to build a shared understanding of the project with your team, other internal stakeholders, and with potential cooperating organizations that may be providing letters of support.

Clarify the problem space and project goals. Articulate the need for the project and include available input from practitioners in the field to support your case. Explain who and what your project will affect, and how. How will this project build on, or differ from, what has been done already?

Research funding opportunities. Your project should align with the mission, vision, and program areas of your potential funder. Understand what each funder is looking for, the difference they are aiming to make in the world, and make a case for how your project will contribute to their vision and mission.

Concisely frame your project design. Consider using a logic model or other method to outline the *resources* you'll need to implement your project, the *activities* that will be done during the project, and the *outputs, outcomes,* and longer-term *impact* that will result from the work. Use this framework to inform your project budget, timeline, and evaluation plan.

Avoid the "curse of knowledge." Ask a few people who are unfamiliar with the project to review what you have written and provide feedback on the concept, structure, and flow of your proposal. Have your final round of copyediting or proofreading done by someone with fresh eyes.

Reach out to funders when possible. Inform yourself about if and/or how each funder wants to be approached. If they welcome contact, get in touch with program staff according to their stated guidelines. If possible, connect with a program officer to discuss your concept well before submitting your proposal to see if it is a good fit for their funding priorities. They often have tips for strengthening a submission, or may provide suggestions for other funding opportunities.

It takes a team. Explain why your organization is qualified to take on this work. Describe how your staff's skills, experience, and expertise will ensure the project is successful.

Collaborate to amplify impact. Are there organizations you should partner with? Can they help implement the project, disseminate results, or provide subject matter expertise? A letter of commitment or support from them will strengthen—or may be required for—your application. Consider offering a template letter they can customize that includes a description of your project and their role in it.

Measure and assess. How will you evaluate your work? Describe the instruments you will use to determine your success. What quantifiable results are you aiming for, and how will you measure success?

Communicate your results broadly. Think beyond your target community, even if the program was local. Your peers and others around your region and country can also learn from your experiences, challenges, and successes. Create a dissemination plan outlining how and where you will promote and publish your findings.

Teitel (2018, para. 2) provides eight tips "to increase the likelihood of your next proposal getting funded." According to the Grantsmanship Center (https://www.tgci.com), reviewers of proposals are most interested in the purpose and definition of the project, the priority of the project, the financial information, the background of the requesting organization, the personnel, and evaluation of the project. The Grantsmanship Center also offers free resources on grant proposal basics, essentials for getting the grant, advice on locating funders, and how to manage a grant if you are successful. There are several questions that a foundation likely will consider when reviewing a proposal:

1. Is the proposal problem solving?
2. Is the problem important?
3. Is this the appropriate foundation?
4. Is the proposal innovative?
5. Will the project become self-supporting?
6. Can the proposing group do the work?

7. Is the project demonstrative (i.e., can it be used as a model)?
8. How will the program be evaluated?
9. Is the amount of money requested sufficient?

Another key to obtaining funding is identifying research areas that are considered timely. From time to time, "inventories" or agendas of needed research studies have been produced and may be of some assistance in the identification of topics likely to be seen as relatively high priorities by funding agencies. Here are some resources that highlight possible topics:

- ACRL's *Academic Library Impact: Improving Practice and Essential Areas to Research* (Connaway et al. 2017)
- ACRL's *Open and Equitable Scholarly Communications: Creating a More Inclusive Future* (Maron et al. 2019)
- ALSC's *National Research Agenda for Library Service to Children (Ages 0–14)* (2019)
- *Artificial Intelligence (AI) in Strategic Marketing Decision-Making: A Research Agenda* (Stone et al. 2020)
- *Close Encounters of the Digital Kind: A Research Agenda for the Digitalization of Public Services* (Lindgren et al. 2019)
- "Exploring the Library's Contribution to the Academic Institution: Research Agenda"
- "IoT and AI for Smart Government: A Research Agenda" (Kankanhalli, Charalabidis, and Mellouli 2019)
- "Moving the EBLIP (Evidence Based Library & Information Practice) Community's Research Agenda Forward" (Eldredge, Holmes, and Ascher 2015)

SUMMARY

The proposal is as essential to successful research as the outline is to good writing. It represents what should be the careful planning that precedes a well-conceived research study. The proposal should spell out, to a reasonable degree, the details of a proposed research project and serve as a guide to which the researcher may refer as they carry out the study.

In terms of format, most research proposals are essentially the same. The elements generally included are the title page, abstract, literature review, hypothesis or research questions, assumptions, definitions, research design, data analysis, budget if appropriate, anticipated results, limitations, and references. A timetable can be quite useful in keeping the research project on schedule and may be appended or integrated throughout the proposal.

A variety of characteristics can increase the attractiveness of a proposal. Most of these attributes result from the proposal being well written and from the author using an appropriate, effective format with well-chosen and documented references to relevant literature in the proper citation style. Perhaps most important, the proposal should be clear, straightforward, and succinct.

A variety of features may detract from a research proposal. They range from unsound hypotheses to excessive budgets, with the most common problems being: poorly written, inexplicit proposals; unsound designs; irrelevant topics; and unqualified investigators. It is key for any research proposal to be as free of detracting features as possible, but this is particularly crucial for proposals for sponsored research.

REFERENCES

ACRL Research Planning and Review Committee. 2019. *Environmental Scan 2019.* Chicago: Association of College and Research Libraries.

Babbie, Earl R. 2021. *The Practice of Social Research.* 15th ed. Boston: Cengage Learning.

Connaway, Lynn Silipigni. 2005. "A Research Funding Opportunity for Library and Information Science Faculty: The OCLC/ALISE Library and Information Science Research Grant Program." *Journal of Education for Library and Information Science* 46(3): 258–65. https://doi.org/10.2307/40323849.

Connaway, Lynn Silipigni, William Harvey, Vanessa Kitzie, and Stephanie Mikitish. 2017. *Academic Library Impact: Improving Practice and Essential Areas to Research.* Chicago: Association of College and Research Libraries.

Covey, Stephen R. 1990. *The 7 Habits of Highly Effective People.* New York: Fireside/Simon & Schuster.

Eco, Umberto. 2015. *How to Write a Thesis.* Cambridge, MA: The MIT Press.

Eldredge, Jonathan D., Heather N. Holmes, and Marie T. Ascher. 2015. "Moving the EBLIP Community's Research Agenda Forward." *Evidence Based Library and Information Practice* 10(2): 170. https://doi.org/10.18438/B8J60S.

Gerding, Stephanie K., and Pamela H. MacKellar. 2017. *Winning Grants: A How-to-Do-It Manual for Librarians.* 2nd ed. Chicago: Neal Schuman/ALA Editions.

Harrod, Leonard Montague. 2005. *Harrod's Librarians' Glossary and Reference Book: A Directory of Over 10,200 Terms, Organizations, Projects and Acronyms in the Areas of Information Management, Library Science, Publishing and Archive Management.* Edited by Raymond John Prytherch. Aldersshot, UK, and Burlington, VT: Ashgate.

Islam, M. Rezaul. 2018. *Social Research Methodology and New Techniques in Analysis, Interpretation, and Writing.* Hershey, PA: IGI Global.

Kankanhalli, Atreyi, Yannis Charalabidis, and Sehl Mellouli. 2019. "IoT and AI for Smart Government: A Research Agenda." *Government Information Quarterly* 36(2): 304–9. https://doi.org/10.1016/j.giq.2019.02.003.

Khosrow-Pour, Mehdi, and IGI Global. 2013. *Dictionary of Information Science and Technology.* 2nd ed. http://0-services.igi-global.com.oasis.unisa.ac.za/resolvedoi/resolve.aspx?doi=10.4018/978-1-4666-2624-9.

Landau, Herbert B. 2011. *Winning Library Grants: A Game Plan.* Chicago: American Library Association.

Leedy, Paul D., Jeanne Ellis Ormrod, and Laura Ruth Johnson. 2019. *Practical Research: Planning and Design.* 12th ed. New York: Pearson Education.

Levine-Clark, Michael, and Toni Carter Dean. 2013. *ALA Glossary of Library and Information Science.* Chicago: American Library Association.

"Library Trends|JHU Press." n.d. Accessed November 18, 2020. https://www.press.jhu.edu/journals/library-trends.

Lindgren, Ida, Christian Østergaard Madsen, Sara Hofmann, and Ulf Melin. 2019. "Close Encounters of the Digital Kind: A Research Agenda for the Digitalization of Public Services." *Government Information Quarterly* 36(3): 427–36. https://doi.org/10.1016/j.giq.2019.03.002.

Marcinkowski, Mike, and Matthew Schuelke. 2017. "Introduction to NIH Grants." Saint Louis University.

Maron, Nancy, Rebecca Kennison, Paul Bracke, Nathan Hall, Isaac Gilman, Kara J. Malenfant, Charlotte Roh, and Yasmeen Shorish. 2019. *Open and Equitable Scholarly Communications: Creating a More Inclusive Future.* Chicago: Association of College and Research Libraries.

Maxwell, Nancy Kalikow. 2014. *The ALA Book of Library Grant Money.* 9th ed. Chicago: American Library Association.

"National Leadership Grants for Libraries." n.d. Institute of Museum and Library Services.

"National Research Agenda for Library Service to Children." 2019. Association for Library Service to Children.

"Public Libraries Respond to the Opioid Crisis with Their Communities." 2020. WebJunction. February 26. https://www.webjunction.org/explore-topics/opioid-crisis.html.

Sohn, Emily. 2019. "Secrets to Writing a Winning Grant." *Nature* 577(7788): 133–35. https://doi.org/10.1038/d41586-019-03914-5.

Staines, Gail M. 2016. *Go Get That Grant! A Practical Guide for Libraries and Nonprofit Organizations.* 2nd ed. Lanham, MD: Scarecrow Press.

Stone, Merlin, Eleni Aravopoulou, Yuksel Ekinci, Geraint Evans, Matt Hobbs, Ashraf Labib, Paul Laughlin, Jon Machtynger, and Liz Machtynger. 2020. "Artificial Intelligence (AI) in Strategic Marketing Decision-Making: A Research Agenda." *The Bottom Line* 33(2): 183–200. https://doi.org/10.1108/BL-03-2020-0022.

Strunk, William, and E. B. White. 2019. *The Elements of Style.* 4th ed. New York: Pearson.

Teitel, Martin. 2018. "A Foundation Insider's Eight Tips to Help You Win Your Next Grant." https://trust.guidestar.org/a-foundation-insiders-eight-tips-to-help-you-win-your-next-grant.

"Write Your Research Plan | NIH: National Institute of Allergy and Infectious Diseases." n.d. Accessed November 19, 2020. http://www.niaid.nih.gov/grants-contracts/write-research-plan.

4

Principles of Quantitative Methods

Inductive reasoning contributed to the development of what is known as the scientific method or the scientific method of inquiry (SMI). This approach to the discovery of knowledge, which arose during the Renaissance, gained major support in the sixteenth century. Many scholars still consider the SMI the most valid method for resolving unanswered questions and solving problems. There are other viewpoints, however. Budd (1995), for example, argues that the SMI is too positivist in nature, and that library and information science (LIS) needs more research that is based on a different epistemological foundation—one that is less concerned with universal laws and invariant relationships.

There is a general consensus among researchers regarding the basic pattern of the SMI, but specific elements do vary. Leedy and Ormrod, with Johnson (2019), describe the SMI as a means by which insight into an undiscovered truth is sought by (a) identifying the problem that will provide the goal of the research, (b) developing a tentative hypothesis, (c) gathering the data needed to resolve the problem, and (d) empirically testing the hypothesis by analyzing and interpreting the data.

Babbie (2021), who sees the SMI as a combination of inductive and deductive methods, depending on the research phase, summarizes the basic steps of the scientific method as (a) theory, (b) operationalization of concepts, and (c) observation. Frankfort-Nachmias, Nachmias, and DeWaard point out that "each stage influences the development of *theory* and is influenced by it in turn" (2015, 17).

Some believe that LIS has little formal theory of its own (McKechnie and Pettigrew 2002); others call for more LIS research to advance practice and theory (Hernon 1996; Riggs 1994). Budd (2001) reminds us that "general progress only occurs when there has been deep critical investigation into the workings of our field." This means that one must study the intellectual foundations of the LIS field. This type of reflection will influence not only our research, but also the development of systems and services for the practice of LIS. Before beginning the research process, basic epistemological and ontological assumptions and presuppositions should be considered because our assumptions and presuppositions influence how we approach and conduct research in the social and behavioral sciences.

FORMULATING HYPOTHESES

Definitions of Hypothesis

The second major step in the standard SMI is the formulation of one or more theoretical hypotheses. A variety of definitions of "hypothesis" found in the literature reflect slightly different perspectives or emphases. Babbie defines the hypothesis as "a specified testable expectation about empirical reality that follows from a more general proposition" (2021, 43). Leedy, Ormrod, and Johnson define a research hypothesis as "a logical conjecture, a reasonable guess, an educated conjecture" (2019, 5) that provides a framework for the design of a research project and the collection of data. Mouly considered a hypothesis to be "a tentative generalization concerning the relationship between two or more variables of critical interest in the solution of a problem under investigation" (1963, 62). A concise and understandable definition of hypothesis is "a tentative answer to a research problem that is expressed in the form of a clearly stated relationship between independent and dependent variables" (Frankfort-Nachmias, Nachmias, and DeWaard 2015, 55). Merriam-Webster ("Definition of Hypothesis" n.d.) defines hypothesis as "a tentative assumption made in order to draw out and test its logical or empirical consequences." "Regardless of any specific definition, hypotheses provide a tentative or working explanation of some phenomenon, extend knowledge, offer an unambiguous and relational statement of the extent of a relationship between variables, present a statement that is testable, and guide the conduct of research" (Hernon and Schwartz 2013, 85).

A hypothesis can be given more than one label based on its role in a given research context or its intrinsic properties. Some examples of these labels that you may find in the research are the following:

1. **Working or research hypothesis:** Helps to delimit and guide the study. This hypothesis begins a research study.
2. **Final hypothesis:** Reflects the findings of the research study. It often is synonymous with the study's final conclusion.
3. **Particular hypothesis:** Explains a specific fact or situation; for example, "not all college students are skilled library users."
4. **Causal hypothesis:** States that there is a causal relationship between two or more variables (i.e., that a particular factor or condition determines or affects another factor or condition).

5. **Null hypothesis:** Asserts that there is no real relationship between or among the variables in question. It involves the supposition that chance, rather than an identifiable cause, has produced some observed result. It is used primarily for purposes of statistical hypothesis testing.

6. **Alternative hypothesis:** Asserts that there is a relationship between or among the variables in question. In statistical hypothesis testing, the alternative hypothesis is the rival of the null hypothesis, as they are by definition mutually exclusive. An alternative hypothesis is occasionally called a "minor" or "secondary" hypothesis, though the latter, which has less well-accepted concepts, seems to suggest something quite different.

7. **Inductive hypothesis:** Moves from the particular to the general, or a generalization based on observation.

8. **Deductive hypothesis:** Shifts from the general to the particular, or a hypothesis derived from a theory.

9. **Nondirectional hypothesis:** Indicates that a relationship or difference exists between variables but says nothing about the direction of the relationship. For example, one might hypothesize that there will be a significant relationship between students' grade point averages and their use of library resources. Note that this hypothesis is nondirectional because it does not try to characterize the direction of the relationship (cf. "library users will have significantly *higher* grade point averages than nonusers").

10. **Directional hypothesis:** Indicates that a relationship or difference exists between variables while clearly stating the direction of that relationship. For example, it could logically be hypothesized that the assignment of term papers results in significantly *more* library use by certain students.

11. **Bivariate hypothesis:** Proposes a relationship between two phenomena or variables.

12. **Multivariate hypothesis:** Proposes a relationship among more than two phenomena or variables.

13. **Univariate hypothesis:** Concerns only one phenomenon or variable. A univariate hypothesis proposes a relationship between a data sample and its underlying population (probability distribution). For example, we may hypothesize that a random sample of students who participated in our survey on library services were drawn from a population consisting of 50 percent women and 50 percent men.

The hypotheses listed above are not mutually exclusive. For example, one might begin a study with a research hypothesis that proposes a causal relationship between two variables and indicates which variable affects the other.

Mouly (1978, 38) defined a model as "a descriptive analogy designed to help visualize a complex phenomenon." It is no wonder that Hernon and Schwartz (2013, 85), editors of *Library & Information Science Research*, stated that when reviewing manuscripts and reading published research, they "notice that some researchers have problems in formulating, testing, and interpreting hypotheses."

Sources of Hypotheses

As previously suggested, one of the most convenient and logical sources of hypotheses is a theory, since it can be considered to be a broad hypothesis or a set of subhypotheses. However, theories seldom, if ever, simply appear when needed. They are a result of one's in-depth knowledge of a specific field or discipline that requires staying current in the research, theories, and literature within the field or discipline. Indeed, the findings of other studies reported in the literature are excellent sources of hypotheses. Existing and assumed relationships reported in research results often provide the basis for formulating hypotheses. Similarly, certain relationships often can be observed in a work setting; such observations or hunches frequently lead to more formal hypotheses.

Pilot or exploratory studies also are good sources of hypotheses. Mouly stated that some amount of data gathering, such as the recall of past experience, the review of related literature, or a pilot study, must precede the formulation and refinement of the hypothesis (Hernon and Schwartz 2013, 64). Another source of hypotheses is the assumption that if two situations agree with one another in one or more respects relevant to the problem in question, they probably will agree in other respects. Such an assumption may be restated as one or more hypotheses.

Developing the Hypothesis

Again, the formulation of a hypothesis ideally begins with consideration of a theory, and more specifically, one or more components of a theory. But at the very least, this process starts with a set of specific facts or observations, which the researcher is attempting to explain. Generally, this explanation, or hypothesis, will be written as a statement of a possible relationship between two or more variables.

The basis for the hypothesis almost always rests on one or more assumptions. The most closely related assumption and the hypothesis are considered to constitute the premises from which the facts to be explained must be inferred logically. In some research only the most basic assumption is referred to as the premise. Basic assumptions are assumed, for the purposes of a research study, to be true and therefore are not tested during the research.

Basic assumptions should not be confused with methodological assumptions. The former help to support or explain the hypothesis. For example, a hypothesis that predicts that older people are less likely to use information technology than are younger people might be partially explained by the assumption that older people have more anxiety regarding the use of technology. In conducting a study on the use of information technology by different age groups, one might make the methodological assumption that adequate numbers of people of different ages will be willing to participate in the study.

Once the hypothesis and basic assumptions are identified, it is possible to develop additional explanations of relationships between or among the variables in specific situations. These additional explanations constitute, in effect, alternative hypotheses.

The most viable hypothesis must then be identified by evaluating the various alternative hypotheses and eliminating the less effective ones. One guiding principle is the law of parsimony (also known as "Occam's razor"): when confronted with two or more hypotheses that are roughly equivalent in terms of descriptive or predictive power, one should choose the hypothesis that relies on the fewest assumptions. Other characteristics of good hypotheses are identified below, but in the next section the major components of the hypothesis, the variables, are considered.

Variables

A *variable* in a research project is "any characteristic, experience, behavior, or outcome of interest that has two or more distinct values" (Leedy, Ormrod, and Johnson 2019, 421). Variables, or factors, can be labeled in a variety of ways depending on the nature of the relationship between or among them. For example, in a causal relationship the factor (or factors) typically identified first in the hypothesis is referred to as the *independent variable*. Other labels used for the independent variable include the predictor variable and the experimental variable. This is the variable that determines, influences, or produces the change in the other main factor.

The second main factor (or factors) in the causal hypothesis is usually referred to as the *dependent variable* or the subject variable. This variable is dependent on or influenced by the independent variable(s). The statement of the hypothesis should at least imply the nature of the relationship between the independent and dependent variables. For example, "the *more* library instruction a college student receives, the *more* they will use the college library."

However, hypotheses often take the form of conjectural statements, such as "librarians are as assertive as other professional groups" or "the information needs of researchers are different from those of practitioners" (Hernon and Schwartz 2013, 15). Thus, the independent and dependent variables always are not as easily identified as perhaps they should be. Given below are the titles of ten studies. Try to identify the independent and dependent variables within each title listed below. For example, "assertiveness training" would appear to be the independent variable and "job satisfaction" the dependent variable in the study title, *A note on the contribution of assertiveness training to job satisfaction of professional librarians.*

1. *A study of the relationship of role conflict, the need for role clarity, and job satisfaction for professional librarians.*
2. *Library design influences on user behavior and satisfaction.*
3. *An investigation of the relationships between quantifiable reference service variables and reference performance in public libraries.*

4. *The impact of differing orientations of librarians on the process of children's book selection: a case study of library tensions.*
5. *Journal selection and journal usage in academic libraries.*
6. *The effect of retrieval ranking on the access of selected science titles.*
7. *Implications of title diversity and collection overlap for interlibrary loan among secondary schools.*
8. *The attitudes of adults toward the public library and their relationships to library use.*
9. *Early libraries in Louisiana: a study of the Creole influence.*
10. *The Great Depression: its impact on forty-six large American public libraries; an inquiry based on a content analysis of published writings of their directors.*

These are the independent and dependent variables for the ten study titles:

Title number 1: independent variable, role conflict; dependent variables, need for role clarity and job satisfaction.
Title number 2: independent variable, library design; dependent variables, user behavior and satisfaction.
Title number 3: independent variable, quantifiable reference service variables; dependent variable, reference performance.
Title number 4: independent variable, differing orientations of librarians; dependent variable, process of children's book selection.
Title number 5: independent variable, journal selection; dependent variable, journal usage.
Title number 6: independent variable, ranking of titles retrieved; dependent variable, access of selected science titles.
Title number 7: independent variables, title diversity and collection overlap; dependent variable, interlibrary loan among secondary schools.
Title number 8: independent variable, attitudes of adults toward the public library; dependent variable, library use.
Title number 9: independent variable, Creole influence; dependent variable, early libraries in Louisiana.
Title number 10: independent variable, Great Depression; dependent variable, large American public libraries.

As can be seen from these examples, relationships between variables often are indicated by the use of such terms as "influence," "impact," and "effect." But such clues are not always present, and they do not always convey the specific nature of the relationship or distinguish between independent and dependent variables. A hypothesized relationship may not even include independent and dependent variables as such. The researcher may not be knowledgeable enough about the research problem to predict that one variable causes another. For example, does an increase in grade point average cause an increase in library use, or vice versa? In a given study, a variable might logically be viewed as either an independent or a dependent variable, or neither. Other types of variables include the following:

Intervening variable: any variable that occurs in the causal chain between some independent variable and its dependent variable. It also serves as an independent variable for the dependent variable. For example, one might hypothesize that library instruction (the independent variable) causes more library use (the dependent variable), when in actuality, library instruction produces greater confidence (the intervening variable), which in turn causes more library use.

Antecedent variable: a variable that occurs prior to some already identified or hypothesized independent variable. In the previous example, had confidence been initially identified as the independent variable, then library instruction could have been thought of as the antecedent variable.

Extraneous variable: a variable at first perceived as the real cause of some effect when it was, in actuality, only a coincidental correlate of that effect. It can also be defined as a variable that influences both the independent and the dependent variables so as to create a spurious association between them that disappears when the extraneous variable is controlled. (Extraneous variables are discussed in more detail in the section on experimental research methods.)

Component variable: two or more variables that represents the same variable. For example, reference questions and book loans are components of a variable called library use.

Conditioning or moderating variable: a variable that represents the conditions under which a hypothesized relationship between other variables holds true. For example, more library instruction might cause more library use *only if* the instruction is relevant to the interests or needs of the learner.

Confounding or interfering variable: another influence that may affect the dependent variable, but one in which the researcher is not interested.

Concepts

In order to organize data to perceive relationships among variables, the researcher must first make use of concepts. A *concept* may be defined as an abstraction from observed events or a shorthand representation of a variety of facts. Its purpose is to simplify thinking by subsuming a number of events under one general heading (Selltiz, Wrightsman, and Cook 1981, 41). Library use is a concept representing or abstracting the many characteristics and types of library use. As indicated in the earlier example, there are a variety of specific kinds of library use, such as reading, browsing, and using physical or virtual space.

Not only can concepts be broken down into more concrete elements, but they also can be elevated to more abstract levels. These higher-level concepts, often referred to as *constructs*, generally represent such phenomena as attitudes, perceptions, and roles. For a specific phenomenon, the conceptual hierarchy would range from the construct, at the most abstract level, to the concept, and finally to the variable at the most concrete level.

It should be noted at this point that the greater the distance between the concepts or constructs and the facts to which they are supposed to refer, the greater the possibility they may be misunderstood or inaccurately used. In addition, constructs, due to their greater abstractedness, are more difficult to relate to the phenomena they are intended to represent. Therefore, it is important to define carefully the concepts and constructs, both in abstract terms and in terms of the operations by which they will be represented in the study. The former may be considered formal or *conceptual definitions*; the latter are referred to as working or *operational definitions.*

In providing a conceptual definition of a phenomenon such as "library use," the researcher would no doubt rely heavily on the already established definition as reflected in other studies. If a conceptual definition did not already exist, researchers would need to develop their own, keeping it consistent, where possible, with current thought and attempting to link it to the existing body of knowledge using similar concepts or constructs.

In order to carry out the planned research, the investigator must translate the formal definitions of the concepts into observable or measurable events (i.e., variables) via working definitions. Most concepts cannot be directly observed, so they must be broken down into more concrete phenomena that can be measured.

Some argue that working definitions should state the means by which the concept will be measured and provide the appropriate categories. While this may not be a necessary part of the actual definition, at some point this step will be necessary, and the working definition should at least imply how the concept will be measured.

Returning to the example of library use, one could formally define library use, as did Zweizig (1977, 3), as "the output of libraries, the point at which the potential for service becomes kinetic." While this may be a suitable conceptual definition, it does little to suggest how one would actually measure library use. Consequently, the researcher would need to develop one or more working definitions in order to operationalize "library use."

More than one working definition for a concept is generally considered to be desirable, if not necessary. A given concept may be too complex to be reduced to a single measurable phenomenon. In addition, having more than one working definition for a concept helps to increase the reliability of the findings, as the different measurements tend to serve as cross-checks for one another. For example, if a person were found to own a library card, which could be one definition of library use, but were found never to use the library, then one would question the validity of using card ownership to represent library use. The researcher would be better advised to utilize a variety of working definitions, including borrowing and downloading books, accessing databases and journals, asking reference questions, requesting interlibrary loans, and so forth.

Again, at some point the researcher would need to specify exactly how the activities specified by the working definitions would be measured. For example, will only subject, as opposed to directional, reference questions be counted? What categories, such as research, ready reference, policy and procedural, and holdings, will be used to organize the questions? It should be kept in mind that working definitions usually are considered adequate only to the extent that the instruments or procedures based on them gather data that constitute satisfactory indicators of the concepts they are intended to represent. So, if the asking of reference questions does not represent the kind of library use that the researcher had in mind, then obviously it should not be used.

One other note of caution: in developing both conceptual and working definitions, one should avoid so-called *spurious definitions*. These are circular definitions, which tend to define terms using those same terms. If one defined "library use" as "using the library," then one would be providing a circular definition of no real value to the researcher or reader.

Desirable Characteristics of Hypotheses

In addition to representing the simplest possible explanation of a specific phenomenon or relationship, an ideal hypothesis should possess several other characteristics, including the following:

1. **Generalizability, or universality:** A hypothesis with this trait should hold up in more than one situation. On the other hand, valid hypotheses can be formulated legitimately for specific situations.
2. **Compatibility with existing knowledge:** A hypothesis is more likely to be generalizable if it has been based on the findings of other studies. The hypothesis should not be isolated from the larger body of knowledge.
3. **Testability:** The suitability of the hypothesis for empirical testing may be its most important characteristic. Regardless of its other traits, if it cannot be tested adequately, it is of little or no value. It even can be argued that the hypothesis should imply how it can be tested.
4. **Invariability:** The relationship stated in the hypothesis should not vary over a reasonable period of time.
5. **Causality:** The ideal hypothesis states a relationship that is causal in nature (i.e., that the independent variable[s] actually causes or determines one or more dependent variables). Many researchers also argue that the hypothesis should be predictive. Hillway (1964, 128) stated that "the success of a theory [of which the hypothesis is a part] for predictive purposes constitutes one of the most useful criteria by which it may be judged."

Unfortunately, often it is not possible in the social sciences to formulate hypotheses that are causal or predictive in nature. Social science researchers frequently have to settle for associative type hypotheses, or hypotheses that state a correlational but not causal relationship between two or more variables. For example, one may argue that as a student's library use increases, his or her grades improve, without being prepared to contend that greater library use actually causes the improvement in grades. It could be that some other factor, such as an interest in reading, is causing both the library use and the high grades. The concept of causality is discussed in greater detail in the section on experimental research.

Goldhor (1972, 59) among others, argued that a good hypothesis should contain a "causal element" that explains why it is thought that the hypothesized relationship holds true. An example of a causal element is: the more a person is interested in a hobby, the more likely that person is to browse the web for information about that hobby, because the development of a hobby calls for knowledge, skills, and expertise available from other hobbyists through Facebook, Pinterest, and blog postings.

It may well be that the causal element is synonymous with the most basic assumption, or premise of the hypothesis. Regardless of the terminology used, however, the process of identifying why the relationship exists is an important one, producing several benefits. For example, the researcher cannot hope to explain why a certain relationship exists without acquiring a thorough understanding of the phenomenon under study. Explaining why a relationship holds true forces the investigator to go beyond mere description of it. Consideration of causality also forces the researcher to distinguish between the independent and dependent variables. Otherwise, one cannot state which factor causes which. Finally, after specifying why a relationship exists, the researcher is more likely to be able to predict what the hypothesized relationship will produce.

Testing the Hypothesis

In testing the validity of a hypothesis, researchers typically employ the deductive method, in that they begin with a theoretical framework, formulate a hypothesis, and logically deduce what the results of the test should be if the hypothesis is correct. This is usually accomplished in two stages.

First, the researcher deductively develops certain logical implications (also known as logical consequences and criteria), which, when stated in operational terms, can help to reject or support the hypothesis. These logical implications should indicate evidence that must be collected and must be valid for an adequate test. Considering our hypothesis regarding library instruction and library use, several criteria could logically represent library use or provide evidence of use. Operationally defined, such criteria could include the number of visits to the library, the number of e-books and journal accesses and/or downloads, the number of books borrowed, and so forth.

The second basic step in testing a hypothesis involves actually subjecting it to a trial by collecting and analyzing relevant data. For example, one would at this point collect data on the subjects' actual library use, as evidenced by criteria already established. This stage requires the use of one or more criterion measures in order to evaluate the evidence that has been collected. "The choice of the criterion measure is crucial: not only must it be reliable and valid, it also must be sufficiently sensitive to detect changes as they occur" (Mouly 1978, 69). If one were using the number of visits to the library as evidence of library use, it would be important to detect all library visits, not just some of them. It also might be necessary to determine types of library visits, whether virtual or physical, and the purpose for and duration of each visit, for example.

As previously indicated, in order to measure library use adequately, it probably would be necessary to measure it in more than one way (i.e., employ more than one operational definition). If more than one operational definition is considered, then it follows that more than one logical consequence can be expected and that more than one criterion measure must be employed. Establishment of "the truth of an hypothesis in the absolute sense is not accomplished until all possible logical consequences have been tested and the hypothesis becomes a law" (Goldhor 1972, 81). Until a hypothesis is tested in every appropriate situation, the researcher is at best building support for the hypothesis, not proving it. In effect, each logical consequence can provide several different bases for testing the same hypothesis or relationship.

Causality also plays an important role in the testing of hypotheses. As Goldhor (1972, 86) noted,

> The testing or verification of an hypothesis is strengthened or augmented by analysis of available relevant data so as to show (1) that they agree with predictions drawn logically from the one hypothesis, (2) that they do not also confirm the consequences of alternative hypotheses, and (3) that they involve points in a logical chain of cause and effect.

Consideration of the causal relationship (when it exists) forces the investigator to employ or measure consequences that will provide evidence of the nature of the hypothetical relationship. This usually can be accomplished by utilizing data collection procedures and criterion measures that have the ability to support or reject the hypothetical cause of the relationship. For example, if college students who had high grades and who were heavy users of the library were found to be using the library strictly for recreational reading, one probably would have to reject the hypothesis and consider some phenomenon other than library use to be the cause of their high grades. Such a finding might suggest other possible relationships, however.

At this point, two reminders appear to be in order. One, it should not be forgotten that the hypothesis should be related to existing knowledge as closely as possible. This caveat also applies to the findings resulting from the testing of the hypothesis. This process is crucial if research is to build on previous studies and not merely produce fragmentary, unrelated bits of data.

Two, it is important to remember that scientific research should produce a cyclical trajectory from facts to hypotheses, to laws, to theories, and back to facts as the basis for the testing and refinement of more adequate hypotheses. In other words, the research process should never end; it should merely continue to build on previous research and to shape and reshape its findings.

An appropriate question to ask at this point is whether a hypothesis is always possible and/or helpful. It is not always possible, desirable, or justifiable to develop a formal hypothesis for a research study. This is particularly the case for exploratory research in areas too undeveloped to provide the basis for formally stated hypotheses and for most qualitative research. A formal research hypothesis can even be a hindrance to exploratory research, and the investigator may have more to gain by entering into an exploratory study with few preconceived ideas. It may not be possible, or at least not advisable, to predict relationships and outcomes of exploratory research, because doing so may bias the researcher and encourage neglect of potentially important information.

Also, when fact-finding alone is the purpose of the study, which often is the case with descriptive surveys, there may be little use for a hypothesis. At the very least, however, the researcher should have some "research questions" that they are attempting to answer and that will help, in lieu of a hypothesis, to guide the research. Some researchers distinguish between "descriptive research questions," which ask what is the amount or extent of a given variable, and "explanatory research questions," which ask how or whether certain variables are related. The following are examples of the former: How many students use the academic library during specific time periods? What are the subject majors of the users of an academic library? The following are examples of the latter: Is there a relationship between the student academic success and how often they use the academic library? Is there a relationship between the subject majors of students and the types of reference questions they ask? It is probably safe to say, however, that most major studies, particularly those involving some interpretation of facts, should incorporate a research hypothesis. "Not the facts alone, but the conclusions that we can draw from them must be regarded as the chief objective of research" (Hillway 1964, 131). Without the rigorous testing of a valid hypothesis, fully generalizable conclusions are not possible.

VALIDITY AND RELIABILITY

As one develops and conducts a research study, one should always be concerned with its validity and reliability. Generally speaking, research is considered to be valid when the conclusions are true, and reliable when the findings are repeatable. But validity and reliability are actually requirements for both the design and the measurement of research. Regarding the design, the researcher should ask whether the conclusions are true (valid) and repeatable (reliable) (Judd, Smith, and Kidder 1991, 49). Measurement, of course, is the process of ascertaining the dimensions, quantity, or capacity of something, and it is closely related to the notion of operational definitions previously discussed. "More specifically, *measurement* is a procedure where a researcher assigns numerals—either numbers or other symbols—to empirical properties (variables) according to a prescribed set of rules" (Frankfort-Nachmias, Nachmias, and DeWaard 2015, 139). Research design is the plan and structure of the research framework. It is influenced by the nature of the hypothesis, the variables, the constraints of the real world, and so forth. Research design must occur at the beginning of a research project, but it involves all of the steps that follow.

Validity of Research Design

"Validity is a multi-faceted word or concept" (Hernon and Schwartz 2009, 73), and there are at least three types of validity as it relates to the design of research. One is referred to as *internal validity*. Briefly stated, a research design is internally valid if it accurately identifies causal relationships, if any, and rules out rival explanations of the relationships. Internal validity is particularly crucial to experimental research design.

Research design is considered to have *construct validity* if the variables being investigated can be identified and labeled properly. The design should permit the specification of the actual cause and effect and the identification of the concepts or constructs involved. (A somewhat different view of construct validity is considered in the discussion of validity as it relates to the measurement process.)

The third kind of validity critical to the design of research is *external validity*. Research has external validity or generalizability when its conclusions are true or hold up beyond the confines of a particular study. In other words, the findings should be generally true for studies conducted under a variety of circumstances or conditions (e.g., other times, people, places). The quality of external validity can best be determined by replicating a study or retesting to see if the results will be repeated in another setting. This aspect of validity is similar to the concept of reliability.

Validity in Measurement

In brief, the extent to which an instrument measures what it is designed to measure indicates the level of validity of that measure. Data collection instruments may be high in reliability and low in validity, or vice versa. For example, a test intended to measure the effect of library skills on library use might actually be measuring the influence of instructors on library use, and it would therefore be low in validity. On the other hand, repeated applications of the test, in comparable circumstances, may produce essentially the same results, indicating high reliability. Ideally, the instrument would be high in both validity and reliability.

As is the case for reliability, correlation coefficients can be calculated for the validity of an instrument. Reliability coefficients are correlations between identical or similar methods, while validity coefficients are correlations between dissimilar methods based on dissimilar operational definitions but measuring the same concepts. In other words, the validity coefficient indicates the extent to which independent instruments or observations measure the same thing.

One example of a method for calculating the validity of an instrument involves the multitrait-multimethod matrix, which is a table of correlations for two or more traits measured by two or more methods. The matrix should produce relatively high correlations between scores that reflect the same trait measured by different methods, while the correlations obtained from measuring two different traits with different instruments or measuring traits with the same instrument should be low. If two separate tests, measuring two different concepts, are highly correlated, then the two concepts are probably not truly separate and distinct.

For some standardized tests, such as IQ and personality tests, reliability and validity scores have been calculated based on past applications and validation studies and are available in the literature. For many tests or instruments, and obviously for newly developed ones, however, scores are not available. Reliability scores can be calculated by correlating the scores for repeated tests. The method used to evaluate the validity of an instrument is determined by the type of validity with which one is concerned.

The standard texts on research methods do not evidence unanimity in their categorization of validity. A careful reading of several works, however, suggests that the terminology and classification schemes vary more than the types of validity themselves. What follows is hopefully at least a consensual overview of the basic types of validity as they relate to measurement.

Logical Validity

Logical validity is generally based on expert judgment. It includes content validity and face validity. *Content* validity represents the degree to which an instrument measures a specific content area. For example, a test designed to measure a student's mastery of library skills must measure what the student was supposed to learn.

In order to be adequate, content validity must contain both item validity and sampling validity. *Item* validity reflects whether the items of the instrument or test actually represent measurement in the intended content area. Does a question about how to search for information about a subject in a web browser actually measure a student's information literacy? *Sampling* validity is concerned with how well the instrument samples the total content area. A test of library skills should not be limited to library users' ability to discover materials. The test should include exercises to measure if the users are able to evaluate the websites and resources that they have found.

Face validity is similar to content validity, and the terms are sometimes used interchangeably. Face validity is a sort of catchall term often used rather loosely. It has been defined as "the degree to which a test appears to measure what it claims to measure." Face validity usually is based on the opinion of subject experts who have been asked to evaluate an instrument. This method of determining validity is quite subjective, but sometimes it is the only feasible one available.

Empirical Validity

The second basic type of validity regarding measurement has been referred to as empirical and criterion-related validity. In contrast to logical validity, empirical validity is based on external, objective criteria. It includes concurrent validity and predictive validity.

Concurrent validity indicates the degree to which the scores on a test or other data collection instrument are related to the scores on another, already validated, test administered at the same time, or to some other valid criterion (e.g., grade point average) available at the same time. Concurrent validity also represents the ability of an instrument to discriminate among people who are known to differ. For instance, in developing an instrument to measure *how* people use an academic library, one would expect it to distinguish between undergraduate and graduate students, as there already is evidence indicating that their library use differs. If members of these two groups "scored" the same on the test, then there would be a good chance that the test was actually measuring something other than types of library use—perhaps simply frequency.

Predictive validity has to do with the degree to which an instrument can identify differences that will evidence themselves in the future. If one were predicting that frequent library users were more likely to go on to graduate school than were infrequent or nonusers, then subsequent observations should support that prediction. A greater proportion of the people who scored relatively high on an initial library use questionnaire should then be found enrolled in graduate school at a later date.

Construct Validity

It is possible for validity of measurement to be based on both logical judgment and external criteria. Such validity is usually known as construct validity. The definition of construct validity sounds like the definition of face validity, in that construct validity represents the extent to which an instrument measures the concept or construct that it is intended to measure. As is the case with face validity, when selecting a test or instrument to employ in a research study, it is important to choose carefully one that accurately measures the construct of interest. This selection process should be based on the judgment of subject experts. Unlike face validity, however, construct validity requires more than expert opinion for determination. In order to ensure construct validity, it must be demonstrated that an instrument measures the construct in question and no other. In operational terms, construct validity requires that two or more measures of different constructs, using similar instruments, produce low correlations (i.e., *discriminant* validity) and that two or more measures of the same construct result in high correlations, even though different instruments are used (i.e., *convergent* validity). In other words, an instrument should be capable of measuring the construct (as represented by appropriate variables) it is supposed to measure, of distinguishing the construct from others, and of measuring other constructs simultaneously. The multitrait-multimethod matrix discussed earlier is one method for determining the convergent and discriminant validity of an instrument and thereby measuring its construct validity.

Reliability of Research Design

If the design of a research study is reliable, then its findings should be repeatable or replicable and generalizable. Exact replications of the study, including specific procedures, can be made to assess the reliability of the design. Conceptual replications of only the ideas or concepts can be used to evaluate the external validity of the design.

Reliability in Measurement

As previously stated, research requires that one be able to measure concepts and constructs as represented by variables, which often are translated into, or operationally defined as, a set of categories or a scale. Unfortunately, virtually all measurement is imperfect. Consequently, a measurement, or observed score, comprises the true score (which may never be known) and the error of measurement, or the discrepancy between the observed and the true scores. A measurement is generally considered to be reliable when the error component is reasonably small and does not fluctuate greatly from one observation to another. Thus, reliability can be defined as the degree to which an instrument accurately *and* consistently measures whatever it measures. In short, a reliable data collection instrument is one that is relatively free from measurement error.

There are methods for assessing the reliability or *stability* of measurement techniques. One of the most commonly used methods results in what is known as a test-retest correlation. When researchers employ this technique, they use the same data collection instrument to observe or collect scores twice for the same group of subjects. The instrument should be administered at different times but under equivalent conditions. The two sets of scores are then correlated to see how consistent or reliable the instrument was in measuring the variables. The smaller the error of measurement, the more likely the correlation will be high.

If it is not feasible to repeat the measurement process, or if the *internal consistency* or homogeneity of the test is doubtful, other methods can be used to determine the reliability of the instrument. For example, in utilizing the split-half method, the researcher splits the measuring instrument into two sets of questions or items after it is administered. The scores on the two halves are then correlated to provide an estimate of reliability. The instrument should be split in equivalent halves, each of which is representative of the total. This can be done by assigning the odd-numbered items to one set and the even-numbered items to the other, or by using some random assignment technique. Keep in mind, however, that a data collection instrument may have been designed to measure one variable or several variables.

Other methods for assessing the reliability of measurement include the average item-total correlation, in which each item's score is correlated with the total score and the coefficients are averaged. With a technique called the average interitem correlation, each item is correlated with every other item, and the average of the coefficients represents a measure of internal consistency and indicates how well the items all measure the same construct. If these conditions do exist, then the test-retest correlation of the total score will be higher than the test-retest correlation of the individual items. When data are gathered by observers, it is important that their observations agree if they observed the same phenomena. *Intercoder reliability* (also known as *interrater reliability*) refers to the extent to which two or more observers agree.

Reliability also can be expressed in terms of the *standard error of measurement*, which is an estimate of how often one can expect errors of a given size. It is calculated using the following formula:

$$SE_m = \sqrt{SD}\ 1 - r$$

where

SE$_m$ = standard error of measurement
SD = standard deviation of scores
r = reliability coefficient

A small standard error of measurement indicates high reliability and vice versa.

In considering the reliability of the data collection tool, one must, as has been stated, be concerned with the amount of measurement error. It also is essential that the instrument measure only the constructs of interest, not a variety of others. Otherwise it is difficult, if not impossible, to know which construct, or variable, to credit for the magnitude of the score.

A reasonable question to ask at this point would be: What is a satisfactory reliability coefficient? Ideally, every score or observation should have a reasonably high correlation with the construct or variable measured, but the determination of what constitutes a "high" correlation must be somewhat subjective. This question is comparable to asking what constitutes a high correlation between two variables. Both answers depend on a variety of factors. Regarding measurement, it should be noted that the reliability is always contingent on the degree of uniformity of the given characteristics in the population. The more homogeneous the population with regard to the variable in question, the more reliable the instrument is likely to be. For example, if an instrument has been designed to measure library use, and library use varies little among the subjects being studied, the instrument should be able to measure use consistently.

The level of reliability needed by a researcher also will vary according to the desired degree of distinction among cases. High reliability is more important, or at least more difficult to achieve, when making fine discriminations among cases than when merely identifying extremes. If the latter is all that is desired, a relatively crude measurement device should suffice. If a librarian merely wished to know what proportion of the library's users were children, young adults, and adults, then users could be observed and assigned to one of the three broad categories. If it were important to know exact ages, then users would have to be asked for that information on a questionnaire or during an interview. The resultant set of categories or the measurement scale would contain the number of ages reported and would require a more reliable data collection instrument.

Scales

The level of discrimination is in large part a function of the measurement scale used by the research instrument. *The American Heritage Dictionary* (The American Heritage Dictionary n.d.) defines scale as "a progressive classification, as of size, amount, importance, or rank; a relative level or degree." There generally are four types of measurement scales used in the research instrument:

1. **Nominal scale:** The nominal or categorical scale consists of two or more named categories into which objects, individuals, or responses are classified. For example, a survey of academic library users could employ a nominal scale for the purpose of categorizing users by subject major. The simplest nominal scale is the dichotomous scale, which has only two values, such as yes-no or true-false. The important

characteristic of the nominal scale is that the categories are qualitative, not quantitative.

2. **Ordinal scale:** An ordinal scale defines the relative position of objects or individuals with respect to a characteristic, with no implication as to the distance between positions. This type of scale is also referred to as a "rank order." Attitude or Likert-type scales are examples of ordinal scales. It should be noted, however, that some researchers do consider Likert-type scales to be interval level scales. For example, one could rank order users' level of satisfaction on a scale such as the following:

1	2	3	4	5
Very Dissatisfied	Dissatisfied	Neutral	Satisfied	Very Satisfied

But one could not assume that the distance from "Very Dissatisfied" to "Dissatisfied" is the same as the distance from "Neutral" to "Satisfied." In other words, the second range might represent a greater change than the first range.

3. **Interval scale:** The interval scale provides a ranking of positions, as does the ordinal scale, but the intervals of measurement are equal. In addition, the interval scale has a zero point, below which scores are given a negative value, if they occur. A temperature scale is an example of an interval scale. Interval level data are less common than ordinal data in the social sciences.

4. **Ratio scale:** The ratio scale allows one to compare the magnitude of responses or measurements. It is comparable to the interval scale, except that it has an absolute zero, below which values cannot occur. Frequency of library use could be considered to be ratio level data; in analyzing such information, one would be able to correctly state, for example, that one person has used the library twice as often as another. Ratio level data are relatively rare in the social sciences, because few scales actually have true zero points.

When considering the issue of measurement, it should be kept in mind that measurement presupposes theory. In order for any measurement to have meaning, one must have a solid understanding of the relationship between the variable and the underlying construct that it represents. Kidder (1981, 139) referred to this relationship as "epistemic correlation." To some extent, epistemic correlation can be established by developing an intuitive theory regarding the relationship and identifying a second variable that also stands for the construct. If a significant epistemic correlation exists, then there should be a correlation between each variable and the construct, and between the two variables.

ETHICS OF RESEARCH

Ethics are of importance to social and behavioral research, especially when the research involves human subjects. Unfortunately, unethical practices seem to have become more common, or at least more difficult to detect, in recent years (Coates 2014, 598–601; Davison and Martinsons 2011, 288–293; Metcalf 2016). An increasing number of research studies are conducted by large groups of researchers, making it harder to observe misconduct and attribute it to the appropriate person(s). Experimental replication, a traditional safeguard against unethical conduct, is more problematic given the size, cost, and complexity of many contemporary studies. The proliferation of journals has resulted in less stringent editing, and more of what is published is going unchallenged (Beall 2013; Bornmann, Nast, and Daniel 2008; Heneberg 2014). At the same time, the rate at which scientific journal articles are being retracted has increased significantly over the last several years (Lam 2015). Finally, what is ethical practice and what is not is not always clear-cut.

General Guidelines

A book by Joan E. Sieber (1992) provided a reasonably comprehensive, but succinct, guide to planning ethical research. In her opening chapter, she commented:

> The ethics of social research is not about etiquette; nor is it about considering the poor hapless subject at the expense of science or society. Rather, we study ethics to learn how to make social research "work" for all concerned. The ethical researcher creates a mutually respectful, win-win relationship with the research population; this is a relationship in which subjects are pleased to participate candidly, and the community at large regards the conclusions as constructive.

Or, as Hoyle, Harris, and Judd (2001) note, the issue of ethics often comes down to balancing the costs of questionable practices against the potential benefits of the research. Sieber's first chapter includes a discussion of institutional review boards (IRBs), also known as human subjects committees, human investigation committees, and human subjects review boards. The US government requires that all universities and other organizations that conduct research involving human subjects and that receive federal funding for research involving human subjects (virtually all universities granting doctoral degrees) must have an IRB. "The purpose of the IRB is to review all proposals for human research before the research is conducted to ascertain whether the research plan has adequately included the ethical dimensions of the project" (Sieber 1992, 5). IRBs exist to help ensure that no harm will come to human subjects, that they are informed of and consent to the protocol of the research study, and that their confidentiality or anonymity will be protected. Miller and Salkind's textbook (2002, 100–17) on research design includes facsimiles of the IRB documents used by the University of Kansas. Those documents address submission criteria, application forms, audio and video recording of subjects, payment to subjects, subject selection considerations, implied consent, inclusion of research instruments, deception of subjects, the review process, and so forth. Readers who want to know more about IRBs may wish to consult *The IRB Reference Book* (Russell-Einhorn and Puglisi 2001).

Many professional associations have guidelines for ethical research. Miller and Salkind's book (2002) provides a reprint of the *Code of Ethics* published by the American Sociological Association. That code covers issues such as professional competence, integrity, respect for people's rights, dignity and diversity, social responsibility, ethical standards, harassment, conflicts of interest, disclosure of financial support and relevant relationships, confidentiality, and the publication process (Miller and Salkind 2002). The other chapters in the book by Sieber (1992) covered the research protocol (proposal), general ethical principles, voluntary informed consent and debriefing (interaction with subjects immediately following their participation in the research), privacy, confidentiality, deception, elements of risk, benefits, research on children and adolescents, and community-based research on vulnerable urban populations and AIDS. Sieber's appendix includes sample consent and assent forms for use with older children. Schutt (2019, 244) also provides several examples of consent forms.

A number of other standard textbooks on research methods in the social and behavioral sciences devote space to ethics in research. Hoyle, Harris, and Judd (2001), for example, give considerable attention to the ethical implications of research. Johanson (2002, 67) states, "It is impossible for any research to avoid ethics. They are inextricably entwined." He then takes a rather philosophical approach to ethics in research, discussing social ideals and research and principles and ethical codes. He also addresses some of the more pragmatic concerns such as ethics committees and the publishing of research results. Johanson (2002) provides several useful examples or case studies relating to the links among practice, ethics, and research. Chapter 9 of this book discusses ethics in the context of qualitative research.

Schutt (2019, 244) deals with ethical issues in experimental research and in survey research separately. He notes, "Deception is an essential part of many experimental designs. . . . As a result, contentious debate continues about the interpretation" of research ethics. He then discusses the issue of deception in more detail and next considers the question of how much subjects may be harmed by the way benefits are distributed as part of a field experiment.

In his section on ethics in survey research, Schutt (2019, 301) points out that "special care must be taken when . . . sensitive personal questions are to be asked." He notes that many surveys employ questions that could prove damaging to the subjects if their answers were disclosed, and in such cases it is critical to preserve subject confidentiality, if not anonymity. Schutt stresses that the "cover letter or introductory statement must be credible. The letter should establish that the research is being conducted by a researcher or organization that the respondent is likely to accept as a credible, unbiased authority" (Schutt 2019, 279) and "point out that the respondent's participation is completely voluntary" (Schutt 2019, 280). The cover letter or opening statement should also disclose the researcher's affiliation and the project's sponsors and identify any possible harm to, or benefits for, subjects.

A book by Kimmel (1988) focuses on ethics in applied social research. Kimmel covers many of the same topics treated by other textbooks, but there is a particularly useful chapter on special problems in applied settings. One section of that chapter discusses some of the ethical issues in organizational research, which often deals with issues such as personnel evaluation, program evaluation, and the implementation of interventions designed to improve employee performance and relations. Such activities are quite susceptible to ethical abuse. Kimmel also addresses some of the unanticipated consequences of prevention research. For example, a preventive intervention designed to increase worker productivity might cause psychological harm. Kimmel concludes the chapter with a consideration of ethical issues that may arise after the research is completed, related to possible consequences of applying the results, misuse of the new knowledge, and responsibilities of the applied social researcher.

Ethical issues can arise regarding the use and reporting of the results of statistical analysis related to the researcher's biased use and/or interpretation of statistical techniques and data. Other ethical issues have to do with "the level of effort researchers should make to ensure that no errors in their research or in the writing up of their results will appear in print or in distributed electronic form" (Kimmel 1988, 200). Krathwohl (2004, 217) raises two possible ethical issues related to ownership of the data: availability of the data to others for secondary analysis and apportionment of credit on publication. Issues that can be reduced with the adoption of institutional research data management and reuse plans and policies that provide guidelines addressing data protection, including the anonymization and participant consent for secondary data analysis (Tripathy 2013).

Goetz makes a case for making dark data (the data that did not support the researchers' hypotheses) openly accessible for further analysis. He premises his discussion on the idea of publication bias, "where science gets skewed because only positive correlations see the light of day" (Goetz 2007).

Guidelines for Library and Information Science Professionals

Since LIS has adopted methodologies from other disciplines, it has had to focus on research ethics. Several books and articles have been concerned, at least in part, with ethical issues specific to LIS practitioners and researchers. Lynn Westbrook (2000), for example, in her book on the analysis of community information needs, incorporates guidelines for ethical practices as appropriate. These guidelines stress that anonymity, or confidentiality, of everyone involved must be maintained; that library services should never appear to depend on patron participation in the study; and that no harm should come to any subject (Westbrook 2000, 47). She reminds the reader that, on completion of the study, all confidential data should be destroyed, including interview transcripts, lists of subject names, and observation notes, and that both electronic and paper files should be weeded as much as possible. Westbrook also stresses the importance of emphasizing ethical practices when training staff to conduct information needs analyses.

In his article on the ethical considerations of information professionals, Thomas J. Froehlich (1992) discussed the ethical issues that can arise when decisions are being made about who should publish research results and take the credit. Other issues related to the publication process can include plagiarism, falsification or fabrication of data, dual submissions of manuscripts to journals, and duplicate publication of identical or largely identical manuscripts without permission from the editors (Froehlich 1992, 309). However, the use of text-matching software can be used to detect and flag plagiarism. Plagiarism as an issue pertinent to the LIS field was addressed by a panel at the 2014 iConference, which included publishers, editors, reviewers, and researchers (Greifeneder et al. 2014). Elizabeth Wager (2014) argues that publishers, editors, academic societies, and research institutions also have ethical responsibilities for published research and should develop and enforce policies that address the fabrication of data and plagiarism. Chapter 9 of a book by Hauptman (2002) includes ethical issues related to research and publication by academic librarians.

Smith (1994) focuses on the ethics of research about the uses of information provided by librarians. In other words, to what extent are librarians justified in investigating the information use activities of patrons in order to improve information services provided to them? What are the ethics of user studies? Smith (1994, 64–67) noted that there is a need for guidelines for research on user needs and information use but that such guidelines should not scare practitioners away from "the serious evaluation and research that needs to be conducted if librarians are to serve the public and to preserve the profession."

Carlin (2003, 14), while pointing out the need for more consideration of the place of ethics in LIS research, presents several cases and debates from other disciplines to raise the visibility of research ethics for researchers in LIS. He also discusses the possibility of an "ethics of interdisciplinarity" and stresses the importance of being accountable for the presentation of research strategies and accurately distinguishing between primary and secondary sources.

Ethics for Research in the Digital Environment

As Case and Given (2016) indicate, a relatively new ethical issue involves use of the internet for research. "The ubiquity of information exchange on the internet, for example, has led to discussion among researchers regarding the ethics of collecting public submissions to mailing lists, discussion boards, websites, and social media" (Case and Given 2016, 234). Some researchers use postings on social media for their research to collect and analyze the data and report the findings. This raises the question of whether or not the subjects have been *fully informed* that they are being studied, especially if the context of the posts is personal. Some consider these postings on social media to be equivalent to editorials and opinion pieces in journalistic writings. However, with the constantly changing technology environment, it is critical for researchers to continually assess the ethical implications of their work (Case and Given 2016).

The Association of Internet Research (AoIR) (2019) approved ethical guidelines for internet research in 2019. The guidelines provide detailed information on conducting ethical research using data available on the internet, such as on social media sites (Fiesler and Proferes 2018). The guidelines also address ethical pluralism and cross-cultural awareness that include ethical framework. One of the frameworks addressed is feminist ethics. Luka and Millette (2018) propose practices of feminist ethics of care in social media research. This means that "researchers pay particular attention to relationality, mutual care, reciprocity, and respect between participant and researcher" (Warfield et al. 2019). Researchers also must be aware and respect how participants self-identify and use the participants' choice of pronouns when referring to themselves. These characteristics are important in all research settings, but critically important in internet research, especially in visual internet research using social media sites such as YouTube, Instagram, and Snapchat. Since these sites are heavily visual, smart phones often are used to record, photograph, and post.

This widespread use of smart phones and other smart devices by researchers for data collection poses additional issues concerning individual privacy. See the discussion of these issues in text box 4.1 by Vivek Singh.

Text Box 4.1: Behavioral Analytics of Socio-Mobile Data

Vivek Singh

Today there are more than 6 billion smart phones collecting rich personal information about human behavior at scales and resolutions never feasible before. With the emergence of devices for health tracking (e.g., Fibits), smart homes (e.g., Alexa, Nest), and smart watches (e.g., Apple watch), I anticipate a future where every glance, heartbeat, emotion, movement, and social interaction of a person can be digitally captured and shared with the community *if the person chooses to do so*. I take this watershed moment to be similar to when the telescopes were first invented. The emergence of data about planets and their movements fundamentally transformed human understanding about the physical universe. Emerging mobile phone and sensor data may have a similar effect on our understanding of the social sciences, allowing us to test, validate, and potentially refine multiple theories related to human behavior.

While supporting research ranging from better emotional well-being to personalized health, these data also bring to the fore the issue of *privacy*. For example, my colleagues and I have shown that just three additional pieces of spatiotemporal information can be enough to uniquely identify an individual's spending traces among millions of other customers (Montjoye et al. 2015). In another work, similar spatiotemporal traces have been shown to predict depression (Huckins et al. 2018). While I strongly believe in the positive potential of such data—for example, for early detection of Alzheimer's disease (Tung et al. 2014)—these examples highlight the need for us to carefully examine our understanding of privacy in mobility data and also have an informed discussion on the ethics surrounding the use of such data. "With great powers, come great responsibilities," as they say, and a simple yardstick I would suggest is, "would I be comfortable if I were one of the subjects of this study?"

References

Huckins, Jeremy F., Alex W. daSilva, Rui Wang, Weichen Wang, Elin L. Hedlund, Eilis I. Murphy, Richard B. Lopez, et al. 2018. "Fusing Mobile Phone Sensing and Brain Imaging to

Assess Depression in College Students." *BioRxiv*, September, 276568. https://doi.org/10 .1101/276568.

Montjoye, Yves-Alexandre de, Laura Radaelli, Vivek Kumar Singh, and Alex "Sandy" Pentland. 2015. "Unique in the Shopping Mall: On the Reidentifiability of Credit Card Metadata." *Science* 347(6221): 536–39. https://doi.org/10.1126/science.1256297.

Tung, James Yungjen, Rhiannon Victoria Rose, Emnet Gammada, Isabel Lam, Eric Alexander Roy, Sandra E. Black, and Pascal Poupart. 2014. "Measuring Life Space in Older Adults with Mild-to-Moderate Alzheimer's Disease Using Mobile Phone GPS." *Gerontology* 60(2): 154–62. https://doi.org/10.1159/000355669.

As social media sites, such as "message boards, social networks, patient forums, Twitter, blogs, and Facebook" (Golder et al. 2017) and "biomedical technology provide increased monitoring capability of overt behavior and physical responses, we can expect more challenges to the boundaries of acceptable research" (Case and Given 2016, 234). The use of the internet and social media sites has increased awareness of individuals' privacy. With the use of cookies, tracking individuals' demographic data and search patterns on commercial websites, even if the individuals do not make purchases on the site, large amounts of personal data are being collected. Combine the mass collection of aggregated personal data with the fact that many individuals did not give consent or gave consent to collect the data without fully understanding the implications and the need for ethical data collection practices and guidelines becomes evident.

Since most existing guidelines for ethical research were not developed with such information technologies in mind, e-research introduces new challenges, such as access rights and legal ownership of the data; intellectual property rights; and data security, storage, and curation (Mutula 2011). Social media research brings different challenges associated with "the legal and ethical implications of empirical research using APIs for data collection" (Lomborg and Bechmann 2014, 256) and the data mining and analysis of social media networks (Neuhaus and Webmoor 2012). Schultze and Mason (2012) suggest a framework for conducting internet research that encourages researchers to ask questions about whether the study deals with "human subjects as opposed to digital material."

Traditional human subjects research requires informed consent and direct contact with study participants, who have agreed to be studied and are aware they are being studied. The European Union has adopted the General Data Protection Regulation, referred to as the GDPR. This regulation gives individuals control over their personal data and "applies to the processing of personal data wholly or partly by automated means" ("Material Scope" n.d.) However, internet research is outside of the scope of the regulations; "for example, in the United States, the use of publicly available data (e.g., tweets) may not meet the criteria of research involving human subjects" (Fiesler and Proferes 2018, 1). This uncertainty of requirements for participants of internet research may lead to research misconduct.

RESEARCH MISCONDUCT

As Krathwohl states, ethical standards are, in effect, a constraint on research; and they can be divided "into two aspects: (1) the legal and institutional constraints designed to protect the people from whom data are gathered and (2) the responsibility of the individual researcher for proper conduct above and beyond legalities. The former, covered by U.S. federal regulations, ensures that the researcher's institution provides adequate safeguards for the protection of human subjects in all federally funded research" (2004, 204). Hence, the IRBs discussed previously.

In addition to IRBs, many universities have policies and procedures regarding research misconduct. Wayne State University, in Detroit, Michigan (2010), for example, has an online document that provides necessary definitions and procedures "for investigating and reporting instances of alleged or apparent research misconduct."

In spite of the guidelines and codes of ethics for research, scientific/ research misconduct can and still does occur. The "Commission on Research Integrity, which was created as part of the National Institutes of Health Revitalization Act of 1993, proposed new procedures for addressing scientific misconduct" (Burke et al. 1996, 199). The Office of Research Integrity (ORI) has been reviewed and revised periodically, with a new regulation, "Public Health Service Policies on Research Misconduct," that came into effect in 2005 (2005). Redman (2017) calls for a review of the Commission on Research Integrity to develop sustainable standards addressing bias and the irreproducibility in research. The public may presume that professions are self-regulating. "However, the effectiveness of self-regulation in the academic profession is currently being challenged" (Braxton and Bayer 1994, 351). There is at least a perception that research misconduct in LIS is less of a problem than it is in other fields, "principally because the stakes are not terribly high in LIS, as compared with fields such as biology, physics, medicine, and the like" (Burke et al. 1996, 200). Or as Wiberley stated, "there is less of it than in other fields that have greater funding or greater prestige. The greater the stakes, the more incentive there is to cheat" (Burke et al. 1996, 200).

But what is scientific or research misconduct, and how is it defined? Wayne State University's policy (2010) regarding research misconduct applies to "fabrication, falsification, plagiarism fabrication, falsification, or plagiarism in proposing, performing, or reviewing research, or in reporting research results. . . . Misconduct does not include honest error or differences of opinion." Altman and Hernon (1997, 2) noted an agreement among professional organizations, governmental agencies, and scientists "that fabrication, falsification, or plagiarism in proposing, performing, or reporting research constitute scientific misconduct."

LIS professionals desiring more information about scientific and research misconduct are encouraged to consult *Research Misconduct*, edited by Altman and Hernon (1997). Chapters in that work address such issues as misconduct and the scholarly literature, implications of misconduct for bibliographic instruction, and implications of research misconduct for libraries and librarians. Also included are appendices that reference codes of ethics from professional societies, guidelines for instructions to authors, and sources helpful for information about cases of research misconduct.

Another useful resource is the *Journal of Information Ethics*, devoted to research ethics. Articles treat, among other topics, information ethics in the workplace, the lure of research misconduct, the influence of academic departments/disciplines on misconduct, federal actions against plagiarism, misconduct involving digital imaging, and the legal aspects of research misconduct.

SUMMARY

As previously stated, a research project that adheres to the basic SMI consists of certain stages; this chapter has considered four of them: identification or development of the theory; identification of the problem; formulation of the hypothesis; and measurement as related to validity, reliability, and level. A research project is not likely to succeed unless careful attention has been paid to these steps. Yet it is tempting for the researcher to slight, if not ignore, these steps in order to get involved in the design of the study and the collection and analysis of data. Unfortunately, such research generally is less meaningful than it could be. Researchers should recognize that the time that goes into the conceptual development and planning of a research study is time well spent, and it will result in fewer problems in the later stages of the research. As has been written elsewhere, "A question well-stated is a question half answered" (Isaac and Michael 1995, 36). The last section addressed the important issues of ethics in research, including the ethical considerations of conducting research in the digital environment, and research misconduct.

REFERENCES

Altman, Ellen, and Peter Hermon. 1997. *Research Misconduct: Issues, Implications, and Strategies*. Greenwich, CT: Praeger.

The American Heritage Dictionary. n.d. "Definition of Scale." Accessed June 13, 2020. https://ahdictionary.com/word/search.html?q=scale.

Association of Internet Researchers. 2019. "AoIR Interent Research Guidelines 3.0.Pdf." https://aoir.org/reports/ethics3.pdf.

Babbie, Earl R. 2021. *The Practice of Social Research*. 15th ed. Boston: Cengage.

Beall, Jeffrey. 2013. "Unethical Practices in Scholarly, Open-Access Publishing." *Journal of Information Ethics* 22(1): 11–20. https://doi.org/10.3172/JIE.22 .1.11.

Bornmann, Lutz, Irina Nast, and Hans-Dieter Daniel. 2008. "Do Editors and Referees Look for Signs of Scientific Misconduct When Reviewing Manuscripts? A Quantitative Content Analysis of Studies That Examined Review Criteria and Reasons for Accepting and Rejecting Manuscripts for Publication." *Scientometrics* 77(3): 415–32. https://doi.org/10.1007/s11192-007-1950-2.

Braxton, John M., and Alan E. Bayer. 1994. "Perceptions of Research Misconduct and an Analysis of Their Correlates." *The Journal of Higher Education* 65(3): 351–72. https://doi.org/10.2307/2943972.

Budd, John M. 1995. "An Epistemological Foundation for Library and Information Science." *The Library Quarterly: Information, Community, Policy* 65(3): 295–318.

Budd, John M. 2001. *Knowledge and Knowing in Library and Information Science: A Philosophical Framework*. Lanham, MD: The Scarecrow Press.

Burke, Mary, Min-min Chang, Charles Davis, Peter Hernon, Paul Nicholls, Candy Schwartz, Debora Shaw, Alastaor Smith, and Stephen Wiberley. 1996. "Editorial: Fraud and Misconduct in Library and Information Science Research." *Library & Information Science Research* 18: 199.

Carlin, Andrew P. 2003. "Disciplinary Debates and Bases of Interdisciplinary Studies: The Place of Research Ethics in Library and Information Science," 16.

Case, Donald O., and Lisa M. Given. 2016. *Looking for Information: A Survey of Research on Information Seeking, Needs, and Behavior*. Bingley, UK: Emerald Group.

Coates, Heather. 2014. "Ensuring Research Integrity: The Role of Data Management in Current Crises." *College & Research Libraries News* 75(11): 598–601. https://doi.org/10.5860/crln.75.11.9224.

Davison, Robert M., and Maris G. Martinsons. 2011. "Methodological Practice and Policy for Organisationally and Socially Relevant IS Research: An Inclusive–Exclusive Perspective." *Journal of Information Technology* 26(4): 288–93. https://doi.org/10.1057/jit.2011.19.

"Definition of Hypothesis." n.d. Accessed October 29, 2020. https://www.merriam-webster.com/dictionary/hypothesis.

Fiesler, Casey, and Nicholas Proferes. 2018. "'Participant' Perceptions of Twitter Research Ethics." *Social Media + Society* 4(1): 2056305118763366. https://doi.org/10.1177/2056305118763366.

Frankfort-Nachmias, Chava, David Nachmias, and Jack DeWaard. 2015. *Research Methods in the Social Sciences*. 8th ed. New York: Worth.

Froehlich, Thomas J. 1992. "Ethical Considerations of Information Professionals." *Annual Review of Information Science and Technology (ARIST)* 27: 291–324.

Goetz, Thomas. 2007. "Freeing the Dark Data of Failed Scientific Experiments." *Wired*, September 25. https://www.wired.com/2007/09/st-essay-3.

Golder, Su, Shahd Ahmed, Gill Norman, and Andrew Booth. 2017. "Attitudes toward the Ethics of Research Using Social Media: A Systematic Review." *Journal of Medical Internet Research* 19(6): e195. https://doi.org/10.2196/jmir.7082.

Goldhor, Herbert. 1972. *An Introduction to Scientific Research in Librarianship*. Urbana, IL: University of Illinois, Graduate School of Library Science.

Greifeneder, Elke, Lynn Silipigni Connaway, Jiang Tingting, Michael Seadle, Debora Weber-Wulff, and Dietmar Wolfram. 2014. "Where Does Originality End and Plagiarism Start? Discussing Plagiarism in Information Science." In *IConference 2014 Proceedings*. iSchools. https://doi.org/10.9776/14418.

Hauptman, Robert. 2002. *Ethics and Librarianship*. Jefferson, NC: McFarland & Company.

Heneberg, Petr. 2014. "Parallel Worlds of Citable Documents and Others: Inflated Commissioned Opinion Articles Enhance Scientometric Indicators." *Journal of the Association for Information Science and Technology* 65(3): 635–43. https://doi.org/10.1002/asi.22997.

Hernon, Peter. 1996. "Editorial: Publishing Research." *The Journal of Academic Librarianship* 22(1): 1–2. https://doi.org/10.1016/S0099-1333(96)90026-9.

Hernon, Peter, and Candy Schwartz. 2009. "Reliability and Validity." *Library & Information Science Research* 31(2): 73–74. https://doi.org/10.1016/j.lisr.2009.03.001.

Hernon, Peter, and Candy Schwartz. 2013. "Editorial: Hypotheses—An Overview." *Library & Information Science Research* 35(2): 85–87.

Hillway, Tyrus. 1964. *Introduction to Research*. 2nd ed. Boston: Houghton Mifflin.

Hoyle, Rick H., Monica J. Harris, and Charles M. Judd. 2001. *Research Methods in Social Relations*. 7th ed. Fort Worth, TX: Cengage Learning.

Isaac, Stephen, and William B. Michael. 1995. *Handbook in Research and Evaluation: A Collection of Principles, Methods and Strategies Useful in the Planning, Design, and Evaluation of Studies in Education and Behavioral Sciences*. 3rd ed. San Diego: EdITS.

Johanson, Graeme. 2002. "Ethics in Research." In *Research Methods for Students, Academics and Professionals: Information Management and Systems*, edited by Kirsty Williamson, 67. Wagga Wagga, Australia: Charles Sturt University, Center for Information Studies.

Judd, Charles M., Eliot R. Smith, and Louise H. Kidder. 1991. *Research Methods in Social Relations*. Fort Worth, TX: Harcourt Brace Jovanovich.

Kidder, Louise H. 1981. *Research Methods in Social Relations*. 4th ed. New York: Holt, Rinehart and Winston.

Kimmel, Allan J. 1988. "Ethics and Values in Applied Social Research." In *Applied Social Research Methods*. Vol. 12. Newbury Park, CA: Sage.

Krathwohl, David R. 2004. *Methods of Educational and Social Science Research: An Integrated Approach*. 2nd ed. Long Grove, IL: Waveland Press.

Lam, Bouree. 2015. "A Scientific Look at Bad Science." *The Atlantic*, September. https://www.theatlantic.com/magazine/archive/2015/09/a-scientific-look-at-bad-science/399371.

Leedy, Paul D., Jeanne Ellis Ormrod, and Laura Ruth Johnson. 2019. *Practical Research: Planning and Design*. 12th ed. New York: Pearson Education.

Lomborg, Stine, and Anja Bechmann. 2014. "Using APIs for Data Collection on Social Media." *The Information Society* 30(4): 256–65. https://doi.org/10.1080/01972243.2014.915276.

Luka, Mary Elizabeth, and Mélanie Millette. 2018. "(Re)Framing Big Data: Activating Situated Knowledges and a Feminist Ethics of Care in Social Media Research." *Social Media + Society* 4(2): 2056305118768297. https://doi.org/10.1177/2056305118768297.

"Material Scope." n.d. Intersoft Consulting. *General Data Protection Regulation (GDPR)* (blog). Accessed October 29, 2020. https://gdpr-info.eu/art-2-gdpr.

McKechnie, Lynne, and Karen E. Pettigrew. 2002. "Surveying the Use of Theory in Library and Information Science Research: A Disciplinary Perspective." *Library Trends* 50(3): 406–17.

Metcalf, Joseph. 2016. "Human-Subjects Protections and Big Data: Open Questions and Changing Landscapes." Council for Big Data, Ethics, and Society. https://bdes.datasociety.net/wp-content/uploads/2016/10/Human-Subjects-Lit-Review.pdf.

Miller, Delbert C., and Neil J. Salkind, eds. 2002. *Handbook of Research Design and Social Measurement*. 6th ed. Thousand Oaks, CA: Sage.

Mouly, George J. 1963. *Educational Research*. New York: American Book Company.

Mouly, George J. 1978. *Educational Research: The Art and Science of Investigation*. Boston: Allyn & Bacon.

Mutula, Stephen M. 2011. "Ethics and Trust in Digital Scholarship." *The Electronic Library* 29(2): 261–76. https://doi.org/10.1108/02640471111125212.

Neuhaus, Fabian, and Timothy Webmoor. 2012. "Agile Ethics for Massified Research and Visualization." *Information, Communication & Society* 15(1): 43–65. https://doi.org/10.1080/1369118X.2011.616519.

"Public Health Service Policies on Research Misconduct; Final Rule." 2005. *Federal Register* 70(94): 28369–400. PMID: 15898182.

Redman, Barbara K. 2017. "Commentary: Legacy of the Commission on Research Integrity." *Science and Engineering Ethics* 23(2): 555–63. https://doi.org/10.1007/s11948-016-9753-6.

Riggs, Donald E. 1994. "Losing the Foundation of Understanding." *American Libraries* 25(5): 449.

Russell-Einhorn, Michele K., and Thomas Puglisi. 2001. *Institutional Review Board (IRB) Reference Book: Protecting the People Who Volunteer to Participate in Research.* [Washington, DC]: PricewaterhouseCoopers.

Schultze, Ulrike, and Richard O. Mason. 2012. "Studying Cyborgs: Re-Examining Internet Studies as Human Subjects Research." *Journal of Information Technology* 27(4): 301–12. https://doi.org/10.1057/jit.2012.30.

Schutt, Russell K. 2019. *Investigating the Social World: The Process and Practice of Research.* 9th ed. Thousand Oaks, CA: Sage.

Selltiz, Claire, Lawrence S. Wrightsman, and Stuart W. Cook. 1981. *Research Methods in Social Relations.* 3rd ed. New York: Holt, Rinehart and Winston.

Sieber, Joan E. 1992. *Planning Ethically Responsible Research: A Guide for Students and Internal Review Boards.* Newbury Park, CA: Sage.

Smith, Martha M. 1994. "Survival and Service: The Ethics of Research on the Uses of Information Provided by Librarians." *North Carolina Libraries* 65: 64–67.

Tripathy, Jaya Prasad. 2013. "Secondary Data Analysis: Ethical Issues and Challenges." *Iranian Journal of Public Health* 42(12): 1478–79.

Wager, Elizabeth. 2014. "Publication Ethics: Whose Problem Is It?" *Insights* 25(3): 294–99. https://doi.org/10.1515/prilozi-2015-0004.

Warfield, Katie, Jamie Hoholuk, Blythe Vincent, and Aline Dias Camargo. 2019. "Pics, Dicks, Tits, and Tats: Negotiating Ethics Working with Images of Bodies in Social Media Research." *New Media & Society* 21(9): 2068–86. https://doi.org/10.1177/1461444819837715.

"Wayne State University Policy and Procedure Regarding Research Misconduct, Executive Order 89–4." 2010. Wayne State University: University Policy. https://policies.wayne.edu/administrative/10-01-research-misconduct.

Westbrook, Lynn. 2000. *Identifying and Analyzing User Needs: A Complete Handbook and Ready-to-Use Assessment Workbook.* New York: Neal-Schuman.

Zweizig, Douglas L. 1977. "Measuring Library Use." *Drexel Library Quarterly* 13(3): 3–15.

5

Survey Research and the Questionnaire

"Survey research typically employs a face-to-face interview, a telephone interview, or a written questionnaire" (Leedy, Ormrod, and Johnson 2019, 153). These data collection techniques or instruments are most commonly, but not exclusively, used to collect data for the survey research method. The questionnaire is described in this chapter. Other types of survey research data collection techniques are included in other chapters of the book. The interview is discussed in chapter 11, and observation is included in chapter 12. These are data collection techniques or instruments, not research methodologies, and they can be used with more than one methodology. Observation is the possible exception, in that some texts do treat observational research as both a technique and a methodology. Regardless of what they are called, the purpose of these techniques is to collect data. Achievement tests, aptitude tests, and so forth, of course, often are used to collect data for educational research and to assess or evaluate performance, ability, knowledge, and behavior.

Survey refers to a group of research methods commonly used to determine the present status of a given phenomenon. The basic assumption of most survey research is that by carefully following certain scientific procedures, one can make inferences about a large group of elements by studying a relatively small number selected from the larger group. For example, if one wanted to learn the opinions of all academic librarians in the United States about information literacy, one could study a sample of several hundred librarians and use their responses as the basis for estimating the opinions of all of them.

SURVEY RESEARCH

To *survey* means to look at or to see over or beyond or, in other words, to observe. *Observations* made during the course of a survey are not limited to those of the physical type, however, and techniques commonly used for collecting survey data are considered later in this chapter.

As just indicated, a key strength of survey research is that, if properly done, it allows one to generalize from a smaller group to a larger group from which the subgroup has been selected. The subgroup is referred to as the *sample*, and techniques for drawing samples are discussed in considerable detail in chapter 6. The larger group is known as the *population*; it must be clearly defined, specifically delimited, and carefully chosen.

The observations or measurements made during survey research, or any other kind of research, generate *data*, or information. These data are particularly susceptible to *bias* introduced as a result of the research design (and at other stages in the research process), which is considered here and throughout the book.

Major Differences between Survey Research and Other Methods

As has been noted, survey research has characteristics common to most other research methods, but it also exhibits certain important differences. For example, survey research is used to gather contemporary data, while historical research is primarily concerned with past data. Some argue that historical research is less bound to the scientific method of inquiry (SMI), although the data collection and analyses of the historical method are structured and rigorous.

In contrast to experimental research, survey research does not enable the researcher to manipulate the independent variable, provides less control of the research environment, and therefore is not considered capable of definitely establishing causal relationships. On the other hand, survey research is better suited than experimental research to studying a large number of cases, especially those that are geographically dispersed. Also, survey research is generally considered to be more appropriate for studying personal factors and for exploratory analysis of relationships.

Types of Survey Research

In selecting a method, and a type of survey research in particular, the investigator must keep in mind the problem under consideration, the sources of the desired information, the nature of the data to be collected, and the major purpose of the research. For example, if the purpose of the study is to formulate a problem for a more precise investigation or to develop more formal hypotheses, then a formative or exploratory type of survey may be in order.

Exploratory Survey Research

An exploratory survey study, often conducted as qualitative research, can increase the researcher's familiarity with the phenomenon in question. It can help to clarify concepts, establish priorities for future research, identify new problems, and gather information with practical applications, although such results cannot always be anticipated. Following are specific kinds of exploratory research surveys:

> *Literature survey.* Literature surveys or reviews are in some respects exploratory in nature, in that they often focus on developing hypotheses, based on previous research that may suggest further investigation. Literature surveys may stand alone, but more often they are part of a larger study, in which case they are considered to be supportive of the research that follows rather than as research studies themselves.
>
> *Experience survey.* Experience surveys, as the name suggests, gather and synthesize the experiences of specialists and/or practitioners in a particular field. They too are exploratory, in that their aim is to identify relationships between variables and not to provide an accurate picture of current or best practices (Selltiz, Wrightsman, and Cook 1959). The researcher's primary interest is in gaining provocative ideas and useful insights (i.e., suggestions for future research, rather than specific statistics). Experience surveys, as well as suggesting hypotheses, can provide information on the feasibility of doing further research. For example, they can provide information on where the facilities for research can be obtained, which factors can and cannot be controlled, and whether or not the necessary data are readily available. Experience surveys also may help to establish priorities for research and to summarize the knowledge of practitioners regarding the effectiveness of various methods and procedures, or best practices in a particular field.
>
> *Analysis of insight-stimulating examples.* Where there is little experience to serve as a guide, researchers have found the intensive study of selected examples to be a useful method of stimulating insights and suggesting hypotheses for future research. This method differs from the case study approach in that it tends to be more intensive and narrower in scope. The types of examples or cases likely to be of most value depend on the problem under study, but in general, cases that provide sharp contrasts or have striking features tend to be the most useful.

Speaking of exploratory surveys in general, it is important to remember that they merely suggest insights or hypotheses; they cannot test them. By selecting examples that have special characteristics, one no longer has cases that are typical, but may, instead, constitute a biased sample. In addition, exploratory studies do not provide enough control of extraneous variables, nor should they, to permit the testing of a specific relationship. An exploratory study should be the first step of the research process, followed by the testing of hypotheses to determine if the findings are generalizable.

Descriptive Survey Research

A second general type of survey research is descriptive research. In this chapter the focus is on the collection and analysis of quantitative data. However, some of the topics discussed in this chapter also are relevant to qualitative data. Leedy (1980, 76) described this method as "appropriate for data that are quantitative in nature and that need statistical assistance to extract their meaning." Researchers often use "survey research methods" and "descriptive research" synonymously.

Other Types of Survey Research

There are several other types of survey research that appear in the literature. These include:

- **Cross-sectional study:** A typical survey, such as a Gallup poll, designed to measure one or more phenomena across a sample representative of the population or the whole population.
- **Trend study:** A survey conducted over a period of time so as to measure trends, patterns, or changes. The trend study may be treated as a *longitudinal* study.
- **Cohort study:** A survey conducted to collect data from the same population more than once. The same people are not surveyed, but the subjects are selected from the same population.
- **Panel study:** A survey designed to collect data from the same sample of subjects, often over time. The panel study may be treated as a *longitudinal* study.
- **Approximation of a longitudinal study:** An attempt to simulate a true longitudinal study by asking people to recall past behavior and activities.
- **Parallel samples study:** A survey of separate samples regarding the same research problem. For example, a study of university library use might necessitate surveying both students and faculty.
- **Contextual study:** A survey of a person's environment, conducted to learn more about the person. For example, a study of a person's information use might benefit from a consideration of the information resources available to that person.
- **Sociometric study:** A comprehensive survey of more than one group, including the interrelationships among the groups. For example, a thorough study of children's literature might entail surveying authors, critics, publishers, librarians, parents, and children.
- **Critical incident study:** An in-depth examination of a specific event or activity rather than a broad survey of many occurrences; similar to the "analysis of insight-stimulating examples" described above (Golden 1982, 5). The critical incident technique (CIT) was developed by John C. Flanagan as part of his work on behavior studies in the United States (US) Army Air Forces during World War II (Flanagan 1954).

To learn more about these specific types of studies, standard texts on survey research can be consulted. Many of these are referenced in this chapter.

Basic Purposes of Descriptive Survey Research

Usually the basic purposes of descriptive survey research are to describe characteristics of the population of interest, estimate proportions in the population, make specific predictions, and test associational relationships. They also can be used to *explore* causal relationships. Looking first at describing the population, it should be kept in mind that a description of characteristics of the population is often based on a description of the characteristics of a (hopefully) representative sample—hence the importance of the sampling technique.

Having identified characteristics of the population, it then becomes important to estimate (if using a sample) their proportions in the population. Without such data, one can say little about the significance of the traits. For example, it may be interesting to learn that some academic librarians hold subject master's degrees, but little can be done to interpret the possible impact of this phenomenon without knowing what percentage of all academic librarians hold subject master's degrees.

Information regarding characteristics or proportions also is necessary to make predictions about specific relationships. In the course of the study just alluded to, one may find that a high percentage of libraries with an acquisitions budget of a certain size employ librarians with subject master's degrees. On the basis of such data, the researcher may be prepared to predict that, in most cases, libraries having an acquisitions budget over a certain amount will indeed have librarians with subject master's degrees.

The researcher may wish to go a step further and "test" the relationship between budget size and librarians' credentials. The testing of a relationship between two or more variables is described in greater detail later in this chapter, but it should be noted here that some tests are more rigorous than others. The consensus is that descriptive survey research can consider but not test causal relationships, and that it can test associational relationships. In other words, by using a survey, the researcher may find that libraries with large acquisitions budgets do tend to have more librarians with subject master's degrees, but such a study legitimately could conclude only that there seemed to be a correlation between budget size and librarians' credentials, not that budget size caused librarians with subject master's degrees to be hired. Other factors or variables, such as degree of departmentalization and faculty role in the selection of materials, could have had as much or more influence than budget size on the criteria for hiring certain librarians. As the survey research study could not control these other variables, it could not test a causal relationship. As discussed previously, the relationship must make sense conceptually as well, regardless of the methodology or technique used.

Yet descriptive survey research, while usually less rigorous than experimental research, is stronger than exploratory research for testing relationships between variables. In gaining rigorousness, however, it tends to lose flexibility. In short, it tends to provide a suitable method for studying specific phenomena.

Basic Steps of Survey Research: An Overview

Formulating objectives. As is true of any research, in selecting the method (and in designing the techniques to be employed) one must consider the objectives of the study, or how the data will be used. In turn, the objectives should be based on the problem to be investigated or the questions to be answered. The important concern here is that the method selected be precise enough to ensure that the data collected will be relevant to the question or problem under study.

Selecting data collection techniques. Having selected the method (e.g., survey, historical, experimental), the next basic step is to select or design the specific technique or techniques to be used to collect the necessary data. Such techniques as observation, interviews, and questionnaires often are used, but if no suitable technique already exists, then a new one must be devised.

This stage is a critical point at which safeguards against bias and unreliability should be introduced. As Leedy, Ormrod, and Johnson (2019, 181) warn, "bias can creep into a research project in a variety of subtle ways." It can be easily overlooked by even the most careful and conscientious researcher (Leedy, Ormrod, and Johnson 2019); therefore, the researcher should safeguard the data from the influence of bias. Leedy, Ormrod, and Johnson define bias as "any influential factor that distorts the data obtained or conclusions drawn" (2019, 181). Bias can enter into a study at several points, including during sampling and data collection activities. Bias is difficult, if not impossible, to avoid completely, but at the very least it should be minimized. When bias does appear to exist, the researcher should acknowledge its presence and indicate how it affects the results of the study. Examples of such occurrences are provided where these topics are discussed in this chapter.

It is important to pretest the data collection tool at this time. This step is covered in the section on questionnaires, but the desirability of pretesting applies to all data collection techniques.

Selecting the sample. Another activity, treated at length in chapter 6, is the selection of the sample, a necessary step for all surveys based on portions of a population. It is worth reemphasizing here, however, that findings based on a sample should provide a reasonably accurate representation of the conditions for the total group, and consequently considerable attention must be given to the sampling technique.

It also is worth noting that when deciding the representativeness of the sample to the total group, the researcher should consider both statistical and practical differences between the sample and the total group. For example, in comparing libraries of a sample with their total group on collection size, one may find that a difference of a few thousand volumes in collection size is a statistically significant difference. If one were looking at small, or possibly even medium-sized, libraries, this statistical difference might be noteworthy. But if one were studying large university library collections of 2 million volumes or more, a difference of a few thousand volumes would probably have no real significance, regardless of what the statistics indicated. In other words, the average size of the sample library collections might differ from the average collection size of the population being sampled, but one still could have a reasonably accurate or representative sample for most purposes.

Collecting the data. Having selected an appropriate data collection tool and the sample to which it will be applied, the next basic step is to collect the data. If one is conducting a relatively large survey, there is a good chance that it will be necessary to employ one or more researchers or research assistants who are responsible for gathering the data. These research team members should be well trained in the techniques of data collection and should be familiar with the specific tool being used in the study.

Throughout the survey research project, those collecting the data should be supervised closely, and checks should be established to help ensure that all data collection is accurate and unbiased. As soon as possible after collection, the data should be checked for completeness, comprehensibility, consistency, and reliability. This step often is referred to as "cleaning" the data, and a thorough cleaning of possibly "dirty" data can prevent numerous problems in subsequent statistical analysis. Cleaning the data can involve everything from simply reading the results, to looking for surprising responses and unexpected patterns, to verifying or checking the coding of the data. If transcripts are part of the data collection tools, whether text or audio or video (that are transcribed to text or used as recorded), they also will need to be reviewed and revised to be sure no participant identifying information is included and any garbled or unintelligible transcriptions are corrected.

Analyzing and interpreting the results. The process of analyzing the data gathered basically involves coding the responses or placing each item in the appropriate category (more on this later); tabulating the data; and calculating appropriate statistical computations. It is advisable to improve the economy of the study by planning these steps well in advance and in considerable detail. As indicated previously, it also is important to provide safeguards against error. This can be accomplished in part by checking the reliability of the coders and by checking the accuracy of the tabulations and statistical analysis.

Looking ahead to the interpretation phase, it is useful to be systematic in describing the treatment of the data. The researcher should state clearly and specifically what data are needed to resolve the problem, where they are located, and how they were obtained. The researcher also should describe fully the different steps that will be taken to interpret the data. In addition, the researcher should try to ensure that the statistics calculated have a rational base (i.e., explain why these statistical analyses were chosen; their limitations, if any; and how they will be used). Finally, the researcher should distinguish between the mere presentation of the data and the interpretation of the data. The former is basically descriptive in nature; the latter involves analysis and explanation.

Survey Research Designs

The most straightforward type of survey research is descriptive; it is designed to ensure that the sample is reasonably representative of the population about which the researcher wishes to generalize and that the relevant characteristics have been accurately measured.

Where more than mere description and simple tabulations are desired, for example, in an analytical survey, it may be necessary to develop a more sophisticated design. A common design for survey research, which facilitates the analysis of relationships, is known as the "static-group comparison." It is quite similar to a so-called preexperimental design and can be diagrammed as follows:

$$\frac{X \quad O}{O}$$

With more than one level of X, the design becomes

$$\frac{X_1 \quad O_1}{X_2 \quad O_2}$$

This design depicts two groups, as indicated by the two lines or rows, with two levels of X. The "independent" variable, X, could represent age, X_1 retired adults, and X_2 middle-aged adults. The "dependent" variable, O, could represent library use, with O_1 representing library use for the retired adults and O_2 representing library use for the middle-aged adults. In other words, the Os represent observations or measurements of the dependent variable: library use.

The line between the two groups means that they naturally are occurring groups, or that X is a naturally occurring condition, in this case, age. This is in contrast to the manipulated independent variables, discussed in the section on experimental research in this chapter.

In analyzing the results of a survey employing the latter example of a static-group comparison design, the researcher would compare the O scores of the comparison groups to determine whether there is a relationship between X and O. In other words, does one age group seem to use the library more than the other?

The difficulty in interpreting the results of a static-group comparison is that there is a real possibility that other differences between the two groups also may be affecting library use. For example, retired adults may have more leisure time than middle-aged adults and therefore may be more inclined to use libraries. Or, had the middle-aged adults been found to be heavier library users, it might have been because they tended to have higher incomes and that something about higher income encourages library use.

As has been stated, the best that survey research can demonstrate is correlational or associational relationships, and correlation does not demonstrate causation. On the other hand, correlation is necessary for causation, so evidence of a strong correlation between two variables would strengthen the case for causation.

A second, relatively common example of a survey research design is known as the "panel design." The panel design is a slightly stronger design than the static-group comparison because it takes into account the time sequence and changes over time by collecting data on the Xs and Os at two or more times. The panel design is diagrammed as follows:

$$\frac{X_{11}\, X_{12}\, X_{13}\, O \ldots X_{12}\, X_{13}\, O \ldots X_{12}\, O}{X_{21}\, X_{22}\, X_{23}\, O \ldots X_{22}\, X_{23}\, O \ldots X_{22}\, O}$$

The first of the two subscripts on the Xs indicates the level of the "independent" variable, for example, for gender—male and female. The second subscript represents the variable identification. For example, X_{11} could represent males with a certain level of income, X_{12} males with a certain educational background. The Os represent the "dependent" variable or, in this example, frequency of library use. The line continues to indicate naturally occurring groups. The fact that the Xs and Os occur more than once in each group indicates that the data are collected and observations are made more than once for at least some of the variables.

In analyzing the results of survey research employing this design, the researcher may conclude that females, in conjunction with certain levels of income, education, and age, are more likely to use libraries than males with comparable values on those variables. But the researcher should draw such conclusions cautiously, as the time intervals may not be adequate to allow the Xs to effect changes in library use and, once again, there may be other important group differences affecting library use that have not been taken into account. Such designs do, however, help the researcher to understand and analyze relationships between variables and to generalize from natural processes that have occurred. While they cannot establish causation, they can help to build a case for it.

Survey research has been used in library and information science (LIS) research for a variety of purposes. Survey research has been effective for use and user studies, state-of-the-art surveys, and library performance evaluations. It also is one of the most used methods in the LIS literature (Case and Given 2016; Connaway 2015; Luo and McKinney 2015; Togia and Malliari 2017; Vakkari 2008). Before conducting survey research, Lance (2017) recommends that the researcher ask "what do I need to know, and do data on this already exist? If the answer to the latter is yes, don't do another survey." A book by Fink provides a useful step-by-step guide to conducting surveys in any discipline (Fink 2017).

Survey Research Costs

Survey research tends to be relatively inexpensive, at least if the sample or population being surveyed is not large, but still it often is desirable to reduce its costs. Recommended guidelines for reducing survey costs include the following:

- Shorten the length of data collection.
- Reduce the number of follow-ups.
- Limit pilot or pretesting to a small number of participants.
- Shorten the time spent developing data collection instruments by adapting already existing instruments.
- Make the instrument as short as possible.
- Use nonmonetary incentives to encourage respondents.
- Minimize staff costs.
- Shop around for the least expensive supplies and equipment.
- Reduce the number of survey activities.
- Minimize the amount of time each activity takes (Fink 2013, 140).

THE QUESTIONNAIRE

Prequestionnaire Planning

The planning that should precede the design of a questionnaire is not that different from the planning that should go into the early development of a research study. The process is presented here in brief outline form as a way of reviewing the major steps and of emphasizing decisions that should be made before the data collection instrument is selected or designed.

1. Define the problem (and purpose).
2. Consider previous, related research and the advice of experts.
3. Hypothesize a solution to the problem (or at least identify research questions, the answers to which will shed some light on the problem).
4. Identify the information needed to test the hypothesis. This step should include deciding which aspects of the problem will be considered and planning ahead to the presentation and analysis of the data. Deciding how the data will be organized, presented, and analyzed can significantly influence what types of data will have to be collected. It may be useful at this point to construct so-called dummy tables, or tables presenting the important variables with hypothetical values, to help anticipate possible problems regarding presentation and analysis.
5. Identify the potential respondents or subjects. Practical questions should be asked at this point, such as, "Are the potential respondents accessible? Are they likely to respond?"
6. Select the best or most appropriate technique for collecting the necessary data. Here the researcher should consider the relevant advantages and disadvantages of the questionnaire, interview, observation, and other techniques in relation to the more general methodology to be used.

To some extent, research findings are affected by the nature of the data collection technique used. Findings strongly affected by the technique can lose their validity. Consequently, a researcher may elect to use two or more techniques and methods to test hypotheses and/or measure variables; this process often is referred to as *triangulation*. Burgess (1984, 146) believed that triangulation implies "the notion of three points of view within a triangle"; therefore, Gorman and Clayton (2005) suggest using the term "mixed methods" "to allow the researcher to use a range of methods, data, investigators and theories within any study." For example, information about library use could be collected with questionnaires, interviews, documentary analysis, and observation. Consistent findings among the different data collection techniques would suggest that the findings are reasonably valid. Discrepancies among the results would indicate a need for further research. Morgan (2006, 168–82) provides a discussion of the various approaches for combining qualitative and quantitative methods, as well as identifying the challenges of combining the two methods, and these are discussed in more detail in chapter 2.

Advantages of the Questionnaire

The questionnaire, which the *American Heritage Dictionary of the English Language* defines as "a form containing a set of questions, especially one addressed to a statistically significant number of subjects as a way of gathering information for a survey" ("Questionnaire" 2020), offers several important advantages over other techniques or instruments for collecting survey data, among which are the following:

- The questionnaire, especially the mail, email, online, and telephone/cell phone questionnaire, tends to encourage frank answers. This is in large part because it is easier for the researcher to guarantee anonymity for the respondent when using one of these types of questionnaire. In addition, the respondent can complete the questionnaire without the researchers being present. Thus, the questionnaire can be quite effective at measuring attitudes (see fourth bullet below for another consideration).
- The characteristics of the questionnaire that help to produce frank answers also eliminate interviewer bias. This is not to say that the questions could not be worded in a biased manner, but that there is no style of verbal presentation that can influence the response. The problem of biased questions is a serious one and is treated in greater detail later.
- Another way of stating the second advantage is that the fixed format of the questionnaire tends to eliminate variation in the questioning process. Once the questions have been written in their final version and included in the questionnaire, their contents and organization will not change. However, this does not rule out the possibility of respondents interpreting a particular question in different ways.

- The manner in which mail, email, and online questionnaires are distributed and responded to also allow them to be completed, within limits, at the leisure of the participants. This encourages well thought out, accurate answers. On the other hand, if the researcher is more interested in obtaining spontaneous or immediate reactions, as in an attitudinal survey, then the relatively large amount of time allotted for completion of the questionnaire could be a disadvantage.
- Questionnaires can be constructed so that quantitative data are relatively easy to collect and analyze.
- Questionnaires can facilitate the collection of large amounts of data in a relatively short period of time. Questionnaire-based surveys of several thousand people are not unusual, and responses typically are expected within one to two weeks.
- Last, but not least, questionnaires usually are relatively inexpensive to administer.

Disadvantages of the Questionnaire

While the advantages of the questionnaire seem to outweigh the disadvantages, there are several disadvantages that should be noted:

- Use of the mail questionnaire eliminates personal contact between the researcher and the respondent. However, this also can be seen as an advantage because, as previously stated, the absence of direct contact eliminates interviewer bias from the questioning process.
- Studies indicate that people who are highly opinionated regarding the subject of a questionnaire are more likely than others to be motivated enough to complete and return it. This phenomenon tends to result in a biased sample or return, as the less opinionated members of the sample will be underrepresented and may have certain characteristics in common.
- Questionnaires may be more difficult for uneducated participants to complete, again possibly resulting in a biased return. Researchers can minimize this problem by keeping their audience in mind when developing the questionnaire and writing the questions.
- In general, there simply seems to be resistance to mail questionnaires and less use of this type of questionnaire. However, the mail questionnaire still is discussed in research methods books (Babbie 2021; Leedy, Ormrod, and Johnson 2019; Schutt 2019). In the extreme case, this can result in some participants attempting to "sabotage" a survey by purposefully responding incorrectly to some questionnaire items. This problem can be alleviated through appropriate research design, specific techniques of which are mentioned later in this chapter.
- Nonresponse rates are relatively high for mail, email, and online questionnaires, although online surveys often first use another survey method to recruit participants. Since survey respondents are usually female, more educated, and older than those who do not respond to surveys, nonresponses reduce the sample size and may introduce

sampling error by eliminating a subset of the population. The researcher should correct for sampling bias incurred from nonresponse or minimize nonresponse rates by combining several data collection techniques (Burkell 2003).

- If the questionnaire is distributed electronically, it will reach only those who have access to and are comfortable using email, the internet, and technology.

See Wolff's (Wolff-Eisenberg 2015a, 2015b) "blog posts about the survey administration process and ways to ultimately increase survey completion rates." Wolff, Manager, Surveys and Research, at Ithaka S+R, provides practical tips for administering the questionnaire, such as the best words to use in the subject line when emailing an online survey, what to include in the signatory of the message, and other tips on the mechanics of creating the documentation for disseminating email questionnaires.

Constructing the Questionnaire

Proper construction of the questionnaire is essential to its success. In general, the researcher must consider the information needed to answer the research questions and the characteristics of the participants. The former concern is dealt with first. See tips for constructing a questionnaire in text box 5.1 by Peggy Gallagher.

Text Box 5.1: Questionnaires

Peggy Gallagher

As a reference librarian early in my career, I learned that asking the right questions is paramount to understanding the true information need before diving into resources to find an answer. The same is true in conducting research, whether it be medical, legal, social science, or market research, asking the right questions—and asking them in a way that leads to meaningful answers—can lead to breakthroughs.

Questionnaires can be used for both quantitative and qualitative research needs. Asking a well-formed close-ended question can help quantify the prevalence of a certain attribute (e.g., how many students indicate they consider the library a "safe space" on campus). Following that question with an open-ended one can help qualify how students define what a "safe space" means to them.

While using open-ended questions can lead to insightful findings (and provide some juicy quotes to illustrate those findings), the data analysis on the back end is more involved and time-consuming. Careful consideration should be given to how much effort will be needed to elicit findings from each question when designing a questionnaire.

Here are a few pitfalls to avoid when designing questionnaires:

- Ask about only one attribute at a time. For example, in the statement "*I found the course engaging and informative,*" a survey respondent will not know how to answer if they found the course engaging but not informative, or vice versa.

> • In single-choice questions, be sure the answer options are mutually exclusive. Otherwise, make the question multiple-choice. For example, if asking about a respondent's role, and the answers include *student*, *library staff*, *faculty*, *researcher*, or *other*, it is feasible that a respondent could play many of these roles.
>
> For an example of a rather long, complex, but effective survey instrument and the findings that were derived from its use, please see the following:
>
> Bryant, Rebecca, Anna Clements, Pablo de Castro, Joanne Cantrell, Annette Dortmund, Jan Fransen, Peggy Gallagher, and Michele Mennielli. 2018. *Survey Instrument: Practices and Patterns in Research Information Management: Findings from a Global Survey*. Dublin, OH: OCLC Research. https://doi.org/10.25333/P9JT-W154.
> Bryant, Rebecca, Anna Clements, Pablo de Castro, Joanne Cantrell, Annette Dortmund, Jan Fransen, Peggy Gallagher, and Michele Mennielli. 2018. *Practices and Patterns in Research Information Management: Findings from a Global Survey*. Dublin, OH: OCLC Research. https://doi.org/10.25333/BGFG-D241.

Type of Question According to Information Needed

In selecting or writing specific types of questions, researchers first must consider what kind of data they need. The major types of questions, according to the kind of information needed, include the following:

- **Factual questions:** Questions used to ascertain such things as the respondents' age, gender, and so forth. This is probably the most straightforward type of questionnaire item.
- **Opinion and attitude questions:** Questions intended to determine individuals' ideas, inclinations, prejudices, convictions, and so forth. They tend to be considerably more subjective than factual questions and are more difficult to validate externally. Questionnaires used for an attitudinal survey are usually known as "attitude scales" or "indexes."
- **Information questions:** Questions designed to measure the respondent's knowledge about some topic. They typically require the greatest response time.
- **Self-perception questions:** Questions quite similar to attitude questions but restricted to individuals' opinions about themselves.
- **Standards of action questions:** Questions used to determine how respondents would act in certain circumstances. For example, one may ask library users how they would react to a new library service or a change in hours.
- **Questions about actual past or present behavior:** Questions that potentially fall within some of the categories of questions already identified but tend to be narrower in that they focus on behavior. For example, the kind of information gathered to describe past or present behavior could be factual, attitudinal, or informational in nature. Behavioral questions also tend to be rather subjective but usually become more

valid as they become more specific. Data on past and present behavior can serve to some extent as a predictor of future behavior.

- **Projective questions:** Questions that allow respondents to answer questions indirectly by attributing their personal beliefs and attitudes to others. In other words, they permit the respondents to indicate how they would react to some question or situation by reporting how peers, colleagues, and others would react in the same situation. This technique can be particularly useful for eliciting responses on a topic about which participants may be reluctant to express their own, true feelings openly or directly. For example, certain public librarians could be asked how their colleagues feel about censorship, with the researcher assuming that the attitudes of the respondents are similar to the attitudes of the colleagues. The researcher must be aware, however, that such measures may be weak in validity as indicators of the characteristics they are designed to measure.

Projective questions are considered to be a type of indirect method of questioning people and require only minimal cooperation on the part of the individuals being studied. Hoyle, Harris, and Judd (2002) discuss a variety of specific projective methods, as well as several more structured indirect tests. The reader interested in learning more about indirect assessment should consult Hoyle, Harris, and Judd (2002), keeping in mind that the validity and reliability of indirect methods are open to question. Such techniques are probably most appropriate for exploratory research.

All or most of the items in a questionnaire may be focused on one specific topic and, in aggregate, be considered to constitute a *scale* for the topic of interest. In the typical survey in LIS, however, the questionnaire likely will consist of a variety of questions addressing a number of components of a broader topic.

Type of Question According to Form

In selecting or designing questionnaire items, the researcher must consider the question format to best obtain the desired information. The form of the question in turn determines the method of response. The researcher must decide which response format will be the easiest for the respondent while still producing adequate, definite, and uniform answers. Whenever possible, it is recommended that consistent response formats be employed. This design results in less confusion for the respondent and makes speedier replies possible.

There are two basic types of questions: open-ended and fixed-response questions. *Open-ended* or *unstructured questions* are designed to permit free responses from participants rather than ones limited to specific alternatives. They are especially useful for exploratory studies and "are called for when the issue is complex, when the relevant dimensions are not known, or when the interest of the researcher lies in exploration of a process or of the individual's formulation of an issue" (Selltiz, Wrightsman, and Cook 1959).

On the negative side, as there is almost no limit to the possible responses to an open-ended question, these answers are usually more difficult to categorize and analyze than responses to structured questions. Open-ended questions also may discourage responses because they typically take longer to answer.

Examples of open-ended questions are:

What resources did you use?
What made you choose these resources instead of others?
What made these resources easy or difficult to use (White and Connaway 2011)?

Fixed-response or *structured questions*, also known as closed questions, limit the responses of the participant to stated alternatives. The possible responses may range from a simple "yes" or "no," to a checklist of possible replies, to a scale indicating various degrees of a particular response.

Structured questions have several advantages and disadvantages in comparison with unstructured questions. Structured questions more easily accommodate precoding, in that the possible responses are generally known and stated. The precoding, in turn, facilitates the analysis of the data gathered by the questions. Precoding essentially involves anticipating responses, establishing numerical codes or symbols for the various responses, and including the codes on the questionnaire. An example of a precoded questionnaire item follows:

Did you simply take the first answer/solution you were able to find? 1. Yes 2. No (White and Connaway 2011)

In this example, the respondent would be asked to choose the number representing his or her answer. A one or a two, whichever the response happens to be, would be entered into the dataset for future analysis. (This technique is discussed in greater detail in chapter 8.) The use of precoded forms is sometimes referred to as direct data entry or DDE. The respondent in this example could have been asked to choose "yes" or "no" rather than choose a code. If using an online survey software program, the questionnaire can be set up to code the responses. If the researcher does not use a software program, after receiving the completed questionnaire, the researcher would have to assign a numerical code to that response and enter it, thus adding an extra step to the analysis process.

Other advantages to the structured question format include the fact that responses to structured questions tend to have more reliability than responses to unstructured questions. This occurs because there is a limited set of responses and thus less potential for variation from test to test. Fixed-alternative questions also have the advantages of being "standardizable," simple to administer, and more easily understood by the respondent in terms of the dimensions along which the answers are sought. Having fixed responses also helps to ensure that the answers are given in a frame of reference that is relevant to the purpose of the inquiry.

Among the disadvantages of the structured question is a real possibility that a limited set of possible replies can force respondents to select inaccurate answers. None of the choices may correspond exactly with the participant's position, or they may not allow for qualification. Having an "other" category can alleviate this problem somewhat, but respondents may tend to limit their answers to those provided rather than utilizing the "other" option.

Similarly, a closed question may force a statement of opinion on an issue about which the respondent does not have one. The inclusion of a "don't know" or "no opinion" type response can help to provide an indication of no opinion, but again the respondent may be inclined to give a more definite response. The omission of possible responses also can introduce bias. For example, in a question asking individuals to check the online sources they use regularly, the list may be biased toward traditional online sources rather than more innovative, social-oriented ones, in that more options are provided for one or the other orientation. Again, an "other" category does not completely eliminate this problem.

Providing possible answers also can help the respondent to cover up a certain amount of ignorance. The respondents will be able to provide a reasonable answer even when they know nothing about the subject. Whether this is a problem depends on the nature of the study.

In conclusion, "closed questions are more efficient where the possible alternative replies are known, limited in number, and clear-cut. Thus, they are appropriate for securing factual information . . . and for eliciting expressions of opinion about issues on which people hold clear opinions" (Selltiz, Wrightsman, and Cook 1959, 262). In practice, a combination of structured and unstructured questions can be most efficient. In addition, two surveys, or a survey followed by a survey of a subsample, can effectively utilize both types of questions and thereby complement one another. For example, following a survey based on structured questions, a subsample could be studied in greater depth with unstructured questions.

Structured questions come in a variety of specific formats, including the following:

1. A checklist, each item of which requires a response. (An example is provided for this and each of the other types of structured questions to follow.)

   Have you experienced any of the following advantages in the environment of chat reference? [Yes, No, N/A]

   > Anonymity (a layer of separation between librarian and user)
   > Personal sense of greater connection to user
   > Elimination of geographic boundaries
   > Obtaining email address or name from user
   > Personal convenience (i.e., working from home)
   > Less physical pressure, as users are not physically present
   > Excitement of working in a high-tech environment
   > Pleasure of receiving more varied and interesting questions
   > Ease of understanding users' reactions (Radford and Connaway 2005)

2. A checklist of items, one or more of which represents the "best" answer.

Which of the following about being online do you worry about most? (Check all that apply.)

Concerns about levels of privacy
Connecting with people I have never met face-to-face
A desire not to be perceived as vain or egotistical
The risk of wasting time
Other: _____ (White and Connaway 2011)

3. A checklist of items with subdivisions or categories.

What is the highest grade of school you have completed? (Circle/click on one number.)

Grade school	01	02	03	04	05	06	07	08
High school			09	10	11	12		
College or technical school			13	14	15	16		
Postgraduate		17						

4. A checklist of bracketed or grouped responses.

What is your age?

12–14
15–18
19–28
29–35
36–45
46–55
56–65
65+ (Radford and Connaway 2005)

5. Fill in the blank. The information desk is on the _____ floor of the library.

Scaled Responses

A variety of questions utilize scales of one type or another in order to obtain responses. One kind of scale is the *rating scale*. Specific rating scales, with examples, include the following:

1. Please compare the following specific aspects of your experiences as a chat reference provider. [Five-point scale in each case, Excellent, Very good, Good, Fair, Poor, N/A]

My ability to conduct a reference interview is:
My ability to receive and respond to users' feedback is:
My ability to provide the best service and resources is:
My ability to communicate with users is:
My ability to deal with time pressures is:

My ability to follow up on users' queries later is:
My ability to provide user access to databases is:
My sense of professional satisfaction is: (Radford and Connaway 2005)

An itemized rating scale often has a category representing "no opinion" or "undecided."

2. A graphic rating scale. This, too, is a scale designed to collect ordinal-level data, but unlike the specific category scale, the graphic scale allows the respondent to check anywhere along a continuum on a paper questionnaire.

For each of the following statements, indicate your degree of agreement by placing a checkmark on the continuum.

a. The library does an adequate job of teaching students how to use its collections.

```
|_____|_____|_____|
```
Strongly agree   Strongly disagree

b. The library's collection usually is adequate to meet my needs.

```
|_____|_____|_____|
```
Strongly agree   Strongly disagree

The second and third points along the continuum could have been labeled as "Agree" and "Disagree," but doing so might have encouraged respondents to limit their responses to four labeled checkpoints. Such scales typically have from four to seven categories or checkpoints and often are used for measuring attitudes. It may be desirable to include a response for "undecided" or "no opinion." Careful consideration must be given to the placement of such a category, however, since its location on the continuum determines its point value. (If it were placed in the middle of the graphic scale given above, its value would be three. If placed at the end, its value might be one or five.) If the code for the value is treated as a real number, then the value of statistics such as those representing the average can be misleading and the results of the data analysis difficult to interpret.

3. A rank-order or comparative rating scale.

Please rank, in order of importance, the following types of library services.

(Record "1" for the most important, through "5" for the least important.)

_____ Information literacy programs
_____ Reference services
_____ Circulation services
_____ Maker spaces
_____ Group study rooms

Ranking type questions are not always recommended and should be used carefully. They become especially difficult for the respondent to deal with when many items are listed.

Other scaling methods use multiple responses or measurements and combine the responses into a single-scale score. Multiple-item scales can be categorized as differential, summated, and cumulative.

According to Hoyle, Harris, and Judd (2002), *multiple-item scales*, even more so than rating scales, can help to reduce the complexity of data. They also hold more potential for testing hypotheses and are considered to have better validity and reliability.

A *differential scale*, often referred to as a Thurstone type scale, utilizes a series of statements or items with equidistances between them. Each item receives a value point equidistant from those immediately preceding and following it. The respondents are asked to check each statement with which they agree or the two or three statements that best represent their positions. Statements about a public library might include the following examples:

Statement	Scale value
I believe the public library is an important agency for educating citizens.	1.0
I believe the public library plays a major role as a cultural agency.	1.5
I believe the public library duplicates educational services provided elsewhere.	7.4
I believe the public library is of value only for recreational reading.	8.2

The statements would represent favorable and unfavorable attitudes toward the public library and would be arranged in a random order. The respondent's overall attitude would be the mean of the scale values of the items with which the individual respondent agreed.

Differential scales do have certain disadvantages. They are time consuming to develop since it is difficult to design questions that truly represent values equidistant from one another. In addition, it is difficult to avoid rater or compiler bias in developing questions utilizing differential scales.

Summated scales also consist of a series of statements or items, but no effort is made to distribute them evenly along a continuum. In fact, only items that are favorable or unfavorable to the attitude of interest are used (unless a "no opinion" type of response is included). The Likert scale is one of the most commonly used summated scales. See tables 5.1 and 5.2 for examples of a Likert scale.

In the examples above, the sum of responses to the items indicating the degree to which an academic, public, or other library participates in the activities related to reduced inequalities, minus the sum of responses to the items the library used to do this but no longer do, never has done this, or not sure, would constitute the scale score. The response values would be those values assigned to "we do this on a regular basis," "we do this on occasion or as the

Table 5.1.   Example of Likert Scale: Academic Library

Please indicate the degree to which your library participates in the following activities related to reduced inequalities (the United Nations Sustainable Development Goal (n.d.) (SDG) 10):

Academic Library	We do this on a regular basis (e.g., daily, weekly, monthly, etc.)	We do this on occasion or as the need arises	We used to do this but no longer do	We have never done this	Not sure
Offer **programs, services, and/or collections** to promote awareness and education around diversity (e.g., beliefs, socioeconomic and educational status, race, gender, sexual orientation, physical ability, age, etc.).					
Provide inclusive physical facilities (gender-neutral restrooms, feminine hygiene products, physically accessible facilities).					
Implement policies to ensure diverse staffing and leadership.					
Provide employee training around equity, diversity, and inclusion.					
Implement services/programs designed to reduce inequality based on gender, age, race, ethnicity, religion, etc.					
Implement vocabularies and metadata policies designed to reduce bias.					
Provide meals as part of a structured program on campus or in partnership with community agencies					

Table 5.2.   Example of Likert Scale: Public or Other Library

Public or Other Library	We do this on a regular basis (e.g., daily, weekly, monthly, etc.)	We do this on occasion or as the need arises	We used to do this but no longer do	We have never done this	Not sure
Offer **programs, services, and/or collections** to promote awareness and education around diversity (e.g., beliefs, socioeconomic and educational status, race, gender, sexual orientation, physical ability, age, etc.).					
Provide inclusive physical facilities (gender-neutral restrooms, physically accessible facilities, etc.).					
Implement policies to ensure diverse staffing and leadership.					
Provide employee training around equity, diversity, and inclusion.					
Implement services/programs designed to reduce inequality based on gender, age, race, ethnicity, religion, etc.					
Implement vocabularies and metadata policies designed to reduce bias.					
Provide services and/or facilities specifically for the homeless.					

need arises," and so forth. Likert-type scales are often used with individual, nonsummated scales as well. (See the examples of itemized rating and graphic scales given above.)

The major disadvantage of summated or Likert-type scales is that they do not permit one to say anything about the exact amount of differences in attitudes since they represent an ordinal scale of measurement. For example, one could not say that a respondent who checked "strongly disagree" was twice as unfavorable toward some library service as a respondent who checked "disagree." Some do argue that the data collected by a Likert-type scale are, for all practical purposes, interval level, and proceed to analyze the data accordingly. A more conservative, rigorous approach would not permit making this assumption.

The third basic category of multiple-item scales utilized in questionnaires is the *cumulative scale*. It consists of a series of statements with which the respondent indicates agreement or disagreement; however, the items are related to each other, so one "should" respond to subsequent items in a manner similar to preceding ones. It is generally assumed that cumulative scales represent the ordinal level of measurement. Examples of cumulative scales are the Bogardus-type scale, used for measuring social attitudes, and the Guttman scale, also known as "scale analysis" or "the scalogram method." As was the case with the Likert scale, all items or statements must be either clearly favorable or unfavorable to the topic. A unique feature of the cumulative scale is that none of the respondents should give a negative response before a positive response or a positive response after a negative response.

A specialized scale that shares some of the characteristics of the summated scales is the *semantic differential scale*. This scale provides pairs of antonyms and synonyms, along with five- to seven-step rating scales. See table 5.3 for an example of a semantic differential scale.

To obtain the respondent's overall rating of the library, the researcher would sum the total value of each column and divide by the number of rows (five).

All of these scales possess one or more weaknesses. As previously noted, one common problem is the determination of the neutral position when provided. Another is the conceptual validity of assigning one value or point that represents a person's attitude along a continuum when, in fact, a wide range of values may be more accurate.

Self-ratings are subject to a variety of limitations resulting from personal bias and the subjectivity of the questions. Ratings by others can suffer from

Table 5.3. Example of Semantic Differential Scale

For each pair of items below, what number comes closest to describing the conditions of your public library? (Circle/click on one number on each line.)

	Extremely	Moderately	Neither	Moderately	Extremely	
a. Pleasant	1	2	3	4	5	Unpleasant
b. Clean	1	2	3	4	5	Dirty
c. Organized	1	2	3	4	5	Disorganized
d. Helpful	1	2	3	4	5	Unhelpful
e. Available when needed	1	2	3	4	5	Unavailable when needed

certain *systematic errors*, which decrease the validity and reliability of the results. One of these, the *halo effect*, occurs when the respondents generalize the rating from one item to another in an unconscious attempt to make their ratings consistent. This phenomenon is especially likely to occur when a general, all-encompassing question is asked before more specific questions on the same topic. For example, if a respondent answers positively to a general question about a library, the respondent is more likely to give positive responses to subsequent questions about specific services of the same library. Another constancy error, the *generosity error*, involves the rater's overestimating the desirable qualities of subjects. A third systematic error, the *contrast error*, results when respondents tend to view persons as different from themselves on the trait being rated. A variety of other factors relating to the construction and administering of questions can decrease the reliability of their scales. These problems are considered elsewhere in this text where applicable.

Having selected a specific form of response, the researcher must make other decisions regarding that particular format. If a researcher has decided to utilize the check answer, then the researcher must decide if it would be best to provide dichotomous, multiple-choice, or scaled responses. The researcher should develop a checklist that includes enough alternatives and mutually exclusive categories, which means there should be (within limits) a category for every possible response, and no response should require more than one category to contain it. For many fixed-response questions, the researcher must decide whether to provide a "don't know" response option. There is a difference of opinion about the desirability of doing this, but a good case can be made for providing that option when it is reasonable to expect that some respondents will not have an opinion or any knowledge on which to base an answer.

Question Content and Selection

Having decided on the type(s) of questions to be employed in terms of the information needed to answer the research questions and the form of response desired, the researcher must next decide what specific questions to ask and consider their content and wording. The researcher first should determine whether a specific question actually is necessary or will be useful. If the answer is "no," the question should not be included. If the answer is "yes," how many questions are needed on that particular topic to obtain the necessary information? One should never ask more questions than are absolutely necessary.

One technique that can help the researcher avoid unnecessary and redundant questions, while asking those that are necessary, is to construct a variable-question matrix. This matrix simply is a table with the questions numbered across one edge and the variables across an adjoining edge. Corresponding boxes or cells are then checked when there is a question about a variable. If several cells are checked for any one variable, it may suggest that more questions are being asked about that topic than is necessary. Too few or no checks for a variable would raise the opposite concern.

Another question that researchers should ask themselves is whether the respondents can be expected to have the information needed to provide an answer. Perhaps a question needs to be more concrete, specific, or related to the respondents' personal experiences. On the other hand, the question should be general enough that it is free from spurious concreteness or specificity; that is, it should not be more specific than it sounds.

In general, a question should not be biased, or at least it should be accompanied by a question designed to balance any emphasis or perspective. The researcher also should avoid questions that are misleading because of unstated assumptions or unanticipated implications.

Last but not least, the researcher should be satisfied that each question asks only one question. This is a common occurrence in questionnaires, and yet it does not receive the attention that it deserves. Consider the following real questionnaire item as an illustration: "Ability to describe the various theories of learning and assess their relevance to particular adult learning situations." In this case, the respondents were asked to rate the degree to which they agreed with this statement. But what if one agreed with "describing the various theories" but disagreed with "assessing their relevance?" Obviously, a single response could not represent both of these attitudes. In addition, a question containing more than one concept presents difficulties for subsequent analysis and interpretation.

Question Wording

The way in which the contents of questionnaire items are worded also can affect their validity and reliability. Consider the following two questions:

Do you think the United States should forbid public speeches against democracy?
Do you think the United States should not allow public speeches against democracy?

In 1940, these two forms of this attitude question were asked in a "split-ballot" experiment using two comparable national samples. Although there seems to be no real difference between forbidding and not allowing something, in one sample, 54 percent of the respondents said the United States should forbid speeches against democracy, but in the other, 75 percent said the government should not allow such speeches. It appears that the variation in wording significantly affected the responses to essentially the same question. This test was replicated in the mid-1970s, and again there was a difference between samples of about 20 percent (*ISR Newsletter* 1982, 6–7).

During the Watergate scandal, Gallup polls never found a majority of Americans to be in favor of "impeaching" President Nixon; however, a majority never failed to favor impeachment when defined as an "indictment" or a decision to bring the president to trial before the Senate. For discussions of how words can be interpreted differently in library settings, the reader may wish to consult articles written by Bookstein (1985) and Kidston (1985).

It is therefore a good idea to avoid questions that tend to be misunderstood because of difficult or unclear wording. Such questions can result from the use of biased and emotionally laden terms. In general, it also is a good idea not to use slang, jargon, and technical terms. It is even possible for some words to be objectionable to certain respondents, thereby biasing their answers or resulting in their not completing the questionnaire.

In most cases, questionnaire items should be impersonal, but whether they should request information directly or indirectly depends on the type of information needed. When the researcher doubts that subjects will be willing or able to give accurate information about themselves, indirect methods of collecting data may be necessary. However, the validity of indirect methods tends to be more suspect, and they sacrifice precision and reliability in the interest of breadth and depth of information.

In constructing questionnaire items, one should be careful that the wording used in certain questions does not bias responses to later questions. To help alleviate this problem, as well as others previously mentioned, it is important to provide clear definitions of key terms where needed. The researcher must avoid making too many assumptions about the respondent's knowledge or the likelihood that all respondents will interpret important terms in the same way (Bookstein 1982).

Sequencing of Questionnaire Items

Even the sequencing of questions can influence how they are answered. Changes in question order can produce "context errors" resulting in substantial differences in responses to the same question. In a 1979 study, a question was asked about whether a pregnant woman should be allowed "to obtain a legal abortion if she is married and does not want any more children" (*ISR Newsletter* 1982, 7). When this question was asked alone, responses were considerably more favorable than when it followed a question about allowing abortion if "there is a strong chance of serious defect in the baby." During the US presidential campaign in 1992, voters were asked to name their favorite candidate in a two-way race between George H. W. Bush and Bill Clinton and in a three-way race among Bush, Clinton, and Ross Perot. Perot always fared better if the three-way question was asked last rather than first.

Due to the effects of "context," it is important to maintain the same order of questions if a survey is being repeated in order to investigate trends. Within a single study, the researcher should consider whether a question is likely to be influenced by the context of the preceding questions. Also, is the question led up to in a natural way? Does it occur too early or too late with regard to arousing sufficient interest and avoiding undue resistance?

It is generally recommended that questions with a similar context be placed together. Another rule of thumb is to sequence the questions from the general to the specific. Particular topics may dictate other sequences, however. The first question generally is considered to be the most crucial one, and it has a relatively large influence on the response rate. Therefore, it should be clearly related to the topic, interesting, neutral, and easy to answer. The first question also should be well constructed, and it is usually desirable for it to be one that all subjects can answer.

Sources of Error

Before continuing with the outline of the procedures for developing a questionnaire, it may be worthwhile to consider some of the types of questionnaire error not already discussed. Some of the more common types of error or bias, not all of which are limited to questionnaires, are the following:

Researcher bias. In essence, this bias results from the researcher's unconsciously developing the questionnaire in a manner that will increase the likelihood of obtaining the desired results.

Sponsorship bias. This bias results from the researcher's, hopefully unconscious, attempt to produce research results that will please the outside agency funding the research. A researcher may well be suspected of such bias if his or her research is sponsored by an agency with vested interests in certain outcomes.

Imperfections of design. Weaknesses in the design of the questionnaire can result in biased or inaccurate responses. Such imperfections include haphazard sequencing, inadequate instructions, and a failure to explain the purpose and scope of the study.

Respondent interpretations. As previously implied, varying interpretations of the "facts" and key terms by the respondents also can result in inaccurate answers.

Time lapse. It has been found that answers to the same question tend to vary over time even when not directly affected by the passage of time. It must be realized that perceptions, attitudes, and so on are not static in most cases.

Circumstances. A variety of factors, such as carelessness and mood of the respondent, ambiguous questions, "unthinking" answers, and general resistance to questionnaires, can produce inaccurate responses.

Response bias. Error can result from the response rate being low, and thus the final sample ends up less representative than originally conceived. Some of the steps that can be taken to minimize response bias include using questionnaires only when one is reasonably certain that the subjects are interested in the topic, making responses confidential or anonymous, sending reminders to complete questionnaires, providing gift or cash incentives to encourage responses (some incentives can be included with an email or online questionnaire by initiating a trigger for the gift when the questionnaire is completed and submitted), and being realistic about eligibility criteria for subjects.

Reactive insight. There is a growing concern that as subjects participate in surveys over time, especially in surveys dealing with sensitive topics, they may begin to rethink their lives, attitudes, and so forth. This activity could then result in the participants' being biased in certain areas and less representative of their larger populations.

Preparing the First Draft

Much of the preceding section relates, of course, to the preparation of the first draft of the questionnaire. As suggested above, the researcher must decide on the sequence of questions that best serves his or her purpose. In some cases, this may result in the questions being sequenced in the most logical arrangement.

This may mean ordering the items from the general to the particular, or the best arrangement may be by subject. For example, a questionnaire about the administration of a library could be categorized by staff, services, collections, budget, and so forth. Questions within these sections could then be ordered from the most general to the most particular. When the topic changes noticeably, it is a good idea to provide a lead-in statement as a transition.

On the other hand, the researcher may wish to achieve the optimal psychological sequence, which may not be the same as the most logical arrangement. This can be an important consideration when a questionnaire contains sensitive questions, or questions that ask for rather confidential information, or questions that take a lot of time to answer. Such questions can prompt a person to quit answering a questionnaire and return it partially finished or worse yet, discard it. But if these questions occur near the end of the questionnaire, the respondent is more likely to go ahead and complete the questionnaire because of the time and effort already invested in it.

In light of the types of errors discussed above, the best psychological sequence also may mean that questions that are likely to bias questions that follow should be located at or near the end of the questionnaire. This will at least reduce the error or bias that they introduce into the study.

In preparing the first draft of the questionnaire, the researcher may decide that some questions are of such a nature that respondents are unlikely to answer them accurately or honestly. In this case, the researcher should consider incorporating some "cross-check" questions to determine the reliability of certain questions. Cross-check questions are those that ask for the same information as one or more others, but each is worded differently. If the respondents answer essentially the same question differently, then one must question their reliability. Keep in mind, however, as previously discussed, the wording of a question can affect its responses. In addition, respondents may be irritated, or even insulted, if they detect the use of cross-check questions. Such a reaction can affect their responses to the questionnaire as a whole and bias the results.

Evaluating the Questionnaire

Once the first draft of the questionnaire has been completed, and before it actually is pretested, it is a good idea to get one (or more) expert's opinion of the questionnaire. A person who is an expert in research methodology can help to catch methodological weaknesses in the instrument, such as faulty scales and inadequate instructions. A person who is familiar with the topic of the questionnaire can help in assessing the face validity of the questions. Do they make sense, are they easy to understand, do they ask what they are supposed to be asking?

The Pretest

After obtaining an informal evaluation of the questionnaire, it should be pretested fully. This pretest is sometimes referred to as a "pilot study," although pilot study is actually more synonymous with "exploratory study." A pretest gives the researcher an opportunity to identify questionnaire items that tend to be misunderstood by the participants or do not obtain the information that is needed. But in addition to testing the actual questionnaire items, the pretest should include interviews with some or all of the pretest participants or at least incorporate one or more open-ended questions about the questionnaire. Interviews and/or open-ended questions are necessary in order for the respondents to have ample opportunity to point out problem questions, that is, questions that were not understood, poor instructions, too time consuming or difficult to complete, and unnecessary or missing questions, and to give their general reactions to the instrument. Pretest participants sometimes are encouraged to call the researcher if they wish to make additional comments about the questionnaire.

The pretest also offers certain advantages beyond helping to refine the data collection instrument. It can permit a preliminary testing of the hypothesis, point out a variety of problems not anticipated relating to design and methodology, facilitate a practice run of the statistical procedures to be used, and perhaps even indicate that the final study may not produce any meaningful results and therefore should be rethought or abandoned.

Ideally, the pretest sample should be as scientifically selected as the sample for the final study. That is, it should be randomly selected and of an adequate size to permit generalizations to the population. In actual practice, pretest samples are seldom so rigorously selected. Sometimes known as "samples of several," they often are in effect nonprobability, convenience samples, selected because of their members' proximity and willingness to participate. But the pretest sample should be reasonably representative of the final study group, or there is little value in conducting the pretest.

Researchers also should be careful that they do not view the pretest as a mere formality. This means that if the pretest does turn up any problems, the questionnaire should be revised accordingly. If substantial problems are found, resulting in significant revisions, another pretest should be conducted. This process should continue until the researcher is prepared to move to the final study with a questionnaire that does not represent an instrument that is significantly different from the last one pretested.

As the researcher evaluates the results of the pretest, there are some good questions to ask: Did each of the items measure what it was intended to measure? Were all of the words understood? Did all respondents similarly interpret all questions? Did each fixed-response question have an answer that applied to each respondent? Were some questions regularly skipped or answered unintelligibly?

Final Editing

Having been pretested, the questionnaire is ready for final editing before distribution. It is recommended that the title of the study or survey be placed at the top of the questionnaire. The organization will benefit from the employment of an outline format in lettering and numbering sections and questions. If the researcher uses software to create and disseminate an online survey, the formatting will be done programmatically. If the researcher is using a paper questionnaire, the questions on each page should be arranged so that there is adequate white space among them and in the margins. Adequate lines or spaces should be left for responding to open-ended questions. Nothing frustrates the respondent more than being asked to provide answers for which there is inadequate room. One less-than-ideal solution to this is asking the respondent to use the back side of the page when necessary on paper questionnaires or providing adequately sized text boxes for online question versions.

The general rule is that the questionnaire should be as short as possible in order to encourage complete responses. Other factors, such as the respondent's motivation, which is affected by his or her interest in the topic and probability of benefiting from the study, may make a longer questionnaire feasible.

There are a number of steps one can take to keep the questionnaire length to a minimum. First, while instructions must be clear, they also should be kept as brief as possible. Second, if the questionnaire is to be mailed, it can be typed in a small font. Third, relatively long questionnaires can be printed on both sides of the sheet, in order to at least minimize the thickness of the instrument. Finally, and for other reasons as well, the questionnaire should ask only for information not already held by the researcher. Unnecessary and redundant questions should be avoided. It is a waste of the respondent's time to supply information already held by the researcher or readily available from other sources, and if the respondent becomes aware of being asked to do so, there is a greater chance that the questionnaire will not be completed and returned or submitted.

In order to facilitate accurate, easy responses, the researcher should strive for simplicity in word use and question construction. As much as possible, the questionnaire's response format should be consistent. For example, the respondent should be asked to "circle the number" or "check the appropriate box" or "click on the number" throughout as much of the questionnaire as is appropriate. Changing formats can create some confusion as well as increase the response time. It typically requires more than one format to obtain all needed information, such as age and job, however, and some researchers argue that switching formats helps to keep the respondent alert and to avoid response patterns. The respondent's accuracy generally will increase if factual questions are tied to a definite time period. For example, rather than asking a person how often they use a library during a typical year, it may be better to ask how often they used the library between January and December of the preceding year.

Other measures that will help both the researcher and the respondent is to keep open-ended questions to a minimum in *self-administered* questionnaires. While they may be necessary in certain types of studies, they are more susceptible to inconsistencies in interpretation and unreliable responses. As previously indicated, the analysis will be expedited by utilizing as much precoding as possible, and this is not practical with open-ended questions.

It may be useful to screen out respondents who should not answer certain questions. This will save response time for the participant and analysis time for the researcher. One technique for doing this involves the use of filter questions or skip patterns. A filter question may, for example, ask the respondents if they have used the library's reference service during the preceding twelve months. If the answer is no, then the respondent may be asked to skip the next few questions pertaining to reference services and go on to those asking about the collection. Skip patterns can easily be automated in an online questionnaire by deleting questions if a specific answer is checked or by not allowing an answer to be inserted if the question does not correspond to the previous answer. A graphic format may be utilized by drawing a line to the next pertinent question so as to avoid any confusion, if using a paper questionnaire. An illustration of this method follows:

1. Did you try any new approaches to finding information? (Choose only one)
   Yes (Skip to question two)
   No (Skip to question four)
2. What new approaches did you try? (White and Connaway 2011)

Finally, the questionnaire should have a thank-you note at the end and repeat the instructions for how and by when the questionnaire should be returned/submitted. An accompanying letter or email might have contained this information but could have been misplaced or deleted.

Cover Email or Letter with Introductory Information

In most cases, a cover email or letter should accompany the questionnaire or link to the online questionnaire. Its basic purpose is to provide introductory information by briefly explaining the purpose of the study, any benefits to the respondents, and to stress the importance of each person responding. In some situations, such as with instruments designed to measure certain values indirectly, it may be necessary to be somewhat vague, if not actually misleading, about the scope of the study. This does present ethical concerns, however, and in general it is best to be open regarding the purpose of the study. It is not easy to conceal the true nature of a study, and if respondents become aware that they have been misled, they are not likely to view the questionnaire favorably. Those receiving the introductory information and questionnaire generally appreciate being told how they were selected to participate in the study. Miller and Salkind (2002, 123) also suggest including in the cover letter a statement that informs the respondents that by returning the questionnaire they are consenting to participate in the study. A consent form or a statement informing the respondents that submission of the online questionnaire is consent to participate should be included in the cover email or introduction to the online questionnaire.

If one can be used legitimately, it is a good idea to employ a letterhead, whether it is an online or mail survey, to lend some authority to the study. Cover email and letters should be written in a friendly, but professional, style.

Individuals are more likely to complete the questionnaire if the cover email or letter stresses the potential usefulness of the study for the respondent. Along those lines, it may help to offer each respondent the results, or at least a summary of the results, of the study. To avoid having to distribute any more results than necessary, it is a good idea to ask respondents to indicate whether they wish to receive some report of the study results. Instead of promising to send results of the study to respondents, the researcher may simply emphasize that results will be disseminated via the professional literature or via a web page and include the URL, or state that the URL will be distributed when the results are available.

Another useful technique for increasing the response rate, as well as helping to ensure frank answers, is to guarantee confidentiality and/or anonymity for all respondents. The researcher should keep in mind, however, that confidentiality and anonymity do not mean the same thing. Confidentiality merely assures the respondent that their replies and name will not be associated publicly. Anonymity requires the use of techniques that make it impossible for anyone, including the researcher, to link a respondent with their answers. The latter is more difficult to achieve, especially in the online environment, and it should not be promised to the respondents unless it is actually going to be provided (see chapter 9 for more detail on informed consent, confidentiality, and anonymity).

Distribution of the Questionnaire

There are three main methods of administering the survey questionnaire. It can be self-administered, which means that the respondents are asked to complete the questionnaire themselves; administered face-to-face to respondents by researchers; or administered to respondents via the telephone by interviewers. The self-administered questionnaire can be disseminated via email, online, mailed, or handed out in person.

Online questionnaire. In the relatively recent past, surveys have been designed for participants to enter their responses directly into a computer; however, in the late 1980s and early 1990s email questionnaires were used more often because of the ease of transmission, the immediacy of the delivery, and the low cost of distribution. These early survey instruments were text-based and allowed for no interactivity. They basically were paper questionnaires delivered electronically resulting in a different method of dissemination for the paper questionnaire. The internet became more accessible and more popular in the mid-1990s and made multimedia and interactive surveys possible. Online surveys also make it possible to "micro-target respondents" and to "create multiple surveys simultaneously" (Bertot 2009, 119). Most of the online survey programs are cloud-based and are able to handle a variety of question types, a variety of answer display options, branches and filters, fills, computations, range and edit checks, and error resolution. Online surveys can be especially useful for surveying populations for which there is no list and for exploratory research, and they tend to provide quicker response times and less time to administer than do paper surveys.

Email and online surveys can be designed to automate skip patterns and automatically validate answers. Online surveys can be designed to skip questions, based on the respondents' answers to previous questions, and to validate the respondents' answers to identify missed questions or unusable answers. These automated functions help to reduce measurement errors. An example of skip logic used by OCLC in an online questionnaire addressing the United Nations SDGs follows:

1. **How familiar are you with the United Nations Sustainable Development Goals (SDGs)?**
   - Very familiar (I have actively taken part in activities and/or discussions around the SDGs)
   - Familiar (I have read about the SDGs and know a little bit about them)
   - Somewhat familiar (I have heard about the SDGs but do not know much about them)
   - Not familiar (I had not heard about the SDGs prior to this) **[Skip to Q9]**
2. **How did you first learn about the SDGs? [If answered Very familiar, Familiar, or Somewhat familiar on Q1]**
   - IFLA
   - ALA
   - ASIS&T
   - United Nations
   - Partner institution
   - Conference or event
   - OCLC
   - News source
   - Colleague
   - Friend
   - Not sure
   - Other (Please specify)
3. **To what degree, if any, has your library incorporated the SDGs into your strategic planning?**
   - We have not incorporated the SDGs into our strategic planning **[Skip to Q9]**
   - We have considered the SDGs as part of our strategic planning efforts but do not explicitly reference them **[Skip to Q9]**
   - We have explicitly referenced the SDGs in our strategic plans
   - Not sure **[Skip to Q9]**

It also is possible to embed a survey into a website. Wakeling et al. (2017) embedded a survey into WorldCat.org to learn the demographics of those using the system, what these users were trying to find, and how the types of searches used to find the resources, that is, known-item, unknown-item, or institutional information (holdings) searches. There were 2,918 responses to this survey embedded into WorldCat.org.

There are numerous commercial and open source electronic survey tools available. These tools enable researchers to create and administer surveys online and in a cloud-based environment. The survey responses are stored in that the cloud and can be accessed online or downloaded into software programs. Two popular software programs for survey research are SurveyMonkey

(2020) and Qualtrics (2020). These software platforms enable the researcher to design the online questionnaire and offer templates, collect responses, and analyze the results. The software enables researchers to gather data from chatbots, apps, mobile devices, social media sites, embedded into websites, etc. They also enable researchers to share updated responses to online surveys in real time. Hinchliffe and Wolff-Eisenberg (2020a) shared live results of the responses to a survey on academic library response to COVID-19 on the web. See the live results of the survey at https://surveys.ithaka.org/results/public /aXRoYWthLVVSX3E5c3lDWkJzM0ZEVDd4Zi01ZTY5NmZkZDcxZjA3ZjAwMT A0ZmM3ZmY=#/pages/Page_5b80c888-79df-4993-affa-aa746f5f55ee (Hinchliffe and Wolff-Eisenberg 2020b). For those interested in embedding a survey into a website, there is a short, informative article by Cederman-Haysom (2020) that provides three easy ways to do this in SurveyMonkey.

The sources of error for online questionnaires include those discussed above for the mail survey. The lack of coverage for online surveys is the most readily identifiable source of error. One problem with email surveys is acquiring email address lists, but the internet and social media have made it possible to acquire convenience samples without having to know respondents' email addresses. To maintain confidentiality and anonymity of the respondents' names, researchers should strip the respondents' email addresses from their submitted surveys. Schonlau, Fricker, and Elliot (University of Ljubljana (Slovenia) Faculty of Social Sciences n.d.) recommend that the respondents be assured that all survey data are encrypted and saved to a private server in order to retain the respondents' privacy. Miller and Salkind (2002, 123) state that it is possible that someone other than the intended recipient may see the subjects' responses; therefore, the subjects should be informed that while every effort will be made to retain their privacy and confidentiality, it cannot be guaranteed. In addition, online surveys often can be flagged as spam by internet service providers. To avoid this problem, a unique, confidential identifier can be assigned to each person being asked to participate in the study, or each individual can be given a unique URL for accessing the questionnaire. In addition to privacy issues, email addresses often cannot be randomly selected and online surveys require access to technology; therefore, underrepresenting people who do not have access to technology, that is, internet service, computers, tablets, or mobile phones, who tend to have lower income and less education, or those who do not spend a lot of time on the internet or who do not feel comfortable using technology.

However, online surveys are inexpensive to disseminate, can reach global participants relatively quickly, and enable automated follow-up requests to respondents. Frankfort-Nachmias, Nachmias, and DeWaard state, "Online surveys provide better response rates than some of the other methods" (2015, 206), which is an advantage to the other types of surveys discussed in this chapter. The WebSM website is dedicated to the methodological issues of web surveys (Schutt 2019; University of Ljubljana (Slovenia) Faculty of Social Sciences n.d.).

Mail questionnaire. Unless the questionnaire is designed as a self-mailer, or is to be emailed or electronically submitted to the researcher, it should be accompanied by a self-addressed, stamped, return envelope. Again, almost anything that will help to encourage responses is worth doing. In deciding when to mail the questionnaire, the researcher should take into account common vacation periods and other such factors that may affect how quickly individuals are likely to respond. If one were mailing questionnaires to university faculty members and asking that they be completed and returned within ten days, it obviously would not be wise to mail them just before semester break. A timetable can be quite useful for keeping track of when certain activities relating to the distribution of the questionnaire should take place.

Whether disseminating a mail, email, or online questionnaire, the researcher should expect to have to conduct one or more follow-up mailings in order to reach an adequate response rate. In so doing, the researcher must first decide how long to wait before distributing a follow-up mailing. This decision will depend on how long the participants were given to respond to the first mailing. The response period should be long enough to avoid rushing the participants but short enough that they do not forget about the questionnaire. One to two weeks usually is considered to be a reasonable period of time.

A second decision relating to the follow-up is whether another copy of the questionnaire should be included with the reminder letter. Once again, any device that will help to increase the number of responses should be considered. Obviously, the more duplicate questionnaires mailed, the greater the costs for the researcher. The cost of postage is not an issue with the email or online questionnaire; however, there still are costs associated with the researcher's time. Those receiving a follow-up with no questionnaire are not likely to take the time to write for another copy if they have lost the first one. Some experts recommend designing the follow-up to be as eye-catching as possible, through the use of clever letters, humorous pictures, and so on. Items such as free pencils, books, and so forth are sometimes offered with the follow-up to encourage responses.

Another important decision regarding follow-up mailings concerns whether to send them to all participants in the study or only to those who have not yet responded. In order to avoid sending follow-up questionnaires to all participants, one must maintain some sort of record of returns. The most common method of keeping track of who has returned his or her questionnaire, unless respondents are asked to write their names, is to code each questionnaire. This is usually done by placing somewhere on each questionnaire a number that represents each participant in the survey. When a questionnaire is returned, the code number is noted, and the corresponding name is checked as having returned the questionnaire.

This method, however, has a serious drawback when utilized in a study guaranteeing anonymity. People are becoming more aware of this technique and realize that a number or code on their questionnaire probably means the researcher will be able to associate their answers with their names. Consequently, they may well doubt the researcher's promise to maintain anonymity, if given. As a result, they may refuse to answer the questionnaire, or at least the validity of their responses may be weakened.

One method for dealing with the need to maintain a record of who has returned a questionnaire in order to avoid sending follow-up questionnaires to all participants, while still assuring anonymity, involves the use of postcards. A postcard can be sent with each questionnaire with a code number for, or the name of, each participant. No identifier is put on the questionnaire itself. The participant is asked to mail the postcard separately but at about the same time that the questionnaire is returned. The researcher will thus receive something indicating who has returned their questionnaire but will not be able to associate a particular response with an individual, or at least not on the basis of code numbers.

Another technique involves removing the respondent's name from a master list upon receipt of the questionnaire. Having done so, if any identifier is removed from the questionnaire, there is no longer any way to associate responses with names of respondents. When a follow-up questionnaire is mailed or emailed, it only is sent to those names remaining on the master list. If either of these two techniques is to be used for follow-up mailings, it probably is a good idea to explain it briefly in the cover letter.

No matter how many steps one takes to maximize the response to a questionnaire, there still is a good chance that the response rate will be lower than what was desired, especially with a mail questionnaire. One rule of thumb has been that a response rate of at least 75 percent is needed if one wants to be able to assume that what was learned about the respondents is reasonably equivalent to what would have been learned about all the individuals included in the survey had everyone responded. Seventy-five percent is a rather high threshold, however, and many surveys have gathered reliable data with lower response rates. The critical issue is how much the nonrespondents differ from those who did respond. An acceptable response rate can be lower for a homogeneous population than for a heterogeneous one. If one is concerned about the response rate, then it is advisable to learn as much as possible about the nonrespondents, at least on the key variables, to determine how much they differ from the respondents. Information can be obtained about nonrespondents by, for example, examining other sources of data such as census reports, checking the findings of studies of the same population, and conducting telephone interviews with nonrespondents.

In-person questionnaire. For local assessments and self-studies, paper questionnaires can be distributed in-person and used to evaluate services, programs, events, and instruction. These are typically handed out at service desks or at the beginning of presentations and classes. If collected before participants leave the room, for example, after a public library after-school program or an academic library information literacy instruction (ILI) session, often close to 100 percent participation can be achieved. When surveys are distributed at service points, an incentive, such as entry into a drawing for a prize, can help to increase return percentage. Questionnaires should be made available in languages other than English for communities with large foreign or immigrant populations, if possible. One drawback of this type of distribution is that it does not survey potential users, only those who physically come to the library and attend its programs. However, valuable assessment and longitudinal data can be gathered if questionnaires are well-designed and both distributed and collected systematically. It is recommended that these types of questionnaires be planned in advance to anticipate high-use or high-traffic times, and that stratified collection periods, such as mornings, evenings, and weekends, be included.

SUMMARY

This chapter provides an overview of survey research, including descriptive surveys. Guidance and tips for constructing and distributing the question-naire are included with examples.

"The strength of survey research is in answering questions of fact and in assessing the distributions of the characteristics of populations" (Kidder 1981, 80). It does not permit causal inferences, although it can facilitate the analysis of relationships between variables, particularly correlational relationships. Survey research is typically weak on internal control or validity, but if based on random sampling, it is strong in external validity. This is because survey research generally concerns itself with naturally occurring variables in natural settings.

When conducting survey research, researchers have several data collection techniques at their disposal. This chapter has considered one of the most commonly used techniques: the questionnaire.

Questionnaires frequently are used for obtaining information about a person's perceptions, beliefs, attitudes, and so forth. As the web has become more widely available and popular, it is being utilized to distribute question-naires and to conduct interviews.

In developing the questionnaire, the researcher must make decisions regarding the specific types of questions to be used. These decisions are greatly affected by the kinds of information needed and whether the study is exploratory in nature. Throughout the design process, the researcher must be particularly careful not to introduce bias into the study. Even the sequencing of questions can affect their accuracy. The only reliable way to ensure that the results of survey research can be generalized from a sample to a population or beyond a single study is to draw a representative sample.

REFERENCES

Babbie, Earl R. 2021. *The Practice of Social Research*. 15th ed. Boston: Cengage.

Bertot, John Carlo. 2009. "Web-Based Surveys: Not Your Basic Survey Anymore." *The Library Quarterly* 79(1): 119–24. https://doi.org/10.1086/593960.

Bookstein, Abraham. 1982. "Sources of Error in Library Questionnaires." *Library Research* 4(1): 85–94.

Bookstein, Abraham. 1985. "Questionnaire Research in a Library Setting." *Journal of Academic Librarianship* 11(1): 24–28.

Burgess, Robert G. 1984. *In the Field: An Introduction to Field Research*. Contemporary Social Research 8. London: Routledge.

Burkell, Jacquelyn. 2003. "The Dilemma of Survey Nonresponse." *Library & Information Science Research* 25(3): 239–63. https://doi.org/10.1016/S0740-8188(03)00029-X.

Case, Donald O., and Lisa M. Given. 2016. *Looking for Information: A Survey of Research on Information Seeking, Needs, and Behavior.* Bingley, UK: Emerald Group.

Cederman-Haysom, Tim. 2020. "3 Easy Ways to Survey Your Website Visitors." SurveyMonkey. https://www.surveymonkey.com/curiosity/3-easy-ways-survey-website-visitors.

Connaway, Lynn Silipigni. 2015. "Research Challenges: The Pathway to Engagement and Progress." Presented at the the ILL International Seminar on LIS Education and Research: Challenges of LIS Research, Barcelona, Spain, June 4.

Fink, Arlene G. 2013. *How to Conduct Surveys: A Step-by-Step Guide.* 5th ed. Los Angeles: Sage.

Fink, Arlene G. 2017. *How to Conduct Surveys: A Step-by-Step Guide.* 6th ed. Thousand Oaks, CA: Sage.

Flanagan, John C. 1954. "The Critical Incident Technique." *Psychological Bulletin* 5: 327–58.

Frankfort-Nachmias, Chava, David Nachmias, and Jack DeWaard. 2015. *Research Methods in the Social Sciences.* 8th ed. New York: Worth.

Golden, Gary. 1982. *Survey Research Methods.* Chicago: ACRL.

Gorman, G. E., and Peter Clayton. 2005. *Qualitative Research for the Information Professional: A Practical Handbook.* 2nd ed. London: Neal-Schuman.

Hinchliffe, Lisa, and Christine Wolff-Eisenberg. 2020a. "First This, Now That: A Look at 10-Day Trends in Academic Library Response to COVID19." *Ithaka S+R* (blog). https://sr.ithaka.org/blog/first-this-now-that-a-look-at-10-day-trends-in-academic-library-response-to-covid19.

Hinchliffe, Lisa, and Christine Wolff-Eisenberg. 2020b. "First This, Now That: A Look at 10-Day Trends in Academic Library Response to COVID19—Live Results." Live Results.

Hoyle, Rick H., Monica J. Harris, and Charles M. Judd. 2002. *Research Methods in Social Relations.* 7th ed. Fort Worth, TX: Cengage Learning.

ISR Newsletter. 1982. "Questions and Answers."

Kidder, Louise H. 1981. *Research Methods in Social Relations.* 4th ed. New York: Holt, Rinehart and Winston.

Kidston, James S. 1985. "The Validity of Questionnaire Responses." *The Library Quarterly* 55(2), 133–50.

Lance, Keith Curry. 2017. "Constructing the Questionnaire: How Do I Develop a Survey If I Have No Idea Whre to Being?" In *Research Methods in Library and Information Science,* 6th ed., Lynn Silipigni Connaway and Marie L. Radford. Santa Barbara, CA: Libraries Unlimited.

Leedy, Paul D. 1980. *Practical Research: Planning and Design.* 2nd ed. New York: Macmillan.

Leedy, Paul D., Jeanne Ellis Ormrod, and Laura Ruth Johnson. 2019. *Practical Research: Planning and Design.* 12th ed. New York: Pearson Education.

Luo, Lili, and Margaret McKinney. 2015. "JAL in the Past Decade: A Comprehensive Analysis of Academic Library Research." *The Journal of Academic Librarianship* 41(2): 123–29. https://doi.org/10.1016/j.acalib.2015.01.003.

Miller, Delbert C., and Neil J. Salkind, eds. 2002. *Handbook of Research Design and Social Measurement.* 6th ed. Thousand Oaks, CA: Sage.

Morgan, David L. 2006. "Practical Strategies for Combining Qualitative and Quantitative Methods: Applications to Health Research." In *Emergent Methods in Social Research,* edited by Sharlene Hesse-Biber and Patricia Leavy, 165–82. Thousand Oaks, CA: Sage.

"Online Survey Software—Qualtrics." 2020. Qualtrics. https://www.qualtrics.com /core-xm/survey-software.

"Questionnaire." 2020. In *The American Heritage Dictionary of the English Language*, 5th ed. Houghton Mifflin Harcourt. https://ahdictionary.com/word /search.html?q=questionnaire.

Radford, Marie L., and Lynn Silipigni Connaway. 2005. "Seeking Synchronicity: Evaluating Virtual Reference Services." OCLC. https://www.oclc.org/content /research/areas/user-studies/synchronicity.html.

Schutt, Russell K. 2019. *Investigating the Social World: The Process and Practice of Research*. 9th ed. Thousand Oaks, CA: Sage.

Selltiz, Claire, Lawrence S. Wrightsman, and Stuart W. Cook. 1959. *Research Methods in Social Relations*. Rev. ed. New York: Holt, Rinehart and Winston.

"SurveyMonkey: The World's Most Popular Free Online Survey Tool." 2020. SurveyMonkey. https://www.surveymonkey.com.

Togia, Aspasia, and Afrodite Malliari. 2017. "Research Methods in Library and Information Science." In *Qualitative versus Quantitative Research*, Vol. Chapter 3, edited by Sonyel Oflazoglu, 43–64. Rijeka, Croatia: InTech. http://dx .doi.org/10.5772/intechopen.68749.

"United Nations Sustainable Development Goals." n.d. United Nations. Accessed November 9, 2020. https://sdgs.un.org/goals.

University of Ljubljana (Slovenia) Faculty of Social Sciences. n.d. "WebSM.Org—Web Survey Methodology." Accessed June 28, 2020. http://www.websm.org.

Vakkari, Pertti. 2008. "Trends and Approaches in Information Behaviour Research." *Information Research* 13(4). http://www.informationr.net/ir/13 -4/paper361.html.

Wakeling, Simon, Paul Clough, Lynn Silipigni Connaway, Barbara Sen, and David Tomás. 2017. "Users and Uses of a Global Union Catalog: A Mixed-Methods Study of WorldCat.Org." *Journal of the Association for Information Science and Technology* 68(9): 2166–81. https://doi.org/10.1002/asi.23708.

White, David S., and Lynn Silipigni Connaway. 2011. "Digital Visitors and Residents: What Motivates Engagement with the Digital Information Environment." Funded by JISC, OCLC, and Oxford University. https://www.oclc.org /research/areas/user-studies/vandr.html.

Wolff-Eisenberg, Christine. 2015a. "Survey Administration Best Practices: First Steps." *Ithaka S+R* (blog). August 25. https://sr.ithaka.org/blog/survey -administration-best-practices-first-steps.

Wolff-Eisenberg, Christine. 2015b. "Survey Administration Best Practices: Crafting Effective Communications." *Ithaka S+R* (blog). October 14. https://sr .ithaka.org/blog/survey-administration-best-practices.

6

Sampling

Sampling is one of the most crucial steps in survey research. Rigorous sampling methods have been developed and used primarily within the context of survey research. However, sampling techniques are relevant to other research methods, such as experiments, observations, and content analysis.

BASIC TERMS AND CONCEPTS

Before considering some standard techniques of sampling, it is important to have an understanding of the following basic terms and concepts related to sampling.

Universe. the theoretical aggregation of all units or elements that apply to a particular survey. For example, if one were surveying librarians, the study universe would include all librarians, regardless of type, location, and so forth. Universe is not frequently used today; it often is used synonymously with "population."

Population. the total of all cases that conform to a prespecified criterion or set of criteria. It is more specific or better defined than a universe and is in effect a designated part of a universe. For example, American academic librarians would be part of the universe of librarians and could represent the population for a survey study. The population is the aggregation of units to which one wishes to generalize the results of a research study. Selection of the population must precede the selection of the sample, assuming a sample is to be drawn, and is crucial to the success of the sampling stage. Selection of the population must be done carefully with regard to the selection criteria, desired size, and parameters. It is also important to consider costs, in terms of time and money, when selecting a population. If the population is too large or expensive to manage, then the study is handicapped from the start. Obviously, the members of the population must be readily accessible to the researcher; otherwise, it will be difficult, if not impossible, to collect the necessary data.

169

Population stratum. a subdivision of a population based on one or more specifications or characteristics. A stratum of the population of all American academic librarians could be those with a collection of at least one million volumes or with a budget of a certain size.

Element. an individual member or unit of a population. Each academic librarian would be an element of the population of academic librarians. The total number of elements of a population is usually designated by capital N.

Census. a count or survey of all the elements of a population and the determination of the distribution of its characteristics. A complete census is usually not possible, or at least is impractical and unnecessary, so typically a sample of the population rather than the entire population is surveyed

Sample. a selection of units from the total population to be studied. It is usually drawn because it is less costly and time consuming to survey than is the population, or it may be impossible to survey the population. However, one can never be absolutely certain how representative a sample is of its population, unless a census is also made, which would obviate using the sample. The concept of representativeness is crucial to sampling and is treated in greater depth later in this chapter.

Case. an individual member of the sample. The total number of cases in a sample is usually designated by lowercase n.

Sampling frame. the actual list of units from which the sample, or some part of the sample, is selected. It is often used interchangeably with "population list." One problem with email surveys was acquiring email address lists, but the internet has made it possible to select samples without having to know respondents' email addresses (Babbie 2021).

TYPES OF SAMPLING METHODS

It is useful to distinguish between two basic types of sampling methods: probability sampling and nonprobability sampling. Probability sampling is the more scientific of the two methods, and the bulk of this section is devoted to that technique. Nonprobability sampling is considered first.

Nonprobability Sampling

With a nonprobability sample, the researcher cannot state the probability of a specific element of the population being included in the sample. In fact, one cannot be assured that a specific element has any probability of being included in the sample. Therefore, nonprobability samples suffer from important weaknesses. When selection probabilities are unknown, one cannot make legitimate use of statistical inference. That is, a nonprobability sample does not permit generalizing from the sample to the population, because the researcher has no assurance that the sample is representative of the population. Nor can the researcher, relying on a nonprobability sample, evaluate the risks of error involved in making inferences about the sample.

On the other hand, nonprobability samples usually are easier and cheaper to obtain than are probability samples, and for some purposes, such as where the focus is on the sample itself, may be quite adequate. "Samples of several" are commonly used for pretests. In some cases, nonprobability samples may be the only feasible samples. There are measures one can take to try to improve the representativeness of nonprobability samples. These techniques are referred to when discussing some of the different kinds of nonprobability samples that follow.

Accidental, convenience, or availability sample. In utilizing an accidental sampling technique (also referred to as convenience or availability sampling), the researcher selects the cases that are at hand until the sample reaches a desired, designated size. If one wished to conduct an academic library user study, one might elect to survey library users as they entered or exited the library, on a first-come, first-served basis. There would be little or no preferential selection of respondents.

Obviously, there would be relatively little, if any, assurance that the sample was reasonably representative of the library's users. The researcher is unable to assure that the accidental sample was not atypical. The researcher might query users during some other time period and end up with quite different responses. Accidental sampling is seldom adequate for any kind of survey.

Quota sample. A type of nonprobability sample that improves somewhat on the accidental sample is the quota sample, in which the researcher takes steps to ensure that the significant, diverse elements of the population are included. The quota sample method also attempts to ensure that the different elements are included in the sample in the proportions in which they occur in the population. The researcher who wishes to survey the users of an academic library would take measures to ensure that the sample includes the same percentages of faculty, graduate students, and so on as exist in the entire academic community. Or the researcher may choose to sample the same number of persons representing each element of the population, and then to assign them a weight according to their portion of the total population. The latter technique obviously requires knowledge of the proportions of the population according to each element.

Among the problems inherent in quota sampling is difficulty determining that the proportions for each element are accurate. Second, biases may exist in the selection of cases representing the various elements, even though their proportion of the population might have been accurately estimated. For example, the researcher sampling academic library users may survey the correct proportions of senior undergraduate students, graduate students, and so forth, but for some reason may tend to query those inclined to be more competent library users. If one were investigating library skills, such a bias would be damaging to the validity of the study.

Yet quota samples, while they should be used cautiously, are useful for exploratory studies, as are other nonprobability sampling techniques. Quota sampling often is used for public opinion surveys.

Snowball sample. Some refer to this type of sampling as accidental sampling. It is an appropriate method to use when members of the population are difficult to identify and locate, such as migrants and homeless individuals or those belonging to possibly stigmatized or at-risk groups, such as abused women. The researcher contacts members of the population who can be identified and located and then asks these individuals to provide information to identify other members of the population to participate in the research. This type of sampling is cumulative, hence the name, snowball sampling (Babbie 2021). It is used in exploratory research since the technique can result in "samples with questionable representativeness" (Babbie 2021, 193). It is commonly used in qualitative research where representativeness is not a goal.

Purposive sample. At times it may seem preferable to select a sample based entirely on one's knowledge of the population and the objectives of the research. In designing a survey of the directors of large university libraries who are in the process of developing new and adapted online and in-person programs and services based on the impact of the COVID-19 pandemic, the researcher may decide that the easiest way of obtaining a sample of such librarians would be to select librarians known to the researcher to be making such changes.

The researcher would be making the assumption that such a sample would be reasonably typical of all university librarians involved in developing new and adapted online and in-person services. Unfortunately, such an assumption may not be justified. There is no assurance that a purposive sample is actually representative of the total population. Any sampling method not utilizing random selection is susceptible to bias.

Self-selected sample. As the label suggests, a self-selected sample is a group of cases, usually people, who essentially have selected themselves for inclusion in a study. A researcher might, for example, publish a notice in a professional journal asking individuals to volunteer to submit certain information or to participate in some other way. Again, there is a strong possibility that these volunteers would not be representative of the entire population to which they belong.

Incomplete sample. An incomplete sample, while not originally intended to be a nonprobability sample, in effect becomes one. For example, if a large percentage of the cases selected does not respond or participate in a study, then assurance that the sample is representative of the population is quite possibly lost, even though the sample may have been selected randomly. Another example of an incomplete sample is one drawn from an incomplete population list. Again, the sample may have been drawn randomly, but as the faulty list was in effect biased or not fully representative of the population, the sample must be considered unrepresentative and, in effect, a nonprobability sample.

Probability Sampling

As previously indicated, the primary purpose of sampling is to select elements that accurately represent the total population from which they were drawn. Probability sampling enhances the likelihood of accomplishing this objective and also provides methods for estimating the degree of probable success; that is, it incorporates probability theory, which provides the basis for estimating population parameters and error (Babbie 2021). The crucial requirement of probability sampling is that every element in the population has a known probability of being included in the sample. A discussion of major types of probability sampling follows.

Simple random sample (SRS). This is the basic sampling method of survey research. This technique gives each element in the population an equal chance of being included in the sample. It also makes the selection of every possible combination of elements equally likely. In other words, if the population or sampling frame were five hundred elements, in drawing an SRS of that population one should be as likely to include elements one and three as two and four, or one and two, and so forth.

In order for the probabilities of including each element and each combination of elements to be equal, it is necessary that there be independence from one draw to the next. The selection of any element should have no effect on the chances of remaining elements being selected. But this condition cannot be met fully unless the sampling is done with replacement. In sampling with replacement, the researcher would place every element back in the population list after it was selected for the sample so that it is again available for selection. If replacement is not done, then the remaining elements would not have the same likelihood of being drawn as did the elements already selected. The remaining population would decrease in number as elements were selected, and those still in the population would have an increasingly greater chance of being selected. Similarly, the likelihood of every combination being selected would not remain constant, because as some elements were removed from the population and not replaced, certain combinations would no longer be possible.

However, if the elements selected for the sample are subsequently put back in the population list (after making note that they are now a part of the sample), then there is the possibility that some of them may be selected for the sample again. This practice presents practical problems, so sampling with replacement is not often done. This normally does not invalidate the sample, however, as the sample usually represents a relatively small percentage of the population, and the chances of any element being selected two or more times is slight. But if the sample is as much as one-fifth the size of the population, technically one should introduce correction factors if possible. However, samples drawn without replacement do tend to be more representative.

There are mathematical formulas that can be used to correct for sampling without replacement, but if the sample represents a relatively small proportion of the population, use of a formula is unnecessary. In addition, exact correction factors are seldom known. Yet if correction does seem to be warranted, using such formulas is generally preferable to sampling with replacement and taking a chance of drawing some elements more than once. Those readers interested in correction formulas should refer to a standard text on sampling.

Selecting the simple random sample (SRS). There are several techniques available for selecting an SRS. Traditional methods include the roulette wheel or lottery-type approach. Such methods have been criticized as being at least potentially biased, or not fully random, however, because of physical or logistical imperfections. For example, if one were drawing ping pong balls from a large bowl or revolving drum, there is the possibility that the balls might not have been adequately mixed to begin with and that those placed in the container early, or late, have a greater chance of being selected. Consequently, it is advisable to consider other, more reliable techniques.

One recommended method commonly used for drawing an SRS involves the use of a table of random numbers. A well-known example is the Rand Corporation's *A Million Random Digits* (see table 6.1 for an illustrative page). A table of random numbers is simply that: a listing of randomly arranged numbers. There are numerous open access random number generators available online. In effect, the computer numbers the elements in the population, generates its own series of random numbers, and provides the list of elements selected. Computer generation of samples is particularly useful when drawing very large samples or working with large populations. Calculator.net ("Random Number Generator" 2020) and Random.org ("RANDOM.ORG—List Randomizer" 2020) offer free random number generators. Random.org offers many different types of random generators, including randomizing lists of names, email addresses, telephone numbers, etc. The basic steps involved in using such a table are as follows:

1. The first step would be to number sequentially the elements of the population. For example, a population of five hundred elements would be numbered from 1 to 500, so that each element now has a unique number.
2. The next step is to determine how many of the elements are to be selected for the sample. Techniques for determining a desirable sample size are discussed below; for now assume that a decision has been made to draw a sample of fifty.
3. As there are three-digit numbers in the population, it will be necessary to select three-digit numbers from the table in order to give every element a chance of being selected.
4. The next step is to choose the starting point in the table and the pattern for moving through the table. Pure chance must determine the starting point. A simple way of selecting the starting point is to close one's eyes and place a pencil point on the table. The number under or nearest the pencil point then becomes the starting point.
5. For ease of illustration, suppose that the pencil came down at the head of the fifth column of the table. As three-digit numbers must be selected, one could then consider, along with the 7, the next two digits, and 732 becomes the first number to be considered for the sample. It would also be possible to move down the column from 7 and consider 722 as the first three-digit number. Regarding the pattern of movement, one could proceed from there across to the right, or left, down, or diagonally through the table. All that matters is to be consistent.
6. As stated, 732 will be considered first for the sample. But as it is larger than any number in the population (the largest is 500), it will

have to be rejected or ignored. Assuming one has decided to move down the three-digit column to the bottom and then back up to the top of the next three-digit column, the next number to be considered would be 204. The number 204 does fall within the population, so the element represented by 204 would be included in the sample. This process would continue until fifty elements had been selected. If sampling without replacement, one would skip numbers that have already been included in the sample.

If the population list or sampling frame is in an electronic file, a random sample can be selected by a computer.

Systematic sample. A method of selecting a random sample that is considered by most to be as reliable and accurate as simple random sampling is systematic sampling. This technique involves taking every nth element from a list until the total list has been sampled. For example, the researcher may have a population list of one thousand elements and decide to select every tenth element for the sample. This would be a sampling interval of ten and would result in a sampling ratio of 1:10 and a sample of one hundred. The list should be considered to be circular, in that the researcher would select every nth name, beginning with a randomly chosen starting point and ending with the first name of the interval immediately preceding the starting point.

However, with systematic sampling not every combination of elements has an equal chance of being drawn. So, if the list is not randomly arranged, such as is the case with an alphabetical listing, the sample would not be random. For some variables or problems, however, an alphabetical arrangement would have no relevance and could be treated as a randomly arranged list. For example, ranked lists such as lists of personnel, and hierarchically arranged, or cyclical lists, such as lists of houses, can easily produce biased samples. To elaborate on the first example, if one were selecting every tenth individual from an organization's personnel list arranged by department and rank within the department, and if the departments had approximately the same number of employees, then the sample might tend to include people of the same rank. If these individuals tended to have certain characteristics in common, then the sample would be biased. In short, systematic sampling is generally as satisfactory as SRS, but only if the population list exhibits no trends or patterns.

Stratified random sample. In selecting this type of sample, one must first divide all of the population elements into groups or categories and then draw independent random samples from each group or stratum. This technique represents a modification of simple and systematic random sampling, in that it reduces the number of cases needed to achieve a given degree of accuracy or representativeness. The strata should be defined in such a way that each element appears in only one stratum. Different sampling methods may be used for different strata. For example, a stratified random sample may be drawn from one stratum and a systematic sample from another.

There are two basic types of stratified random samples—proportional and disproportional. In drawing a proportional stratified sample, one would draw

Table 6.1. Random Numbers

10 09 73 25 33	76 52 01 35 86	34 67 35 48 76	80 95 90 91 17	39 29 27 49 45
37 54 20 48 05	64 89 47 42 96	24 80 52 40 37	20 63 61 04 02	00 82 29 16 65
08 42 26 89 53	19 64 50 93 03	23 20 90 25 60	15 95 33 47 64	35 08 03 36 06
99 01 90 25 29	09 37 67 07 15	38 31 13 11 65	88 67 67 43 97	04 43 62 76 59
12 80 79 99 70	80 15 73 61 47	64 03 23 66 53	98 95 11 68 77	12 17 17 68 33
66 06 57 47 17	34 07 27 68 50	36 69 73 61 70	65 81 33 98 85	11 19 92 91 70
31 06 01 08 05	45 57 18 24 06	35 30 34 26 14	86 79 90 74 39	23 40 30 97 32
85 26 97 76 02	02 05 16 56 92	68 66 57 48 18	73 05 38 52 47	18 62 38 85 79
63 57 33 21 35	05 32 54 70 48	90 55 35 75 48	28 46 82 87 09	83 49 15 56 24
73 79 64 57 53	03 52 96 47 78	35 80 83 42 82	60 93 52 03 44	35 27 38 84 35
98 52 01 77 67	14 90 56 86 07	22 10 94 05 58	60 97 09 34 33	50 50 07 39 98
11 80 50 54 31	39 80 82 77 32	50 72 56 82 49	29 40 52 41 01	52 77 56 78 51
83 45 29 96 34	06 28 89 80 83	13 74 67 00 78	18 47 54 06 10	68 71 17 78 17
88 68 54 02 00	86 50 75 84 01	36 76 66 79 51	90 36 47 64 93	29 60 91 10 62
99 59 46 73 48	87 51 76 49 69	91 82 60 89 28	93 78 56 13 68	23 47 83 41 13
65 48 11 76 74	17 46 85 09 50	58 04 77 69 74	73 03 95 71 86	40 21 81 65 44
80 12 43 56 35	17 72 70 80 15	43 31 82 23 74	21 11 57 82 53	14 38 55 37 63
74 35 09 98 17	77 40 27 72 14	43 23 60 02 10	45 52 16 42 37	96 28 60 26 55
69 91 62 68 03	66 25 22 91 48	36 93 68 72 03	76 62 11 39 90	94 40 05 64 18
09 89 32 05 05	14 22 56 85 14	46 42 72 67 88	96 29 77 88 22	54 38 21 45 98
91 49 91 45 23	68 47 92 76 86	46 16 28 35 54	94 75 08 99 23	37 08 92 00 48
80 33 69 45 98	26 94 03 68 58	70 29 73 41 35	53 14 03 33 40	42 05 08 23 41
44 10 48 19 49	85 15 74 79 54	32 97 92 65 75	57 60 04 08 81	22 22 20 64 13
12 55 07 37 42	11 10 00 20 40	12 86 07 46 97	96 64 48 94 39	28 70 72 58 15
63 60 64 93 29	16 50 53 44 84	40 21 95 25 63	43 65 17 70 82	07 20 73 17 90
61 19 69 04 46	26 45 74 77 74	51 92 43 37 29	65 39 45 95 93	42 58 26 05 27
15 47 44 52 66	95 27 07 99 53	59 36 78 38 48	82 39 61 01 18	33 21 15 94 66
94 55 72 85 73	67 89 75 43 87	54 62 24 44 31	91 19 04 25 92	92 92 74 59 73
42 48 11 62 13	97 34 40 87 21	16 86 84 87 67	03 07 11 20 59	25 70 14 66 70
23 52 37 83 17	73 20 88 98 37	68 93 59 14 16	26 25 22 96 63	05 52 28 25 62
04 49 35 24 94	75 24 63 38 24	45 86 25 10 25	61 96 27 93 35	65 33 71 24 72
00 54 99 76 54	64 05 18 81 59	96 11 96 38 96	54 69 28 23 91	23 28 72 95 29
35 96 31 53 07	26 89 80 93 54	33 35 13 54 62	77 97 45 00 24	90 10 33 93 33
59 80 80 83 91	45 42 72 68 42	83 60 94 97 00	13 02 12 48 92	78 56 52 01 06
46 05 88 52 36	01 39 09 22 86	77 28 14 40 77	93 91 08 36 47	70 61 74 29 41
32 17 90 05 97	87 37 92 52 41	05 56 70 70 07	86 74 31 71 57	85 39 41 18 38
69 23 46 14 06	20 11 74 52 04	15 95 66 00 00	18 74 39 24 23	97 11 89 63 38
19 56 54 14 30	01 75 87 53 79	40 41 92 15 85	66 67 43 68 06	84 96 28 52 07
45 15 51 49 38	19 47 60 72 46	43 66 79 45 43	59 04 79 00 33	20 82 66 95 41
94 86 43 19 94	36 16 81 08 51	34 88 88 15 53	01 54 03 54 56	05 01 45 11 76

Source: The RAND Corporation. 1955. *A Million Random Digits*. Glencoe, II.: Free Press.

176

the same percentage from each stratum. If there were one thousand elements in a population, divided into ten strata of one hundred each, and if one desired a total sample of one hundred, then ten elements, or 10 percent, would be drawn from each stratum. It is more likely, however, that the strata would not all have the same number of elements. In that case, the same percentage would still be taken from each stratum, but the resulting numbers would vary.

If a researcher were to stratify all public libraries in a state according to budget size, it is probable that there would be different numbers of libraries in each group. But if the groups were roughly equal in their number of libraries, and if the categories tended to be internally homogeneous, then it would be reasonable to select the same percentage of libraries from each stratum or to use a constant sampling rate. Doing so would produce a *proportional stratified sample*, with libraries of certain budget sizes being included in the sample in the same proportions in which they occur in the population.

On the other hand, if there were considerable variations within individual strata, or if some strata were so small as to be in danger of barely being represented in the total sample, if at all, the researcher would be well advised to draw a *disproportional stratified sample*, sometimes referred to as *optimum allocation*. In order to do this, the researcher would draw approximately the same number of elements from each stratum regardless of its size. In order to do this, it would be necessary to use different sampling fractions or to select different percentages of cases from the strata. Consequently, some cases would represent a greater percentage of the sample than of the population. "Optimum precision is attained if sampling fractions in the different strata are made proportional to the standard deviations in the strata" (Lakner 1998).

This method would provide enough cases per category to allow meaningful comparisons among categories. As is true for proportional stratified sampling, it would help to assure a more representative total sample than might be expected with simple or systematic random sampling. Unlike proportional sampling, it could do so even when the groups are lacking in internal homogeneity. Disproportional stratified random sampling also can be used to take a relatively large sample from the stratum from which it is cheapest to gather data. In an interview survey of libraries, for example, this may be the group of libraries closest to the researcher. However, the increase in precision over proportional stratified sampling tends to be small, and optimizing the sample for group comparisons means the sample is no longer optimal for estimating the total population.

The choice of stratification variables typically depends on which ones are available and which ones are presumably related to the variables that one wants to represent accurately. Returning to the survey of public libraries within a state, it may well be that the researcher would decide to stratify public libraries by known budget size on the assumption that budget size would correlate with collection size—the actual variable to be studied, but yet to be determined. In other words, stratifying on budget size would help to ensure that there would be proper representation of collection sizes, and other variables, related to budget size. In general, the stratified sample would be more

Table 6.2.   Proportional and Disproportional Stratified Sampling

Strata/Samples	Library Budget in Thousands of Dollars			
	0–100	101–250	251–500	501
Strata	100	300	400	200 (N = 1,000)
Proportional sample	10	30	40	20 (n = 100)
	10%	10%	10%	10%
Disproportional sample	25	24	24	24 (n = 97)
	25%	8%	6%	12%

representative of a number of variables than would an SRS taken for the same purpose.

Table 6.2 presents stratification figures for a hypothetical population of one thousand public libraries. As can be seen in the first row, one hundred libraries have budgets of $100,000 or less, three hundred libraries have budgets of $101,000–$250,000, and so forth. If one were to draw a proportional stratified sample using a uniform sampling ratio of 10 percent, then the sample would contain ten libraries with budgets of $100,000 or less, and so forth. The researcher might conclude, however, that a sample of ten is too small to be very reliable and that comparisons of samples of such disparate size might be chancy. Therefore, the researcher might decide to vary the sampling ratio across strata in order to end up with samples of about the same size (see the bottom line, where sampling ratios vary from 6 to 25 percent). With either sampling technique, the total sample contains about one hundred cases.

A statistical note: when computing estimates of means and estimating standard errors for disproportional stratified samples, one should compute values separately for each of the strata and then weight them according to the relative size of the stratum in the population. This is not necessary for proportional stratification, as it is in effect "self-weighting." In addition, it should be recognized that in theory one cannot make legitimate use of various nonparametric statistical tests, such as tests for the significance of correlation, or analysis of covariance, without substantial modifications. Unfortunately, statistical textbooks seldom address this issue.

Cluster sample. In social science research, it is not unusual to encounter situations in which the populations cannot be listed easily for sampling purposes. Examples include the populations of countries and states, or all college students within the United States. When it is impossible or impractical to compile an exhaustive list of the elements of a total population, cluster sampling may be used effectively.

Essentially, the technique of cluster sampling involves dividing a population into clusters or groups and then drawing a sample of those clusters. The population might already be grouped into subpopulations, and cluster sampling becomes merely a matter of compiling a list of the subpopulations, or clusters, and selecting a random sample from them. For example, while a list of a city's residents may not exist, people do live on discrete blocks. Therefore, one could draw a sample of city blocks, compile lists of persons residing on those blocks, and then sample the people living on each block.

In using cluster sampling, it is desirable that each cluster's units be as heterogeneous as possible, but that characteristics of the clusters themselves be similar. This is particularly important if all members of each selected cluster are to be included in the final sample. Yet typically the elements constituting a given natural cluster within a population are more homogeneous than are all the elements of the total population. Therefore, relatively few elements may be needed to represent a natural cluster, while a relatively large number of clusters will be required to represent the diversity of the total population. The more heterogeneous the clusters, the fewer will be needed. "With a given total sample size, however, if the number of clusters is increased, the number of elements within a cluster must be decreased, and vice versa," (Babbie 2021, 220) unless the clusters are known to be especially heterogeneous.

Cluster sampling may be either single-stage or multistage. Single-stage cluster sampling occurs only once. In the earlier example involving the selection of city blocks, all elements or persons residing on each block would be included in a single-stage design. In a two-stage design, the simple random sampling of city blocks would be followed by a random sampling of the persons living on the blocks. Or, in a more complex design, a sampling of census tracts could be followed by a random sampling of smaller clusters of blocks, followed by a sampling of individual houses, and conclude with a sampling of persons living in those houses. A combination of probability and nonprobability sampling may be used in multistage sampling, but the researcher should keep in mind the likely loss of accuracy with nonrandom sampling.

The sampling procedure illustrated in figure 6.1 is a combination of cluster, stratified, and simple random sampling that has been employed by the Institute for Social Research at the University of Michigan. The procedure involves the following steps:

1. The entire geographical area of the forty-eight contiguous states is divided into small areas called *primary sampling units* (PSUs). The PSUs are usually counties, metropolitan areas, or telephone exchange areas. A stratified random sample of about seventy-five PSUs is selected from the total list.
2. Each PSU is stratified into large cities, smaller cities and towns, and/or rural areas. Each unit within a stratum is referred to as a *sample place*, and one or more sample places are selected from each stratum.
3. Each sample place is divided into *chunks*, which are distinct areas such as blocks. A number of chunks are randomly selected from each sample place.
4. The chunks are broken down into *segments*, which are areas containing from four to twelve dwelling units. Segments are then randomly drawn from each chunk.

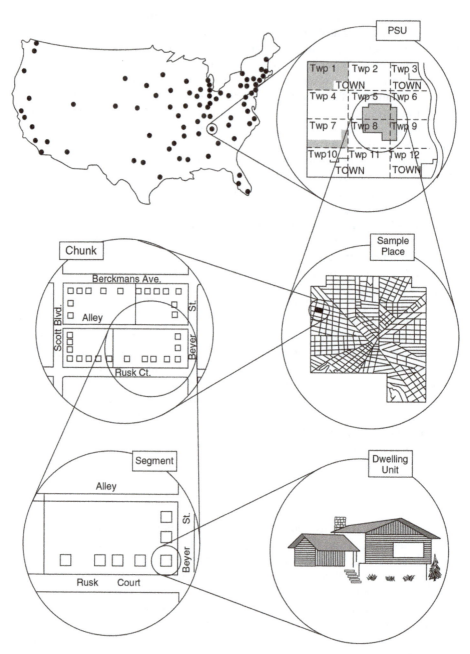

Figure 6.1. Cluster Sampling Method
From *Survey Research Center, Interviewer's Manual,* rev. ed. Ann Arbor: Institute for Social Research, University of Michigan, 1976, p. 8–2.

5. *Dwelling units*, selected from each segment, constitute the final sample. A city directory can be used to obtain telephone numbers for the dwelling units so chosen.

As previously noted, cluster sampling may be the only feasible or practical design where no population list exists. It also tends to be a cheaper sampling method for large surveys. But multistage cluster sampling does sacrifice accuracy because sampling error can occur at each stage. In a two-stage sampling design, the initial selection of clusters is subject to sampling error, and the sampling of elements within each cluster is subject to error. The researcher must decide if the greater efficiency gained from cluster sampling is worth the greater risk of sampling error and must attempt to minimize the error by optimizing the number of clusters and elements selected. Theoretically, cluster sampling necessitates using special statistical formulas, especially when the clusters are of greatly differing sizes. Again, a text on sampling should be consulted if more information about this issue is desired.

With the popularity of social media, such as blogs, Twitter, Facebook, and Snapchat, researchers are building communities to freely discuss issues. These communities provide opportunities for researchers to have access to individuals who may not respond to other types of data collection methods or who have particular characteristics. Blair and Blair (2014) discuss using social media for survey sampling. Using social media to recruit study respondents can be an advantage for longitudinal studies, because the researcher can reconnect with and track respondents through these sites. Since social media often include personal information about individuals, it can be less expensive to recruit respondents, especially individuals with specific characteristics, through these sites. However, these individuals only represent a small percentage of the population who are comfortable using this medium to communicate; therefore, researchers should use social media as sample frames only when they represent the intended target groups, to avoid bias. Macri and Tessitore (2011) suggest using some type of quota or convenience sampling when targeting Facebook users for sampling.

The widespread use of mobile phones, and in particular smart phones, has impacted survey research, since respondents can be reached not only on landlines, but anywhere on mobile phones. The use of smart phones also has made it possible to contact individuals via email, text, or voice and to develop apps for disseminating questionnaires. "It is estimated that more than 5 billion people have mobile devices, and over half of these connections are smartphones . . . [However,] a median of 76% across 18 advanced economies surveyed have smartphones, compared with a median of only 45% in emerging economies" (Silver 2019). This means that if a researcher uses the smart phone for dissemination of a questionnaire to the general population, another mode of distribution should be used in conjunction with the phone.

See table 6.3 for a simplified outline of the summarization of the characteristics of major random sampling techniques. This may be helpful when developing a sampling frame.

Table 6.3.   Population Characteristics and Appropriate Random
Sampling Techniques

Population Characteristics	Example of Population Type	Appropriate Sampling Technique
A general homogeneous mass of individual units	First-year students of a private university	Simple random sampling (systematic sampling if the population list is long)
Definite strata, each as internally homogeneous as possible and of approximately the same size	All undergraduate students of a private university; each level represents a stratum	Proportional stratified sampling
Definite strata, some of which are quite small and/ or internally heterogeneous	All public libraries in a state, stratified by budget size, resulting in an upper budget category containing only a few libraries	Disproportional stratified sampling
Clusters whose group characteristics are similar, but whose elements or internal characteristics are quite heterogeneous	A population consisting of the users of the major urban public libraries in the nation; the libraries tend to be similar, but their users vary widely in characteristics	Cluster sampling

DETERMINING THE SAMPLE SIZE

The general rule of thumb for the size of the sample is, quite simply, the larger the better. Babbie suggests that probability samples of less than one hundred are not likely to be very representative of the population (Babbie 2021). Yet there is no point in utilizing a sample that is larger than necessary; doing so unnecessarily increases the time and money needed for a study. There are at least four general criteria that can help to determine the necessary sample size. The first is the degree of precision required between the sample and the population. The less accuracy needed, the smaller the necessary sample. The second is the variability of the population, which influences the sample size needed to achieve a given level of accuracy or representativeness. In general, the greater the variability, the larger the sample needed. (Statistics commonly used to estimate the variability of a population are noted in chapter 8.) A third is the method of sampling to be used, which can affect the size of the appropriate sample. As noted in the discussion of random sampling, stratified sampling requires fewer cases to achieve a specified degree of accuracy than does simple or systematic random sampling. The fourth criterion is the way in which the results are to be analyzed, which influences decisions about sample size. Samples that are quite small place significant limitations on the types of statistical analyses that can be employed.

Use of Formulas

Statistical formulas have been developed for calculating appropriate sample sizes. They typically take into account the confidence level, which relates to the probability of the findings, or differences between samples, being due to chance rather than representing a real difference. The confidence level is equal to one minus the level of significance, or one minus the probability of rejecting a true hypothesis. Formulas also consider the degree of accuracy with which one wishes to estimate a certain characteristic of the population and the variability of the population, usually as represented by its estimated standard deviation—a standard measure of dispersion. The greater the spread of scores about the mean, the larger the standard deviation.

$$n = \frac{S^2}{[S_1 E_1(\bar{x})]^2}$$

One such formula is stated as follows:

where

n = sample size
S = standard deviation of the variable or characteristic of the population (estimated)
$S_1 E_1(\bar{x})$ = standard error of the mean or sampling error.

The difficulty in using formulas is that S, the population's standard deviation, must be estimated. It is known only if the total population is analyzed, therein eliminating the need for taking a sample. In addition, if the sample represents a large proportion of the population, a finite population correction has to be included. "Usually, sampling units have numerous attributes, one or more of which are relevant to the research problem" (Frankfort-Nachmias, Nachmias, and DeWaard 2015, 145). Therefore, if more than one variable is to be studied, a sample that is adequate for one variable may not be satisfactory for another. One should consider the variability of all of the variables; the sample size tends to increase as the number of variables increases.

A proportional allocation formula, based on the assumption that a characteristic occurred 50 percent of the time, was used by Krejcie and Morgan (1970) to develop a table of sample sizes for given population sizes. This table is presented here (see table 6.4) but, as previously noted, a variety of factors can influence desirable sample size. A table of sample sizes may represent a rather simplistic, and quite possibly conservative, method for ascertaining a sample size. Again, there is seldom much justification for using a sample that is larger than necessary.

Table 6.4 does not require any calculations. To obtain the required sample size, one need only enter the table at the given population size (e.g., 9,000) and note the adjacent sample size (368). Figure 6.2 illustrates the relationship between sample size and total population. This figure and the table indicate that as the population size increases, the rate of requisite increase in sample size decreases.

Table 6.4. Table for Determining Sample Size from a Given Population

N	S	N	S	N	S
10	10	220	140	1,200	291
15	14	230	144	1,300	297
20	19	240	148	1,400	302
25	24	250	152	1,500	306
30	28	260	155	1,600	310
35	32	270	159	1,700	313
40	36	280	162	1,800	317
45	40	290	165	1,900	320
50	44	300	169	2,000	322
55	48	320	175	2,200	327
60	52	340	181	2,400	331
65	56	360	186	2,600	335
70	59	380	191	2,800	338
75	63	400	196	3,000	341
80	66	420	201	3,500	346
85	70	440	205	4,000	351
90	73	460	210	4,500	354
95	76	480	214	5,000	357
100	80	500	217	6,000	361
110	86	550	228	7,000	364
120	92	600	234	8,000	367
130	97	650	242	9,000	368
140	103	700	248	10,000	370
150	108	750	254	15,000	375
160	113	800	260	20,000	377
170	118	850	265	30,000	379
180	123	900	269	40,000	380
190	127	950	274	50,000	381
200	132	1,000	278	75,000	382
210	136	1,100	285	1,000,000	384

Note: N is population size, S is sample size. The degree of accuracy = 0.05.

From Krejcie, Robert V., and Daryle W. Morgan, "Determining Sample Size for Research Activities," *Educational and Psychological Measurement* 30 (Autumn 1970): 608.

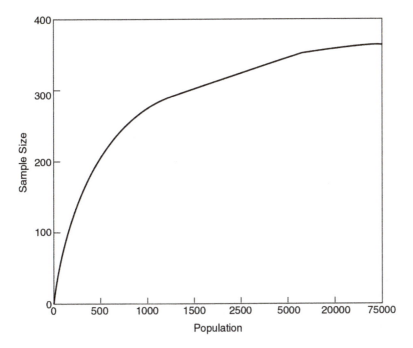

Figure 6.2. Relationship between Sample Size and Total Population
Adapted from Krejcie, Robert V., and Daryle W. Morgan, "Determining Sample Size for Research Activities," *Educational and Psychological Measurement* 30 (Autumn 1970): 609.

To calculate the optimal sample size when dealing with a continuous variable such as age, one could use the following formula:

$$n = \frac{z^2 s^2}{E^2}$$

where

n = sample size
z = z score for desired confidence level (see chapter 8 for a discussion of
   z scores)
s = standard deviation
E = allowable error.

Readers wanting to know more about determining sample size may wish to refer to works by Kraemer and Thiemann (1987), Hernon (1994), and Cohen (1988). The latter provided several tables of sample sizes as functions of the type and power (the probability that a statistical test will yield statistically significant results) of the statistical test being used.

Sample size calculators also are freely available on the internet. Both Creative Research Systems (http://www.surveysystem.com/sscalc.htm) and SPH analytics (https://www.sphanalytics.com/sample-size-calculator-using-percentage

-values) provide sample size calculators that will determine the sample size and the confidence level.

Sampling Error

Formulas also are available for estimating the "sampling error" or, as it is often referred to, the "standard error of the mean." The standard error of the mean represents how much the average of the means of an infinite number of samples drawn from a population deviates from the actual mean of that same population. For example, if a population consisted of fifty libraries with collections averaging 500,000 volumes, one should be able to draw all possible sample combinations of ten libraries, average the means of all the samples, and end up with 500,000 volumes as the mean of the sampling distribution. If the mean of the sampling distribution were based on a limited number of samples, it is possible that it would deviate somewhat from the actual population mean, thus indicating some sampling error.

If the population is large relative to the sample, the formula for calculating the standard error of the mean, or in fact the standard deviation of the sampling distribution of the means, is as follows:

$$S_1E_1(\bar{x}) = \frac{S}{\sqrt{n}}$$

where

S = the standard deviation of the population
N = the number of elements in the population
n = the number of cases in the sample

If the sample represents a relatively small proportion of the population, or if the population standard deviation is not known and must be estimated, as is usually the case, then modified versions of the formula must be used. The formula for the first situation is as follows:

$$S_1E_1(\bar{x}) = \sqrt{\frac{S^2}{n} \cdot \frac{N-n}{N-1}}$$

where

S = the standard deviation of the population
N = the number of elements in the population
n = the number of cases in the sample

The formula for the standard error of the mean, where the population standard deviation is not known, requires substituting an unbiased estimate (s), or the standard deviation of the sample, for the standard deviation of the population (S). "The term *unbiased estimate* refers to the fact that as one draws more and more samples from the same population and finds the mean of all these unbiased estimates, the mean of these unbiased estimates approaches the population value" (Nachmias and Nahmias 1981, 425).

The formula for the standard deviation of the sample is as follows:

$$s = \sqrt{\frac{\sum_{i=1}^{n}(x_i - \bar{x})^2}{n-1}}$$

where

x_i = sample score
x = sample mean
n = the number of cases in the sample

Dividing by $n - 1$ instead of n is done to reduce bias or, according to some texts, to help compensate for a small sample. The value for s can then be substituted for S in the first formula given for calculating the standard error of the mean:

$$S_1 E_1(\bar{x}) = \frac{s}{\sqrt{n}}$$

As previously indicated, there is a point of diminishing returns with regard to the sample size and sampling error. Starting with a sample of one person and then increasing the sample size, the accuracy of the sample will improve rapidly up to about 500 cases. Beyond 500, a relatively large increase in the number of cases is needed in order to increase significantly the accuracy of the sample. For example, if 600 cases are drawn for the sample, the amount of sampling error involved is about 4 percent. To decrease this to 3 percent, it would be necessary to increase the sample size to 1,067; to reduce error to 2 percent requires an increase to 2,401 cases. In other words, after a certain point is reached, increasing the sample size will increase the researcher's workload without appreciably improving the accuracy of the sample. Thus, the researcher is well advised to base his or her decision regarding sample size on desired precision and confidence levels, and not to decide arbitrarily that some percentage of the population represents an optimal sample size. (See figure 6.3 for an illustration of the relationship between sample size and error in this example.)

Again, one of the main purposes for selecting and analyzing samples is to obtain information about the population from which the sample has been drawn. "If an unbiased sample were taken from the population, it would be hoped that the sample mean would be a reasonable estimate of the population mean. Such an estimate is known as a *point estimate* but it is unlikely that the mean of a sample will be identical to the mean of the population" (Simpson

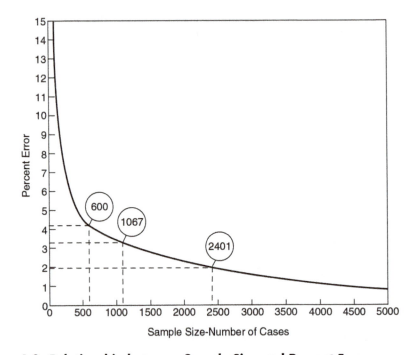

Figure 6.3. Relationship between Sample Size and Percent Error
From Benson, Dennis K., and Jonathan L. Benson, *A Benchmark Handbook: Guide to Survey Research Terms*, Columbus, OH: Academy for Contemporary Problems, 1975, p. 2.

1988, 44). Statisticians often content themselves with calculating *interval esti-mates* or the ranges within which the actual population means are likely to fall.

Other Causes of Sampling Error

The size of a sample, or more specifically having too few cases, is not the only cause of sampling error. A variety of factors can contribute to a sample's being less representative of its population than is satisfactory. If not guarded against, bias of one sort or another easily can compromise a research study. Bias is particularly a problem with nonrandom samples, as there is less of a safeguard against personal attitudes, preferences, and so forth affecting the researcher's selection of cases. For example, if a researcher were selecting library users for an interview on library services, there may be the inclination, if even unconsciously, to slight persons of color, who appeared to be unskilled library users, or were not well dressed.

Even utilizing probability or random sampling techniques, the unwary researcher can end up with a biased or inaccurate sample. This problem includes any techniques used by the researcher resulting in each element in the list not having an equal chance of being included.

Nonsampling Error

The information gathered from a sample can be inaccurate as a result not only of the inaccuracy or the lack of representativeness of the sample, but also of errors of measurement. For example, in responding to a questionnaire or interview, individuals may lie about their age or report figures inaccurately, for a variety of reasons. Nonsampling error is difficult to estimate but generally, as sample size goes up, so does nonsampling error. Another way of stating this relationship is that as sampling error decreases, nonsampling error tends to increase. Since sampling error generally decreases as sample size increases, one is faced with some conflict between sampling and nonsampling error. Some sort of balance is usually desirable, and the largest sample size possible is not necessarily the best.

SUMMARY

This chapter provides an overview of sampling methods, sampling error, and nonsampling error. The most common, and one of the best, techniques for selecting a representative sample is simple random sampling. Depending on certain characteristics of the population, or on the purpose of the research, other probability techniques may be preferable in a given situation.

Concerns include the size of the sample and sampling error. There are formulas for estimating these properties, but again, the nature of the population and the purpose of the research should be considered. There are no absolute criteria for sample size and sampling error. What is satisfactory for one study may not be for another. There may even be occasions in which nonprobability sampling is preferable to probability sampling, but the researcher should keep in mind that the generalizability of studies using nonprobability samples is open to serious question.

REFERENCES

Babbie, Earl R. 2021. *The Practice of Social Research*. 15th ed. Boston: Cengage.

Blair, Edward, and Johnny Blair. 2014. *Applied Survey Sampling*. Thousand Oaks, CA: Sage.

Cohen, Jacob. 1988. *Statistical Power Analysis for the Behavioral Sciences*. 2nd ed. Hillsdale, NJ: Routledge.

Frankfort-Nachmias, Chava, David Nachmias, and Jack DeWaard. 2015. *Research Methods in the Social Sciences*. 8th ed. New York: Worth.

Hernon, Peter. 1994. "Determination of Sample Size and Selection of the Sample: Concepts, General Sources, and Software." *College & Research Libraries* 55: 171–79. https://doi.org/10.5860/crl_55_02_171.

Kraemer, Helena Chmura, and Sue Thiemann. 1987. *How Many Subjects? Statistical Power Analysis in Research*. Newbury Park, CA: Sage.

Krejcie, Robert V., and Daryle W. Morgan. 1970. "Determining Sample Size for Research Activities." *Educational and Psychological Measurement* 30 (Autumn): 608.

Lakner, Edward. 1998. "Optimizing Samples for Surveys of Public Libraries: Alternatives and Compromises." *Library & Information Science Research* 20(4): 321–42. https://doi.org/10.1016/S0740-8188(98)90026-3.

Macri, Esther, and Christiano Tessitore. 2011. "Facebook Sampling Methods: Some Methodological Proposals." Presentation presented at the New Techniques and Technologies for Statistics, Brussels, Belgium, February 22.

Nachmias, David, and Chava Nachmias. 1981. *Research Methods in the Social Sciences*. 2nd ed. New York: St. Martin's Press.

"Random Number Generator." 2020. https://www.calculator.net/random-number -generator.html.

"RANDOM.ORG—List Randomizer." 2020. https://www.random.org/lists.

Silver, Laura. 2019. "Smartphone Ownership Is Growing Rapidly Around the World, but Not Always Equally." Pew Research Center. *Pew Research Center's Global Attitudes Project* (blog). https://www.pewresearch.org/global /2019/02/05/smartphone-ownership-is-growing-rapidly-around-the-world -but-not-always-equally.

Simpson, Ian S. 1988. *Basic Statistics for Librarians*. 3rd ed. London: Library Association.

7

Experimental Research

Experimental research often is labeled the most rigorous of all research methods and "as the 'gold standard' against which all other designs are judged" (Trochim 2006). If experimental research is done well, it is the best method for testing cause and effect relationships (internal validity). A review of the literature indicates that the use of this research method in library and information science (LIS) research studies is becoming more prevalent. Chu analyzes a total of 1,162 scholarly publications in the *Journal of Documentation* (JDoc), the *Journal of the Association for Information Science and Technology* (JASIST), and *Library & Information Science Research* (LISR) from 2001 to 2010 and identifies the research methods used. She reports that the JDoc sample of publications used experimental research (13.4 percent) about the same amount as questionnaires and interviews. The largest percentage (31 percent) of articles published in JASIST and the lowest percentage (9 percent) of articles published in LISR during this time period used experimental research methods (Chu 2015). Togia and Malliari (2017) analyzed 440 LIS articles published in five journals. They found that 78 percent of the articles reported empirical research, with 4.4 percent of these reporting the use of experiments, with the greatest number of these studying information retrieval. Ma and Lund (2020) analyzed 3,422 articles in LIS published in 2006, 2012, and 2018. They reported that the "experiment was consistently the most utilized research method, more commonly associated with information science/systems studies" (2020, 7). Before discussing experimental research methods per se, causality, a concept that is crucial to experimental research, is considered.

CAUSALITY

Simply stated, causality suggests that a single event (the "cause") always leads to another single event (the "effect") (Selltiz, Wrightsman, and Cook 1959, 80). Anderson (1986, 9) noted that "causes and consequences concentrate on the relationships between phenomena—how one phenomenon affects another." In the social sciences, at least, the focus is normally on a variety of determining factors that increase the probability of a certain event occurring, rather than on a single factor. Goldhor (1972, 87) even argued that the "demonstration of causality in any rigorous sense is philosophically impossible," and he suggested that causality and "explanation" can be used interchangeably. Yet an understanding of causality is essential to the proper testing of causal hypotheses or relationships and is useful in designing research studies to be as rigorous as possible.

The Conditions for Causality

In attempting to confirm causality in a relationship, one must consider the so-called conditions or factors that may exist. A *necessary condition* is one that must occur if the phenomenon of which it is a cause is to occur. That is to say, if X, the independent variable, is a necessary condition of Y, the dependent variable, Y will never occur unless X occurs. For example, if information literacy instruction (ILI) was a necessary condition of effective library use, then the latter would never occur unless ILI had been provided.

A *sufficient condition* is one that always is followed by the phenomenon that it "causes." In other words, if X is a sufficient condition of Y, then whenever X occurs, Y always will occur. If ILI were a sufficient condition of effective library use, then after an individual received appropriate ILI, they would begin using the library effectively.

A condition may or may not be both necessary and sufficient for the occurrence of a phenomenon. (If both, Y would never occur unless X had occurred, and whenever X occurred, Y would occur also.) In the example provided, one can see that it is quite possible for neither condition to exist. Information literacy instruction probably is not a necessary condition for effective library use, as a user may teach himself or herself to use the library; and it certainly is not a sufficient condition, as effective library use does not always follow ILI, regardless of how well it is presented.

As previously noted, in the social sciences especially, a variety of factors tend to cause or influence any one dependent variable. The example of effective library use is a good case in point. In addition to ILI, effective library use might be affected by motivation, intelligence, previous experiences, role models, peer pressure, and so forth. In short, the researchers rarely find a single factor or condition that is both necessary and sufficient to cause an event, so they are well advised to consider other types of conditions.

One type of condition that can be considered, in addition to necessary and sufficient conditions, is the *contributory condition*. Contributory conditions increase the probability that a certain phenomenon will occur, but they do not make it certain. So, if library instruction were considered to be the factor likely to have the strongest effect on library use, then the other factors named, such as peer pressure, might be considered contributory conditions. And in fact, the combination and interaction of all of the relevant factors or independent variables would probably best explain effective library use.

The picture is further complicated by the fact that certain variables will represent contributory conditions in some situations but not in others. Again, social science concepts tend to be complex, and the interaction of variables, or how they affect one another and combine influences, must be taken into account. The conditions under which a given variable is a contributory cause are referred to as *contingent conditions*. In the previous example, the various factors suggested as likely causes of effective ILI might be so only if the library's services, spaces, and online and physical collections were strong. In other words, the environment may increase or decrease the influence of certain variables.

The researcher also should be aware of the possibility of *alternative conditions* that might make the occurrence of a certain phenomenon more likely. Alternative conditions, in essence, are the different forms that a given factor or variable may take and how the factor's influence is affected by its form. Information literacy instruction can be provided in different formats, and it may be that one type of ILI would promote effective library use and another would not. For example, library orientation may be inappropriate for graduate students and have no real effect on how they use the library, while instruction in the use of the literature of a certain discipline may greatly improve their library use effectiveness. In turn, the alternative conditions would continue to be affected by other contributory conditions, such as how well the library is able to support research in the specific area of graduate study.

A less commonly discussed factor, *mechanism*, refers to the conditions that create the causal connection, or the intervening variables. Consideration of the mechanism helps us understand how variation in the independent variable(s) results in variation in the dependent variable(s). This condition seems to be conceptually similar to the contingent condition discussed earlier, in that it is concerned with the context in which the cause has its effects.

Bases for Inferring Causal Relationships

Unfortunately, as Goldhor implied, it usually is impossible to demonstrate directly that one variable causes another variable, either by itself or in combination with other variables. As a result, the social science researcher normally has to infer a causal relationship between two or more variables based on the data gathered (Goldhor 1972, 87).

One type of evidence for inferring a causal relationship is known as *concomitant variation*. Evidence of concomitant variation, or covariation when there are two variables, indicates that the independent variable (X) and the dependent variable, or assumed effect (Y), are associated in the way predicted by the causal hypothesis. For example, one might have hypothesized that as the amount of ILI is increased, the level of information literacy skills will increase.

The relationship just specified is an example of a positive one. A relationship in which both variables decrease simultaneously is in effect a positive relationship as well. Other possible relationships include a negative or inverse relationship, in which as one variable decreases, the other increases (or vice versa), and a curvilinear relationship, in which the degree to which one variable affects the other tends to diminish beyond a certain point.

In the case of a hypothesis that predicts that the independent variable is a contributory condition of the dependent variable, the "logical consequence" would be that Y would appear in more cases where X is present than in cases where it is not present. So, if it were hypothesized that ILI is a contributory condition of effective library use, then persons who had received ILI would be more likely to be effective library users than those who had not received ILI. But one would not be able to assume that every person who had received ILI would be an effective library user. Other types of causal hypotheses (e.g., X is a necessary cause of Y) would call for other patterns of associations between the independent and the dependent variables.

A second basis for inferring a causal relationship between two variables is the *time order* of occurrence of the variables. To establish the necessary time order requires evidence that the dependent variable did not occur before the independent variable. One could not support a hypothesis predicting a necessary causal relationship between ILI and effective library use if it were found that the effective library use was occurring before the student received any ILI.

The third basis for inferring a causal relationship is nonspuriousness or evidence *ruling out other factors* as possible causes of the dependent variable. However, such evidence merely helps to provide a reasonable foundation for inferring that X is or is not a cause of Y. It cannot absolutely confirm a relationship, because the researcher may have overlooked one or more other factors that are actually the determining conditions. The process of ruling out other factors, or controlling for the effects of extraneous variables, is considered further in upcoming sections of this chapter.

In conclusion, there are certain conditions that should exist, and certain kinds of inferences that must be made, in order to support causal relationships. The most effective method for collecting the necessary evidence, or testing a causal hypothesis, is the experiment.

CONTROLLING THE VARIABLES

Certain characteristics or capabilities are essential to the experimental research method. Virtually all quantitative research requires the measurement of variables, but experimental research necessitates the control and manipulation of certain variables as well. In addition, the variables must vary under different conditions, or have at least two values; otherwise, they are not considered variables. The independent variable is the experimental variable, also referred to as the cause or causal variable and the predictor variable. It is the variable that the researcher manipulates. Organismic variables are variables such as age and income, which often are treated as independent variables, but over which the researcher has no real control. The dependent variable often is known as the effect, the subject variable, or the criterion variable. It is "caused," or at least affected, by the independent variable.

True experimental manipulation also requires the use of at least one experimental group and one comparison or control group, each consisting of an appropriate number of subjects. The experimental group receives the experimental treatment, and the comparison group receives no treatment, thereby creating an independent variable with at least two values. The dependent variable is represented by the measurement of the effect of the experimental treatment, and several dependent variables or measures of effect may be used.

If one were conducting an experiment to measure the effect of ILI on library use, ILI would be the independent variable, and library use would be the dependent variable. The two values for ILI could be the provision of instruction to the experimental group and no instruction for the comparison group. The dependent variable could be measured by a tally of the frequency of library use for the members of both groups. Another dependent variable could be types of reference questions asked by members of the two groups.

One of the difficulties in exerting adequate control in an experiment is the fact that typically there are a variety of extraneous independent variables that conceivably are influencing or causing the dependent variable(s), in addition to those being investigated. Extraneous variables also can influence both the independent and the dependent variables and thus create a spurious association between them. In order to isolate the effects that the experimental variable or variables are having, the researcher must control the extraneous independent variables, which could include, in the most recent example, assignments made by instructors, increased "marketing" by the library, and so forth.

There are three major techniques for controlling the influence of extraneous variables, two of which are intended to equate the experimental and comparison groups prior to the experiment. One technique involves holding the other variables constant by matching or selecting subjects with the same traits for the experimental and comparison groups. That is, as a subject is selected for the experimental group, another one that is quite similar in all characteristics or variables that are relevant or capable of affecting the dependent variable is selected for the comparison group. For example, after a subject had been selected for the experimental group in a study on the effects of ILI, then a subject with a comparable IQ, previous library experience, GPA, age, and so forth would be assigned to the comparison group. It is difficult to identify all relevant variables when matching subjects, but the researcher may derive some consolation from the fact that key variables tend to correlate highly with other, unidentified variables.

If the subjects are not completely equivalent going into the experiment, the extraneous variables may be controlled statistically during the analysis stage. However, this approach is less reliable than others, as it is done ex post facto, or after the experiment. No amount of statistical control can completely undo the preceding effects of other factors. And it is effective at all only if the relevant extraneous variables are identified and properly measured.

Random Assignment

The third and best technique for equating two or more groups before the experimental treatment begins is referred to as random assignment or randomization (not to be confused with random sampling or selection). It is a

procedure used after the sample is selected but before the experimental treatment is applied. It involves randomly assigning the subjects in the total sample to the experimental and comparison groups. Specific techniques used for
random assignment are often essentially the same as those used for selecting
random samples. The researcher may elect, for example, to use a table of random numbers, to employ a computer to generate a list of random numbers, or
to draw names from a hat.

One can assume, however, that the groups are equivalent only within certain probability levels. But "equating" the experimental and comparison
groups is essential for making causal inferences about the effects of the experimental treatment. It improves the external validity, or generalizability, of the
experiment, as well as its internal validity, or the dependability of the results.
Random assignment does not necessarily control for the effects of the experimental setting. The researcher must take other steps to eliminate or minimize
the influence of such factors as the mode of instruction, quality of tests, and
interaction of subjects.

INTERNAL VALIDITY

Briefly defined, internal validity "refers to the possibility that the conclusions drawn from experimental results may not accurately reflect what went
on in the experiment itself" (Babbie 2021, 239). Stated more positively, it is
"the conclusiveness with which the effects of the independent variable are
established in a scientific investigation, as opposed to the possibility that
some confounding variables may have caused the observed results" (Kidder
1981, 447).

Generally speaking, the greater the control the experimenter has over the
experiment, including the extraneous variables, the greater the internal validity. The greater the control, however, the more artificial or unnatural is the
setting and the lower the external validity. (This relationship is referred to
again when discussing experimental designs.)

Threats to Internal Validity

Internal validity is crucial to the dependability of the results of an experiment, and it is closely related to replicability. It indicates the extent to which
the experiment adequately tested the treatment under study by helping to
rule out rival explanations and ensuring freedom from bias. In short, internal
validity provides confidence that the observed effect on the dependent variable
is actually due to the independent variable.

Unfortunately, a number of factors can jeopardize the internal validity of
experimental research. Those factors most frequently cited in standard texts
are the following:

1. History, or specific events, in addition to the experimental treatment
   or variable, which occur between measurements of the dependent

variable. During an experimental study of the effects of ILI on the frequency of library use, subjects might be exposed to some event or influence such as a midterm exam that would encourage them to use the library more than usual. The researcher might then be uncertain about how much of the increase in library use was caused by the midterm exam and how much by the ILI provided.

2. Maturation, or processes *within* the subjects operating as a function of time, such as growing older or more mature. During the course of the experiment just referred to, the subjects might naturally develop into more frequent library users regardless of any ILI received.

3. Testing, or the effects of taking a test on the scores of subsequent testing. In an ILI experiment, students would tend to do better on a second test of information literacy skills simply because they had already taken the test.

4. Instrumentation, or the process wherein changes in the techniques used for the measurements, or changes in the persons making the measurements, affect a second set of measurements or observations. For example, if a pretest on library use measured use as the number of *materials used in the physical library*, and a second test measured it as the number of *materials used in the digital library*, then the second measurement probably would be different simply because the method of measurement had been changed.

5. Statistical regression, which is the phenomenon wherein extreme scores obtained on a first test tend to gravitate toward the mean on subsequent tests. This is especially significant when groups have been selected on the basis of their extreme scores. If subjects in one group achieved extremely high scores on a test of information literacy skills, and subjects in a second group earned exceptionally low scores, the odds are that many of the subjects in both groups would tend to be closer to the mean score on a retest. Again, this event would confound the effects of any ILI provided between tests.

6. Biases in differential selection of subjects for the comparison groups. If a researcher selected students for the comparison group (the group not receiving any ILI) who were not likely to evidence much use of the library, then the researcher would be guilty of biasing the experiment in favor of the experimental treatment. The students in the experimental group (those receiving ILI) probably would use the library more than those in the comparison group, with or without ILI, but it might appear that ILI was having a positive effect.

7. Experimental mortality, or the differential loss of subjects from the comparison group. If during the course of an experiment students who tended to be infrequent library users, perhaps because of their area of study, dropped out of the comparison group, then the remaining members might produce scores higher than would be normal. Such an occurrence would suggest that ILI was having less effect than it actually was, because the difference in scores between the experimental and comparison groups would be less than expected.

8. Interaction of selection and other sources of invalidity. The results of interaction can be mistaken for the effects of the experimental variable. For example, the students selected for the experimental group might have been exceptionally receptive to ILI because they had matured intellectually during the experiment. Therefore, their retest scores would be higher than their pretest scores, and the gain probably would be attributed to the ILI received. At least some, if not all, of the increase in test scores could have resulted, however, solely from the intellectual maturation that had taken place.

To repeat, these threats to internal validity, if not controlled, may well produce effects confounded with the effect of the experimental stimulus (Campbell and Stanley 1963, 5). Types of experimental designs that can help to control these extraneous variables are discussed later.

EXTERNAL VALIDITY

Before taking up specific types of experimental designs, external validity, the second type of validity important to successful experimental research, is considered. External validity is important because it relates to "the generalizability of experimental findings to the 'real' world" (Babbie 2021, 241). Hoyle, Harris, and Judd (2002, 32) defined external validity as "the extent to which one can generalize the results of the research to the populations and settings of interest in the hypothesis."

Threats to External Validity

Unfortunately, as Campbell and Stanley (1963, 5) noted, the question of external validity is never completely answerable. As is the case with internal validity, certain experimental designs can help to maximize external validity. The major factors jeopardizing external validity, or representativeness, are the following:

- The reactive or interactive effect of testing. This occurs when a *pretest* increases or decreases the subject's sensitivity or responsiveness to the experimental variable, thus making the results unrepresentative of the general, or unpretested, population from which the subjects were selected. If students were pretested on their information literacy skills, given ILI for one semester, and then tested again on information literacy skills, there is a good chance that their skills would be higher on the retest. However, the researcher would have to question how much of the increase in skills was due to the pretest's making the students more aware of, for example, library services and resources and therefore more likely to improve their library use with or without the ILI.
- The interaction effects of selection biases and the experimental variable. This threat is similar to the sixth threat to internal validity listed

above. It simply means that one must be careful not to select experimental subjects who are likely to be more receptive to the experimental variable than is the general population. For example, if one selected English honors students for an experiment on the effects of ILI, there is a chance that they would be more motivated to utilize ILI than average English students. Consequently, the ability to generalize the results of the study to other, more typical, students would be diminished.

- The reactive effects of the experimental arrangements, which can prevent the researcher from being able to generalize about the effect of the experimental variable on persons exposed to it in nonexperimental settings. In other words, the experimental environment, or elements thereof, might have been influencing the subject along with, or instead of, the experimental treatment. Behavior in the laboratory has a tendency not to represent accurately what would happen in similar circumstances in real life. A well-known example of this phenomenon is the classic Hawthorne study, in which workers in experiments conducted from 1924 to 1932 at the Hawthorne Works factory near Chicago became more productive whenever they were studied, regardless of whether their working conditions improved or worsened, simply because they were aware that they were being observed (Landsberger 1958).

- Multiple treatment interference, which may occur whenever more than one experimental treatment is applied to the same subjects, basically because the effects of prior treatments do not entirely disappear. For example, if a student were given different types of ILI, one after another, they would tend to have a cumulative effect on the student's information literacy skills. Consequently, it would be difficult for the researcher to distinguish between the effects of any one mode of ILI and those of the others.

In summary, the threats to external validity basically are interaction effects, involving the experimental treatment and some other variable. On the other hand, the factors jeopardizing internal validity are those that directly affect the dependent variables or scores. They are factors which by themselves can produce changes that might be mistaken for the results of the experimental treatment (Landsberger 1958, 16).

EXPERIMENTAL DESIGNS

In spite of the challenges associated with creating equivalent groups, controlling for the threats to internal and external validity, and establishing adequate control over the experimental setting, experimental research holds significant potential for the resolution of library-related problems. As has been noted, the testing of causal hypotheses increases one's ability to explain why certain phenomena occur, and experimental research may be the method best equipped for such testing. Survey research methods, for example, are not able to provide the researcher with enough control over extraneous variables to be able to say with any certainty that one variable is the direct cause of another. In a survey of students' library usage, one could ask them why they used the library, but data gathered in that manner would at best allow the establishment of associational relationships. For a number of reasons, even including a desire to please the researcher, the subject might attribute more influence to the ILI than was warranted.

As previously indicated, a variety of designs can be employed for experimental research, and the stronger they are, the better they can minimize or control the various threats to internal and external validity. Some of the designs appropriate for true experiments, or those experiments designed to investigate causal relationships while exercising considerable control and utilizing random assignment, are considered first.

True Experimental Designs

1. The Pretest-Posttest Control Group Design. One of the classic, true experimental designs is usually referred to as the pretest-posttest control group design. As will be evident after a few examples, the standard names of basic designs tend to describe them rather well, but diagrams point out their major features even more clearly. The diagram for this design appears as follows:

$$R \quad O_1 \quad X \quad O_2$$
$$R \quad O_3 \quad \quad O_4$$

In this illustration, and in the others that follow, the X symbolizes the experimental treatment or independent variable or cause. The O represents the process of observation or measurement of the dependent variable or effect. These observations can take the form of questionnaires, tests, interviews, and so forth. Each row represents one group of subjects; the left-to-right direction indicates the temporal order, and Xs and Os vertical to one another occur simultaneously. The R indicates that the subjects in the group so designated have been randomly assigned to their treatment or lack of treatment.

Therefore, this first diagram indicates that there are two groups, both randomly assigned. Both groups have been pretested and retested, but only the first group received the experimental treatment. The random assignment means that the two groups should be equivalent, or nearly so. This experimental design is considered strong because it controls for all eight of the threats to internal validity. For example, history is controlled because historical events that might have produced a change from O_1 to O_2 also would produce a comparable change from O_3 to O_4. In other words, due to random assignment, the groups are equivalent and should be equally affected by historical events, especially if the experiment is controlled as carefully as possible. For example, a study conducted as a double-blind experiment, in which the person administering the experimental treatment does not know who the subjects are and the subjects do not realize they are part of an experiment, will be proportionately stronger in internal validity. In the ILI study, assignments given to students outside the experimental setting should have similar effects on both groups. The other threats to internal validity would be controlled in essentially the same manner.

The pretest-posttest control group design is not as effective at controlling the threats to external validity. The interaction of testing and X remains a concern, because attitudes and behavior may be affected by the pretest. The design's ability to control the interaction of selection biases and X is questionable. It should account for differences between the experimental and control groups, but the results may still be atypical due to the nature of the subjects selected. This design's control of reactive arrangements is probably less than satisfactory also. There remains a good possibility that phenomena such as the Hawthorne effect may influence the effect of X. Multiple treatment interference is not an issue here, because only one experimental treatment is involved.

In summary, this particular design is stronger in internal validity than in external validity. This suggests that the researcher could be confident that the experimental treatment, not extraneous variables, caused the measured effects; however, the researcher would have to be cautious in generalizing the results to other groups, as they might have been unique for those particular subjects.

2. The Solomon Four-Group Design. A second standard, true experimental design is referred to as the Solomon four-group design. It is diagrammed as follows:

$$
\begin{array}{llll}
R & O_1 & X_1 & O_2 \\
R & O_3 & & O_4 \\
R & & X_2 & O_5 \\
R & & & O_6
\end{array}
$$

As can be seen, this design involves four randomly assigned, or equivalent, groups, two of which receive the experimental treatment, and two of which are given posttests only.

This design "scores" the same on internal validity as does the pretest-posttest control group design because it controls all eight threats. It is better than the pretest-posttest control group design in controlling the factors that jeopardize external validity, in that it is able to control the interaction of pretesting and X. It can do this because one experimental group and one control group are not pretested, thus allowing the researcher to measure the effects of the experimental treatment without the "contamination" of a pretest. It also benefits from the fact that the effect of X can be determined in four ways: the differences between O_2 and O_1, O_2 and O_4, O_5 and O_6, and O_1 and O_3. In short, this design is somewhat stronger than the pretest-posttest control group design and should be used in preference to it when possible.

3. The Posttest-Only Control Group Design. The posttest-only control group design diagrams the same as the last two groups of the Solomon four-group design and appears as follows:

$$
\begin{array}{lll}
R & X & O_1 \\
R & & O_2
\end{array}
$$

This design is not used as frequently as it deserves to be, perhaps because of its lack of a pretest. Yet one can assume that the two groups are equivalent at the start of a study because of the random assignment, and a pretest should not be necessary to confirm that assumption. In fact, this design achieves the same control of internal and external validity as does the Solomon four-group design, but without the necessity of establishing four groups. Therefore, it is in some ways preferable to the Solomon four-group design, as well as to the pretest-posttest control group design. Not having pretests, however, precludes the researcher's being able to calculate differences in the dependent variable before and after the experiment, or gain scores.

4. Factorial Designs. The three preceding designs are examples of designs capable of accommodating only one independent and one dependent variable. Factorial designs can deal with two or more independent variables and one dependent variable. They tend to be higher in external validity than other true experimental designs, because they can consider more independent variables and can measure interaction. As can be seen in the following example, a factorial design contains every possible combination of the independent variables.

$$
\begin{array}{cccc}
R & X_1 & X_2 & O_1 \\
R & X_1 & & O_2 \\
R & & X_2 & O_3 \\
R & & & O_4
\end{array}
$$

Not only would this design allow the researcher to measure the specific effects of the two independent variables on the dependent variable, but it should give some indication of the interaction of X_1 and X_2. In other words, it controls for multiple treatment interference.

A simpler factorial design is as follows:

$$
\begin{array}{ccc}
R & X_1 & O_1 \\
R & X_2 & O_2 \\
R & & O_3
\end{array}
$$

This is a multivariate equivalent of the pretest-posttest control group design. It does not measure the interaction of treatments, but that should be unnecessary, as no one group receives more than one treatment. There may be some situations, such as in ILI experiments, however, in which one would be interested in knowing if the different modes of instruction had any cumulative effects on information literacy skills or library use.

True Experiments and Correlational Studies

Having discussed the essential criteria for true experimental research and having looked at a few examples of true experimental designs, it should be kept in mind that it is not always possible to assign people to experimental treatments in a laboratory-like setting. For example, if one were designing a study to test the effects of ILI provided to English literature students on their use of the library, in most cases it would not be possible to assign particular students to the sections designated to receive and not to receive ILI. The researcher probably would have to accept the two groups as they already were constituted. Thus, there would be no assurance that the two groups were equivalent.

Consequently, much social research is correlational, or associational, in nature. This type of research may permit one to predict change in one variable based on knowledge about another variable, but it would not allow the establishment of a causal relationship between the variables. Correlational studies tend to be relatively high in external validity but relatively low in internal validity and therefore less able to account for rival explanations of a relationship.

Essentially true experiments can be conducted in real-life settings, assuming the controls are adequate. Such experiments often are referred to as field experiments. They tend to be less artificial than laboratory-type experiments but still may lose validity if the subjects are aware that they are being studied.

Reiterating a point previously made, properly conducted true experiments should be high in internal validity. This means that the researcher should be quite confident that the experimental treatment was the cause of the observed effect. True experiments have less external validity, however. That is, true experiments are poor representations of natural situations. More specifically, they provide a relatively artificial test of the hypothesis, tend to be low in generalizability, and often produce relatively little descriptive data about the population, unless the subjects are unusually representative.

Difficulties to Be Avoided. In order to design an experiment that will be as reliable and valid as possible, the researcher should attempt to avoid

- relying too heavily on a single experiment,
- using poorly designed or faulty data collection instruments,
- not identifying all of the variables that may affect the results,
- not choosing subjects that are as representative of the population as possible,
- introducing experimenter bias,
- introducing subject bias,
- making the subjects aware of the hypothesis being tested through unconscious signaling or behavior, or
- using an insufficient number of subjects.

Evaluating the Experiment. In evaluating the design and results of an experiment, there are several points to consider. First, the experiment should have the ability to test a null hypothesis, which suggests that there is no relationship between the variables being studied. Second, the experiment should be sensitive. That is, it should be able to detect relatively small effects or differences. Increasing the number of subjects, which decreases the chance of random or experimental error, and exerting additional control, such as by matching subjects, help to increase the experiment's sensitivity. The selection of subjects can be facilitated with the use of power charts, which provide the number of subjects for each group, given the effects of power or sensitivity of the experiment, the effect size, and the significance level (Keppel and Wickens

2004). "The experiment is planned so that the size of each treatment group provides the greatest sensitivity that the effect on the outcome is actually due to the experimental manipulation in the study" (Creswell 2008, 157). The formulas used for determining optimal sample sizes for surveys are of limited use for experiments.

In evaluating the results of the experiment, the researcher should assess the reliability of the data and their external validity, or generalizability. Last, but not least, the significance or importance of the results should be considered.

Preexperimental Designs. If random assignment of subjects and laboratory-like control are not possible, it will be necessary for the researcher to use a preexperimental or quasi-experimental design. Preexperimental designs are those designs that not only lack random assignment but have few observation points as well. A few examples of preexperimental designs follow.

1. The One-Shot Case Study. The one-shot case study, which can be diagrammed simply as $X O$, is an extremely weak design. As there only is one group, there is no basis for comparison of subjects who have received and have not received the experimental treatment.

With neither random assignment nor pretests, this design is susceptible to numerous alternative influences or threats to its internal validity. It is threatened particularly by history, maturation, selection biases, and experimental mortality. Regarding external validity, this design is unable to control for interaction between selection biases and the experimental variable. For practical reasons, however, the one-shot case study is used fairly frequently.

2. The One-Group Pretest-Posttest Design. The one-group pretest-posttest design represents a slight improvement over the one-shot case study, because it incorporates a pretest, or one more observation point. It appears as follows:

$$O_1 \quad X \quad O_2$$

If posttest scores are higher than the pretest scores, this design should rule out selection biases as a rival explanation. It does not, however, control for the effects of history, maturation, testing, instrumentation, interaction of selection and other factors, and quite possibly statistical regression. It also is about as weak as the one-shot case study at controlling threats to external validity.

3. The Static-Group Comparison. Another preexperimental design, which improves a bit more on the preceding designs, known as the static-group comparison, diagrams as follows:

Group 1	X	O_1
Group 2		O_2

As can be seen, this design utilizes two groups rather than one, each of which is observed once. The line, however, as well as the absence of Rs, indicates that the groups occurred naturally and were not based on random assignment. In other words, "this is a design in which a group which has experienced X is compared with one which has not, for the purposes of establishing the effect of X" (Campbell and Stanley 1963, 12). An example of naturally occurring groups might be two English literature classes, to which the researcher was unable to assign particular students and which already had experienced some level of an experimental variable such as ILI. Since the researcher was unable to create two equivalent groups, there is no assurance that the two groups had experienced the same amount of the experimental variable or that the experimental treatment actually produced the differences, if any, in the final group scores. Differences in group scores might have resulted entirely because one or the other group was atypical.

Consequently, as the researcher using this design cannot be certain whether X actually caused O, or natural selection did, the static-group comparison is at best a correlational design. The X represents what the subjects naturally brought to the study, and the researcher can only ascertain that there is some sort of association between the variables in question. The static-group comparison often is considered to be a survey design.

To its credit, the static-group comparison does control relatively well several threats to internal validity: history, testing, instrumentation, regression, and possibly maturation. It is not considered to be capable of controlling the threats to external validity.

Quasi-Experimental Designs

A type of experimental design that represents an improvement over preexperimental designs, including those just considered, is the quasi-experimental design, which usually includes naturally occurring groups, but often involves more than one group and typically has more observation points than do preexperimental designs. The employment of naturally occurring groups means there is no random assignment of subjects to the control and experimental groups.

Quasi-experimental designs are not as strong as those for true experiments. As they do not have randomly assigned treatment and comparison groups, comparisons must be made with nonequivalent groups or with the same subjects in one group prior to and after treatment. In most cases the independent variable(s) cannot be fully manipulated by the researcher. Quasi-experimental designs also have less control than do true experiments but are able to rule out more threats to internal validity than preexperiments can. If the quasi-experimental design is strong enough to rule out many of the threats to internal validity, it may be used to infer cause and effect (Hoyle, Harris, and Judd 2002, 126). A few examples of quasi-experimental designs follow.

1. The Time-Series Design. The time-series design is an example of a single-group quasi-experimental design. It takes this form:

$$O_1 \quad O_2 \quad O_3 \quad O_4 \quad X \quad O_5 \quad O_6 \quad O_7 \quad O_8$$

As a comparison will reveal, this design represents an extension of the one-group pretest-posttest design $(O_1 \, X \, O_2)$. The longer sequence of observation points helps to control for additional factors jeopardizing internal validity, such as maturation and testing, because it allows one to examine trends in the data before, at the time of, and after the experimental treatment. Graphing the Xs and Os can help to reveal any patterns that might exist. For example, if one were testing the information literacy skills of students and learned that their skills were regularly rising even before X, or ILI, was applied, one would have to question the apparent effects of ILI.

The time-series still is relatively weak in external validity. It does possibly control for interaction of selection biases and reactive arrangements.

2. The Equivalent Time-Samples Design. A second single-group quasi-experimental design, the equivalent time-samples design, employs two equivalent measurements, one when the experimental variable is present and another when it is not, and then repeats the sequence. This design diagrams as follows:

$$X_1 \ O \ X_0 \ O \ X_1 \ O \ X_0 \ O$$

This type of design is particularly useful when the effect of the experimental treatment is expected to be of transient or reversible character (e.g., ILI or environmental conditions within the library). This arrangement is relatively high on internal validity but low on external validity because of the effects of multiple treatment interference.

3. The Pretest-Posttest Nonequivalent Control Group Design. This multiple-group design has some of the features of the static-group comparison and the one-group pretest-posttest design. As can be seen from the following diagram, it provides pretest information and a comparison group, but the groups are not fully matched or randomly assigned and thus cannot be assumed to be equivalent.

Group 1	O_1	X	O_3
Group 2	O_2		O_4

The comparison group would be selected for its similarity to the experimental group, however. Its major advantage over the static group comparison is that one can measure preexisting differences between the groups. It is used widely in educational research.

4. The Multiple Time-Series Design. A second multiple-group, quasi-experimental design is the multiple time-series design. It is the multiple-group counterpart of the time-series design and could be diagrammed thus:

Group 1	O_1	O_2	O_3	O_4	X	O_5	O_6	O_7	O_8
Group 2	O_1	O_2	O_3	O_4		O_5	O_6	O_7	O_8

Assuming that the groups were exposed to the same historical conditions, this design should control for the effects of history. It is considered to be a useful design for conducting research in schools.

Ex Post Facto Designs

Ex post facto designs are a weaker type of quasi-experimental design. They are designed to simulate real experimentation by using a static-group type comparison such as this

$$\frac{X \quad O}{O}$$

to accomplish a pre-X equation of groups by matching on pre-X characteristics *after* the members of the groups have experienced the experimental variable. Perhaps, for example, one has assumed the directorship of a library soon after the library gave some sort of ILI to all first-year English students. It might be tempting to try to determine whether the information literacy skills of those students were better than those of other first-year students not given ILI. The experimental group, those students who received ILI, is in effect already established. In order to *simulate* a real experiment, the librarian must attempt to establish a comparison group of students equivalent to those in the "experimental group." It would be necessary, therefore, to identify students comparable to those students who had received ILI. The librarian must try to match the two groups of students on every relevant trait, such as previous training in information literacy skills. As Mouly (1978, 257) stated, "this is experimentation in reverse, and it is very difficult to match subjects on enough variables to rule out other influences." The researcher has no control over events that have already occurred and can never be certain how many factors might have been involved.

In spite of the fact that quite a few significant studies have employed ex post facto analysis, such designs can be weak. Yet they sometimes represent the only feasible approach for investigating a particular question. Specific types of ex post facto analysis include case studies and the so-called causal-comparative studies.

Internet-Based Experiments

The use of web applications for conducting Internet-based experiments has become more prominent, especially in some of the social sciences. This technique allows researchers to collect large amounts of data from widely dispersed people and locations at minimal cost. On the other hand, Internet-based experiments have relatively weak internal controls creating threats to internal validity, construct validity, and external validity; therefore, measures need to be taken to address biased samples, biased returns, and low response rates (Bar Ilan and Peritz 2002). ". . . converging evidence shows that Internet-based research methods often result in qualitatively comparable results to traditional methods (e.g., (Krantz and Dalal 2000; Luce et al. 2007; Buchanan, Johnson, and Goldberg 2005), even in longitudinal studies (Hiskey and Troop 2002"; Reips and Krantz 2010, 197–98).

There are several good resources for designing internet-based experiments available online. One of these online tools is http://wextor.org. It guides the researcher through the process of creating the customized web pages needed for an experiment. Another good online resource for designing internet-based experiments is https://www.socialpsychology.org/expts.htm ("Online Social Psychology Studies" 2020). The site includes links to research projects, resources for conducting research, how-to guides, and software. Additional information about the methodology of internet-based experiments can be found in an article by Reips (2007) and another by Reips and Krantz (2010).

SUMMARY

Experimental research is generally considered to be the most rigorous of the basic research methods. Unlike historical and survey methods, experimental research is considered capable of supporting causal relationships. It is able to do so primarily because, at least in the case of true experiments, it employs equivalent comparison groups, permits manipulation of the experimental variable, and controls alternative causes of the dependent variable. Experimental methods can be used to examine questions such as the effect of ILI on student achievement, the effect of changes in library spaces on user behavior, and users' reactions to different modes of library services.

Experimental studies have been criticized for being artificial and for not reflecting real-life situations. However, designs, other than true experimental designs, can be used to allay this problem. One of these alternatives, the preexperimental design, is the weakest type of experimental design, but is higher in external validity. The second alternative, the quasi-experimental design, represents a compromise between preexperiments, which are low in internal validity, and true experiments, which are high in internal validity. Stated somewhat differently, it is a compromise between maximizing internal validity and external validity. It is a good choice of design when a natural setting is used, when random assignment of subjects is not feasible, and when the independent or experimental variable cannot be manipulated fully (e.g., when the independent variable represents a demographic variable or a process of natural selection).

There are an almost unlimited number of quasi-experimental designs; researchers are not restricted to those already developed by others but also may create their own. The amount of control built into a quasi-experimental design can vary, but it almost always is less than that of true experimental designs. Consequently, the results of quasi-experimental designs tend to be more subject to incorrect interpretation.

REFERENCES

Anderson, James A. 1986. *Communication Research: Issues and Methods.* New York: McGraw-Hill.

Babbie, Earl R. 2021. *The Practice of Social Research.* 15th ed. Boston: Cengage Learning.

Bar Ilan, Judit, and Bluma C. Peritz. 2002. "Informetric Theories and Methods for Exploring the Internet: An Analytical Survey of Recent Research Literature." *Library Trends* 50: 371–92.

Buchanan, Tom, John A. Johnson, and Lewis R. Goldberg. 2005. "Implementing a Five-Factor Personality Inventory for Use on the Internet." *European Journal of Psychological Assessment* 25(3): 115–27. https://doi.org/10.1027/1015 -5759.25.3.211.

Campbell, Donald T., and Julian C. Stanley. 1963. *Experimental and Quasi-Experimental Designs for Research.* Chicago: Rand McNally.

Chu, Heting. 2015. "Research Methods in Library and Information Science: A Content Analysis." *Library & Information Science Research* 37(1): 36–41. https://doi.org/10.1016/j.lisr.2014.09.003.

Creswell, John W. 2008. *Research Design: Qualitative, Quantitative, and Mixed Methods Approaches.* 3rd ed. Thousand Oaks, CA: Sage.

Goldhor, Herbert. 1972. *An Introduction to Scientific Research in Librarianship.* Urbana: University of Illinois, Graduate School of Library Science.

Hiskey, Syd, and Nicholas A. Troop. 2002. "Online Longitudinal Survey Research: Viability and Participation." *Social Science Computer Review* 20(3): 250–59. https://journals.sagepub.com/doi/abs/10.1177/089443930202000303 ?casa_token=KFGLU9PUIRkAAAAA:DDiLqOGrwloFKfVK0w3uOS9P6vELaQ Opvw0AoDoJqr0bL0_yXvvlgO6nAZgR5j9lk4HQw_ahN2Q.

Hoyle, Rick H., Monica J. Harris, and Charles M. Judd. 2002. *Research Methods in Social Relations.* 7th ed. Fort Worth, TX: Cengage Learning.

Keppel, Geoffrey, and Thomas D. Wickens. 2004. *Design and Analysis: A Researcher's Handbook.* 4th ed. Upper Saddle River, NJ: Pearson.

Kidder, Louise H. 1981. *Research Methods in Social Relations.* 4th ed. New York: Holt, Rinehart and Winston.

Krantz, John H., and Reeshad Dalal. 2000. "Validity of Web-Based Psychological Research." In *Psychological Experiments on the Internet*, edited by Michael H. Birnbaum, 35–60. San Diego: Academic Press. https://doi.org/10.1016 /B978-012099980-4/50003-4.

Landsberger, Henry A. 1958. *Hawthorne Revisited: Management and the Worker: Its Critics, and Developments in Human Relations in Industry.* Cornell University.

Luce, Kristine H., Andrew J. Winzelberg, Smita Das, Megan I. Osborne, Susan W. Bryson, and C. Barr Taylor. 2007. "Reliability of Self-Report: Paper versus Online Administration." *Computers in Human Behavior*, Including the Special Issue: Avoiding Simplicity, Confronting Complexity: Advances in Designing Powerful Electronic Learning Environments 23(3): 1384–89. https://doi.org /10.1016/j.chb.2004.12.008.

Ma, Jinxuan, and Brady Lund. 2020. "The Evolution of LIS Research Topics and Methods from 2006 to 2018: A Content Analysis." *Proceedings of the Association for Information Science and Technology* 57(1): e241. https://doi.org/10 .1002/pra2.241.

Mouly, George J. 1978. *Educational Research: The Art and Science of Investigation.* Boston: Allyn & Bacon.

"Online Social Psychology Studies." 2020. Social Psychology Network. https:// www.socialpsychology.org/expts.htm.

Reips, Ulf-Dietrich. 2007. "The Methodology of Internet-Based Experiments." In *The Oxford Handbook of Internet Psychology*, edited by Adam N. Joinston, Katelyn McKenna, Tom Postmes, and Ulf-Dietrich Reips, 373–90. Oxford, UK: Oxford University Press.

Reips, Ulf-Dietrich, and John H. Krantz. 2010. "Conducting True Experiments on the Web." In *Advanced Methods for Conducting Online Behavioral Research.*, edited by Samuel D. Gosling and John A. Johnson, 193–216. Washington, DC: American Psychological Association. https://doi.org/10.1037/12076 -013.

Selltiz, Claire, Lawrence S. Wrightsman, and Stuart W. Cook. 1959. *Research Methods in Social Relations*. Rev. ed. New York: Holt, Rinehart and Winston.

Togia, Aspasia, and Afrodite Malliari. 2017. "Research Methods in Library and Information Science." In *Qualitative versus Quantitative Research,* edited by Sonvel Oflazoglu, Chapter 3. Rijeka, Croatia: InTech. http://dx.doi.org/10 .5772/intechopen.68749.

Trochim, William M. K. 2006. "Experimental Design." *Research Methods Knowledge Base*. 2nd ed. Last modified March 10, 2020. https://conjointly.com /kb/experimental-design.

8

Analysis of Quantitative Data

STATISTICAL ANALYSIS

Statistical analysis, or "statistics," is concerned with the development and application of methods and techniques for organizing and analyzing data (usually quantitative) so that the reliability of conclusions based on the data may be evaluated objectively in terms of probability. There are two major areas or types of statistics: theoretical and applied. The former is concerned with the mathematical aspects of statistics; the latter involves the practical applications of statistics and is the focus of this chapter. Hence, statistics is a valuable tool for both researchers and practitioners (Vaughan 2001).

A knowledge of basic statistics is imperative in LIS, both to the research producer and research consumer, just as it is in any social science or in any field that relies on empirical evidence for the development of principles (Wallace 1985).

This text does not attempt to teach readers how to conduct a statistical analysis. However, it does indicate the kinds of things that statistical analysis can and cannot do, while emphasizing the care that should be exercised in using statistics. Specific examples are given for the major types of analysis. In no way do these examples represent a comprehensive listing of all the statistical tests that may be employed. Readers looking for other relatively nonmathematical, nonthreatening introductions to statistics may wish to refer to Klein and Dabney (2013), Vickers (2009), Wheelan (2013), Urdan (2017), Silver (2020), Van Belle (2011), Reinhart (2015), Boslaugh (2012), and Gonick and Woolcott Smith (2015). Texts written primarily for library and information professionals include those by Patten (2018), Wildemuth (2017), and Friedman (2015). The *Dictionary of Statistics and Methodology* is an excellent resource for "readers trying to inform themselves about research terms and concepts so they can be effective consumers and, potentially, producers of research" (Vogt and Johnson 2016, xvi).

Data Mining

Libraries and other information agencies have had to embrace and adopt ever-changing technology, including social networking, data mining, text mining, data analytics, and log analysis. To facilitate and utilize these technological innovations, libraries must employ personnel who have backgrounds in not only library and information science (LIS), but also computer science, statistics, linguistics, machine learning, and mathematics. This type of research requires the integration of "the scientific method with activities that are more similar to product development than to basic research" (Powell 1995, 327).

Librarians are particularly interested in utilizing appropriate methods to evaluate their services and systems. Online searching, for example, has been evaluated with traditional research methods and techniques such as questionnaires, interviews, focus group interviews, observation, and experiments. A less common method, protocol analysis, has been found useful for studying information-seeking behaviors. Protocol analysis has been called "the thinking aloud technique" because it represents an analysis of subject searchers' thoughts as they perform their subject searches at the catalog (Peters 1991, 151). During a protocol analysis, the user verbalizes the decisions and behaviors that they are performing to search the catalog. Audio and video recording often are used to record the activity being analyzed, and screen capture is available through simulation software. As a type of obtrusive observation, the process itself can affect the behavior being analyzed, but using a camera is likely to be less intrusive than direct human observation (Wiedenbeck, Lampert, and Scholtz 1989, 25–26).

It often is difficult to recruit subjects for protocol analysis research projects, and this data collection method is time consuming; therefore, only two or three subjects may be included for each user group. Researchers may have assumptions about user behaviors or preferences skewing their observations and reporting of the protocols. It also is challenging to interpret and use the data generated by protocols unless behaviors are identified and defined, and quantitative metrics are developed prior to the initiation of the protocols (Covey 2002, 25).

In contrast, data mining utilizes computer programs and software to analyze large datasets for the identification of patterns and relationships. It not only is unobtrusive but also takes advantage of the technology that is being evaluated. Data analytics enables the researcher to make inferences and to develop conclusions based on what the researcher already knows. See text box 4.1, Behavioral Analytics of Socio-Mobile Data, by Vivek Singh, included in chapter 4.

Log Analysis

One type of data mining is log analysis, sometimes referred to as transaction log analysis, transaction monitoring, search log analysis, or query log analysis. Log analysis is the examination of the records and data that online systems (such as online catalogs) and search engines are able to record and monitor. It can take the form of macroanalysis, which is concerned with aggregate use data and patterns, and microanalysis, which focuses on the dynamics of individual search patterns. The log analysis methodology can be used to study scholarly communication and productivity in bibliometric studies by analyzing the logs of online journals and databases and to help researchers understand the behaviors of users of online information retrieval systems. The rationale of the analyses is for the development of information retrieval systems that will better fulfill the needs of users, based on their actual search behaviors. Peters (1996), however, believed that log analysis has been underutilized in practice where it can provide data for library managers to develop systems and services for library users. Banks (2000) suggested that practicing library managers could use online catalog usage log data to schedule reference service staff based on the high and low usage patterns during a specified time period.

Since logs provide a record of the search strategy employed by users without interfering with the searcher, an analysis of transaction logs can reflect users' actual online search experiences. The analysis of the logs that focus on search often are referred to as search log analysis or query log analyses. This methodology clearly demonstrates how users employ search strategies rather than how users describe their search strategies. There also is no chance of the interference of interviewer bias in the data collection.

In addition to the report of search type and failure and success rates and search method types, errors and problems are also calculated for most of the studies. Unfortunately, the search types, failure or success rates, and errors or problems are not defined or calculated consistently throughout the published literature, and the data provided from each system are not standardized (Tolle 1983). In addition to these disadvantages, the individual users are not identifiable from the transaction logs, and it is often difficult or impossible to determine when one searcher ends a search session and another begins a session. It is also impossible to discern from the transaction logs who is doing the search and why. See text box 8.1, Log Analysis, by Jim Jansen, for more information on log analysis.

For these reasons, it often is useful to incorporate the log analysis method with other data collection methods. Nielsen (1986) linked log analysis data with user demographic data, as did Millsap and Ferl (1993), and Connaway, Budd, and Kochtanek (1995). Using a questionnaire, Connaway, Budd, and Kochtanek interviewed subjects after they completed their online searches. This enabled the researchers to link the logs (subjects' search behaviors) with demographic data. Connaway et al. (2019) updated the methodology developed by Connaway, Budd, and Kochtanek (1995), by capturing cloud-based library discovery layer search logs and interviewing fourteen individuals about their search sessions. Customized protocols were developed for each of the interview participants using the critical incident technique (Flanagan 1954). The information from the semistructured interviews was then used to inform a bulk log analysis to better understand how many search sessions resulted in the access of materials, and the features of the session that made access more likely. The results of using this combined data collection method confirmed that user logs can contain incomplete or misleading evidence of user activity and provide only part of the user's behavior. Interview protocols that are customized based on log analysis can elicit more detailed insights into user experience and behavior.

Using log data in conjunction with semistructured interviews of individuals' online searching behaviors can inform how library and information professionals set up information systems and design information literacy instruction based on individuals' needs and behaviors.

Wakeling, Clough, Connaway, Sen, and Tomás (2017) investigated the use and users of WorldCat.org using a multimethod approach—focus group interviews, an online survey, and log analyses. Structuring a study in this way allows for the search behaviors to be analyzed in relation to the searchers' experience with online systems, educational background, reason for the search, and so on, thus requiring the researcher to infer less about the nature of the search and maintaining the validity of the study.

Text Box 8.1: Log Analysis

Jim Jansen

Log analysis is a versatile data-driven methodology for directly deriving metrics concerning the *who, what, when, where,* and *how* (the 4WH) people engage with technology. Leveraging advanced methods and secondary data, one can move close to 5WH by discerning the *why* driving the engagement. A variety of online technologies widely leveraged log analysis for better user insights.

Along with subareas such as search log analysis and weblog analysis, the log analysis method is an especially appealing experimental procedure that one can relate to theoretical constructs grounded in behaviorism. Still, it is also a practical methodology that concerns itself with factors, including key performance indicators (KPIs) for organizations, such as libraries and businesses, to understand users.

There are at least two attributes that make log analysis essential and valuable as a method for those researching or managing the use of online technology. First, log analysis is naturalistic (i.e., not in a lab). Therefore, you get real behaviors from real users using real systems interacting with needed information. Log analysis is everything that a lab study is not. (Note: I acknowledge that one can use log analysis in a lab study.) Second, log analysis has few volume bounds. Once your technology is set up, it is just as easy to collect a billion records as it is to obtain a million. You can get to the point where your sample is pretty close to your population, which is a fantastic advantage in quantitative statistical analysis.

Like any method, there are some pitfalls to avoid. One, do not underestimate the amount of time, effort, or energy it takes to do data cleaning and preparation. This phase can easily take 80 percent of your time, with the analysis consuming the remaining 20 percent. Two, in the investigation, log data is a type of trace data (i.e., hints of life that people leave behind as they go about their daily business). As such, the meaning of such data is susceptible to researcher bias.

Recommended Further Reading

Blokdyk, Gerardus. 2018. *Google Analytics: A Complete Guide—2019 Edition*. 5STARCooks.
Gil, Carlos. 2019. *The End of Marketing: Humanizing Your Brand in the Age of Social Media and AI*. London: Kogan Page.
Jansen, Bernard J. (Jim). 2009. "Understanding User-Web Interactions via Web Analytics." *Synthesis Lectures on Information Concepts, Retrieval, and Services* 1(1): 1–102. https://doi.org/10.2200/S00191ED1V01Y200904ICR006.

Jansen, Bernard J., Joni O. Salminen, and Soon-Gyo Jung. 2020. "Data-Driven Personas for Enhanced User Understanding: Combining Empathy with Rationality for Better Insights to Analytics." *Data and Information Management* 4(1): 1–17. https://doi.org/10.2478/dim-2020-0005.

Rogel-Salazar, Jesus. 2020. *Advanced Data Science and Analytics with Python.* Boca Raton, FL: Chapman & Hall/CRC.

Salminen, Joni, Soon-Gyo Jung, Shammur Chowdhury, Sercan Sengün, and Bernard J. Jansen. 2020. "Personas and Analytics: A Comparative User Study of Efficiency and Effectiveness for a User Identification Task." In *Proceedings of the 2020 CHI Conference on Human Factors in Computing Systems,* 1–13. CHI '20. New York: Association for Computing Machinery. https://doi.org/10.1145/3313831.3376770.

Log analysis may be, and often is, used in conjunction with other research methods; for example, log data can be matched with questionnaire and interview data, as discussed above. Research utilizing unobtrusive log analysis, like any research method that is unobtrusive, does not inform those being studied that they are being observed, which may raise ethical questions related to the invasion of privacy.

With the emergence of consumer and social media sites, as well as the number of daily online searches, the amount of information and data that are being generated, collected, and analyzed is overwhelming. The term "big data" "describes the data challenges that we are facing and going to face" (Song and Zhu 2016, 364). Data science is the discipline that attempts to address and make sense of big data, as is discussed in the next section.

Data Science

"Data, technologies, and people are the three pillars of data science" (Song and Zhu 2016, 364). The data can be structured or unstructured, and the technologies include "Hadoop ecosystems, NoSQL, in-memory computing, data mining, machine learning, cloud computing and 'people' include computer scientists, statistician, domain experts, data scientists, and business analyzers" (Song and Zhu 2016, 366). Information scientists also can play a crucial role in data science since there is a need for individuals who understand structured and unstructured data, technology, and people—the users—of data and systems. This brings in information retrieval, information-seeking behaviors, and user interface design. Based on these needs, there is much discussion and development of curricula for data science education in LIS programs (Burton and Lyon 2017; Burton et al. 2018; Lyon 2012; Lyon and Brenner 2015; Lyon and Mattern 2015, 2017; Semeler, Pinto, and Rozados 2019; Song and Zhu 2016; Wang 2018).

Machine Learning and Artificial Intelligence

Data science includes the analysis of historical data to develop models for forecasting, and data scientists use machine learning algorithms to make predictions. "Machine learning involves observing and studying data or experiences to identify patterns and set up a reasoning system based on the findings" (Chatterjee 2020). Using statistical models, machines can learn independent techniques based on patterns and clusters derived from large datasets. Machine learning is a subset of artificial intelligence (AI) that "combines large amounts of data through iterative processing and intelligent algorithms to help computers learn automatically" (Chatterjee 2020) using logic and decision trees. Some examples of AI are voice assistants and chatbots, while examples of machine learning include recommender systems used in library and media streaming systems, like Spotify and Netflix. Machine learning also is being tested to generate library metadata (Boman 2019).

Text mining or text analytics "is an artificial intelligence technology that uses natural language processing (NLP) to [normalize unstructured] data for analysis or to drive machine learning (ML) algorithms" ("What Is Text Mining, Text Analytics and Natural Language Processing?" 2019). Text mining makes it possible to analyze large collections of written documents using algorithms and other computer applications. Rathore and Roy (2014) used text mining to develop a topic model for more relevant results for users' searches. See text box 8.2, Text Mining by Jiqun Liu, for more information on text mining.

Text Box 8.2: Text Mining

Jiqun Liu

Text-mining techniques are useful for extracting meaningful patterns and features from unstructured text data of varying types. In my research on information retrieval, text-mining techniques (especially for the topic modeling methods) allow me to identify hidden topics, sentimental features, and task properties from users' queries, pages visited, and usefulness feedback during web searches. The implicit topical and task-related knowledge learned from observable interactions can enhance our understanding of user characteristics, as well as the context of information retrieval, and thereby inform the simulation, design, and evaluation of task-aware search recommendations.

For researchers using text mining, the very first step is to get familiar with textual data and problem space. Based on the nature of the problem (e.g., identifying an unknown pattern in conversational interaction or statistically verifying a hypothesis) and the properties of datasets (e.g., size, feature types available, or data distribution across different groups), a researcher could select an appropriate model or develop knowledge and skills needed for addressing the research problem. A common pitfall to avoid for beginners is starting with a complex, fancy model and trying to fit the problem into it. There is no one-size-fits-all model that can magically produce "good results" in all circumstances. It is the research problem that determines the right tool for the job.

In addition, to better release the potential of text-mining techniques, researchers need to properly preprocess their "dirty" data before analysis, such as removing stop words, stemming, excluding irrelevant records, and so on. When working with datasets from various sources, researchers have to extract text and structure so that they can have the textual format needed for further analysis and synthesis. Many existing packages with built-in functions (e.g., NLTK package in Python) can help speed up the process of data cleaning. Two good examples of text-mining applications include studies by Metzler and Croft (2005), and Mukherjee, Kumar, Liu, Wang, Hsu, Castellanos, and Ghosh (2013).

References

Metzler, Donald, and W. Bruce Croft. 2005. "A Markov Random Field Model for Term Dependencies." In *Proceedings of the 28th Annual International ACM SIGIR Conference on Research and Development in Information Retrieval, 472–79.* SIGIR '05. New York: Association for Computing Machinery. https://doi.org/10.1145/1076034.1076115.

Mukherjee, Arjun, Abhinav Kumar, Bing Liu, Junhui Wang, Meichun Hsu, Malu Castellanos, and Riddhiman Ghosh. 2013. "Spotting Opinion Spammers Using Behavioral Footprints I Proceedings of the 19th ACM SIGKDD International Conference on Knowledge Discovery and Data Mining." *Proceedings of the 19th ACM SIGKDD International Conference on Knowledge Discovery and Data Mining.* https://dl.acm.org/doi/abs/10.1145/2487575.2487580?casa_token=NCr2tXcXYs8AAAAA:qu_yJDxl_okhnQByQNBs0jagCfIO9f5_WBZ4GJuqvOGYNkPpa7PCHMaX5Ps6zbLrHcBpJTPZ8ms.

Bibliometrics

Bibliometrics is a special type of documentary research or inquiry into the tools of LIS that uses mathematics and statistics. It has been defined as "the application of mathematics and statistical methods to books and other media of communication" (Ferrante 1987, 201). It also has been referred to as "a series of techniques that seek to quantify the process of written communication" (Ikpaahindi 1985, 163) and as "the quantification of bibliographical data" (White 1985, 35). Related terms are scientometrics, informetrics, altmetrics (alternative metrics, which include counts and occurrences of tweets, cites, downloads, and views), cybermetrics, webometrics, and librametrics, all considered bibliometric measurements. The main distinction between them is the type of data used for the analyses (Roemer and Borchardt 2014).

The early bibliometric studies produced three basic laws: (1) Bradford's Law of Scatter, which describes how the literature of a subject area is distributed in its journals and which forms the basis for calculating how many journals contain a certain percentage of the published articles; (2) Lotka's Law, a formula for measuring/predicting the productivity of scientific researchers; and (3) Zipf's Law, which describes the frequency of the appearance of certain words or, more specifically, suggests that people are more likely to select and use familiar, rather than unfamiliar, words. See Wallace (1989) and Osareh (1996) for useful overviews of the origins of bibliometrics.

Following early research, bibliometrics branched into quantitative analyses, qualitative studies, and most recently, studies combining quantitative and qualitative methods. Bibliometric research, especially if quantitative, involves the application of mathematical formulas and considerable counting and statistical analysis. Bibliometric analyses have greatly benefited from the availability of computerized bibliographic databases, citation indexes, and statistical programs.

One of the most common types of bibliometric research is concerned with citations. Citation analysis is essentially concerned with "who cites whom" (Martyn and Lancaster 1981, 52). The three basic concepts of citation analysis are (1) "direct citation, which establishes the relationship between documents and the researchers who use them" (White 1985, 35–42); (2) bibliographic coupling, where the reference lists of two documents share one or more of the same cited documents (Smith 1981); and (3) "co-citation, which occurs when two citations are cited together" (White 1985, 39).

Applications of bibliometric research identified by White (1985), von Ungern-Sternberg (1989), Wallace (1989), Osareh (1996), and others include:

- improving the bibliographic control of a literature;
- identifying a core literature, especially journals;
- classifying a literature;
- tracing the spread of ideas and growth of a literature;
- designing more economic information systems and networks;
- improving the efficiency of information-handling services;
- predicting publishing trends;
- describing patterns of book use;
- developing and evaluating library collections; and
- evaluating journal performance (e.g., citation impact).

Big data have made the different types of bibliometric research very popular. "Altmetrics gives authors data like article pageviews and number of downloads, along with social media, and article sharing indicators of impact that complement citation-based metrics" (Roemer and Borchardt 2014). It provides ways for researchers to track and document impact across a wide array of media and platforms (Dihman 2015). There are several introductory articles on altmetrics (Bringham 2014; Careless 2013; Ming-Yueh and Ling-Li 2014; Piwowar 2013; Roemer and Borchardt 2015a; Scardilli 2014) and multiple papers describing practical uses of altmetrics in libraries (Aung, Erdt, and Theng 2017; Aung et al. 2019; Bar-Ilan et al. 2018; Barnes 2015; Crotty 2014; Didegah, Bowman, and Holmberg 2018; Keita 2012; Konkiel 2013; Konkiel and Scherer 2013; Levine 2014; Liu and Adie 2013; Michalek, Buschman, and McEvoy 2014; Roemer and Borchardt 2015b; Sugimoto et al. 2017; Taylor 2013; Zuccala et al. 2015).

Björneborn and Ingwersen (2004, 1217) defined webometrics as "the study of the quantitative aspects of the construction and use of information resources, structures and technologies on the Web drawing on bibliometric and informetric approaches." "Informetrics investigates characteristics and measurements of persons, groups, institutions, countries; publications and information sources; disciplines and fields; and information retrieval processes" (Bar Ilan and Peritz 2002, 371). These methods are used to study web documents, sites, information retrieval tools (such as search engines), and user studies. Abrizah et al. (2014) analyzed more than five thousand informetrics papers published from 1948 to 2012 to identify productivity, citation impact, and coauthorship, which exemplifies both the breadth and depth of this research method.

"Scientometrics analyses the quantitative aspects of the production, dissemination and use of scientific information with the aim of achieving a better understanding of the mechanisms of scientific research as a social activity" according to Chellappandi and Vijayakumar (2018, 6), who provide an introduction to metric studies—scientometrics, cybermetrics/webometrics, informetrics, altmetrics, and bibliometrics. See text box 8.3, Social Tagging, by Melissa Adler to learn how social tagging can be used to study social activity.

Text Box 8.3: Social Tagging

Melissa Adler

The Dewey Decimal Classification, Wikipedia, and Twitter are all systems that have been designed to assemble, organize, and facilitate access to the world's knowledge. While these and other library and information systems have sprung from different worldviews, very often they have a common aim based in the belief that global systems can connect people who might not otherwise meet, and that communication across cultural and political borders will lead to understanding and social progress. They all function by channeling information via categories (of users, genres, topics, places, etc.) and their associations. Twenty-first-century systems have afforded more opportunities for users to categorize data in social media through social tagging, increasingly in the specific form of hashtags.

Twitter has become an especially fruitful space for mining user-generated hashtags to understand how they organize conversations and draw people together (or apart). #BlackLivesMatter stands as a key example of how a movement can be fueled and organized through social media, and the hashtag itself has offered an entry into studying sentiment analysis, algorithmic cultures, social movements, and classification research. To my mind, hashtags are compelling for their capacity to organize information and action in real time in online spaces that reach across communities and geographic regions. And they serve as both a counterexample and exemplar of global knowledge organization systems. Unlike the relatively static systems like the Dewey Decimal or Library of Congress Classification systems, hashtags have a greater capacity to shift in meaning and use, depending on their context, users, and audiences. Rather than working from within the system as part of a relatively hidden infrastructure and being developed by a few "expert" classifiers, hashtags function because they are visible, are generated by the people creating content, and there is greater potential for diversity of voices.

#BlackLivesMatter can certainly be viewed as a categorizing technique that resists the colonial structures that support so many information communication technologies. From library shelves to commercial search engines, the classifications that organize information are too frequently based on assumptions that consumers and producers of information are white, and the systems reinforce heteropatriarchal norms and values. At the same time, hashtags become uniform identifiers that are understood and used by broad and/or local publics in a global, commercial system. And they have a capacity to normalize and politicize in ways that resemble the more traditional systems. Viewing the various ways of organizing through names and categories shows that these processes do not simply take place in and reflect historical and political contexts, but they shape and frame discourses, priorities, and worldviews. While it's true that social media and hashtags are new phenomena, it is crucial to understand their attendant tensions and affordances in the context of a long history of desires and priorities that fuel library and information technologies and their categorizing techniques.

Recommended Reading

Adler, Melissa. 2020. "Afterword: The Strangeness of Subject Cataloging." *Library Trends* 68(3) (April 2): 549–56. https://doi.org/10.1353/lib.2020.0005.

Adler, Melissa, and Lindsey M. Harper. 2018. "Race and Ethnicity in Classification Systems: Teaching Knowledge Organization from a Social Justice Perspective." *Library Trends* 67(1): 52–73. https://doi.org/10.1353/lib.2018.0025.

Bonilla, Yarimar, and Jonathan Rosa. 2015. "#Ferguson: Digital Protest, Hashtag Ethnography, and the Racial Politics of Social Media in the United States." *American Ethnologist* 42(1): 4–17. https://doi.org/10.1111/amet.12112.

The interest in bibliometric research continues. A cursory examination of *JASIS&T* from 2003 through 2020 identified approximately 1,400 published papers addressing the topics of bibliometrics, webometrics, altmetrics, and informetrics. Bibliometrics has been used to evaluate humanities and social sciences research using Google Scholar data (Bornmann et al. 2016); to apply the h-index to the top video content creators on YouTube (Hovden 2013); to identify the frequency, nature, and depth of use of Michel Foucault's work by LIS scholars retrieved in LIS journal databases (Dewey 2020); to study the growth of items included in the Web of Science (Hu, Leydesdorff, and Rosseau 2020); to predict future research impact at different career states based on social networks (Zuo and Zhao 2020); and to identify the 500 most cited articles in LIS for a thirty-seven-year period (Wusu and Lazarus 2018). The bimonthly newsletter *Research Trends* provides "up-to-the minute insights into the state of science through thought-provoking articles based on bibliometric data" ("Scopus Powers 'Research Trends'" n.d.). Recognizing that "bibliometrics emerged as a field in its own right" almost forty years ago, *Research Trends* interviewed Wolfgang Glänzel, of the Expertisecentrum O&O Monitoring in Leuven, Belgium. Glänzel stated in an interview that "the quantity and quality of bibliometric tools have increased and improved considerably during the last three decades" (Geraeds and Kamalski 2010). However, he identified three major challenges of bibliometrics: (1) the need for a different approach to bibliometric research to accommodate the different publication and citation practices of humanities and social science researchers; (2) "the development of web-based tools" (Geraeds and Kamalski 2010) to document and reproduce results of scholarly communication has not kept pace with the changes in electronic communication made available by the internet and open-access publishing; and (3) the lack of capability to model and measure the social impacts of communication outside research communities. In other words, bibliometric and citation analysis are not without their limitations and potential problems. The three basic laws identified above have not held up in every situation where they have been applied. A number of people have concerns about using citation counts to evaluate the scholarship of researchers because of issues such as self-citation and incomplete citation databases. Sound bibliometric analysis can be followed by faulty interpretation, and quantity and quality of citations are not necessarily related. Treating web links as citations begs questions of validity because of variability in the search engines, the lack of quality control, and the automatic replication of links. Altmetrics also has been subject to similar criticisms as bibliometrics. However, since altmetrics utilizes "a new array of metrics based on consumption, user engagement, and quality, altmetrics tools claim to offer a broader picture of influence for researchers within and across specialties" (Roemer and Borchardt 2014).

ROLE OF STATISTICS

Generally speaking, statistical analysis may be used to accomplish four basic tasks. First, statistics may indicate the central point around which a mass of data revolves. Second, they may show how broad or diverse the spread can be for a mass of data. Third, statistics may reveal how closely or distantly certain features within the mass of data are related, as well as whether a relationship even exists. Fourth, they may indicate the degree to which the facts might have occurred by mere chance, or whether there is a probability of their having been influenced by some factor other than pure chance (Leedy 1980, 141). The last function is accomplished with statistical tests of the hypothesis.

In short, the basic purpose of statistical analysis is to summarize observations or data in such a manner that they provide answers to the hypothesis or research questions. Statistics facilitate drawing general conclusions based on specific data. Stated somewhat differently, "the field of statistics involves methods for describing and analyzing data and for making decisions or inferences about phenomena represented by the data" (Frankfort-Nachmias and Nachmias 2008, 320). Both methods, even the second one concerning making inferences, are essentially methods of analysis and should be distinguished from interpretation. Interpretation of the results follows the analysis stage, and the purpose is to search for the broader meaning of the results by linking them to other available knowledge.

CAUTIONS IN USING STATISTICS

In addition to keeping in mind that the statistical analysis cannot provide the interpretation, the researcher should be aware of other concerns in using statistics. For example, the nature of the data to a large extent determines the statistical techniques that can be used legitimately. That is to say, certain techniques are appropriate for use with categorical data, others with ordinal data, and so forth. Specific examples illustrating this principle are provided later in this chapter. In addition, the more controlled the research setting, the less is the need, in general, for certain statistical techniques. Most, if not all, of the important relevant variables are already controlled, and replication of the study is less likely to produce different results.

Statistical analysis is necessary for most research studies involving quantitative data and is particularly crucial at the sampling and analysis stages. The analysis process should be planned well in advance in order to anticipate problems that may be encountered. The analysis of a study is shaped, to a considerable extent, before the data are collected.

The anticipation of the analysis process determines what kinds of data will be needed. For example, a researcher may wish to determine if there is a significant difference between the average frequency of library use of students who have and have not received information literacy instruction (ILI). In order to do so, the researcher will need to employ an appropriate statistical test, such as the difference of means test. As the difference of means test requires interval level data, the researcher must be certain to measure the frequency of library use on an interval scale. Simply ranking users as high, moderate, or low would not be adequate in this case. Once the data have been collected, there is little potential for changing them, and the researcher is at that point limited to certain statistical techniques.

The conceptual development of a research study should not, however, be dictated by the statistical techniques to follow. In the example given above, the researcher should decide on the most valid measure of library use, then apply the best statistical methods available. They should not decide to use factor analysis, for example, and then proceed to force the data into that technique, regardless of its appropriateness. Sophisticated statistical analysis cannot substitute for early, sound conceptual development.

STEPS INVOLVED IN STATISTICAL ANALYSIS

Regardless of the specific techniques or tests employed, there are certain basic steps common to virtually all statistical analyses. Those steps are discussed briefly here before taking a more detailed look at the major types of analysis.

The Establishment of Categories

To organize and analyze the data collected for a study, it is necessary to place them in categories. The identification or establishment of categories should take place before the data are gathered. The actual categorization of the data takes place during or after the collection process. In establishing categories, four basic rules or guidelines should be followed:

1. The set of categories or values (i.e., the classification scheme) for any one variable should be derived from a single classificatory principle, which is determined by the research question or hypothesis being investigated. For example, if one were studying the relationship between the number of years of experience that staff have in answering reference questions and reference performance, two sets of categories would be needed. Each staff member's number of years of experience answering reference questions would be categorized according to the number of years of experience and would represent a ratio level scale. Reference performance could be categorized according to the percentage of reference questions

answered correctly, another ratio scale. Another variable might be the type of reference question. Questions could be assigned to a set of nominal categories. For example, the authors published results of a longitudinal study that divided virtual reference queries into nine types: subject search, ready reference, procedural, no question, holdings, research, inappropriate, directional, and reader's advisory. The article "Not Dead Yet! A Longitudinal Study of Query Type and Ready Reference Accuracy in Live Chat and IM Reference" provides a definition and attribution for each category plus verbatim examples (Radford and Connaway 2013).

2. Each set of categories should be exhaustive. That is, it should be possible to place every observation in one of the categories of the set. This does not preclude the use of a miscellaneous or catchall category, such as "other." However, if one finds it necessary to place a substantial number of observations in an "other" category, or if a large percentage of such observations seem to have certain characteristics in common, the establishment of one or more additional categories should be considered. It is generally preferable to establish as many categories as possible and, if necessary, reduce or combine them later.

3. The categories within each set should be mutually exclusive. This means that it should not be possible to place a specific observation correctly in more than one category. Returning to the categorization of reference questions, every reference question received should logically fit into one, but no more than one, of the categories. It should not, for example, be possible for a question to be placed accurately in both the directional category and the research category. If it is conceivable to do so, then the categories are not adequately defined or the observations are not accurate.

4. Last, but not least, the development of categories should be based on a sound knowledge of the subject matter and an anticipation of likely responses. A person establishing categories for reference questions should have had enough reference experience, and have done enough reading about the topic, to be able to predict the types of questions that will appear in a study and establish categories accordingly. In the aforementioned article, seven of the nine categories for virtual reference questions were derived from previous research. Only two new categories were added, "no question" and "inappropriate," as these were found to be present in the data, but not previously described in the literature (Radford and Connaway 2013, 7).

Coding the Data

Once the categories have been established and data "assigned" to them, it is necessary to convert the new data or responses to numerical codes, so that they can be tabulated or tallied. These codes are, in turn, assigned to specified locations in data files, particularly if programmatic data analysis is planned. A codebook is useful for describing the locations of variables and for indicating the codes assigned to the categories or values of each variable, such as Yes = 1;

No=2. However, if the original responses are already numerical, such as test scores or volume counts in libraries, then they do not need to be assigned new codes, unless they are being recoded or assigned to groupings.

One of the most important considerations in coding is reliability. Problems of reliability in coding can result from inadequacies in the data. For example, a poorly worded questionnaire item may not produce enough relevant information for the purpose of the study. Answers to questions that actually ask more than one question are, of course, difficult, if not impossible, to code accurately. Problems with the categories also may lead to a lack of reliability, particularly if they do not meet the basic guidelines outlined above. Inaccuracies can emerge during the coding process itself as a result of observations being assigned to the wrong category. For that reason, it is important to see that coders are adequately trained and to verify or check the accuracy of their work. As noted in the section in chapter 5 on questionnaire construction, precoding can help to minimize coding errors and thus increase reliability.

In coding the data, researchers traditionally have transcribed the observations or scores for each individual or case from the data collection instrument to coding or transfer sheets. Once the coding sheets were complete, the researcher could work directly from the coding sheets, if analyzing the data manually. (See the codebook in table 8.1.) Today researchers usually analyze the data programmatically, often using statistical packages and data analysis software.

When coding *mail surveys*, which most likely will be in hard copy, researchers may scan and upload the data files; however, directly inputting the data into a computer program may be the most efficient method for coding. The software may display each question and prompt the researcher to input the response. Some researchers use a database management program to control data entry. The majority of statistical programs now enable uploading a data file or entering the data directly into the statistical program using some sort of data editor. More specifically, the program prompts the person entering data for each response, checks the response to ensure that it is valid for that variable, and then saves the response in the proper data file. Statistical programs often store data in proprietary formats, making it difficult to share data and to analyze them in multiple programs. Therefore, it often is better to enter the data into a database or spreadsheet so that they may be used in multiple statistical packages and shared. As discussed in chapter 5, many researchers are optimizing the opportunities made available to them online via the internet. Web-based and email surveys enable inputting responses directly into the software program when respondents submit their questionnaires for analysis. SurveyMonkey is one of the more popular survey packages currently being used and supports social media surveys, mobile surveys, survey templates, etc. ("SurveyMonkey: The World's Most Popular Free Online Survey Tool" 2020).

After the data have been prepared and saved in electronic format, they then can be analyzed using a software program such as those identified later in this chapter. The manuals that accompany these programs explain how to create data files that can be manipulated by the particular software and how to calculate certain statistics by executing appropriate commands. Some of the manuals even explain how to reformat data files originally created for analysis by another statistical package. Those individuals wanting to read

Table 8.1.   Codebook: Digital Literacy Instruction Sessions

Column	Label	Variables
A	ID with author's initials	
B	Rate technology skills	1 = poor 2 = fair 3 = average 4 = good 5 = excellent
C	Confident before class	1 = poor 2 = fair 3 = average 4 = good 5 = excellent
D	Confident after class	1 = poor 2 = fair 3 = average 4 = good 5 = excellent
E	Level of knowledge before class	1 = poor 2 = fair 3 = average 4 = good 5 = excellent
F	Level of knowledge after class	1 = poor 2 = fair 3 = average 4 = good 5 = excellent
G	Look for more health information	1 = yes 2 = no
H	If no, provides explanation	1 = explanation
I	Rate instructor	1 = poor 2 = fair 3 = average 4 = good 5 = excellent
J	Attend another class	1 = yes 2 = no
K	If no, provides explanation	1 = yes

(*continued*)

Table 8.1.   (continued)

Column	Label	Variables
L	Previous guest lectures	1 = yes 2 = no
M	Previous information literacy training	1 = yes 2 = no
N	Come to other programs	1 = yes 2 = no
O	If no, provides explanation	1 = yes
P	Age	1 = under 20 2 = 21–40 3 = 41–60 4 = 61–80 5 = 81+
Q	Gender	1 = male 2 = female 3 = genderqueer 4 = transgender 5 = prefer not to answer 6 = other
R	Education	1 = high school 2 = community college 3 = university
S	Computer at home	1 = yes 2 = no
T	Email	1 = yes 2 = no
U	Engage in social media	1 = yes 2 = no
V	Search internet	1 = yes 2 = no
W	Other	1 = yes Blank if no response

more about the coding process may wish to refer to Wetcher-Hendricks (2014). Stephanie Mikitish discusses the importance of collecting, coding, and analyzing data in text box 8.4, Statistical Analysis.

Text Box 8.4: Statistical Analysis

Stephanie Mikitish

As a former researcher/librarian at Rutgers University and now as a data analyst at the Library of Congress, statistical analysis appeals to me. I can utilize it to describe, explore, and demonstrate in an objective manner, and on a large scale, the effects that the resources, services, and programming that these libraries offer have on the communities that they serve. I would advise researchers interested in statistical analysis to learn enough about each method to ensure that they are utilizing it appropriately and effectively.

Appropriate utilization means choosing the best method and adhering to the norms of collecting data, performing, and reporting on the results of the analysis. Statistical Associates Publishing (2012) offers excellent resources for applying and reporting on many statistical analyses. Collaborating with scholars in and reading the methodology sections of articles/dissertations in library and information science (LIS), education, computer science, psychology, statistics, and political science can provide more specific examples for utilizing these methods. I recommend studying measures of central tendency for describing data, regression and ANOVA for testing hypotheses about the data, and cluster and factor analyses for exploring relationships between data. Pew Research Center (2013), Data.gov (2020), and the Inter-University Consortium for Political and Social Research (2020) offer library-related datasets to practice utilizing these analyses.

Just as important as appropriate utilization is effective utilization, which means that results are presented so that that an audience without a statistical background can understand and care about them. More specifically, the significant/nonsignificant findings and effect sizes should be contextualized for the audience. I recommend Keller (2015) for examples of simple descriptions of various analyses and soliciting feedback from members of your target audience on the effectiveness of your drafts/practice publications/presentations.

As data-driven decision making becomes more expected, the interest in and use of statistical analyses will increase. When utilized appropriately and effectively, these methods are useful tools for LIS professionals and researchers to incorporate in their studies.

References

"Data.Gov." 2020. Data.Gov. https://www.data.gov.
DC 20036USA202-419-4300 | Main 202-857-8562 | Fax 202-419-4372 | Media. 2013. "July 18–Sept. 30, 2013—Library Typology." Pew Research Center: Internet, Science & Tech. https://www.pewresearch.org/internet/dataset/september-2013-library-typology.
"Inter-University Consortium for Political and Social Research." 2020. https://www.icpsr.umich.edu/web/pages.
Keller, Dana K. 2015. *The Tao of Statistics: A Path to Understanding (with No Math)*. 2nd ed. Thousand Oaks, CA: Sage.
Statistical Associates Publishing. 2012. http://www.statisticalassociates.com/booklist.htm.

ANALYZING THE DATA: DESCRIPTIVE STATISTICS

Once the data are ready to be analyzed, the researcher can choose to use descriptive statistics, inferential statistics, or both. Descriptive statistics provide an overall view of your findings and should be the first step in data analysis to determine other analyses that will be undertaken and to explain your findings. Aytac and Slutsky examine 1,778 research articles published in thirteen LIS journals from 2008 to 2012. They report that "'descriptive' statistical analysis was the most frequently used technique among the articles with 74.0% (560)" (Aytac and Slutsky 2014, 150). Descriptive statistics may be a predominant type of data analysis in LIS research because they do provide an overview of the research findings and they can provide at least six basic functions.

First, at the most basic level, the statistical analysis can indicate how many persons, objects, scores, or whatever achieved each value (or fell into each category) for every variable that was measured. These calculations are usually reported in tables known as *frequency distributions*. Common types of frequency distributions are simple or absolute, cumulative, percentage, and grouped distributions.

Second, when it may be difficult to grasp the overall meaning of frequency distribution tables, pictorial representations can be used to portray a variety of characteristics of the cases or individuals with respect to the variable or variables measured. This process typically involves the use of one or more data displays such as bar graphs or charts, pie charts, histograms, and frequency polygons (see figures 8.1, 8.2, 8.3, and 8.4). Graphical representations generally sacrifice some detail in an effort to improve communication of data, but the loss of detail may well be desirable and justifiable. Graphs are especially useful for displaying the findings of a research study that has a large number of cases. Graphing and visualization data have become easier in recent years because of the widespread availability of data analysis and spreadsheet programs. Tufte has authored several interesting and useful books about the visual display of quantitative information (Tufte 2016, 2018a, 2018b, 2019).

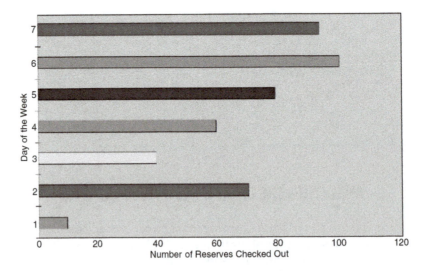

Figure 8.1. Bar Graph/Chart

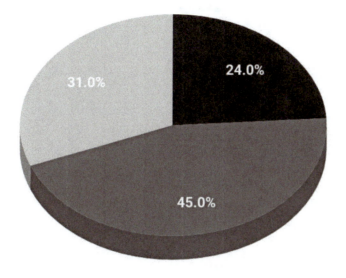

● **Audiovisual**   ● **Monographs**   ● **Serials**

Figure 8.2. Pie Chart

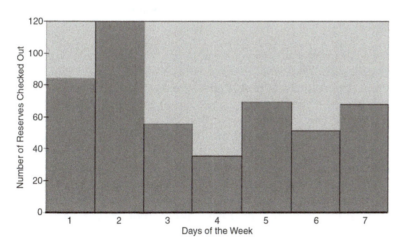

Figure 8.3. Histogram

Third, descriptive statistics are capable of characterizing what is typical in a group of cases. Such statistics, referred to as measures of *central tendency*, commonly include the mean, the median, and the mode. The (arithmetic) *mean* is what is commonly called the average. It is the sum of the scores divided by the total number of cases involved. The *median* is the value of the middle item when the scores are arranged according to size. The *mode* refers to the category or score that occurs most frequently.

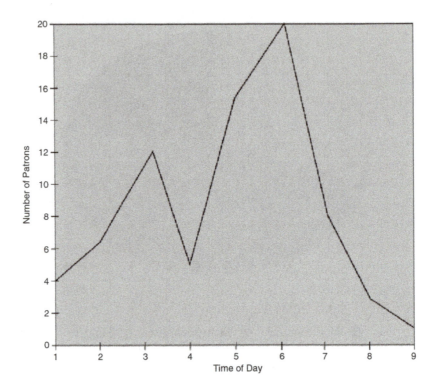

Figure 8.4. Frequency Polygon

Fourth, descriptive statistics can indicate how widely cases in a group vary. These statistics are known as measures of *dispersion* or *variability*; examples include the range of scores (the highest score minus the lowest score), their mean deviation (the arithmetic mean of the absolute differences of each score from the mean), the standard deviation (the square root of the arithmetic mean of the squared deviations from the mean), and the variance (the mean squared deviation).

The standard deviation is one of the most frequently used measures of dispersion, but it is also one of the more difficult to comprehend. As noted above, it reflects the amount of deviation from the mean for the observed scores. Stated differently, it is the positive square root of the variance. Its size increases whenever the size of the deviation scores increases. It is a useful measure of dispersion because, in many distributions of scores, one knows what percentage of the scores lie within plus or minus one, two, and three standard deviations. Its usefulness is enhanced because its units of measure are the same as those of the original data. The standard deviation is useful for comparing groups.

Assume, for example, that a survey of a public library's users found that their ages ranged from three to sixty years, their mean age was forty-five, and the standard deviation was three. We would thus know that 67 percent of the users fell between one standard deviation, or three years, or between the ages of forty-two to forty-eight, and so on for two and three standard deviations.

The formula for the standard deviation is as follows:

$$S = \sqrt{\frac{\sum X_i^2}{N}}$$

where $\sum X_i^2$ equals the total of the squared deviation scores, and N equals the number of cases.

Fifth, descriptive statistics can measure the relationship between or among the different variables in the data. These are generally referred to as correlational or associational statistics. They have the ability to allow prediction of one variable based on another, but they cannot be used to establish causal relationships. Correlation coefficients are, of course, correlational or descriptive statistics, but they also are often treated as inferential statistics; they are discussed in the section of this chapter that treats that type of statistical test.

Another common type of correlational statistic is the cross-tabulation or bivariate frequency. Bivariate frequencies are the products of tables in which two variables have been cross-classified. The tables consist of rows and columns, where the categories or values of one variable are labels for the rows, and the categories of the second variable are labels for the columns. By convention, the independent variable usually is the column variable, and the dependent variable usually is the row variable.

The calculation and analysis of bivariate frequencies is an essential step in discovering or testing relationships between variables, so an example of a bivariate table is presented and discussed next. In reading table 8.2, one should first note the title and headings in order to learn what information is contained in the table. In this example, the title and headings indicate that the table summarizes data on annual frequency of library use and age. It also is apparent that the data have been grouped or categorized in ranges. Each range represents a value for the respective variable.

Table 8.2.   Frequency of Library Use by Age

Library Use per Year	Age				
	1–12	**13–25**	**26–50**	**51+**	**Total**
0–5	6	12	15	40	73
	9%	15%	25%	43%	25%
6–12	10	13	12	35	70
	16%	16%	20%	38%	24%
13–24	25	30	12	10	77
	39%	38%	20%	11%	26%
25+	23	25	20	7	75
	36%	31%	34%	8%	25%
Total	64	80	59	92	295
	100%	100%	100%	100%	100%

As indicated previously, the reader probably can assume that the column variable, age, is the independent variable, and the row variable, library use, is the dependent variable.

The reader should check at the bottom of the table to see if the source for the data is identified. Knowing the source helps the reader to assess the reliability of the data. If the source is not given at the foot of the table, it should be indicated at the appropriate place in the text. Remember that every table should be referred to within the text and summarized or highlighted in some fashion.

Next, the reader should determine in which direction the percentages have been calculated. It is important to know whether the percentages have been calculated down the columns or across the rows. This can be learned by noting where the "100%" values have been placed. In table 8.2, the percentages have been calculated down the columns. It is possible to calculate percentages in both directions.

Finally, the reader should compare the percentage differences in the table in order to determine the extent to which relationships, if any, exist between the variables. Comparisons always are made in the direction opposite to the one in which the percentages were calculated. In table 8.2, the reader would examine percentages across rows in order to determine whether given levels of library use significantly varied according to age. In looking at the first row, one can see that 9 percent of those who were between the ages of one and twelve used the library zero to five times, 15 percent of those aged thirteen to twenty-five used the library zero to five times, and so forth. An examination of the entire row indicates that the older age groups tended to exhibit less library use, in that higher percentages of them fell into the lowest library use category. The relative percentages in the other rows tend to support this conclusion. The only noteworthy anomaly is represented by the percentage of persons aged twenty-six to fifty who used the library twenty-five or more times (34 percent). An occasional anomaly does not necessarily weaken a pattern or resulting conclusion, but it generally is worth further consideration for the insights it may provide.

The figures in the "total" column indicate what percentages of the total number of cases fell into the different ranges of library use. The figures across the "total" row indicate the numbers and percentages of persons who occurred in each age category. The numbers in the final column and row are referred to as marginals, or univariate frequencies. They are purely descriptive in nature. The numbers within the individual cells are the cross-tabulations or bivariate frequencies. They are the figures that can help to point out relationships, as they represent the cases that have certain values for both variables. For example, the six cases in the first cell represent persons who were aged one to twelve *and* who used the library zero to five times during the preceding year. By examining such figures, the reader may detect a pattern of covariation, or a relationship between two variables. In this case, use tended to decrease as age increased. Barnes (1985) has a useful chapter on preparing and analyzing tables for those wanting to read more about this topic. Most statistical software and spreadsheet programs provide methods for easily displaying statistical analyses in tables and charts.

The sixth basic function that descriptive statistics can perform is to describe the difference between two or more groups of individuals. This really is no more than a special case of showing the relationship between two variables. Such uses of descriptive statistics often involve measures of central tendency. For example, if one had measured the library skills of two groups of students, it could be revealing to compare the mean scores of the two groups. If the two groups had received different types of instruction, such a comparison could help to indicate the superior instructional method.

ANALYZING THE DATA: INFERENTIAL STATISTICS

In contrast to descriptive statistics, which simply summarize and describe the data (though, as indicated above, they can at least suggest relationships), inferential statistics can perform certain more sophisticated functions. They are most commonly used to predict or estimate population *parameters* or characteristics based on random sample *statistics* and to test hypotheses using tests of statistical significance to determine if observed differences between groups or variables are "real" or merely due to chance. Inferential statistics help one to make inferences and judgments about what exists on the basis of only partial evidence.

Using inferential statistics as first described, one could measure the loss rate for a sample of books and then predict the loss rate for the entire population or collection based on the sample statistic. Applying inferential statistics in the second manner, one could test the relationship between loss rate and circulation loan periods by analyzing the difference in loss rates for two groups of books: one housed in a library with a long loan period and one in a library with a short loan period. In evaluating the difference, if any, it would be necessary to determine if the difference were too large to be due merely to chance, rather than to the effects of different loan periods.

It is important to remember that statistical methods are used to test the null hypothesis (or the "hypothesis of no relationship"), as opposed to the research hypothesis, which does predict a relationship (usually a positive one). Null hypotheses are necessary to avoid the "fallacy of affirming the consequent" (i.e., researchers are only able to eliminate false hypotheses rather than accept true ones). In other words, demonstrating that B occurred does not mean that theory A is necessarily true, or that A caused B. One must eliminate other theories before concluding that A is true. Stated yet another way, to support a hypothesis that two or more variables are related, one must first demonstrate that they are not unrelated. Or one must demonstrate that it is safe to conclude that the null hypothesis is wrong, so as to conclude that the variables really are related. Demonstrating that the null hypothesis is unlikely to be true before concluding that there is a real relationship also helps to rule out chance as the cause of the relationship.

Accepting the null hypothesis as true means that (a) any observed difference or relationship is not statistically significant and is probably due to chance or sampling error, and (b) the research hypothesis is not supported. Rejecting the null hypothesis means that the research hypothesis is supported.

Both of these applications of inferential statistics are based on an assumption of random sampling and on probability theory, and the researcher should have a good understanding of their basic concepts. Random sampling is discussed in chapter 6. Probability theory relates to the mathematical likelihood of an event occurring. Central to probability theory is the assumption that while repeated events will exhibit a certain pattern over time, individual or short-time events tend to differ from overall long-term patterns of events. For example, if one flips a coin enough times in a fair manner, the law of large numbers should take effect, and the result should end up with roughly 50 percent of the flips being heads and 50 percent being tails. On the other hand, ten flips of the coin might well produce as few as three or four or as many as seven or eight heads.

If the difference between the outcome (say six heads out of ten tosses) and 50 percent was small, then one might attribute the difference to chance. If nine of ten flips resulted in heads, then one might suspect that something was amiss and that some variable, such as a defective coin, was affecting or biasing the outcomes of the coin flips. Fortunately, "the mathematical theory of probability provides a basis for evaluating the reliability of the conclusions we reach and the inferences we make when we apply statistical techniques to the collection, analysis, and interpretation of quantitative data" (Huntsberger 1977, 71). As probability theory plays such a crucial role in statistical analysis, the reader is encouraged to consult one or more standard statistics texts on this subject.

Inferential statistics themselves are of two basic types: parametric statistics or tests and nonparametric statistics or tests. Either type should be used only when certain conditions exist. There have been multiple longitudinal studies of the types of statistical analyses used in LIS literature. These studies provide a synopsis of how the LIS research landscape has evolved and changed.

Dilevko (2007, 209) examines "research articles published between 2001 and 2005 that academic and public librarians are most likely to read" to determine the extent to which inferential statistics were used. He compares these results to the results of studies conducted in the 1970s and 1980s (Dilevko 2007). He reports that there has been "an increase in the use of inferential statistics" in the 475 articles examined. Of the 135 documented uses of inferential statistics in the articles, 36 different inferential statistics were used. The inferential statistics that had more than a total of five occurrences in the articles were "T-tests (21), chi-square (20), Pearson's r (16), multiple regression (9), one-way ANOVA (9), reliability coefficients (7), and post hoc tests (6)" (Dilevko 2007, 217). The majority of the articles using inferential statistics were authored by librarians or library management personnel.

Aytac and Slutsky (2014) report that after descriptive statistical analysis, correlational analysis (n=41, 5.3 percent), inferential statistical analysis (n=32, 4.2 percent), and multiple analysis (n=20, 2.6 percent) are the next most used methods of statistical analysis in the thirteen LIS journals published from 2008 to 2012. They also report significant differences in the use of quantitative versus qualitative data analysis techniques by practitioners and contributors. In their sample of articles, practitioners (n=319, 72.8 percent) and contributors (n=81, 73.6 percent) primarily employed quantitative data analysis techniques. "Academics used both quantitative (n = 120, 58.5%) and qualitative (n = 44, 21.5%) as well as both analyses in one single study (n = 41, 20%)" (Aytac and Slutsky 2014, 151). The authors report that both the practitioners and collaborators in the sample most often used quantitative data analysis techniques, specifically descriptive statistics (practitioners, n = 360, 82.2 percent; collaborators, n = 81, 73.6 percent) (Aytac and Slutsky 2014). However, the academic researchers in the sample used both correlational statistics (n = 19, 9.3 percent) and inferential statistics (n = 16, 7.8 percent). The use of correlational and inferential statistics in this sample of LIS publications was lower than the use of descriptive statistics.

Zhang, Wang, and Zhao (2017) review research papers published between January 1999 and December 2013 in six top-ranking LIS journals. There were 5,175 qualifying papers and of these, 1,497 papers used statistical methods. They report that inferential statistical methods were used in the majority of the papers (1,308), followed by predictive statistical methods (851), and 523 papers that reported using other methods. Of these, parametric statistics are used in 1,408 of the papers and nonparametric statistics were used in 751 of the papers. The authors conclude that "research studies using statistical methods in the field have increased steadily" (Zhang, Wang, and Zhao 2017, 1084).

Togia and Malliari (2017) analyze a random sample of 440 articles published from 2011 to 2016 in five LIS research journals that had the highest impact factor in Ulrich's Serials Directory. They report that 28.4 percent of the articles used descriptive statistics while 18.5 used inferential statistics. If both descriptive and inferential statistics were used in an article, only the inferential statistics were reported.

Zhang Wang, and Zhao (2017) analyze 1,821 papers from six LIS research journals recommended by domain experts, in publication for at least nineteen years, online full-text access, and impact factor published between 1999 and 2017. The majority of the papers used parametric inferential statistics (1,023), followed by nonparametric inferential statistics and predictive statistics correlation methods (both 823), and predictive statistical regression methods (377).

Parametric Statistics

When data are assumed to have a probability distribution that can be specified by some set of parameters (e.g., a normal distribution or binomial distribution), parametric statistics can be used to infer the values of those parameters and to perform certain kinds of inferences that depend on assumptions about the underlying distribution. Before making an assumption about the probability distribution of data, it is important to compare the structure of the data with the expected structure of the distribution. For example, when the data of a normal distribution are plotted on a graph, they should produce a curve that is symmetrical and unimodal (see figure 8.5); its mean, median, and mode should all coincide; and there should be a constant area, or proportion of cases, between the mean and an ordinate that is a given distance from the mean in terms of standard deviations. Slightly more than two-thirds of the

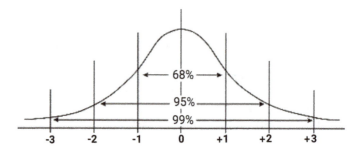

Figure 8.5. Normal Curve

cases should fall within plus or minus (±) one standard deviation of the mean, slightly more than 95 percent within plus or minus two standard deviations, and almost all cases within plus or minus three standard deviations.

However, if the sample drawn from the population has one hundred or more cases, the normality assumption almost always can be relaxed. That is, a normal population is not required, as the sampling distribution of sample means is likely to be normal. This is a result from probability theory known as the "central limit theorem." In fact, "no matter how unusual a distribution we start with, provided N [the sample size] is sufficiently large, we can count on a sampling distribution that is approximately normal" (Blalock 1979, 183). It is sampling distributions, not populations, that form the basis for tests of significance. (See the section on sampling error in chapter 6 for a definition of the "mean of the sampling distribution.")

If the sample size falls somewhere between fifty and one hundred, and if there is evidence that departure from normality is not great, then statistical tests of this type can be used with some confidence. If the sample is less than thirty, the researcher should use such tests cautiously unless the approximation to normality is known to be good (Blalock 1979, 187).

Parametric tests with normally distributed data also assume that the variance of each group in question is similar and that the samples are randomly drawn. In addition, they require that the data being analyzed are primarily interval or ratio level data.

Parametric tests are relatively powerful, or likely to detect a difference between groups if a difference really exists. The power of a test is directly related to its ability to eliminate false null hypotheses. Power may be defined as one minus the probability of a type II error. (A type II or "beta error" is the error of failing to reject a null hypothesis when it is actually false; a type I or "alpha error" is the error of rejecting a true null hypothesis. When the probability of one type increases, the other decreases.)

Following are some examples of frequently used parametric tests that can be used on normally distributed data:

1. *Z test.* This test, using standard scores, tests the difference between a group's results and the results that would be expected due to chance alone. Or, stated somewhat differently, it is used to determine whether

the mean of a sample is significantly different from the mean of the population from which it is taken. (A standard, or Z, score is relative to the mean and measured in standard deviation units. It equals the deviation from the mean divided by the standard deviation.) A Z test could be used, for example, to decide whether the physical condition of a sample of DVDs selected from a library's collection is representative of the physical condition of the entire collection in general.

2. *Student's t-test.* This test can be used in place of the Z test where there is still only one group but where, in contrast to the Z test, the standard deviation of the population is not known.

3. *Difference of means.* This commonly used statistical test utilizes the t statistic and determines if the statistical difference between the mean scores of two groups is significant. It does not require the population standard deviations to be known.

4. *Analysis of variance (ANOVA).* This statistical test represents an extension of the difference of means test. It utilizes the F statistic (a ratio of variances), and it tests for differences among the means of more than two samples or groups. Strictly speaking, ANOVA could be used to compare just two groups, but it would produce the same results as a t-test in that case. Multiple analysis of variance (MANOVA) is designed for situations in which one needs to test relationships that involve more than one dependent variable.

5. *Post hoc tests.* These test "the statistical significance of differences between group means" that have an overall difference calculated after an ANOVA or a regression analysis (RA) has been done (Vogt 2005, 241).

   a. Tukey's HSD (Honestly Significant Difference) test is used to examine the pattern of mean difference and can be used with more than two groups. The HSD score is the within-group variability and is part of the ANOVA result. It is compared with all of the possible pairs of means to determine if there is a significant difference between the HSD score and each mean difference.

   b. The Scheffé test is a test of significance used for multiple comparisons of means in an ANOVA. It is good for comparing unequal cell sizes and "tends to err on the side of underestimating significance" (Vogt 2005, 241).

6. *Reliability coefficient.* This statistic indicates the reliability of a measurement, that is, a test, scale, and so forth. It ranges from zero (completely unreliable when observed variance is attributed to random error) to one (completely reliable).

   a. Cronbach's α is a "measure of internal reliability or consistency of the items in an instrument that have more than two answers, such as Likert scales" (Vogt 2005, 71).

   b. The Kuder-Richardson test "measures the internal consistency or reliability of tests in which items have only two possible answers" (Vogt 2005, 166), such as yes/no or true/false.

7. *Pearson's product-moment correlation coefficient (r).* This test generally is referred to as simply the correlation coefficient; it measures the

degree of linear association between two variables or the extent to which changes in one value correspond with changes in another value. It can range from negative one to positive one. A negative coefficient indicates a negative relationship, or, as one variable increases, the other decreases (or vice versa). A positive value indicates a positive relationship, or, as one variable increases, the other increases, or they both decrease. A coefficient of zero, or near zero, means that there is little or no linear relationship between the variables. Use of this statistic requires interval level data. Referring back to a concern about the physical condition of DVDs, one could measure the correlational relationship between the number of times certain DVDs are borrowed and the number of times they must be replaced.

Relationships between two variables can be plotted on a graph, which is usually called a scattergram. A straight line can then be plotted that relates specific values of one variable to values of the other. In figure 8.6 the scores of one of the variables are represented on the abscissa (horizontal line), and the scores of the second variable are represented on the ordinate (vertical line). For example, the X value on the horizontal axis could be the number of items checked out; the Y value on the vertical axis could be the length of visit. When two variables are highly correlated, the plotted points tend to be very close to the straight line, and as previously noted, the correlation coefficient would be close to one. This line is called a line of regression, and the equation of this line is called a regression equation.

A major aim of quantitative research is prediction. When two variables are correlated, regression equations can be used to predict what value of variable Y would most likely be associated with a given value of X. Regression analysis itself is considered next. See text box 8.5, Ordinary Least Squares: Regression Analysis, by Christopher Cyr for more detail about regression analysis.

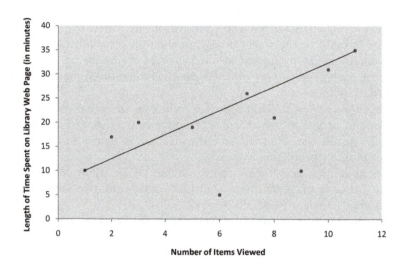

Figure 8.6. Scatter Diagram with a Regression Line

8. *Regression.* This type of analysis, as is the case for correlation, can be used for descriptive and inferential purposes. In the former case, Pearson's correlation coefficient is used as the basis for developing a simple linear regression equation to predict the value of one variable when the value of the other variable is known. As an inferential technique, linear regression can be used to generalize findings from a sample to the population from which the sample was randomly selected. For example, using data collected from a sample, one could predict that a certain percentage increase in the length of time one spends on the library web page would result in a certain percentage increase in the number of items viewed.

Regression, and correlation, analysis can be used with two variables or "can readily be extended to include any number of interval scales [variables], one of which can be taken as dependent and the remainder independent" (Blalock 1979, 451). Utilizing multiple regression analysis, one could measure a number of characteristics of reference librarians and use those as a basis for predicting how successful a reference librarian would be in answering reference questions.

Text Box 8.5: Ordinary Least Squares: Regression Analysis

Christopher Cyr

There is a common (and possibly apocryphal) anecdote in statistics that claims, in New York City, there is a correlation between ice cream sales and the crime rate. Does that mean that one of these things has a causal relationship with the other? Common sense suggests probably not. If one does not cause the other, then what could account for this correlation? The answer is that there is a third variable, temperature, that has a causal relationship with both of them. People eat more ice cream when it is warmer outside, and crime rates also tend to go up in the summer months. How do we account for cases like this (known as a spurious correlation), where two variables appear to be related, but only because a third variable has a causal impact on both of them?

Regression analysis is a technique that allows us to account for these types of relationships, and it does a lot more than that. With regression, we can see both the significance of a relationship (or the likelihood that the relationship is caused by random statistical noise rather than a genuine relationship) and the magnitude of the relationship (or how much of an impact one variable has on another). We also can include controls, which allow us to see the independent relationship that two variables have when others are held constant. In the example above, when temperature is included as a control, the relationship between ice cream sales and the crime rate becomes statistically insignificant.

There are many different types of regression analysis, but most researchers who use it begin with a technique called Ordinary Least Squares (OLS). Given certain assumptions, OLS is considered to be the best linear unbiased estimator of the relationship between the variables included in a statistical model. An OLS model will allow you to predict the value of a variable of interest (also known as the dependent variable) based on the equation below.

$$Y_i = B_0 + B_1(X_1) + B_2(X_2) + B_3(X_3) + E_i$$

Y_i represents the value of the dependent variable, and X_1-X_3 are the values of the independent variables in the model. A model can include more than three X variables, though adding too many can create problems. B_0 represents the constant (or Y intercept), and B_1-B_3 represent the coefficients (or slopes) for their corresponding X variables. E_i represents the error term, or the part of Y_i that is not predicted by the model.

OLS regression can help us answer a lot of questions in library and information science, where many variables of interest might be highly correlated with each other. For example, a 2017 study on the impact of library instruction on information literacy skills, which used a sample of students from two different campus, used OLS to control for the fact that the likelihood of having library instruction differed across the two campuses (Luetkenhaus et al. 2017). OLS is also useful for calculating the magnitude of the effect that a variable has. For example, a 2020 study of the impact of open education resources on student success used OLS to determine "if a course with 50 students enrolled moved from a $100 textbook to an open education resource—or even just put that textbook on reserve—we predict one more student would pass the course every semester" (Wimberley, Cheney, and Ding 2020).

One pitfall to be aware of as you begin working with OLS regression is the assumptions involved in the model. These assumptions are rarely perfectly met, and most of the other regression techniques are meant to address which specific assumptions are violated. In my experience, when using regression analysis, there is usually another model that better fits the data that you are analyzing than OLS, and which specific model depends on how your dependent variable is measured and distributed. OLS offers a great starting point for working with regression, but it is good to be aware of its limitations and ways that other models can address these limitations (e.g., maximum likelihood estimation).

References

Luetkenhaus, Holly, Erin Hvizdak, Corey Johnson, and Nicholas Schiller. 2017. "Measuring Library Impacts through First Year Course Assessment." *Communications in Information Literacy* 11(2): 339–53. https://doi.org/10.15760/comminfolit.2017.11.2.6.

Wimberley, Laura, Elizabeth Cheney, and Yi Ding. 2020. "Equitable Student Success via Library Support for Textbooks." *Reference Services Review* (ahead-of-print). https://doi.org/10.1108/RSR-03-2020-0024.

Nonparametric Statistics

In contrast to parametric statistics, nonparametric statistics are considered to be distribution-free. That is, they do not require the assumption of an underlying parametrized distribution (e.g., a normal population) and therefore are often used with smaller samples. As they involve weaker assumptions, they are less powerful than the parametric tests and require larger samples in order to yield the same *level of significance*. The level of significance is the probability of rejecting a true hypothesis. It usually is set at .05 or .01, which means that the null hypothesis, or the prediction of no relationship, is to be rejected if the sample results are among the results that would have occurred no more than 5 percent, or 1 percent, of the time. Stated somewhat differently, a significance level of .05 means that there is a 5 percent probability that the researcher will reject a hypothesis that actually is true.

Nonparametric tests are usually, but not always, used with ordinal level data. Following are five common examples:

1. *Chi-square test (X^2).* This test is useful for determining if a statistically significant relationship exists between two categorical variables. If the population is known to be normally distributed, chi-square can be treated as a parametric statistic and frequently is used for causal, comparative studies. The process for calculating a chi-square is essentially the same as described in the section on bivariate frequencies, and it produces the same kind of cross-classification. It can indicate only if there is a significant relationship; statistics such as Cramer's V must be used to determine the strength of any relationships. Returning again to our concern about the physical condition of a library's book collection, we might use a chi-square test to determine whether there is a significant relationship between the location of books and their condition (as assigned to categories). Pearson's chi-square test is the best known one.
2. *Mann-Whitney U-test.* This is one nonparametric equivalent of the difference of means test and is used to test for a significant difference between two groups. It cannot be used unless the population is symmetric about its median.
3. *Wilcoxon Sign test.* This test can be used instead of the Mann-Whitney when the data are not symmetrical. It also is useful in determining the significance of the difference between two correlated groups.
4. *Spearman rank-order correlation, or Spearman's ρ.* This is a nonparametric correlation coefficient that can be calculated for ranked or ordinal level data. It is interpreted in the same manner as Pearson's correlation coefficient.
5. *Kruskal-Wallis test.* This nonparametric alternative to analysis of variance is appropriate when one has a number of independent random samples and an ordinal scale level of measurement.

Selecting the Appropriate Statistical Test

As has been indicated for most of the examples given above, the various statistical tests must meet certain conditions before being appropriate for use. For example, certain tests call for a normal population, others for a particular level of measurement (see chapter 4 for a consideration of basic measurement scales). Most of the examples presented here were intended for the analysis of either one group or two groups. There also are statistical tests intended for more than two variables; such techniques are referred to as multivariate analyses and include multiple regression and factor analysis. One also should consider the primary purpose of the research in choosing statistics—that is, whether it is descriptive or analytical in nature. Other questions relate to the need to distinguish between independent and dependent variables and to the sampling method used.

These and other kinds of questions should be answered before selecting a statistical test. Otherwise, an inappropriate test may be used and thereby invalidate the results of the analysis. The selection of a proper statistic can be facilitated by using some sort of decision tree to systematize the process. An example of the use of decision trees in selecting appropriate statistical tests can be found in a booklet published by the SAS Institute (Andrews, Klem, and O'Malley 1998). In using this guide, one starts by noting how many variables are involved, then continues along the "branches" of the decision tree, answering questions at each decision point. Eventually one arrives at a box that will contain a statistical technique, measure, or test appropriate to the situation. The same information is available in most standard statistical texts, but in a less compact, sequential format. Statistical programs are widely available and provide assistance to researchers in identifying and selecting the appropriate statistical tests.

The next section works through an example of how a statistical test might be selected and used to test a hypothesis. Suppose an experiment had been conducted to test the effects of ILI on the library skills of certain university students. The researcher established two groups of randomly selected students. One group of students was given ILI during the course of the study; one group received no instruction. At the end of the experiment, the information literacy skills of the students in both groups were measured with a test. The mean test score of the experimental group (instruction) was 85; the mean score of the control group (no instruction) was 65. Thus, the difference between mean test scores was 20. The research hypothesis for the study predicted that there would be a significant difference between the mean scores. The implicit null hypothesis was that there would not be a statistically significant difference.

In this scenario, two groups have been observed, and the mean information literacy skills scores for two groups of subjects have been calculated. It is assumed that the two groups were drawn independently from a normally distributed population (all of the students enrolled at the university) in terms of their information literacy skills, but the standard deviation for the population is not known. The test scores represent ratio-level data. Prior to the study it was determined that ILI would be considered the independent variable and information literacy skills (scores) the dependent variable. Thus, the difference of means t-test is identified as an appropriate and legitimate statistic for testing the hypothesis.

As indicated, there is a difference of 20 points between the mean test scores of the two groups. The question is whether 20 points represent a statistically significant difference. In order to answer this question, one must first select the significance level and critical region to be used with the test. Assume that the .01 level of significance was selected, which means that the test would have a 1 percent chance of rejecting the null hypothesis when it actually is true. Or, as previously stated, it is the probability of making a type I error.

In selecting the *critical region*, the researcher is deciding whether one or both tails of the sampling distribution will be used to determine whether the hypothesis will be accepted or rejected. (If normal, the sampling distribution would resemble the curve in figure 8.5.) If the researcher is able to predict the direction of the relationship, it is advisable to use a one-tailed test so all of the critical region can be concentrated in one end of the curve. If the direction of the relationship cannot be predicted, a two-tailed test is preferable. In this case, one expects BI to increase library skills, so a one-tailed test is selected. Since the significance level is .01, the critical region would be the extreme right 1 percent of the curve or distribution. If the outcome falls into that area, then the null hypothesis would be rejected, with a 1 percent chance of having made an error.

Next, one must calculate the value of "t" for the difference of means test. This can be done using the appropriate formula or computer program. Once computed, the t value must be checked in a table of t values to determine whether it is statistically significant (or a computer program can be used to do this). If the value is equal to or greater than the value in the table for the appropriate level of significance and "degrees of freedom," then it is deemed statistically significant, or not likely to have occurred by chance. For many statistical tests, the number of degrees of freedom (df) is defined as one less than the size of the sample, or n -1. Therefore, the researcher is justified in rejecting the null hypothesis of no relationship and at least tentatively accepting the research hypothesis. It can be concluded, therefore, that ILI does appear to have a positive impact on the library skills of certain university students. If the t value is lower than the corresponding one in the table this would, of course, dictate the opposite conclusion.

CAUTIONS IN TESTING THE HYPOTHESIS

In using statistics to test hypotheses, one always must keep in mind that statistical inferences are based on probability, and one can never rely on statistical evidence alone for a judgment of whether a hypothesis is true. Such a decision must be based on the presuppositions or conceptual basis of the research as well.

It also is important to remember that a single statistical "acceptance" of a hypothesis does not prove it to be true with absolute certainty. It is seldom, if ever, possible to accept a hypothesis outright as the single correct one, since there are a large number of additional hypotheses that also could be accepted. One simply decides, based on the statistical results, that a hypothesis should not be rejected. This does provide some support for the hypothesis.

Meta-analysis generally refers to a set of statistical procedures used to summarize and integrate many studies that focused on the same issue. An article by Chow (1987) provided a critique of meta-analysis. Ke and Cheng (2015) develop a framework for the study of the meta-analysis in LIS. Although the findings indicate that meta-analysis has potential as an LIS research method, the authors identify a number of challenges that must be addressed before widespread adoption of the method.

An older, but still useful, Sage publication presented an overview of meta-analysis in social research (Glass, McGaw, and Smith 1981). The first author of this book, Glass (2000), stated in a 2000 paper, "Meta-analysis needs to be replaced by archives of raw data that permit the construction of complex data landscapes that depict the relationships among independent, dependent and mediating variables." Now that some journals require that the raw data used for the publication of the research findings must accompany the paper, these archives of raw data are becoming more readily available.

Even when statistical tests or the results of other studies suggest that there is a consistent difference or relationship between groups or variables, this finding still does not explain the reason for the relationship. In order to make causal inferences, one must meet assumptions over and above those required for establishing the existence of a statistical relationship.

The old saying "Correlation does not prove causation . . . is meant to remind us that an association between two variables might be caused by something other than an effect of the presumed independent variable on the dependent variable—that is, it might be a spurious relationship" (Schutt 2015, 205–6). An example of spurious relationship is "if we measure children's shoe sizes and their academic knowledge . . . we will find a positive association. However, the association results from the fact that older children have larger feet as well as more academic knowledge. Shoe size does not cause knowledge, or vice versa" (Schutt 2015, 206). This phenomenon also is referred to as *confounding* the dependent and independent variables. Again, only a sound understanding of the conceptual basis for an apparent relationship can explain its nature; statistics alone cannot.

Other caveats regarding the use of statistics include the fact that a statistically significant result is not necessarily socially or practically significant. Differences of a few thousand volumes between two university library collections could produce significant statistical differences, but in the context of multimillion volume collections, such a difference holds little if any practical significance.

Finally, "weighted data, missing data, small sample sizes, complex sample designs, and capitalization on chance in fitting a statistical model are sources of potential problems in data analysis" (Andrews, Klem, and O'Malley 1998, 1). When one of these situations exists, statistics should be used with extra caution.

STATISTICAL ANALYSIS SOFTWARE

"Today, quantitative analysis is almost always done by computer programs such as SPSS and MicroCase" (Babbie 2021, 416). Depending on the methodology, the data often are inherently numerical and easily uploaded into statistical software packages. With the use of online questionnaires, the data can be transported into statistical software programs as soon as the respondents submit the completed survey. Numerical data can be submitted to statistical software programs on personal computers (PCs), servers, and in the cloud. As computing power increases, statistics programs are continually being updated.

Using a statistical package via servers or the cloud is an efficient technique for analyzing large amounts of data. There are multiple examples of these types of statistical software packages, such as Statsols, formerly BMDP, which no longer is available. Statsols provides nQuery, which is the platform for clinical trial research (Statsols n.d.). The software calculates sample size and statistical analysis.

Another comprehensive statistical package for data analysis is SAS. It was designed "for use by business analysts, statisticians, data scientists, researchers, and engineers" ("SAS/STAT Software Fact Sheet" 2017). SAS/ STAT provides more than ninety procedures for statistical analysis and the capability to output data visualizations. There are modules for analytics for the web, social media, and marketing as well as Text Miner software. SAS offers cloud solutions and can be operated through a graphical interface, or via application programming interfaces (APIs). The SAS base system for PCs supports statistical analysis, as well as report writing, in a variety of formats for data management and retrieval.

Minitab is a relatively easy-to-use statistical and graphical analysis software package ("Minitab Statistical and Process Management Software for Six Sigma and Quality Improvement" n.d.). MicroCase, another statistical analysis and data management system, was developed for social science researchers and is available for PCs ("MicroCase" n.d.).

One of the most popular statistical packages is IBM's SPSS. The SPSS system is a comprehensive, versatile, and relatively easy-to-use statistical software platform for statistical analysis, report writing, tabulation, and general-purpose data management. It provides a suite of modules containing numerous statistical procedures, from simple tables to multivariate analyses. Other SPSS features are modelers, predictive analytics for big data, prescriptive analytics, a variety of data import and export modes, and data support for Python and R programming languages, and SPSS is available for use on PCs and servers, such as Linux systems. There are cloud service offerings and social media analytics software and a graphical user interface. IBM offers multiple SPSS products for academic and business statistics that include a basic set of modules for calculating a number of standard statistics as well as programs for more advanced statistics, graphic analysis, and data management. A multitude of tutorials, webinars, and other resources also are available for SPSS ("SPSS Statistics—Resource Library | IBM" n.d.).

Qualtrics is a web-based survey tool that enables the development, dissemination, and analysis of survey data ("Online Survey Software—Qualtrics" 2020). Tableau is used in academia and industry to provide interactive analytics to display data (Ackermann, Goek, and Plagman 2019).

R is a programming language and an environment where one is able to implement statistical analyses and produce graphics ("R: What Is R?" n.d.). R is available for free and is similar to some of the functionality of SPSS.

SYSTAT is another comprehensive statistics, graphics, and data management software package ("About Systat Software, Inc." n.d.). SYSTAT, as is true of some of the other packages developed for the PC, provides statistical and graphics capabilities.

Some basic statistical tools are available online only, such as the Rice Virtual Lab in Statistics ("Rice Virtual Lab in Statistics (RVLS)" n.d.). A statistics text and resource list and a simple analysis lab into which a user may paste small datasets also are available online.

In using computers for statistical analysis, one should be careful that the ease of doing so does not waste the researcher's time. With the possible exception of some exploratory research, the investigator should avoid indiscriminately generating all sorts of analyses without any consideration of relevant concepts, theories, and hypotheses. As is the case with manual analyses, researchers should be certain that they have a thorough understanding of the statistical procedures used. A book by Nardi (2005) is intended to assist readers in the interpretation of basic statistics, graphs, and tables that are commonly found in academic writing.

VISUALIZATION AND DISPLAY OF QUANTITATIVE DATA

"A picture often is worth some unmeasurable quantity of words . . . [graphs] are useful particularly for exploring data because they show the full range of variation and identify data anomalies that might be in need of further study" (Schutt 2015, 313). Quantitative data lends itself well to visualizations; therefore, quantitative research usually includes graphs, tables, and figures for displaying findings as they succinctly summarize your findings. Visual displays and depictions of the data should be exactly that—understandable without words. Creating visualizations of the data should be done during the data collection and analysis phases of the research as well as in the interpretation and dissemination of the findings.

"Quantitative researchers have software packages that can develop publishable tables, graphs, and charts" (Miles, Huberman, and Saldaña 2020, 104). It is possible to create pivot tables in SPSS ("Pivot Tables" 2014) and Qualtrics ("Online Survey Software—Qualtrics" 2020). Graphs, charts, and figures can

Table 8.3. Total Respondents by Library Type (N = 705)

Library Type	Number of Responses	Percent of Responses
Education: University/Higher Education	468	66%
Public	60	9%
Research	43	6%
Education: Community College/Technical School	36	5%
Special (corporate, law, medical, other)	25	4%
Government (federal, state, local; all but national libraries)	23	3%
Education: school (K–12)	16	2%
National	13	2%
Museum/Archive/Cultural Heritage	7	1%
Education: other	7	1%
Consortia	4	1%
Other	3	<1%

be created using the SPSS Chart Builder ("Building Charts" 2014), and Qualtrics ("Results-Reports Visualizations—Qualtrics Support" n.d.) has the capability to automatically create visualizations from reports as well as custom visualizations. SPSS offers tutorials for creating charts and tables ("Using the Chart Builder Gallery" 2014). Visme, a data presentation and visualization tool designed for educators and marketing and business professionals, also provides the capability to add animation to static data visualizations.

Tableau often has been used to display data in the LIS literature, although it is considered by some to be expensive with an unappealing layout (Ackermann, Goek, and Plagman 2019; Datig and Whiting 2018; Guhde 2019; Guo 2019; Hall and Clarke 2019; Klein, Kinsley, and Brooks 2019; Lewellen and Plum 2016; Murphy 2013; Puckett-Rodgers, Layton, and King 2019). Microsoft Office programs, such as Word and Excel, also can be used to create tables and graphs.

The following visualizations and displays of quantitative data provide examples of the possibilities for displaying data.

Table 8.3 depicts the number and percent of responses from the different library types to an online survey on open content.

Figure 8.7 is a way to display the roles of the research and university library respondents of an online open content survey in percentages, highlighting that half of the respondents were in leadership roles.

Figure 8.8 is a similar depiction of data as figure 8.7. However, figure 8.8 is displaying the percentages of duplication rates for books held by the Research Libraries UK (RLUK) consortia within the consortia compared to the duplication rates for the books held by RLUK compared to all library holdings in WorldCat.

Figure 8.9 displays multiple data points from different numbers of respondents of the open content online survey.

Figure 8.10 exemplifies a way to display quantitative data on a map with the circles sized to scale to depict the number of distinct print book publications in each mega-region.

In figure 8.11 the quantitative data for the collective print collection is visually represented by increasing the scale. At a glance, "it is evident that smaller groupings of libraries cannot provide full coverage of the holdings of larger groupings" (Lavoie, Dempsey, and Malpas 2020, 990).

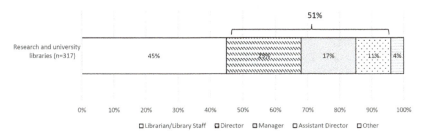

Figure 8.7. Lead Contributor Level of Responsibility: Research and University Libraries (n = 317)

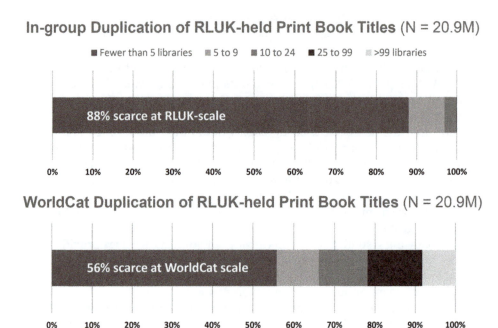

Figure 8.8. RLUK Collective Print Book Collection: Duplication Rates

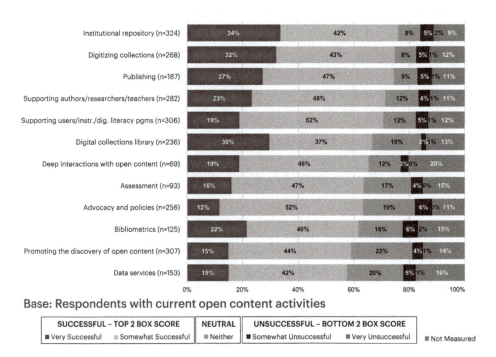

Figure 8.9. Successfulness of Open Content Activities: Research and University Libraries

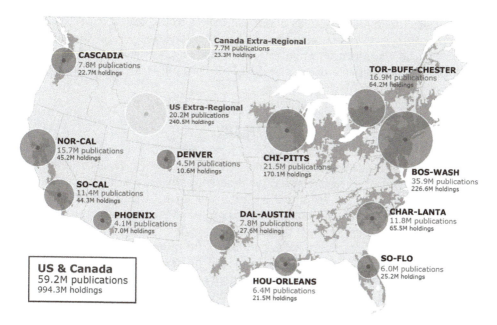

Data represents print book holdings in WorldCat as of January 2019. Circles are scaled to reflect the number of distinct print book publications in each mega-region.

Figure 8.10. US and Canadian Mega-Regional Collective Print Book Collections

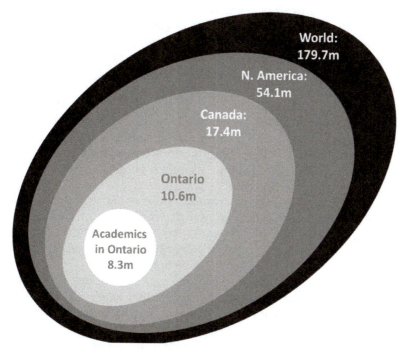

Figure 8.11. Scaling the Collective Print Book Collection: A Canadian Perspective

These are just a few examples of different ways to display quantitative data. There are many other examples available in the literature and in the different statistical and visualization programs. "Graphic displays will help draw attention to important aspects of your findings and simplify interpretation of basic patterns" (Schutt 2015, 564).

SUMMARY

Statistical methods generally are used for descriptive purposes and for statistical inference. Descriptive statistics deal with the tabulation of data; their presentation in tabular, graphical, or pictorial form; and the calculation of descriptive measures. Inferential statistics are used for making inductive generalizations about populations, based on sample data, and for testing hypotheses. Both types of statistics permit interpreting quantitative data in such a way that the reliability of conclusions based on the data may be evaluated objectively by means of probability statements.

With the availability of vast amounts of data created from online consumer and social media sites and search engines data science has emerged as the discipline that attempts to address and make sense of big data. Data scientists use machine learning algorithms to develop models for forecasting. Text mining, an AI technology, is the analysis of large collections of written documents using algorithms and other computer applications

Data mining, log analysis, bibliometrics, citation analysis, altmetrics, webometrics, and informetrics are other unobtrusive data collection and analysis methods. The discussion in this chapter of these methods and their uses in LIS only is an introduction and does not explain how to use these methods. If readers are interested in learning more about these methods, it will be necessary to refer to other texts and articles that more thoroughly address them.

The typical basic steps in statistical analysis are categorizing the data, coding the data, and calculating the appropriate statistics. Descriptive statistics, if calculated, can characterize what is typical in a group, indicate how widely cases in the group vary, show the relationships between variables and groups, and summarize the data. Inferential statistics can estimate population parameters and test the significance of relationships between and among variables.

Certain inferential statistics are classed as parametric statistics, and they require the assumption of a normal population. Others are considered nonparametric or distribution-free statistics. The requirements for using specific statistics of either kind tend to vary somewhat, and the researcher should carefully avoid using statistical tests inappropriately.

There are cautions in utilizing statistics. Perhaps the most important principle to keep in mind is that statistics, whether generated manually or by a computer, cannot substitute for early, sound conceptual development of the research design and statistical analysis. Even the most sophisticated, comprehensive statistical packages simply "crunch" numbers, with no real regard for the underlying theories and hypotheses. It is left to the researcher to determine which statistical techniques represent valid methods of analyzing the data. The final interpretation of the analysis must be done by the investigator; statistics can only facilitate the process.

Finally, this chapter provides an overview of visualizing and displaying data. In addition to bar charts and graphs there are more sophisticated information visualization and display options. There are multiple statistical and visualization software programs for creating different ways of displaying and representing the data. The visualization and display of quantitative data can be used throughout the different phases of the research to identify relationships, patterns, and anomalies and to articulate the findings in a clear and concise way.

REFERENCES

"About Systat Software, Inc." n.d. SYSTAT. Accessed July 10, 2020. https://systatsoftware.com/about.

Abrizah, A., Mohammadamin Erfanmanesh, Vala Ali Rohani, Mike Thelwall, Jonathan M. Levitt, and Fereshteh Didegah. 2014. "Sixty-Four Years of Informetrics Research: Productivity, Impact and Collaboration." *Scientometrics* 101(1): 569–85. https://doi.org/10.1007/s11192-014-1390-8.

Ackermann, Eric, Sara Goek, and Emily Plagman. 2019. "Outcome Measurement in Academic Libraries: Adapting the Project Outcome Model." In *Proceedings of the 2018 Library Assessment Conference: Building Effective, Sustainable, Practical Assessment*, edited by Sue Baughman, Steve Hiller, Katie Monroe, and Angela Pappalardo, 1–14. Washington, DC: Association of Research Libraries.

Andrews, Frank M., Laura Klem, and Patrick M. O'Malley. 1998. *Selecting Statistical Techniques for Social Science Data: A Guide for SAS Users*. Cary, NC: SAS Institute.

Aung, Htet Htet, Mojisola Erdt, and Yin-Leng Theng. 2017. "Awareness and Usage of Altmetrics: A User Survey." *Proceedings of the Association for Information Science and Technology* 54(1): 18–26. https://doi.org/10.1002/pra2.2017.14505401003.

Aung, Htet Htet, Han Zheng, Mojisola Erdt, Ashley Sara Aw, Sei-Ching Joanna Sin, and Yin-Leng Theng. 2019. "Investigating Familiarity and Usage of Traditional Metrics and Altmetrics." *Journal of the Association for Information Science and Technology* 70(8): 872–87. https://doi.org/10.1002/asi.24162.

Aytac, Selenay, and Bruce Slutsky. 2014. "Published Librarian Research, 2008 through 2012: Analyses and Perspectives." *Collaborative Librarianship* 6(4): Article 6. https://digitalcommons.du.edu/collaborativelibrarianship/vol6/iss4/6.

Babbie, Earl R. 2021. *The Practice of Social Research*. 15th ed. Boston: Cengage Learning.

Banks, Julie. 2000. "Are Transaction Logs Useful? A Ten-Year Study." *Journal of Southern Academic and Special Librarianship* 1(3): 1–7. http://southernlibrarianship.icaap.org/content/v01n03/banks_j01.html.

Bar-Ilan, Judit, Stefanie Haustein, Staša Milojević, Isabella Peters, and Dietmar Wolfram. 2018. "Peer Review, Bibliometrics and Altmetrics—Do We Need Them All?" *Proceedings of the Association for Information Science and Technology* 55(1): 653–56. https://doi.org/10.1002/pra2.2018.14505501073.

Bar Ilan, Judit, and Bluma C. Peritz. 2002. "Informetric Theories and Methods for Exploring the Internet: An Analytical Survey of Recent Research Literature." *Library Trends* 50: 371–92.

Barnes, Annie S. 1985. *Social Science Research: A Skills Handbook*. Bristol, IN: Wyndahm Hall Press.

Barnes, Cameron. 2015. "The Use of Altmetrics as a Tool for Measuring Research Impact." *Australian Academic & Research Libraries* 46(2): 121–34. https://doi.org/10.1080/00048623.2014.1003174.

Belle, Gerald van. 2011. *Statistical Rules of Thumb*. Somerset, N J: Wiley-Interscience.

Björneborn, Lennart, and Peter Ingwersen. 2004. "Toward a Basic Framework for Webometrics." *Journal of the American Society for Information Science and Technology* 55(14): 1216–27. https://doi.org/10.1002/asi.20077.

Blalock, Hubert M., Jr. 1979. *Social Statistics*. Rev. ed. New York: McGraw-Hill.

Boman, Craig. 2019. "An Exploration of Machine Learning in Libraries." In *Artificial Intelligence and Machine Learning in Libraries* 55(1), edited by Jason Griffey, 21–25. Chicago: ALA TechSource. https://www.alastore.ala.org/content/artificial-intelligence-and-machine-learning-libraries.

Bornmann, Lutz, Andreas Thor, Werner Marx, and Hermann Schier. 2016. "The Application of Bibliometrics to Research Evaluation in the Humanities and Social Sciences: An Exploratory Study Using Normalized Google Scholar Data for the Publications of a Research Institute." *Journal of the Association for Information Science and Technology* 67(11): 2778–89. https://doi.org/10.1002/asi.23627.

Boslaugh, Sarah. 2012. *Statistics in a Nutshell: A Desktop Quick Reference*. 2nd ed. Sebastopol, CA: O'Reilly Media.

Bringham, Tara J. 2014. "An Introduction to Altmetrics." *Medical Reference Services Quarterly* 33(4): 438–47.

"Building Charts." 2014, October 24. www.ibm.com/support/knowledgecenter/sslvmb_23.0.0/spss/base/chart_creation_container.html.

Burton, Matt, and Liz Lyon. 2017. "Data Science in Libraries." *Bulletin of the Association for Information Science and Technology* 43(4): 33–35. https://doi.org/10.1002/bul2.2017.1720430409.

Burton, Matt, Liz Lyon, Chris Erdmann, and Bonnie Tijerina. 2018. "Shifting to Data Savvy: The Future of Data Science in Libraries." Project Report. University of Pittsburgh.

Careless, James. 2013. "Altmetrics 101: A Primer." *Information Technology* 30(2): 1–36.

Chatterjee, Marina. 2020. "Data Science vs Machine Learning and Artificial Intelligence." GreatLearning. November 4. https://www.mygreatlearning.com/blog/difference-data-science-machine-learning-ai.

Chellappandi, P., and C. S. Vijayakumar. 2018. "Bibliometrics, Scientometrics, Webometrics/Cybermetrics, Informetrics and Altmetrics—An Emerging Field in Library and Information Science Research." *Shanlax International Journal of Education* 7(1): 5–8.

Chow, Siu L. 1987. "Meta-Analysis of Pragmatic and Theoretical Research: A Critique." *The Journal of Psychology* 121(3): 259–71. https://doi.org/10.1080/00223980.1987.9712666.

Connaway, Lynn Silipigni, John M. Budd, and Thomas R. Kochtanek. 1995. "An Investigation of the Use of an Online Catalog: User Characteristics and Transaction Log Analysis." *Library Resources & Technical Services* 39(2): 142–52.

Connaway, Lynn Silipigni, Chris Cyr, Brittany Brannon, Peggy Gallagher, and Erin M. Hood. 2019. "Speaking on the Record: Combining Interviews with Search Log Analysis in User Research." *Submitted for Review*.

Covey, Denise Troll. 2002. *Usage and Usability Assessment: Library Practices and Concerns*. Washington, DC: Digital Library Federation and Council on Library and Information Resources.

Crotty, David. 2014. "Altmetrics: Finding Meaningful Needles in the Data Haystack." *Serials Review* 40(3): 141–46.

Datig, Ilka, and Paul Whiting. 2018. "Telling Your Library Story: Tableau Public for Data Visualization." *Library Hi Tech News* 35(4): 6–8. https://doi.org/10.1108/LHTN-02-2018-0008.

Dewey, Scott Hamilton. 2020. "Foucault's Toolbox: Use of Foucault's Writings in LIS Journal Literature, 1990–2016." *Journal of Documentation* 76(3): 689–707. https://doi.org/10.1108/JD-08-2019-0162.

Didegah, Fereshteh, Timothy D. Bowman, and Kim Holmberg. 2018. "On the Differences between Citations and Altmetrics: An Investigation of Factors Driving Altmetrics versus Citations for Finnish Articles." *Journal of the Association for Information Science and Technology* 69(6): 832–43. https://doi.org/10.1002/asi.23934.

Dihman, Anil Kumar. 2015. "Bibliometrics to Altmetrics: Changing Trends in Assessing Research Impact." *Journal of Library & Information Technology* 35(4): 310–15.

Dilevko, Juris. 2007. "Inferential Statistics and Librarianship." *Library & Information Science Research* 29(2): 209–29. https://doi.org/10.1016/j.lisr.2007.04.003.

Ferrante, Barbara Kopelock. 1987. "Bibliometrics: Access in Library Literature." *Collection Management* 2 (Fall): 201.

Flanagan, John C. 1954. "The Critical Incident Technique." *Psychological Bulletin* 5: 327–58.

Frankfort-Nachmias, Chava, and David Nachmias. 2008. *Research Methods in the Social Sciences.* 7th ed. New York: Worth.

Friedman, Alon. 2015. *Statistics for Library and Information Services: A Primer for Using Open Source R Software for Accessibility and Visualization.* Lanham, MD: Rowman & Littlefield.

Geraeds, Gert-Jan, and Judith Kamalski. 2010. "Bibliometrics Comes of Age—Research Trends." *Research Trends.* https://www.researchtrends.com/issue15-january-2010/research-trends-7.

Glass, Gene V. 2000. "Meta-Analysis at 25." https://www.gvglass.info/papers/meta25.html.

Glass, Gene V., Barry McGaw, and Mary Lee Smith. 1981. *Meta-Analysis in Social Research.* Beverly Hills, CA: Sage.

Gonick, Larry, and Woollcott Smith. 2015. *The Cartoon Guide to Statistics.* Rev. ed. New York: William Morrow.

Guhde, Emily. 2019. "Step Aside, Tableau: The Pros and Cons of Analyzing and Reporting Ithaka S+R Survey Results Using Google Data Studio." In *Proceedings of the 2018 Library Assessment Conference: Building Effective, Sustainable, Practical Assessment,* edited by Sue Baughman, Steve Hiller, Katie Monroe, and Angela Pappalardo, 71–80. Washington, DC: Association of Research Libraries.

Guo, Jin Xiu. 2019. "Smart Data, Smart Library: Assessing Implied Value through Big Data." In *Proceedings of the 2018 Library Assessment Conference: Building Effective, Sustainable, Practical Assessment,* edited by Sue Baughman, Steve Hiller, Katie Monroe, and Angela Pappalardo, 40–47. Washington, DC: Association of Research Libraries.

Hall, Kristin, and Janet H. Clarke. 2019. "Communicating Library Impact through the Assessment Website." In *Proceedings of the 2018 Library Assessment Conference: Building Effective, Sustainable, Practical Assessment,* edited by Sue Baughman, Steve Hiller, Katie Monroe, and Angela Pappalardo, 127–42. Washington, DC: Association of Research Libraries.

Hovden, Robert. 2013. "Bibliometrics for Internet Media: Applying the h-Index to YouTube." *Journal of the American Society for Information Science and Technology* 64(11): 2326–31. https://doi.org/10.1002/asi.22936.

Hu, Xiaojun, Loet Leydesdorff, and Ronald Rosseau. 2020. "Exponential Growth in the Numbers of Items in the WOS." *International Society for Scientometrics and Informetrics* 16(2): 32–38.

Huntsberger, David V. 1977. *Elements of Statistical Inference.* 4th ed. Boston: Allyn & Bacon.

Ikpaahindi, Linus. 1985. "An Overview of Bibliometrics: Its Measurments, Laws, and Their Implications." *Libri* 35 (June): 163.

Ke, Qing, and Ying Cheng. 2015. "Applications of Meta-Analysis to Library and Information Science Research: Content Analysis." *Library & Information Science Research* 37(4): 370–82. https://doi.org/10.1016/j.lisr.2015.05.004.

Keita, Bando. 2012. "Almetrics: Alternative Ways of Measuring Scholarly Impact Based on the Social Web." *Journal of Information Processing & Management/ Joho Kanri* 55(9): 638–46.

Klein, Grady, and Alan Dabney. 2013. *The Cartoon Introduction to Statistics.* New York: Hill & Wang.

Klein, Jesse, Kirsten Kinsley, and Louis Brooks. 2019. "Building a 'Library Cube' from Scratch." In *Proceedings of the 2018 Library Assessment Conference: Building Effective, Sustainable, Practical Assessment*, edited by Sue Baughman, Steve Hiller, Katie Monroe, and Angela Pappalardo, 359–70. Washington, DC: Association of Research Libraries.

Konkiel, Stacy. 2013. "Altmetrics: A 21st Century Solution to Determining Research Quality." *Online Researcher* 37: 11–15.

Konkiel, Stacy, and Dave Scherer. 2013. "New Opportunities for Repositories in the Age of Altmetrics." *Bulletin of the American Society for Information Science and Technology* 39(4): 22–26. https://doi.org/10.1002/bult.2013.1720390408.

Lavoie, Brian, Lorcan Dempsey, and Constance Malpas. 2020. "Reflections on Collective Collections." *College & Research Libraries* 81(6): 981–96. https://doi.org/10.5860/crl.81.6.981.

Leedy, Paul D. 1980. *Practical Research: Planning and Design.* 2nd ed. New York: Macmillan.

Levine, Emil. 2014. "Libraries in the Digital Age: Qualitative Methods and Altmetrics in Assessments." *Information Today* 31(7): 10–11.

Lewellen, Rachel, and Terry Plum. 2016. "Assessment of E-Resource Usage at University of Massachusetts Amherst: A MINES for Libraries® Study Using Tableau for Visualization and Analysis (RLI 288, 2016)." https://publications.arl.org/jca85v.

Liu, Jean, and Euan Adie. 2013. "Five Challenges in Altmetrics: A Toolmaker's Perspective." *Bulletin of the American Society for Information Science and Technology* 39(4): 31–34. https://doi.org/10.1002/bult.2013.1720390410.

Lyon, Liz. 2012. "The Informatics Transform: Re-Engineering Libraries for the Data Decade." *International Journal of Digital Curation* 7(1): 126–38. https://doi.org/10.2218/ijdc.v7i1.220.

Lyon, Liz, and Aaron Brenner. 2015. "Bridging the Data Talent Gap: Positioning the ISchool as an Agent for Change." *International Journal of Digital Curation* 10(1): 111–22. https://doi.org/10.2218/ijdc.v10i1.349.

Lyon, Liz, and Eleanor Mattern. 2015. "Applying Translational Principles to Data Science Curriculum Development." In *IPres 2015 Proceedings*, 9. Chapel Hill, NC. http://d-scholarship.pitt.edu/27159.

Lyon, Liz, and Eleanor Mattern. 2017. "Education for Real-World Data Science Roles (Part 2): A Translational Approach to Curriculum Development."

International Journal of Digital Curation 11(2): 13–26. https://doi.org/10 .2218/ijdc.v11i2.417.

Martyn, John, and F. Wilfrid Lancaster. 1981. *Investigative Methods in Library and Information Science: An Introduction.* Arlington, VA: Information Resources Press.

Michalek, Andrea, Mike Buschman, and Kathleen McEvoy. 2014. "Analyze This: Altmetrics and Your Collection." *Against the Grain* 26(2): 80–81. https://doi .org/10.7771/2380-176X.6734.

"MicroCase." n.d. Spring Arbor University—Services. Accessed November 14, 2020. https://serviceportal.arbor.edu/TDClient/1958/Portal/Requests/ServiceDet ?ID=18894.

Miles, Matthew B., A. Michael Huberman, and Johnny Saldaña. 2020. *Qualitative Data Analysis: A Methods Sourcebook.* 4th ed. Thousand Oaks, CA: Sage. https://www.vitalsource.com/products/qualitative-data-analysis-matthew -b-miles-v9781506353081.

Millsap, Larry, and Terry Ellen Ferl. 1993. "Research Patterns of Remote Users: An Analysis of OPAC Transaction Logs." *Information Technology and Libraries* 12: 321–43.

Ming-Yueh, Tsay, and Tseng Ling-Li. 2014. "An Introductory Review of Altmetrics." *Journal of Educational Media & Library Sciences* 51: 91–120.

"Minitab Statistical and Process Management Software for Six Sigma and Quality Improvement." n.d. Minitab Inc. Accessed June 29, 2020. http://www .minitab.com/en-us.

Murphy, Sarah Anne. 2013. "Data Visualization and Rapid Analytics: Applying Tableau Desktop to Support Library Decision-Making." *Journal of Web Librarianship* 7(4): 465–76. https://doi.org/10.1080/19322909.2013.825148.

Nardi, Peter M. 2005. *Interpreting Data.* Boston: Pearson.

Nielsen, Brian. 1986. "What They Say They Do and What They Do: Assessing Online Catalog Use Instruction through Transaction Monitoring." *Information Technology and Libraries* 5(1): 28–34.

"Online Survey Software—Qualtrics." 2020. Qualtrics. https://www.qualtrics.com /core-xm/survey-software.

Osareh, Farideh. 1996. "Bibliometrics, Citation Analysis and Co-Citation Analysis: A Review of Literature I." *Libri* 46(3): 149–58. https://doi.org/10.1515/libr .1996.46.3.149.

Patten, Mildred L. 2018. *Understanding Research Methods: An Overview of the Essentials.* 10th ed. New York: Routledge, Taylor & Francis Group.

Peters, Thomas. 1996. "Using Transaction Log Analysis for Library Management Information." *Library Administration & Management* 10 (Winter): 20–25.

Peters, Thomas A. 1991. *The Online Catalog: A Critical Examination of Public Use.* Jefferson, NC: McFarland.

"Pivot Tables." 2014, October 24. www.ibm.com/support/knowledgecenter /sslvmb_24.0.0/spss/base/pivot_container.html.

Piwowar, Heather. 2013. "Introduction Altmetrics: What, Why and Where?" *Bulletin of the American Society for Information Science and Technology* 39(4): 8–9. https://doi.org/10.1002/bult.2013.1720390404.

Powell, Ronald R. 1995. "Research Competence for Ph.D. Students in Library and Information Science." *Journal of Education for Library and Information Science* 36(4): 319–29.

Puckett-Rodgers, Emily, Denise Layton, and Kat King. 2019. "Participatory Data-Gathering and Community Building." In *Proceedings of the 2018 Library Assessment Conference: Building Effective, Sustainable, Practical Assessment,* edited by Sue Baughman, Steve Hiller, Katie Monroe, and

Angela Pappalardo, 235–44. Washington, DC: Association of Research Libraries.

"R: What Is R?" n.d. Accessed November 14, 2020. https://www.r-project.org /about.html.

Radford, Marie L., and Lynn Silipigni Connaway. 2013. "Not Dead Yet! A Longitudinal Study of Query Type and Ready Reference Accuracy in Live Chat and IM Reference." *Library & Information Science Research* 35(1): 2–13. https:// doi.org/10.1016/j.lisr.2012.08.001.

Rathore, Abhishek Singh, and Devshri Roy. 2014. "Performance of LDA and DCT Models." *Journal of Information Science* 40(3): 281–92. https://doi.org/10 .1177/0165551514524678.

Reinhart, Alex. 2015. *Statistics Done Wrong: The Woefully Complete Guide*. San Francisco: No Starch Press.

"Results-Reports Visualizations—Qualtrics Support." n.d. Accessed November 14, 2020. https://www.qualtrics.com/support/survey-platform/reports-module /results-section/visualizations/visualizations-overview.

"Rice Virtual Lab in Statistics (RVLS)." n.d. Rice Virtual Lab. Accessed June 29, 2020. http://onlinestatbook.com/rvls.html.

Roemer, Robin Chin, and Rachel Borchardt. 2014. "Keeping Up with . . . Altmetrics." Text. Association of College & Research Libraries (ACRL). http://www .ala.org/acrl/publications/keeping_up_with/altmetrics.

Roemer, Robin Chin, and Rachel Borchardt. 2015a. "Chapter 1. Introduction to Altmetrics." *Library Technology Reports* 51(5): 5–10.

Roemer, Robin Chin, and Rachel Borchardt. 2015b. "Altmetrics and the Role of Librarians." *Library Technology Reports* 51(5): 31–37.

"SAS/STAT Software Fact Sheet." 2017.

Scardilli, Brandi. 2014. "An Introduction to Altmetrics." *Information Technology* 31(9): 11–12.

Schutt, Russell K. 2015. *Investigating the Social World: The Process and Practice of Research*. 8th ed. Los Angeles: Sage.

"Scopus Powers 'Research Trends.'" n.d. Accessed November 13, 2020. https:// www.elsevier.com/about/press-releases/science-and-technology/scopus -powers-research-trends.

Semeler, Alexandre Ribas, Adilson Luiz Pinto, and Helen Beatriz Frota Rozados. 2019. "Data Science in Data Librarianship: Core Competencies of a Data Librarian." *Journal of Librarianship and Information Science* 51(3): 771–80. https://doi.org/10.1177/0961000617742465.

Silver, Nate. 2020. *The Signal and the Noise: Why Most Predictions Fail but Some Don't*. New York: Penguin Press.

Smith, Linda C. 1981. "Citation Analysis." *Library Trends* 30(85): 83–106.

Song, Il-Yeol, and Yongjun Zhu. 2016. "Big Data and Data Science: What Should We Teach?" *Expert Systems* 33(4): 364–73. https://doi.org/10.1111/exsy .12130.

"SPSS Statistics—Resource Library | IBM." n.d. Accessed November 14, 2020. https://www.ibm.com/products/spss-statistics/resources.

Statsols. n.d. "Platform for Optimizing Clinical Trial Design | Classical & Adaptive Trials." Accessed November 14, 2020. https://www.statsols.com/nquery.

Sugimoto, Cassidy R., Sam Work, Vincent Larivière, and Stefanie Haustein. 2017. "Scholarly Use of Social Media and Altmetrics: A Review of the Literature." *Journal of the American Society for Information Science and Technology* 68(9): 2037–62. https://asistdl.onlinelibrary.wiley.com/doi/full/10.1002/asi.23833 ?casa_token=VmauSqcitgwAAAAA%3A_mEUheEmngHlo32Iu1e74HtW8qRylv 99YTpinphDTPQ-Nqu1MJ10vnoPeenqMqXyjFxtBZM0HdiU.

"SurveyMonkey: The World's Most Popular Free Online Survey Tool." 2020. SurveyMonkey. https://www.surveymonkey.com.

Taylor, Mike. 2013. "Exploring the Boundaries: How Altmetrics Can Expand Our Vision of Scholarly Communication and Social Impact." *Information Standards Quarterly* 25(2): 27–32.

Togia, Aspasia, and Afrodite Malliari. 2017. "Research Methods in Library and Information Science." In *Qualitative versus Quantitative Research,* edited by Sonyel Oflazoglu, Vol. Chapter 3, 43–64. Rijeka, Croatia: InTech. http://dx.doi.org/10.5772/intechopen.68749.

Tolle, John E. 1983. *Current Utilization of Online Catalogs: A Transactional Log Analysis.* Vol. 1. Dublin, OH: OCLC Office of Research.

Tufte, Edward R. 2016. *Visual and Statistical Thinking: Displays of Evidence for Making Decisions.* Cheshire, CT: Graphics Press.

Tufte, Edward R. 2018a. *Envisioning Information.* Cheshire, CT: Graphics Press.

Tufte, Edward R. 2018b. *The Visual Display of Quantitative Information.* 2nd ed. Cheshire, CT: Graphics Press.

Tufte, Edward Rolf. 2019. *Visual Explanations: Images and Quantities, Evidence and Narrative.* Cheshire, CT: Graphics Press.

Ungern-Sternberg, Sara von. 1989. "Teaching Bibliometrics." *Journal of Education for Library and Information Science* 39(1): 76–80.

Urdan, Timothy C. 2017. *Statistics in Plain English.* 4th ed. New York: Routledge.

"Using the Chart Builder Gallery." 2014, October 24. www.ibm.com/support/knowledgecenter/sslvmb_23.0.0/spss/tutorials/bcharttut_gallery.html.

Vaughan, Liwen. 2001. *Statistical Methods for the Information Professional: A Practical, Painless Approach to Understanding, Using, and Interpreting Statistics.* Medford, NJ: Information Today.

Vickers, Andrew J. 2009. *What Is a P-Value Anyway? 34 Stories to Help You Actually Understand Statistics.* Boston: Pearson.

Vogt, W. Paul, ed. 2005. *Dictionary of Statistics & Methodology: A Nontechnical Guide for the Social Sciences.* 3rd ed. Thousand Oaks, CA: Sage.

Vogt, W. Paul, and R. Burke Johnson. 2016. *The Sage Dictionary of Statistics and Methodology: A Nontechnical Guide for the Social Sciences.* 5th ed. Thousand Oaks, CA: Sage.

Wakeling, Simon, Paul Clough, Lynn Silipigni Connaway, Barbara Sen, and David Tomás. 2017. "Users and Uses of a Global Union Catalog: A Mixed-Methods Study of WorldCat.Org." *Journal of the Association for Information Science and Technology* 68(9): 2166–81. https://doi.org/10.1002/asi.23708.

Wallace, Danny P. 1985. "The Use of Statistical Methods in Library and Information Science." *Journal of the American Society for Information Science* 36(6): 402–10. https://doi.org/10.1002/asi.4630360610.

Wallace, Danny P. 1989. "Bibliometrics and Citation Analysis." In *Principles and Applications of Information Science for Library Professionals,* edited by John N. Olsgaard, 10–26. Chicago: American Library Association.

Wang, Lin. 2018. "Twinning Data Science with Information Science in Schools of Library and Information Science." *Journal of Documentation* 74(6): 1243–57. https://doi.org/10.1108/JD-02-2018-0036.

Wetcher-Hendricks, Debra. 2014. *Analyzing Quantitative Data: An Introduction for Social Researchers.* Hoboken, NJ: Wiley.

"What Is Text Mining, Text Analytics and Natural Language Processing?" 2019. Linguamatics. August 28. https://www.linguamatics.com/what-text-mining-text-analytics-and-natural-language-processing.

Wheelan, Charles. 2013. *Naked Statistics: Stripping the Dread from the Data.* New York: Norton.

White, Emilie C. 1985. "Bibliometrics: From Curiosity to Conventions." *Special Libraries* 76: 35.

Wiedenbeck, Susan, Robin Lampert, and Jean Scholtz. 1989. "Using Protocol Analysis to Study the User Interface." *Bulletin of the American Society for Information Science* 15(5): 25–26.

Wildemuth, Barbara M. 2017. *Applications of Social Research Methods to Questions in Information and Library Science.* 2nd ed. Santa Barbara, CA: ABC-CLIO.

Wusu, Oluwaseyi H., and Nneka G. Lazarus. 2018. "Major Trends in LIS Research: A Bibliometric Analysis." *Library Philosophy and Practice* 22.

Zhang, Jin, Yanyan Wang, and Yuehua Zhao. 2017. "Investigation on the Statistical Methods in Research Studies of Library and Information Science." *The Electronic Library* 35(6): 1070–86. https://doi.org/10.1108/EL-02-2016-0042.

Zuccala, Alesia A, Frederik T. Verleysen, Roberto Cornacchia, and Tim C. E. Engels. 2015. "Altmetrics for the Humanities: Comparing Goodreads Reader Ratings with Citations to History Books." Edited by Stefanie Haustein and Cassidy R. Su. *Aslib Journal of Information Management* 67(3): 320–36. https://doi.org/10.1108/AJIM-11-2014-0152.

Zuo, Zhiya, and Kang Zhao. 2020. "Understanding and Predicting Future Research Impact at Different Career Stages—A Social Network Perspective." *Journal of the Association for Information Science and Technology,* 1–19. https://doi.org/10.1002/asi.24415.

9

Principles of
Qualitative Methods

INTRODUCTION TO QUALITATIVE METHODS

In chapters 4 through 8 the focus is on quantitative methods; the next four chapters put the spotlight on qualitative approaches. Claims for the power of qualitative approaches center on their use as a "*strategy for discovery*, for *exploring new ideas*, and for *developing hypotheses*" (Miles, Huberman, and Saldaña 2020, 8) as opposed to hypothesis testing, as generally seen in quantitative methods. Qualitative methods have long been of interest to librarians, as the growing body of literature using these frameworks can attest. However, barriers such as inadequate training and ongoing perceptions within the broader research community that qualitative methods are more subjective and not as scientific or rigorous as quantitative approaches continue (Radford 2011). Denzin and Lincoln (2018, 2) assert that "the methodological struggles of the 1970s and 1980s, fights over the very existence of qualitative research, while part of a distant past, are very much alive in the second decade of the new millennium. They are present in the tenure battles that are waged every year for junior faculty when their qualitative research is criticized for not being scientific."

Within library and information science (LIS), Galliers and Huang conducted a pilot study using interviews and a grounded theory approach to investigate training in qualitative methods in the information systems area, which is allied to the LIS discipline. They found that the positivist paradigm and quantitative methods continue to dominate the field and explored the impact on scholarship of the lack of education in qualitative methods (Galliers and Huang 2012). In a textual analysis of 500 peer-reviewed articles regarding use of qualitative approaches in information science, Cibangu found that only 5.6 percent of authors mentioned qualitative methods in their abstract.

Cibangu (2013, 194) concluded that there should be "tighter and long-term investment" in qualitative methods and advocated "a clearer and less fragmentary use of qualitative research in the increasingly interdisciplinary research setting of information science." Suarez (2010, 75) developed an assessment framework to evaluate the worth of qualitative methods in helping library practitioners for evidence-based LIS practice and concluded that "results obtained from qualitative research projects can be applied as evidence to support library practice." This text endeavors to demystify qualitative methods and argues that they are worth pursuing to investigate a range of LIS problematics, as well as to help in constructing theory (Cibangu 2013, 213).

To start with some basic definitions, Corbin and Strauss (2014, 1), who are highly distinguished qualitative researchers, best known for grounded theory analysis, defined methodology as "a way of thinking about and studying social phenomena." They defined methods as the "techniques and procedures for gathering and analyzing data" (Corbin and Strauss 2014, 1). More specifically, this chapter is concerned with qualitative research, which is characterized as: "A form of research in which a researcher(s) or designated coresearcher(s) collects and interprets data, making the researcher as much a part of the research process as participants and the data they provide" (Corbin and Strauss 2014, 1). Qualitative analysis is comprised of "thought processes that go on when interpreting data and assigning concepts to stand for meaning" (Corbin and Strauss 2014, 57).

Denzin and Lincoln (2018, 10) make a distinction between research and inquiry, noting that "*qualitative research* is a situated activity that locates the observer in the world. Qualitative research consists of a set of interpretive, material practices that make the world visible. These practices transform the world. They turn the world into a series of representations, including fieldnotes, interviews, conversations, photographs, recordings, and memos to the self. At this level, qualitative research involves an interpretive naturalistic approach to the world. This means that qualitative researchers study things in their natural settings, attempting to make sense of or interpret phenomena in terms of the meanings people bring to them." Another definition of qualitative methods is that it is "a type of scientific research" which shares these characteristics with quantitative research as an investigation that:

- seeks answers to a question
- systematically uses a predefined set of procedures to answer the question
- collects evidence
- produces findings that were not determined in advance
- produces findings that are applicable beyond the immediate boundaries of the study. (Mack et al. 2005, 2)

Sometimes qualitative research is defined by what it is not, in comparison to quantitative methods (i.e., qualitative methods are not mathematical, or produce findings not derived from statistical procedures or quantification). Qualitative methods are not seen to be in direct opposition to quantitative methods in this textbook, as is explored in the section on mixed methods in chapter 2. Although these methods are viewed as fundamentally different, they are not fundamentally opposed. They can be used in combination or in conjunction. Some researchers, though, may see these methods as dichotomous. Qualitative methods differ from quantitative methods primarily in these dimensions: analytical objectives, types of questions posed, data collection instruments used, types of data produced, and degree of flexibility of research design (Mack et al. 2005, 2).

Chapter 1 points out that qualitative methods are inductive and more subjective than quantitative methods, which are deductive and more objective. Qualitative approaches believe that there can be multiple paths to truth; quantitative seeks the singular "Truth" of the positivistic paradigm. The inductive data analysis can be seen as a process, in which categories or themes are found in the data, which lead to knowledge claims and are used to develop theory. Qualitative research looks to develop hypotheses rather than test them. It features an ongoing process of elaboration and interpretation of concepts or categories. These new understandings are characterized by complexity, ambiguity, and rich depth. So, in contrast to quantitative methods, qualitative frameworks are employed to gain a deeper understanding of the context (e.g., culture, organization, events) through use of a relatively small number of participants, rather than a numerical description of a large sample of a population. They "seek to preserve form and content of human behavior and to analyze its qualities, rather than subject it to mathematical or formal transformations" (Lindlof and Taylor 2011, 45). Qualitative methods address these types of questions: (a) How do participants gain meaning from surroundings and events? (b) How do their meanings impact or influence their behavior? (c) What patterns emerge from multiple participants, or a combination of interviews and observation? (d) What do these patterns help to explain about the given context?

STRENGTHS OF A QUALITATIVE APPROACH

Miles, Huberman, and Saldaña (2020, 8) note that a major strength of qualitative data is precisely in its focus on "*naturally occurring, ordinary events in natural settings*, so that we have a strong handle on what 'real life' is like." Further, the data are "collected in close proximity to a specific situation," which they refer to as "*local groundedness*." The discovery of any given phenomena is explored within the local context. Another valuable aspect is that qualitative research allows for the exploration and understanding of "latent, underlying, or nonobvious issues" (Miles, Huberman, and Saldaña 2020, 8) within this local context that may not be easily found in quantitative approaches and that are more flexible, as methods can be changed and/or adapted as data collection proceeds. Additionally, qualitative data, when gathered and analyzed properly, also have the following strengths:

- Richness and holism, able to uncover complexity including "'thick descriptions' of the sort that Geertz advocated in his benchmark book: *The Interpretation of Cultures* (Geertz 1973, 3–20; Miles, Huberman, and Saldaña 2020, 8).

- Collection during "*a sustained period*" which goes "far beyond snap-shots of 'what?' or 'how many?' to just how and why things happen as they do—and even *assess causation* as it actually plays out in a par-ticular setting (Miles, Huberman, and Saldaña 2020, 8).
- Ability to determine the "*meanings* people place on the ,events, pro-cesses, and structures of their lives and for connecting those mean-ings to the *social world* around them" (Miles, Huberman, and Saldaña 2020, 8).

ROLE OF THE RESEARCHER

As highlighted in the Corbin and Strauss quote above, the role of the researcher is key as a fundamental part of the research instrument, present as an interpreter throughout the observations, interviews, or other data gath-ering. This role is in contrast to quantitative approaches, in which the researcher may be absent during an experiment, or treatment (e.g., adminis-tration of survey questionnaire) although present before and afterward. The qualitative researcher is thus the "human instrument" of data collection with the goal of understanding the participant's point of view, with the focus on discovery, rather than verification of a monolithic truth.

Concerns about subjectivity are seen as unwarranted in qualitative meth-ods in which the researchers' individual contribution through inductive rea-soning is seen as a resource to be valued, rather than as a source of bias (that would be unwelcome). Richards (2005, 25) suggested qualitative researchers have been recently advised to eschew the word "bias," "since it has been given very specific meanings and warnings in the context of qualita-tive sampling and error estimation." She argued though, that "the goal of most qualitative research is to learn from the data. But researchers don't have empty minds. Indeed, one of the special hazards and excitements of working with qualitative researchers is that they are likely to have strong val-ues and commitment to their topic. So good research design will always take into account what's known already, and will build into the design the ways this knowledge can and will be used and tested" (Richards 2005, 25–26). According to Mehra (2002), researchers must be aware of "biases, blind spots and cognitive limitations" and that this awareness is as important as their theoretical expertise.

Additionally, Mehra (2002) argued that the researcher makes many deci-sions along the way which greatly influence every part of a project: "A research-er's personal beliefs and values are reflected not only in the choice of methodology and interpretation of findings, but also in the choice of a research topic. In other words, what we believe in determines what we want to study." Several scholars note that true objectivity on the part of a researcher, includ-ing quantitative researchers, is unobtainable. Patton (1990, 169–83) sug-gested that it is more likely that one can obtain a state of "empathic neutrality," rather than objectivity. Richards imaginatively described self-aware scholars as those who are able to reflect on what "baggage" they bring, similar to the need to declare contents of luggage before boarding an international flight. "If you don't declare it, you will take in, surreptitiously, assumptions or expectations that will colour what you see and how you see it. Throughout the research, aim to maximize the usefulness, and ensure the testing of those ideas" (Richards 2005, 26).

During the course of a project, one's perspective as a researcher may shift as "a perceptible change occurs in your grasp of the social life under study" (Lindlof and Taylor 2019, 122). These shifting perspectives include the insider/participant (emic lens) and outsider/researcher (etic lens). The emic lens is usually sought in ethnographies and participant observations and privileges the viewpoint of the member of the culture or social group under study. The researcher seeks to walk in another's shoes and also discover what the meaning of the footwear is to that individual (Lindlof and Taylor 2019, 122). Therefore, "when we achieve an emic competency, we are able to describe the actors' world through the meanings they attribute to their own culture and communications" (Lindlof and Taylor 2019, 122). The etic lens, on the other hand, evaluates the view of the social scene through "the categories provided by our disciplinary knowledge and theory" (Lindlof and Taylor 2019, 123). Many times, qualitative data are coded and analyzed through use of a category scheme derived from and building on previous research (Connaway, Radford, and OCLC Research 2011; Radford 2006; Radford et al. 2020). These perspectives are not mutually exclusive and can be used in combination to yield a nuanced and a multidimensional view of the research context at hand. One valuable thing to consider is, what are your emic and etic perspectives? For example, for a scholar who also may be (or has been) a practicing librarian, what insider paradigms are held? How are the data that are collected interpreted within this paradigm? One way to minimize this effect might be to assemble a varied research group, with data coders who are not part of the insider group. For example, in a study of library jargon in live chat reference transcripts, coders with a master's degree in library science may not be able to recognize words as jargon that the lay person would (Connaway, Radford, and OCLC Research 2011). Alternatively, one may also want to include emic perspectives when studying aspects of complex issues such as inclusion, diversity, and social justice research. Does your emic perspective permit you to understand the perspective of the community you are studying? Should a varied research group be assembled that includes insiders as well as outsiders?

THE UNDERLYING ASSUMPTIONS OF NATURALISTIC WORK

Distinguishing qualitative research is as much about the perspective as it is about method. It is a way of thinking about and seeing social reality, which is why a discussion about underlying assumptions is central to this chapter.

As noted above, one important piece of the puzzle for qualitative research is that the natural setting is revered, rather than as within the experimental paradigm in which variables are manipulated to see the effects on subjects, or data are collected in surveys that generally strip away much of the context in pursuit of generalizable findings for a large population. Outliers usually are discarded in quantitative methods. In qualitative methods, the participants or respondents are queried about their interpretations of the meanings of settings and situations. So, the natural context is integral, and exceptions or outliers are thought to add valuable contributions to the richness of the description.

Chapter 2 explored basic domain questions including distinctions for the naturalistic work that have to do with epistemological (centered on the nature and origin of knowledge) and ontological (centered on the nature of being) foundations. The underlying ideology for qualitative approaches is that human behavior in any given context only can be explicated by the participants, with their highly subjective interpretations.

One of the traditions that underlie the naturalistic approach is social constructionism, which highlights "how humans actively use symbolic resources to *objectify, circulate,* and *interpret* the meaningfulness of their existence and their environments" (Lindlof and Taylor 2019, 63). Meanings thus become accepted (or not) by groups, and then adopted by formal institutions as "*preferences, techniques,* and *policies*" (Lindlof and Taylor 2019, 63). Subsequently, origins of meanings can become fixed for future generations. Currently, scholars using this perspective focus on how "*symbols, discourse,* and *media* operate in this process" (Lindlof and Taylor 2019, 63).

Another key component is the narrative voice of the respondent. According to Miles, Huberman, and Saldaña (2020, 324), qualitative data, including participant quotes, "represents and presents data vividly about the study's phenomenon of interest." The uniqueness of each participant's voice is captured in qualitative inquiry and provides the vividness and credibility that makes for compelling and interesting reading. This narrative voice is captured and revealed to readers in the liberal use of participant verbatim quotes in illustrating findings, which may be in the form of emergent categories or themes, as further discussed in chapter 12.

ETHICAL CONCERNS

Because of the nature of qualitative inquiry, the majority of the time researchers gather data through direct contact with respondents, as shall be discussed in the below section on data-gathering techniques, as well as in chapters 10, 11, and 12. Since this is the case, qualitative methods demand a deep sensitivity on the part of the researcher, and a heightened awareness of the complex nature of ethical concerns that surround naturalistic approaches. Ethics has to do with one's moral philosophy, an understanding of what action to take in a given situation, as well as a consideration of right versus wrong behavior.

The ethical treatment of research subjects is of utmost importance to individual institutions, such as universities or colleges, as well as LIS funding agencies. These entities also usually have policies on research with human subjects, and many require Human Subjects Certification. For examples, members of the Big Ten universities require all individuals involved in research with human subjects, including principal investigators, coinvestigators, and other study personnel, to complete Collaborative IRB Training Initiative (CITI) certification. Institutional review boards (IRBs) generally prescribe ethical actions or "procedural ethics" that include necessary or universal protections for participants. These include: "do no harm; avoid deception; get informed consent; ensure privacy and confidentiality" (Tracy 2013, 243).

A model of a comprehensive discussion of research ethics, including a detailed *Code of Ethics* (1999) is available from the American Sociological Association (ASA) website. This code includes six general principles centering on (a) professional competence; (b) integrity; (c) professional and scientific responsibility; (d) respect for people's rights, dignity, and diversity; (e) social responsibility; and (f) human rights ("Code of Ethics and Policies and Procedures of the ASA Committee on Professional Ethics" 1999, 2). It also includes a list of nineteen ethical standards, centering on the above areas of the general principles, with topics such as: delegation and supervision, conflicts of interest, public communication, informed consent, and plagiarism ("Code of Ethics and Policies and Procedures of the ASA Committee on Professional Ethics" 1999, 2–3). Additional highly recommended resources on ethics in qualitative methods have been written by Hammersley and Traianou (2012); Flynn and Goldsmith (2013); and Sieber and Tolich (2013). According to Bailey (2018), there are three major ethical areas of concern that are relevant to field research, depending on the research context: (a) informed consent, (b) deception, and (c) confidentiality. Each of these is discussed below.

INFORMED CONSENT

According to the *ASA Code of Ethics* (1999), informed consent is a "basic ethical tenant of all research involving human subjects, including sociological research." It is required when "data are collected from research participants through any form of communication, interaction, or intervention" or in cases when data concerning participants are being collected "in a private context where an individual can reasonably expect that no observation or reporting is taking place" ("Code of Ethics and Policies and Procedures of the ASA Committee on Professional Ethics" 1999, 12–13). So, if people have a reasonable expectation of being in a private space, one must obtain informed consent (such as in a private office or inside their home). If, on the other hand, data are being collected by observation in a public place (such as at a library service desk, or in a public study area), informed consent may not be needed. If, however, one is interviewing participants, even in a public place, consent must be gotten. A good rule of thumb is when recording equipment is being used, when individuals are being singled out for study via observation or any form of interviewing, when the expectation on a participant's part is for privacy, and whenever in doubt, ask for signed consent. Furthermore, for the *ASA Code of Ethics,* informed consent consists of the following information: "As part of obtaining informed consent, sociologists inform prospective research participants or their legal representatives of the nature of the research. They indicate to them that their participation or continued participation is voluntary; they inform them of significant factors that may be expected to influence their willingness to participate (e.g., possible risks and benefits of their participation); and they respond to questions from them. Also, if relevant, sociologists explain that refusal to participate or withdrawal from participation in the research involves no penalty, and explain any foreseeable consequences of declining or withdrawing, when necessary" ("Code of Ethics and Policies and Procedures of the ASA Committee on Professional Ethics" 1999, 12).

There should be two copies of the informed consent form, both signed by the participant and the researcher. One copy goes to each, and researchers keep their copy until the research project has concluded. Some granting agencies require forms to be kept in a secure place for up to three years. See text box 9.1 for a sample interview consent form.

Text Box 9.1: Sample Interview Consent Form

Consent to Take Part in A Research Study

TITLE OF STUDY: Reference in the Time of COVID-19: Transforming Essential User Services

Principal Investigator: Marie L. Radford, PhD

This consent form is part of an informed consent process for a research study, and it will provide information that will help you decide whether you want to take part in this study. It is your choice to take part or not. After all of your questions have been answered and you wish to take part in the research study, you will be asked to sign this consent form. You will be given a copy of the signed form to keep. Your alternative to taking part in the research is not to take part in it.

Who is conducting this research study, and what is it about?

You are being asked to take part in research being conducted by Marie Radford, PhD, chair and professor of the Department of Library and Information Science at the School of Communication & Information at Rutgers, The State University of New Jersey, and Laura Costello, MLIS, virtual reference librarian at Rutgers University Libraries. The purpose of this study is to understand how libraries adapted their user services as a result of the physical service closures and service reductions related to the COVID-19 global pandemic.

What will I be asked to do if I take part?

The interview will take about 60 minutes to complete. We anticipate twenty-five to thirty subjects will take part in the study. The interview will take place via video software (e.g., Skype, WebEx, Zoom) and will use audio and video recording to enable researchers to create a transcript of the interview for analysis. This recording will only be used within the research team and will be stored securely for the duration of the research and then deleted.

What are the risks and/or discomforts I might experience if I take part in the study?

The questions in this interview will focus on your institution's response to the COVID-19 pandemic and your experiences providing service to users through the service changes brought by the pandemic. We do not anticipate that this topic will cause risk or discomfort. Breach of confidentiality is a risk of harm, but a data security plan is in place to minimize such a risk. Also, some questions may make you feel uncomfortable. If that happens, you can skip those questions or withdraw from the study altogether. If you decide to quit the interview, your responses will NOT be saved.

Are there any benefits to me if I choose to take part in this study?

There are no direct benefits to you for taking part in this research. You will be contributing to knowledge about the library response to COVID-19, and your participation may help libraries adapt to service changes in the future.

Will I be paid to take part in this study?

You will receive a $30 gift card for your participation in this study, which will be delivered via email after your interview.

How will information about me be kept private or confidential?

All efforts will be made to keep your responses confidential, but total confidentiality cannot be guaranteed. Your name and institutional affiliation may be collected during the interview. The identifiable information will not be stored with your interview transcript. Instead, your responses will be assigned a subject number which will be stored separately from your identifiable information so others will not know which responses are yours. We will securely store the key code linking your responses to your identifiable information in a separate password-protected file, which will be destroyed after data analysis is complete and study findings are professionally presented or published.

No information that can identify you will appear in any professional presentation or publication.

What will happen to information I provide in the research after the study is over?

The information collected about you for this research will not be used by or distributed to investigators for other research.

What will happen if I do not want to take part or decide later not to stay in the study?

Your participation is voluntary. If you choose to take part now, you may change your mind and withdraw later. In addition, you can choose to skip interview questions that you are not comfortable answering or stop the interview at any time. You may also withdraw your consent for use of responses you provided during the interview, but you must do this in writing to the PI Marie Radford.

Who can I call if I have questions?

If you have questions about taking part in this study, you can contact the principal investigator:

Marie L. Radford, PhD
Chair and Professor, Department of Library and Information Science
Rutgers, the State University of New Jersey
4 Huntington St., New Brunswick, NJ 08901
Office: DeWitt Rm 206
848-932-8797 (o)
732-932-6919 (fax)
mradford@comminfo.rutgers.edu

If you have questions about your rights as a research subject, you can contact the IRB director at: (732) 235-2866 or the Rutgers Human Subjects Protection Program at (973) 972-1149 or email us at humansubjects@ored.rutgers.edu.

Please keep this consent form if you would like a copy of it for your files.

AGREEMENT TO PARTICIPATE

1. Subject consent:
I have read this entire consent form, or it has been read to me, and I believe that I understand what has been discussed. All of my questions about this form and this study have been answered. I agree to take part in this study.

Subject Name (printed): _____

Subject Signature: _____ Date: _____

2. Signature of Investigator/Individual Obtaining Consent:
To the best of my ability, I have explained and discussed all the important details about the study including all of the information contained in this consent form.

Investigator/Person Obtaining Consent (printed): _____

Signature: _____ Date: _____

DECEPTION

Deception in qualitative research is a critical concept and strictly is to be avoided with rare exceptions. It can be defined as being dishonest and/or misleading to participants in getting them to believe something that is not true, or not quite true. This can occur in a number of ways. "For example, deception results when people are not told that they are participating in a study, are misled about the purpose or details of the research, or are not aware of the correct identity or status of the researcher" (Bailey 2018, 23). In such cases, it is obvious that informed consent cannot be obtained, since the participant does not have full or accurate information. According to Bailey (2018, 23), there are debates about how much deception, if any, is acceptable. There are examples for this ongoing controversy, about deceptive practices in qualitative research. The most often cited one was conducted by Humphreys and published in an award-winning book in 1970. He conducted covert research in a men's restroom without revealing his identity or that he was conducting research, and deliberately changing his appearance for health interviews (Humphreys 1970, 20–21). There can be arguments for and against the use of deception, although the ASA guidelines state that deceptive techniques are not to be used. There are degrees of seriousness of deception, and the *Code for Ethics*, however, does describe some exceptions. "Sociologists do not use deceptive techniques unless they have determined that the following conditions have been met: (1) the research involves no more than minimal risk to research participants; (2) deception is justified by the study's prospective scientific, educational, or applied value; (3) equally effective alternative procedures that do not use deception are not feasible; and (4) they have obtained the approval of an authoritative body with expertise on the ethics of social science research such as an institutional review board" ("Code of Ethics and Policies and Procedures of the ASA Committee on Professional Ethics" 1999). Additionally, the *ASA Code of Ethics* stipulates that participants must be debriefed to explain any possible misconceptions at the end of the research project. Most research in LIS does not engage in deception, although sometimes textual information can be manipulated in the case of experimental research. One minimal form of deception using surrogates, rather than actual users, has been used in several unobtrusive and obtrusive studies in LIS, including the "secret shopper" variety and those using master's students to evaluate services (Crowe and Bradshaw 2016; Divelko 2000; Durrance 1989, 31–36; Hernon and McClure 1986, 37–41; Nilsen 2004).

The touchstone here is to abide by the researcher's IRB standards and to consult mentors and advisers if there is any doubt about the ethics of any deception, even that which is considered to be minimal.

CONFIDENTIALITY AND ANONYMITY

Confidentiality is one of the basic ethical principles of research with human subjects. It is defined as "the safeguarding of information obtained in confidence during the course of the research study" (Wallace 2010). Or as "an explicit or implied guarantee by a researcher to a respondent in social science research whereby the respondent is confident that any information provided to the researcher cannot be attributed back to that respondent" (Jamison n.d.).

Corbin and Strauss (2014) noted that: "Researchers should explain to participants that anything they say or do will be kept confidential; all identifying information will be removed from transcription and field notes; and if there are recordings, once the transcription is completed the recording will be erased or deleted." Generally, as detailed in the sample, above, there is an explicit statement of confidentiality in the consent form. Guarantee of confidentiality is essential since it allows the participant to speak freely without worry about being identified later when the research is reported or published. This is, of course, especially vital for controversial or personal topics, such as health concerns, or within-institution evaluations. A closely related concept is that of anonymity, which "is the protection of a research participant's or site's identity" (Wallace 2010). In cases of true anonymity, the researcher is unaware of the participant's identity. This unawareness of a participant's identity is impossible for face-to-face (FtF) data collection, as is the case with individual and focus group interviews, case studies, and observations, but possible for online data collection, such as some social media or chat conversations, in which the user has a masked identity or username (Taylor 1999). In focus group interviews conducted within an organization, such as a particular library or library system, neither anonymity or true confidentiality can be promised. Respondents can be asked to keep everything said confidential, but all should be instructed that this is not guaranteed. Trevisan and Reilly suggested that there should be a more nuanced approach to the privacy of participants. They advocated for allowing "the use of direct quotes when it is unlikely to prove harmful to the user but also sets out to provide the maximum level of anonymity possible for those who divulge sensitive information in these semi-public spaces" (Trevisan and Reilly 2014, 1131). Data collected from social media posts should be modified so that they cannot be traced back to an individual by a keyword search (Markham and Buchanan 2012). For more depth on the topic of ethics, refer to these highly recommended resources: *Essentials of Thinking Ethically in Qualitative Research* (Van den Hoonaard and Van den Hoonnaard 2013), *Making Data in Qualitative Research: Engagements, Ethics, and Entanglements* (Ellingson and Sotirin 2020), *and The SAGE Handbook of Qualitative Research Ethics* (Iphoofen and Tolich 2018).

DATA-GATHERING TECHNIQUES

There are numerous techniques in qualitative data collection. As mentioned in chapter 1, interviews and observations are among the most popular qualitative methods used in LIS research. Interviews include both individual and focus group variety, and these are covered in depth in chapter 11. Observations, ethnographic field notes, and diaries as sources of data are discussed in chapter 12. Denzin and Lincoln (2018, 9) said that "there are separate and detailed literatures on the many methods and approaches that fall under the category of qualitative research, such as case study, politics and ethics, participatory inquiry, interviewing, participant observation, visual methods, and interpretive analysis. They also added analysis of artifacts, documents, and records; autoethnography; applied ethnography; and textual analysis to the list of qualitative methods (Denzin and Lincoln 2018, 12). Written diaries and personal journals are one type of textual data that are considered in qualitative research, but others include books, reports, letters, transcripts of audio and video recordings, brochures, researcher's notes and memos, and online text such as website content, social media such as blogs and tweets, email, chats, and more. For example, Haberl and Wortman innovatively used two data-gathering techniques, interviews plus photo elicitation, to inform their development of a library spaces business plan at a large public library. To understand how sixteen people used library spaces at five different library branches, interviewees were asked to take photos to be used during individual interviews (Haberl and Wortman 2012). Advances in technology are creating opportunities for new modes of data collection. For example, in her dissertation, Barriage used a mobile photography device (PixStori) for children ages five to seven, that enabled them to take pictures and add a voice recording in her study of the ways they experienced information relating to their individual areas of strong interest. She followed up with photo-elicitation conversations that discovered how children think and feel about information (Barriage 2018).

Barney Glaser (2011), one of the founders of the grounded theory approach, has famously said: "All is data." In referring to this quote, Charmaz commented: "Yes, everything you learn in the research setting(s) or about your research topic can serve as data. However, data vary in quality, relevance for your emerging interests, and usefulness for interpretation. Researchers also vary in their ability to discern useful data and in their skill and thoroughness in recording them" (Charmaz 2014, 29). Because qualitative questions are usually multifaceted ones, it is necessary to collect rich and complex data, and to have a flexible research design, that allows for collection of additional data, as necessary. An interview might lead to a site visit (observation), and once at the site the respondent might share textual data such as reports or emails. For example, in the Seeking Synchronicity grant project (Connaway, Radford, and OCLC Research 2011), three anticipated focus group interviews quickly expanded, when the results of the first group with teenagers proved to be surprising and much different than those with older participants, leading to two additional focus group interviews with this demographic (Radford and Connaway 2007). Richards (2015, 36) defines qualitative data as "the 'stuff' you work with, the records of what you are studying. The research identifies events or accounts as data by selecting and using them as evidence in analysis." So data can be your individual interview or focus group interview transcript, or transcripts of live chat reference sessions, or ethnographic field notes and memos, One characteristic of qualitative data is that they often are voluminous and "messy." According to Richards (2015, 35), "Making qualitative data is ridiculously easy. The challenge is not so much making data but rather making useful, valuable data, relevant to the question being asked, and reflecting usefully on the process of research." Qualitative data tend to expand rapidly: "The records of research events grow in unpredictable ways, as new sources of data present themselves" (Richards 2015, 35). It is true that "the time commitment for analysis of qualitative data is, in reality, much greater than that for many quantitative techniques" (Radford 2011, xii). For the novice researcher, it might be hard to imagine what transcripts of 15- to 20-hour-long interviews, or three, 2-hour focus group interviews with a dozen participants each might look like. Once one is deep into a project with a corpus like these of a large amount (piles?) of qualitative data to analyze, it soon can hit home that the data are not "neat" or easily organized for analysis, as is generally the case for quantitative data. "Qualitative data records can be highly varied in origin and style, uneven in detail and unalike in source and reliability. . . . A researcher seeking to learn from the data, rather than test a theory already arrived at, will usually be helped by having more than one way of looking at what is being studied" (Richards 2015, 35). In the case of having multiple ways or methods for investigation, as in when mixed methods and triangulation are employed, it is not likely that the data will be uniform. The benefits, however, of taking a qualitative or mixed-method approach to inquiry, are deserving of the extra effort in time for data collection and analysis, because of the highly nuanced and heuristically rich results.

RESEARCH DESIGN

Keeping in mind the research question(s), the goal of the design process is to consider this crucial question: "What do I need to know in order to answer *this* question" (Richards 2015, 41)? There is no denying that purely quantitative methods are valuable tools, but often it is difficult to make sense of statistical or numerical results. "For example, how *specifically* can services be improved when people have consistently rated library service as 'Excellent' when asked in quantitative surveys? What does this 'Excellent' rating mean? Why has it been chosen by the respondent? What factors were most important in selecting this 'Excellent' rating" (Radford 2011, xi)? Qualitative methods, or a mixture of qualitative and quantitative methods woven together skillfully, can get at these crucial shades of meanings from participants' point of view.

Research design is an art, rather than a science. According to Maxwell (2013, 4), there are five components in the design process that include the following:

- **Establishing goals:** Why is this study being undertaken, and why is it worthwhile?
- **Developing the conceptual framework:** What is already known? What previous research and theory can inform this study?
- **Articulating research questions:** What specifically will the study help to understand?
- **Selecting methods:** What will be done to answer the research questions?
- **Testing validity:** How might results be wrong?

The first three of Maxwell's steps are addressed in this chapter. One contribution of Maxwell's (2013, 4) approach that is different from other views of research design is that his model is not driven by creation of research questions as the initial step, but rather to see the above five components as working together, with research questions being central, and both affected by and informed by all of the others. Chapter 10 addresses the selection of qualitative methods and establishing validity, and chapter 2 discusses mixed-method designs.

Establishing Goals

Maxwell (2013) suggested that there are three types of goals for qualitative research: personal, practical, and intellectual. Marshall and Rossman (2016) articulate a different trio of purposes for qualitative research, including: exploratory (investigating phenomena that are not well understood); explanatory (explaining patterns related to the phenomena and identifying relationships among these); and descriptive (documenting and describing the phenomena). The main thing to consider, even at the start of a research project, is: what is the reason that the project is being undertaken? It is critical to consider the end product from the very beginning: what does the researcher envision as the desired outcome? Research projects do not exist in a vacuum. They usually are part of a research agenda, an ongoing series of smaller investigations that are generally focused on a larger goal (or broader problematic) and may wind up constituting a brief period of time, or may evolve over time to become the life's work of the researcher. Chapter 1 introduces some of the reasons (e.g., achieving tenure or promotion, completing a master's or PhD thesis, satisfying unbridled curiosity, answering burning questions) that are bound up in decisions to engage in research and in which problematics present themselves as worthy subjects. Taking on a project that will result in a publication or two is driven by a different goal than completing a dissertation for a PhD. Beginning researchers frequently first engage in research that is directed by someone else (e.g., a professor with grant money to hire student workers, a colleague who invites you into a work-related research project, a dissertation adviser) and then move to develop their own work. It is useful to begin working under a mentor who can teach you practical research skills and guide decision making. Those who become excited about the thrill of discovery and find research enjoyable and challenging soon find that they want to embark on their own research to pursue their own goals.

Whatever the project to be undertaken, begin with the end in mind. Setting clear goals from the onset will help keep it on track and lead to purposeful decisions along the way.

DEVELOPING THE CONCEPTUAL FRAMEWORK

Another major part of the research design is the conceptual framework. "Conceptual frameworks are simply the current and evolving version of the researcher's 'map' of the qualitative territory being investigated" (Miles, Huberman, and Saldaña 2020, 15). The conceptual framework describes "either graphically and/or in narrative form, the main things to be studied—for example, the key factors, variables, phenomena, concepts, participants—and the presumed interrelationships among them—as a *network*" (Miles, Huberman, and Saldaña 2020, 15). Conceptual frameworks are critically important as they articulate the "argument about why the topic one wishes to study matters, and why the means proposed to study it are appropriate and rigorous" (Ravitch and Riggan 2012, 7). According to Ravitch and Riggan (2012, 10–13), there are three components to the conceptual framework: personal interests (the researcher's motivation and epistemological/philosophical frame); topical research (existing scholarship on the subject); and theoretical framework. The idea of the conceptual framework is to identify and stipulate the perspective of the researcher as well as the key components of the study and their relationships—specifically detailing what is to be included (as well as what will not be included) (Marshall and Rossman 2016). It also can be thought of as partially being a boundary-setting exercise. Initially it may be difficult to have a concrete idea of the interworkings of the interrelationships, so the conceptual framework may be revised several times throughout the research process. Miles, Huberman, and Saldaña (2020,15) make a distinction between theoretical frameworks and conceptual frameworks as follows: "a theoretical framework utilizes theory/theories and their constituent elements as the presumed 'working model' that drives the investigation and analysis of a social phenomenon. But a conceptual framework is a more inductively derived and evolutionary model that can certainly include aspects of the theoretical, but primarily incorporates case- or site-specific variables, concepts, contexts, participants and so on. In other words, a conceptual framework grounds itself in the local elements of a particular, unique study: a theoretical framework abstracts a study's ideas based on the literature." The deep reading involved in developing the literature review and selecting theoretical frames, as chapters 2 and 3 describe, are valuable in informing the structure and are woven within the main features of the conceptual framework.

DEVELOPING RESEARCH QUESTIONS

In contrast to quantitative methods that generally are hypothesis-driven, qualitative research most often addresses research questions or sensitizing concepts in the case of grounded theory. "This is because most qualitative studies are concerned with the interpretation and critical analysis of meanings rather than the causal explanation of variables. In addition, qualitative researchers are known to alter the destinations of their studies while en route; this is much more difficult to do with hypotheses" (Lindlof and Taylor 2019, 167). The research questions are usually derived from the rigorous literature review and examination of possible theoretical frameworks, or arise from a more grounded-theory approach (see chapter 10 for more on grounded theory). The classic umbrella question of interest for qualitative researchers, especially ethnographers, is often framed as: "What is going on here?" (Lindlof and Taylor 2019, 130). Research questions are defined as "open-ended questions (or statements) that articulate the empirical expectations of the study" (Lindlof and Taylor 2019, 167). Research questions can be difficult to construct; many beginning researchers will revise theses many times in consultation with advisers or mentors, so some advice is to not get too attached to initial research questions. Initially, at the very beginning of a project, the goal is not to formulate the "right question" as in a hypothesis statement, but rather to start with one to three open questions, suggested by the literature or theoretical framework, that are initial statements of what one is interested in finding out about (Tracy 2013). These can be refined, restated, discarded, or added to later.

Miles, Huberman, and Saldaña (2020, 22) explained the purpose of research questions as follows: "They tell me what I want to know most or first; my collection of data will be more focused. I am also beginning to make some implicit sampling decisions. I will look only at *some* participants in *some* contexts dealing with *some* issues. The questions also begin to point me toward data-gathering methods—observations, interviews, and document collection. Finally, the research questions begin to operationalize the conceptual framework and make the initial theoretical assumptions even more explicit."

To help readers to understand a more concrete idea of research questions, below are some examples from one grant project and several published qualitative studies in the LIS context.

Research Questions for Focus Group and Individual Interviews in the Public Library Context

Williamson, Bannister, and Sullivan (2010) sought to identify the information needs of retired baby boomers (BB) and how the Australian public library (PL) system can respond to these information needs. Data collection and analysis involved qualitative coding of transcriptions from interviews with focus group interviews (seven in total, with eight to ten baby boomers in each group), and individual interviews with seventeen community gatekeepers, including librarians and community organizers.

Research questions:

1. What are the similarities and differences between BBs and the generations before and after that make BBs the 'crossover' generation an appropriate label?
2. What will be the impact of the retirement of the BBs on the PL, particularly on (a) use of resources; (b) BBs' social needs; and (c) volunteering? (Williamson, Bannister, and Sullivan 2010, 180)

Research Questions for Mixed-Methods Study with Focus Group and Individual Interviews in the Academic Library Context

Nitecki and Abels (2013) addressed a research gap within the assessment literature by focusing on measuring how clients of an academic library value its services, rather than the role the library assumes (e.g., archive). The authors utilized a framework for inquiry, referred to as the "five-whys" to determine root factors, referred to as causes, which contribute to the institutional perception of the value a library provides its community, referred to as effects. Mixed-methods analysis was performed on transcripts of in-person interviews with ten faculty members and focus group interviews of six library advisory members.

Research questions:

1. What effects of the library do faculty most value?
2. What are perceived causes of these valued effects?
3. What variations among the causes faculty identify for valued effects emerge from use of the five-whys inquiry? (Nitecki and Abels 2013, 320)

Research Questions for Focus Group and Individual Interviews in a High School Context

An exploratory study conducted by Singh, Radford, Huang, and Furrer (2017) investigated the effects of emerging phone apps (such as Instagram, Twitter, Facebook, and Snapchat) on cyberbullying behaviors in high school settings. Data were collected from three focus group interviews and eleven individual interviews. Qualitative data analysis was conducted that applied and built on an existing coding scheme for cyberbullying.

Research questions:

1. What effect does the increasing prevalence of image and video content, compared to text, in messaging apps have on cyberbullying among high school students?

2. What effect does the perceived ephemerality of messages have on cyberbullying among high school students?
3. What effect do other features of emerging mobile apps (e.g., location-based interactions, anonymity) have on cyberbullying among high school students? (Singh, Radford, Huang, and Furrer 2017)

Research Questions for a Mixed-Methods Grant Project Using Transcript Analysis, Individual Interviews, and Design Sessions in the Consortial Live Chat Virtual Reference Context

Cyber Synergy: Seeking Sustainability through Collaboration between Virtual Reference and Social Q&A Sites (Radford, Connaway, and Shah 2011), a grant project funded by IMLS, Rutgers, and OCLC, explored maintaining quality and long-term viability of virtual reference services (VRS) by investigating what could be learned through social question-answering (SQA) services. There were three data collection and analysis phases: (1) a longitudinal analysis of 500 VRS transcripts and 1,000 SQA transcripts, (2) qualitative coding of in-depth interviews with ~150 information professionals and key users of SQA and VRS, and (3) qualitative coding of three design sessions with seventeen information professionals, policy makers, and systems experts to gather their knowledge and opinions as well as to explore options for developing new hybrid SQA and VRS systems.

Research questions:

1. What is the current state of VRS quality compared to longitudinal data and to Q&A Sites?
2. How can VRS become more collaborative, within and between libraries, and tap more effectively into librarians' subject expertise?
3. Can VRS be more sustainable through collaboration with SQA services?
4. How can we design systems and services within and between VRS and SQA for better quality and sustainability? (Radford, Connaway, and Shah 2011)

Research Questions for a Mixed-Methods Study Using a Questionnaire and Individual Interviews Investigating Chat Virtual Reference in the Time of COVID-19

Radford, Costello, and Montague (2020, 2021) explored the impact of the COVID-19 pandemic on academic live chat and other virtual reference services (VRS)through twenty-eight semistructured individual interviews and two longitudinal questionnaires, one focused on the early days of the pandemic (March–August, 2020) and the other focused on the fall 2020 semester (September to December, 2020). The 300 questionnaires were completed by academic librarians across the United States who directed and/or participated in live chat services during the pandemic. The research questions were developed following a review of LIS crisis communication scholarship and took a theoretical stance from Goffman (1967).

Research questions:

1. What has been the impact on academic live chat reference services due to the COVID-19 pandemic?
   1a. What plans/policies did libraries have in place for crisis planning for reference services, including virtual services? Were these adequate?
   1b. What changes have libraries put in place regarding virtual reference services to respond to the pandemic?
2. How have questions to live chat reference services changed during the pandemic?
3. What changes have taken place, if any, during the pandemic in the experience of live chat reference encounters, especially relating to relational aspects from the viewpoint of librarians and service users?

All of the above examples are included to illustrate viable research questions within a variety of contexts. They generally are open questions (as opposed to closed or yes/no questions) and focus specifically in the area of the research topic and goals. As noted above, development of research questions is an iterative process, and questions may evolve during the proposal and literature review. In fact, sometimes one or more research questions can be developed post hoc, in the midst of data analysis (Radford et al. 2017).

Once you have your research questions developed, the next step is to figure out which method of data collection will help you to address these questions. Chapters 10, 11, and 12 provide more information about the panoply of qualitative methods that are available.

RESEARCH DESIGN IN ONLINE ENVIRONMENTS

Library presence in online environments are proliferating, especially in the wake of the COVID-19 pandemic, which requires additional considerations with regard to research design for institutions wishing to track digital service use and assess its worth. The impact of COVID-19 had a sudden and extensive impact on service delivery; in mid-March 2020, most universities had to rapidly move classes online, and physical libraries across America quickly switched to online-only delivery of essential services including instruction and reference (Hinchliffe and Wolff-Eisenberg 2020). VRS use surged (Radford, Costello, and Montague 2021). Social media presence in libraries also has seen extraordinary growth in recent years. Weller (2015) provided an overview of critical challenges in the area of social media research and ways to address these. In addition, the availability of digital texts has presented qualitative researchers with a vast data store to tap into, such as collections of websites and social media archives (e.g., Twitter feeds, blog postings, and online forums). Lomborg (2012) detailed methodological, ethical, and technical challenges, strengths, as well as limitations, for research using social media archives. Research is emerging that uses online data sources to examine issues such as social media site availability in academic libraries (Collins and Quan-Haase 2014; De Jager-Loftus and Moore 2013; Harrison et al. 2017) and public libraries (Forcier, Rathi, and Given 2013; Hofschire and Wanucha 2014) through a variety of mixed methods, as explored in the next section.

New Modes for Online Data Collection

As discussed in chapter 10, technological innovation has enabled qualitative data to be collected online, including participation in individual and focus group interviews and analysis of social media data, all of which requires additional provisos for ensuring privacy and informed consent (Fiesler and Proferes 2018; Kinder-Kurlanda and Zimmer n.d.; Kitzie 2019). Web-based tools have seen a rapid increase in use in LIS research in recent years, including applications such as programs, sites, and open source initiatives (Hall et al. 2019; Saha 2019). During the COVID-19 pandemic, face-to-face data collection for interviews became impossible. As the United States went into lockdown, researchers wanting visual contact that was precluded with phone calls turned to video conferencing software such as Zoom, Web-Ex, Skype, Microsoft Teams, and other similar products. One benefit of using these products was that they frequently would enable a full recording to be captured easily. These systems also had their limitations, of course, one being difficulty with video or audio feeds, and the need for greater wi-fi bandwidth ("Johnson: What's That Again?" 2020). Additionally, there were privacy concerns and technological difficulties.

Today there are more options for qualitative data collection than ever before, driven by technology and the fluidity of emergent sites such as social media platforms (e.g., see text box 9.2). As people's behaviors and practices change, researchers continually are devising and trying out innovative and exciting modes for online data collection.

Text Box 9.2: Investigating Young People's Information Interactions on Health Topics in Social Media

Leanne Bowler

How might young people be using interactive, participatory social media services to search for, locate, and use health information? We explored this question by looking at *Yahoo! Answers*, a popular social question and answer (Social Q&A) site that provides open-source information for the online community (Bowler et al. 2012, 2013; Oh et al. 2013). In *Yahoo! Answers*, both the questions and the answers can be from an anonymous source—a situation that offers benefits *and* risks to those who seek information privately on a sensitive topic. We know that teens who suffer from eating disorders are reluctant to speak directly to a medical professional about the extent of their symptoms, or to seek diagnosis or treatment (Katzman et al. 2010), and *Yahoo! Answers*, might be one place they go to find information.

Social media content can be freely available on the web, and often in vast quantities. A considerable effort is needed to process the data before it is usable for data analysis. In our study, we used *Yahoo! Answers Application Programming Interface* (API), to gather questions on eating disorders that had been posted to *Yahoo! Answers* between December 2005 and April 2011. This resulted in a dataset of 3,111 questions. This dataset was reduced to 2,230 questions when we removed questions where the asker self-identified as an adult, questions that had no answers, and duplicate questions. As data analysis proceeded, we created a set of categories to help narrow the data field further.

Some words of caution with regard to using anonymous content from social media are needed here, even if that content is publicly available. First of all, there is no guarantee that the people who generate content in social media are who they say they are. That is why in our study into teen use of *Yahoo! Answers*, we chose a topic that interests teens and then triangulated the data from *Yahoo! Answers* with face-to-face interviews with teens.

Secondly, the identity of users of social media services can sometimes be discerned quite easily. When this happens, I feel the data shouldn't be referenced or quoted, even if identifiers have been removed, since your audience can easily locate the data themselves online.

Researchers may see content in social media that immediately threatens the well-being of someone. Before embarking on a study using user data from social media, researchers should, with the help of their institution's ethics committee or institutional review board, work out the boundaries and procedures for reporting these situations. Often the social media service itself provides guidelines.

User-generated content on the web presents a valuable opportunity to explore young peoples' online information interactions, particularly on sensitive topics. But care should always be taken. Behind the data are real people, some of whom may be unaware of how their online interactions can be viewed and used by others.

Research about teens and their use of social media, particularly in their search for health information, is more relevant than ever. In a recent study that I conducted with teens about their interactions with COVID-19 information, participants indicated that social media has been an information source for them during the pandemic (the results will be submitted for publication). Although the data source for this more recent study was interviews, not user-generated content, the findings indicate that further research in social media and health information is needed.

References

Bowler, Leanne, Eleanor Mattern, Wei Jeng, Jung Sun Oh, and Daqing He. 2013. "'I Know What You Are Going through': Answers to Informational Questions about Eating Disorders in Yahoo! Answers: A Qualitative Study." *Proceedings of the American Society for Information Science and Technology* 50(1): 1–9. https://doi.org/10.1002/meet.14505001057.

Bowler, Leanne, Jung Sun Oh, Daqing He, Eleanor Mattern, and Wei Jeng. 2012. "Eating Disorder Questions in Yahoo! Answers: Information, Conversation, or Reflection?" *Proceedings of the American Society for Information Science and Technology* 49(1): 1–11. https://doi.org/10.1002/meet.14504901052.

Katzman, Deborah K., Nuray O. Kanbur, and Cathleen M. Steinegger. 2010. "Medical Screening and Management of Eating Disorders in Adolescents." In *The Oxford Handbook of Eating Disorders*, edited by W. Stewart Agras, 267–91. New York: Oxford University Press.

Oh, Jung Sun, Daqing He, Wei Jeng, Eleanor Mattern, and Leanne Bowler. 2013. "Linguistic Characteristics of Eating Disorder Questions on Yahoo! Answers—Content, Style, and

Emotion." *Proceedings of the American Society for Information Science and Technology* 50(1): 1–10. https://doi.org/10.1002/meet.14505001068.

For further reading, see these other examples of Social Q&A research on sensitive health topics:

Bae, Beom Jun, and Yong Jeong Yi. 2017. "What Answers Do Questioners Want on Social Q&A? User Preferences of Answers about STDs." *Internet Research* 27(5): 1104–21. https://doi.org/10.1108/IntR-08-2016-0245.

Pater, Jessica A., Lauren E. Reining, Andrew D. Miller, Tammy Toscos, and Elizabeth D. Mynatt. 2019. "'Notjustgirls': Exploring Male-Related Eating Disordered Content across Social Media Platforms." In *Proceedings of the 2019 CHI Conference on Human Factors in Computing Systems*, 1–13. CHI '19. New York: Association for Computing Machinery. https://doi.org/10.1145/3290605.3300881.

Yi, Yong Jeong. 2018. "Sexual Health Information-Seeking Behavior on a Social Media Site: Predictors of Best Answer Selection." *Online Information Review* 42(6): 880–97. https://doi.org/10.1108/OIR-06-2017-0204.

SUMMARY

This chapter asserts that qualitative approaches are valuable in investigating a range of LIS problematics, as well as helpful in constructing theory. Qualitative methods are inductive and more subjective than quantitative methods and can be used successfully in conjunction with them. Qualitative methods address these types of questions: (a) How do participants gain meaning from surroundings and events? (b) How do their meanings impact or influence their behavior? (c) What patterns emerge from multiple participants, or combination of interviews and observation? (d) What do these patterns help to explain about the given context?

Qualitative research involves an interpretive, naturalistic approach to the world that recognizes both the insider/participant (emic lens) and the outsider/researcher (etic lens). These perspectives are not mutually exclusive and can be used in combination to yield a nuanced and a multidimensional view of the research context at hand. Additionally, qualitative researchers study phenomena in their natural settings, adopting an underlying ideology that human behavior in any given context only can be explicated by the participants, with their highly subjective interpretations. Qualitative methods demand a deep sensitivity on the part of the researcher, and a heightened awareness of the complex nature of ethical concerns that surround naturalistic approaches. This chapter also provides an overview of three major ethical areas of concern that are relevant to field research, depending on the research context: informed consent, deception, and confidentiality.

There are numerous techniques in qualitative data collection, and new methods are seen to be emerging. As mentioned in chapter 1, interviews and observations are among the most popular qualitative methods used in LIS research. Other techniques include case study, diaries, visual methods, interpretive analysis, autoethnography, applied ethnography, textual analysis, and analysis of artifacts. Because qualitative questions usually are multifaceted ones, it is necessary to collect rich and complex data and to have a flexible research design that allows for collection of additional data, as necessary.

The goals or purposes for qualitative research include exploratory, explanatory, and descriptive, most often addressing research questions as opposed to quantitative hypotheses. The research questions usually are derived from the rigorous literature review and examination of possible theoretical frameworks or arise from a more grounded-theory approach.

Research design takes into account the research questions, conceptual/ theoretical frameworks, methods, participant groups, and ethical concerns. One way to test the design is to conduct a pilot study. Additional information about qualitative methods is found in the chapters that follow.

REFERENCES

Bailey, Carol R. 2018. *A Guide to Qualitative Field Research*. 3rd ed. Thousand Oaks, CA: Sage.

Barriage, Sarah Corinne. 2018. "Examining the Red Thread of Information in Young Children's Interests: A Child-Centered Approach to Understanding Information Practices." Rutgers University—School of Graduate Studies. https://doi.org/10.7282/T3MP56QC.

Charmaz, Kathy. 2014. *Constructing Grounded Theory*. 2nd ed. Thousand Oaks, CA: Sage.

Cibangu, Sylvain K. 2013. "A Memo of Qualitative Research for Information Science: Toward Theory Construction." *Journal of Documentation* 69(2): 194–213. https://doi.org/10.1108/00220411311300048.

"Code of Ethics and Policies and Procedures of the ASA Committee on Professional Ethics." 1999. Washington, DC: American Sociological Association. https://www.asanet.org/sites/default/files/savvy/images/asa/docs/pdf/Codeof Ethics.pdf.

Collins, Gary, and Anabel Quan-Haase. 2014. "Are Social Media Ubiquitous in Academic Libraries? A Longitudinal Study of Adoption and Usage Patterns." *Journal of Web Librarianship* 8(1): 48–68. https://doi.org/10.1080/19322909 .2014.873663.

Connaway, Lynn Silipigni, Marie L Radford, and OCLC Research. 2011. *Seeking Synchronicity: Revelations and Recommendations for Virtual Reference*. Dublin, OH: OCLC Research.

Corbin, Juliet, and Anselm Strauss. 2014. *Basics of Qualitative Research: Techniques and Procedures for Developing Grounded Theory*. 4th ed. Thousand Oaks, CA: Sage.

Crowe, Kathryn, and Agnes Kathy Bradshaw. 2016. "Taking a Page from Retail: Secret Shopping for Academic Libraries." *Evidence Based Library and Information Practice* 11(1): 40–56. https://doi.org/10.18438/B85S6H.

De Jager-Loftus, Danielle P., and Abby Moore. 2013. "#gathercreateshare: How Research Libraries Use Pinterest." *Internet Reference Services Quarterly* 18(3–4): 265–79. https://doi.org/10.1080/10875301.2013.840714.

Denzin, Norman K., and Yvonna S. Lincoln. 2018. *The Sage Handbook of Qualitative Research*. 5th ed. Los Angeles, CA: Sage.

Divelko, Juris. 2000. *Unobtrusive Evaluation of Reference Service and Individual Responsibility: The Canadian Experience*. Westport, CT: Ablex.

Durrance, Joan C. 1989. "Reference Success: Does the 55 Percent Rule Tell the Whole Story?" *Library Journal* 114(7): 31–36.

Ellingson, Laura L., and Patty Sotirin. 2020. *Making Data in Qualitative Research: Engagements, Ethics, and Entanglements*. Abingdon, UK: Routledge.

Fiesler, Casey, and Nicholas Proferes. 2018. "'Participant' Perceptions of Twitter Research Ethics." *Social Media + Society* 4(1): 2056305118763366. https://doi.org/10.1177/2056305118763366.

Flynn, Leisa R., and Ronald E. Goldsmith. 2013. *Case Studies for Ethics in Academic Research in the Social Sciences*. Thousand Oaks, CA: Sage.

Forcier, Eric, Dinesh Rathi, and Lisa M. Given. 2013. "Knowledge Management and Social Media: A Case Study of Two Public Libraries in Canada." *Journal of Information & Knowledge Management* 12(4): 1350039. https://doi.org/10.1142/S0219649213500391.

Galliers, Robert D, and Jimmy C Huang. 2012. "The Teaching of Qualitative Research Methods in Information Systems: An Explorative Study Utilizing Learning Theory." *European Journal of Information Systems* 21(2): 119–34. https://doi.org/10.1057/ejis.2011.44.

Geertz, Clifford. 1973. "Thick Description: Toward an Interpretive Theory of Culture." In *The Interpretation of Cultures*, edited by Clifford Geertz, 3–20. New York: Basic Books.

Glaser, Barney G. 2011. *The Grounded Theory Perspective: Conceptualization Contrasted with Description*. Mill Valley, CA: Sociology Press.

Goffman, Erving. 1967. *Interaction Ritual: Essays on Face-to-Face Interaction*. Oxford, England: Aldine.

Haberl, Valerie, and Beth Wortman. 2012. "Getting the Picture: Interviews and Photo Elicitation at Edmonton Public Library." *LIBRES: Library and Information Science Research Electronic Journal* 22(2): 1–20.

Hall, Nathan, Zack Lischer-Katz, Matt Cook, Juliet Hardesty, Jennifer Johnson, Robert McDonald, and Tara Carlisle. 2019. "Challenges and Strategies for Educational Virtual Reality: Results of an Expert-Led Forum on 3D/VR Technologies across Academic Institutions," December. https://doi.org/10.6017/ital.v38i4.11075.

Hammersley, Martyn, and Anna Traianou. 2012. *Ethics in Qualitative Research*. Thousand Oaks, CA: Sage.

Harrison, Amanda, Rene Burress, Sarah Velasquez, and Lynnette Schreiner. 2017. "Social Media Use in Academic Libraries: A Phenomenological Study." *The Journal of Academic Librarianship* 43(3): 248–56. https://doi.org/10.1016/j.acalib.2017.02.014.

Hernon, Peter, and Charles R. McClure. 1986. "Unobtrusive Reference Testing: The 55 Percent Rule." *Library Journal* 111(7): 37–41.

Hinchliffe, Lisa Janicke, and Christine Wolff-Eisenberg. 2020. "First This, Now That: A Look at 10-Day Trends in Academic Library Response to COVID19." *Ithaka S+R* (blog). March 24. https://sr.ithaka.org/blog/first-this-now-that-a-look-at-10-day-trends-in-academic-library-response-to-covid19.

Hofschire, Linda, and Meghan Wanucha. 2014. "Public Library Websites and Social Media." *Computers in Libraries* 34(8): 4–9.

Humphreys, Laud. 1970. *Tearoom Trade: Impersonal Sex in Public Places*. New York: Aldine de Gruyter.

Iphoofen, Ron, and Martin B. Tolich. 2018. *SAGE Handbook of Qualitative Research Ethics*. Thousand Oaks, CA: Sage. https://www.textbooks.com/SAGE-Handbook-of-Qualitative-Research-Ethics-18-Edition/9781473970977/Ron-Iphofen.php.

Jamison, Wes. n.d. "Confidentiality in Social Science Research." WPI Projects Program. http://www.wpi.edu/Academics/Projects/confidentiality.html.

"Johnson: What's That Again?" 2020. *The Economist*.

Kinder-Kurlanda, Katharina, and Michael Zimmer. n.d. *Internet Research Ethics for the Social Age: New Challenges, Cases, and Contexts*. New York: Peter Lang.

Kitzie, Vanessa. 2019. "'That Looks Like Me or Something i Can Do': Affordances and Constraints in the Online Identity Work of US LGBTQ+ Millennials." *Journal of the Association for Information Science and Technology* 70(12): 1340–51. https://doi.org/10.1002/asi.24217.

Lindlof, Thomas R., and Bryan C. Taylor. 2011. *Qualitative Communication Research Methods*. 3rd ed. Thousand Oaks, CA: Sage.

Lindlof, Thomas R., and Bryan C. Taylor. 2019. *Qualitative Communication Research Methods*. 4th ed. Los Angeles: Sage.

Lomborg, Stine. 2012. "Researching Communicative Practice: Web Archiving in Qualitative Social Media Research." *Journal of Technology in Human Services* 30(3–4): 219–31. https://doi.org/10.1080/15228835.2012.744719.

Mack, Natasha, Cynthia Woodsong, Kathleen M. MacQueen, Greg Guest, and Emily Namey. 2005. *Qualitative Research Methods: A Data Collector's Field Guide*. Research Triangle Park, NC: Family Health International. https://www.fhi360.org/sites/default/files/media/documents/Qualitative%20Research%20Methods%20-%20A%20Data%20Collector's%20Field%20Guide.pdf.

Markham, Annette, and Elizabeth Buchanan. 2012. "Recommendations from the AoIR Ethics Working Committee (Version 2.0)." Association of Internet Researchers. http://www.aoir.org/reports/ethics.pdf.

Marshall, Catherine, and Gretchen B. Rossman. 2016. *Designing Qualitative Research*. 6th ed. Thousand Oaks, CA: Sage.

Maxwell, Joseph A. 2013. *Qualitative Research Design: An Interactive Approach*. Thousand Oaks, CA: Sage.

Mehra, Beloo. 2002. "Bias in Qualitative Research: Voices from an Online Classroom." *The Qualitative Report* 7(1): 1–19.

Miles, Matthew B., A. Michael Huberman, and Johnny Saldaña. 2020. *Qualitative Data Analysis: A Methods Sourcebook*. 4th ed. Thousand Oaks, CA: Sage. https://www.vitalsource.com/products/qualitative-data-analysis-matthew-b-miles-v9781506353081.

Nilsen, Kirsti. 2004. "The Library Visit Study: User Experiences at the Virtual Reference Desk." *Information Research* 9(2). http://informationr.net/ir/9-2/paper171.html.

Nitecki, Danuta A., and Eileen G. Abels. 2013. "Exploring the Cause and Effect of Library Value." Edited by J. Stephen Town. *Performance Measurement and Metrics* 14(1): 17–24. https://doi.org/10.1108/14678041311316103.

Patton, Michael Quinn. 1990. *Qualitative Evaluation and Research Methods*. 2nd ed. Newbury Park, CA: Sage.

Radford, Marie L. 2006. "Encountering Virtual Users: A Qualitative Investigation of Interpersonal Communication in Chat Reference." *Journal of the American Society for Information Science and Technology* 57(8): 1046–59. https://doi.org/10.1002/asi.20374.

Radford, Marie L. 2011. "Foreword." In *Using Qualitative Methods in Action Research: How Librarians Can Get to the Why of Data*, edited by Douglass Cook and Leslie Farmer, xi–xii. Chicago: ACRL.

Radford, Marie L., and Lynn Silipigni Connaway. 2007. "'Screenagers' and Live Chat Reference: Living up to the Promise." *Scan* 26(1): 31–39.

Radford, Marie L., Lynn Silipigni Connaway, Stephanie Mikitish, Mark Alpert, Chirag Shah, and Nicole A. Cooke. 2017. "Shared Values, New Vision: Collaboration and Communities of Practice in Virtual Reference and SQA." *Journal of the Association for Information Science and Technology* 68(2): 438–49. https://doi.org/10.1002/asi.23668.

Radford, Marie L., Lynn Silipigni Connaway, and Chirag Shah. 2011. "Cyber Synergy: Seeking Sustainability through Collaboration between Virtual Reference and Social Q&A Sites." Grant Proposal. Institute of Museum and Library Services (IMLS): Rutgers University and OCLC. http://citeseerx.ist.psu.edu/viewdoc/download?doi=10.1.1.434.1004&rep=rep1&type=pdf.

Radford, Marie L., Laura Costello, and Kaitlin Montague. 2020. "Chat Reference in the Time of COVID-19: Transforming Essential User Services." Presented at the Proceedings of the ALISE Annual Conference.

Radford, Marie L., Laura Costello, and Kaitlin Montague. March 2021, in press. "Surging Virtual Reference Services: Covid-19 a Game Changer." *College & Research Libraries News,* 82(3).

Radford, Marie L., Vanessa Kitzie, Stephanie Mikitish, Diana Floegel, Gary P. Radford, and Lynn Silipigni Connaway. 2020. "'People Are Reading Your Work,' Scholarly Identity and Social Networking Sites." *Journal of Documentation* (ahead-of-print). https://doi.org/10.1108/JD-04-2019-0074.

Ravitch, Sharon M., and Matthew Riggan. 2012. *Reason and Rigor: How Conceptual Frameworks Guide Research.* Thousand Oaks, CA: Sage.

Richards, Lyn. 2015. *Handling Qualitative Data: A Practical Guide.* 3rd ed. Thousand Oaks, CA: Sage.

Saha, Biswajit. 2019. "Web Based Tools: Emerging Paradigms in the Field of Academic Research." *International Journal of Information Dissemination and Technology* 9(3): 136. https://doi.org/10.5958/2249-5576.2019.00029.3.

Sieber, Joan E., and Martin B. Tolich. 2013. *Planning Ethically Responsible Research.* Thousand Oaks, CA: Sage.

Singh, Vivek K., Marie L. Radford, Qianjia Huang, and Susan Furrer. 2017. "'They Basically Like Destroyed the School One Day': On Newer App Features and Cyberbullying in Schools." Presented at the Proceedings of the 2017 ACM Conference on Computer Supported Cooperative Work and Social Computing (CSCW), New York.

Suarez, Doug. 2010. "Evaluating Qualitative Research Studies for Evidence Based Library and Information Practice." *Evidence Based Library and Information Practice* 5(2): 75–85. https://doi.org/10.18438/B8V90M.

Taylor, T. L. 1999. "Life in Virtual Worlds: Plural Existence, Multimodalities, and Other Online Research Challenges." *American Behavioral Scientist* 43(3): 436–49. https://doi.org/10.1177/00027649921955362.

Tracy, Sarah J. 2013. *Qualitative Research Methods.* Oxford, UK: Wiley-Blackwell.

Trevisan, Filippo, and Paul Reilly. 2014. "Ethical Dilemmas in Researching Sensitive Issues Online: Lessons from the Study of British Disability Dissent Networks." *Information, Communication & Society* 17(9): 1131–46. https://doi.org/10.1080/1369118X.2014.889188.

Van den Hoonaard, Willy Carl, and Deborah Kestin Van den Hoonnaard. 2013. *Essentials of Thinking Ethically in Qualitative Research.* Walnut Creek, CA: Left Coast Press.

Wallace, Peggy. 2010. *Encyclopedia of Case Study Research.* Thousand Oaks, CA: Sage. http://methods.sagepub.com/reference/encyc-of-case-study-research/n9.xml.

Weller, Katrin. 2015. "Accepting the Challenges of Social Media Research." *Online Information Review* 39(3): 281–89. https://doi.org/10.1108/OIR-03-2015 -0069.

Williamson, Kirsty, Marion Bannister, and Jen Sullivan. 2010. "The Crossover Generation: Baby Boomers and the Role of the Public Library." *Journal of Librarianship and Information Science* 42(3): 179–90. https://doi.org/10 .1177/0961000610368917.

10

Analysis of Qualitative Data

DATA ANALYSIS TOOLS AND METHODS

Chapter 9 set the stage by giving an overview of the principles of qualitative methods and covering the topic of research design. This chapter focuses attention on the analysis of qualitative data, which some see as a mysterious process wherein findings arise from the data as if by some mystical means. Quite the contrary; a strong qualitative design has incorporated a rigorous process for identifying participants, for data collection, and for analysis, as described at length in basic qualitative research texts (Aggarwal and Zhai 2012; Charmaz 2014; Corbin and Strauss 2014; Marshall and Rossman 2016; Miles, Huberman, and Saldaña 2013; Miles, Huberman, and Saldaña 2020; Richards 2015; Tracy 2013; Wildemuth 2017). During the research design process, the researcher must think ahead to figure out what the data to be collected should look like and consequently how they will be analyzed. This book advocates that the end point (answering the research questions, informing theoretical construction) should be firmly in mind prior to collecting any data. Data analysis begins early in the research process, concurrently with data collection (Miles, Huberman, and Saldaña 2020). Since time and resources are finite, if the data to be collected do not address the research questions or point toward theory development, they are superfluous and should not be gathered at all. Consider this data sample from the "Seeking Synchronicity" project, which is a response to an open-ended online survey question that was formulated using the critical incident technique (CIT) (Flanagan 1954): "Remember a time when you had an unsuccessful encounter with the reference librarian. Describe this time and can you recall/describe exactly what made it unsuccessful?" It was provided from a nonuser, or potential user, of virtual reference services (VRS) who had used physical libraries and was nineteen to twenty-eight years old:

It was a while ago, but I asked the reference librarian where to find books relating to a certain topic I was studying in school at the time and she just kind of said "over there" and pointed. . . . She did not seem engaged or interested in truly helping me find the books and didn't really care that I never found them, I was w[a]ndering all over looking and she just sat there. . . . She did not seem interested in helping me, let alone exhaust all of her means for doing so. Ever since then, I usually avoid that person and go to the one who has helped me successfully.

In using the CIT, the researcher generally asks about an experience that is memorable, in this case an unsuccessful experience, although one could also ask for a successful experience or any other experience, leaving it up to the participant to decide what was most memorable (Radford 2006a). The researcher using the CIT would have anticipated data that look like the above, a brief paragraph that tells a story about a particular time when the participant (in this case) encountered a reference librarian and had an unsuccessful outcome. Another CIT question for this participant also would ask about an occasion when a reference librarian encounter was successful. The form of the data would closely follow this vignette, although the substance of the encounter, and in particular what the participant has to say about what made it unsuccessful, could not be anticipated exactly. Some constructs that can be used in making sense of the above data sample follow:

- context/setting/situation
- events
- perspectives
- time constraints
- process
- activity
- strategies
- relationships
- social structures and conventions
- rituals related to politeness

Just thinking about the data in terms of these aspects (and perhaps the reader can think of others to add to this list) can be useful, and a strong theoretical basis for data interpretation, as discussed in chapters 2 and 10, can provide a wedge or starting point for analysis, as will be seen as this chapter unfolds.

The purpose of qualitative data analysis is to identify patterns and themes in the data, to discover relationships and insights into the key issue or problem that is being investigated. Thus, data can be seen to inform the creation of theoretical possibilities. The aim of qualitative data analysis goes beyond description, to delving into a deeper understanding of the phenomenon. One characteristic of qualitative analysis is that it is not rigid or static, but an iterative process, which involves multiple and careful reading of the data to sensitize the researcher who is looking for these patterns, identifying categories, themes, and dimensions of these categories and their properties. "The process of bringing order, structure, and interpretation to a mass of collected data is messy, ambiguous, time-consuming, creative, and fascinating. It does not proceed in a linear fashion; it is not neat" (Marshall and Rossman 2016).

As patterns and themes begin to take shape, the researcher has to remain sensitive, to avoid taking one paradigmatic stance toward the data and their interpretation. "Sensitivity stands in contrast to objectivity. It means having insight as well as being tuned in to and being able to pick up on relevant issues, events, and happenings during collection and analysis of the data. Sensitivity requires that a researcher take the role of the other—walk, so to speak, in that other person's shoes—and try to discern the meaning of words and actions of participants" (Corbin and Strauss 2014). Therefore, researchers must have a reverence for qualitative data, one that privileges data to speak for themselves explicitly, not implicitly.

STAGES IN DATA ANALYSIS

Qualitative data can take multiple formats and vehicles (e.g., audio recordings, transcripts, photographs, field notes of observations, diaries, tweets, videos). If analysis begins with the first step, the first piece of data collected, and is an iterative process that may double back on itself, are there distinct stages that can be delineated? The following sections propose to provide a road map to such a winding journey.

Preparing and Processing Data for Analysis

The basic "raw" data of recordings, field notes, or text typed into an online survey (as in our example above from the CIT question) "must be processed before they are available for analysis" (Miles, Huberman, and Saldaña 2020, 62). This process encompasses the careful write-up of formal versions of field notes, adding comments and depth to sketchy excerpts, correcting mistakes, and making the notes sensible for the researcher, as well as for other members of a research team or doctoral committee. Sometimes this may require translation, which poses another layer of complexity in analysis (Marshall and Rossman 2016). It may mean doing the labor to make sure that confidentiality is maintained and that the participant cannot be identified in summaries, reports, and publications. Processing may involve de-identifying data, by removing identification items including names, institutions, email addresses, and so forth, from electronically captured data, such as social media captures or live chat transcripts. For social media captures, it also may be necessary to reword posts, to protect the identity or privacy of participants. Interview participants must be assigned code names or numbers to protect confidentiality, and these must be kept in a secure and separate place. Some granting agencies require destruction of these records, as well as all data and transcriptions, usually three years after completion of the project. It may not be readily apparent to the beginner, but this stage involves a substantial time commitment and will take "roughly three to five times as much time for processing and ordering the data as the time you needed to collect them. Just one substantive week at a field site often can result in something like hundreds of pages of typed-up field notes, interview transcripts, documents, and ancillary materials" (Miles, Huberman, and Saldaña 2020).

Recordings of individual or focus group interviews also must be further processed by the researcher, who "listens to or watches the recording, makes notes, selects excerpts" and usually transcribes the recording into text (Miles, Huberman, and Saldaña 2013, 71. The transcription process is viewed by some as an onerous chore to be delegated to a paid transcriber (if funds permit) or to be slogged through by the researcher. This part of data preparation is often experienced as a waste of time or a delay to the beginning of the true analysis process. However, if the idea is adopted that data analysis begins with data collection, analysis can be fruitfully developed further during the transcription process. It is recommended here that researchers, especially novices, do as much of the transcription themselves as possible. Transcribing individual or focus group interviews or other speech can be accomplished manually or by recording in different video and conferencing applications, such as WebEx, Teams, Zoom, and Skype as well as using apps available for smart phones, laptops, and tablets that enable files to be imported into software applications that greatly facilitate transcription by converting speech into text (Marshall and Rossman 2016; Paulus, Lester, and Dempster 2014). Rushing through the data analysis stage can be detrimental to the ultimate findings, and it is important for the researcher to remain close to the original data through repeated experiences of listening to or viewing recordings of the participants. Vivid examples (or "juicy quotes") can be identified at this stage, and the researcher can begin to note themes or categories to be explored later.

Another important part of the preparation process involves deciding whether or not you will use data analysis software, and if so, selecting and learning how to use it. Richards suggests that starting early to master the software package of choice is urgent for two reasons: (1) there will not be time later, and (2) the software is needed from the beginning. On the lack of time later, she notes: "As soon as your project is underway, data will build up, and if you are still unable to use your software's tools, learning them will distract you, while delaying learning them will mean some data records are handled manually, some with software, and the project is inconsistent from the start" (Richards 2015, 27). Regarding the second reason, she says: "Your software will provide the container for your data and ideas, and the tools for exploring the relationships between data and ideas. From the first ideas, and the first data, you should be able to handle storage and management deftly with software" (Richards 2015, 27). In addition, the software can assist in data management over the life of the project, especially since qualitative data are complex and nuanced by situation and context (Richards 2015).

Computer-Assisted Qualitative Data Analysis Software (CAQDAS)

The CAQDAS packages help to provide a place to contain all data sources and have multiple affordances, especially for large datasets common in qualitative projects. There is a growing number of these products available, in both proprietary and open-source versions. More information including tutorials, and free trials of these, are available on the product websites.

The most popular proprietary products are thought to be:

- ATLAS.ti (http://atlasti.com/free-trial-version)
- MAXQDA (https://www.maxqda.com/qualitative-analysis-software #Demodownload)
- NVivo (http://www.qsrinternational.com/Trial)

Other proprietary software packages include Dedoose, QDA Miner, QDA Miner Lite, Qiqqa, Quirkos, Tansana (recommended for video data analysis), andXSight. Open-source software includes Aquad, Cassandre, CLAN, Coding Analysis Toolkit (CAT), Compendium, and RQDA ("Computer-Assisted Qualitative Data Analysis Software" 2020). As their popularity has grown steadily, resources for those wishing to learn more about the use of these packages have become available, most notably a book by Jackson and Bazeley (2019) on using NVivo, which has a chapter on analysis of data from Twitter, Facebook, YouTube, and web pages.

Common features of all these packages include creating and applying codes. Some (including NVivo and RQDA) have advanced features that support such enhancements as enabling queries (to explore data to discover patterns, connections, etc.), supporting visualizations (to create charts, models, maps, and cluster analyses), and delivering reports (to document and export findings). It is important to understand the limitations of these packages, however, the chief one being that they do not do the mental/intellectual work of the data analysis. "No mechanism can replace the mind and creativity of the researcher. Still, computers can serve as tools" (Marshall and Rossman 2016, 226). They can help the researcher with the mechanics of data analysis. "Computer software can assist the analysis phase because they facilitate making and writing observational notes, editing, coding, storing, searching and retrieval, linking data, writing memos, analyzing content, displaying data, drawing and verifying conclusions, building theory, mapping graphics, and writing reports" (Marshall and Rossman 2016, 227). This is not directly comparable to what quantitative packages like SPSS do for numerical data, since these run sophisticated statistical analyses on data. In the case of qualitative products, all of the analysis must be done by the researcher. As Marshall and Rossman (2016, 228) pointedly note: "We caution that software is only a tool to help with some of the mechanical and management aspects of analysis; the difficult analytical work must be done by the researcher's own internal hard drive!"

Nevertheless, CAQDAS are extremely useful for analyzing data from surveys, individual and focus group interviews, observations, and any type of textual data (e.g., transcripts, tweets, blogs, social media postings). Files can be imported in text, tables, images, sound, and video formats.

What are some advantages and disadvantages to using or not using qualitative data analysis software? There are some justifications for using manual techniques for analysis of data, especially if the research design calls for a relatively small amount of data to be collected. Manual analysis consists of using pencil and paper or a basic word processing program (e.g., Microsoft Word) or a spreadsheet (e.g., Microsoft Excel) to house data and track analysis, such as assigning codes. Within Word, for example, the track changes feature can be used to highlight and code text in comment boxes, although this endeavor becomes difficult with large datasets as coding progresses, as discussed below.

Following are some advantages of using manual processes for coding and data analysis:

- It's free! There are labor costs for the researcher's time, but no funds are needed for purchase of sophisticated software packages that may be expensive. If the researcher has very limited funds and no institutional access to or grant funds to buy software packages, manual coding may be the only option. Some open source products mentioned above may come "free," although they require technical knowledge and sometimes programming knowledge, as is the case for RQDA.
- There is no technology learning curve. Qualitative packages can require an investment of a considerable amount of time to learn how to use them effectively.
- One can just jump in. Related to the previous item, without much preparation time beyond the processing of data, such as editing field notes, converting audio or video to text, and physical organization of data. Once processing is completed, analysis can start immediately.
- It feels easier (not really). Manual coding might feel as if it is easy, but as data collection and analysis progress, manual systems become cumbersome.

Disadvantages of using manual processes for coding and data analysis include the following:

- Code changes are difficult and time consuming. This is perhaps the most important drawback of manual systems. Initial coding may seem simple, but what happens when a code changes, becomes combined with other codes, or is eliminated? Painstaking edits must be made for each time the initial code was used.
- Comparison of different types of data is cumbersome. Within software packages, links can be made across different data modes, which is more difficult or impossible for manual systems.
- It is challenging for teamwork. Individual coding is one thing; when working in teams, some members might not be physically collocated, so sharing analysis and comparing coding and sharing data become extremely problematic for manual coding.
- Intercoder reliability (ICR) is painstaking to determine. Software packages provide tools and reports for comparing codes and analysis. Computing this by hand is strenuous and time consuming.

Advantages of using CAQDAS for coding and data analysis include the following:

- It enables ease of assigning and changing codes. One of the most important features of qualitative software is the ability to assign and change codes easily and globally. As data analysis progresses, codes can be easily combined, changed, eliminated, renamed, and so forth. Some products use "drop and drag" features for quick coding. Colored bars in NVivo allow the researcher to see where coding has been completed, levels of density, and more.

- It provides the ability to connect different data types. Qualitative software has the capability to code disparate data formats such as transcripts and audio files.
- It enables links between data and demographic information. Suppose the researcher wants to know what only the female participants in a series of interviews had to say about a particular theme, or all those older or younger than a certain age. In manual coding it would be possible, but time consuming, to cross-code these types of demographic data for comparison.
- It offers the availability of advanced functions, such as those mentioned above: creating and applying codes, queries, visualizations, delivering reports, and theoretical modeling. Text search can help researchers find and code commonly occurring words and the frequency of these.
- It offers tutorials. To help with training, these packages provide tutorials to those who have purchased them. In addition, training is available via webinar and in person. Many academic institutions will have user groups that can provide additional support.
- It offers the ability to add annotations and memos that can be searched and aggregated to the data.
- It enables a team of researchers to have access to common datasets and analysis tools, regardless of location.
- It calculates ICR. A report can be run that compares coding among several researchers and computes percentages of agreement.

Some disadvantages of using CAQDAS for coding and data analysis include the following:

- It can be costly. Software packages can be very expensive to purchase, and they require purchase of updates and subscriptions over time. Some universities may purchase site licenses for students, staff, and faculty members or provide discounted pricing.
- It may involve a steep learning curve. Time needs to be invested to learn and to stay up to date with software upgrades.
- Software may be buggy. Some programming glitches exist that prove to be challenging. The best practice to cope with this type of problem, which may result in loss of data or coding, is to make backups frequently and to keep multiple backups in different virtual and physical places.

Smith et al. (2019) used NVivo to analyze qualitative data from 391 surveys and one focus group to review its support program for graduate students at the University of Otago Library. To investigate how academic libraries could better support first-generation college students, Bussell used NVivo to analyze surveys from fifty-nine libraries across all fifty states. Their work resulted in a list of recommendations that include "assigning liaisons for first-generation programs, working to create an inclusive and affirming library environment, designing library spaces that support the multiple social roles and identities of first-generation students," and more (Bussell 2020, 242). Another example of a project that used NVivo software can be found in the work of Ross (2011), who performed a grounded analysis of eighteen individual interviews with library directors from the Appalachian area of the eastern part of America. Ross sought to discover how nonresidents used public libraries and to explore strategies and policies that library directors used to serve this population. The authors have used NVivo software for data analysis of two large grant projects (Connaway, Radford, and OCLC Research 2011; Radford, Connaway, and Shah 2011). The "Seeking Synchronicity" (Connaway, Radford, and OCLC Research 2011) project spanned three years and involved analysis of a large amount of qualitative, longitudinal data collected via individual and focus group interviews, surveys, and live chat virtual reference sessions. The research team, composed of researchers, faculty, PhD and MLIS students, and technology support, was located in several states. Without using a package such as NVivo, data analysis with massive datasets among such a large team would have been nearly impossible.

For this project (Radford et al. 2019), the qualitative data analysis process consisted of seven steps:

1. Conduct and transcribe interviews, focus groups, and randomly select live chat transcripts.
2. Develop initial codebook using etic codes from previous projects and the literature review, building emic codes that are found as analysis goes along (more on etic and emic codes and codebooks is found later in this chapter).
3. Load transcripts and insert codebook into NVivo.
4. Conduct initial coding of a portion of the data by each team member (20 percent overlap for each coder), and run the intercoder reliability check in NVivo. Discuss and make adjustments as needed to codebook and coding process.
5. Code transcripts in NVivo, continuing to adjust codebook. Identify "juicy quotes" that are illustrative of emerging codes.
6. Complete data analysis, exporting results, running reports, comparing findings across types of data.
7. Conduct intercoder reliability check, again discussing and making adjustments as needed.

NVivo also was used by Lingel (2011) in research on urban immigrants' information tactics using interviews and participatory mapping, and by Sibbald et al. (2013), who used mixed methods including survey and social network analysis and semistructured interviews. Yadamsuren and Heinström (2011) also reported using NVivo to assist in analysis of twenty interviews accompanied by think-aloud sessions to study individuals' reactions to online news.

Scales (2013) used ATLAS.ti to analyze student assignments, and shares rare insights as to how other researchers can use this package in the qualitative analysis process, including its organization and functions. Henczel investigated the impact of national library associations on the profession, libraries, and members. She interviewed fifty-two participants from four national library associations and created digital recordings, which were transcribed for analysis. She noted that "ATLAS.ti qualitative analysis software was chosen for this study as it provided a systematic approach to analyzing unstructured data including text, video and audio files" (Henczel 2014, 122).

Researchers at Radford University and Longwood University used ATLAS.ti to study the use of mystery shoppers for service improvement at the reference desk. They performed quantitative and qualitative analysis on survey data:

> Each topic within a comment was identified and assigned a one or two word "code" that captured the essence of the topic (e.g., "approachable") and a "tag" designating the code as "favorable" (þ) or "unfavorable" (2) (e.g., "approachable þ"). ATLAS.ti qualitative analysis software or Excel was used to code the comments. The resulting codes, along with their definitions and examples of each were recorded in a code list common to both libraries. A combined total of 110 valid comments generated 168 code/tag combinations. These code/tag combinations were then organized by meta-analysis category. (Kocevar-Weidinger et al. 2010, 35)

One example in the LIS literature was found that used the open-source product RQDA. Burns and Bossaller conducted nine semistructured interviews with academic librarians to study communication overload. They note that they transcribed the interview recording into text and that this free software "facilitates coding, category building, and project management. [They] used this software to code and annotate the transcripts as well as maintain project logs, notes, and memos" (Burns and Bossaller 2012, 603).

For projects that will generate a large amount of data from interviews, text files (such as transcripts), or open-ended survey data, or for longitudinal research or studies with teams/individuals at multiple locations, CAQDAS are highly recommended. The affordances greatly outweigh the drawbacks for those who have access at their institutions, or monetary resources to purchase them, or the technical skills needed for the open-source products.

Deciding Whether to Use Qualitative Software

Richards asks "Should you use qualitative software? And replies "Well, of course. All researchers will use some software. But should you use one of the specialist packages for qualitative work? Before taking that step, seriously reflect on the other ways you use computers, for communicating, reflecting, reporting, searching and exploring. These are the tasks associated with qualitative analysis. Do some thinking about which of these tools please you and help you, which extend your skills, and which impede your life and work. Approach the specialist software in this context. Do you need them? Do these packages offer to improve or impede your knowledge of data and your ability to explore data records and see patterns and meanings?" (Richards 2015, 27). Richards also notes that "most qualitative researchers now use some specialist software, and most probably should" (Richards 2015, 27).

However, it should be noted that the use of CAQDAS has been controversial, with early enthusiasts in the mid-1990s believing that these products were the "silver bullet" for superior qualitative analysis. Later, the "snake oil" metaphor arose as a "push-back" on using software for analysis, with some articulating the dark side of these packages that mechanize the process, pulling the data away from the researcher. More recently, it has been acknowledged that CAQDAS is not without flaws, but that it can be used appropriately, with due caution being taken by the researcher to stay close to the data. Jackson and Bazely's approach "acknowledges the potential for mutual influence between researcher and software and urges us to let go of the fear that the software is hijacking the process. We still need to learn more about the contexts in which software influences us and with what results" (Jackson and Bazeley 2019, 4–6). For more on this controversy, see text box 10.1. For an example of a project that used NVivo for data analysis, see text box 10.2.

Text Box 10.1: CAQDAS Methodological Concerns

Diana Floegel

Data analysis software are often presented as convenient and efficient tools for qualitative and quantitative researchers. While such software can certainly be useful, especially if we have large datasets or if we work on projects with multiple analysts, they raise a number of methodological concerns that are worth noting.

First, we can discuss *epistemic* concerns. Depending on our epistemic orientation, software is not appropriate for all forms of analysis. Computer Assisted Qualitative Data Analysis Software (CAQDAS) such as NVivo and Dedoose further remove our data from their initial source: by definition, the programs process and then reproduce recordings, transcripts, and other files in new formats (Biernacki 2012). This means that we, as researchers, are farther removed from our data than when we conduct manual analyses. If we approach research from epistemic orientations that require a close dialog between ourselves and our data, such as constructivism (Dey 1999), software may not be appropriate because they create additional physical barriers between us and our research.

Second, we can discuss *analytical* concerns. Data analysis software are often best suited for deductive analytic approaches, especially in a qualitative realm (Miles, Huberman, and Saldaña 2013). This is because their features encourage a top-down approach to applying and developing codes. Further, the design of these systems often encourages granular and descriptive coding; in all likelihood, you will end up with an expansive codebook if you use data analysis software. While this is not always a problem in and of itself, it can lead us to chiefly develop descriptive analyses, thus stalling more in-depth theoretical analyses (Corbin and Strauss 2008).

Finally, it is worth mentioning *classificatory* concerns, which feed into the above-mentioned problems. Some data analysis software (such as Qualtrics) offer data collection features in addition to or in tandem with analytic capabilities. These data collection features are typically infused with normative epistemic and aesthetic orientations. Take, for example, a survey question that asks someone to report their gender. Quantitative survey software like Qualtrics often suggest categoric responses—"male, female, other"—that enforce the gender binary. Though these can be overridden, if used, such responses affect both data collection and analysis, and they are violent toward nonbinary people. As this example demonstrates, software programs are not neutral, but are, in fact, infused with (often normative) values.

References

Biernacki, R. 2012. *Reinventing Evidence in Social Inquiry: Decoding Facts and Variables.* London: Palgrave Macmillan.

Corbin, Juliet M., and Anselm L. Strauss. 2008. *Basics of Qualitative Research: Techniques and Procedures for Developing Grounded Theory.* 3rd ed. Thousand Oaks, CA: Sage.

Dey, Ian. 1999. *Grounding Grounded Theory: Guidelines for Qualitative Inquiry.* Illustrated ed. San Diego: Emerald.

Miles, Matthew B., A. Michael Huberman, and Johnny Saldaña. 2013. *Qualitative Data Analysis: A Methods Sourcebook.* 3rd ed. Thousand Oaks, CA: Sage.

Text Box 10.2: Using NVivo to Build a Model Describing the Health Information Practices of LGBTQIA+ Communities in South Carolina

Vanessa Kitzie

A significant body of research demonstrates how social and structural factors produce health disparities among LGBTQIA+ communities (IOM 2011; James et al. 2016; ODPHP 2014). Less is known about the relationship between these factors and how communities seek, use, and share health information. My research team interviewed thirty LGBTQIA+ community leaders in South Carolina (SC) to understand this relationship.

We hand-coded three verbatim interview transcripts sentence-by-sentence using a combination of initial, process, and in vivo coding (Charmaz 2014). We met several times to discuss emergent codes and resolve coding discrepancies. These open codes formed the basis for nodes we created in NVivo. We coded four additional transcripts during this open coding phase in NVivo, using the *Quick Code* feature. The *Coding Comparison* feature allowed us to easily see the similarities and differences between how each team member was applying the codes. We used this information to further refine them. We then coded the rest of the transcripts, identifying broader coding categories (parents) under which we nested our open codes (children). Following this axial coding process, we used the *Concept Map* feature to engage in selective coding. We specified the relationships between these coding categories. See table 10.1 for coding examples at each stage. The coding process resulted in a conceptual model describing how social and structural factors, which we called contextual conditions (Gibson and Martin 2019), produce risks, or anticipated harms, and barriers, or experienced harms. In turn, risks produce health information practices that protect an individual or community from anticipated harms. In contrast, barriers produce health information practices that defend an individual or community against harms being experienced (Kitzie, Wagner, and Vera 2020).

Table 10.1. Example of Codes at Each Stage

Open Codes	Axial Codes	Selective Code
Sharing "health care horror stories "Sharing personal experiences with self-prescribing to prevent harm to other community members	Word of mouth	Community defensive information practices
Going to the same doctor as other community members Getting tested due to community-based social media awareness campaign	Making decisions based on prior community experience	
Avoiding health care to prevent being misgendered Avoiding therapist who is a "front" for conversion therapy	Collectively avoiding known harmful sources	

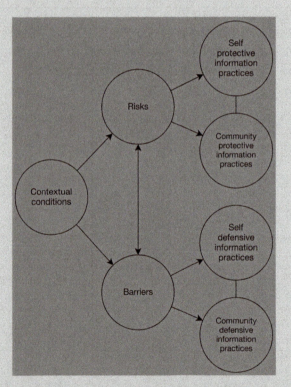

Figure 10.1. A Conceptual Model Describing the Health Information Practices of SC LGBTQIA+ Communities Created Using NVivo's Conceptual Map Feature

References

Charmaz, Kathy. 2014. *Constructing Grounded Theory*. Thousand Oaks, CA: Sage.

Gibson, Amelia N., and John D. Martin. 2019. "Re-Situating Information Poverty: Information Marginalization and Parents of Individuals with Disabilities." *Journal of the Association for Information Science and Technology* 70(5): 476–87. https://doi.org/10.1002/asi .24128.

IOM. 2011. "The Health of Lesbian, Gay, Bisexual, and Transgender People: Building a Foundation for Better Understanding." Washington, DC. https://doi.org/10.17226/13128.

James, Sandy, Jody Herman, Susan Rankin, Mara Keisling, Lisa Mottet, and Ma'ayan Anafi. 2016. "The Report of the 2015 U.S. Transgender Survey." National Center for Transgender Equality. https://ncvc.dspacedirect.org/handle/20.500.11990/1299.

Kitzie, Vanessa L., Travis L. Wagner, and A. Nick Vera. 2020. "'In the Beginning, It Was Little Whispers . . . Now, We're Almost a Roar': Conceptualizing a Model for Community and Self in LGBTQ+ Health Information Practices." In *Sustainable Digital Communities*, edited by Anneli Sundqvist, Gerd Berget, Jan Nolin, and Kjell Ivar Skjerdingstad, 15–31. Lecture Notes in Computer Science. Cham, Switzerland: Springer International. https://doi.org/10 .1007/978-3-030-43687-2_2.

ODPHP. 2014. "Lesbian, Gay, Bisexual, and Transgender Health." Healthy People 2020. https://www.healthypeople.gov/2020/topics-objectives/topic/lesbian-gay-bisexual-and -transgender-health?topicid=25.

STRATEGIES FOR DATA ANALYSIS

The nitty-gritty of qualitative research is found in approaches to coding textual data. There are two dominant ways to conceptualize this process. The first of these is what is known as the "grounded theory" approach, in which no prior set of categories or themes is imposed on the data; instead, the categories are developed from the data using the constant comparative method (see below). The second approach involves finding, developing, using, adopting, or expanding a category scheme that already exists in the literature and applying this scheme to the data the researcher has collected (Alomari, Sandhu, and Woods 2014; Sonnenwald et al. 2014). This type of analysis is especially useful in applying previously developed theory either from LIS or from a related discipline to a new context, with a different type of participants, or in a longitudinal work. Let us consider the grounded theory (inductive approach) first and then move on to discuss the use of established coding schemes (deductive approach).

Grounded Theory

Grounded theory arose from the work of Glaser and Strauss (Corbin and Strauss 2014; Glaser 1967, 1992), who developed and published this method in their landmark book *The Discovery of Grounded Theory* and subsequent monographs that had an enormously influential impact on qualitative methods. Grounded theory involved a 360-degree turnaround from positivist research, which starts with a hypothesis derived from existing theory and collects data to prove or disprove it, moving in a deductive fashion. In grounded theory, the theory arises in a systematic, inductive way using data to construct theory. One of the most clear, practical, and comprehensive discussions of grounded theory principles and the process of coding data is found in Kathy Charmaz's (2014) *Constructing Grounded Theory*. Charmaz stated that "grounded theory methods consist of systematic, yet flexible guidelines for collecting and analyzing qualitative data to construct theories from the data themselves. Thus, researchers construct a theory 'grounded' in their data. Grounded theory begins with inductive data, invokes iterative strategies of going back and forth between data and analysis, uses comparative methods, and keeps you interacting and involved with your data and emerging analysis" (Charmaz 2014, 1). For Charmaz, actions distinguish researchers. Hence grounded theorists:

- Conduct data collection and analysis simultaneously in an iterative process.
- Analyze actions and processes rather than themes and structure.
- Use comparative methods.
- Draw on data (e.g., narratives and descriptions) in service of developing new conceptual categories.
- Develop inductive abstract analytic categories through systematic data analysis.
- Emphasize theory construction rather than description or application of current theories.
- Engage in theoretical sampling.
- Search for variation in the studied categories or process.
- Pursue developing a category rather than covering a specific empirical topic (Charmaz 2014, 15).

Grounded theory has found its way into a broad array of social science research, and Mansourian (2006) found a considerable number of studies that have successfully applied grounded theory in LIS research. Hicks used a constructivist grounded theory approach in a study of mitigating risk in information literacy. Data sources included semistructured interviews and photo-elicitation methods in investigating language learners overseas and their information literacy practices. This work "provides a theoretically rich exploration of language-learner information literacy practices while further identifying the importance of time, affect and information creation within information literacy research and practice as well as the need for the continued theorization of information literacy concepts" (Hicks 2020, 126). Tan's (2010) article on grounded theory is recommended, as it gives practical advice and provides a discussion of four common problems for inexperienced LIS scholars: (a) the use of grounded theory as a method or methodology, (b) how the literature review should be used, (c) how a coding strategy should be developed, and (d) identifying the theory that is generated. In addition, González-Teruel and Abad-Garcia (2012) provided an overview of grounded theory research in the area of information behavior and find that most of these studies explore health information contexts. Perhaps the benchmark study using grounded theory in this discipline is by Constance A. Mellon (1986), an early adopter in LIS who used this method to develop theory related to library anxiety as part of her dissertation research. Also, grounded theory has been used effectively to construct Ellis's (1993) information-seeking model. See text box 10.3 for a discussion of constructivist grounded theory. The next section of this chapter discusses developing a coding strategy using the constant comparative method.

Text Box 10.3: Constructivist Grounded Theory

Diana Floegel

Grounded theory was first articulated as such by Glaser and Strauss (1967a). Their original text is epistemically divided between positivist and constructivist approaches to the methodology. Since its publication, two camps of grounded theory have developed: classical grounded theory, which aligns with Glaser's positivist orientation, and constructivist grounded theory, which aligns with Strauss's constructivist orientation (Wilson and Hutchinson 1996). Constructivist grounded theory is a highly reflexive methodology wherein the researcher is in constant dialog with their data, consistently interrogating their own place within every step of the project and acknowledging that their own perspectives will shape findings (Dey 1999).

Constructivist grounded theory is a flexible and interpretive approach to describing phenomena of interest via simultaneous data collection and analysis (Charmaz 2014). The methodology culminates in the development of middle-range theoretical contributions that describe the causes and consequences of phenomena, as well as the conditions under which they occur (Dey 1999). As a methodology, it is methods-agnostic, meaning we choose our methods based on our phenomenon of interest and developing analysis. It is perhaps unfortunate that Glaser and Strauss's original text is epistemically inconsistent and widely cited for its approach to inductive analysis, as this confluence of circumstances has arguably led many a scholar to label their research "grounded theory" when they in fact use inductive analysis that may or may not include constant comparison (Suddaby 2006). For the sake of the methodology and our scholarship, it is important that we only define our research as constructivist grounded theory when we truly deploy the methodology; there is no such thing as a "grounded theory approach" or "grounded theory light."

There are six components of constructivist grounded theory:

1. **Develop middle-range theory**: Grounded theory should be employed in order to develop theory where theory lacks (Glaser and Strauss 1967b), or to expand existing theoretical frameworks (Costello 2017; Gibson and Martin 2019).
2. **Inductive analysis**: We should analyze our data inductively; grounded theorists do not deductively apply frameworks or coding schemes from prior literature to their data. However, we do identify *sensitizing concepts* as we develop our phenomena of interest and throughout our study as part of theoretical sampling. Sensitizing concepts demonstrate where theoretical gaps exist, where further theory development is needed, and how our work is situated among prior literature (Charmaz 2014; Dunne 2011). Inductive analysis in a grounded theory study involves three overlapping coding stages: (1) open coding, where we develop in vivo codes that are often gerunds from our data (this may be called "verbing"); (2) axial coding, where we group our codes into analytical categories; and (3) focused or theoretical coding, where we further abstract our categories into theoretical constructs (Charmaz 2014). Coding is not a linear process: as we continue to collect and analyze data, we move flexibly between all three stages, deconstructing and reconstructing categories and constructs in order to address negative cases (Lincoln and Guba 1985).

3. **The constant comparative method**: We often say that data collection and analysis occur "simultaneously" in constructivist grounded theory. This is a bit of a misnomer; really, we collect and analyze data *iteratively* so that there are not separate "data collection" and "data analysis" phases of the methodological process. This is called constant comparison, or the constant comparative method (Charmaz 2014).

4. **Theoretical sampling**: Theoretical sampling is arguably the most important and most overlooked component of constructivist grounded theory (Draucker et al. 2007). In constructivist grounded theory work, we do not begin with a predetermined sampling strategy based on populations or other data sources of interest. Instead, we begin to collect and analyze data related to our phenomenon of interest (often, but not always, via semistructured interviews), then we determine where to next collect data based on the *theoretical* directions our work takes us (Glaser and Strauss 1967b). During theoretical sampling, we may need to ask new questions, collect data from new sources, or design new studies in order to pursue developing categories and constructs, address negative cases in our data, and reach theoretical saturation. Theoretical sampling should happen iteratively, alongside inductive analysis and constant comparison, so that we pursue data based on our developing analysis.

5. **Memoing**: Memoing allows us to trace our analytic processes throughout our work (Charmaz 2014). Memos do not need to be formal, and may in fact be most useful when they are spontaneous (Charmaz 2014). As we progress throughout our study, memos should become more complex, integrating our data, sensitizing concepts, and developing codes, categories, and constructs (Charmaz 2014). Memos may include *actor memos* that describe our participants and/or the systems and institutions we examine, as well as how they interact; *process memos* that describe our methodological processes and decision making; and *analytic memos* that track our developing analyses.

6. **Assessing trustworthiness**: It is difficult to determine when a grounded theory study is over: the constructivist epistemic that underscores the methodology means that we will never claim to conclusively develop a generalizable theory (Lincoln and Guba 1985). However, we do use a suite of methods to ensure that our works' theoretical contribution is *trustworthy*, or robust and transferable (Lincoln and Guba 1985). This suite includes *member-checking*, or continuing to communicate with participants throughout our data collection and analysis in order to ask them further questions and solicit their input on developing findings (Miles, Huberman, and Saldaña 2015); *peer debriefing*, or a combination of formal and informal critical discussions about our developing findings with knowledgeable people (Lincoln and Guba 1985); and *negative case analysis*, or identification of deviant cases in our data that suggest we need to continue theoretical sampling (Draucker et al. 2007; Lincoln and Guba 1985). In sum, trustworthiness checks should help us determine when we reach a reasonable degree of *theoretical saturation* (Low 2019).

It is key to note that these components overlap. True constructivist grounded theory is iterative—it does not happen in discrete parts or steps. It is also difficult! The text provided here is a brief overview. When considering constructivist grounded theory, be sure to read the works cited below, and remember that deploying the methodology takes a great deal of practice.

References

Charmaz, Kathy. 2014. *Constructing Grounded Theory*. Thousand Oaks, CA: Sage.
Costello, Kaitlin Light. 2017. "Social Relevance Assessments for Virtual Worlds: Interpersonal Source Selection in the Context of Chronic Illness." *Journal of Documentation* 73(6): 1209–27. https://doi.org/10.1108/JD-07-2016-0096.

Dey, Ian. 1999. *Grounding Grounded Theory: Guidelines for Qualitative Inquiry*. Bingley, UK: Emerald Group.

Draucker, Claire B., Donna S. Martsolf, Ratchneewan Ross, and Thomas B. Rusk. 2007. "Theoretical Sampling and Category Development in Grounded Theory." *Qualitative Health Research* 17(8): 1137–48. https://doi.org/10.1177/1049732307308450.

Gibson, Amelia N., and John D. Martin. 2019. "Re-Situating Information Poverty: Information Marginalization and Parents of Individuals with Disabilities." *Journal of the Association for Information Science and Technology* 70(5): 476–87. https://doi.org/10.1002/asi.24128.

Glaser, Barney G., and Anselm L. Strauss. 1967a. *The Discovery of Grounded Theory: Strategies for Qualitative Research*. New York: Aldine.

Glaser, Barney G., and Anselm L. Strauss. 1967b. *The Discovery of Grounded Theory: Strategies for Qualitative Research*. New York: Aldine.

Lincoln, Yvonna S., and Egon G. Guba. 1985. *Naturalistic Inquiry*. Thousand Oaks, CA: Sage.

Low, Jacqueline. 2019. "A Pragmatic Definition of the Concept of Theoretical Saturation." *Sociological Focus* 52(2): 131–39.

Miles, Matthew B., A. Michael Huberman, and Johnny Saldaña. 2015. *Qualitative Data Analysis: A Methods Sourcebook*. 4th ed. Thousand Oaks, CA: Sage.

Suddaby, Roy. 2006. "From the Editors: What Grounded Theory Is Not." *Academy of Management Journal* 49(4): 633–42. https://doi.org/10.5465/amj.2006.22083020.

Wilson, Holly Skodol, and Sally Ambler Hutchinson. 1996. "Methodologic Mistakes in Grounded Theory." *Nursing Research* 45(2): 122–24. https://doi.org/10.1097/00006199-199603000-00012.

CONTENT ANALYSIS

Content analysis is an umbrella term that "was originally developed to analyze text such as journal articles, newspapers, books, responses to questionnaires, and transcribed interviews." Since then it has "also been used to analyze graphical, aural, and video messages" (Wildemuth 2017, 307). There are two types, quantitative and qualitative. Below, the qualitative version that features the inductive derivation of codes, categories, and thematic patterns is described.

The Constant Comparative Method and Coding Data

A major strategy for analysis of qualitative data is the use of the constant comparative method, which embraces "constant comparisons" defined as "the analytic process of comparing different pieces of data against each other for similarities and differences" (Corbin and Strauss 2014, 85). It requires the researcher to ask continually: "What is this piece of data saying?" "Is this idea different from or similar to the next segment?" This involves comparing and aggregating pieces of data on the basis of similar characteristics and beginning the process of sorting these into interim groups or emerging themes. According to Charmaz, there are two phases for grounded theory coding: initial coding (which Corbin and Strauss (2014, 85) call open coding) and focused coding (which involves theoretical application and development). The goal of coding is to attach labels to data segments that capture what each segment is about. "During initial coding we study fragments of data—words, lines, segments, and incidents—closely for their analytic import. From time to time, we may adopt our participants' telling terms as codes. Initial coding continues the interaction that you shared with your participants while collecting data but brings you into an interactive analytic space" (Charmaz 2014, 107). Grounded theory approaches move from using data to create codes, to grouping them into concepts, and then grouping them into larger, theoretical categories. Following initial coding, in the focused coding stage, "telling initial codes" are chosen and/or new codes are developed that combine "numerous initial codes" (Charmaz 2014, 138). Charmaz (2014, 138) asserts that "while engaging in focused coding, we typically concentrate on what we define as the most useful initial codes and then we test them against extensive data." Thus, "focused coding requires decisions about which initial codes make the most analytic sense to categorize your data incisively and completely" (Charmaz 2014, 138).

Charmaz (2014, 190) also is a proponent of identifying "in vivo codes," which are codes that come "directly from your respondents' discourse" or "voice." She defined these as "codes that researchers adopt directly from the data, such as telling statements they discover in interviews, documents, and the everyday language used in a studied site" (Charmaz 2014, 343). She identified three kinds of "in vivo codes":

- general terms that the participant describes as being something everyone "knows" and points to "significant meanings";
- an "innovative term" used by a respondent, which succinctly expresses an important point of view; and
- "insider shorthand terms" used by the participant's group. (Charmaz 2014, 343)

It is recommended that novice researchers pay especially close attention to the voice of participants and seek "in vivo codes" in the data analysis process. These allow scholars to stay close to the data and to remain "grounded" by these data in analysis. Also, it is advisable to be on the lookout for "juicy quotes" (Di Gregorio 2000) to capture that can be used later to illustrate categories and definitions and to bring the participant's voice into the analysis, write-up, and later, in publication. Use of juicy quotes in reports and articles brings the research to life and enables the reader to hear the participant's voice, which adds validity to the findings. Merely stating codes and themes without representative or vivid quotes not only is dull, but also removes the findings to a level of abstraction that makes it difficult for readers to process.

One of these other ways to conceptualize coding is found in the work of Corbin and Strauss (2014) and is also discussed extensively by Miles, Huberman, and Saldaña (2020, 86), who wrote that "coding is not just something you do to "get the data ready" for analysis, rather . . . it is a form of early and continuing analysis that drives ongoing data collection." Corbin and Strauss (2014, 57) defined coding as "denoting concepts to stand for meaning" and concepts as "words used by analysts to stand for interpreted meaning." The goal of coding is ultimately data reduction and theory construction, by identifying possible patterns and distilling and sorting the data for making comparisons with other data segments. The overarching aim is to categorize phenomena found in the data themselves: identifying, naming, abstracting, and relating.

However, Corbin and Strauss contended that there is a difference between coding and analysis, in that analysis embraces a broader effort and refers to "both the concept and the thought processes that go behind assigning meaning to data. Analysis is exploratory and gives consideration to different possible meanings in data" (Corbin and Strauss 2014, 58). Corbin and Strauss further asserted that open coding (also referred to as initial coding) is the process by which categories and properties are discovered in data through an iterative process of reviewing the data line by line, paragraph by paragraph. The process of identifying concepts requires painstaking work by the researcher, who repeatedly queries the data. Asking questions is a fundamental analytical strategy that is useful at every analytical stage and enables scholars to

- probe as needed,
- develop initial answers,
- think "outside the box" of their own filters, and
- become knowledgeable about their data. (Corbin and Strauss 2014, 90–91)

Additional analytical techniques are described in depth by Miles, Huberman, and Saldaña, who discussed level of analysis (e.g., word, phrase, sentence, or paragraph). They suggested strategies such as the "flip-flop," in which the researcher queries the data and participants to discover the opposite so as to better understand perspective (e.g., if focus is on what is easy, consider what is difficult). Another example is to pay close attention to the warning or red flag and be careful in interpreting words like everyone, always, never, and so forth. It is recommended that the researcher then probe for contradictory or opposite cases. If something always happens, what would it look like if it did not happen that way (Miles, Huberman, and Saldaña 2020)? Identifying patterns for concepts also requires the researcher to keep a detailed record of analysis, including marginal notations, memos (Charmaz 2014), an unstructured list of concepts, and a structured list of coded concepts (especially when coding large volumes of data, discussed above in the section on CAQDAS).

Miles, Huberman, and Saldaña drew attention to a distinction between deductive versus inductive coding. The section above describes inductive coding that arises from the data through the constant comparison method. "One method of creating codes is developing a provisional 'start list' of codes prior to field work—*deductive* or a priori coding. The list comes from the literature review, conceptual framework, list of research questions, hypotheses, problem areas, and/or key variables that the researcher brings to the study" (Miles, Huberman, and Saldaña 2020, 74). This list may be small, with twelve provisional codes, or may extend up to fifty or more codes. These can be entered into CACDAS programs, usually before any data are uploaded (Miles, Huberman, and Saldaña 2020, 74). Here are some examples from the LIS research in which deductive coding (or a combination of deductive and inductive coding) was used:

- Investigation of communities of practice (CoP) in virtual reference and social question and answer (SQA) services, in which codes from the CoP framework were applied to interview data (Radford et al. 2017).
- Using codes derived from the theories of information poverty and stigma to examine the information practices of individuals who have or are considering extreme body modifications (Burnett, Subramaniam, and Gibson 2009).
- Employing concepts of bounded rationality, rational choice theory, gratification theory, and time as a context in information seeking, to examine how individuals employ convenience in their information-seeking behaviors (Lingel and Boyd 2013).

Theme Analysis

During the process of category development and coding, themes are generally identified by grouping similar categories into larger categories and naming these as such. Major themes emerge in the process of grouping categories together and paying attention to the amount of data coded into each category. Usually, the themes that are returned to again and again in the data become the major themes, and those falling underneath these, as related topics, become "subthemes" or minor themes. An example can be found in the work of one of the authors, who studied virtual reference encounters and grouped categories of interpersonal communication instances found in live chat transcripts into a detailed category scheme that included high-level themes such as "Facilitators" and "Barriers" and into subthemes derived from a theoretical framework, which included "Content-Related Facilitators," "Relational Facilitators," "Content-Related Barriers," and "Relational Barriers" (Radford 1999, 2006a). The examples below from the "Cyber Synergy" grant project provide additional illustrations of coding practices.

Cyber Synergy Grant, Online Survey Magic Wand Question: Example of Coding Scheme

The authors were coprincipal investigators with Shah for the grant project previously mentioned above: "Cyber Synergy: Seeking Sustainability through Collaboration between Virtual Reference and Social Q&A Sites" (Radford, Connaway, and Shah 2011). One phase of this project involved telephone interviews with fifty-one users of virtual reference or SQA sites. This project addressed the following four research questions:

- RQ1. What is the current state of virtual reference services (VRS) quality compared to longitudinal data and to SQA websites?
- RQ2. How can VRS become more collaborative within and between libraries and tap more effectively into librarian[s'] subject expertise?
- RQ3. Can VRS be more sustainable through collaboration with SQA services?
- RQ4. How can we design systems and services within and between VRS and SQA for better quality and sustainability?

The telephone interviews were designed to inform RQ2, RQ3, and RQ4 and included the following question, which was known as the "magic wand question": If you had a magic wand and could create a site for all your information-seeking needs, what would it look like? Who would be answering your questions?

As the team of interviewers was conducting the interviews, each of them typed the responses into SurveyMonkey. The interviewers endeavored to capture verbatim answers, rereading replies after typing them. Table 10.2 shows a partial list of the raw telephone interview data.

Once all the interviews were completed, the principal investigators worked together to review the data through repeated readings and to create a hierarchy of initial codes. Table 10.3 shows one of the early frameworks for the coding scheme for the magic wand question. Note that these are categories that are grounded in the data, not imposed by a previous theoretical or conceptual framework.

Working back and forth from the data, the principal investigators highlighted portions of the data and affixed initial codes to these. Table 10.4 shows a partial sample at this stage. The notes to the left are from one coder and indicate that these could be used as examples to illustrate a particular code. After a second coder worked through a portion of the data, areas of disagreement were identified and then discussed to resolve differences in order to ensure intercoder reliability (ICR), sometimes referred to as interrater reliability (IRR).

Table 10.5 shows what the final codebook looked like with the definitions, examples from the data, and "n" counts of how many of the respondents' data contained this code.

Table 10.6 displays one particularly notable quote from the magic wand question, which was identified as a "juicy quote," not because it was representative of any of the categories but because it was particularly descriptive and creative, different from the other data.

These examples and tables 10.2 to 10.6 are included to illustrate coding practices. The following sections discuss additional approaches to coding data.

Discourse Analysis

Budd has divided discourse analysis (DA) into two different approaches: content analysis in the form of "linguistic-based analysis," which is discussed

Table 10.2.   Magic Wand Partial Raw Data from Phone Interviews

Participant No.	Q. If you had a magic wand and could create a site for all your information-seeking needs, what would it look like? Who would be answering your questions?
P3	I haven't seen a site, maybe because I haven't searched for it. . . . I'd like to see a site similar to Angie's List with tons of experts in the field ready to answer your questions vs. the general public. It'd be awesome! It'd be like a "Your Expert Ready for Hire." You could just click on there and have them answer it. A lot of times, I'll get responses back that are totally asinine and off the wall, so you get a lot of stuff you have to troll through. It's not worth pursuing that avenue. If there was a site and the person was an expert in history, that'd be great. I say Angie's List because I assume they wouldn't do it for free.
P6	I think that there would be all different areas and divided into different subjects, with someone with a doctorate or high standard of credentials whom I could trust when using their information. I think a 24-hour immediate response instead of waiting for someone to post a response to your question, where you are guaranteed a response. I mean, overall it would just be a very easy to use a site that is accessible to anyone, but the core thing is that it would be divided by subject.
P7	It could probably look like a site, there'd be different links that could take you to different pages of the website, like professor's advice or medical advice. A doctor might not be able to answer something you need in another area, so it would offer more specific ways to find your answer. I think a range of people could contribute to it, probably people who are in the professions if they know more about it. Maybe an area for opinions from average people, you know, students.
P10	Pharmacy-wise, I would have a clinical pharmacist on the other end. In general, if there were a web wizard where all the information was put in by experts. It would be easy to use with an option to get more information when necessary.
P11	It would be similar to a website like Yahoo. I would usually want teachers and professors answering the questions, maybe graduate students, too.
P12	It'd probably have a lot of categories, so if I had a question about sports or cars or education, I would click on that tab and there'd be a bunch of frequently asked questions answered by experts.
P14	I guess it would definitely have a search bar like Google. The reference sources we use online like EBSCO so you could have different sections based on where you wanted to get your information from, for example, opinion-based, reference, journals, just broken up into different subgroups so you could look specifically where you would like to find your information.

(continued)

Table 10.2.   (continued)

Participant No.	Q. If you had a magic wand and could create a site for all your information-seeking needs, what would it look like? Who would be answering your questions?
P15	I think there's already a site like that for me, except it's not free. Have you ever heard of Cramster? It basically has solutions through textbooks and all the explanations of how to do everything. There's also other students or professors who answer questions for you. I would still be using it if it stayed free, but it's not anymore. It had all the math and science textbooks on there.
P17	It'd probably look very similar to Google, like a mass search engine with so many topics. Depending on the topic, I'd try to find people well versed in that area, people who work with the product and use it all the time, they'd be the ones answering the questions. I'd definitely do a call feature. If you go to Google and you type a certain chain of restaurants in your area, it has the option to call or get directions or the website, so my site would have something like that also.
P18	Like Ask Jeeves? I hated Ask Jeeves. I mean, I kind of like the way Yahoo! Answers does it. Maybe when you go to type in your question, as soon as you type in a subject matter, underneath it could scroll down different options that people have asked already, then immediately scroll down and find the topic. Let's say you select painting and then type in "impasto," then it might pop up "artists that have used impasto," then you could immediately go down and click that answer. Kind of like an FAQ but it pops up right away. Then the more words you type in the more specific the answer gets. Not a lot of noticeable advertisements. Everyone could answer, like they do on Yahoo! Answers. Everyone has a certain type of knowledge. The other day I typed in "How did Reagan fix the economy?" and someone put a very specific answer and most people below kind of tweaked it or agreed with what that person said. You take evaluating which part of the answer is accurate, and you could look up more stuff and match up what other people have said that they all agree on. I would hope that there would be some sort of filters, so deleting or reporting joking answers. I like the way Yahoo! Answers [works].

above, and "culturally or socially based discursive practices," such as those that Foucault has developed. Budd (2006, 65) notes that both of these types of analyses have potential for LIS and recommends the increased use of discourse analytic methods. The overarching premise of DA is to question and explore the relationship of the library as an institution and/or LIS as a field of research within a larger social and cultural context (Budd 2006, 65–82). Current LIS research using DA also seeks to shed light on how sociological, philosophical, and other critical literatures might be used as lenses to investigate

Table 10.3.   Magic Wand Initial Coding Categories and Themes

Code No.	Code/Category	Definition	Examples	n
I	**Who answers**			
I A	Experts			
I B	Anyone			
II	**Qualifications**			
II A	Education	Degree (e.g., PhD, MD, JD)		
II B	Who verifies credentials			
II B 1	By site			
II B 2	External party	e.g., BBB		
II C	Experience	Life or occupational experience		
III	**Look like existing site**			
III A	Yahoo! Answers			
III B	Google			
III C	Cramster			
III D	Chegg			
IV	**Site structure**			
IV A	Forum	Threaded discussions, archival		
IV B	One search box	Algorithm matches to previously asked questions		
IV C	Categories	Hierarchical subject index		
V	**Cost to use**			
V A	Free			
V B	Paid	Includes paying for a different level of service		
VI	**Rewards/recognition for answerers**			
VII	**Communication**			
VII A	Asynchronous			
VII B	Synchronous			
VII B 1	Skype			
VII B 2	IM/Chat			

(continued)

Table 10.3.   (continued)

Code No.	Code/Category	Definition	Examples	n
VII B 3	Phone			
VIII	**Display**			
VIII A	Avatars			
VIII B	Colors			
VIII C	Uncluttered			
IX	**Convenient**			

Table 10.4.   Magic Wand Partial Data Showing Initial Code Analysis

Coder 1	Participant No.	Questions and Responses	Good Examples
		Q. If you had a magic wand and could create a site for all your information-seeking needs, what would it look like? Who would be answering your questions?	
IA1, IIA3, IIIB	P3	I haven't seen a site, maybe because I haven't searched for it. . . . I'd like to see a site similar to Angie's List with tons of experts in the field ready to answer your questions vs. the general public. It'd be awesome! It'd be like a "Your Expert Ready for Hire." You could just click on there and have them answer it. A lot of times, I'll get responses back that are totally asinine and off the wall, so you get a lot of stuff you have to troll through. It's not worth pursuing that avenue. If there was a site and the person was an expert in history, that'd be great. I say Angie's List because I assume they wouldn't do it for free.	
IIB3, F	P6	I think that there would be all different areas and divided into different subjects, with someone with a doctorate or high standard of credentials who I could trust when using their information. I think a 24-hour immediate response instead of waiting for someone to post a response to your question, where you are guaranteed a response. I mean, overall it would just be a very easy to use site that is accessible to anyone, but the core thing is that it would be divided by subject.	IIF

(continued)

Table 10.4.   (continued)

Coder 1	Participant No.	Questions and Responses	Good Examples
IIB3, IA1,IIB1	P7	It could probably look like a site, there'd be different links that could take you to different pages of the website, like professor's advice or medical advice. A doctor might not be able to answer something you need in another area, so it would offer more specific ways to find your answer. I think a range of people could contribute to it, probably people who are in the professions if they know more about it. Maybe an area for opinions from average people, you know, students.	
IA1, IB1, IIC	P10	Pharmacy-wise, I would have a clinical pharmacist on the other end. In general, if there were a web wizard where all the information was put in by experts. It would be easy to use with an option to get more information when necessary.	
IIA, IA1, IB1	P11	It would be similar to a website like Yahoo. I would usually want teachers and professors answering the questions, maybe graduate students, too.	
IIB3, IIB4	P12	It'd probably have a lot of categories, so if I had a question about sports or cars or education, I would click on that tab and there'd be a bunch of frequently asked questions answered by experts.	IIB4
IIA2, IIB2, IIB3	P14	I guess it would definitely have a search bar like Google. The reference sources we use online like EBSCO so you could have different sections based on where you wanted to get your information from, for example, opinion-based, reference, journals, just broken up into different subgroups so you could look specifically where you would like to find your information.	
IIA3, IA1, IB1	P15	I think there's already a site like that for me, except it's not free. Have you ever heard of Cramster? It basically has solutions through textbooks and all the explanations of how to do everything. There's also other students or professors who answer questions for you. I would still be using it if it stayed free, but it's not anymore. It had all the math and science textbooks on there.	

(continued)

Table 10.4.   (continued)

Coder 1	Participant No.	Questions and Responses	Good Examples
IIA2, IB3	P17	It'd probably look very similar to Google, like a mass search engine with so many topics. Depending on the topic, I'd try to find people well versed in that area, people who work with the product and use it all the time, they'd be the ones answering the questions. I'd definitely do a call feature. If you go to Google and you type a certain chain of restaurants in your area, it has the option to call or get directions or the website, so my site would have something like that also.	
IA1, IA2	P18	Like Ask Jeeves? I hated Ask Jeeves. I mean, I kind of like the way Yahoo! Answers does it. Maybe when you go to type in your question, as soon as you type in a subject matter, under-neath it could scroll down different options that people have asked already, then immediately scroll down and find the topic. Let's say you select painting and then type in "impasto," then it might pop up "artists that have used impasto," then you could immediately go down and click that answer. Kind of like an FAQ but it pops up right away. Then the more words you type in the more specific the answer gets. Not a lot of noticeable advertisements. Everyone could answer, like they do on Yahoo! Answers. Everyone has a certain type of knowledge. The other day I typed in "How did Reagan fix the economy?" and someone put a very specific answer and most people below kind of tweaked it or agreed with what that person said. You take evaluating which part of the answer is accurate and you could look up more stuff and match up what other people have said that they all agree on. I would hope that there would be some sort of filters, so deleting or reporting joking answers. I like the way Yahoo! Answers [works].	

Table 10.5.   Magic Wand Codebook with Definitions, Examples, and Counts

Code No.	Code/Category	Definition	Examples with Participant Number	No. of Responses*
I	Who answers			
I A	Type	What type of person answers.		
I A 1	Experts	Person answering must have expertise to post answer.	"I would probably want someone who has some sort of expertise in that subject, not just some random guy who thinks he's right" (P65).	34
I A 2	Crowd	Anyone can answer.	"I think it'd be all different types of people, maybe ordinary people and then their qualifications and experience after" (P37).	8
I B	Qualifications		"Subject experts would answer the questions, show their qualifications and experience, and indicate why their input would be helpful" (P33).	1
I B 1	Education	Person answering has formal training/ education.	"I would say professors because they're more educated, they know what they're talking about" (P25).	20
I B 2	Experience	Person is working or has experience that would make them experts, but not necessarily formal education or training.	"Hopefully people who know a lot about the topic who have definite real world experience" (P31); "I guess the people I would have answering it is different people with experience in a variety of different backgrounds." (P54).	10
I B 3 a	Who verifies		"They would be verified professionals" (P41).	1

(continued)

Table 10.5. (continued)

Code No.	Code/Category	Definition	Examples with Participant Number	No. of Responses*
I B 3 b	Site	The site verifies or displays credentials.	"If there was a website administrator that could say who the person was (e.g., a professor or a director of something)" (P36); "Surely you could have a screening mechanism" (P48).	5
I B 3 c	Other	An organization external to the site verifies credentials.	"I look for an accredited place instead of some random you know blog or something [like Better Business Bureau]" (P51)	1
II	Interface			
II A	Looks like existing site	Sites are named		
II A 1	Google		"I think that the only thing I would probably have is similar to Google where there's a search or 'ask your question here,' that eliminates a lot of that not knowing where to go" (P54).	8
II A 2	Other		"It would probably look like Wikipedia" (P39).	8
II A 3	Yahoo!		"I like the format of Yahoo! Answers" (P57).	6
II B	Site structure	Features of the site.		
II B 1	Categories	Info organized into facets.	"I want it to be multiple categories and subjects" (P50).	13
II B 2	Search box	Includes a search bar.	"It would probably be very easy to read a search bar in the top where you could type in your question" (P53).	8

(continued)

Table 10.5.   (continued)

Code No.	Code/Category	Definition	Examples with Participant Number	No. of Responses*
II B 3	Forum	Includes threaded discussions.	"It would probably be a mashup of a forum, a wiki site, and a live chat service" (P20).	3
II B 4	FAQ	Includes an FAQ.	"I would click on that tab and there'd be a bunch of frequently asked questions answered by experts" (P12).	1
II C	Display	How the site looks.		1
II C 1	Colors	Respondent suggests colors for the site.	"My favorite colors are orange and yellow and red, so I'd design it out of those colors" (U-49); "Blue appeals to people's eyesight" (P62).	4
II C 2	Avatars	Site and/or people answering have an image representing them.	"Would want this for health-related or life questions, definitely it would be a grandmother. For research questions, a very well educated person, like a professor" (P42).	2
II C 3	Tags	Users can tag questions or answers.	"I would put in there some kind of tag service, so people answering questions or reading answers could put a tag on there" (P19).	1
II C 4	Rating	Users can rate answers.	"I like that Yahoo! includes the rating of the answer, especially if there is more than one answer to the question" (P19).	1
II D	Communication	How the askers and answers communicate.		
II D 1	Asynchronous		"Yes, [I] would like to have a video posted to follow (for a recipe). 'This is how I cook this dish'" (P40).	5

(continued)

Table 10.5. (continued)

Code No.	Code/Category	Definition	Examples with Participant Number	No. of Responses*
II D 2	Synchronous	"I could ask an expert and be able to get answers in real time" (P35).	3	
II D 2 a	Skype		"Something like Skype would be very helpful to communicate better" (P45).	3
II D 2 b	IM/Chat	"Maybe instant messaging with subject experts would be nice" (P41).	2	
II D 2 c	Phone	"You have to pay to chat with the experts over the phone" (P50).	1	
II E	Convenient	The site is easy to use.	"It'd be very very user friendly and simple to work with" (P68).	10
II F	Fast	The responses are returned quickly.	"I think a 24-hour immediate response instead of waiting" (P6).	2
II G	Follow-up	The site allows for the original asker or others to ask additional questions on the topic.	"If you felt like the answer didn't fulfill what you're looking for, you could always try a second person that would come up so you could get a second opinion and different sources" (P55).	2
III	Cost to use	How much askers would have to pay.		
III A	Free		"I would want it to be free! Not everyone can afford some of this stuff" (P29).	3

(continued)

Table 10.5.   (continued)

Code No.	Code/Category	Definition	Examples with Participant Number	No. of Responses*
III B	Paid		"Maybe people could create an account where they pay each month, I would monetize it because I think people would use it" (P24).	2
III C	Tiered	For further expert analysis, the asker would have to pay.	"Some of these sites I go on you can type your question, but I would add a hotline where you can chat with these experts who are real, but there will be an additional fee" (P50).	1
IV	Rewards/ recognition for answerers		"People post their questions on there and they get points for it or rewards if you post the answer" (P29).	2

*The last column refers to the number of participants whose response was coded into the corresponding code/category.

Table 10.6.   Example of Juicy Quote for Magic Wand Question

P42	Oh that's crazy! [laughter] I would say like a grandmother, like an elderly person, or maybe experienced person, like a grandmother type would be a person answering the question. Nature scene in the background, like kind of a leafy woods type scenery with sunlight streaming through the leaves, symbolizing wisdom. When I clicked in, I'd be talking to grandma. Would want this for health-related or life questions, definitely it would be a grandmother. For research questions, a very well educated person, like a professor. Background kinda like a book shelf. Color of screen like bindings on a book, like a library. Maybe a woman, in her mid-50s. To learn about qualifications, I would like to see an "about link," which would drop down where the qualifications and certifications for that person would be given. [Probe what is lacking in the services you use?] The self-assurance of who is giving you the information for the questions you are asking is not there in present services. These people answering are too anonymous, even the librarians. I don't know what their areas of expertise are.

epistemological and ontological assumptions and factors that contribute to research approaches, including those of the methods themselves.

Qualitative data collection usually is accomplished through case studies, analysis of library and/or institutional documentation, interview transcripts, researcher's personal experience, participant observation, or ethnography.

Discourse analysis also can use quantitative methodology, but this appears to be rare; although one article was found that used latent semantic analysis (LSA) as a technique to explore selected discourse from organizations including the International Federation of Library Associations and Institutions (IFLA), the American Library Association (ALA), and the Turkish Librarians' Association (TLA), finding that there is a positive relation among these (Üniversitesi and Darvish 2010).

Following is a range of examples of research contexts in LIS that have used qualitative approaches to DA as a method of analysis:

- Assessment of the biases communicated via library-based processes, such as classification of Welsh art materials, through a hermeneutic and interpretive approach (Ragaller and Rafferty 2012).
- Examination of adoption of commercial models for libraries, such as the bookstore model (such as Book Industry Standards and Communications), and potential consequences for public service institutions of adopting this model as it relates to values, standards, terminologies, and impact on users (Martínez-Ávila and Kipp 2014).
- Exploration of the values and standards underlying library practices and role of the use of space in a public library context from a sociological perspective (Čepič 2012).
- Investigation of the discourses regarding internet access in Singapore (Kay Heng Heok and Luyt 2010).
- Analysis of the concept of information poverty using a close reading of LIS journal articles from 1995 to 2005, in which the findings reveal four discursive procedures: (a) economic determinism, (b) technological determinism and the "information society," (c) historicizing the "information poor," and (d) the LIS profession's moral obligation and responsibility (Haider and Bawden 2007).
- Exploration of the role and identities of school librarians in a DA study as part of a larger ethnographic study of collaborations between teachers and a school librarian (Kimmel 2011).
- Investigation of stereotypes, such as of librarians and libraries, in popular culture, including, books, film, television, and graphic novels (Radford, Radford, and Alpert 2015).
- Theoretical exploration of gendered expectations and literacy of language arts teachers in a graduate adolescent literature class using a social constructionist framework. Findings have implications for librarians "to examine and redefine our current strategies for motivating readers and recommending library materials" (Brendler 2014).

Wildemuth (2017) further discusses how DA is framed in LIS providing a detailed analysis of two examples from the work of Radford and Radford (1997), as well as Frohmann (1997). She carefully delineates the essential steps that are taken in DA as suggested by the classic text by Potter and Wetherell (1987) as follows:

- "Construct your research question . . ."
- "Select a sample of discourse to study . . ."

- "Collect the records and documents you will analyze . . ."
- "Code the data . . ." (Wildemuth 2017, 333).
- "Analyze the data by "close reading and rereading of the texts . . ."
- "Validate your findings" (Wildemuth 2017, 334).

Critical Approaches

Critical approaches are contained within Budd's (2006) categorization of discourse analysis methods that involve "culturally or socially based discursive practices." These interpretive frameworks facilitate critical explorations of LIS issues, including questioning the institutional discourses guiding librarianship and LIS research. Who participates in these discourses? Who is not included within them? These are two types of questions often asked when employing this method.

According to Creswell and Poth, critical approaches fundamentally embrace critical theoretical frames that can be viewed as shaped through the paradigmatic interpretive lens of postmodern perspectives (see chapter 2). "Critical theory perspectives are concerned with empowering human beings to transcend the constraints placed on them by race, class, and gender. Researchers need to acknowledge their own power, engage in dialogues, and use theory to interpret or illuminate social action. Central themes that a critical researcher might explore include the scientific study of social institutions and their transformations through interpreting the meanings of social institutions and their transformations through interpreting the meanings of social live; the historical problems of domination, alienation, and social struggles, and a critique of society and the envisioning of new possibilities" (Creswell and Poth 2016; Fay 1987; Morrow and Brown 1994; Soyini, 2020).

As described below, and seen in the numerous examples cited here, critical methods embrace a variety of allied theoretical approaches, subtheories, applications of the work of critical thinkers, and analysis of different types of textual or mediated data. Data sources can include text (books, articles, graphic novels, comic books (Radford, Radford, and Alpert 2015), newspapers, etc.), media (film (Radford and Radford 2003), television, photographs, radio, etc.), and online sources (YouTube clips, blogs, social media postings, online discussion groups, etc.). Critical researchers interrogate the data sources using the lens of chosen theoretical frames or philosophical writings, similar to literary analysis. Montgomerie's edited monograph, *Critical Methods in Political and Cultural Economy,* is recommended as guide to critical methodology that "demonstrate[s] how methods are transformative and reimagines research strategies as both an embodied practice and a social process" (Montgomerie, 2017). Additionally, Compton, Meadow, and Schilt's (2018) edited book describes queer methods that are used in sociology.

Wiegand issued a call to action for LIS scholars in an article published in *The Library Quarterly* in 1999 to address "tunnel vision and blind spots" in LIS history and to look outside of traditionally narrow theoretical and methodological frames to apply a broader spectrum of thought to LIS problematics, including that of postmodern thinkers. Following the publication of this article, a special issue of *The Library Quarterly,* in 2003, featured articles that applied the work of thinkers such as Bourdieu, Foucault, Hall, and Gramsci (Budd 2003; Raber 2003; Radford 2003; Radford and Radford 2003). Budd (2003) wrote about Bourdieu's concept of power, the goals of praxis (i.e., interpretive, ethical social action), and cultural production, noting: "If, as Wayne Wiegand claims, librarianship is afflicted by tunnel vision and blind spots, the task facing the profession is broadening perspective to encompass potentially fruitful work done in other disciplinary fields."

More recently, there has been a steady growth in LIS publications that take a critical approach (Cooke 2019; Fritch 2018; Tewell 2018). Critical theory includes such frameworks as feminist theory, critical race theory, queer theory, and disability theories (Creswell and Poth 2016). These frames can be blended, as exemplified by Adler (2016), who brings knowledge organization scholars "into dialogue with critical race theorists, indigenous studies scholars, and queer theorists around conversations about reparations and reparative reading practices . . . identifies specific cases, including #BlackLivesMatter, indigenous subject headings and classifications, and the Digital Transgender Archives as models for taxonomic reparations."

"Queer theory is characterized by a variety of methods and strategies relating to individual identity . . . it explores the myriad complexities of the construct, identity, and how identities reproduce and 'perform' in social forums" (Creswell and Poth 2016). Drabinski (2013) applies queer theory to cataloging practices and the politics of correction. Bryant, Bussel, and Halpern (2019) investigated gender identity and performance as a professional resource. Extending Ettarh's work (2014) on intersectionality and librarianship, Floegel and Jackson (2019) utilize the matrix of domination as a framework through which to examine how libraries can reflect and reify oppression in overlapping structural, disciplinary, hegemonic, and interpersonal domains. Wagner and Crowley (2020) used a critical discourse analysis (CDA) approach informed by queer theory to consider exclusionary practices directed toward trans and gender-nonconforming individuals in academic library facilities. They note that "Crucially, CDA does not only address how these power relations are reproduced in discourse but does so with an explicit stance and aim of critiquing them. In other words, CDA aims to investigate critically social inequality as expressed and legitimized primarily through language, but constitutive of other discursive practices such as signs, gestures, and text. In this, the critical discourse analyst takes an explicit stance towards the issues, institutions, and power structures that are at play" (Wagner and Crowley 2020).

As Adler's work demonstrates, a key area of development in LIS is the application of critical race theory that "focuses theoretical attention on studying and transforming the relationship between race, racism, and power" (Delgado and Stefancic 2012, 3). "Race and racism is deeply embedded within the framework of American society" (Creswell and Poth 2016, 30), which has been historically suppressed or sanitized in accounts of librarianship (Wiegand 2020). LIS scholars are using critical race theory in interpretive analyses of a variety of problematics that consider the Library Bill of Rights (Bocchicchio-Chaudhri 2019), the LIS curriculum (Gibson, Hughes-Hassell, and Threats 2018), issues of neutrality and social justice (Gibson et al. 2017), antiracism

(Hudson 2017), minority librarians in higher education (Johnson 2016), and diversity in children's books (Mabbott 2017) and in law libraries (Watson 2019).

A growing body of work is investigating critical approaches to librarianship and to information literacy. Drabinski notes that "critical librarianship offers a framework for thinking about our work that asks how library structures came to be and what ideologies underpin them. Viewing librarianship through this frame allow us to imagine new and better worlds on our way to making them" (Drabinski 2019, 49). Others, such as Cooke (2019) and Fritch (2018), also apply critical theory to LIS pedagogy and information literacy.

A few overviews of critical theoretical approaches have appeared recently that are very useful. For example, Audunson et al. (2019) have compiled an overview of public libraries as an infrastructure for a sustainable public sphere. Lawrence (2020) also has an article that uses critical theory to address "the problem of oppressive tastes in the public library."

Additionally, Dewey has provided a detailed summary and analysis of the use of Foucault's work in LIS, highlighting the pioneering contributions of Radford, and Radford and Radford (Dewey 2020; Radford 1992, 1998, 2003; Radford and Radford 1997; Radford and Radford 2001; Radford and Radford 2003; Radford and Radford 2005; Radford, Radford, and Lingel 2012, 2015, 2018). Dewey conducted a bibliometric content analysis of 105 LIS journals, published from 1990 to 2016 to investigate whether and to what depth Foucault's ideas are explored within 1,062 articles he inspected. He concluded that "most uses of Foucault are brief or in passing. In-depth explorations of Foucault's works are comparatively rare and relatively little-used by other LIS scholars" (Dewey 2020, 689).

Conversation Analysis

Conversation analysis (CA) is an approach to analyzing talk that is captured in natural settings that has become well established in the disciplines of communication, sociology, linguistics, ethnomethodology, ethnography, and social psychology (Sidnell and Stivers 2016). "A primary aim of CA is to lay out the basic sense-making practices and regularities of interaction that form the basis for everyday communication, in both informal and professional settings" (2008, 175). It highlights the importance of context and revealing regularities of social conduct through examining particular episodic interactions (Mandelbaum 2008, 175–88). Two recommended texts that detail the specifics on coding data for CA are by (1) Cliff and (2) Sidnell and Stivers. Basically, the method involves the creation of transcripts, audio or video recordings of normal conversations, which are then coded using rigorous and conventional annotation techniques (Sidnell and Stivers 2016). CA concerns itself with two foundations, namely "*action*" or "the things we do with words—and *sequence*—'a course of action implemented through talk'" (Schegloff 2007). Although it has not been used extensively in LIS, CA is perceived as a fruitful method for examining language-related contexts within the field, including explorations of how different mediated modes (such as asynchronous, FtF, and live chat) may affect communication and for assessing the ethical implications of reference interviews.

One example from LIS is found in the work of Savolainen, who used CA to investigate talk in a do-it-yourself online forum by analyzing twenty discussion threads. This article has value in applying CA to studying asynchronous online dialog and elaborating Schegloff's CA model for organization of sequence in conversation (Savolainen 2019).

Another notable use of CA was by Epperson and Zemel, who studied live chat reference and assert that this method is useful to analyze services that rely on communication between librarian and library user, such as reference. They believed that use of CA escapes the "tendency to impose analytic categories and classificatory schemes that obscure the extremely situated and collaborative nature of reference work" (Epperson and Zemel 2008).

Here are additional examples of research contexts in LIS that have used CA as a method of analysis:

- Investigation of communication problems in live chat-based reference transcripts (Dempsey 2016; Radford 2006a; Radford et al. 2011; Ulvik and Salvesen 2007).
- Inquiry into the information-seeking and questioning behavior of young female children in family interactions (Barriage and Searles 2015b).

Regardless of what qualitative methods are used for data collection and analysis, it is critical that the researcher keep in mind standards for validation and quality. Qualitative methodology, although flexible and naturalistic, has acceptable standards of quality that are described in the section below.

ENSURING INTEGRITY AND QUALITY

How do you ensure integrity? What is quality in qualitative research? How does one ensure that one's work will be seen as valid, credible, and useful by others? According to Marshall and Rossman, criteria for judging quality that were taken from more quantitative research were initially also adopted for qualitative research, and they named "reliability, validity, objectivity, and generalizability" as touchstones. However, they noted that more recently there has been a challenge to these "canonical standards" in the postmodern era, in which other standards have become generally accepted (Marshall and Rossman 2016, 43). As might be expected, much has been written on quality standards in qualitative research, some of it contentious. Grounded theory scholars Corbin and Strauss described quality qualitative research as having the following characteristics:

- It makes intuitive sense that resonates with the readers' and participants' life experiences.
- It is compelling, clearly written, and logical in organization and conclusions, and makes readers think and want to read and learn more.

- It is substantial, provides insight, and shows sensitivity both to the topic and to the participants.
- It is innovative, moving beyond the ordinary (Corbin and Strauss 2014).

Trustworthiness also is a traditional measure of quality for qualitative methods (Marshall and Rossman 2016). Does the reader find results to be credible? Do they trust and believe the findings? Experts such as Lincoln and Guba (1985) and Sandelowski (1986) chose to include truth value (i.e., adequate representation of multiple constructions of reality), applicability (i.e., fit or transferability), and consistency (i.e., dependability; enabling other researchers to follow method) as necessary to assessments of quality. Another standard is comparability, related to applicability, which considers whether the researcher clearly and fully describes characteristics of the group studied in the concepts generated that will enable comparisons to other groups (although generalizability is not a goal) (LeCompte and Goetz 1982). Closely related to this idea is translatability, or the ability for others to make comparisons confidently. This means that the researcher was careful to explain the methods used, to describe analytic categories, and to provide details on the characteristics of the group studied (LeCompte and Goetz 1982).

Primary Techniques for Ensuring Integrity and Avoiding Analytic Bias

In qualitative research, the role of the researcher includes interpretation of data for the sake of validity; however, it is important to strive to avoid *analytic* bias. Corbin and Strauss noted that it is the nature of qualitative research to be subjective and to have some researcher bias built in. They contended that this is not entirely bad, "especially when it comes to choosing the research problem, setting the research question and choosing the audience for whom to write." So an LIS researcher would choose to explore, research, and publish in LIS areas of interest. Corbin and Strauss further explained: "It is when it comes to analysis that perspectives, biases, and assumptions can have their greatest impact. The impact comes in the meaning given to data, the concepts used to stand for that meaning, the questions that are asked, and the comparisons that are made" (Corbin and Strauss 2014, 46).

According to Miles, Huberman, and Saldaña (2020, 291), there are two possible sources of bias: (1) "the effects of the researcher on the case" and/or (2) "the effects of the case on the researcher." They describe four archetypical types of analytic bias:

Holistic fallacy: "Interpreting events as more patterned and congruent than they really are, lopping off the many loose ends of which social life is made—that is, sloppy research." (Miles, Huberman, and Saldaña 2020, 289)

Elite bias: "Overweighting data from articulate, well-informed, usually high-status participants and underrepresenting data from less articulate, lower-status ones." (Miles, Huberman, and Saldaña 2020, 289)

Personal bias: "The researcher's personal agenda, personal demons, or personal 'axes to grind,' which skew the ability to represent and present field work and data analysis in a trustworthy manner." (Miles, Huberman, and Saldaña 2020, 289)

Going native: "Losing your perspective . . . being co-opted into the perceptions and explanations of local participants." (Miles, Huberman, and Saldaña 2020, 289)

Miles, Huberman, and Saldaña (2020, 289) described a variety of tactics for assessing the quality of data, avoiding bias, and testing and confirming findings: (a) checking for representativeness, (b) weighing evidence, (c) making if-then tests, (d) getting feedback from informants, and (e) checking "unpatterns" (e.g., outliers, extreme cases, surprises, negative evidence).

Another extremely useful strategy for ensuring quality results is the use of triangulation by using a variety of data sources and a research design with multiple methods in which the problem that is being studied is approached through use of several qualitative techniques, or a mix of qualitative and quantitative methods. See chapter 9 for a discussion of mixed methods and triangulation.

Intercoder Reliability and Validity

Another important element for ensuring validity is the discovery and assignment of codes or themes within the data. Qualitative analysis can be undertaken by a single researcher or in teams, as in collaborative or grant-funded work. In either case, validity checks must be performed on the analysis, and an important strategy for this assessment is the intercoder reliability (ICR) check, also known as interrater reliability or interjudge reliability. According to Lavrakas (2008), "Intercoder reliability refers to the extent to which two or more independent coders agree on the coding of the content of interest with an application of the same coding scheme." Whether creating codes or discovering in vivo codes during the process of coding data, it is important to remember that it is inadequate to have only one coder. Using a second or third trained person to code a portion of the data (approximately 20 percent is a standard adopted by the authors) ensures that codes are not subjectively assigned. Performing ICR checks helps to answer the questions: How do you know that the codes assigned are valid? Are the coding instructions and definitions of the codes clear? Can someone else sort the data into the codes with enough agreement that this method and the results can be seen as valid?

This important process consists of two or more coders comparing their identification of data and sorting them into codes and then comparing results and determining a percentage of agreement. Generally, 75 to 85 percent is regarded as an acceptable minimum, and it is the authors' experience that when seeking publication for articles reporting coded qualitative data using teams, journal editors and other reviewers may prefer to see 85 percent or better scores. If initial ICR scores are found to be low, coders need to discuss each code to resolve differences. This process can be used to improve the final score, and the standard practice is to then report both the initial score and the score after discussion. According to Bakeman and Quera, there are three important reasons for performing tests of ICR. They asserted: "Observer accuracy is rightly called the *sine qua non* of observational research, and there are at least three major reasons why it is essential: first, to assure ourselves that the coders we train are performing as expected; second to provide coders with accurate feedback they need to improve . . . ; and third, to convince others, including our colleagues and journal editors, that they have good reason to take our results seriously" (Bakeman and Quera 2011).

The ICR may be calculated in many ways; among the most popular are Cohen's (Cohen 1960) Kappa, Scott's (1955) pi, Krippendorff's (1980) Alpha, and Holsti's (1969) Coefficient of Reliability. Cohen's Kappa is one of the most commonly used statistics for point-by-point observer agreement. It is a summary measure that determines how well two observers agree when asked to independently code data using a shared codebook. Therefore, it is a summary of how well coders agree when applying codes to data. It is preferable to a straight percentage of agreement, because it takes into consideration the possibility that agreement on codes could have occurred by chance alone. It represents the total frequency of agreement minus the expected frequency of agreement by chance, divided by the total units coded minus the expected frequency of agreement by chance. Kappa value falls in a range between negative one and one, with negative values not meaningful and a value of zero occurring purely by chance. Agreement that falls between 40 and 60 percent is moderate agreement, 60–80 percent is thought to be good, and scores higher than 80 percent are seen as a very good agreement rate (Zaiontz n.d.). The Kappa calculation almost always will be lower than the probability of observed agreement (they are only equal when agreement between coders is perfect). The Kappa score almost never will be a negative value, but when it is, the coders must ask themselves why they are disagreeing at worse than chance levels (Bakeman and Quera 2011).

As noted in the section above on CAQDAS software that is used to analyze qualitative data, Cohen's Kappa is calculated in NVivo by running a coding comparison query and can be computed for multiple coders who are not necessarily physically collocated. Some researchers choose to compute ICR using more than one measure and then report all scores in their reports or publications. An example from LIS research is by Hughes (2014), who reported both a Cohen's Kappa score and Krippendorff's Alpha in a content analysis of reference transactions, including location-based and subject-based questions to help in staffing decision making.

One additional recommendation is that it is an excellent idea to conduct ICR tests early in the coding process, for example, after coding one interview transcript, or approximately 5 percent of the data. One does not want to learn the hard way that once a large amount of data has been coded, it is a major effort to go back and recode if the decision was made to wait to calculate the level of coding agreement. It is much easier, less stressful, and less time consuming to do this early in the initial coding process and to make adjustments, especially when working with a group of coders, such as on a large grant project.

Visualization and Display of Qualitative Data

Closely connected to qualitative data analysis is ways in which the researcher constructs visualizations and displays of the findings. Display can be defined as "a visual format that presents information systematically (and sometimes evocatively) so the user can draw conclusions and take needed action" (Miles, Huberman, and Saldaña 2020, 104). Definitions of information visualization in LIS are "grounded in the visual elements, and in particular pictorial or graphical formats. Its key use has been identified as its ability to help decision makers see analytics, further helping them to comprehend difficult concepts and even identify new patterns . . . Information visualization is easier for the brain to process than other forms of data, such as reports or spreadsheets" (Chen 2017).

Traditionally, data visualization has been most closely associated with quantitative research that involves numbers (think bar charts, graphs, tables, and pie charts that are easily created using spreadsheets such as Excel, as discussed in chapter 8). However, there is a growing body of literature on visual representations of qualitative data that is being embraced in the social sciences, including LIS. Miles and Huberman (1994) pioneered the use of matrices and network displays in their early work in the social sciences, and continue to champion these, plus have added graphics to this list with coauthor Saldaña more recently. The way that a researcher chooses to create data visualizations is thought of as integral to the analysis process that is to be considered as a first step, rather than a last step that is done just prior to finishing a report, project, or publication. Display is conceived of as an aid to analysis "the chances of drawing and verifying conclusions are much greater than for extended text, because the display is arranged coherently to permit careful comparisons, detection of differences, noting of pattern and themes, seeing trends, and so on" (Miles, Huberman, and Saldaña 2020, 104). According to Miles, Huberman and Saldaña, these are the three most important display modes for qualitative data: "1) Matrices, with defined rows and columns, 2) Networks, a series of nodes or bins with links (lines and arrows) between them, and 3) Graphics, consisting of a wide array of other visual devices in various forms and formats" (Miles, Huberman, and Saldaña 2020, 103–18).

Chandler, Anstey, and Ross (2015, 4) note that CAQDAS, introduced above in this chapter, and other types of software and technological developments have further enabled researchers to create visualizations that include the above three modes, plus "word clouds, and word trees" which have all "become more common in qualitative dissemination efforts." Chandler et al. cite a study by Verdinelli and Scagnoli that analyzed three years of publications in three top qualitative research journals to see what types of qualitative data displays were used and found "most common were matrices, networks, flowcharts, boxed displays, and modified Venn diagrams, followed by taxonomies, ladders, metaphorical visual displays, and decision tree modeling" (Chandler, Anstey, and Ross 2015, 6; Verdinelli and Scagnoli 2013). Additionally, Chandler et al. advocate the use of combining infographics and innovative modes such as using audio clips that can be embedded in written manuscripts, poster and oral presentations, to effectively convey a qualitative "story."

In LIS, the term "information visualization" (IV or InfoVis) has been widely adopted. There is a special issue of *Library Technical Reports* (Chen 2017) on information visualization that overviews its use in library settings. Ostergren et al. (2011, 531) argue that InfoVis is also a field of study that is "a central, integrated component of study in Information Science," and, as such, it should be deeply studied in iSchool curricula. They surveyed iSchools to see what software is being taught (for both qualitative and quantitative displays) and found a large number including "Tableau, Spotfire, GGobi, R, Mathematica, prefuse, Many Eyes, DreamWeaver, protovis, Flare, gnuplot and various forms of mind-mapping software, both proprietary and open source." They also found that this software was used to create a wide range of visualizations as follows: "networks (social and bibliographic), tree and mind maps, charts, graphs, temporal visualizations, geographics, geographic information systems (GIS), thematic overlays (Google Earth), trend analysis, time series, multi-dimensional graphics, algorithmic based visualizations and science mapping (knowledge domain visualizations)" (Ostergren et al. 2011, 532). They conclude that information visualization is "useful for any form of research, in any discipline" and that it can be a "tool for data analysis (using visual means of representing large data sets in ways that reveal patterns) and data communication (traditional graphs and charts are a form of information visualization which can be made significantly more effective when produced with an appreciation for the principles of IV)" (Ostergren et al. 2011, 535).

Hofschire, who is the director of the Library Research Service at the Colorado State Library, wrote a practical, useful, and highly accessible article, "Data Visualization on a Budget: Simple Tips, Techniques, and Low-Cost Tools," designed for those who are new to InfoVis and may lack large sums of money to purchase propriety software. She notes that "The saying 'a picture is worth a thousand words' certainly rings true when it comes to data visualizations. Recently, we have been bombarded with statistics about COVID-19, and some of the most impactful and digestible information has come in the form of visualizations—for example, the ubiquitous 'flatten the curve' charts." As information professionals, "many of us regularly report data about our work, including operational statistics (circulation, database use, etc.) and the results of user research, to demonstrate the impacts of our services. How can we take advantage of the power of data visualization to maximize the impact of this reporting" (Hofschire 2020, 19)? She suggests that the first step is to "think about where you can take the opportunity to show—i.e., visualize the information—rather than just telling" (Hofschire 2020, 20). The free or low-cost tools she recommends include: Microsoft Office 365 or Google Sheets/Slides for "creating charts . . . designing presentations, reports and infographics." For finding icons, she recommends use of the Microsoft Office 365 icon library, Adobe Spark, or the Noun Project website "that can be used with a variety of software, to seamlessly customize and add any icon from its vast library to your visualization" (Hofschire 2020, 22). Also, she recommends Infogram (free, or via subscription for advanced features), which has templates for "infographics, reports, slides, social media posts, and more" and Adobe Spark, which adds video slideshows to the

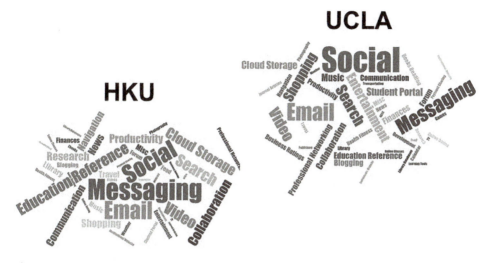

Figure 10.2. Word Clouds
Connaway, Kitzie, Hood, and Harvey 2017, 24.

Infogram list (Hofschire 2020, 22). Finally, she notes that working to visualize data "can be fun" (Hofschire 2020, 22).

A creative use of information visualization is found in the work of Gibson and Kaplan, who used a place-based approach to explore information practices of parents of individuals with disabilities to identify examples of information seeking and sharing. They used a combination of tables, figures, and visual models to clearly display their qualitative findings. Most notably they use a display that resembles an archery target to depict their "Spatial Information Seeking Zone Model" (Gibson and Kaplan 2017).

As another example, one investigation of research on the geospacial web (e.g., Google Earth and Google Maps), Elwood (2011) concludes that "Geoweb research should continue to rely on a diverse range of visualization practices and visual methods . . . [and] we must continue utilizing these new conceptual resources in creative and integrative ways."

When undergraduate and graduate students and faculty at the University of California–Los Angeles (UCLA) and Hong Kong University (HKU) completed the visitors and residents (V&R) mapping exercise, the research team was able to identify their different modes of engagement with technology, apps, and websites in word clouds. See figure 10.2. The study participants categorized the different forms of engagement they used for both their personal and professional activities and if they engaged as visitors or residents.

[T]he Visitors see the web as a series of tools. They decide what they want to achieve, chose an appropriate online tool to do the job, then log-off. They leave no social trace of themselves online. The Residents live a proportion of their lives online. They see the web as a place where they can express themselves and spend time with people. Residents will have a profile on a social networking platform and aspects of their persona, or digital identity, maintaining a presence even when they are not online. The premise of this project is that V&R is a continuum in which the way participants interacted with the digital and non-digital world were more Visitor or Resident depending on their personal motivations and the context and situation at the time. (Connaway, Lanclos, and Hood 2013, 290)

In The Many Faces of Digital Visitors & Residents report (2017) the OCLC research team used a decision tree algorithm that would take the V&R maps created by librarians and students and determine whether the map was created by a librarian or a student "by answering a cascade of questions that it learns based on training data" (Connaway, Kitzie, Hood, and Harvey 2017, 25). The results of the first decision tree created by the algorithm, which correctly identified seventy-eight of the eighty-three maps, are depicted in figure 10.3.

There are different ways of graphically depicting timelines. These vary in the difficulty of creating the graphic and in the complexity of visualizing the data. Figure 10.4 (Lavoie, Dempsey, and Malpas 2020) is a timeline illustrating the collective collection studies conducted by OCLC Research indicating highlights of the findings from the studies.

Cycle diagrams can represent themes and subthemes of the findings to readers at a glance. Figure 10.5 (Bryant, Dortmund, and Lavoie 2020) is an example of a cycle diagram that visually represents the major themes and subthemes for successful intracampus social interoperability identified by the study participants.

As discussed above, information visualizations are integral to analysis and reporting qualitative research, especially since "in this highly visual culture, showing rather than telling can make a more effective and memorable impact on our audience" (Miles, Huberman, and Saldaña 2020, 104).

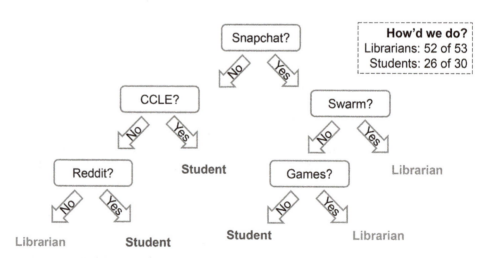

Figure 10.3. Fixed-Depth Decision Tree Classifiers
Connaway, Kitzie, Hood, and Harvey 2017, 43.

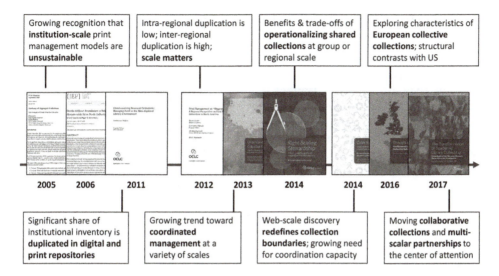

Figure 10.4. Timeline of Selected OCLC Research Collective Collection Reports and Trends
Lavoie, Dempsey, and Malpas 2020.

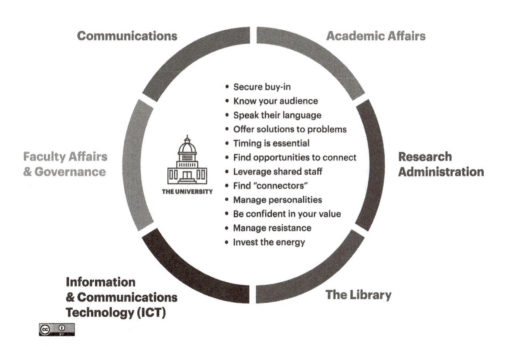

Figure 10.5. Key Takeaways about Successful Intracampus Social Interoperability
Bryant, Dortmund, and Lavoie 2020, 33.

CONCLUSION: MORE TO LEARN ON DATA ANALYSIS AND CODING

Data analysis takes three Ps: persistence, patience, and practice. Analysis and coding are iterative processes, involving careful and repeated reading of data, intense attention to nuances uncovered in the analysis process, and an ongoing willingness to be open to the data and to revise analysis and coding schemes during the process.

Working closely with a mentor who has experience coding and analyzing qualitative data is invaluable to the novice. Do not be afraid to ask for help early and often. During the literature review period, be alert to discover existing coding schemes and theoretical constructs. Finding an existing coding scheme that has a firm basis in an established theory can be a huge breakthrough. The grounded theory approach can be taken if the phenomenon of interest is largely unstudied, but frequently there is extant work that can be applied, perhaps extended, by new research in different contexts and situations. Another highly recommended tactic is to conduct a small pilot study and to start by analyzing a small amount of data. What codes and categories can be found in initial analysis? Is this the type of data needed to answer the research questions? Can access be obtained for the target participant group? Are the right questions being asked of participants? Which questions are most important? Which can be dropped? Pending completion of the pilot study, the data collection method, instruments, and procedures can be revised. Codes can be developed and applied from pilot study to main study. As additional data are collected, pause and revise procedures as needed. When categories have reached saturation and the research questions are answered, that is the time to stop, complete the writing process, and publish or present results, as covered in chapters 3 and 15.

SUMMARY

Qualitative data analysis constitutes a rigorous process beginning with data collection. A strong theoretical basis for data interpretation could provide a starting point not only for informing analysis, but also to undergird the study conceptualization and design. The purpose of qualitative data analysis is to inform the creation of theoretical possibilities by discovering relationships and insights into the phenomena studied. Analysis constitutes an iterative process in which the researcher must demonstrate sensitivity to how emerging themes and patterns relate to what the overall data communicate and thus privilege the data implicitly, rather than explicitly.

This chapter reviews how to prepare and process data for analysis, including a discussion of methods to capture the data and different software to analyze the data. The chapter then delves into data analysis, or coding textual data. Two dominant ways to conceptualize this process are grounded theory, in which no prior set of categories informs how the data are categorized and described, and using and adopting/extending a preexisting coding scheme that is applied to the data collected. The researcher may choose to code deductively, solely using this scheme, or deductively and inductively, in which codes underneath the high-level, preexisting theoretical categories are informed by the data. The constant comparative method represents a major strategy for inductive analysis. This method requires the researcher to compare and aggregate pieces of data by similar characteristics and begin to sort them into groups that represent emerging themes. Of key importance to this method are in vivo codes, which derive directly from the voices of participants, rather than being imposed by the researcher. The chapter provides examples of how both inductive and deductive methods are used to derive or assess coding categories and themes, as well as examples of codebooks summarizing these resultant categories and themes.

Other methods of qualitative analysis are discussed also. These methods include conversation analysis, which has not been used extensively in LIS but provides a fruitful area for future research that examines language-related contexts within the field. Discourse analysis, which envelops conversation analysis and cultural and social discursive practices, is discussed as well. Additionally, this chapter will provide an overview of critical approaches.

To ensure quality in qualitative research, this chapter recommends employing measures such as trustworthiness, or whether the reader finds the results to be credible; comparability, or whether the researcher provides a description that enables comparisons to other groups; and translatability, or the ability to make these comparisons confidently. These measures provide an overall indication of how well the researcher explained the methods used, described analytic categories, and provided details on the characteristics of the group studied. For ensuring integrity, the chapter recommends avoiding analytic bias, or the meaning researchers assign to the data based on their own perspectives, biases, and assumptions. Some useful strategies for exercising such avoidance are to check for representativeness, weigh evidence, make if-then tests, get feedback from informants, and use a research design with multiple methods or modes of data collection. The researcher can maintain both quality and integrity by testing the data for validity between how different individuals assign codes or themes within the data. This assessment is achieved by calculating ICR. Multiple measures to perform this calculation are reviewed. The authors recommend conducting ICR early in the coding process so as not to have to learn the hard way once a large amount of data have been collected and having to go back and recode based on a misaligned coding agreement.

Finally, this chapter provides an overview of information visualization and display, stressing that these techniques can be used in the early stages of data collection to help detect patterns and represent relationships in the data and in the latter stages, to help present data in an easily understood and visually compelling way.

REFERENCES

Adler, Melissa. 2016. "The Case for Taxonomic Reparations." *Knowledge Organization* 43(8): 630–40. https://doi.org/10.5771/0943-7444-2016-8-630.

Aggarwal, Charu C., and ChengXiang Zhai. 2012. *Mining Text Data.* New York: Springer Science & Business Media.

Alomari, Mohammad Kamel, Kuldeep Sandhu, and Peter Woods. 2014. "Exploring Citizen Perceptions of Barriers to E-Government Adoption in a Developing Country." *Transforming Government: People, Process and Policy* 8(1): 131–50. https://doi.org/10.1108/TG-05-2013-0013.

Audunson, Ragnar, Svanhild Aabø, Roger Blomgren, Sunniva Evjen, Henrik Jochumsen, Håkon Larsen, Casper Hvenegaard Rasmussen, Andreas Vårheim, Jamie Johnston, and Masanori Koizumi. 2019. "Public Libraries as an Infrastructure for a Sustainable Public Sphere: A Comprehensive Review of Research." *Journal of Documentation*, May. https://doi.org/10.1108/JD-10-2018-0157.

Bakeman, Roger, and Vicenc Quera. 2011. *Sequential Analysis and Observational Methods for the Behavioral Sciences.* Cambridge: Cambridge University Press.

Barriage, Sarah C., and Darcey K. Searles. 2015. "Astronauts and Sugar Beets: Young Girls' Information Seeking in Family Interactions." Presented at the Association for Information Science and Technology (ASIS&T), Saint Louis, November 6.

Bocchicchio-Chaudhri, Celeste. 2019. "Bringing Critical Race Theory to the Library Bill of Rights." In *Social Justice and Activism in Libraries: Essays on Diversity and Change*, edited by Su Epstein, Vera Gubnitskaia, and Carol Smallwood, 129–36. Jefferson, NC: McFarland.

Brendler, Beth M. 2014. "Diversity in Literary Response: Revisiting Gender Expectations." *Journal of Education for Library and Information Science* 55(3): 223–40.

Bryant, Rebecca, Annette Dortmund, and Brian Lavoie. 2020. "Social Interoperability in Research Support: Cross-Campus Partnerships and the University Research Enterprise." Dublin, OH: OCLC Research.

Bryant, Tatiana, Hilary Bussell, and Rebecca Halpern. 2019. "Being Seen: Gender Identity and Performance as a Professional Resource in Library Work." *College & Research Libraries* 80(6): 805–26. https://doi.org/10.5860/crl.80.6.805.

Budd, John. 2006. "Discourse Analysis and the Study of Communication in LIS." *Library Trends* 55(1): 65–82. https://doi.org/10.1353/lib.2006.0046.

Budd, John M. 2003. "The Library, Praxis, and Symbolic Power." *The Library Quarterly* 73(1): 19–32. https://doi.org/10.1086/603373.

Burnett, Kathleen, Manimegalai Subramaniam, and Amelia Gibson. 2009. "Latinas Cross the IT Border: Understanding Gender as a Boundary Object between Information Worlds." *First Monday* 14(9). https://firstmonday.org/ojs/index.php/fm/article/view/2581/2286.

Burns, Sean C., and Jenny Bossaller. 2012. "Communication Overload: A Phenomenological Inquiry into Academic Reference Librarianship." *Journal of Documentation* 68(5): 597–617. https://doi.org/10.1108/00220411211255996.

Bussell, Hilary. 2020. "Libraries Support First-Generation Students through Services and Spaces, but Can Do More." *Evidence Based Library and Information Practice* 15(1): 242–44. https://doi.org/10.18438/eblip29689.

Čepič, Ana Vogrinčič. 2012. "Libraries Today, Libraries Tomorrow: Contemporary Library Practices and the Role of Library Space in Light of Wider Social Phenomena—Sociological Perspective." *Knjiznica* 56(4): 95–107.

Chandler, Rasheeta, Erica Anstey, and Henry Ross. 2015. "Listening to Voices and Visualizing Data in Qualitative Research: Hypermodal Dissemination Possibilities." *SAGE Open* 5(2): 2158244015592166. https://doi.org/10.1177/2158244015592166.

Charmaz, Kathy. 2014. *Constructing Grounded Theory.* 2nd ed. Thousand Oaks, CA: Sage.

Chen, Hsuanwei Michelle. 2017. "Information Visualization Principles, Techniques, and Software." *Library Technology Reports* 53(3): 8–16.

Cohen, Jacob. 1960. "A Coefficient of Agreement for Nominal Scales." *Educational and Psychological Measurement* 20(1): 37–46. https://doi.org/10.1177/001316446002000104.

Compton, D'Lane R., Tey Meadow, and Kristen Schilt. 2018. *Other, Please Specify*. Oakland: University of California Press. https://www.ucpress.edu/book/9780520289277/other-please-specify.

"Computer-Assisted Qualitative Data Analysis Software." 2020. In *Wikipedia*. https://en.wikipedia.org/w/index.php?title=Computer-assisted_qualitative_data_analysis_software&oldid=946158912.

Connaway, Lynn Silipigni, Vanessa Kitzie, Erin M. Hood, and William Harvey. 2017. "The Many Faces of Digital Visitors & Residents: Facets of Online Engagement." Dublin, OH: OCLC Research.

Connaway, Lynn Silipigni, Donna Lanclos, and Erin M. Hood. 2013. "'I Find Google a Lot Easier Than Going to the Library Website.' Imagine Ways to Innovate and Inspire Students to Use the Academic Library." In *Proceedings of the Association of College & Research Libraries (ACRL) 2013 Conference*. Vol. 289–300.

Connaway, Lynn Silipigni, Marie L. Radford, and OCLC Research. 2011. *Seeking Synchronicity: Revelations and Recommendations for Virtual Reference*. Dublin, OH: OCLC Research.

Cooke, Nicole A. 2019. "Leading with Love and Hospitality: Applying a Radical Pedagogy to LIS." *Information and Learning Sciences* 120(1/2): 119–32. https://doi.org/10.1108/ILS-06-2018-0054.

Corbin, Juliet, and Anselm Strauss. 2014. *Basics of Qualitative Research: Techniques and Procedures for Developing Grounded Theory*. 4th ed. Thousand Oaks, CA: Sage.

Creswell, John W., and Cheryl N. Poth. 2016. *Qualitative Inquiry and Research Design: Choosing among Five Approaches*. Thousand Oaks, CA: Sage.

Delgado, Richard, and Jean Stefancic. 2012. *Critical Race Theory: An Introduction*. 2nd ed. New York: New York University Press.

Dempsey, Paula R. 2016. "'Are You a Computer?' Opening Exchanges in Virtual Reference Shape the Potential for Teaching." *College & Research Libraries* 77(4). https://doi.org/10.5860/crl.77.4.455.

Dewey, Scott Hamilton. 2020. "Foucault's Toolbox: Use of Foucault's Writings in LIS Journal Literature, 1990–2016." *Journal of Documentation* 76(3): 689–707. https://doi.org/10.1108/JD-08-2019-0162.

Di Gregorio, Silvana. 2000. "Using NVivo for Your Literature Review." Presented at the Strategies in Qualitative Research: Issues and Results from Analysis Using QSR Nvivo and Nud*Ist, The Institute of Education, London, September 29.

Drabinski, Emily. 2013. "Queering the Catalog: Queer Theory and the Politics of Correction." *The Library Quarterly* 83(2): 94–111. https://doi.org/10.1086/669547.

Drabinski, Emily. 2019. "What Is Critical about Critical Librarianship?" *Publications and Research*, April. https://academicworks.cuny.edu/gc_pubs/537.

Ellis, David. 1993. "Modeling the Information-Seeking Patterns of Academic Researchers: A Grounded Theory Approach." *The Library Quarterly* 63(4): 469–86. https://doi.org/10.1086/602622.

Elwood, Sarah. 2011. "Geographic Information Science: Visualization, Visual Methods, and the Geoweb." *Progress in Human Geography* 35(3): 401–8. https://doi.org/10.1177/0309132510374250.

Epperson, Terrence W., and Alan Zemel. 2008. "Reports, Requests, and Recipient Design: The Management of Patron Queries in Online Reference Chats." *Journal of the American Society for Information Science and Technology* 59(14): 2268–83. https://doi.org/10.1002/asi.20930.

Ettarh, Fobazi. 2014. "Making a New Table: Intersectional Librarianship." *In the Library with the Lead Pipe* (blog). /2014/making-a-new-table-intersectional -librarianship-3/.

Fay, Brian. 1987. *Critical Social Science: Liberation and Its Limits*. Ithaca, NY: Cornell University Press.

Flanagan, John C. 1954. "The Critical Incident Technique." *Psychological Bulletin* 5: 327–58.

Floegel, Diana, and Lorin Jackson. 2019. "Recasting an Inclusive Narrative: Exploring Intersectional Theory." In *Proceedings of the 2019 Association for College & Research Libraries Conference*, 412–20.

Fritch, Melia Erin. 2018. "Teaching as a Political Act: Critical Pedagogy in Library Instruction." *Educational Considerations* 44(1). https://doi.org/10.4148 /0146-9282.1868.

Frohmann, Bernd. 1997. "'Best Books' and Excited Readers: Discursive Tensions in the Writings of Melvil Dewey." *Libraries & Culture* 32(3): 349–71.

Gibson, Amelia, Sandra Hughes-Hassell, and Megan Threats. 2018. "Critical Race Theory in the LIS Curriculum." In *Re-Envisioning the MLS: Perspectives on the Future of Library and Information Science Education*, edited by Johnna Percell, Lindsay C. Sarin, Paul T. Jaeger, and John Carlo Bertot, 44B:49–70. *Advances in Librarianship*. Bingley, UK: Emerald. https://doi.org/10.1108 /S0065-28302018000044B005.

Gibson, Amelia N., Renate L. Chancellor, Nicole A. Cooke, Dahlen Sarah Park, Shari A. Lee, and Yasmeen L. Shorish. 2017. "Libraries on the Frontlines: Neutrality and Social Justice." *Equality, Diversity and Inclusion: An International Journal* 36(8): 751–66. https://doi.org/10.1108/EDI-11-2016-0100.

Gibson, Amelia N., and Samantha Kaplan. 2017. "Place, Community and Information Behavior: Spatially Oriented Information Seeking Zones and Information Source Preferences." *Library & Information Science Research* 39(2): 131–39. https://doi.org/10.1016/j.lisr.2017.03.001.

Glaser, Barney G. 1992. *Basics of Grounded Theory Analysis*. Mill Valley, CA: Sociology Press.

Glaser, Barney G., and Anselm L. Strauss. 1967. *The Discovery of Grounded Theory: Strategies for Qualitative Research*. London: Aldine.

González-Teruel, Aurora, and M. Francisca Abad-García. 2012. "Grounded Theory for Generating Theory in the Study of Behavior." *Library & Information Science Research* 34(1): 31–36. https://doi.org/10.1016/j.lisr.2011.02.006.

Haider, Jutta, and David Bawden. 2007. "Conceptions of 'Information Poverty' in LIS: A Discourse Analysis." *Journal of Documentation* 63(4): 534–57. https:// doi.org/10.1108/00220410710759002.

Henczel, Susan. 2014. "The Impact of Library Associations: Preliminary Findings of a Qualitative Study." *Performance Measurement and Metrics* 15(3): 122–44. https://doi.org/10.1108/PMM-07-2014-0025.

Hicks, Alison. 2020. "Moving beyond the Descriptive: The Grounded Theory of Mitigating Risk and the Theorisation of Information Literacy." *Journal of Documentation* 76(1): 126–44. https://doi.org/10.1108/JD-07-2019-0126.

Hofschire, Linda. 2020. "Data Visualization on a Budget: Simple Tips, Techniques, and Low-Cost Tools." *Computers in Libraries* 40(5).

Holsti, Ole R. 1969. *Content Analysis for the Social Sciences and Humanities*. Reading, MA: Addison-Wesley.

Hudson, David James. 2017. "On 'Diversity' as Anti-Racism in Library and Information Studies: A Critique." *Journal of Critical Library and Information Studies* 1(1). http://dx.doi.org/10.24242/jclis.v1i1.6.

Hughes, Annie M. 2014. "Content Analysis of Reference Transactions Provides Guidance Regarding Staffing of Library Service Points." *Evidence Based Library and Information Practice* 9(2): 31–33. https://doi.org/10.18438/B8NK6S.

Jackson, Kristi, and Pat Bazeley. 2019. *Qualitative Data Analysis with NVivo*. 3rd ed. Thousand Oaks, CA: Sage.

Johnson, Kelli. 2016. "Minority Librarians in Higher Education: A Critical Race Theory Analysis." Dissertation, Huntington, WV: Marshall University. https://mds.marshall.edu/etd/1019.

Kay Heng Heok, Adrian, and Brendan Luyt. 2010. "Imagining the Internet: Learning and Access to Information in Singapore's Public Libraries." *Journal of Documentation* 66(4): 475–90. https://doi.org/10.1108/00220411011052911.

Kimmel, Sue K. 2011. "'Consider with Whom You Are Working': Discourse Models of School Librarianship in Collaboration." *School Library Media Research* 14: 133–52. http://www.ala.org/aasl/sites/ala.org.aasl/files/content/aaslpubs andjournals/slr/vol14/SLR_Volume_14.pdf#page=133.

Kocevar-Weidinger, Elizabeth, Candice Benjes-Small, Eric Ackermann, and Virginia R. Kinman. 2010. "Why and How to Mystery Shop Your Reference Desk." *Reference Services Review* 38(1): 28–43. https://doi.org/10.1108/00907321011020707.

Krippendorff, Klaus. 1980. *Content Analysis: An Introduction to Its Methodology*. London: Sage.

Lavoie, Brian, Lorcan Dempsey, and Constance Malpas. 2020. "Reflections on Collective Collections." *College & Research Libraries* 81(6): 981–96. https://doi.org/10.5860/crl.81.6.981.

Lavrakas, Paul. 2008. *Encyclopedia of Survey Research Methods*. Thousand Oaks, CA: Sage. http://dx.doi.org/10.4135/9781412963947.n228.

Lawrence, E. E. 2020. "On the Problem of Oppressive Tastes in the Public Library." *Journal of Documentation* (ahead-of-print). https://doi.org/10.1108/JD-01-2020-0002.

LeCompte, Margaret D., and Judith Preissle Goetz. 1982. "Problems of Reliability and Validity in Ethnographic Research." *Review of Educational Research* 52(1): 31–60. https://doi.org/10.3102/00346543052001031.

Lincoln, Yvonna S., and Egon G. Guba. 1985. *Naturalistic Inquiry*. Thousand Oaks, CA: Sage.

Lingel, Jessa, and danah boyd. 2013. "'Keep It Secret, Keep It Safe': Information Poverty, Information Norms, and Stigma." *Journal of the American Society for Information Science and Technology* 64(5): 981–91. https://doi.org/10.1002/asi.22800.

Lingel, Jessica. 2011. "Information Tactics of Immigrants in Urban Environments." *Information Research* 16(4): paper 500. http://www.informationr.net/ir/16-4/paper500.html.

Mabbott, Cass. 2017. "The We Need Diverse Books Campaign and Critical Race Theory: Charlemae Rollins and the Call for Diverse Children's Books." *Library Trends* 65(4): 508–22. https://doi.org/10.1353/lib.2017.0015.

Mandelbaum, Jenny. 2008. "Conversation Analysis Theory." In *Engaging Theories in Interpersonal Communication: Multiple Perspectives*, edited by Leslie A. Baxter and Dawn O. Braithwait. Thousand Oaks, CA: Sage.

Mansourian, Yazdan. 2006. "Adoption of Grounded Theory in LIS Research." *New Library World* 107(9/10): 386–402. https://doi.org/10.1108/03074800610702589.

Marshall, Catherine, and Gretchen B. Rossman. 2016. *Designing Qualitative Research*. 6th ed. Thousand Oaks, CA: Sage.

Martínez-Ávila, Daniel, and Margaret E. I. Kipp. 2014. "Implications of the Adoption of BISAC for Classifying Library Collections." *Knowledge Organization* 41(5): 377–92. https://doi.org/10.5771/0943-7444-2014-5-377.

Mellon, Constance A. 1986. "Library Anxiety: A Grounded Theory and Its Development." *College & Research Libraries* 47(2): 160–65.

Miles, Matthew B., and A. Michael Huberman. 1994. *Qualitative Data Analysis: An Expanded Sourcebook*. 2nd ed. Thousand Oaks, CA: Sage.

Miles, Matthew B., A. Michael Huberman, and Johnny Saldaña. 2013. *Qualitative Data Analysis: A Methods Sourcebook*. 3rd ed. Thousand Oaks, CA: Sage.

Miles, Matthew B., A. Michael Huberman, and Johnny Saldaña. 2020. *Qualitative Data Analysis: A Methods Sourcebook*. 4th ed. Thousand Oaks, CA: Sage. https://www.vitalsource.com/products/qualitative-data-analysis-matthew-b-miles-v9781506353081.

Montgomerie, Johnna, ed. 2017. *Critical Methods in Political and Cultural Economy*. Milton Park, Abingdon, UK: Routledge. https://www.routledge.com/Critical-Methods-in-Political-and-Cultural-Economy/Montgomerie/p/book/9781138934276.

Morrow, Raymond A., and David D. Brown. 1994. *Critical Theory and Methodology*. Thousand Oaks, CA: Sage.

Ostergren, Marilyn, Jeff Hemsley, Miranda Belarde-Lewis, and Shawn Walker. 2011. "A Vision for Information Visualization in Information Science." In *IConference '11: Proceedings of the 2011 IConference on*, 531–37. Seattle: ACM Press. https://doi.org/10.1145/1940761.1940834.

Paulus, Trena M., Jessica N. Lester, and Paul G. Dempster. 2014. *Digital Tools for Qualitative Research*. London: Sage.

Potter, Jonathan, and Margaret Wetherell. 1987. *Discourse and Social Psychology: Beyond Attitudes and Behaviour—Open Research Online*. London: Sage .http://oro.open.ac.uk/24334.

Raber. 2003. "Librarians as Organic Intellectuals: A Gramscian Approach to Blind Spots and Tunnel Vision." *The Library Quarterly* 73(1): 33–53. https://doi.org/10.1086/603374.

Radford, Gary P. 1992. "Positivism, Foucault, and the Fantasia of the Library: Conceptions of Knowledge and the Modern Library Experience." *The Library Quarterly* 62(4): 408–24. https://doi.org/10.1086/602496.

Radford, Gary P. 1998. "Flaubert, Foucault, and the Bibliotheque Fantastique: Toward a Postmodern Epistemology for Library Science." *Library Trends* 46(4): 616–34.

Radford, Gary P. 2003. "Trapped in Our Own Discursive Formations: Toward an Archaeology of Library and Information Science." *The Library Quarterly* 73(1): 1–18. https://doi.org/10.1086/603372.

Radford, Gary P., and Marie L. Radford. 2001. "Libraries, Librarians, and the Discourse of Fear." *The Library Quarterly* 71(3): 299–329. https://doi.org/10.1086/603283.

Radford, Gary P., and Marie L. Radford. 2005. "Structuralism, Post-Structuralism, and the Library: De Saussure and Foucault." *Journal of Documentation* 61(1): 60–78. https://doi.org/10.1108/00220410510578014.

Radford, Gary P., Marie L. Radford, and Mark Alpert. 2015. "Slavoj Žižek, Rex Libris, and the Traumatic Real: Representations of the Library and the Librarian in a Modern Comic Book Series." *Journal of Documentation* 71(6): 1265–88. https://doi.org/10.1108/JD-08-2014-0116.

Radford, Gary P., Marie L. Radford, and Jessica Lingel. 2012. "Alternative Libraries as Discursive Formations: Reclaiming the Voice of the Deaccessioned
Book." *Journal of Documentation* 68(2): 254–67. https://doi.org/10.1108
/00220411211209221.

Radford, Gary P., Marie L. Radford, and Jessica Lingel. 2015. "The Library as
Heterotopia: Michel Foucault and the Experience of Library Space." *Journal of Documentation* 71(4): 733–51. https://doi.org/10.1108/JD-01-2014
-0006.

Radford, Gary P., Marie L. Radford, and Jessa Lingel. 2018. "Transformative
Spaces: The Library as Panopticon." In *Proceedings of the 2018 IConference:
Transforming Digital Worlds*, edited by Gobinda Chowdhury, Julie McLeod,
Val Gillet, and Peter Willett, 10766: 684–92. Cham, Switzerland: Springer
International. https://doi.org/10.1007/978-3-319-78105-1_79.

Radford, Marie L. 1999. *The Reference Encounter: Interpersonal Communication
in the Academic Library.* Publications in Librarianship 52. Chicago: Association of College and Research Libraries, A Division of the American Library
Association.

Radford, Marie L. 2006a. "The Critical Incident Technique and the Qualitative
Evaluation of the Connecting Libraries and Schools Project." *Library Trends*
55(1): 46–64. https://doi.org/10.1353/lib.2006.0051.

Radford, Marie L. 2006b. "Encountering Virtual Users: A Qualitative Investigation
of Interpersonal Communication in Chat Reference." *Journal of the American
Society for Information Science and Technology* 57(8): 1046–59. https://doi
.org/10.1002/asi.20374.

Radford, Marie L., Lynn Silipigni Connaway, Stephanie Mikitish, Mark Alpert, Chirag Shah, and Nicole A. Cooke. 2017. "Shared Values, New Vision: Collaboration and Communities of Practice in Virtual Reference and SQA." *Journal of
the Association for Information Science and Technology* 68(2): 438–49.
https://doi.org/10.1002/asi.23668.

Radford, Marie L., Lynn Silipigni Connaway, and Chirag Shah. 2011. "Cyber Synergy: Seeking Sustainability through Collaboration between Virtual Reference and Social Q&A Sites." Grant Proposal. Institute of Museum and Library
Services (IMLS): Rutgers University and OCLC. http://citeseerx.ist.psu.edu
/viewdoc/download?doi=10.1.1.434.1004&rep=rep1&type=pdf.

Radford, Marie L, Vanessa Kitzie, Diana Floegel, Lynn Silipigni Connaway, Jenny
Bossaller, and Sean Burns. 2019. "NVivo Inspiration: Investigating Com-
puter Assisted Qualitative Data Analysis." Presented at the iConference,
Washington, DC.

Radford, Marie L., and Gary P. Radford. 1997. "Power, Knowledge, and Fear: Femi-
nism, Foucault, and the Stereotype of the Female Librarian." *The Library
Quarterly* 67(3): 250–66. https://doi.org/10.1086/629951.

Radford, Marie L., and Gary P. Radford. 2003. "Librarians and Party Girls: Cultural Studies and the Meaning of the Librarian." *The Library Quarterly* 73(1):
54–69. https://doi.org/10.1086/603375.

Radford, Marie L., Gary P. Radford, Lynn Silipigni Connaway, and Jocelyn A.
DeAngelis. 2011. "On Virtual Face-Work: An Ethnography of Communication
Approach to a Live Chat Reference Interaction." *The Library Quarterly* 81(4):
431–53. https://doi.org/10.1086/661654.

Ragaller, Irene, and Pauline Rafferty. 2012. "Biases in the Classification of Welsh
Art Material: Dispersion, Dilettantism and Depreciation." *Aslib Proceedings:
New Information Perspectives* 64(3): 262–73. https://doi.org/10.1108
/00012531211244563.

Richards, Lyn. 2015. *Handling Qualitative Data: A Practical Guide*. 3rd ed. Thousand Oaks, CA: Sage.

Ross, Sheri V. T. 2011. "Non-Resident Use of Public Libraries in Appalachia." *Library Management* 32(8/9): 540–52. https://doi.org/10.1108/014351211 11187905.

Sandelowski, Margarete. 1986. "The Problem of Rigor in Qualitative Research." *Advances in Nursing Science* 8(3): 27–37. https://doi.org/10.1097/00012272 -198604000-00005.

Savolainen, Reijo. 2019. "Seeking and Sharing Information Dialogically: A Conversation Analytic Study of Asynchronous Online Talk." *Journal of Documentation* 75(3): 530–49. https://doi.org/10.1108/JD-09-2018-0140.

Scales, B. Jane. 2013. "Qualitative Analysis of Student Assignments: A Practical Look at ATLAS.Ti." Edited by Jennifer Rosenfeld and Raida Gatten. *Reference Services Review* 41(1): 134–47. https://doi.org/10.1108/0090732131130 0956.

Schegloff, Emanuel A. 2007. *A Sequence in Interaction: A Primer in Conversation Analysis*. New York: Cambridge University Press.

Scott, William A. 1955. "Reliability of Content Analysis: The Case of Nominal Scale Coding." *The Public Opinion Quarterly* 19(3): 321–25.

Sibbald, Shannon L., C. Nadine Wathen, Anita Kothari, and Adam M. B. Day. 2013. "Knowledge Flow and Exchange in Interdisciplinary Primary Health Care Teams (PHCTs): An Exploratory Study." *Journal of the Medical Library Association: JMLA* 101(2): 128–37. https://doi.org/10.3163/1536-5050.101 .2.008.

Sidnell, Jack, and Tanya Stivers, eds. 2016. *The Handbook of Conversation Analysis*. Cambridge, England: Cambridge University Press.

Smith, Shiobhan Alice, Antje Lubcke, Dean Alexander, Kate Thompson, Christy Ballard, and Fiona Glasgow. 2019. "Listening and Learning: Myths and Misperceptions about Postgraduate Students and Library Support." *Reference Services Review* 47(4): 594–608. https://doi.org/10.1108/RSR-03-2019-0019.

Sonnenwald, Diane H., Hanna Maurin Söderholm, Gregory F. Welch, and Bruce A. Cairns. 2014. "Illuminating Collaboration in Emergency Health Care Situations: Paramedic-Physician Collaboration & 3D Telepresence Technology." *Information Research* 19(2). http://www.informationr.net/ir/19-2/paper618 .html#.Xv9jw2pKgUR.

Soyini, Madison D. 2020. *Critical Ethnography: Method, Ethics, and Performance* 3rd ed. Thousand Oaks, CA: Sage.

Tan, Jin. 2010. "Grounded Theory in Practice: Issues and Discussion for New Qualitative Researchers." *Journal of Documentation* 66(1): 93–112. https:// doi.org/10.1108/00220411011016380.

Tewell, Eamon C. 2018. "The Practice and Promise of Critical Information Literacy: Academic Librarians' Involvement in Critical Library Instruction." *College & Research Libraries* 79(1): 10–34. https://doi.org/10.5860/crl.79.1.10.

Tracy, Sarah J. 2013. *Qualitative Research Methods*. Oxford, UK: Wiley-Blackwell.

Ulvik, Synnøve, and Gunhild Salvesen. 2007. "Ethical Reference Practice." *New Library World* 108(7/8): 342–53. https://doi.org/10.1108/03074800710 763635.

Üniversitesi, Aralık, Orta Doğu Teknik, and Hamid Darvish. 2010. "Intellectual Freedom and Libraries: A Quantitative Discourse Analysis." *Bilgi Dunyasi/ Information World* 11(2): 444–49.

Verdinelli, Susana, and Norma I. Scagnoli. 2013. "Data Display in Qualitative Research." *International Journal of Qualitative Methods* 12(1): 359–81. https://journals.sagepub.com/doi/full/10.1177/160940691301200117.

Wagner, Travis L., and Archie Crowley. 2020. "Why Are Bathrooms Inclusive If the Stacks Exclude? Systemic Exclusion of Trans and Gender Nonconforming Persons in Post-Trump Academic Librarianship." *Reference Services Review* (ahead-of-print). https://doi.org/10.1108/RSR-10-2019-0072.

Watson, Margaret. 2019. "Diversity and the Post-Colonial Law Library." *Legal Information Management* 19(3): 126–30. https://doi.org/10.1017/S1472669619000367.

Wiegand, Wayne A. 2020. "Sanitizing American Library History: Reflections of a Library Historian." *The Library Quarterly* 90(2): 108–20. https://doi.org/10.1086/707669.

Wildemuth, Barbara M. 2017. *Applications of Social Research Methods to Questions in Information and Library Science.* 2nd ed. Santa Barbara, CA: ABC-CLIO.

Yadamsuren, Borchuluun, and Jannica Heinström. 2011. "Emotional Reactions to Incidental Exposure to Online News." *Information Research* 16(3). http://www.informationr.net/ir/16-3/paper486.html.

Zaiontz, Charles. n.d. "Cohen's Kappa." Real Statistics Using Excel. Accessed July 3, 2020. http://www.real-statistics.com/reliability/interrater-reliability/cohens-kappa.

11

Individual and Focus Group Interviews

This chapter covers two purposeful and particular types of interview that have a long-standing and ongoing popularity as data-collecting techniques for qualitative research: individual and focus group interviews. Interviews should be familiar to even the fledgling qualitative researcher. Certainly, all students, library professionals, and researchers have some awareness of the general process and most likely have participated in many interviews of different types. These may include job interviews, journalistic interviews, and perhaps having been an observer or participant in a focus group interview.

The individual interview (also known as the one-on-one interview) is discussed first, as it shares many characteristics with focus groups and because "intensive interviewing has become the most common source of qualitative data" (Charmaz 2014, 18). As noted in chapter 1, existing research in library and information science (LIS) frequently features interviews, which were found to be the most-often-used method in Greifeneder's (2014) analysis of articles on information behavior or information seeking in the *Journal of the Association for Information Science and Technology* (JASIS&T), *Information Research, Journal of Documentation*, and the *iConference Proceedings* (2012–2014). Ullah and Ameen (2018, 57) preformed a meta-analysis of reviews of LIS research methods and found that individual interviews and focus group interviews were second in popularity to survey questionnaires for data collection, which was also found to be the case in previous research by Julien, Pecoskie, and Reed. Their analysis of 749 articles indexed in *Library Literature and Information Science Full-Text* from 1999 to 2008 revealed that interviews were also the second-most-used method, following survey questionnaires (Julien, Pecoskie, and Reed 2011, 19).

Why use interviews in data collection? "One of the major purposes of the qualitative interview [is] *generating factual information about the world*, especially about things or processes that cannot be observed effectively by other means" (Lindlof and Taylor 2019, 221). Additional purposes of the individual interview for qualitative research are numerous and include the following:

- Understanding participants' *"experience, knowledge, and/or worldviews"* and perspectives, which are "achieved in three forms of interview talk: stories, accounts, and explanations" (Lindlof and Taylor 2019, 223).
- Discovering participants' language forms. (How do they talk about things? What words and expressions are used?)
- Finding out about the past.
- Validating and verifying information obtained from other sources.
- Attaining efficient data collection (Lindlof and Taylor 2019).

Another important purpose for interviews is to obtain "juicy quotes" and *in vivo* codes (Charmaz 2014) that can vividly illustrate a research finding and bring (perhaps otherwise abstract) findings to life. For example, one interviewee from a grant-funded research study, Cyber Synergy, when asked about referrals for reference questions within their area of subject knowledge, said: "It was the kind of question where I could give an okay answer and I knew this colleague could give a great answer" (Radford, Connaway, et al. 2017, 348). The verbatim quote is a more interesting way to bring the data to life than just listing the category name, which might be "referral to colleague."

What types of problematics are appropriate for interviews to be used for data collection? As previously noted, interviews are used when it is important to gather the perceptions, opinions, and accounts of experiences of members of your selected participant group(s). In academic library settings, interviews have been used for the following problematics, with the number (if available) and type of participants listed:

- Investigation of perceptions and behaviors in creating and maintaining scholarly identity using social networking sites (SNS) (thirty individuals, ten academic librarians, ten doctoral students, ten faculty) (Radford et al. 2020).
- Exploration of adaptive measures for implementing and operating a 24-hour schedule (five library managers) (Bowman 2013).
- Examination of the challenges and ways to improve applications of "fair use," including interpretations of copyright law (sixty-five librarians) (Butler 2010).
- Analysis of preparation for new catalogers (twenty-two new professional catalogers) (Dulock 2011).
- Study of innovation in academic libraries (six university librarians) (Jantz 2012).
- Investigation of the value of research (twenty-three library administrators) (Perkins and Slowik 2013).
- Research on how university commuter students use library space (seven university students) (Bauer 2020).

Similarly, in public library settings interviews have been used for the following topics of investigation. Eight public libraries in the United States were studied to identify how they partnered with the local community to respond to the opioid crisis (Allen et al. 2019). Case studies included the researchers visiting the libraries for one or two days to review the libraries' materials, policies, procedures, etc. and to conduct sixty-four individual interviews (eight library directors or assistant directors, seven library managers, eight library frontline staff, eight library board members, nine community partner directors, six community partner frontline staff, and eighteen community members who had been affected by opioid misuse).

- Exploring the role of public libraries in the lives of immigrant women (nine female immigrants to Norway from Iran, Afghanistan, and Kurdistan) (Audunson, Essmat, and Aabø 2011).
- Research on e-government service roles of public libraries; collaborations among community groups, government agencies, and organizational leaders; and community influences of these services and collaborations (7,260 libraries responded to survey, interviews with state library staff from seven libraries and site visits of these libraries) (Bertot et al. 2013).
- Impact study of the 2008–2009 recession on UK libraries (four public library authorities) (Child and Goulding 2012).
- Analysis of consumer health information services (twenty library staff members) (Flaherty 2013).
- Examination of how elderly patrons perceive and use library spaces (six library staff members) (Sikes 2020).
- Study of application of digitization of local heritage (twelve local studies librarians and three other key informants) (Smith and Rowley 2012).
- Evaluating the value of therapeutic reading groups (fourteen members of therapeutic reading groups) (Walwyn and Rowley 2011).

The authors along with other collaborators also have used interviews to discover users' perceptions of virtual reference services (VRS) and social question-answering (SQA) sites (fifty virtual reference and SQA users) (Kitzie, Connaway, and Radford in press).

The variety of uses for interviews may be surprising. These examples from published studies that use interviews to elicit information in both academic and public library contexts illustrate two important features of interviews as data collection techniques: (1) they can be used for an extremely varied range of problematics, and (2) they allow the researcher to carefully select participants/respondents of a larger population that have particular knowledge or experience with the phenomena of interest. It also is apparent that large numbers of informants are not necessary, especially for exploratory investigations that are seeking initial, preliminary information, not seeking to generalize to a larger population (as is the case in quantitative research). The published studies cited above reported findings from data analysis of interviews with a low of four participants to a high of sixty-five, with most below sixteen.

In qualitative interviewing, there are several recognized distinct types of interviews, which include the ethnographic interview, informant interviews, respondent interviews, and narrative interviews. The ethnographic interview is "also known as an *informal conversational interview, situational conversation,* or *go-along*" and are the "most spontaneous and least structured form of interviewing. It typically occurs in a cultural scene while the investigator is busy hanging out with the people being studied" (Lindlof and Taylor 2019, 225). See also Kusenbach (2003), Patton (1990), and Schatzman and Strauss (1973). Spradley (2016) provides a detailed discussion of the ethnographic interview for those who are interested in more information. The informant interview involves discovering people who have the knowledge needed to understand a particular research problematic. They are called informants because they inform the investigator "about the cultural scene: its history, customs, and rituals; its issues problems, and challenges; the identities, backgrounds, and actions of key players," etc. (Lindlof and Taylor 2019, 227). Respondent interviews usually are used as a sole data collection method and are designed to "elicit open-ended responses" from interview schedules that "follow a standard order so that responses can be compared across the subjects in a sample" (Lindlof and Taylor 2019, 229). Finally, narrative interviews are "uniquely concerned with *entire stories*" as opposed to eliciting part of the story as do other types of interviews that seek to extract "facts, themes, issues, references to people and places, for later reassembly into analytic categories" (Lindlof and Taylor 2019, 231).

Another way of classifying the different types of interviews is by three levels of structure: (1) unstructured (in which the participant is in control of the process and the researcher's role is to listen and clarify), (2) semistructured (in which control is shared and questions are open-ended), and (3) structured (in which highly controlled questioning is determined by the researcher) (Bailey 2018; Wildemuth 2017). In qualitative research, most interviews are "relatively informal, semi-structured events" (Lindlof and Taylor 2019, 225). These types of interviews involve developing an initial list of questions, but allowing flexibility and leeway to insert probe questions, as needed, in response to what the interviewee has to say.

One of the first steps in developing a standardized structured or semistructured interview is the development of the list of questions to be asked, also known as the *interview schedule*. The techniques for constructing questionnaires and structured interview schedules are quite similar (see chapter 4).

Kvale and Brinkmann (2015, 160–64) provides this typology of interview questions, with examples:

- **Introducing questions:** Broad openers such as "Can you tell me about . . . ?" "Do you remember an occasion when . . . ?"
- **Follow-up questions:** Involve direct reference or repetition of what has just been said.
- **Probing questions:** Digging deeper, as in "Could you say something more about that?" "Can you give a more detailed description of what happened?"
- **Specifying questions:** Asking for more detail or elaboration: "What did you think then?" "What did you actually do when you felt a mounting anxiety?"

- **Direct questions:** Getting right to the heart of the topic: "Have you ever received money for good grades?" "When you mention competition, do you then think of a sportsmanlike or a destructive competition?"
- **Indirect questions:** Asking about other people, such as "How do you believe other students regard the competition for grades?" "Did you ever hear of anyone cheating at your university?"
- **Structuring questions:** Used when a theme is exhausted by breaking off long, irrelevant answers: "I would now like to introduce another topic: . . ."
- **Silence:** Pausing that gives the interviewees time to think and reflect. Active listening (nodding, saying uh huh, etc.) will help to encourage additional comments or continuation.
- **Interpreting questions:** Asking the interviewee to provide more explanation: "You then mean that . . . ?" "Is it correct that you feel that . . . ?"

As is true for questionnaires, it is highly recommended that interview schedules be pretested, and the pretest should provide the respondents with ample opportunity to comment on the questions. Poorly constructed questions will confuse the respondents, stall their thinking, reduce the depth of the data, and convince them that the study is less useful, and may cause the interviewee to go off topic (Kvale and Brinkmann 2015, 160–64).

In developing interview questions, it is extremely important to not go off track with questions or to ask irrelevant questions. One highly recommended step in developing the questions is to make sure that each of the interview questions will help to find the answer or illuminate at least one of the research questions. Placing a list of the interview questions next to the research questions and connecting (or mapping) these together is an important exercise. Any interview questions that do not directly connect to a research question should be discarded. Similarly, if it is found that no interview questions exist to address/answer any of the research questions, then additional interview questions must be added. Do not forget to also include demographic questions (such as gender, age, educational level, ethnicity, work experience, etc.) for any information that will be useful in later analysis. Usually demographic questions are asked at the beginning of the interview, with the least intrusive questions first. Like surveys, asking for personal information (including a person's age) may be off-putting as initial questions. Age ranges can be used to soften the effect. Again, do not collect any information that does not have a purpose for analysis, but be sure to collect particular information that is needed before the end of the interview. It is often difficult, or sometimes impossible, to get back to a respondent later if demographic information is found to be missing.

An additional step in the development of the interview involves the training of interviewers. Even if a researcher is working with experienced interviewers, he or she needs to become familiar with the particular questions. The same interviewers should be involved in the pretest as in the final interview. Training is important since, as Kvale and Brinkmann assert, "Interview research may to some appear a simple and straightforward task. It seems quite easy to obtain a sound recorder and ask someone to talk about his or her experiences regarding some interesting topic or to encourage a person to tell his or her life story. It seems so simple to interview, but . . . it is hard to do well. Research interviewing involves a cultivation of conversational skills that most adult human beings already possess by virtue of being able to ask questions, but the cultivation of these skills can be challenging" (Kvale and Brinkmann 2015, 4).

As alluded to above, selection of the right participants also is key to obtaining relevant and valid results. Recruiting the wrong participants can spell disaster for a project, just as recruiting the right participants can lead to success. Consider the goal of the study and who would be the best type of person to provide rich data to address the research question. One tried and true technique to help in recruitment is the incentive; providing a gift card, chance to win a prize (such as the top tech gadget of the moment), or other compensation is often critical in getting a sufficient number of respondents to interview. There are ethical and budget implications for these incentives, so it is important to plan for this expense in drafting grant proposals or setting up a research project (see chapter 3 for more information on budgeting). Sometimes it is necessary to be creative if budgets are tight. Deciding how many people to interview is an important part of the planning process and may be driven by budget realities, as well as available time of the researchers to conduct the interviews, transcription (if needed), and the analysis. These constraints may dictate the number of interviews, although ideally the number of interviews conducted should be fluid, with a target of perhaps ten to fifteen, with more added if data categories do not reach saturation. In other words, one should continue to interview as long as new information is being garnered. Once the interviewer hears very similar responses over and over, it is time to stop. For a large project, it is possible that fifty or more individual interviews can be conducted, but this usually requires a team of researchers who can assist in conducting the study and analyzing the results (Radford and Connaway 2005).

Regarding ethical considerations, Spradley discusses the set of professional responsibilities put forth by the Council of the American Anthropological Association (AAA) who "adopted a set of principles to guide ethnographers when faced with conflicting choices" such as "should I tape record what an informant says or merely make a written record? How will I use the data collected and will I tell informants how it will be used" (Spradley 2016, 34)? The AAA has updated their Code of Ethics which contains seven Principles of Professional Responsibility which are: "1) Do No Harm; 2) Be Open and Honest Regarding Your Work; 3) Obtain Informed Consent and Necessary Permissions; 4) Weigh Competing Ethical Obligations Due Collaborators and Affected Parties; 5) Make Your Results Accessible; 6) Protest and Preserve Your Records; and 7) Maintain Respectful and Ethical Professional Relationships" ("AAA Ethics Blog: Principles of Professional Responsibility (American Anthropological Association)—Archaeological Ethics Database" n.d.) Each of these is elaborated on in the AAA Ethics Blog. Spradley translates these to his list of ethical principles: "consider informants first; safeguard informants' rights, interests, and sensitivities; communicate research objectives; don't exploit informants; and make reports available to informants" (Spradley 2016, 34–39).

Also, Kvale and Brinkmann (2015, 83–102) provide an excellent chapter on "Ethical Issues of Interviewing," which covers guidelines for informed consent, privacy, confidentiality, consequences, the role of the researcher, and learning ethical research behavior.

Determining who should be interviewed first involves determining a target group and then choosing a sample. "Qualitative researchers usually work with small samples of people, nested in their context and studied in-depth—unlike quantitative researchers, who aim for larger numbers of context-stripped cases and seek statistical significance" (Miles, Huberman, and Saldaña 2020, 27). In qualitative research, purposeful sampling rather than random sampling is generally used (although some researchers use mixed random and purposeful sampling) (Miles, Huberman, and Saldaña 2020; Wengraf 2001). Some of the elements or desired characteristics of participants will determine what type of purposeful sampling is selected, and there is a large range of sampling strategies for qualitative methods. Following are some of the most common types (Wengraf 2001, 28):

- convenience sample
- homogeneous sample
- maximum variation sample
- typical case
- critical case
- confirming or disconfirming case
- stratified sampling (e.g., by time of week, month, or year)
- snowball sampling (also known as chain or opportunistic)
- criterion sampling
- theory-based sampling (also known as theoretical sampling)
- extreme or deviant cases
- politically important cases

Many LIS researchers use a convenience sample; however, if other than a pilot study is being done, it is better if the sample is chosen for more research-driven or theoretical reasons, such as finding typical or critical cases. Snowball sampling can be used when it is difficult to find the right participants, perhaps because they are not easily found with the usual recruitment methods such as using listservs, flyers, Facebook ads, and pop-up surveys at service points. It involves starting with one participant and letting that person lead you to others. Theoretical sampling is used when the concepts or themes derived from the data drive the selection of participants and data collection. It differs from other forms of sampling in that it involves deliberate selection and seeking of data to inform a developing or extant theory. Also, it is used to refine and enlarge theoretical categories. It is more about investigating concepts and seeking variation than representativeness (Charmaz 2014; Corbin and Strauss 2014).

CONDUCTING THE INDIVIDUAL INTERVIEW

There are seven stages in the interview process, according to Kvale and Brinkmann (2015):

- **Thematizing:** clarifying the interview's purpose and the concepts to be explored.
- **Designing:** defining clearly the process to be used including ethical considerations.
- **Interviewing:** conducting the interview.
- **Transcribing:** creating a written verbatim text of the interview.
- **Analyzing:** figuring out the meaning of data in relation to the study's research questions.
- **Verifying:** determining the reliability and validity of data.
- **Reporting:** telling others about the findings.

When the point is reached to conduct an interview, it is critical to establish good rapport with the participant. The interviewer should attempt to create a friendly, nonthreatening atmosphere. Much as one does with a cover letter, the interviewer should give a brief, casual introduction to the study; stress the importance of the person's participation; and assure anonymity, or at least confidentiality, when possible. The interviewer should answer all legitimate questions about the nature of the study and produce appropriate credentials on request. They should be prepared to respond to such questions as: How did you happen to pick me? Who gave you my name? Who are you?

When possible and appropriate, the researcher should set up the interview well in advance, and, of course, the interviewer should appear for the interview punctually. There are two very important aspects of the interview context: time and location. First, it is important to make sure that the time will work for the interviewee; a rushed interview because the participant has inadequate time can be a disaster (Lindlof and Taylor 2019, 237–51; Spradley 2016, 51). Second, the location should be both comfortable and protected so that confidentiality can be maintained (Lindlof and Taylor 2019, 238). It is important that the location be free from distractions like children and pets. A barking dog is annoying and can make later transcription of an interview difficult.

Some researchers recommend sending the list of questions to the participant before the scheduled interview. Some interviewees may request this, especially if they have tight schedules and wish to maximize the interview time. This may be inadvisable, however, if the interviewer is particularly concerned about obtaining frank, spontaneous responses, since giving respondents too much time to consider answers is likely to reduce their candidness.

If the interview has been scheduled ahead of time, it is a good idea to confirm the date by telephone or email and to send a reminder several days before the interview. Visual aids, such as photos, or in some cases short videos, may be used to facilitate the questioning or improve the recording of responses. It is always important to obtain informed consent; most academic institutions require this as part of the institutional review board (IRB) requirements for research with human subjects, and if you are planning to publish results, most scholarly journals also require this. As part of informed consent, it is desirable to obtain the interviewee's permission to use the information in the resulting research report, with the assurance that confidentiality will be strict and that identity will be masked.

If the interviewee's responses are to be recorded, his or her written permission to do so should also be obtained in advance. If using audio/digital recording, equipment must be checked ahead of time and extra batteries and/or an extension cord may be needed. The interviewer may also take brief notes, but this may be disruptive and should be kept to a minimum. It is important for the interviewer to be paying attention rather than concentrating on capturing data; thus, the audio recorder is highly recommended.

Following the interview, the researcher may wish to create a verbatim transcript of the interview, for analysis purposes. One may want to submit a typescript of the questions and responses to the interviewee for confirmation of the accuracy of the answers. It should be made clear, however, that the respondent is not to use this opportunity to revise the meaning or the substance of their answers.

When asking the questions, the interviewer should avoid rephrasing questions for the interviewee. One of the advantages of interviews is the inherent personal contact, but one must be careful that this does not become a liability. Expansions or revisions of questions, or unnecessary explanations, in effect result in different questions being asked of different participants. Consequently, comparisons of responses become invalid. For similar reasons, the interviewers should not alter the sequence of the questions from respondent to respondent, nor should they omit questions. As discussed previously, the context of the question can affect or bias its response. And as was true for questionnaires, the interviewer should avoid asking more than one question at a time. In contrast to mail, email, or online questionnaires, the reactions of the researcher can affect the respondent's answers. The interviewer must be careful not to show surprise or other emotions as a result of any of the interviewee's responses. Such reactions can bias future responses of the participant.

In obtaining or encouraging responses, the interviewer may find it necessary to repeat certain questions. This should not present a problem so long as the interviewer does not significantly change the wording of such questions. In order to obtain an adequate response from the interviewee, it may on occasion be necessary for the interviewer to ask the respondent to elaborate on his or her reply. If done carefully, this should be legitimate, but one should always avoid putting words into the respondent's mouth. The interviewees' responses should represent their thoughts alone, not a combination of theirs and the interviewer's. To obtain as many responses as possible, the interviewer must also learn how to deal with "don't knows." Often people need a certain amount of encouragement before they will respond fully to a particular question. There is a fine line, however, between encouraging a response and helping to word it or forcing an answer where there should not be one. Consequently, one should be conservative or cautious in encouraging a response when the interviewee seems reluctant to provide one. Probing for complete answers can take the form of repeating the question (with the caveats given above), making an expectant pause, repeating the respondent's answer, making reassuring remarks, asking for further clarification, and asking neutral questions such as: Anything else? Any other reason? Could you tell me more about that?

As is the case with questionnaires, it is desirable to precode the answer sheets when possible. This is feasible only with fixed or structured responses, of course. Free-answer responses should be recorded verbatim, if at all possible, to facilitate subsequent analysis and to prevent the loss of data. Digital recorders provide one relatively easy method of capturing answers word for word. It is a good idea to record responses during the interview and to use the respondent's verbatim words (rather than summaries or paraphrases). If any probes for more complete answers are used, they should be noted. For example, the participant might give a partial or general answer to a specific question, so the interviewer might say: "Can you tell me more about this?" or "Can you be more specific?"

If you are providing an incentive, such as a gift card, it is important to get a signed receipt or email confirmation, especially in the case of grant-supported research, in which the funder may require proof that participants received the incentives.

Recent published studies have used interviews in a variety of ways that exemplifies how they can be used alone and in combination with other methods of data collection and analysis, as illustrated by the below examples.

- Cox, Pinfield, and Rutter (2019, 418) conducted interviews with thirty-three library directors to "capture a snapshot of perceptions of the potential impact of AI [Artificial Intelligence] on academic libraries and to reflect on its implications for library work." Their findings provided insights "on impacts of AI on search and resource discovery, on scholarly publishing, and on learning" and challenges that "included libraries being left outside the focus of development, ethical concerns, intelligibility of decisions and data quality. Some threat to jobs was perceived." Additionally, potential roles for libraries were identified and the "paradigm of the intelligent library" was offered to embrace AI for academic library contexts (Cox, Pinfield, and Rutter 2019, 418).
- Conrad and Tucker (2019, 397) conducted in-depth semistructured interviews, which included an in-depth review and application of the hybrid card sorting method to "demonstrate how incorporating hybrid card-sorting activities into interviews can enable deeper participant reflections and generate rich data sets to increase understanding." They concluded that "using either open or fixed designs, or hybrid variations, card-sort activities can make abstract concepts more tangible for participants, offering investigators a new approach to interview questions with the aid of this interactive, object-based technique" (Conrad and Tucker 2019, 397).
- Dalmer combined interviews with textual analyses in a methodological piece featuring an institutional ethnography within the context of health information practice research. "Drawing from a library and information science study that combined interviews and textual analyses to examine the social organisation of family caregivers' health-related information work," they conclude "with an overall assessment of what institutional ethnography can contribute to investigations of health information practices" and offer "a new method of inquiry" (Dalmer 2019, 703).

- Gibson and Martin held interviews from twenty-four mothers whose children had Down syndrome and/or autism spectrum disorder (ASD), using a constructivist grounded theory approach (Charmaz 2014) taking a critical perspective, which draws on "concepts from critical disability theory, critical race theory, and critical work within information and library science." They apply Chatman's (1996) theory of information poverty, to develop the concept of information inequities, and propose applications "for the development and design of systems and service models intended to provide access to information and services for individuals with disability" (Gibson and Martin 2019).
- Moniarou-Papconstantinou used semistructured interviews with forty-one LIS undergraduate students from three universities in Greece. Their purpose is "to examine how LIS students position themselves in their field of study and the resources they use in processes of meaning-making." Findings "showed that the academic knowledge content of the object, the assignment of scientific characteristics to it, the signifier of the book, the form of professional practice and, above all, technology are the most prominent resources among those that most young people utilized in their effort to negotiate the symbolic class (i.e., the dominant cultural categories which give meaning to the social world)" (Moniarou-Papaconstantinou 2020).

Additional examples can be found in the LIS literature, further illustrating the versatility of the interview method (Jaeger et al. 2015; Lingel and Boyd 2013; Oxley 2013).

Telephone Individual Interviews

Other important ways to conduct interviews are via the telephone or in virtual environments (see below). Telephone interviews can be used alone or in tandem with face-to-face (FtF) interviews or observations, as was done by Flaherty, who used telephone interviews to follow up on in-person interviews and site visits (Flaherty 2013). Connaway, Radford, and OCLC Research (2011) used telephone interviews as part of a multiphase IMLS grant project to study virtual reference in conjunction with focus groups and online surveys. Frey and Oishi (1995) have authored a book *How to Conduct Interviews by Telephone and in Person* that is a good resource for telephone-interviewing techniques.

Computer-assisted telephone interviewing (CATI) was first introduced in 1971 but gained more popularity in the early 1990s with the introduction of computer-assisted FtF interviewing (Couper et al. 2002, 557). CATI can facilitate team research projects with multiple interviews, collecting and organizing information about the call history for a particular informant, expediting the interview process ("Online Interviewing" n.d.). It is quite popular with survey researchers, especially those seeking a large and randomized sample. There are various CATI practices, but it basically involves the automatic dialing of computer-generated random digit telephone numbers and an interviewer equipped with a headset and the script and questions displayed on a computer monitor. When the respondent answers the telephone, the interviewer begins asking the questions and inputs the respondent's answers into the computer. The data are automatically prepared for analysis (Babbie 2021).

One major disadvantage of the telephone interview is that the process obviously favors those people who have telephones. Although mobile cell telephone ownership seems to be ubiquitous these days, there still are a number of people who do not own telephones, especially among the poor, elderly, less educated, and those living in rural areas. The Pew Research Center ("Mobile Phone Technology Fact-Sheet" n.d.) has estimated that as of June 12, 2019, 4 percent of American adults do not have cell telephones, while 19 percent do not own smart phones. Consequently, a sample of telephone subscribers would tend to underrepresent poor and rural households, thus producing a "digital divide that persists even as lower-income Americans make gains in tech adoption" (Anderson and Kumar 2019) that may weaken a particular study. Yet another challenge is that a growing number of people who use cell telephones may no longer have a landline telephone in their homes and so might be particularly difficult to access for a survey. There are concerns that the demographics of wireless-only households are different from those of others, perhaps "underconnected," through reliance on cell-phone-only access to the internet (Anderson and Kumar 2019). Response rates may be lower for cell telephone users than for landline telephone owners. This problem is made worse by the fact that unlisted/call blocked telephone numbers are becoming more common.

In comparison with the FtF interview, the person being interviewed over the telephone can more easily forget an appointment than an FtF appointment or might refuse the call for a number of reasons (e.g., they are on another call, may be driving, do not feel like talking, forgot that their phone is silenced). In addition, it is easier for telephone interviewees to terminate the interview abruptly, before it is finished. Therefore, the response rate tends to be a bit lower for telephone than for FtF interviews. Also, telephone responses lack many nonverbal cues, such as raised eyebrows, frowns, or smiles, which are helpful in interpreting FtF responses.

Like the researcher-administered questionnaire, the telephone interview tends to combine the advantages and disadvantages of the mail questionnaire and the FtF interview. Among the advantages of telephone/online video interviews are the following: (1) they tend to provide significant savings in actual time and cost in contrast to the FtF interview; (2) they can be conducted more quickly after an event has occurred; (3) it is generally easier to supervise, train, and monitor the staff for a telephone/online video interview than for a FtF interview (telephone interviewing does require some special skills, however, that should be incorporated in the training); and (4) they lend themselves to a certain amount of computer assistance. A growing number of recent research studies in LIS have used Skype, Teams, Zoom, or other online platforms to collect data.

Online/Virtual Individual Interviews

Babbie (2021) provided a list of survey research techniques that have developed because of advances in technology. Use of virtual interviews is growing, especially during the COVID-19 pandemic, when FtF interviews became hazardous, and includes those conducted via video (such as Zoom, Webex, or Skype) and those via chat (synchronous) or email (asynchronous). However, because more and more interviews are being conducted using information and communication technologies (ICTs), these techniques deserve special attention.

Online interviews are defined by Maddox as "a structured conversation, consisting of the question set, an interviewer, an interviewee and the technology used to conduct and record the interview. What makes them different to an in-person interview is: The role of the technology in facilitating real-time co-presence and interactivity [and] the approach the interviewer takes to build rapport and curate the conversation" (Maddox 2020, 6). Adding to a crowd-sourced document titled "Doing Fieldwork in a Pandemic," Maddox asserts that there is a growing body of work on conducting online interviews and that these can be facilitated through "mundane everyday communicative practices and objects" such as mobile phones, laptops, Skype, Zoom, text chat that enable "audio-visual interactivity and textual synchronicity" (Maddox 2020). She also provides information on designing questions and the steps to take while conducting the interview.

There are ethical and safety issues to consider when conducting online interviews. Online systems such as Zoom, Skype, and other platforms are not 100 percent secure. As Caroline Are (2019) notes: "Online interviewing is not a flawless technique to research data and to protect participants. However, it is a valid means of research when all others fail to grant at least some degree of protection." During the COVID-19 pandemic, travel was prevented/difficult/risky, and FtF interviewing was not safe. "As Chiumento, Machin, Rahman and Frith conclude: 'In settings that are unstable, the concept of researchers protecting participants becomes less applicable, with the assumptions of ideal field sites where researchers are the ones in a position of control no longer holding true. [. . .] In these cases, online interviewing is an alternative format when the "ideal" of in-person interviewing becomes impossible'" (Chiumento et al. 2018).

Online interviewing via email or live chat presents time savings as well, when compared to FtF interviews, but involves a different set of challenges. There are many differences between FtF and virtual interviews. The online interview utilizes ICTs and computer-mediated communication (CMC), which allow humans to interact directly with each other in synchronous or real time using screens, text, and keyboards.

One advantage of email is having the interview data already converted to text, eliminating the time and expense of transcription of audiotapes. However, email is asynchronic and does not allow for much back and forth if, for example, the respondent does not understand the question, or if the interviewer would like to probe on a particular answer. Another disadvantage is that there always is wait time for the researcher to get a response, and it is easy for respondents to ignore email.

Email can be used, however, in cases where telephone or online video interviews are not possible due to different time zones, if interviewing a population (such as deaf or hard of hearing, or English language learners) who may prefer text to audio communication, or when interviewees simply prefer the anonymity afforded by virtual environments. Researchers have used virtual interviewing to investigate internet use and culture, the demographics and characteristics of internet users, experiences with distance learning, and general human behavior (Gubrium et al. 2012).

Like email, live chat interviewing has the advantage of producing a transcript, and unlike email, it is synchronous, taking place in real time. Live chat allows for give and take and for probe questions to be inserted as needed. There is some time lost in the typing process, although skilled typists can be nearly as fast as speech, but cross-checking occurs frequently when questions and answers get out of sync. However, many nonverbal communication channels, such as facial expression and vocal tone, are missing. "In the disembodied interview all the subtle visual, nonverbal cues which can help to contextualize the interview in a FtF scenario are lost. Representations of these cues (using shortcuts like abbreviations such as LOL [for laughing out loud], emoticons and emojis, all caps, etc.) can be used, although these are not as expressive as vocal, facial, and body cues" (Ross, Nilsen, and Radford 2009).

Advantages of Individual Interviews

In contrast to the mail or electronic questionnaire, the interview has distinct advantages. Perhaps most important, it almost always produces a better response rate. The sample of persons actually participating in the study tends to represent a large percentage of the original sample and is therefore more representative of the population than would be a sample representing a relatively low response rate. Apparently, the personal contact of the interview helps to encourage, or put more pressure on, people to respond fully. Consequently, it also is possible to employ interview schedules of greater length than comparable questionnaires, without jeopardizing a satisfactory response rate.

According to Maddox, online live interviews have these advantages:

- Live interviews allow for the interviewer to seek clarification and follow threads of the conversation.
- They also allow for the ability of the interviewer to check that they understand the meaning of what the participant has said.
- Online interviews mean that you can conduct a real time interview, with another person, in a conversational format, but be in different spatial locations and contexts.
- It is possible to conduct anonymous interviews using IRC text chat and some other website interfaces. (Maddox 2020, 6)

The interpersonal contact, whether FtF or virtual, also provides a greater capacity than the mail or electronic questionnaire for the correction of misunderstandings by participants. Again, one must be careful that this capability is not abused and becomes a disadvantage as a result. It is generally believed that the interview is better at revealing information that is complex or emotionally laden. The use of visual aids (such as photographs or videos, taken by the interviewee or provided by the interviewer) can sometimes facilitate presenting and recording complicated information. Another advantage is that the data gathered from email or chat online interviews can be formatted quickly and uploaded easily to data analysis software packages such as NVivo (https://www.qsrinternational.com/nvivo-qualitative-data-analysis-software/support-services/nvivo-downloads) or Atlas Ti (https://atlasti.com). More information on these software analysis programs is provided in chapter 8.

Limitations of the Individual Interview

As with other research methods and techniques, bias presents a real threat to the validity of interviews. Particularly critical is the bias that may be introduced by the interviewer. As previously indicated, some interviewer bias can be avoided by ensuring that the interviewer remains neutral and calm and does not overreact to responses of the interviewee. Other steps that can be taken to help avoid or reduce interviewer bias include having the interviewer dress inconspicuously and appropriately for the environment, holding the interview in a private setting, and keeping the interview as informal as possible. Virtual interviews are thought to diminish the chances of introducing some of these biases, although one of the main biases of interviewing using CMC is the unrepresentativeness of the sample, since not everyone has access to computers and wi-fi or broadband technology. It is key to remember that if conducting a virtual interview, the interviewee may not be seeing you or experiencing the interview in the same way as the interviewer. For example, if the interviewer is using Zoom or Skype on a desktop computer with a large monitor, the interviewee may be using the platform on a smart phone with a different perspective.

Rapport and interpersonal relationships are more difficult to develop in a virtual interview than in person. It is possible to establish a relationship virtually, but it requires a specific skill and can be more challenging than in a FtF or a telephone interview. The interview can be quite expensive in terms of travel and possible long-distance telephone costs, but the virtual Zoom or Skype interview is a more cost-efficient and practical method for conducting in-depth interviews if there is an economical telecommunications system and if the interviewers and researchers are comfortable with and knowledgeable of the technology.

As with the electronic questionnaire discussed above, the virtual interview raises legal and ethical issues. It is difficult to authenticate the responses in an online interview, which necessitates taking steps to ensure that the appropriate person is participating in the interview. Another possible ethical issue is privacy, including the ability for "unobtrusive online research" in which data are collected without the knowledge of participants because it is easily available online, potentially violating informed consent principles (Fielding, Lee, and Blank 2017, 19).

There have been scholars who discuss challenge for qualitative research interviewing, including a "debate over the radical critique of interviewing and the nature of the data it generates" according to Edwards and Holland (2020) who argue that a careful consideration of "the relationship between the interview as a method of data generation for research and the ways of knowing about the world" is "crucial in considering the potentials for the method's practice."

In contrast to what has been covered thus far, there are less-structured interview techniques available to the researcher. The unstructured interview is more flexible than the structured one and most appropriate in the early stages of an investigation and in qualitative studies. It generally is better for studying perceptions, attitudes, and motivation, but it tends to be more difficult to administer and analyze. Examples of less-structured interviews include the focus(ed) group, the clinical interview or personal history, and the nondirective interview. The next section discusses focus group interviews.

FOCUS GROUP INTERVIEWS

Most qualitative interviews take place in the one-on-one fashion, described above. However, group interviews also are popular, including Delphi groups, brainstorming groups, and ethnographic informal interviews of groups that take place in the field (Lindlof and Taylor 2019, 233). The focus group interview is "unquestionably the most popular" among group interviews (Lindlof and Taylor 2019, 233). This technique "originated in marketing studies, but are rapidly being adopted in the social sciences, including information and library science (ILS). Focus group interviews are defined as "small groups of people with particular characteristics convened for a focused discussion of a particular topic" (Hollander 2004, 606; Lindlof and Taylor 2019, 233). The focus group interview technique can be used as a self-contained research method or in combination with other quantitative and qualitative research methods. Focus groups are useful for orienting oneself to a new field; developing ideas and concepts or even generating hypotheses based on informants' insights; evaluating different research sites or study populations; developing and refining research instruments, such as interview schedules and questionnaires; and getting participants' interpretations of results from earlier studies. As a self-contained method, focus groups can be used to explore new research areas or to examine known research questions from the participants' perspective, facilitate complex decision making, and identify and address important issues. The focus group interview may be used instead of the questionnaire or individual interviews, if the research questions warrant use of the method.

Library and information agencies can use the focus group interview method to develop needs assessment, community analysis, and promotional strategies for new services. In LIS research, it can be used to answer research questions concerned with the evaluation of library resources and services, such as online catalogs and e-resources.

What types of problematics are appropriate for focus group interviews? Focus group interviews can and have been used in all types of libraries to obtain information to both get student and faculty input on services and collections, as well as to get librarians' perceptions for strategic planning or other purposes. To provide examples of published research using focus group interviews that have taken place in library settings, following is a list of studies that highlight the problems or issues addressed, with the type of participants listed:

- Discovering the role of library staff to support first-generation students and to understand how their perceptions of library professionals changed over time at Penn State University Libraries (academic libraries—first-generation university students) (Borrelli et al. 2019).
- Understanding whether individuals with disabilities were informed about the services and support that community college libraries made available (community colleges—students with disabilities) (Pontoriero and Zippo-Mazur 2019).
- Examining outreach services in rural public libraries to elderly users, to understand social equity and access issues (public libraries—elderly users) (Sikes 2020).
- Assessing impact of a combined library and writing center initiative (academic libraries—former writing center tutors) (Epstein and Draxler 2020).
- Documenting students' information literacy competencies (academic libraries—upper division undergraduates) (Squibb and Zanzucchi 2020).
- Exploring library book selection decisions and effectiveness (academic library—undergraduate students, faculty, librarians) (Walters et al. 2020).
- Identifying expectations from stakeholder groups for school library programs (school library—stakeholders) (Everhart 2014).
- Exploration of how school librarians can establish and nurture personal learning networks (school library—librarians) (Moreillon 2016).

Another example can be seen in the work of Radford, Connaway, Kitzie, Mikitish, and Floegel (Radford et al. 2018; Radford, Kitzie, et al. 2017; Ross, Nilsen, and Radford 2009), who conducted a series of five focus group interviews along with in-depth transcript analysis to investigate and provide recommendations to mitigate microaggressions to support inclusive information services in libraries. This work builds on previous work by Radford and Connaway (2005), as well as Radford, Connaway, and Shah (2011), which identified relational facilitators and barriers for success in virtual reference. Microaggressions are conceptualized in this work as another barrier to excellent service. The literature defines microaggressions as intentional or nonintentional verbal, behavioral, and environmental indignities toward marginalized groups (Belluomini 2014; Giraldo-Kerr 2017; Sue et al. 2007). Their damaging effects have been observed, but microaggressions are subtle and therefore difficult to identify and address. There is a growing amount of published research on microaggressions in libraries (Sweeney and Cooke 2018), but no studies of microaggressions' presence in virtual library reference service were found during an extensive literature review. However, research on communication behaviors in virtual settings suggests that the anonymity of a virtual presence can heighten microaggressions. Three of the five focus group interviews were conducted with undergraduate academic library users in the northeastern and southern states. The other two were conducted with librarians of color who were in attendance at a library conference in a western state. The data were qualitatively coded using the constant comparative method (Charmaz 2014) and emic/etic coding to expand and enrich the typology that was developed from the transcript analysis, which preceded the focus group interviews. Findings indicated that participants both in the student and librarian groups recounted experiences of microaggressive behavior. Based on the results, guidelines were developed to mitigate microaggressions in virtual and FtF library settings (Ross, Nilsen, and Radford 2009, 203–207).

These examples show the versatility of focus groups in academic, school, and public libraries with respect to both the problems that can be explored and the different types of specific populations and user groups that can be targeted, depending on the study's goals. Note that several of the studies used focus groups in combination with other data collection techniques such as surveys and individual interviews. Connaway and Radford (2007) described the technique and how it was used, along with individual interviews and transcript analysis to study live chat librarians.

In designing a focus group interview, as in individual interviews, the researcher, keeping in mind the objectives of the study, must first identify the target groups, decide who will be interviewed, and recruit participants (Radford 2008, 1–3). Focus groups typically consist of from eight to twelve people (Wildemuth 2017, 262), and it is recommended that an additional two to four participants be "over-recruited" to ensure that the minimum of eight people will show up. Volunteers are often recruited for focus groups (though they may be reimbursed or given a meal, a gift card, or other compensation for their time). As in individual interviews, incentives such as these are desirable to encourage participation, considering that respondents often have busy schedules and many demands on their time. Refreshments generally are a good idea and may be part of the incentive. Busy people, including students, may be enticed to participate in a focus group over lunch. Those working in the nine-to-five business world may be able to attend a breakfast session more easily than lunch. Providing incentives, including refreshments, is often budget-driven, and it is critical to include these in funding requests when developing the research proposal (see chapter 3 for additional information on budgeting).

The interview should be held in a convenient, comfortable, informal location that is conducive to discussion (Stewart and Williams 2005). It may be necessary to use a room that accommodates digital/audio recording and/or observation behind a one-way mirror. Focus groups are usually scheduled for one session of 1 or 2 hours, but it may be necessary to hold more than one session in some cases. It is desirable to select participants who are as representative as possible of their population. It is vital, when possible, to break or stratify groups into smaller, more homogeneous groups. For example, college students could be divided into subgroups of undergraduate, graduate, and professional students. Researchers working with faculty groups may be well-advised to separate postdocs, tenure-track, tenured, and untenured (nontenure track) groups.

One vital consideration for focus groups is who will lead them. Selection of the moderator is crucial to the successful focus group. Preferably, the moderator will be an outside person, one who does not know the participants or have a supervisory position over any of them and who has been trained in focus group techniques. Researchers often want to act as moderators, but there can be ample reasons for using a professional or outside moderator, especially if the researcher knows the participants or may be tempted to use the opportunity for instruction (e.g., with university students) (Shoaf 2003).

Here is a list of some desirable moderator characteristics:

- excellent communication skills
- friendliness, ability to develop quick rapport
- sharp memory and ability to concentrate
- knowledge of group dynamics
- knowledge of when to probe
- restraint

Furthermore, good moderators are able to establish a nonthreatening environment, involve all participants, ask neutral questions, summarize areas of agreement or disagreement, direct (but not control) discussion, listen carefully, probe for more complete responses, and ask open (as opposed to closed or leading) questions. According to Greenbaum, the moderator plays the most critical role in the focus group, one that involves leadership and facilitation of the group so the research objectives are accomplished. The moderator uses techniques to delve into the reasons for attitudes and behaviors, to go below the surface of the answers (Greenbaum 2000).

As in individual interviews, for ethical reasons, before the focus group begins it is always important to obtain informed consent from all participants. The focus group session should open with appropriate introductions and "icebreakers" and then shift to the main questions. The moderator should make introductions and ask participants to briefly introduce themselves. The research project should be described and the role of the focus group interview explained. To avoid problems, it is a good idea to create a safe climate and describe the ground rules at the beginning of the focus group. Participants should be reminded that they must stay for the full length of time to receive compensation, which should be given out at the end and signed for, as usually is required for grant-supported research. It is recommended that guidelines be written on a flip chart that stays in the room on display and be reviewed aloud at the beginning of the focus group session, after introductions. Suggested guidelines include the following:

- This is an open, safe, and secure forum.
- Confidentiality of others should be respected.
- All suggestions are acceptable.
- Be patient with fellow group members (speak one at a time, no interruptions).
- Be an active listener and participant.
- Ask questions if necessary.

The moderator, of course, has the primary responsibility for conducting the interview. "The moderator of the focus group interview plays an important role in its success (or lack of it) . . . [and] is the one who keeps the discussion on track and away from becoming an unfocused conversation . . . achiev[ing] the right balance between controlling the flow of the discussion and allowing the participants free rein" (Wildemuth 2017, 260). Usually, an interview schedule or discussion guide is developed and used, being judicious about not having too many questions that would result in a rushed session where all participants may not get a chance to speak up. Some focus group researchers prefer to identify four or five "themes" or major areas that need to be covered. Four is optimum for a 1- to 2-hour focus group session, and five is the maximum, although it may be tempting to add more. For example, in focus group interviews that might be conducted with members of the public to help in the design of a new public library in an urban setting, four themes could be developed for discussion: spaces; services; collections, including types of media; and programs/events.

The moderator asks questions intended to initiate discussion of pertinent issues and should listen to, not edit or judge, participants' comments. Tent cards with participants' first names written on them large enough to be visible to all are highly recommended, so that people can be called on by their first names, which helps in the transcription process. There are challenges to the moderator that revolve around group dynamics. There usually are talkative people who have to be limited in their dominance of the group by such strategies as asking: "What do others think?" Or by being direct in saying: "Thanks for your input; who else would like to chime in?" The more reserved people must be encouraged through asking: "Could I hear from those who have not yet commented?" And (gently) calling on people by name if necessary: "Skyler, I see that you are shaking your head, can you tell us what you are thinking?" It is crucial for the moderator to be actively listening and to be alert to any problems. Any disruptions or rudeness within the group must be addressed immediately. Having covered the ground rules, it is advised to remind participants of these if, for example, someone is interrupting others or becomes aggressive. Especially in working with groups of adolescents, it is probable that there will be times when the moderator will have to step in quickly to remind participants that they agreed to listen to others and not to interrupt.

Digital/audio recorders often are used to capture focus group data, as in individual interviews, but at some point, these recordings may be transcribed and reduced to a more manageable size. It is highly recommended that an assistant to the moderator be present who takes on a supportive role, although not by directly participating. This person performs a number of functions, such as signing in participants and obtaining informed consent signatures, ensuring equipment is set up and functioning, troubleshooting (in the event of a problem, including latecomers), arranging the room, managing time, and facilitating initial note taking or the summarizing of digital/audio recorded data. In addition, if compensation is being given, such as a gift card, the assistant moderator hands these out and gets signed receipts.

When taking notes, the assistant moderator should attempt to

- trace the threads of an idea throughout the discussion;
- identify the subgroup or individual to whom an idea is important;

- distinguish ideas held in common from those held by individuals;
- capture the vocabulary and style of the group; and
- distinguish, if possible, among perceptions, feelings, and insights. (Wagner and Mahmoodi 1994, 10)

Time management is central to covering all the desired topic themes equally and leaving time at the end for a brief summary of what has been covered and how the data will be used and any "final thoughts" from participants. Time in focus group sessions tends to pass quickly, so moderators and assistant moderators need to be vigilant. It is a courtesy to participants to begin and end on time. As a final wrap-up, the moderator should express appreciation for everyone's time and candor and praise their contributions.

Online/Virtual Video-Based Focus Groups

Video conferencing platforms, such as Zoom, Microsoft Teams, or Webex, have advanced that they now enable virtual, synchronous focus group interviews, and they are increasing in popularity (Browning 2020, 13–14; Daniels et al. 2019). During the COVID-19 pandemic, as was the case for conducting individual interviews, focus group interviews moved online for health-related safety issues, and because travel became potentially hazardous and, in many cases, prohibited by universities and other employers. One advantage to these systems is built-in recording capability so that the sessions can be rewatched and/or transcribed later. If recording capability is not built in, "There is plenty of free software that can help you accomplish this if your chosen video conferencing software does not support it. Some software to help record your screen and audio are OBS Studio, Flashback Express, and Apowersoft (this requires no download, can be done from your browser)" (Browning 2020, 13).

Additional ground rules may need to be set for virtual focus group interviews such as: "Encourage participants to move to a quiet or secluded location, away from distractions. Have them make use of things like text chat or hand raising, since it can be more difficult to interject over a video feed. Ensure before the session starts that everyone is connected successfully (invite them early). Lastly, make sure you obtain video recording consent forms" (Browning 2020, 13)!

ANALYSIS AND REPORTING OF THE FOCUS GROUP INTERVIEW DATA

The information acquired from focus group interviews is generally used to help researchers understand perceptions and attitudes of the target population. The results of focus group interviews cannot be used to generalize an entire population, as the groups may not be representative of their total populations. Instead, the results give one the opportunity to consider a range of responses to questions. The focus group interview permits assessment of nonverbal responses and reveals group interaction patterns. The researcher analyzes the data acquired from the moderator's reports and audio/digitally recorded interview sessions. The analysis begins with getting an overview or global picture of the entire process and involves consideration of words, tone, context, nonverbal communications, responses, and ideas of the interviewees. Typically, analysis begins with listening to the recorded sessions and reviewing transcriptions and any notes from the moderator and assistant moderator.

One of the most prevalent approaches to analyzing focus group data is the content analysis approach, which produces thematic and numerical descriptions of the data. Content analysis is the tallying of mentions of very specific factors. Data either are used to identify in vivo categories (arising from emic, participant responses) and/or patterns that suggest themes and subthemes resulting from repeated readings and listening of recordings, or can be coded into predetermined categories derived from the literature review, theoretical framework, or your previous research, such as a pilot study (etic categories). Often the predetermined categories are derived from theoretical approaches or previous research (e.g., pilot studies) (Radford 1999, 2006; Radford et al. 2020). Segments of coded data can be brief or very extensive, and counts can be reported as percentages or proportions (e.g., "55 percent said" or "the majority of respondents said"). See chapter 8 for more on content analysis, coding, and thematic analysis.

Ethnographic summary is another technique for analyzing focus group interviews and uses data as a basis for summary statements that capture the essence of the responses. Ethnography involves establishing rapport, selecting research participants, transcribing observations and conversations, and keeping diaries, although Geertz believed that none of these techniques or procedures adequately defines the venture. He believed that ethnography is defined by the kind of intellectual effort it is, "an elaborate venture in 'thick description'" (Geertz 1973, 6). Reality, as perceived by the observer, is described in such detail that the reader can experience the total event as if he or she had actually been involved in it. The data must be interpreted in a manner that retains this richness. This thick description, including group interactions, is one of the advantages of the focus group interview method. The ethnographic summary and the content analysis approach are complementary means of analysis, and combining the two approaches brings additional strength to the analysis (Morgan 1988). Ethnography is covered in more detail in chapter 12.

One of the recurring questions that arise with the discussion of the focus group interview technique is its validity and reliability as a research method. "Focus groups are valid if they are used carefully for a problem that is suitable for focus group inquiry" (Morgan 1988, 237). If the researcher deviates from the established procedures outlined above, and if the research questions do not lend themselves to focus group interview methods, the focus group interviews can be invalid. In this way they are similar to other social science methods, in which validity depends not only on the procedures used but also on the context within which the procedures are used (Krueger 2014).

The validity of the analysis of the data collected during the focus group interviews is another concern. If content analysis is used as a method of data analysis, "the validity between the classification schemes, or variables derived from it, and the validity of the interpretation relating content variables to their causes or consequences" is crucial (Weber 1990). This means that in the dissemination and interpretation of the results, the researcher must ascertain that the findings are not generalizable beyond, or dependent on, specific methods, data, or measurements outside the specified study (Weber 1990, 18).

Reproducibility, or intercoder reliability (ICR), can be determined when the same data are coded with the same results by more than one coder. It is important in content analysis because it measures the consistency of understandings or meaning held by two or more coders (Weber 1990, 18). The ICR should be determined when analyzing focus group interview data. If one person examines one set of transcripts, while another concentrates on a different set of transcripts, two perceptions and perspectives of discovery also can be included in the reporting of the results (Morgan 1988). See chapter 10 for a more extensive discussion of ICR.

Advantages of Focus Group Interviews

The main advantage of focus group interviews is the opportunity to observe a large number of interactions on a topic in a limited period of time (Morgan 1988). Focus groups often produce rich data that provide an in-depth understanding of the participants' experiences and meanings. In contrast to most other techniques, focus group interviews are able to benefit from the interactions of more than one respondent.

Focus groups are less formal than individual interviews, although they still can highlight the individual's voice. Capturing "juicy quotes" or illustrative comments is another advantage of focus groups. The synergy of a discussion stimulates unexpected insights and perhaps produces more complete information than would otherwise be obtainable. Focus groups elicit strong and common opinions. An astute moderator will pause and ask: "Is there consensus on this?" when there are many heads nodding in agreement with what one participant says. It is essential to identify and report these key moments of consensus.

The method also can be used with hard-to-reach, underserved, or underrepresented groups, such as potential users of libraries, special needs populations, individuals from underrepresented communities, and children. It is a data-gathering technique that can be useful to both practitioners and researchers when they want to find out not only what a specific group thinks, but why the group thinks what it does. The format gives the moderator a chance to probe and to develop questions and discussions not anticipated by the researcher. The results can be analyzed and reported shortly after the data have been collected (Krueger and Casey 2000).

Wildemuth (2017, 258–59) notes these three strengths of focus group interviews: (a) "participants can compare their views with those of other participants in the group, rather than simply reporting their views to an interviewer"; (b) "their social nature mimics the setting in which people often form their opinions and attitudes. . . . In some cases . . . group members' views will be shifting as they hear and or consider the views of other group members"

(Millward 1995, 258) "the efficiency with which they can be used to generate new ideas" (Gaiser 1997, 259).

Limitations of Focus Group Interviews

Focus group interviews are quite susceptible to bias caused by the interview setting, the moderator, and faulty questions, and of course they are not designed to use a representative (generalizable) sample. The planning, administrative, and financial costs of the sessions can be another disadvantage of the focus group methodology. The cost of the session may include moderator fees, compensation in the form of gift cards or gratuities for the participants, refreshments, room rental, and travel expenses. Transcription of audio/digital recordings is time consuming and can be an added expense if a trained transcriber's services are engaged, although there are many benefits to doing so (Oliver, Serovich, and Mason 2005). These can run $50–$100 or more per hour of recording.

Libraries and other nonprofit organizations can utilize this research technique at less cost by training staff to be moderators and/or transcribers, paying mileage only for the participants, using library facilities for the sessions, and offering refreshments to the participants in lieu of gift cards. In a university setting, sometimes faculty members in departments such as sociology, education, or psychology can be tapped as skilled moderators, and it may be possible to provide compensation in the form of release time or to make other reciprocal arrangements.

As previously noted, the success of the focus group interview depends on the abilities of the moderator. The moderator must be carefully trained in the technique. If the moderator is not capable of directing the participants' discussions to the research questions, the participants can redirect the focus of the interview. The group experience may intimidate and suppress individual differences, causing some participants to withdraw and not participate in the discussions. Focus group interviews also can foster conformity among group members. The group participants can display a collective pattern of defensive avoidance and practice self-censorship by pressuring any member who expresses strong arguments counter to the group's stereotypes or rationalizations. This can intensify group loyalties and rigidly polarize individual opinions. The focus group interview methodology is vulnerable to manipulation by an influential and willful member of the group. Lindlof and Taylor also point out that "the free-wheeling character of focus groups is both its virtue and its potential difficulty. The bounty of talk released in these group sessions is filled with fragmentary thoughts, one-off comments, non sequiturs, and the like" (Lindlof and Taylor 2019, 235). A skillful and trained moderator can control these disadvantages.

Another disadvantage is that the analysis, summarization, and interpretation of responses may be difficult, as is true with individual interview data. Further limitations of focus group data are that they analyze perceptions, not facts, so data are subjective, as is analysis. One preferred way to compensate for these disadvantages is to triangulate and strengthen results by combining more than one data collection method (Radford and Connaway 2005). Miles, Huberman and Saldana (2020, 294) note that "in effect, triangulation is a way to get to the findings in the first place—by seeing or hearing multiple *instances*, of it from different *sources* by using different *methods* and by squaring the finding with others it needs to be squared with." Other scholars agree, recommending that focus group interview results not be used as the sole basis for making policy decisions. Focus group interviews often are used as exploratory techniques, to inform development of a survey, for example, as well as follow-up techniques, to gather more-in-depth information from survey responses or observations. They can provide another highly useful type of data for evidence-based decision making when used in combination with other methods and data analyses.

SUMMARY

This chapter provides a guide to interviews as a data collection technique for qualitative methods, including individual and focus group interviews. There are a variety of different uses for interviews within library contexts, including libraries of all types. Individual interviews can be of three types—unstructured, semistructured, and structured—and are gaining in popularity within qualitative research in LIS to collect perceptions from the targeted participants. This chapter provides guidelines for FtF and virtual interviews, developing the interview schedule, and conducting a pilot study. Sampling techniques are discussed, with attention to the use of purposive sampling in qualitative research, rather than a random technique used in quantitative studies.

Tips and techniques for interviewing are covered, including types of questions and modes of data collection (including in-person, telephone, or virtual data collection via video conferencing, email, and chat). Advantages and disadvantages of interviewing are reviewed. Strengths for individual interviews include better response rates, opportunity to correct misunderstandings, and ability to gather complex or emotionally laden information. Weaknesses include possible presence of bias, difficulty of establishing rapport in virtual interviews, and legal and ethical issues surrounding privacy concerns.

Focus group interviews usually involve eight to twelve people, last 1½ to 2 hours, and are a versatile technique that can be used in all types of libraries and library research. The chapter describes the role of the moderator, who plays a critical role in facilitating the group in order to accomplish research objectives. It is optimal to start broad and narrow down to identify either a semistructured list of questions or four or five themes to discuss while the group meets. Advantages of focus groups include that they can include a large number of participants in a small period of time, present an opportunity for unexpected insights, and provide a good approach for hard-to-reach or underserved groups. Limitations include that they are susceptible to the bias of the moderator, group selection, and faulty questions; they can be costly, although these costs can be reduced by training staff to moderate and transcribe sessions, among other techniques; there is a possibility of conformity among group members; and success relies on a skilled moderator who can identify these issues and correct them.

Data from both individual and focus group interviews are abundant, and usually are processed through use of content analysis to identify patterns and tallies of mentions of specific factors that are found to occur. Analysis can focus on either discovering emergent (emic) themes or coding data into preexisting themes (etic) developed from pilot studies or found in the theoretical or research literature. Ethnographic summary is another approach for analysis in which data are interpreted and presented in a way that maintains their thick description.

For all types of interviews, interpretation and summarization of results are prone to subjectivity; therefore triangulation, combining methods of data collection, is often used to maximize validity.

REFERENCES

"AAA Ethics Blog: Principles of Professional Responsibility (American Anthropological Association)—Archaeological Ethics Database." n.d. Accessed October 25, 2020. http://archaeologicalethics.org/code-of-ethics/american-anthropological-association-aaa-ethics-blog-principles-of-professional-responsibility.

Allen, Scott G., Larra Clark, Michele Coleman, Lynn Silipigni Connaway, Chris Cyr, Kendra Morgan, and Mercy Procaccini. 2019. "Libraries Respond to the Opioid Crisis with Their Communities: Summary Report." https://www.oclc.org/content/dam/research/publications/2019/oclcresearch-public-libraries-respond-to-opioid-crisis-summary-report.pdf.

Anderson, Monica, and Madhumitha Kumar. 2019. "Digital Divide Persists Even as Lower-Income Americans Make Gains in Tech Adoption." *Pew Research Center* (blog). https://www.pewresearch.org/fact-tank/2019/05/07/digital-divide-persists-even-as-lower-income-americans-make-gains-in-tech-adoption.

Are, Caroline. 2019 "Ethical and Practical Challenges of Online Research Interviews." *Humanitarian News Research Network.* https://blogs.city.ac.uk/humnews/2019/03/26/ethical-and-practical-challenges-of-online-research-interviews.

Audunson, Ragnar, Sophie Essmat, and Svanhild Aabø. 2011. "Public Libraries: A Meeting Place for Immigrant Women?" *Library & Information Science Research* 33(3): 220–27. https://doi.org/10.1016/j.lisr.2011.01.003.

Babbie, Earl R. 2021. *The Practice of Social Research.* 15th ed. Boston: Cengage Learning.

Bailey, Carol R. 2018. *A Guide to Qualitative Field Research.* 3rd ed. Thousand Oaks, CA: Sage.

Bauer, Melissa. 2020. "Commuter Students and the Academic Library: A Mixed-Method Study of Space." *Journal of Library Administration* 60(2): 146–54. https://doi.org/10.1080/01930826.2019.1677091.

Belluomini, Ellen. 2014. "Microaggressions and the Internet." SocialWorker.Com. April 2. http://www.socialworker.com/api/content/1c210630-b9c5-11e3-a2d5-1231380a02d9.

Bertot, John Carlo, Paul T. Jaeger, Ursula Gorham, Natalie Greene Taylor, and Ruth Lincoln. 2013. "Delivering E-Government Services and Transforming

Communities through Innovative Partnerships: Public Libraries, Government Agencies, and Community Organizations." *Information Polity* 18(2): 127–38. https://doi.org/10.3233/IP-130304.

Borrelli, Steve, Chao Su, Shenetta Selden, and Lana Munip. 2019. "Investigating First-Generation Students' Perceptions of Library Personnel: A Case Study from the Penn State University Libraries." *Performance Measurement and Metrics* 20(1): 27–36. https://doi.org/10.1108/PMM-07-2018-0018.

Bowman, Adam C. 2013. "24-Hour Academic Libraries: Adjusting to Change." *Journal of Access Services* 10(4): 217–39. https://doi.org/10.1080/15367967 .2013.842342.

Browning, Nathan. 2020. "Online, Synchronous, and Video-Based Focus Group Interviews." In *Doing Fieldwork in a Pandemic* (Crow-Sourced Document), edited by Deborah Lupton, 13–14. https://docs.google.com/document/d/1c lGjGABB2h2qbduTgfqribHmog9B6P0NvMgVuiHZCl8/edit?ts=5e88ae0a.

Butler, Brandon. 2010. "Challenges in Employing Fair Use in Academic and Research Libraries." 273. Research Library Issues: A Bimonthly Report from ARL, CNI, and SPARC.

Charmaz, Kathy. 2014. *Constructing Grounded Theory*. 2nd ed. Thousand Oaks, CA: Sage.

Chatman, Elfreda A. 1996. "The Impoverished Life-World of Outsiders." *Journal of the American Society for Information Science* 47(3): 193–206. https://doi.org /10.1002/(SICI)1097-4571(199603)47:3<193::AID-ASI3>3.0.CO;2-T.

Child, Reetu, and Anne Goulding. 2012. "Public Libraries in the Recession: The Librarian's Axiom." *Library Review* 61(8/9): 641–63. https://doi.org/10 .1108/00242531211292123.

Chiumento, Anna, Laura Machin, Atif Rahman, and Lucy Firth. 2018. "Online Interviewing with Interpreters in Humanitarian Contexts." *International Journal of Qualitative Studies on Health and Well-Being* 13(1): 1444887, quoted in Caroline Are, "Ethical and Practical Challenges of Online Research Interviews," Humanitarian News Research Network. https://blogs.city.ac.uk /humnews/2019/03/26/ethical-and-practical-challenges-of-online-research -interviews.

Connaway, Lynn Silipigni, and Marie L. Radford. 2007. "The Thrill of the Chase in Cyberspace: A Report of Focus Groups with Live Chat Librarians." Informed Librarian Online. http://www.informedlibrarian.com/guestForum.cfm?FILE =gf0701.html.

Connaway, Lynn Silipigni, Marie L. Radford, and OCLC Research. 2011. *Seeking Synchronicity: Revelations and Recommendations for Virtual Reference*. Dublin, OH: OCLC Research.

Conrad, Lettie Y., and Virginia M. Tucker. 2019. "Making It Tangible: Hybrid Card Sorting within Qualitative Interviews." *Journal of Documentation* 75(2): 397–416. https://doi.org/10.1108/JD-06-2018-0091.

Corbin, Juliet, and Anselm Strauss. 2014. *Basics of Qualitative Research: Techniques and Procedures for Developing Grounded Theory*. 4th ed. Thousand Oaks, CA: Sage.

Couper, Mick P., Sue Ellen Hansen, Jaber F. Gubrium, and James A. Holstein. 2002. "Computer-Assisted Interviewing." In *Handbook of Interview Research: Context & Method*, edited by Jaber F. Gubrium, 557. Thousand Oaks, CA: Sage.

Cox, Andrew M., Stephen Pinfield, and Sophie Rutter. 2019. "The Intelligent Library: Thought Leaders' Views on the Likely Impact of Artificial Intelligence on Academic Libraries." *Library Hi Tech* 37(3): 418–35. https://doi.org/10 .1108/LHT-08-2018-0105.

Dalmer, Nicole K. 2019. "Considering the Local and the Translocal: Reframing Health Information Practice Research Using Institutional Ethnography." *Aslib Journal of Information Management* 71(6): 703–19. https://doi.org/10.1108/AJIM-02-2019-0046.

Daniels, Nicola, Patricia Gillen, Karen Casson, and Iseult Wilson. 2019. "STEER: Factors to Consider When Designing Online Focus Groups Using Audiovisual Technology in Health Research." *International Journal of Qualitative Methods* 18 (January): 1–11 https://doi.org/10.1177/1609406919885786.

Dulock, Michael. 2011. "New Cataloger Preparedness: Interviews with New Professionals in Academic Libraries." *Cataloging & Classification Quarterly* 49(2): 65–96. https://doi.org/10.1080/01639374.2011.538910.

Edwards, Rosalind, and Janet Holland. 2020. "Reviewing Challenges and the Future for Qualitative Interviewing." *International Journal of Social Research Methodology* 23(5): 581–92. https://doi.org/10.1080/13645579.2020.1766767.

Epstein, Maglen, and Bridget Draxler. 2020. "Collaborative Assessment of an Academic Library and Writing Center Partnership: Embedded Writing and Research Tutors for First-Year Students." *College & Research Libraries* 81(3): 509–37. https://doi.org/10.5860/crl.81.3.509.

Everhart, Nancy. 2014. "What Do Stakeholders Know about School Library Programs? Results of a Focus Group Evaluation." *School Library Research* 17: 1–14. https://eric.ed.gov/?id=EJ1022550.

Fielding, Nigel G., Raymond M. Lee, and Grant Blank. 2017. *The SAGE Handbook of Online Research Methods.* 2nd ed. Thousand Oaks, CA: Sage.

Flaherty, Mary Grace. 2013. "Consumer Health Information Provision in Rural Public Libraries: A Comparison of Two Library Systems." *The Library Quarterly* 83(2): 155–65. https://doi.org/10.1086/669548.

Frey, James H., and Sabine Mertens Oishi. 1995. *How to Conduct Interviews by Telephone and in Person. The Survey Kit,* Vol. 4. Thousand Oaks, CA: Sage.

Gaiser, Ted J. 1997. "Conducting On-Line Focus Groups: A Methodological Discussion." *Social Science Computer Review* 15(2): 135–44.

Geertz, Clifford. 1973. *The Interpretation of Cultures: Selected Essays.* New York: Basic Books.

Gibson, Amelia N., and John D. Martin. 2019. "Re-Situating Information Poverty: Information Marginalization and Parents of Individuals with Disabilities." *Journal of the Association for Information Science and Technology* 70(5): 476–87. https://doi.org/10.1002/asi.24128.

Giraldo-Kerr, Anna. 2017. "6 Things to Learn about Microaggressions." *Huff Post.* https://www.huffpost.com/entry/six-things-to-learn-about_b_5512057.

Greenbaum, Thomas L. 2000. *Moderating Focus Groups: A Practical Guide for Group Facilitation.* Thousand Oaks, CA: Sage.

Greifeneder, Elke. 2014. "Trends in Information Behaviour Research." *Proceedings of ISIC: The Information Behaviour Conference* 19(4). https://curis.ku.dk/ws/files/137513587/Trends_in_information_behaviour_research.htm.

Gubrium, Jaber F., James A. Holstein, Amir B. Marvasti, and Karyn D. McKinney. 2012. *The SAGE Handbook of Interview Research: The Complexity of the Craft.* Thousand Oaks, CA: Sage.

Hollander, Jocelyn A. 2004. "The Social Contexts of Focus Groups." *Journal of Contemporary Ethnography* 33(5): 602–37.

Jaeger, Paul T., Nicole A. Cooke, Cecilia Feltis, Michelle Hamiel, Fiona Jardine, and Katie Shilton. 2015. "The Virtuous Circle Revisited: Injecting Diversity, Inclusion, Rights, Justice, and Equity into LIS from Education to Advocacy." *The Library Quarterly* 85(2): 150–71. https://doi.org/10.1086/680154.

Jantz, Ronald C. 2012. "Innovation in Academic Libraries: An Analysis of University Librarians' Perspectives." *Library & Information Science Research* 34(1): 3–12. https://doi.org/10.1016/j.lisr.2011.07.008.

Julien, Heidi, Jen (J.L.) Pecoskie, and Kathleen Reed. 2011. "Trends in Information Behavior Research, 1999–2008: A Content Analysis." *Library & Information Science Research* 33 (1):19–24. https://doi.org/10.1016/j.lisr.2010.07.014.

Kitzie, Vanessa L., Lynn Silipigni Connaway, and Marie L. Radford. In press. "'I've Already Googled It, and I Can't Understand It': Users' Perceptions of Virtual Reference and Social Question-Answering Sites." *Reference & User Services Quarterly.*

Krueger, Richard A. 2014. *Focus Groups: A Practical Guide for Applied Research.* Thousand Oaks, CA: Sage.

Krueger, Richard A., and Mary Anne Casey. 2000. *Focus Groups: A Practical Guide for Applied Research.* Thousand Oaks, CA: Sage.

Kusenbach, Margarethe. 2003. "Street Phenomenology: The Go-Along as Ethnographic Research Tool." *Ethnography* 4(3): 455–85.

Kvale, Steinar, and Svend Brinkmann. 2015. *InterViews: Learning the Craft of Qualitative Research Interviewing.* 3rd ed. Los Angeles: Sage.

Lindlof, Thomas R., and Bryan C. Taylor. 2019. *Qualitative Communication Research Methods.* 4th ed. Los Angeles: Sage.

Lingel, Jessa, and danah boyd. 2013. "'Keep It Secret, Keep It Safe': Information Poverty, Information Norms, and Stigma." *Journal of the American Society for Information Science and Technology* 64(5): 981–91. https://doi.org/10.1002/asi.22800.

Maddox, Alexia. 2020. "Doing Online Interviews." https://docs.google.com/document/d/1clGjGABB2h2qbduTgfqribHmog9B6P0NvMgVuiHZCl8/edit?ts=5e88ae0a&usp=embed_facebook.

Miles, Matthew B., A. Michael Huberman, and Johnny Saldaña. 2020. *Qualitative Data Analysis: A Methods Sourcebook.* 4th ed. Thousand Oaks, CA: Sage. https://www.vitalsource.com/products/qualitative-data-analysis-matthew-b-miles-v9781506353081.

Millward, L. J. 1995. "Focus Groups." In *Research Methods in Psychology,* edited by Glynis M. Breakwell, Sean Hammond, and Chris Fife-Schaw, 274–92. London: Sage.

"Mobile Phone Technology Fact-Sheet." n.d. Pew Research Center. Accessed July 2, 2020. https://www.pewresearch.org/internet/fact-sheet/mobile.

Moniarou-Papaconstantinou, Valentini. 2020. "Valuing Studies in Higher Education: Symbolic Means and Strategies of Students Negotiating Their Position in the Library and Information Science Field." *Journal of Librarianship and Information Science* 52(1): 306–14. https://doi.org/10.1177/0961000618799530.

Moreillon, Judi. 2016. "Building Your Personal Learning Network (PLN): 21st-Century School Librarians Seek Self-Regulated Professional Development Online." *Knowledge Quest* 44(3): 64–69.

Morgan, David L. 1988. *Focus Groups as Qualitative Research.* Newbury Park, CA: Sage.

Oliver, Daniel G., Julianne M. Serovich, and Tina L. Mason. 2005. "Constraints and Opportunities with Interview Transcription: Towards Reflection in Qualitative Research." *Social Forces* 84(2): 1273–89. https://doi.org/10.1353/sof.2006.0023.

"Online Interviewing." n.d. Survey System. https://www.surveysystem.com/online-interviewing-cati.htm.

Oxley, Rebecca. 2013. "IDiversity and LIS Education: Student-Based Groups Promoting Cultural Competence as a Vision for the Profession." *The Library Quarterly* 83(3): 236–42. https://doi.org/10.1086/670698.

Patton, Michael Quinn. 1990. *Qualitative Evaluation and Research Methods.* 2nd ed. Newbury Park, CA: Sage.

Perkins, Gay Helen, and Amy J. W. Slowik. 2013. "The Value of Research in Academic Libraries." *College & Research Libraries* 74(2): 143–57. https://doi.org/10.5860/crl-308.

Pontoriero, Catherine, and Gina Zippo-Mazur. 2019. "Evaluating the User Experience of Patrons with Disabilities at a Community College Library." *Library Trends* 67(3): 497–515. https://doi.org/10.1353/lib.2019.0009.

Radford, Marie L. 1999. *The Reference Encounter: Interpersonal Communication in the Academic Library.* Publications in Librarianship 52. Chicago: Association of College and Research Libraries, A Division of the American Library Association.

Radford, Marie L. 2006. "Encountering Virtual Users: A Qualitative Investigation of Interpersonal Communication in Chat Reference." *Journal of the American Society for Information Science and Technology* 57(8): 1046–59. https://doi.org/10.1002/asi.20374.

Radford, Marie L. 2008. "How to Conduct a Focus Group." *Marketing Library Services* 22(1): 1–3.

Radford, Marie L., and Lynn Silipigni Connaway. 2005. "Seeking Synchronicity: Evaluating Virtual Reference Services." OCLC. 2005–2008. https://www.oclc.org/content/research/areas/user-studies/synchronicity.html.

Radford, Marie L., Lynn Silipigni Connaway, Vanessa L. Kitzie, and Diana Floegel. 2018. "Investigating and Mitigating Microaggressions to Support Inclusive Information Services." Presented at the Libraries in the Digital Age (LIDA) conference, Zadar, Croatia, June 13–15, 2018.

Radford, Marie L., Lynn Silipigni Connaway, Stephanie Mikitish, Mark Alpert, Chirag Shah, and Nicole A. Cooke. 2017. "Shared Values, New Vision: Collaboration and Communities of Practice in Virtual Reference and SQA." *Journal of the Association for Information Science and Technology* 68(2): 438–49. https://doi.org/10.1002/asi.23668.

Radford, Marie L., Lynn Silipigni Connaway, and Chirag Shah. 2011. "Cyber Synergy: Seeking Sustainability through Collaboration between Virtual Reference and Social Q&A Sites." Grant Proposal. Institute of Museum and Library Services (IMLS): Rutgers University and OCLC. http://citeseerx.ist.psu.edu/viewdoc/download?doi=10.1.1.434.1004&rep=rep1&type=pdf.

Radford, Marie L., Vanessa L. Kitzie, Lynn Silipigni Connaway, and Diana Floegel. 2017. "'Is It a Journal Title, or What?' Mitigating Microaggressions in Virtual Reference." Presented at ALA/RUSA's New Discoveries in Reference: The 23rd Annual Reference Research Forum, ALA Annual Conference, June 22–27, 2017, Chicago.

Radford, Marie L., Vanessa Kitzie, Stephanie Mikitish, Diana Floegel, Gary P. Radford, and Lynn Silipigni Connaway. 2020. "'People Are Reading Your Work,' Scholarly Identity and Social Networking Sites." *Journal of Documentation* (ahead-of-print). https://doi.org/10.1108/JD-04-2019-0074.

Ross, Catherine S., Kirsti Nilsen, and Marie L. Radford. 2009. *Conducting the Reference Interview.* 2nd ed. New York: Neal-Schuman.

Schatzman, Leonard, and Anselm L. Strauss. 1973. *Field Research: Strategies for a Natural Sociology.* Englewood Cliffs, NJ: Prentice Hall.

Shoaf, Eric C. 2003. "Using a Professional Moderator in Library Focus Group Research." *College & Research Libraries* 64(2): 124–32. https://doi.org/10.5860/crl.64.2.124.

Sikes, Scott. 2020. "Rural Public Library Outreach Services and Elder Users: A Case Study of the Washington County (VA) Public Library." *Public Library Quarterly* 39(4): 363–88. https://doi.org/10.1080/01616846.2019.1659070.

Smith, Lucy, and Jennifer Rowley. 2012. "Digitisation of Local Heritage: Local Studies Collections and Digitisation in Public Libraries." *Journal of Librarianship and Information Science* 44(4): 272–80. https://doi.org/10.1177/0961000611434760.

Spradley, James P. 2016. *The Ethnographic Interview.* Long Grove, IL: Waveland Press.

Squibb, Sara L. Davidson, and Anne Zanzucchi. 2020. "Apprenticing Researchers: Exploring Upper-Division Students' Information Literacy Competencies." *Portal: Libraries and the Academy* 20(1): 161–85. https://doi.org/10.1353/pla.2020.0008.

Stewart, Kate, and Matthew Williams. 2005. "Researching Online Populations: The Use of Online Focus Groups for Social Research." *Qualitative Research* 5(4): 395–416. https://doi.org/10.1177/1468794105056916.

Sue, Derald Wing, Christina M. Capodilupo, Gina C. Torino, Jennifer M. Bucceri, Aisha M. B. Holder, Kevin L. Nadal, and Marta Esquilin. 2007. "Racial Microaggressions in Everyday Life: Implications for Clinical Practice." *American Psychologist* 62(4): 271–86. https://doi.org/10.1037/0003-066X.62.4.271.

Sweeney, Miriam E., and Nicole A. Cooke. 2018. "You're So Sensitive! How LIS Professionals Define and Discuss Microaggressions Online." *The Library Quarterly* 88(4): 375–90. https://doi.org/10.1086/699270.

Ullah, Ahsan, and Kanwal Ameen. 2018. "Account of Methodologies and Methods Applied in LIS Research: A Systematic Review." *Library & Information Science Research* 40(1): 53–60. https://doi.org/10.1016/j.lisr.2018.03.002.

Wagner, Mary M., and Suzanne H. Mahmoodi. 1994. *A Focus Group Interview Manual.* Chicago: American Library Association.

Walters, William H., John Gormley, Amy E. Handfield, Bernadette M. López-Fitzsimmons, Susanne Markgren, Laurin Paradise, and Sarah E. Sheehan. 2020. "Library Book Selection Decisions and Selectors' Effectiveness: Differences among Librarians, Faculty, and Students." *College & Research Libraries* 81(4): 617–45. https://doi.org/10.5860/crl.81.4.617.

Walwyn, Olivia, and Jennifer Rowley. 2011. "The Value of Therapeutic Reading Groups Organized by Public Libraries." *Library & Information Science Research* 33(4): 302–12. https://doi.org/10.1016/j.lisr.2011.02.005.

Weber, Robert Philip. 1990. *Basic Content Analysis.* 2nd ed. London: Sage.

Wengraf, Tom. 2001. *Qualitative Research Interviewing: Biographic Narratives and Semi-Structured Methods.* London: Sage.

Wildemuth, Barbara M. 2017. *Applications of Social Research Methods to Questions in Information and Library Science.* 2nd ed. Santa Barbara, CA: ABC-CLIO.

12

Ethnographic Approaches to Qualitative Research

Wolcott described ethnography as "a way of seeing" (as indicated by the subtitle of his book, *Ethnography: A Way of Seeing*). He also referred to ethnography as a technique and not necessarily a method (Wolcott 1999). Ethnography is a way of seeing how individuals interact and behave in situations by utilizing different qualitative data collection and analysis methods. Asher and Miller (2011) define ethnography as "a collection of qualitative methods that focus on the close observation of social practices and interactions." Rosaldo (quoted in Wolcott) described the research strategy as "deep hanging out" (Rosaldo 1989, 4). When described in these terms, ethnography requires becoming part of a select group, establishing rapport with members of the group, interviewing members of the group, transcribing observations and conversations, and keeping diaries. Geertz (1973, 6) believed that none of these approaches adequately defines the venture; rather, it is a kind of intellectual effort that is "an elaborate venture in 'thick description.'" Although this experience still is documented from the observer's or researcher's perspective, it "allows the researcher to see beyond received understandings of how a certain process or situation is supposed to work or what it is supposed to mean, and learn about the meanings that its participants ascribe to it" (Asher and Miller 2011). Basically, the ethnographic approach helps "the researcher see how members of a group make sense of a situation" (Asher and Miller 2011, 2).

ETHNOGRAPHIC RESEARCH

Ethnographic research provides for the collection of textual, verbal, and visual data. This means that data collection methods can include interviews; visual, audio, and textual diaries; visual and textual journals; and observations.

Industries and corporations such as Microsoft, Google, and Xerox have used approaches for product development and evaluation that are referred to as applied anthropology and include surveys, questionnaires, cognitive mapping, and design sessions. Ethnographic approaches for collecting and analyzing data have become popular in the library and information science (LIS) literature. Of eighty-one LIS user studies articles, reports, and conference presentations that employed ethnographic approaches, "51.9% were published after 2005" (Wakimoto 2013, 96–98). Lanclos and Asher (2016) describe the use of ethnography in library practice. The data collection methods used in the studies included individual and focus group interviews, fieldwork, and observations. For more information about ethnographic research from an anthropologist's perspective, see text box 12.1, On Ethnographic Research: How Do Students Find the Information They Need?, by Andrew D. Asher.

Text Box 12.1: On Ethnographic Research: How Do Students Find the Information They Need?

Andrew D. Asher

As an anthropologist, this question was the motivation for why I started using ethnographic methods to explore libraries and information processes. Because ethnographic methods focus on directly observing, recording, and explaining what people are doing in practice, they are a particularly good strategy for approaching difficult and complex questions like understanding the myriad ways people approach searching for information (Asher, Duke, and Wilson 2013).

For me, the power of ethnographic research derives from its synthetic approach of integrating multiple data sources to create interpretive understandings of social and cultural processes. In this way, ethnographic research is an especially humanistic social science, and uses a constellation of research methods to build knowledge about people's lives by uncovering and learning their stories. Ethnographic research is therefore not just a set of tools, but rather an epistemological stance that seeks to construct a nuanced and holistic portrait of social processes through the diversity of individual experiences.

Ethnographic research methods seek to use people's own categories of analysis as a way of understanding social and cultural processes on their own terms. Researchers using ethnographic approaches must be careful to avoid making assumptions about what they will find, to suspend judgments about people's actions, and to attend to both people's own explanations of the processes being studied as well as analytical or theoretical explanations. While ethnographic methods usually emphasize qualitative data, they should not be seen as opposed to quantitative approaches to research, but instead as a different, and often complementary, way of gathering evidence and discovering meaning within the complexities of human behavior (Boellstorff et al. 2012; Duke and Asher 2012).

Ethnographic research often requires a great deal of time, effort, empathy, and personal engagement from the researcher. However, its payoff is also significant, particularly when given sufficient resources and support to develop long-term and comparative understandings of social context (Lanclos and Asher 2016). By elucidating rich descriptions of the depth and breadth of people's experiences in real situations, ethnographic research is one of the most effective ways to provide answers to the hard questions of "how" and "why" social processes and practices occur.

References

Asher, Andrew D., Lynda M. Duke, and Suzanne Wilson. 2013. "Paths of Discovery: Comparing the Search Effectiveness of EBSCO Discovery Service, Summon, Google Scholar, and Conventional Library Resources." *College & Research Libraries* 74(5): 464–88. https://doi.org/10.5860/crl-374.

Boellstorff, Tom, Bonnie Nardi, Celia Pearce, and T. L. Taylor. 2012. *Ethnography and Virtual Worlds.* Princeton, NJ: Princeton University Press. https://press.princeton.edu/books/hardcover/9780691149509/ethnography-and-virtual-worlds.

Duke, Lynda M., and Andrew D. Asher. 2012. *College Libraries and Student Culture: What We Now Know.* Chicago: American Library Association.

Lanclos, Donna, and Andrew Asher. 2016. "'Ethnographish': The State of the Ethnography in Libraries." *Weave: Journal of Library User Experience* 1(5). https://doi.org/10.3998/weave.12535642.0001.503.

One of the most popular library studies that used both ethnographic and applied anthropology methods for data collection and analysis was conducted at the University of Rochester by Foster and Gibbons (2007). (For a discussion of earlier library studies that used ethnographic methods, see Duke and Asher (2012), *College Libraries and Student Culture: What We Now Know.*) During the course of the study the librarians at the University of Rochester:

- conducted face-to-face (FtF) interviews with students and faculty both in the library and at other campus locations;
- distributed a short questionnaire to undergraduate students who used FtF reference services;
- developed a survey instrument that was used to collect student responses in the library and at other locations on campus, as well as a questionnaire distributed to undergraduate students who came to the reference desk;
- conducted sessions with undergraduate students who designed their ideal library and organized participatory design workshops in which undergraduate students designed their ideal devices for connecting to classwork, people, entertainment, and their library home page;
- recruited students to create photo journals or photo diaries that included twenty specific things, such as their favorite place to study, and then conducted FtF follow-up interviews with the students, who explained the photos; and
- distributed maps for the students to document their movements for an entire day, which are referred to as mapping diaries, and conducted follow-up interviews.

The Ethnographic Research in Illinois Academic Libraries (ERIAL) project was a twenty-one-month study (2008–2010) funded by the Illinois State Library. It included five Illinois university libraries and aimed to identify students' habits and practices when conducting research for their studies ("Home | The

Ethnographic Research in Illinois Academic Libraries" n.d.). ERIAL also included ethnographic approaches for data collection and analysis. "The Project ERIAL web site ("Home | The Ethnographic Research in Illinois Academic Libraries" n.d.) is a goldmine of information on library ethnography" (Kline 2013). (For detailed information on the descriptions, strengths, and weaknesses of the ethnographic data collection methods listed above, see the Project ERIAL website ("Home | The Ethnographic Research in Illinois Academic Libraries" n.d.).

Digital Ethnography

Digital ethnography utilizes the same techniques as described above for ethnography. Duggan (2017) argues that ethnography is a way of studying social and cultural practices that change to reflect everyday cultural practices. Digital ethnography involves conducting ethnographic research in a contemporary world. "It invites researchers to consider how we live and research in a digital, material and sensory environment" (Pink et al. 2016, 2). Ethnography in "the digital environment requires adaptation to account for the nature of digital information (traceable yet ephemeral, easily copied, transmitted quickly and globally)" (Barratt and Maddox 2016, 703).

While some researchers are skeptical of the pursuit of digital ethnography (Duggan 2017; Murthy 2008), others are embracing it while recognizing the challenges (Pink et al. 2016). Lane (2016, 2018, 2020) used digital ethnography to study Harlem teenagers and the adults in their lives by connecting with them both in person and online, becoming a part of their street and digital lives to identify how the digital life of a neighborhood influences personal lives. Barratt and Maddox (2016) conducted digital ethnographic research with drug users and encourage the use of this technique to augment other data collection methods when studying marginalized communities. Standlee (White et al. 2014) proposed that digital ethnology may provide new opportunities for studying young adults who increasingly are using online and digital platforms for interacting. She acknowledges the limitations and challenges of data collection and ethical concerns when studying young adults. LIS researchers also are using digital ethnography techniques to study individuals' behaviors on social media sites, smart phones, etc. Attu and Terras (2017) identified and classified Tumblr-related academic research while Talip et al. (2017) combined online observations of Twitter usage with interviews with IT professionals. Kaskazi describes her research of youth in digital and physical spaces in text box 12.2.

Text Box 12.2: Digital Ethnography and Memoing

Amana Kaskazi

Contemporary research of everyday life necessitates an exploration into the digital spaces in which we communicate, learn, perform, and play.

My research explores civic activities afforded by digital media and the political participatory practices of youth. To conduct my study, I immersed myself in the physical and mediated spaces of teenagers, to better understand the strategies youth use to seek out information, develop an interest and knowledge in political topics and people, and how they communicate and engage in political and civic activities.

I viewed my field site as a network of physical and mediated environments—home, parks, and libraries, as well as group chats and social media platforms—which allowed me to follow my participants as they move across spaces. When conducting my fieldwork, my focus is on my participants and their activities, regardless of the environment. This perspective enables an understanding of the subtleties of their actions and how one space influences interaction in the other. It also enabled a complete immersion into the everyday lives of young people, who fluidly traverse the porous boundaries of physical and digital spaces.

I followed my participants on various social media platforms (Instagram, Twitter, Snapchat, and Tik Tok). One of the benefits of digital ethnography is that online environments are not bound by temporal or spatial limitations, freeing you to explore communication and relationships beyond those you can observe just by being present.

However, researchers must be aware of pitfalls. For example, at the beginning of research I would overlook the role of online spaces or attribute my own use and understanding of those platforms to my participants. While studying a community that you also belong to or a platform that you are familiar with has its benefits, it's important to take an outsider's perspective and ground the analysis in the experiences of the participants.

One way to accomplish this is by taking detailed field notes and memos. My participants would often show and discuss digital content they came across or posted on social media while we were together physically. In those instances, I would ask my participants to take a screenshot or share the content with me on the platform. I also created social media accounts to follow

Figure 12.1. Screenshot of My Instagram Posts throughout My Fieldwork (Amana Kaskazi)

my participants and document the places, spaces, and experiences I had throughout my fieldwork. I viewed these as artifacts and incorporated the photos, screenshots, and videos into my memos to contextualize the artifact and improve my understanding of their digital interactions.

As I mentioned above, I would often take a photo or video during my fieldwork to capture the places and events occurring. I then used these photos and videos as artifacts when writing up my field memos.

Additional Readings

Hine, Christine. 2020. "Ethnographies in Online Environments." In *SAGE Research Methods Foundations,* edited by Paul Atkinson, Sara Delamont, Alexandru Cernat, Joseph W. Sakshaug, and Williams, Richard. London: Sage. https://doi.org/10.4135/9781526421036784565.

Lane, Jeffrey. 2018. *The Digital Street.* Illus. ed. New York: Oxford University Press.

DIARIES

Another ethnographic approach that is used as a qualitative data collection tool is the diary. Diaries can be used "to find out about what patrons do and think, without requiring the constant presence of a researcher" (White et al. 2014). In addition to the mapping and photo diaries discussed above, written and audio diaries or journals often are used in ethnographic studies. However, since these are methods of participant self-reporting, it is beneficial to include other data collection methods, such as direct observation. The written monthly diary was utilized in one of the phases of the three-year longitudinal study described in *The Many Faces of Digital Visitors & Residents: Facets of Online Engagement* (Connaway et al. 2014). However, in an attempt to be less restrictive and to not impose ideas on the diarists, the instructions were very open. The researchers asked the diarists to write about how they engaged in technology and how they got information for both their personal and academic lives. This strategy was not successful. The diarists simply listed web pages and sources, with no explanation of how or why these were chosen. The researchers then developed specific questions that used the critical incident technique (CIT) (Flanagan 1954) (see chapter 10 for the definition and examples of CIT) and gave them to the diarists to be answered and submitted to the researchers each month (Radford 2006).

Written Diarist Submission Form

Participant Name/User Code:

Date:

The University of Oxford and OCLC Research, in partnership with the University of North Carolina, Charlotte, are collaborating on a study to increase understanding of how learners engage with the Web and how educational services and systems can attract and sustain a possible new group of lifelong learners. http://www.oclc.org/research/activities /vandr/default.htm

Thank you for agreeing to take this time to follow up. There are no right or wrong answers. It is not a test. Just be as honest as you can.

You will be compensated upon submission and completion the usual gift card or voucher worth $25/£15 as you have for your diary submissions.

1. Grade Level/Academic Status:

2. Explain a time in the past month when you were SUCCESSFUL in completing an ACA-DEMIC assignment. What steps did you take?

   What resources did you choose to use? Why?

   What made you take these steps?

   What made you choose these resources instead of others?

   What made these resources easy/difficult to use?

   Why do you think your approach worked?

   What new approaches did you try?

   How did you find out about it?

   Did someone tell you or did you find it on your own?

   What made this a good choice for you?

3. Think of a time fairly recently when you struggled to find appropriate resources to help you complete an ACADEMIC assignment. What happened?

   What resources did you choose?

   Why did you choose them?

   What made you take these steps?

   What made you choose these resources instead of others?

   Why do you think this approach did not work?

4. Explain a time in the past month when you were successful in getting what you needed in a PERSONAL situation. What steps did you take?

   What resources did you choose to use? Why?

What made you take these steps?

What made you choose these resources instead of others?

What made these resources easy/difficult to use?

Why do you think your approach worked?

What new approaches did you try?

How did you find out about it?

Did someone tell you or did you find it on your own?

What made this a good choice for you?

5. Explain a time in the past month when you were NOT successful in getting what you needed in a PERSONAL situation. What steps did you take?

What resources did you choose?

Why did you choose them?

What made you take these steps?

What made you choose these resources instead of others?

Why do you think this approach did not work?

6. Tell me something interesting that has happened in the past month in the social media (i.e., bookmarking, RSS web feeds, wikis, blogs, etc.) that you used for ACADEMIC purposes.

What made you use this?

Do you feel that the use of this social media technology was successful/worked for you? Explain why or why not.

7. Tell me something interesting that has happened in the past month in the social media (i.e., bookmarking, RSS web feeds, wikis, blogs, etc.) that you used for PERSONAL situations.

What made you use this?

Do you feel that the use of this social media technology was successful/worked for you? Explain why or why not.

8. What do you have to add to our discussion today about how you got information in the past month for both PERSONAL and ACADEMIC situations?

Thank you again for your time. If you have any questions or concerns, please contact us at:

[Researchers' names, titles, and contact information inserted here.]

Thank you again for your continued participation in our research study.

Please submit this completed document to: [Name, Title, and Contact Information for researcher who collected the data inserted here.]

Source: White, David S., and Lynn Silipigni Connaway. 2011–2014. *Digital Visitors and Residents: What Motivates Engagement with the Digital Information Environment.* Funded by JISC, OCLC, and Oxford University. http://www.oclc.org/research/activities/vandr.html. Reprinted by permission of OCLC.

Advantages of Diaries

Using diaries for data collection has several advantages:

- The inclusion of diaries can broaden the amount of data collected, since the participants are creating the data without the immediate involvement of the researcher.
- Diaries enable the researchers to capture data from the participants' daily lives that may not be readily available because the researchers cannot be with the participants during their everyday lives.

Limitations of Diaries

Diaries also have some limitations:

- The researcher only will receive the information that the participants are willing or have time to share, therefore increasing the possibility of collecting incomplete information.
- If the researcher does not have the opportunity to discuss the diary entries with the participants, there may be insufficient data to fully understand how and why the participants do what they say they do.

To mitigate these limitations, diaries often are used in combination with other data collection instruments, such as interviews and observation.

Mapping

As previously mentioned, the ERIAL project used student-mapping diaries and cognitive mapping to identify how they did research ("Methodology" 2020).

Mapping also has been used with undergraduate students at the University of Richmond (Pukkila and Freeman 2012, 16–19), the University of Connecticut (Cowan 2012), and the American University of Central Asia (Pukkila and Freeman 2012, 40–45). There are different ways of collecting data through mapping. The study participants can be asked to draw maps of their daily activities, such as their use of technology and apps (Connaway et al. 2017) or their movements during a specific time period. Asher et al. (2017) describe a collaborative project using mapping to identify students' spatial experiences on campuses. Gomez describes using teen mappings to identify where they and their families use technologies in their homes and to track their privacy behaviors in text box 12.3.

See figures 12.2, 12.3a, and 12.3b from the digital visitors and residents (V&R) report (Connaway et al. 2017) for examples of the study participants' mappings of their engagement with technology and apps in their personal and institutional (academic, professional, or work) lives. Figure 12.2 represents a participant's map using the V&R app ("Tools: Digital Visitors and Residents Mapping App" 2020), which openly is available on the project web page and also includes a short video tutorial. Figures 12.3a and 12.3b are participants' maps using the V&R mapping exercise sheets (https://www.oclc.org/content /dam/research/activities/vandr/resources/vr-mapping-exercise-sheet -definitions-20190329.pdf) that includes instructions and definitions and also is openly available. These mappings were created by the librarians and library users and prospective users who participated in the digital V&R study (Connaway et al. 2017).

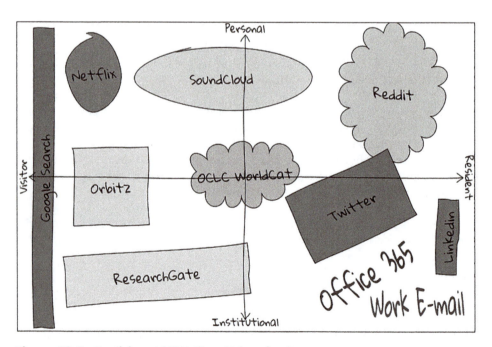

Figure 12.2. Participant V&R Map Using the App

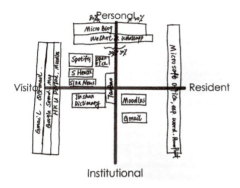

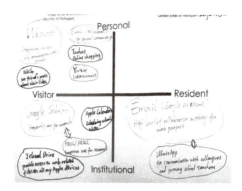

Figure 12.3a. Participant V&R Map Using the Mapping Exercise Sheet

Figure 12.3b. Participant V&R Map Using the Mapping Exercise Sheet

Text Box 12.3: Household Mapping Method

Stefani Gomez

In my study of Puerto Rican and Dominican teens' information practices in the family context, I began my semistructured interviews with a mapping activity adapted from an instrument developed by Katz and Gonzalez (2016). The activity, which asked teens to map out and describe their movements through the spaces where they and their family members used technologies in their homes, helped me, as a researcher, to build rapport and break the ice with the teens. It also provided a context for them to situate the narratives of their technology use in their households in a very literal way. As they traced their routine daily movements through the physical space, it became easy to see how their information and technology practices were influenced and intertwined with other family members and the space itself. The data revealed the teens used their place-based knowledge in combination with context to direct their movement through their homes (Gomez 2017). Satisfying their personal need for privacy and their social role in the family group involved negotiating members' expectations, schedules, and routine movements with their own desires.

The complexity of the task was most pronounced in homes where teens had less space of their own. For example, Lisa and Victoria* were cousins whose families and grandparents temporarily all shared a home. The bedroom they shared with Lisa's younger sister, Camila, was each girl's favorite space to be alone. Though they had never arranged a schedule, they had settled into a routine where both were able to maintain their solitude by shifting their use of technology throughout the household during the day as members relocated. Likewise, the information and activities they engaged with varied depending on where they were and who was in the space. I highly recommend the mapping method coupled with participants' accounts of their maps for researchers interested in investigating the ways that physical space becomes implicated in social and material practices.

References

Gomez, Stefani E. 2017. "Information Practices Relative to Parental Mediation and the Family Context among Puerto Rican and Dominican Teens." Rutgers University—School of Graduate Studies. https://doi.org/10.7282/T3F76GPK.

_____

*Names have been changed to protect participants' privacy.

Katz, Vikki S., and Carmen Gonzalez. 2016. "Toward Meaningful Connectivity: Using Multi-level Communication Research to Reframe Digital Inequality." *Journal of Communication* 66(2): 236–49. https://doi.org/10.1111/jcom.12214.

OBSERVATION

To *observe* means to watch attentively in a scientific or systematic manner. In an observational study, the current status of a phenomenon is determined not by asking, but by observing. Observation is sometimes treated as a research method, sometimes as a data collection instrument to be utilized with a research method. As a data collection instrument, it is used in both basic and applied research and in quantitative and qualitative studies. In applied research, it probably is most frequently used in evaluation. In basic research, it is used with both experimental and survey research designs. Observational methods are central to much qualitative research.

Observation is one of the oldest forms of data collection, but to qualify as scientific observation, it should meet certain criteria. Scientific observation should be systematic, with minimal bias, and strong in usability, reliability, and validity (Mouly 1978). Ethnographers strive for representativeness and informed representations of the behaviors that they think are taking place, since the study of human behavior always is subjective.

Advantages of Observational Research

As a data collection instrument, observation has several important advantages:

- The use of observation makes it possible to record behavior as it occurs in context.
- Observation allows one to compare what people actually did with what they said they did. Participants in a study may consciously or unconsciously report their behavior as different from the way it occurred; the observed behavior may well be more valid.
- Observation can identify behavior, actions, and so forth that people may not think to report because they seem unimportant or irrelevant. It can enable the researcher to examine the relative influence of many factors (Grover and Glazier 1986).
- Through observation, a researcher can study subjects who are unable to give verbal reports (such as very young children).
- The use of observation generally is independent of the subjects' willingness to participate. For example, one could observe how people are using the library catalog without asking them beforehand if they were willing to be observed. However, there are ethical and sometimes legal implications that should be explored before deciding to observe persons without their permission, or at least their awareness.

Limitations of Observational Research

Observational data collection and analysis do suffer from a few limitations. Some of the more important ones are the following:

- It is not always possible to anticipate a spontaneous event and thus be prepared to observe it. Some of the most critical activity in the library's maker spaces or group study rooms, for example, may take place when no one is there to observe it.
- The duration of an event affects the feasibility of observing it. The activities at the reference desk generally are short enough to be easily observed; such would not be the case in trying to observe how a faculty member conducts his or her research.
- Some types of behavior are obviously too private or personal in nature to be observed.
- It generally is somewhat more difficult to quantify observational data than other kinds. Behavior simply cannot always be broken down into neat categories.
- Researcher bias can affect the design of the study and the collection and analysis of the data. Anthropology researchers usually will acknowledge bias and will try to minimize it by working in diverse teams so that different perspectives can be leveraged to gain more information than a single researcher could collect. Involving more than one researcher in the coding of the data and calculating and reporting intercoder reliability (ICR) also can help reduce bias.
- The group that is being studied may not be representative of a larger population.
- Demographic information about the participants may not be available.
- If the participants know that they are being observed, their behavior may be altered ("Commentary on Ethnography, Observational Research, and Narrative Inquiry" n.d.).
- Observation requires the researcher to spend time at the research site and to build relationships with the participants, if the study is obtrusive ("Participant Observation" n.d.).

There essentially are two basic types of observation: unstructured and structured. Both are discussed below.

Unstructured Observation

Unstructured observation is sometimes equated with participant observation, but its most important characteristic reflects the fact that the researcher does not have predetermined sets of categories of behavior to use. Therefore, it is a relatively flexible approach and particularly useful in exploratory research.

In planning unstructured observational research, one must take into account the participants or subjects, the setting, the purpose for the subjects' being where they are, the type of behavior to be observed, and the frequency and duration of the behavior. The researcher must be as well prepared as possible to accurately record the upcoming behavior without going so far as to predesignate specific categories of behavior or to limit the observations to those types of behavior.

Researchers also must decide beforehand what kind of relationship they plan to have with their subjects. The observer may be obtrusive—that is, obviously observing certain behavior and known to the subjects—or unobtrusive. Unobtrusive observation has been conducted in LIS to evaluate FtF reference interactions in public libraries (Cavanagh 2013), to evaluate the accuracy of answers to FtF reference questions in public and academic libraries (Dilevko and Dolan 2000; Hernon and McClure 1986; Richardson 2002; Tewell 2010; Whitlatch 1989; Whittaker 1990), and to explore approachability behaviors of academic reference librarians (Radford 1998). It also has been applied to identify how library space and facilities are used at different times of the day, week, and academic semester or quarter (Bedwell and Banks 2013; Hunter and Ward 2011; Wu and Lanclos 2011).

If the researcher is going to participate in the activities of the subjects, is it going to be in an active or passive role? Finally, the researcher must decide whether the observation will take place with or without the permission of the subjects. Again, ethical considerations come into play here, especially if the observation is to be unobtrusive. (See chapter 9 for additional discussion of these issues.)

In recording unstructured observation, it is best if records are made on the spot and during the event in order to maximize their accuracy. It is best to record observations as unobtrusively as possible, even if the researcher is a participant. Record keeping should not be distracting for the subjects, or it may affect their behavior. Common data collection methods include taking notes and remembering behavior to be recorded later, as soon as possible. The latter tends to be less reliable and less accurate.

Steps can be taken to increase the accuracy of unstructured observations. They include the following:

1. Using two or more observational data collection instruments, such as sound and visual recordings, and then comparing results.
2. Having two or more people observe the same behavior with the data collection instrument and then comparing the results.
3. Being careful to distinguish between actual behavior and perceptions or interpretations of the behavior when taking notes. Researcher bias easily can creep in during this stage.
4. Avoiding involvement in the activity being observed.
5. Being careful not to take behavior for granted.
6. Obtaining reactions from the participants regarding the accuracy of the observations can be useful in situations when the subjects are fully aware of the role of the researcher. But one would have to be careful that doing so did not affect or bias future behavior of the subjects.

Structured Observation

Structured observation is a more formal data collection method, often used in quantitative studies to provide systematic description or to test causal hypotheses. It may be used in field studies or in laboratory-type settings, but it should focus on designated aspects of behavior.

As was the case with unstructured observation, observers must decide in advance what type of relationship should exist between them and the subjects to be observed. Beyond that, the steps involved in planning structured observation are somewhat different from those for unstructured observation.

The most basic step involves developing the observational categories to be employed. (These are set up in advance but may be adjusted later if necessary.) Developing such categories involves defining appropriate, measurable acts, establishing time units or the time length of observations, and anticipating patterns of the phenomena likely to occur. The observer also must decide on his or her frame of reference; for example, will certain behavior be categorized according to a subject's actions or intentions, or by the reactions of others?

Rating scales are used by researchers to record the degree in which specific characteristics or behaviors are demonstrated by the subjects during structured observations. One may use "all-or-none" or dichotomous categories in which the behavior is simply present or absent.

If the researchers can be quite specific about the types of behavior likely to occur, they may elect to utilize sheets with checklists of categories to be coded and cells to be checked as the respective categories of behavior occur. Checklists also may employ symbols to represent certain types of behavior in order to speed up the process of recording observations.

The researcher may choose to use audio and video digital recording technologies, which are readily available on smart phones and tablets and video conferencing platforms, to record observations as accurately as possible. Audio and video recordings are useful for providing an overall view of some behavior, and they permit researchers to analyze the behavior more closely and at convenient times. They do not systematically record or categorize the data; the researcher still must do this. Having the opportunity to review recordings of behavior at a more controlled, slower pace can help to avoid overloading the observer, which is one of the most serious threats to observational accuracy. Otherwise, one must be careful not to assign too much activity to be tracked or recorded to one observer.

Other steps that can be taken to increase the reliability of structured observation, as well as unstructured observation in some cases, include the following:

1. Developing adequate definitions of the kinds of behavior that are to be recorded and being certain that they correspond to the specific concepts to be studied.
2. Training the observers to ensure that they are adequately prepared and that they have confidence in their ability or judgment to check the appropriate categories.

3. Avoiding observer bias. Generally, the observer should take behaviors at their face value and not attempt to interpret their "real" meaning, at least not at the time the observations are made.

The researcher also should be concerned with the validity of the observation, or the extent to which the recorded differences in subjects represent actual differences, rather than the observer's perceptions of differences. Some of the measures that can be taken to improve the accuracy of unstructured observations apply to structured observations as well.

Case Studies

Another approach to gathering ethnographic data is the case study. According to Wildemuth, "In a research context, a case study is defined as a research study focused on a single case or set of cases. . . . We will think of it as a research approach, rather than a specific research design, because a variety of designs and methods of data collection and analysis can be used to accomplish the goals of a particular case study" (2017, 51). An alternative definition comes from Leedy, Ormrod, and Johnson, who define a case study as a "qualitative research design in which a single individual, program, or event is studied in depth for a defined period of time" (2019, 412). Leedy, Ormrod, and Johnson (2019) assert that a case study is often used to learn "more about a little known or poorly understood situation. It can also be appropriate for investigating how an individual or program changes over time, perhaps as the result of certain conditions or events. In either circumstance, it tends to be most useful for generating or providing preliminary support for tentative explanations regarding the phenomenon being studied" (2019, 231). They describe a case study as follows:

> In a typical case study, a researcher collects extensive data on the individual(s), program(s), or event(s) on which the investigation is focused. These data often include observations, interviews, documents (e.g., newspaper articles), past records (e.g., previous test scores), and audiovisual materials (e.g., photographs, videotapes, audiotapes). In many case studies, the researcher spends an extended period of time on site and regularly interacts with the person or people being studied. The researcher also records details about the context surrounding the case or cases of focus, including information about the physical environment and any historical, economic, and social factors that have a bearing on the situation. By portraying such contexts, the researcher helps others who later read the research report to draw conclusions about the extent to which the study's findings might be generalizable to other situations. (Leedy, Ormrod, and Johnson 2019, 231)

Richards (2015) draws a distinction between the single-case focus (within-case analysis) and the comparison between cases (cross-case analysis). She asserts that case studies are useful both at the beginning of a project, early in analysis when "they can be a valuable stimulus to integration," and at the end of a project when they can be used to "illustrate what has been concluded" (Richards 2015, 194). She suggests that one can "treat yourself to a case study not as an end in itself, but as a way-station on the road to bringing it all together" (Richards 2015, 194). Richards also provides advice on doing useful case studies that includes a caution to "never forget the ethics of it all [as] a good case study is far more intrusive and far more recognizable than your account of one participant among many" (2015, 195).

One example of an updated single case study approach that is an example of digital ethnography can be seen in the work of Lane (2020), who studied social relationships among young people in Harlem, NYC, incorporating smart phone data. His ethnographic work uses the case study to "open the social ecology of everyday life" (2020, 2). He evokes "a place-based, starting point to ground ethnographic relationships . . . and departs with youth subjects as they go about their day . . ." (2020, 3). He observes their interactions and use of media, including smart phones and data from "the smartphone itself to collect recorded, phone-based interactions. The researcher interprets that smartphone data (contacts, log activity, and text messages) with the case subject in the context of the ongoing fieldwork. The integration of the technology itself into the deep, ethnographic study of everyday life and media use allows the researcher to become familiar with how young people naturally move across and draw upon multiple, relational, activity setting" (2020, 4).

Lindlof and Taylor (2019, 349) regard the extended case study as a "potent" device that is useful as a type of exemplar characterized as "a sequence of events involving the same actors and settings that occurred over a long period and that demonstrated the operation of a relevant process. . . . In working with these materials, we aspire to craft and deliver an exemplar so that even our chosen group members recognize it as meaningful." Lindlof and Taylor (2019, 350) regard exemplars as forming "a *substructure* for our interpretations. They are the *best evidence* that we can present from our data. Without exemplars, our analytic claims are empty and unpersuasive [italics in original]."

For an authoritative treatment of case study research, Yin (2012) is a recognized expert, who writes in the context of educational scholarship, akin to a range of LIS problematics, especially information literacy instruction.

The case study approach has been used extensively in LIS. One example of an LIS research project that used the case study approach was funded by the Institute for Museum and Library Services (IMLS) and titled *Public Libraries Respond to the Opioid Crisis with their Communities* (2020). This multimethod research, conducted by OCLC and the Public Library Association (PLA), a division of ALA, aimed to investigate the response to the opioid crisis by conducting case studies in eight public libraries across America, as also noted in chapter 14. Other examples of case study research in LIS explore a variety of topics, including: evaluation of health science researchers (Moradi and Dokhani 2020); evaluation of the Innovative Solutions to Homelessness Project (Hill and Tamminen 2020); and using Excel for data visualization in six large universities (LaPolla 2020).

User Experience and Usability Testing

Both user experience (UX) and usability testing often include observational approaches similar to those used in human ethnographic observation. "'User experience' encompasses all aspects of the end-user's interaction with the company, its services, and its products" (Norman and Nielson n.d.). Rohrer provides a useful explanation and description of twenty UX methods and a discussion of "the qualitative vs. quantitative dimension" of UX. He states that "*qualitative* methods are much better suited for answering questions about *why* or *how to fix* a problem, whereas *quantitative* methods do a much better job answering *how many* and *how much* types of questions" (Rohrer 2014). The user interface (UI) only is a *part of the design and of the user experience.* "Usability is a quality attribute of the UI, covering whether the system is easy to learn, efficient to use, [and] pleasant" (Norman and Nielson n.d.). There is an open-access journal dedicated to the subject of UX, the *Journal of Library User Experience* ("Weave Journal of Library User Experience" n.d.), which was started in 2014 at the University of Michigan Library that provides numerous papers on UX in libraries. The Library UX Chicago website has an extensive resource list, articles (Godfrey 2015), and blog posts (Lauersen 2016) addressing the topics. These two sources alone exemplify the popularity of both UX and usability testing in LIS research and practice.

Usability.gov ("User Experience Basics" 2014) provides information on UX basics and resources related to UX. Smashingmagazine.com provides an example of a rainbow spreadsheet (different colors are used to represent study participants' behaviors and reactions) that can be used by a UX team for data collection, which can be formatted into a final report (Sharon 2013). Brodman and Tang provide additional information about UX and usability research in text boxes 12.4 and 12.5.

Text Box 12.4: User Experience (UX)

Kayla Brodman

As I transitioned from commercial brand experience design to library staff and library user experience (UX) design, I brought with me a philosophy that the best user experiences always have clear goals and a solid strategy. The goals should answer: "What is our organization trying to do? Who are we doing it for? What does the end user need? What are they trying to do?" The strategy aligns to how the established goals will be met. If the team does not make conscious decisions that align to the strategy and goals, the experience will not meet user needs or expectations—no matter how usable or beautiful.

UX is more than the usability or visual appeal of an interface. "'User experience' encompasses all aspects of the end-user's interaction with the company, its services, and its products" (Norman and Nielsen n.d.). Look across your organization. Document how a user interacts with both the physical and digital touchpoints. Innovation is identified and brought to life by understanding the successes and gaps of the holistic experience across these touchpoints.

Gain a deeper understanding of and empathize with your users by performing "generative" or exploratory research (also known as discovery, problem-space, or foundational research). Focus on defining their needs, desires, and the range of the experience gaps by using the techniques in the chapters throughout this research methods book. Determine how you can meet those needs by identifying the viability and feasibility—business and technical aspects—to create a user-centric experience as depicted in Figure 12.4 from the IDEO blogpost ("What Is Design Thinking?" n.d.). This is the core of design thinking.

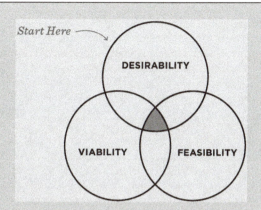

Figure 12.4. What Is Design Thinking?

References

Norman, Don, and Jakob Nielsen. n.d. "The Definition of User Experience (UX)." Nielsen Norman Group. Accessed November 15, 2020. https://www.nngroup.com/articles/definition-user-experience.
"What Is Design Thinking?" n.d. IDEO U. Accessed November 15, 2020. https://www.ideou.com/blogs/inspiration/what-is-design-thinking.

Recommended Reading

Norman, Donald A. 2013. *The Design of Everyday Things*. Rev. ed. Cambridge, MA: MIT Press.

"Evaluating usability involves measuring the degree to which a user can successfully learn and use a system or service . . . usability testing . . . is the observation and analysis of users' behavior while they interact with a system or prototype" (Prasse and Connaway 2008, 215). Usability testing was the catalyst for human-computer interface (HCI) usability studies. The user needs to be involved from the initial design phase through system upgrades.

Text Box 12.5: Usability and User Experience (UX) Research

Rong Tang

As a research method, usability research incorporates the rigor of experimental laboratory tests, the practical flexibility of applied evaluation studies, and a strong flavor of action research that centers on both making recommendations to improve system design and implementing changes. Usability research is also an effective example for mixed-methods research. A standard usability testing session involves three parts: (1) a presession interview, (2) a scenario-and-task-structured test, and (3) a postsession survey. Upon the completion of their study sessions, researchers extract quantitative measures of participants' task performance including task success, time on task, mouse movement, web page changes, etc. In addition, researchers gather qualitative data from participants' think-aloud verbal comments and their posttask and postsession comments on their satisfaction and preferences. Researchers may further code various points in time during task performance when participants seemed confused, hesitated, frustrated, or excited (Song 2018). Moments when participants needed help or were pondering may also be examined. Various types of qualitative data are triangulated with quantitative results in order to achieve a full understanding of user experience and specific usability problems.

The usability method offers powerful empirical insights into user behavior in a rare degree of richness and depth. Typically, a usability session is run by a team of researchers, and recording sessions are complicated by serendipitous factors. Attention to detail and coordination are crucial in preparing and running a session. Data processing and coding often consume great energy and time. Researchers who are just beginning their usability research should not underestimate the importance of planning and the time and resources required to complete a study. In terms of the setting of usability testing, a number of studies demonstrated that synchronous remote testing is as effective as lab-based usability testing in terms of the task completion rate and the number of usability problems identified (Bernheim Brush, Ames, and Newman Davis 2004; Chalil Madathil and Greenstein 2011; Tullis et al. 2002). In the current pandemic situation where in-person research has mostly been suspended, remote usability testing serves as one of the most useful and feasible methods for usability research, including testing COVID-19 tracking tools (Tang et al. 2020).

A major lesson I learned over the years of conducting usability research is that in addition to producing results and recommendations that are practical and timely for stakeholders or general users, it is necessary to pay attention to the scholarly value of your work. Relevant theoretical frameworks might be applied to guide you through analyzing the interplay among behavior variables and interaction patterns. For example, theories of collaboration profiles and processes provided me with meaningful empirical constructs to effectively interpret users' collaboration activities on an interactive tabletop (Tang and Quigley 2014; Tang et al. 2013). In a usability study on PBcore.org website, previous research on performance gaps among user groups and design principles for complex technical websites shed light on the analysis and interpretation of findings (Tang et al. 2018).

References

Bernheim Brush, A. J., Morgan G. Ames, and Janet Louise Newman Davis. 2004. "A Comparison of Synchronous Remote and Local Usability Studies for an Expert Interface l CHI '04 Extended Abstracts on Human Factors in Computing Systems."

Chalil Madathil, Kapil, and Joel S. Greenstein. 2011. "Synchronous Remote Usability Testing: A New Approach Facilitated by Virtual Worlds." In *Proceedings of the SIGCHI Conference on Human Factors in Computing Systems*, 2225–34. CHI '11. New York: Association for Computing Machinery. https://doi.org/10.1145/1978942.1979267.

Tang, Rong, Wenqing Lu, Will Gregg, Steven Gentry, and Stephen E. Humeston. 2018. "Towards a More Inclusive Technical Website: Knowledge Gaps, Performance, Experience, and Perception Differences among Various User Groups." *Proceedings of the Association for Information Science and Technology* 55(1): 494–503. https://doi.org/10.1002/pra2 .2018.14505501054.

Tang, Rong, and Elizabeth Quigley. 2014. "The Effect of Undergraduate Library Users' Dyadic Diversity Attributes on Interactive Tabletop Collaboration, Performance, and Perception." March. https://doi.org/10.9776/14047.

Tang, Rong, Elizabeth Quigley, Jeremy Guillette, and Christopher Erdmann. 2013. "Shared Discovery Using a Library Tool on an Interactive Tabletop: Team Composition, Collaboration

Style and Process." *Proceedings of the American Society for Information Science and Technology* 50(1): 1–15. https://doi.org/10.1002/meet.14505001054.

Tang, Rong, Sanda Erdelez, Emma May, and Yishan Zang. 2020. "The State of Practice of COVID-19 Tracking Systems: An Inventory Study." In *Proceedings of 2020 ASIST Annual Meeting*. https://doi.org/10.1002/pra2.397.

Tullis, Thomas, Stan Fleischman, Michelle Mcnulty, Carrie Cianchette, and Marguerite Bergel. 2002. "An Empirical Comparison of Lab and Remote Usability Testing of Web Sites." January.

Recommended Reading

Tang, Rong, and Yeseul Song. 2018. "Cognitive Styles and Eye Movement Patterns: An Empirical Investigation into User Interactions with Interface Elements and Visualisation Objects of a Scientific Information System." Text. University of Borås. June 15. http://informationr.net/ir/23-2/paper790.html.

Usability testing has been applied in libraries for the development and evaluation of online catalogs and websites. Usability tests also are conducted to evaluate library applications for computers, tablets, and smart phones.

These are some of the library questions that have been addressed in usability tests:

- What is the most effective layout for most users of a web page?
- How can reading from the screen interface be optimized?
- Are users able to find the information that is important to them on the library web page, such as their library account information to find out if they have any overdue items?
- Where is the best placement for the search box on the library web page?
- Is the library web page scalable on a smart phone?

Usability testing also can accommodate more structured, detailed questions, such as the following:

- Can individual personality or cognitive skills predict internet use behavior?
- Can library collection holdings and library data be represented geographically in a way that users are able to understand and that allows them to manipulate the data?
- Can users easily customize and manage discipline-specific content available in an open-source library portal?
- Can users quickly and easily find serials, that is, newspapers, journals, magazines, etc., from a library's website and online catalog (Norlin and Winters 2002, 216)?

Usability tests must be planned, with a timeline, identified goals of testing, the types of individuals needed to participate in the testing, and the recruiting strategy. Becker outlines the purpose, myths, and processes involved in conducting usability testing. She also includes a recommended reading list and examples of possible questions that can be employed for usability testing (Becker 2011). See the following example of a product usability study brief that was developed by OCLC to ensure that the usability team articulates the goals of the usability study with the stakeholders prior to any usability testing. The information is key to aligning the usability team with the stakeholders' goals and collecting the right information to conduct the usability testing. Once the goals are identified and agreed on, the usability study can be conducted through moderated or unmoderated methods to address the areas of investigation.

Example Product Usability Study Brief

Product Goals

To ensure the researcher is aligned with stakeholders.

What is the organization trying to accomplish?
Who is the user?
What are their needs?

Study Goals

To ensure we are providing actionable insights and findings to the team.

User is able to understand how to <insert task>.
User understands where to find <information> on <specific page>.
User understands navigation and labeling.

Issues to Investigate

To ensure all perspectives from the team are captured but are in line with the study goals.

- What is the users' impression of what this page provides?
- What do users want to do on this page?
- How do users get more information about what this site does?
- More importantly, do users want more information about what this site does?
- Are users able to say what this site is?
- Is there anything users don't understand?
- Do users understand the format icons?

Workflows to Test

To ensure that the issues are tested in a context that is meaningful to users.

- Searching for a book, choosing a suitable edition, and determining the fastest way to get it.

Participant Characteristics/Persona Attributes

Factors to consider for screening and recruitment.

Role/Subject Expertise/Technology Expertise/Motivation

- *student*
- *faculty*

- *library reference staff*
- *smart phone user/desktop user*
- *public library user*

Potential Method Approaches

Moderated

- *Moderated studies are helpful for understanding the user's thought process and motivation. They also give the opportunity to probe further during the study.*

Unmoderated

- *Faster because there is no need to coordinate schedules and locations. Quicker to assess a larger sample because users can participate without the moderator in the session; however, allows less flexibility for follow-on questions.*

As new technologies have developed, users' expectations also have changed, making usability testing more important. Usability testing is essential both to determine if users are able to navigate through the systems and applications and to utilize system functionalities and to determine if they even have the desire or need to use the systems and applications. The results of usability testing can not only influence system design but also "identify topics for library information literacy programs" (Prasse and Connaway 2008, 245).

Screen-capturing software often is used to collect the data from usability studies, which usually are audio and video recorded. There needs to be a facilitator, and often an observer and a note taker are present. Wu and Lanclos (Wu and Lanclos 2011) report on a web usability test and provide detailed information on how to prepare and conduct the testing. The notes and screen-captured data must be coded and analyzed.

Usability testing can be done with less technology-oriented methods. These include card sorting or the pile sort method, and wireframes. The pile sort method was introduced by Brim in 1966 when he asked high school students to sort slips of paper with American English role terms, such as mother, teacher, and stockbroker, on them into piles or groups to which they felt the roles belonged (Bernard 2012). The method asks individuals to make lists of relevant topics on a particular subject or provides them with actual cards or slips of paper and then asks them to group the topics into related piles. Card-sorting software tools also are available. The pile sort method has been used with female community college students to identity healthy lifestyle behaviors (Quintiliani et al. 2008). Wireframes are individuals' drawings and sketches or mockups of web pages or interface designs, which can be done on paper, with stencils, or on templates that can be downloaded to smart phones, tablets, and laptops. Wireframes and card sorting or pile sorting can be used to involve users in the design of web pages and can help librarians "build the structure for . . . websites, decide what to put on the homepage, and label categories and navigation" ("Card Sorting" 2013). The site Usability.gov ("What & Why of Usability" n.d.) provides definitions, examples, and instructions on how to plan, conduct, analyze, and report results for several different types of usability tests.

Design Thinking and Participatory Design

Innovation research is discussed in chapter 14, and there is a school of thought that design thinking can support innovation (Chasanidou, Gasparini, and Lee 2015; Liedtka 2015; Patrício, Moreira, and Zurlo 2020; Robbins 2018; Seidel and Fixson 2013; Shpakova, Dörfler, and MacBryde 2020). "Design thinking, an approach to creative problem solving, combines the processes of identifying problems, brainstorming solutions, and prototyping those solutions" (Capdarest-Arest, Opuda, and Stark 2019, 567). Design thinking can be used by librarians for the development of new program services, spaces, organizational processes, and for strategic planning (Clarke, Amonkar, and Rosenblad 2020). During a discussion of the findings of the OCLC project, The New Model Library ("The New Model Library" n.d.), a director of a large metropolitan library in North America stated that design thinking should be used by librarians for planning effective change brought on by the COVID-19 pandemic.

Clarke, Amonkar, and Rosenblad (2020) report that of a total of 272 responses to a survey addressing the interest in and the use of design thinking in library practice, 60.9 percent of the public library respondents and 75.5 percent of the academic librarians were either somewhat familiar or familiar with design thinking. "When asked if they had ever actively used design thinking and methods in their library work, 50 (27% of respondents to that question) answered yes; 70 (38%) answered not sure; and 64 (34%) said no" (Clarke, Amonkar, and Rosenbald 2020, 754). The benefits attributed to using design thinking included "staff benefits (improved problem-solving skills, increased flexibility and ability to rebound from failures, and increased confidence); user benefits (increased opportunities to provide input, collaborate with staff, learn, and feel understood); and overall library benefits (increased awareness and use, streamlined operations, and increased reputation in the user community)" (Clarke, Amonkar, and Rosenbald 2020, 754).

Design thinking also has been used by health sciences librarians to integrate gamification into library instruction (Capdarest-Arest, Opuda, and Stark 2019) and by academic librarians to promote the participation of current and future health professionals in health care hackathons (McGowan 2019).

Although design thinking has been used in library practice and research for programming, planning, UX, physical spaces, and outreach, it may not be utilized to its fullest capacity. Clarke, Amonkar, and Rosenblad (2020) and Clarke (2019) advocate for adding a course on design thinking and methods to the LIS curricula. Most of the respondents to the questionnaire disseminated by Clarke, Amonkar, and Rosenblad (2020) thought that design thinking and methods should be taught in graduate LIS programs as an elective, not a required course.

For those interested in learning more about design thinking and methods, the Design Thinking for Libraries Toolkit is an excellent resource for learning about and implementing design thinking and methods ("Design Thinking for

Libraries" n.d.). The web page includes excellent sources for readings and examples in addition to the toolkit ("About | Design Thinking for Libraries" n.d.).

Another type of closely related research method is participatory design. Participatory design involves the users in the design of technology systems and tools. The method helps researchers to identify individuals' behaviors in their lives. As with community-based participatory research (CBPR) discussed in chapter 14, the individuals involved in the participatory design research help to design and develop the research methodology including data collection and analysis. However, there are differences between the two types of research methods.

> Key differences between CBPR, UCD [user-centered design], and PD [participatory design] relate to their theoretical foundations and to the degree of CBO and community member engagement across project stages. . . . In UCD projects, researchers typically lead the entire effort from study design to dissemination (Ritter, Baxter, and Churchill 2014; Unertl et al. 2016). In PD projects, researchers typically control study design and results dissemination, although end users collaborate in study implementation (Simonsen and Robertson 2013, 295; Unertl et al. 2016). In contrast, CBPR is an all-encompassing research paradigm that defines purposeful engagement among researchers, intended end users, and other stakeholders throughout all stages of a research project. (Unertl et al. 2016, 60; Wallerstein et al. 2005, 682)

Participatory design often is used in health research and with underserved or marginalized populations (Mikesell, Bromley, and Khodyakov 2013). Feng incorporated the cognitive walk-through technique and participatory design methodology with individual interviews. Photos collected by the interviewees were used to frame the questions to examine "how people engage with activity tracking technology and interact with the new types of personal health information generated by the technology" (Feng 2019, 724). Senteio (2019) has used participatory design to identify how older adult African Americans get health information using technology and their social networks. Based on her experience with a participatory design study in an academic library, Morgan (2012) stresses the importance of not only planning a participatory design project, but also of analyzing the data and reporting the findings.

ANALYSIS OF ETHNOGRAPHIC DATA

The data collection methods discussed above are used in ethnographic research studies. The data analysis methods used for the qualitative data collected in diaries, journals, interviews, and mapping are the same as those discussed in chapters 10 and 11. The data must be interpreted in a manner that retains their richness. This "thick description" (Geertz 1973), including group interactions, is one of the advantages of the ethnographic approach. The ethnographic summary and the content analysis approach of open and thematic coding are not conflicting means of analysis.

If quantitative data are collected in the interviews and FtF survey questions, the data analysis methods should be compatible. The analyses most likely will include descriptive statistics but may include inferential statistics, both of which are discussed in chapter 8.

Advantages of Ethnographic Approaches

The following are advantages of ethnographic approaches.

- Ethnographic research is conducted within the context of the culture of the participants and enables the researcher to identity how and why the participants make sense of their surroundings within specific contexts and situations.
- Most of the equipment needed to conduct ethnographic research is inexpensive.
- The results of ethnographic research not only provide insights into behaviors but also provide the opportunity to build relationships with users that can yield richer and unanticipated results.
- The researcher sometimes can quickly document insights from behaviors, even though analyzing the data and writing up the results can be time consuming.
- When ethnographic approaches are embedded in the management, development, and provision of services, the results of the research can be discussed in formal and informal meetings and motivate change to existing services and implementation of new services.
- The collaboration frequently required to conduct ethnographic research in libraries can help to build relationships and draw more and different people from the communities into the library as a source of information about how and why people do their work and search for and use information, as well as attracting new users of the library's offerings.

Limitations of Ethnographic Approaches

The following are limitations of ethnographic approaches.

- Ethnographic research is time consuming; therefore, it can be expensive because of the amount of staff time needed to organize the project and to collect, analyze, and disseminate the data.
- Qualified staff will be needed to organize and conduct the research. If it is not possible to hire the staff needed, it will be necessary to train the existing staff to conduct research using ethnographic approaches. Some academic libraries have worked with faculty and their students to collaborate in studying the role of the library using ethnographic approaches (Hunter and Ward 2011).
- Researcher bias can affect the research process, including data collection and analysis, but can be mitigated by including a group of diverse

researchers to encompass different perspectives and to calculate and report ICR for the coding.

- The findings from ethnographic studies may not be generalizable if there is a small number of participants who are not representative of the population.

SUMMARY

Ethnographic approaches to qualitative research provide the researcher the opportunity to capture members of specific groups' "sense of a situation" (Asher and Miller 2011). The data collection and analysis methods for ethnographic research usually are qualitative, although some data can be quantitative, such as demographic information collected in FtF interviews or prescreening surveys, or data acquired from screen-capturing software. Multiple data collection methods usually are employed and can include audio, visual, and textual diaries or journals; interviews; observation; surveys; user experience (UX); and usability tests. Regardless of the types of data that are collected, the methods of analysis must be compatible with them. The ethnographic researcher must be cognizant of the possible threats to the reliability and validity of the data, as well as any possibility for a breach of ethics.

If the ethnographic research includes a small number of individuals who are not representative of the population, the research is not generalizable. However, this does not have to be the case, nor is it the case in all ethnographic research. The data collected are very rich and can explain how and why individuals of a specific group or groups make decisions and behave the way they do.

Case study is an in-depth research approach that includes multiple data collection and analysis techniques and designs. Case study research includes one or more cases focusing on individuals, programs, or events. Case studies often are used to learn more about a phenomena or situation or how individuals or programs change over time.

UX involves the evaluation of web pages, spaces, and services by targeted users. It is becoming quite popular in the study of user-centered assessment and services and is more encompassing than usability testing, which is a form of ethnographic observation that usually involves the testing of web pages, online catalogs, and other applications. Usability testing is a rigorous process that involves planning. The types of participants must be determined, then they must be recruited and screened. The goals of the usability test must be identified in order for the tasks to be developed. After the tests are conducted, the participants are interviewed again, and then the researchers need to analyze the data from the surveys as well as from the screen captures, audio and visual recordings, and notes taken by the researchers. Once the data are analyzed, they must be interpreted and used to make changes to the tested technologies, services, applications, and web pages.

Design thinking is creative problem solving that includes identifying and brainstorming the problem, culminating with possible solutions. Design thinking has been used in LIS for the development of new programs, services, spaces, and organizational processes, and for strategic planning. There are several excellent sources explaining how to use design thinking in LIS practice and research.

Like CBRD, participatory design is a research method that includes those being studied in the research design, data collection and analysis, and dissemination of the findings. LIS researchers have used participatory design to study how individuals get health information and with marginalized populations.

Ethnographic research can be time consuming and tedious, but this can be said of many research data collection and analysis methods (Asher and Miller 2011). However, the insights and knowledge gained from ethnographic research make the experience worthwhile.

REFERENCES

"About | Design Thinking for Libraries." n.d. Design Thinking for Libraries. Accessed November 17, 2020. http://designthinkingforlibraries.com/about.

Asher, Andrew, Jean Amaral, Juliann Couture, Barbara Fister, Donna Lanclos, M. Sara Lowe, Mariana Regalado, and Maura Smale. 2017. "Mapping Student Days: Collaborative Ethnography and the Student Experience." *Collaborative Librarianship* 9(4): 293–317. https://digitalcommons.du.edu/collaborativelib rarianship/vol9/iss4/7.

Asher, Andrew, and Susan Miller. 2011. "So You Want to Do Anthropology in Your Library?" *The Ethnographic Research in Illinois Academic Librareis (ERIAL) Project* 3: 31.

Attu, Rose, and Melissa Terras. 2017. "What People Study When They Study Tumblr: Classifying Tumblr-Related Academic Research." *Journal of Documentation* 73(3): 528–54. https://doi.org/10.1108/JD-08-2016-0101.

Barratt, Monica J., and Alexia Maddox. 2016. "Active Engagement with Stigmatised Communities through Digital Ethnography." *Qualitative Research* 16(6): 701–19. https://doi.org/10.1177/1468794116648766.

Becker, Danielle. 2011. "Usability Testing on a Shoestring: Test-Driving Your Website." *Information Today.* http://www.infotoday.com/online/may11/Becker -Usability-Testing-on-a-Shoestring.shtml.

Bedwell, Linda, and Caitlin S. Banks. 2013. "Seeing through the Eyes of Students: Participant Observation in an Academic Library." *Partnership: The Canadian Journal of Library and Information Practice and Research* 8(1). https://doi .org/10.21083/partnership.v8i1.2502.

Bernard, Harvey Russell. 2012. *Social Research Methods: Qualitative and Quantitative Approaches.* Thousand Oaks, CA: Sage.

Capdarest-Arest, Nicole, Eugenia Opuda, and Rachel Keiko Stark. 2019. "'Game on!' Teaching Gamification Principles for Library Instruction to Health Sciences Information Professionals Using Interactive, Low-Tech Activities and Design-Thinking Modalities." *Journal of the Medical Library Association: JMLA* 107(4): 566–71. https://doi.org/10.5195/jmla.2019.636.

"Card Sorting." 2013. Usability.Gov. Department of Health and Human Services. October 9. card-sorting.html.

Cavanagh, Mary F. 2013. "Interpreting Reference Work with Contemporary Practice Theory." *Journal of Documentation* 69(2): 214–42. https://doi.org/10 .1108/00220411311300057.

Chasanidou Dimitra, Andrea A. Gasparini, and Eunji Lee. 2015. "Design Thinking Methods and Tools for Innovation." In Marcus A. (ed.), *Design, User Experience, and Usability: Design Discourse*. Lecture Notes in Computer Science, vol. 9186. Springer, Cham. https://doi.org/10.1007/978-3-319-20886-2_2.

Clarke, Rachel I. 2019. "Designing Future Library Leaders: Investigating the Incorporation of Design Thinking and Methods in Master's Level Library Education." In *ALISE 2019 Conference Proceedings*, 48–51. Knoxville, TN. file:///C:/Users/connawal/Downloads/ALISE_2019_Full_Proceedings_Final.pdf.

Clarke, Rachel Ivy, Satyen Amonkar, and Ann Rosenblad. 2020. "Design Thinking and Methods in Library Practice and Graduate Library Education." *Journal of Librarianship and Information Science* 52(3): 749–63. https://doi.org/10.1177/0961000619871989.

"Commentary on Ethnography, Observational Research, and Narrative Inquiry." n.d. Writing@CSU. Accessed July 3, 2020. https://writing.colostate.edu/guides/page.cfm?pageid=1357&guideid=63.

Connaway, Lynn Silipigni, Vanessa Kitzie, Erin M. Hood, and William Harvey. 2017. "The Many Faces of Digital Visitors & Residents: Facets of Online Engagement." Dublin, OH: OCLC Research. https://www.oclc.org/content/dam/research/publications/2017/oclcresearch-many-faces-digital-vandr.pdf.

Cowan, Susan M. 2012. "Assessment 360: Mapping Undergraduates and the Library at the University of Connecticut." https://docplayer.net/1003790-Assessment-360-mapping-undergraduates-and-the-library-at-the-university-of-connecticut.html.

"Design Thinking for Libraries." n.d. Design Thinking for Libraries. Accessed November 17, 2020. http://designthinkingforlibraries.com.

"Digital Visitors and Residents." OCLC. May 4. https://www.oclc.org/research/areas/user-studies/vandr.html.

Dilevko, Juris, and Elizabeth Dolan. 2000. "Government Documents Reference Service in Canada: A Nationwide Unobtrusive Study of Public and Academic Depository Libraries." *Library & Information Science Research* 22(2): 185-222. https://doi.org/10.1016/S0740-8188(99)00053-5.

Duggan, Mike. 2017. "Questioning 'Digital Ethnography' in an Era of Ubiquitous Computing." *Geography Compass* 11(5): e12313. https://doi.org/10.1111/gec3.12313.

Duke, Lynda M., and Andrew D. Asher. 2012. *College Libraries and Student Culture: What We Now Know*. Chicago: American Library Association.

Feng, Yuanyuan. 2019. "The Enhanced Participant-Driven Photo Elicitation Method for Everyday Life Health Information Behaviour Research." *Aslib Journal of Information Management* 71(6): 720–38. https://doi.org/10.1108/AJIM-02-2019-0042.

Flanagan, John C. 1954. "The Critical Incident Technique." *Psychological Bulletin* 5: 327–58.

Foster, Nancy Fried, and Susan Gibbons, eds. 2007. *Studying Students: The Undergraduate Research Project at the University of Rochester*. Chicago: Association of College and Research Libraries. http://www.ala.org/acrl/sites/ala.org.acrl/files/content/publications/booksanddigitalresources/digital/Foster-Gibbons_cmpd.pdf.

Geertz, Clifford. 1973. *The Interpretation of Cultures: Selected Essays*. New York: Basic Books.

Godfrey, Krista. 2015. "Creating a Culture of Usability." *Weave: Journal of Library User Experience* 1(3). https://doi.org/10.3998/weave.12535642.0001.301.

Grover, Robert, and Jack Glazier. 1986. "A Conceptual Framework for Theory Building in Library and Information Science." *Library and Information Science Research* 8(3): 227–42.

Hernon, Peter, and Charles R. McClure. "Unobtrusive Reference Testing: The 55 Percent Rule." *Library Journal* 111, no. 7 (1986): 37–41.

Hill, Teresa, and Katherine A. Tamminen. 2020. "Examining the Library as a Site for Intervention: A Mixed-Methods Case Study Evaluation of the 'Innovative Solutions to Homelessness' Project." *Journal of Library Administration* 60(5): 470–92. https://doi.org/10.1080/01930826.2020.1729626.

"Home." n.d. The Ethnographic Research in Illinois Academic Libraries (ERIAL) Project. Accessed July 3, 2020. http://www.erialproject.org.

Hunter, Gina, and Dane Ward. 2011. "Students Research the Library: Using Student-Led Ethnographic Research to Examine the Changing Role of Campus Libraries." *College & Research Libraries* 72(5): 264–68. https://doi.org/10.5860/crln.72.5.8560.

Kline, Sims. 2013. "The Librarian as Ethnographer: An Interview with David Green." *College & Research Libraries* 74(9): 488–91. https://doi.org/10.5860/crln.74.9.9013.

Lanclos, Donna, and Asher, Andrew. 2016. "'Ethnographish': The State of the Ethnography in Libraries." *Weave: Journal of Library User Experience* 1(5). https://doi.org/10.3998/weave.12535642.0001.503.

Lane, Jeffrey. 2016. "The Digital Street: An Ethnographic Study of Networked Street Life in Harlem." *American Behavioral Scientist* 60(1): 43–58. https://doi.org/10.1177/0002764215601711.

Lane, Jeffrey. 2018. *The Digital Street*. Illus. ed. New York: Oxford University Press.

Lane, Jeffrey. 2020. "A Smartphone Case Method: Reimagining Social Relationships with Smartphone Data in the U.S. Context of Harlem." *Journal of Children and Media* 14(4): 407–21. https://doi.org/10.1080/17482798.2019.1710718.

LaPolla, Fred Willie Zametkin. 2020. "Excel for Data Visualization in Academic Health Sciences Libraries: A Qualitative Case Study." *Journal of the Medical Library Association: JMLA* 108(1): 67–75. https://doi.org/10.5195/jmla.2020.749.

Lauersen, Christian. 2016. "Why Usability Testing Should Be a Part of Regular Library Activity." *The Library Lab* (blog). November 23. https://christianlauersen.net/2016/11/23/ux-in-libraries.

Leedy, Paul D., Jeanne E. Ormrod, and Laura Ruth Johnson. 2019. *Practical Research: Planning and Design*. 8th ed. New York: Pearson.

Liedtka, Jeanne. 2015. "Perspective: Linking Design Thinking with Innovation Outcomes through Cognitive Bias Reduction." *Journal of Product Innovation Management* 32(6): 925–38. https://doi.org/10.1111/jpim.12163.

Lindlof, Thomas R., and Bryan C. Taylor. 2019. *Qualitative Communication Research Methods*. 4th ed. Los Angeles: Sage.

McGowan, Bethany. 2019. "The Role of the University Library in Creating Inclusive Healthcare Hackathons: A Case Study with Design-Thinking Processes." *IFLA Journal* 45(3): 246–53. https://doi.org/10.1177/0340035219854214.

"Methodology." 2020. ERIAL Project. http://www.erialproject.org/project-details/methodology.

Mikesell, Lisa, Elizabeth Bromley, and Dmitry Khodyakov. 2013. "Ethical Community-Engaged Research: A Literature Review." *American Journal of Public Health* 103(12): e7–14. https://doi.org/10.2105/AJPH.2013.301605.

Moradi, Shima, and Firoozeh Dokhani. 2020. "Using the Quadruple Helix Model for Evaluation of Health Science Researches: Case Study of D8 Countries." *Library Hi Tech* 38(4): 723–39. https://doi.org/10.1108/LHT-08-2019-0156.

Morgan, Glenda. 2012. "Of Failure and the Importance of Analysis in Participatory Design." In *Participatory Design in Academic Libraries: Methods, Findings, and Implementations*. Council on Library and Information Resources, Washington, DC, 46–49. https://digitalcommons.colby.edu/cgi/viewcontent.cgi?article=1017&context=faculty_scholarship.

Mouly, George J. 1978. *Educational Research: The Art and Science of Investigation*. Boston: Allyn & Bacon.

Murthy, Dhiraj. 2008. "Digital Ethnography: An Examination of the Use of New Technologies for Social Research." *Sociology* 42(5): 837–55. https://doi.org/10.1177/0038038508094565.

"The New Model Library." n.d. Accessed November 17, 2020. https://www.oclc.org/research/areas/library-enterprise/new-model-library.html.

Norlin, Elaina, and C. M. Winters. 2002. *Usability Testing for Library Websites: A Hands-on Guide*. Chicago: American Library Association.

Norman, Don, and Jakob Nielson. n.d. "The Definition of User Experience (UX)." Nielsen Norman Group. Accessed November 15, 2020. https://www.nngroup.com/articles/definition-user-experience.

"Participant Observation." n.d. OpenLearn Works. Accessed July 3, 2020. https://www.open.edu/openlearncreate/mod/oucontent/view.php?id=13636&section=4.1.

Patrício, Rui, Antonio Carrizo Moreira, and Francesco Zurlo. 2020. "Enhancing Design Thinking Approaches to Innovation through Gamification." *European Journal of Innovation Management* (ahead-of-print). https://doi.org/10.1108/EJIM-06-2020-0239.

Pink, Sarah, Heather A. Horst, John Postill, Larissa Hjorth, Tania Lewis, and Jo Tacchi, eds. 2016. *Digital Ethnography: Principles and Practice*. Los Angeles: Sage.

Prasse, Michael J., and Lynn Silipigni Connaway. 2008. "Usability Testing: Method and Research." In *Academic Library Research: Perspective and Current Trends*, edited by Marie L. Radford and Pamela Snelson, 214–52. Chicago: Association of College and Research Libraries.

"Public Libraries Respond to the Opioid Crisis with Their Communities." 2020. WebJunction. February 26. https://www.webjunction.org/explore-topics/opioid-crisis.html.

Pukkila, Marilyn R., and Ellen L. Freeman. 2012. "Faculty in the Mist: Ethnographic Study of Faculty Research Practices." *Faculty Scholarship*.

Quintiliani, Lisa M., Marci K. Campbell, Pamela S. Haines, and Kelly H. Webber. 2008. "The Use of the Pile Sort Method in Identifying Groups of Healthful Lifestyle Behaviors among Female Community College Students." *Journal of the American Dietetic Association* 108(9): 1503–7. https://doi.org/10.1016/j.jada.2008.06.428.

Radford, Marie L. 1998. "Approach or Avoidance? The Role of Nonverbal Communication in the Academic Library User's Decision to Initiate a Reference Encounter." *Library Trends* 46(4): 699–717.

Radford, Marie L. 2006. "The Critical Incident Technique and the Qualitative Evaluation of the Connecting Libraries and Schools Project." *Library Trends* 55(1): 46–64. https://doi.org/10.1353/lib.2006.0051.

Richards, Lyn. 2015. *Handling Qualitative Data: A Practical Guide*. 3rd ed. Thousand Oaks, CA: Sage.

Richardson, John V., Jr. 2002. "Reference Is Better Than We Thought." *Library Journal* 127(7): 41–42.

Ritter, Frank E., Gordon D. Baxter, and Elizabeth F. Churchill. 2014. "User-Centered Systems Design: A Brief History." In *Foundations for Designing User-Centered Systems: What System Designers Need to Know about People,* edited by Frank E. Ritter, Gordon D. Baxter, and Elizabeth F. Churchill, 33–54. London: Springer. https://doi.org/10.1007/978-1-4471-5134-0_2.

Robbins, Peter. 2018. "From Design Thinking to Art Thinking with an Open Innovation Perspective—A Case Study of How Art Thinking Rescued a Cultural Institution in Dublin." *Journal of Open Innovation: Technology, Market, and Complexity* 4(4): 57. https://doi.org/10.3390/joitmc4040057.

Rohrer, Christian. 2014. "When to Use Which User-Experience Research Methods." Nielsen Norman Group. https://www.nngroup.com/articles/which-ux-research-methods.

Rosaldo, Renato. 1989. *Culture and Truth: The Remaking of Social Analysis*. Boston: Beacon Press.

Seidel, Victor P., and Sebastian K. Fixson. 2013. "Adopting Design Thinking in Novice Multidisciplinary Teams: The Application and Limits of Design Methods and Reflexive Practices." *Journal of Product Innovation Management* 30(S1): 19–33. https://doi.org/10.1111/jpim.12061.

Senteio, Charles R. 2019. "Promoting Access to Health Information: A Method to Support Older African Americans with Diabetes." *Aslib Journal of Information Management* 71(6): 806–20. https://doi.org/10.1108/AJIM-02-2019-0043.

Sharon, Tomer. 2013. "The Rainbow Spreadsheet: A Collaborative Lean UX Research Tool." *Smashing Magazine.* https://www.smashingmagazine.com/2013/04/rainbow-spreadsheet-collaborative-ux-research-tool.

Shpakova, Agnessa, Viktor Dörfler, and Jill MacBryde. 2020. "Gamifying the Process of Innovating." *Innovation* 22(4): 488–502. https://doi.org/10.1080/14479338.2019.1642763.

Simonsen, Jesper, and Toni Robertson. 2013. *Routledge International Handbook of Participatory Design*. New York: Routledge.

Talip, Bazilah A., Bhuva Narayan, Sylvia L. Edwards, and Jason Watson. 2017. "Digital Ethnography as a Way to Explore Information Grounds on Twitter." *Qualitative and Quantitative Methods in Libraries* 5(1): 89–105.

Tewell, Eamon C. 2010. "Accurate Answers to Reference Queries May Be Provided Less Frequently Than Expected." *Evidence Based Library and Information Practice* 5(4): 125–29. https://ejournals.library.ualberta.ca/index.php/EBLIP/article/view/8866/7525.

"Tools: Digital Visitors and Residents Mapping App." 2020. OCLC Research. May 11. https://www.oclc.org/research/areas/user-studies/vandr/tools.html.

Unertl, Kim M., Chris L. Schaefbauer, Terrance R. Campbell, Charles Senteio, Katie A. Siek, Suzanne Bakken, and Tiffany C. Veinot. 2016. "Integrating Community-Based Participatory Research and Informatics Approaches to Improve the Engagement and Health of Underserved Populations." *Journal of the American Medical Informatics Association* 23(1): 60–73. https://doi.org/10.1093/jamia/ocv094.

"User Experience Basics." 2014. Department of Health and Human Services. February 19. user-experience.html.

"Visitors and Residents." 2020. OCLC Research. http://experimental.worldcat.org/vandrmapping/signIn.

Wakimoto, Diana K. 2013. "Ethnographic Methods Are Becoming More Popular in LIS Research." *Evidence Based Library and Information Practice* 8(1): 96. https://doi.org/10.18438/B8BS5P.

Wallerstein, Nina, Bonnie Duran, Meredith Minkler, and Kevin Foley. 2005. "Developing and Maintaining Partnershis with Communities." In *Methods in Community-Based Participatory Research for Health*, edited by Barbara Israel, Eugenia Eng, Amy J. Schulz, and Edith A. Parker, 31–51. San Francisco: Jossey-Bass, A Wiley Imprint.

"Weave Journal of Library User Experience." n.d. Weave Journal of Library User Experience. https://www.weaveux.org.

"What & Why of Usability." n.d. Usability.Gov. Accessed July 3, 2020. https://www.usability.gov/what-and-why/index.html.Wildemuth, Barbara M. 2017. *Applications of Social Research Methods to Questions in Information and Library Science.* 2nd ed. Santa Barbara, CA: ABC-CLIO.

Whitlatch, Jo Bell. 1989. "Unobtrusive Studies and the Quality of Academic Library Reference Services." *College & Research Libraries* 50(2): 181–94.

Whittaker, Kenneth. 1990. "Unobtrusive Testing of Reference Enquiry Work." *Library Review* 39(6): 50–54.

Wolcott, Harry F. 1999. *Ethnography: A Way of Seeing.* Oxford, UK: Altamira Press.

Wu, Somaly Kim, and Donna Lanclos. 2011. "Re-Imagining the Users' Experience: An Ethnographic Approach to Web Usability and Space Design." *Reference Services Review* 39(3): 369–89. https://doi.org/10.1108/00907321111161386.

Yin, Robert K. 2012. *Applications of Case Study Research.* 3rd ed. Thousand Oaks, CA: Sage.

13

Historical Research

This chapter provides an overview of historical research and methods in library and information science (LIS). Some researchers, including some historians, have argued that historical research cannot be considered true scientific research because it does not permit enough precision and objectivity. They assert that it does not have the rigor of such research methods as experimental and survey methods. Others argue that historical research can meet the standards of inquiry of other methods (Mouly 1978). Despite these disagreements, there is a consensus that historical research has much to contribute to LIS. Some scholars believe that the LIS field would benefit from increasing attention to this method (Delsaerdt 2015; Hérubel 2016). One important development is the creation of a new journal in 2017, *Libraries: Culture, History and Society*, which is peer-reviewed and is the official journal of the Library History Round Table (LHRT Journal 2017) of the American Library Association (ALA).

According to Chu and Ke: "Historical method played a dominant role in LIS research until the 1980s. Historical method refers to collecting data by examining, synthesizing, summarizing, and interpreting existing published and unpublished materials related to a historical research problem. Historical method bears some similarity to content analysis because both methods analyze the content of materials for data collection purposes. Historical method differs from content analysis because it deals exclusively with problems of a historical nature" (Chu and Ke 2017; Feehan et al. 1987; Järvelin and Vakkari 1990).

NATURE AND VALUE OF HISTORICAL RESEARCH

To start with a historical perspective, "As used by the Greeks, history meant an inquiry designed to reconstruct past events, and, in a sense, historical research can still be defined as a scholarly attempt to discover what has happened" (Mouly 1978, 157). Currently, historical research, or "documentary research" as it is sometimes labeled (although historical research is not limited to documents), typically goes beyond mere description and attempts to interpret the facts as reconstructed. The historian attempts to give meaning to the facts in light of a relevant theory. The basic purposes of historical research are to "provide a clear perspective of the present" and to facilitate planning for the future by identifying general principles applicable to recurring situations (Mouly 1978, 157). Tosh and Lang (2015) referred to this as "historical awareness," which is based on three principles: difference, context, and process. Difference is the "recognition of the gulf which separates our own age from all previous ages" (Tosh and Lang 2015, 9). Context means that the setting for the subject of the enquiry must be retained (Tosh and Lang 2015, 10). Process is "the relationship between events over time," which makes the events more relevant "than if they were viewed in isolation" (Tosh and Lang 2015, 11).

Chronology

It may be useful at this point to distinguish true historical research from chronology. *Chronology* can be defined as simply the describing of events in the order of their occurrence, a process similar to the older concept of historical research. Chronology is nevertheless important, as it represents the first step in the process of historical research and provides material or data for the steps to follow.

In contrast, true historical research, or *historiography* or intellectual history, is concerned with analyzing and interpreting the meaning of historical events within their contexts. It is the process by which a researcher is able to reach a conclusion about the probable truth of an event in the past by studying objects available for observation in the present (Goldhor 1972, 98).

History has two dimensions, both of which are important to the interpretation of historical data. One dimension is *historical time*, or the chronology that takes into account the spacing of events and patterns. A good example of such a chronology, which is sometimes referred to as a timeline, is *American Library History Literature, 1947–1997*, published in 2000 (Wiegand 2020; Wiegand and comp. 1999). The second dimension is *historical space*, or the geographic location in which events occurred.

Importance of Historical Research to Librarianship

In addition to fulfilling the basic purposes noted above, historical research can make specific contributions to the advancement of LIS. Delsaerdt (2015, 3) advances three reasons why heritage librarians "need to devote themselves to historical research in order to meet the expectations of the library's patrons and to optimize the management of collections." These reasons include: (1) "If you want to maximize service, it is eminently useful to have qualified professionals around who also know the kind of questions researchers have when they approach a library collection; professionals who, furthermore, can fathom the difficulties of being confronted with the specific modalities for consulting historical documents; professionals who, in short, can feel their way into the wishes and expectations of their patrons" (Delsaerdt 2015, 3). (2) "The development of expertise on the level of the book, whether it be hand-written, printed, or digital. The public is entitled to expect . . . that the guardians of this documentary heritage are real experts" (Delsaerdt 2015, 3); and (3) "The field that needs most urgently to be explored in depth by librarians is . . . that of library history" (Delsaerdt 2015, 4).

As Busha and Harter (Busha and Harter 1980, 92) indicated, historical research can contribute to the body of knowledge about librarianship. It can increase our understanding of how, when, and why past events occurred, and it can expand our appreciation of the significance of these events. Busha and Harter also quoted Harris (Harris 1971, 1), who stated that "a clear understanding of the historical definition of the functions of libraries may well contribute to increased communication between libraries." Harris noted that Shera has argued that library history allows librarians to understand the present and to fulfill their social responsibility more effectively (Shera 1952). More specifically, as Gorman and Clayton (Gorman and Clayton 2005, 161) noted, historical research can help to gain historical understanding of the long-term development of library collections, inform budgetary decision making, provide a basis for decisions concerning services, and inform an investigation of changing information culture.

According to the ALA's Library History Round Table (LHRT Journal 2017) Statement on History in Education for Library and Information Science:

> A knowledge of history and an understanding of historical methodology are indispensable elements in the education of library and information professionals. A knowledge of history provides a necessary perspective for understanding the principles and practices of library and information science. Many of the most important issues of our day—including, for example, intellectual freedom, fees for service, service to minorities, access to government information, the role of new technologies, and the place of women in the profession—can only be understood in the light of their historical contexts. And the research process, an essential component of contemporary professional education and practice, can be significantly informed by awareness of both historical precedents and historical methodology.

Hérubel asserts that historical research has gotten short shrift in LIS education. "Library history is increasingly relegated to the margins as information studies, information science, or library science per se occupies precious curricular space for professional training" leading to "professional amnesia" (Hérubel 2016, 14). He argues that "the LIS profession is a practice which privileges professional prerogatives over historical interests, even the history of the LIS profession, and libraries. However, for a profession as ancient as librarianship, it is curious that library history and historians have not garnered their place in the pantheon of academic history" (Collections 2006; Hérubel 2016, 10; Wiegand 2000). He believes that although LIS curricula have largely ignored library history, it "can be found among different disciplines, especially as it touches print culture, and information history" (Hérubel 2016, 14). His analysis finds that historical treatments in LIS from 2004 to 2013 make up 11.6 percent of dissertations and 7.8 percent of journal articles, which he concludes concretizes its marginalization. Additionally, the primary subjects of the journal articles from that time period revolve around two topics: books and library associations, with a considerable drop-off in frequency for the next three topics: publishing, public libraries, and academic libraries.

Hérubel (2016, 12) concludes by calling for invigorated attention to historical research. "To effectively navigate [recent] innovations in approach, methodology, and theory, library historians need to reconceptualize their raison d'être, judiciously incorporating insights and/or techniques originating with humanities and/or social sciences disciplines. Enhancing library history via other disciplines will strengthen library history—moreover, borrowing techniques or methodologies originating in the social sciences or humanities may enhance, or at least amplify, library historians' attempts in enlarging the purview of library history as a scholarly discipline. This can intellectually strengthen library history's position vis-à-vis LIS, mollifying LIS's ahistorical and perceived antipathy to historical scholarship, especially as it focuses on LIS's past."

Both Davis (1998) and Shiflett (2000) have called for the inclusion of LIS history in master's program curricula. They believe that LIS professionals must know and understand the history of the field in a historical context of society and culture to become leaders instead of merely practitioners. By studying history, LIS professionals will look beyond practice and will "strive continuously to raise the standards of the profession and improve the system in which it functions" (Bok 1986, 168–69).

Shiflett (2000, 254–59) suggests utilizing sense-making methodology to teach and learn history. This approach would enable both teachers and students to "make retrospective sense of the situations in which they find themselves and their creations" (Weick 2010, 14). Knowledge and understanding of good historical research can help librarians build on the past in an efficient, effective manner to avoid reinventing the wheel and to develop new theories and systems to advance the profession.

Types of Historical Research

Salevouris and Furay (2015) provide an overview of historical research methods in their practical guide, *The Methods and Skills of History,* and have included a chapter on "Libraries: Real and Virtual." Hillway identified six different types of historical research or documentary study: (1) biographical research, (2) histories of institutions and organizations, (3) the investigation of sources and influences, (4) editing and translating historical documents, (5) studying the history of ideas, and (6) compiling bibliographies. The extent to which these different types are employed depends on the nature of the inquiry and the subject field. Whether they represent true historical research, or the mere compilation of facts, depends on the manner in which they are conducted (Hillway 1964, 159).

This also may be an appropriate place to note that the manner in which historians collect and interpret their data may be somewhat influenced by the historical school of thought to which they adhere. Students of historical research have identified a number of trends in US historiography, for example, ranging from the "providential" perspective of the seventeenth and eighteenth centuries to the more recent "new social history." As Winkler (1984, 5–6) suggested, historians are moving away from new social history and back to an earlier school of thought known as the narrative mode. At the same time, she concluded that narrative history, with its emphasis on how the account is written, is not replacing new social history, with its use of social science analysis techniques. What is happening, according to Winkler, is that scholars are becoming more willing to accommodate a diversity of approaches to conducting and reporting historical research.

SOURCES OF HISTORICAL INFORMATION

The data gathered in historical research can come from a wide variety of sources. Among the more commonly used are the following:

- Official records, such as laws, deeds, annual reports of organizations, charters, circulation data, accession lists, bibliographies, and so forth
- Newspapers and other periodicals
- Eyewitness accounts of events
- Archives
- Manuscripts
- Letters and personal diaries
- Biographies, autobiographies, and memoirs
- Historical studies
- Literary writings
- Oral evidence
- Memorials
- Catalogs
- Schedules, agendas, and so forth
- Archaeological and geological remains (nondocuments)
- Social media posts
- Online discussion groups and forums

Virtually all written sources of historical information can be categorized as either primary or secondary documents. *Primary* sources contain the data that lie closest to the historical event. They are considered to include the testimony of eyewitnesses, or observations made with one of the other senses or by some mechanical device. In most cases, primary sources are the written record of what writers actually observed or the firsthand expression of their thoughts. *Secondary*, or secondhand, sources may be considered virtually everything not viewed as primary. Historians' and others' writings about the past are considered secondary sources, including most textbooks, journal articles, histories, and encyclopedias. The use of primary sources tends to ensure the integrity of a study and to strengthen its reliability. Their use provides the only solid base for conclusions reached in documentary research (Hillway 1964, 147). According to Bates, primary sources "are the raw materials of historical interpretation." They are critical for the consideration of complex historical issues.

Library-related primary sources may include official records, government documents, manuscripts, newspaper articles, letters, and statistics, but whether these sources are truly primary depends on whether they are first-hand accounts. Shiflett (1984, 397) stated that library historians also should consult other primary resources, such as the published proceedings of the ALA since they represent "the collective values of a profession" and the positions of American librarians. Readers particularly interested in sources for library-related research should consult Shiflett's (1984, 385–406) article in *Library Trends*. Statistics, for example, could be based on other, primary sources and thus become secondary sources themselves. The distinction between primary and secondary sources is not as clear-cut as it might at first appear, and it can vary with the authority. Primary sources are defined as being contemporary with the event or thought to which they refer, but different people can define "contemporary" differently. Some prefer a broader definition that recognizes different levels of "primary." For example, a report of a conversation that occurred a week ago would no doubt be primary. A report of that conversation written twenty years later for an autobiography might be considered primary as well, but somewhat less so than the more immediate account. And what about the increasing number of electronic facsimiles? According to Duff and Cherry (2000), some users have expressed concern about the authenticity of web-based digital copies of original documents. Others, however, view facsimiles, whether electronic or photographic, as primary resources for all practical purposes.

It is seldom possible, or even desirable, for historical researchers to base their work entirely on primary sources. Secondary sources may provide important insights and conceptual development not available elsewhere. By synthesizing the existing research literature, secondary sources help to round out the setting or fill in the gaps between primary sources of information and can suggest topics for future research. Because secondary sources do not represent eyewitness accounts, the researcher should keep in mind their limitations and avoid an overreliance on such materials. In evaluating secondary data sources, for example, the researcher should ask questions about the qualifications of the person responsible for the data collection, what data were collected and what they were intended to measure, when the information was collected, the methods that were used to collect the data, and the consistency of the data with data from other sources. See Pozzi's text box 13.1, discussing the use of primary sources for historical research.

Text Box 13.1: Primary Sources Used in Historical Research for Librarianship

Ellen Pozzi

When I visit a library, I find myself wondering about the people who have used it in the past. Historical research enables me to begin to piece together their stories, as I did in my dissertation, "The Public Library in an Immigrant Neighborhood: Italian Immigrants' Information Ecologies in Newark, New Jersey, 1889–1919." In this work, I explored the place of the Newark Free Public Library in Italian immigrants' lives at the turn of the nineteenth to the twentieth century. The primary sources I examined included annual reports, other library records, newspaper clippings, and contemporary journals and books. A critical reading of these sources uncovered some of the voices of library users and led me to create a model of immigrant information ecologies, contributing to an understanding of immigrants' information experiences.

Christine Pawley also pieced together library users' stories in her excellent book *Reading on the Middle Border: The Culture of Print in Late-Nineteenth-Century Osage, Iowa.* She examined reading culture in a midwestern town and connected library history to wider social, cultural, and political events, providing context for the role of the library in society. Books like Pawley's (2009) demonstrate solid research practices and interpretive strategies useful to those new to historical research.

Library circulation records from the late 1800s enriched Pawley's work, but primary sources can be frustratingly incomplete. I found evidence that fourteen Italian or Italian/English newspapers were published for various lengths of time between 1889 and 1919 in Newark but was able to find only two issues of one newspaper. Historical research is time consuming and has no definitive end point. But it is rewarding and contributes to our understanding of contemporary LIS issues by revealing the foundations of today's practices. Knowing the past is essential for charting the future.

References

Pawley, Christine. 2009. *Reading on the Middle Border: The Culture of Print in Late-Nineteeth-Century Osage, Iowa.* Amherst: University of Massachusetts Press.

Pozzi, Ellen. 2013. "The Public Library in an Immigrant Neighborhood: Italian Immigrants' Information Ecologies in Newark, New Jersey, 1889–1919." Rutgers University. https://search .proquest.com/openview/17ff2f53b6f24ffe8b6e3c63966be23d/1?pq-origsite =gscholar&cbl=18750&diss=y.

EVALUATION OF HISTORICAL SOURCES

In selecting specific sources of data for a historical study, it is critical that they be evaluated properly. The researcher should want to know if the sources are relevant to the study, substantial enough to be worthwhile, and competent (i.e., genuine, accurate, and reasonable). The assessment of the last criterion—competency—should involve two basic processes: external criticism and internal criticism.

External Criticism

External criticism, or the gathering of external evidence, is done to determine if a source in fact provides authentic primary data. Are the author, the place, and the date of writing what they purport to be? The process of external criticism is crucial to the credibility of historical research. External criticism may be used interchangeably with textual criticism and usually takes into account the provenance, or origin, of a document. Can the document be traced back to the office or person who supposedly produced it? For example, scholars have long debated the true authorship of at least some of Shakespeare's plays. More recent examples of works whose authenticity has been disputed include de la Peña's diary as it relates to the demise of Davy Crockett, d'Ancona's manuscript about his travels in thirteenth-century China, and even Clement Moore's poem, "'Twas the Night before Christmas."

External criticism often cannot prove the authenticity of a source, but it can provide reasonable confidence that a particular source is authentic. To assess the authenticity of a work, investigators may use bibliographical techniques (see the section on bibliographical research later in this chapter) or draw on expertise in a number of auxiliary disciplines such as linguistics, epigraphy (the study of inscriptions), genealogy, paleography, and heraldry. They may need to utilize certain techniques of the physical sciences, such as chemical analysis of paper and ink. The contents of the document should be examined for consistency with known facts and with information available to the author at the time the document was written. External criticism can involve physical, textual, and bibliographical analysis.

Internal Criticism

Having decided that a document or source is genuine, the researcher should then confirm the validity and reliability of its contents. The concern, at this point, is with what the source says (i.e., its meaning, accuracy, and general trustworthiness). Internal criticism is generally more challenging than external criticism, and it too is often difficult, if not impossible, to achieve with absolute certainty. Many old documents no longer exist in their original forms, and there is no guarantee that their contents have not changed somewhat as they have been copied, translated, and republished over the years. (See the fuller discussion of descriptive bibliography below.)

Babbie states that the more sources "point to the same set of 'facts,' your confidence in them might reasonably increase" (Babbie 2021, 349). He cautions historical researchers to "always be wary of bias in your data sources and, if possible, encourages obtaining "data from a variety of sources representing different points of view" (Babbie 2021, 349) concerning a topic or event. These measures will increase the validity and reliability of the research.

Some evidence of internal validity and reliability can be obtained by considering the reputation and integrity of the author, allowing for the circumstances under which a document was written, and comparing "facts" within a document with the writings of other authors considered to be authoritative. Shafer (1980, 166–67) recommended asking the following questions, among others, when evaluating the internal evidence of a document:

- Do the real meanings of words differ from their literal meanings?
- How well could the author have observed the things he or she is reporting?

- Are there internal contradictions?
- Are any statements inherently improbable?
- Are factual data in agreement with standard reference works?
- Does the document seem to call for further corroboration?

Additional questions could include the following: Did the historian have full access to all of the relevant documents, or were some withheld? Was the author of the document biased? Finally, what significance does the document have as a source of information? Aminzade and Laslett (2016) also have identified a list of questions for historians to use when reading and evaluating documents (Babbie 2021, 349).

BASIC STEPS OF HISTORICAL RESEARCH

Different historians may espouse somewhat different procedures of historical research. For example, one school of thought may emphasize the collection and description of facts, while another may emphasize the interpretation stage. Some believe that a historical study should be guided by a formal hypothesis. Others argue for a more flexible methodology, such as the source-oriented approach, in which historians examine a source or group of sources relevant to their interests and extract whatever is of value, allowing the content of the source to determine the nature of the inquiry (Tosh and Lang 2015, 54). But there seems to be a consensus that historical research generally should meet the same criteria and follow the same procedures as the other basic methods of scientific research (Mouly 1978, 159; Salevouris and Furay 2015, 43). Historical research generally involves the following steps:

- Identification of a problem of historical significance.
- Collection of background information (i.e., literature review of the secondary sources).
- Formulation of a hypothesis when desirable and possible (more on this later).
- Gathering of evidence or data (including verification of the authenticity of the primary sources and the validity and reliability of their contents).
- Organization and analysis of the pertinent data (more often qualitative than quantitative).
- Interpretation of the findings or the drawing of conclusions.
- True historical research tends to resemble a scientific method of inquiry or a problem-oriented approach.

The Hypothesis in Historical Research

Generally speaking, the most significant and useful results of any basic research lie in the generalizations or principles that are derived from the data.

Consequently, historical research, as well as other types of research, especially quantitative designs, may benefit from the incorporation of a hypothesis. Indeed, "the hypothesis is a natural and useful device" in the historical method (Shafer 1980, 176).

More specifically, the use of a hypothesis in historical research helps to increase the objectivity of the study and minimize researcher bias. It also guides the researcher in the collection, analysis, and interpretation of data by indicating what is relevant to the study. The hypothesis provides a basis for considering various factors in relation to one another and for synthesizing them into a generalization or conclusion that puts their overall significance in focus (Mouly 1978, 160). In effect, the use of the hypothesis in historical research amounts to an application of theory.

For example, one could hypothesize that academic libraries have been used to a greater extent when they have had substantive information literacy instruction (ILI) programs than when they have not. Based on this hypothesis, the researcher will know that, at the very least, historical data on use and ILI programs will need to be collected from one or more academic libraries in order to "test" the relationship expressed.

In essence, the hypothesis would be tested by ascertaining the factual truth of specific, relevant events and organizing them to determine whether the presence of the independent variable seemed to have any effect on, or contributed to, the dependent variable. In the example just given, the researcher would attempt to determine whether libraries were more heavily used during periods when they had active ILI programs than when they did not. The measurement of these two variables would be based on how they were operationally defined. As is the case with other research methods, however, one test cannot really prove a hypothesis; but it can lend support to or increase confidence in it.

It can be more difficult to test historical hypotheses than those developed in other types of research. This is largely because historical research is ex post facto in nature, and the researcher obviously has no control over the relevant variables, as they have already occurred. One "cannot re-enact the past but only interpret it" (Goldhor 1972, 111). Nor can the historian always anticipate the facts that will be uncovered as the examination of sources proceeds. Consequently, the historical hypothesis may have to be employed in a more flexible manner than is the case for more structured research.

Causal hypotheses are particularly complex and difficult to establish in historical research, but in spite of being inherently difficult to deal with, causality is often thought to be important to consider in a historical study. Charles A. Beard and Sidney Hook (1946) stated that "no historical account that goes beyond the form of a chronicle can be written without the assumption of causal connection. And no historical chronicle exists in which assumptions of this character are not implicit."

More specifically, considering causality tends to improve the formulation of the hypothesis and the strategies for collecting data. It also promotes the development of generalizations and basic principles. In short, the consideration of causality forces the researcher to move beyond mere description and to reflect on why certain relationships seem to exist. On the other hand, not all historians are in agreement that consideration of causality (and hypotheses) is essential to good historical research.

Collecting the Data

"While historical research is similar to the reviews of literature which precede other forms of research, the historical approach is more exhaustive, seeking out information from a larger array of sources. It also tracks down information that is much older than required by most reviews and hunts for unpublished material not cited in the standard references" (Isaac and Michael 1995). One of the greatest challenges facing historians is the extent to which their research relies on unpublished materials. Many such documents are housed in archives that have developed arrangement and description techniques that differ from those of libraries, and the historian should be well versed in how to identify and access archival collections.

The data collection technique for historical research, or at least for documentary research, involves putting together in a logical fashion the evidence derived from documents or records. This process also often involves the comparing and reconciling of information gathered from two or more sources. Indeed, the use of a variety of sources is considered to be one of the hallmarks of historical research. It is important to note, however, that because of the great volume of data typically collected, it is essential to organize the data as systematically as possible. Before beginning a historical study, the researcher should have a specific plan for the acquisition, organization, storage, and retrieval of the data. *Tertiary* sources, such as library catalogs, periodical indexes, and online repositories of digital archives, are routinely used to identify and access resources. The use of aids such as note cards, bibliography cards, and online citation organizers (e.g., RefWorks, Zotero, and Mendeley); multiple files; and cloud-based services (e.g., DropBox, OneDrive, Box, or Google Drive) can be quite helpful when gathering data from the resources. Storing notes in database files provides advanced search capabilities and enables the researcher to code the data via content analysis. Use of electronic files can also facilitate the use of software for data analysis and for translating, collating, and comparing documents. (See chapter 8 for a discussion of data analysis software.)

Shafer (1980), in his chapter on collecting historical evidence, began with a discussion of recording bibliographical information. He described the process of preparing bibliographic records and noted how critical they are to the overall process. Shafer also highlighted the mechanics of making and analyzing research notes and the importance of using standard methods, and included examples. Shafer reviewed some of the standard bibliographic aids used by historians, including library catalogs, bibliographies, government publication guides and indexes, newspaper and journal indexes, national bibliographies, manuscript and archival guides, dissertation indexes, guides to reference books, booksellers' catalogs, and guides to locations such as union lists. According to Tibbo (2003), other guides to primary resources commonly used by historians include repository websites, bibliographical utilities, and search engines.

The Presentation of Findings

When writing the historical report, the researcher should take care to be objective and to preserve intellectual honesty. This is not to suggest that historical researchers are more prone to partiality than others, but to serve as a reminder that historical research is rather subjective in nature and thus depends on researcher interpretation in data selection and analysis, and it may be susceptible to bias. The report is normally directed to the knowledgeable scholar, and the facts and interpretations should be presented so that the reader can evaluate conclusions in light of documented evidence. The data should be related and integral to the purpose of the study, and clear and unambiguous expression is important.

"The dual aspect of the historical enterprise—the effort to establish what happened and the attempt to explain why things happened in the way they did—explains the twofold task in historical writing: 1) to convey a sense of time or to show chronological development, 2) to analyze and explain the interrelationships of the events studied, to detect underlying patterns, to unify the various elements in a satisfactory whole, which provides a response to the initial research problem, using an analytical style or an approach by topic" (Gorman and Clayton 2005, 175). Thus, historical writings are represented by a variety of literary forms that combine description, narrative, and analysis in different ways and proportions. Description and narrative tend to suffice when the historian merely desires to re-create the past, while analysis is necessary for interpretation of the past. The nature of the subject matter also may influence the literary form of the report.

LIBRARY HISTORY

Historical research in the LIS field has often been referred to as "library history." A comprehensive guide to the literature of American library history was published in 1989 and is available for free on the LRHT website (Davis and Tucker 1989). Shiflett (1984, 402) defined library history as "a rubric that covers a myriad of topics associated with libraries and other information systems. Its major form consists of the traditional library, but it also includes the history of any activity or event that might be part of the domain of library and information science." Busha and Harter (1980, 93) noted that library history is "commonly applied to an account of events that have affected any library or group of libraries, as well as to the social and economic impacts of libraries on their communities." A related, but narrower, area of inquiry is the history of the book. According to Irwin (1958, 3–4), since libraries function within a larger context, library historians should be concerned with "the history not only of scholarship in its narrower sense, but of human civilization and culture and literacy."

Unfortunately, the fact that the history of LIS has been given a special label seems to suggest that it is a special type of history. Some would even argue that it has been an inferior type of history or historical research. In 1952 Shera

(1952, 249) pointed out that library history had evidenced "an excessive preoccupation with antiquarian detail and a provincial point of view." In 1965 Bartlett (1965, 19) argued that "there is never a dearth of library history, but . . . its existence has been consistently marred by a tragic shortage of quality."

Salevouris and Furay (2015, 5) remind us that "without historical perspective we are in danger of falling into the mistaken and perhaps arrogant notion that the problems we face and the solutions we propose are unprecedented and bear no relationship to past human problems. Just one of the contributions history can make is to serve as a useful antidote to such narrow present-mindedness." A review of the more recent literature of library history suggests that the quality of historical research in LIS has improved. (See Davis and Tucker (1989) for a comprehensive guide to the literature of American library history.) As far back as 1978, Kaser (1978, 192) pointed out that "we are vastly better equipped today with sound, rigorous, scholarly understanding than we were a few years ago." Shiflett (1984, 388) stated, "The condemnation of library history as mere antiquarianism is only valid if the short view of history is held."

Examples of historical research in LIS include:

- American women in library service during World War I from 1918 to 1920 (Stauffer 2016).
- Gay and lesbian books in public libraries in the Midwest from 1900 to 1969 (Passet 2012).
- Seventy years of historical dissertation research at the University of Illinois at Urbana-Champaign. (Smith and D'Arpa 2017)

Goedeken (2020) provides an overview of thirty years of American library history through an exploration of the bibliographies of the LHRT. Also, there is an extensive and updated bibliography provided by the ALA LHRT in the semiannual issue of the division's newsletter through 2014 and to the present on the LHRT ("A Publication of the Library History Round Table" n.d.) blog (https://lhrtnews.wordpress.com). The bibliographies published from 1990 through the present are available online as well ("Bibliography of Library History").

As to the future of library history scholarship, the publication of historical research continues to prosper. There continues to be a need for and interest in historical research that considers libraries and other information systems in broad contexts. Almost forty years ago, Hagler (1971, 132) pointed out, there existed a need for more unified interpretations of library history based on comprehensive visions. Wiegand's historical research is a good example of interpretative and rigorous historical research, and he often is referred to as the "dean of American library historians." He published a history of the public library *Part of Our Lives: A People's History of the American Public Library*, and in 2020 he continued his prolific publication record with the article "Sanitizing American Library History: Reflections of a Library Historian" in *The Library Quarterly* (Wiegand 2015).

BIBLIOGRAPHICAL RESEARCH

Another area of scholarly work that some consider to be a special type of historical research is bibliographical research. Others argue that bibliographical research is not true research, at least as prescribed by the scientific method of inquiry. Most would concede, however, that bibliographical research that takes the form of descriptive bibliography certainly comes closer to being true research than does systematic or enumerative bibliography. The latter is not even considered to be true bibliographical research. There is no question, however, that both types of bibliographical work are important scholarly endeavors, which at the very least support the work of "true" researchers or historians.

Systematic Bibliography

Those involved in the compilation of systematic or enumerative bibliographies are concerned with the book (and other materials) as an intellectual entity. Their purpose is to assemble information about individual works into a logical and useful arrangement. The results are one of the following compilations or lists:

- **Universal bibliography:** a bibliography that includes everything published or issued in a subject field regardless of date of publication.
- **National bibliography:** a bibliography that lists everything published (and possibly distributed) in a given country.
- **Trade bibliography:** a bibliography compiled primarily to aid the book trade by supplying information about what books are in print or for sale; when, where, and by whom they were published; and their price.
- **Subject bibliography:** a bibliography that lists materials relating to a specific topic.

Descriptive Bibliography

In contrast to systematic bibliography, descriptive bibliography is concerned with the book as a physical entity or material object. As previously noted, it resembles true research more than does systematic bibliography. Sir Walter Greg once defined descriptive bibliography as follows:

Bibliography is the study of books as tangible objects. It examines the materials of which they are made and the manner in which these materials are put together. It traces their place and mode of origin, and the subsequent adventures which have befallen them. It is not concerned with their contents in a literary sense, but it is certainly concerned with the signs and symbols they contain (apart from their significance) for the manner in which these marks are written or impressed is a very relevant bibliographical fact. And, starting from this fact, it is concerned with the relation of one book to another; the question of which manuscript was copied from which, which individual copies of printed books are to be grouped together as forming an edition, and what is the relation of edition to edition. (Eaton 1964)

A more succinct definition found in the *Oxford English Dictionary* ("Bibliography, n." n.d.) defines bibliography as "the systematic description and history of books, their authorship, printing, publication, editions, etc."

An important function of descriptive bibliography is to describe the "ideal copy," or primary document, and its variants. This process can be broken down into more specific bibliographical research, including the following:

- Analytical bibliography, which is concerned with the physical description of the book to determine the details of the physical process of its manufacturing.
- Textual bibliography, which focuses on certain textual variations between a manuscript and the printed book or among various editions. It is more concerned with the author's words than with the physical aspects of the book.
- Historical bibliography, which deals with the identification of original editions and the placing and dating of individual books.
- Other terms that are sometimes used to represent specific types of descriptive bibliography, or are used as synonyms, are comparative, technical, and critical bibliography.

As was pointed out previously, descriptive bibliographical research is a scholarly activity that may be thought of as historical research in and of itself, but it is also of critical importance to all historians needing assurance of the authenticity and accuracy of their documentary resources. As Ronald McKerrow stated,

> bibliographical evidence will help us to settle such questions as that of the order and relative value of different editions of a book; whether certain sections of a book were originally intended to form part of it or were added afterwards; whether a later edition was printed from an earlier one, and from which; whether it was printed from a copy that had been corrected in manuscript, or whether such corrections as it contained were made in proof, and a number of other problems of a similar kind, which may often have a highly important literary bearing. It will indeed sometimes enable us to solve questions which to one entirely without bibliographical knowledge would appear quite incapable of solution. (Eaton 1964)

Readers interested in learning more about the process of bibliographical research should consult the literature on historical research, reference, and bibliography, including works by Wynar (1967), Robinson (1979), Bowers (2012), Harmon (1998), and Beal (2008). Those interested in examples of bibliographical research may wish to read Eaton's (1964) benchmark article in *Library Trends*.

PROBLEMS IN HISTORICAL RESEARCH

A variety of problems are common to most types of research, but they are particularly important in historical research, including the following:

- Deciding how much data are enough. This is a relatively subjective decision. At one time, historians generally attempted to collect all relevant data; they now tend toward a more selective approach. Yet the historian must continue to avoid overreliance on an insufficient amount of data or evidence. Using too little information can lead to the "argument from silence" (Goldhor 1972, 107). Researchers must be careful not to assume that some event did not occur simply because they are not aware of some record of it.
- Improperly selecting data. Briefly stated, the historian must avoid improper or faulty selection of data, including such tactics as ignoring some data or exaggerating others. Such action will significantly increase the bias in a study.
- Relying too heavily on secondary sources of information. This is particularly likely in studies not dealing with relatively recent events.
- Investigating an overly broad problem. This is difficult to avoid, because historical issues tend to be complex.
- Failing to evaluate adequately the historical data and their sources. (These techniques were addressed in a preceding section.)
- Failing to interpret the data. As previously noted, historical research is most productive when the researcher attempts to synthesize or integrate the facts into meaningful generalizations.
- Reading the present into the past even though the historical data may not support such an interpretation.

Other problems in historical research and criteria for evaluating historical research can be found in the general research guidelines discussed in preceding chapters. In addition, Mouly (1978, 170) has pointed out several criteria for evaluating historical studies. He, and others, emphasized the desirability of a writing style that will attract as well as inform. He called for creating a report that will make a significant contribution on the basis of new knowledge and not simply represent "uninspired hackwork." Finally, Mouly asked that the historical study reflect scholarliness. Again, such criteria are not unique to historical research, but they do seem to receive more attention in this area.

SUMMARY

"Though the methods of historical investigation can be shown to be the appropriate counterparts of the methods used in other sciences to investigate the phenomena that specially concern them, there appears to be a general reluctance to accord to historical conclusions the kind of logical validity that the conclusions of other sciences are deemed to possess" (Stevens 1971, 111). This may be the case because historical research is ex post facto in nature.

The historical researcher must work from evidence back to the event. In addition, the historian usually is in the position of having to investigate exceptionally complex phenomena. Consequently, it is especially difficult for the historian to support causality within a relationship, or even to draw conclusions with a very high level of confidence. For these reasons, it is generally considered advisable for the historical researcher to follow some sort of scientific method of inquiry, including the formulation and testing of a hypothesis and the analysis and interpretation of data. Such processes help to distinguish true historical research from mere chronology.

Regarding the collection of data, it is important for the researcher to draw on primary, rather than secondary, sources as much as possible. It also is crucial that the researcher establish the internal and external validity of his or her sources. Bibliographical research methods often are used for evaluating the latter.

The criteria for evaluating historical research are much the same as those for other methods of research. It is particularly important that historical research be well presented, in a readable but scholarly style. There is a continuing need for genuine historical research in LIS, and the better its presentation, the more impact it is likely to have. To paraphrase Arthur Bestor, there is no logical reason that historical knowledge cannot, in principle, be as exact as knowledge in other sciences and therefore make a real contribution to the advancement of the field (Stevens 1971, 111). Those interested in more information about historical research in LIS should refer to Gorman and Clayton (2005, 160–81), who provide a detailed discussion and examples of historical investigation in information organizations.

REFERENCES

Admin. 2006. "Bibliography of Library History." Text. Round Tables. November 29. http://www.ala.org/rt/lhrt/popularresources/libhistorybib/libraryhistory.

Aminzade, Ron, and Barbara Laslett. 2016. "Reading and Evaluating Documents." In *The Practice of Social Research*, edited by Earl R. Babbie, 357. Belmont, CA: Wadsworth/Cengage Learning.

Babbie, Earl R. 2021. *The Practice of Social Research*. 15th ed. Boston: Cengage.

Bartlett, Richard A. 1965. "The State of the Library History Art." In *Approaches to Library History*, edited by John D. Marshall, 19. Tallahassee: Florida State University Library School.

Beal, Peter. 2008. *A Dictionary of English Manuscript Terminology 1450–2000*. Oxford: Oxford University Press.

Beard, Charles A., and Sidney Hook. 1946. "Problems of Terminology in Historical Writing." In *Theory and Practice in Historical Study: A Report of the Committee on Historiography*, edited by Edward W. Strong, 112. New York: Social Science Research Council.

"Bibliography, n." n.d. In *OED Online*. Oxford University Press. Accessed October 30, 2020. http://www.oed.com/view/Entry/18631.

"Bibliography of Library History." American Library Association. http://www.ala.org/lhrt/popularresources/libhistorybib/libraryhistory.Bok, Derek. 1986. *Higher Learning*. Cambridge, MA: Harvard University Press.

Bowers, Fredson. 2012. *Principles of Bibliographic Description.* Reprint ed. New Castle, DE: Oak Knoll Books.

Busha, Charles H., and Stephen P. Harter. 1980. *Research Methods in Librarianship: Techniques and Interpretation.* Cambridge, MA: Academic Press.

Chu, Heting, and Qing Ke. 2017. "Research Methods: What's in the Name?" *Library & Information Science Research* 39(4): 284–94. https://doi.org/10.1016/j.lisr.2017.11.001.

Collections, Department of Information &, ed. 2006. *Annual Bibliography of the History of the Printed Book and Libraries.* Vol. 31. Annual Bibliography of the History of the Printed Book and Libraries. Springer Netherlands. https://doi.org/10.1007/1-4020-4661-8.

Davis, Donald G. 1998. "Ebla to the Electronic Dream: The Role of Historical Perspectives in Professional Education." *Journal of Education for Library and Information Science* 39(3): 228–35. https://doi.org/10.2307/40324161.

Davis, Donald G., Jr., and John M. Tucker. 1989. *American Library History: A Comprehensive Guide to the Literature.* Santa Barbara, CA: ABC-CLIO.

Delsaerdt, Pierre. 2015. "Heritage Libraries and Historical Research." *Fontes Artis Musicae* 62(1): 1–5.

Duff, Wendy M., and Joan M. Cherry. 2000. "Use of Historical Documents in a Digital World: Comparisons with Original Materials and Microfiche." *Information Research* 6(1): Paper 86. http://informationr.net/ir/6-1/paper86.html.

Eaton, Thelma. 1964. "Bibliographical Research." *Library Trends* 13 (July): 44.

Feehan, Patricia E., Lee W. Gragg, Michael W. Havener, and Diane Kester. 1987. "Library and Information Science Research: An Analysis of the 1984 Journal Literature." *Library & Information Science Research* 9(3): 173–85.

Goedeken, Edward A. 2020. "The LHRT Bibliographies: The First Thirty Years." *Libraries: Culture, History, and Society* 4(1): 81–89. https://doi.org/10.5325/libraries.4.1.0081.

Goldhor, Herbert. 1972. *An Introduction to Scientific Research in Librarianship.* Urbana: University of Illinois, Graduate School of Library Science.

Gorman, G. E., and Peter Clayton. 2005. *Qualitative Research for the Information Professional: A Practical Handbook.* 2nd ed. London: Neal-Schuman.

Hagler, Ronald. 1971. "Needed Research in Library History." In *Research Methods in Librarianship: Historical and Bibliographical Methods in Library Research,* edited by Rolland E. Stevens, 132. Urbana: University of Illinois, Graduate School of Library Science.

Harmon, Robert B. 1998. *Elements of Bibliography: A Guide to Information Sources and Practical Applications.* Lanham, MD: Scarecrow Press.

Harris, Michael H., ed. 1971. *Reader in American Library History.* Washington, DC: NCR Micocard Editions.

Hérubel, Jean-Pierre V M. 2016. "To Honor Our Past: Historical Research, Library History and the Historiographical Imperative: Conceptual Reflections and Exploratory Observations." *Libraries Faculty and Staff Scholarship and Research.* https://docs.lib.purdue.edu/lib_fsdocs/140.

Hillway, Tyrus. 1964. *Introduction to Research.* 2nd ed. Boston: Houghton Mifflin.

Irwin, Raymond. 1958. *The Golden Chain: A Study in the History of Libraries.* London: H. K. Lewis.

Isaac, Stephen, and William B. Michael. 1995. *Handbook in Research and Evaluation: A Collection of Principles, Methods and Strategies Useful in the Planning, Design, and Evaluation of Studies in Education and Behavioral Sciences.* 3rd ed. San Diego: EdITS.

Järvelin, Kalervo, and Pertti Vakkari. 1990. "Content Analysis of Research Articles in Library and Information Science." *Library & Information Science Research* 12(4): 395–421.

Kaser, David. 1978. "Advances in American Library History." In *Advances in Librarianship*, edited by Michael H. Harris, 8:192. New York: Academic Press.

"LHRT Journal." Text. Round Tables. October 8, 2017. http://www.ala.org/rt /library-history-round-table/lhrt-journal.

"LHRT News and Notes—A Publication of the Library History Round Table." n.d. Accessed October 30, 2020. https://lhrtnews.wordpress.com.

Mouly, George J. 1978. *Educational Research: The Art and Science of Investigation.* Boston:Allyn & Bacon.

Passet, Joanne E. 2012. "Hidden in Plain Sight: Gay and Lesbian Books in Midwestern Public Libraries, 1900–1969." *Library Trends* 60(4): 749–64. https:// doi.org/10.1353/lib.2012.0010.

Robinson, A. M. 1979. *Systematic Bibliography.* London: Clive Bingley.

Salevouris, Michael J., and Conal Furay. 2015. *The Methods and Skills of History: A Practical Guide.* 4th ed. Oxford, UK: Wiley Blackwell.

Shafer, Robert J., ed. 1980. *A Guide to Historical Method.* 3rd ed. Homewood, IL: Dorsey Press.

Shera, Jesse H. 1952. "On the Value of Library History." *The Library Quarterly* 22(3): 240–51. https://doi.org/10.1086/617906.

Shiflett, Lee. 1984. "Clio's Claim: The Role of Historical Research in Library and Information Science." *Library Trends* 32: 385–406.

Shiflett, Lee. 2000. "Sense-Making and Library History." *Journal of Education for Library and Information Science* 41(3): 254–59. https://doi.org/10.2307 /40324077.

Smith, Mikki, and Christine D'Arpa. 2017. "What's History Got to Do with It? Seventy Years of Historical Dissertation Research at the School of Information Sciences of the University of Illinois at Urbana-Champaign." *Library Trends* 65(4): 563–88. https://doi.org/10.1353/lib.2017.0019.

Stauffer, Suzanne. 2016. "The Work Calls for Men: The Social Construction of Professionalism and Professional Education for Librarianship." *Journal of Education for Library and Information Science Online* 57(4): 311–24. https://doi .org/10.12783/issn.2328-2967/57/4/5.

Stevens, Rolland E., ed. 1971. *Research Methods in Librarianship: Historical and Bibliographical Methods in Library Research.* Urbana: University of Illinois, Graduate School of Library Science.

Tibbo, Helen. 2003. "Primarily History in America: How U.S. Historians Search for Primary Materials at the Dawn of the Digital Age." *The American Archivist* 66(1): 9–50. https://doi.org/10.17723/aarc.66.1.b120370l1g718n74.

Tosh, Josh, and Sean Lang. 2015. *The Pursuit of History: Aims, Methods and New Directions in the Study of Modern History.* 6th ed. London: Pearson Longman.

Weick, Karl. 2010. *Sensemaking in Organizations.* Reprint ed. Thousand Oaks, CA: Sage.

Wiegand, Wayne A. 2000. "American Library History Literature, 1947–1997: Theoretical Perspectives?" *Libraries & Culture* 35(1): 4–34.

Wiegand, Wayne A. 2015. *Part of Our Lives: A People's History of the American Public Library.* Oxford, England: Oxford University Press.

Wiegand, Wayne A. 2020. "Sanitizing American Library History: Reflections of a Library Historian." *The Library Quarterly* 90(2): 108–20. https://doi.org/10 .1086/707669.

Wiegand, Wayne, and comp. 1999. "Libraries in the U.S. Timeline." *American Libraries* 30(11).

Winkler, Karen J. 1984. "Disillusioned with Numbers and Counting, Historians Are Telling Stories Again." *Chronicle of Higher Education* 28 (June): 5–6.

Wynar, Bohdan S. 1967. *Introduction to Bibliography and Reference Work.* 4th ed. Rochester, NY: Libraries Unlimited.

14

Applied and Community-Based Research

As noted in chapter 1, there is a distinction to be made between basic and applied research. Basic research tends to be theoretical in nature and concerns itself primarily with theory construction, hypothesis testing, and producing new, generalizable knowledge. Applied research tends to be more pragmatic and emphasizes providing information that is immediately usable in the resolution of actual problems, which may or may not have application beyond the immediate study.

On the other hand, both types of research ultimately should add to the existing body of knowledge within a field; in doing so, they may utilize similar methods and techniques. Such utilization is nicely illustrated by the discussion of the evaluation of information storage and retrieval systems in *Guide to Information Science* by Davis and Rush (1980). Davis pointed out that "the interplay between academics [basic researchers] and practitioners [applied researchers] can be extremely valuable," and it should be encouraged (Malenfant 2012). There is no good reason to assume that basic and applied research are mutually exclusive. In fact, basic and applied research can be considered as two parts of a continuum. This has continued to be discussed in the literature. Janes (2013) stated, "academics and practitioners need to play nice." He reiterated that research "can take many forms and be for many purposes" and that collaboration only enhances the impact of the research (Janes 2013). The Association of College and Research Libraries (ACRL) has the Assessment in Action (AiA) program that funds academic librarians to collaborate with faculty to conduct research on student learning and academic success. ACRL published a paper that reports the results of more than 200 of these campus team projects (Malenfant and Brown 2017). The following statement from Sheridan may be more relevant today than it would have been in the past, since librarians often are called on to report on the value of libraries (Barclay 2017; Brown and Malenfant 2016; Cabello and Butler 2017; Connaway et al. 2017; Halpin et al. 2015; Jaeger and Burnett 2010; Malenfant and Brown 2017; Oakleaf 2010; "The Value and Impact of Australian Public Libraries" 2017):

> Although the criteria for merit vary somewhat along the continuum, there is more overlap than typically realized. For example, basic research is judged by its clarity of purpose and interpretation, by its ability to support or refute particular hypotheses, by the incisiveness of the new hypotheses it generates, by the generalizability of the results, and by its technical accuracy, but in addition by the degree to which the results can be utilized in developing a product, a process, or a policy, to mention just a few types of application. (Sheridan 1988, 282)

Applied research, on the other hand, can validate theories and lead to the revision of theories. It "takes the theory and concepts from basic research and, by formal methods of inquiry, investigates 'real world' phenomena" (McClure 1989, 282).

Geographic information system (GIS) technology increasingly has been used in the library and information science (LIS) literature to identify library services by geographic areas (Johnston and Bishop 2011; March 2011; Sin 2011) and to visualize and map user activities in library spaces (Given and Archibald 2015; Mandel 2010; Nazari and Webber 2011). "A GIS is designed for the collection, storage, and analysis of objects and phenomena where geographic location is an important characteristic or critical to the analysis" (Cox and Gifford 1997). While not a basic research method itself, GIS technology is a data collection and analysis tool for research, especially applied research. Libraries have been using geographic information for decision making for the development of services and marketing (Barnes 2013; Brožová and Klimešová 2011; Elliott 2014; Mandel 2010). "The basic operations for GIS spatial analysis are: retrieval, map generalization, map abstractions, map sheet manipulation, buffer generation, polygon overlay and dissolve, measurements, digital terrain analyses, and network analyses" (Cox and Gifford 1997). Ottensmann (1977) discussed how geographic information systems can be employed to analyze patterns of library utilization in public libraries with multiple branches (Ottensmann 1997). Bishop and Mandel (2010) identified uses for GIS in library research, and Meuth and Costa (2011) discussed GIS trends in libraries. Koury, Downing, and Semenza (2012) provided an annotated guide to selected GIS resources. See also text box 2.2, Geographic Information Systems, by Bishop and Mandel in chapter 2.

EVALUATIVE RESEARCH AND ASSESSMENT

Evaluative or evaluation research, as a type of applied research, has as its primary goal not the discovery of knowledge but rather a testing of the application of knowledge within a specific program or project. Thus, it usually is practical or utilitarian in nature, and it generally is less useful than basic research for developing theoretical generalizations. Applegate (2013) authored the book *Practical Evaluation Techniques for Librarians*, which is a how-to manual for library evaluation. In most evaluative studies there is an implicit, if not explicit, hypothesis in which the dependent variable is a desired value, goal, or effect, such as better library skills and higher circulation statistics; the independent variable is often a program or service.

Evaluative research studies typically have a rather large number of uncontrolled variables, as they are carried out in real settings. They usually are limited in terms of time and space, and if the evaluative researchers have a vested interest in the project being evaluated, they are highly susceptible to bias. Two *general types* of evaluative research are summative evaluation and formative evaluation. *Summative*, or outcome, research is concerned with the effects of a program. It tends to be quantitative in nature and often is used as the basis for deciding whether a program will be continued. *Formative*, or process, evaluation, which is done during a program, not following its completion, examines how well the program is working. It often is more qualitative and frequently is used for revising and improving programs. In both types, feedback from program participants is usually considered important. Other broad categories that can encompass a variety of methods are quantitative, qualitative, subjective, and objective evaluation, as well as macroevaluation and microevaluation.

More *specific types* of evaluative research include the use of standards and cost analysis. "When applied to libraries . . . *standards* refer to a set of guidelines or recommended practices, developed by a group of experts that serve as a model for good library service" (Baker and Lancaster 1991, 321). Simple *cost analysis* is basically a descriptive breakdown of the costs incurred in operating an organization. Cost-related techniques more concerned with the assessment of whether monies are being spent in an optimal fashion usually fall into one of two groups: cost-effectiveness studies and cost-benefit analysis. "The term 'cost-effectiveness' implies a relationship between the cost of providing some service and the level of effectiveness of that service. . . . Cost-effective analyses can be thought of as studies of the costs associated with alternative strategies for achieving a particular level of effectiveness" (Lancaster 1993). Some examples of cost-effectiveness measures are the cost per relevant informational resource retrieved, cost per use of a resource, cost per user, cost per capita, and cost by satisfaction level (Lancaster 1993, 267; Matthews 2004).

Cost-effectiveness analysis can be seen as "a truncated form of cost-benefit analysis that stops short of putting an economic value on . . . outcomes [benefits] of programs" (Klarman 1982). "'Cost-benefit,' clearly, refers to a relationship between the cost of some activity and the benefits derived from it. . . . In effect, a cost-benefit study is one that tries to justify the existence of the activity by demonstrating that the benefits outweigh the costs" (Lancaster 1993). A typical cost-benefit analysis involves determining who benefits from and pays for a service, identifying the costs for each group of beneficiaries, identifying the benefits for each group, and comparing costs and benefits for each group to determine if groups have net benefits or net costs and whether the total benefits exceed the total costs.

Tenopir (2013) believed that determining total library value is difficult because every collection or service may be viewed from multiple perspectives during different time periods. She stated that most conceptualizations of value ultimately are concerned with user-centered outcomes, specifically, identifying what library users are able to do because of the academic library and to measure their levels of success. Tenopir described return on investment calculations and open-ended feedback as two of the methods that can be used to provide evidence of library value.

Lancaster identifies the following considerations for cost-benefit analysis (Tenopir 2013):

- Net value approach—the maximum amount the user of an information service is willing to pay minus the actual cost.
- Value of reducing uncertainty in decision making.
- Cost of buying service elsewhere.
- Librarian time replaces user time (i.e., the librarian saves the user time by performing their task).
- Service improves organization's performance or saves it money.

Other kinds of cost analysis, discussed by Weiss (1998) and Matthews (2004), are the following:

- **Cost-minimization analysis:** seeks to determine the least expensive way to accomplish some outcome.
- **Cost-utility analysis:** considers the value or worth of a specific outcome for an individual or society.
- **Willingness-to-pay approach:** asks how much individuals are willing to pay to have something they currently do not have.
- **Willingness-to-accept approach:** asks individuals how much they would be willing to accept to give up something they already have.
- **Cost of time approach:** seeks to determine the most efficient amount of time it takes to accomplish some outcome.

Performance measurement is another specific type of evaluative research. Performance or *output* measures are made to determine what was accomplished as a result of specific programs, services, and resources being available. Performance measures focus on indicators of library output and effectiveness, rather than merely on input such as monetary support, number of books, and number of staff. They clearly are related to the impact of the library on the community, are often concerned with user satisfaction, and can be used with longitudinal as well as current data. Other examples of performance measures have included service area penetration, level of use of facilities and equipment, circulation statistics, availability of materials and staff, and reference service use. Bertot, McClure, and Ryan, Lewis et al., and Bowlby provided examples of performance measures and assessment (Bertot, McClure, and Ryan 2001; Bowlby 2011; Lewis et al. 2013). Although output measures suggest user satisfaction, demand, and performance efficiency, they "do not describe performance or identify the outcomes or benefits resulting from the use of library services and systems" (Connaway 2014).

A variety of techniques can be used for measuring and describing performance; they have included the collection of analytics on the usage of systems and resources, questionnaires, interviews, observations, unobtrusive and virtual reference questions, diaries, consumer panels, and the fulfillment of resource requests. One approach to measuring the performance of libraries and other organizations is benchmarking (see, e.g., Johnson 2019). Benchmarking "represents a structured, proactive change effort designed to help achieve high performance through comparative assessment. It is a process that establishes an external standard to which intended operations can be compared" (Jurow 1993, 120). "Benchmarking not only allows for the establishment of a systematic process to indicate the quality of outputs, but also allows for an organization to create its own definition of quality for any process or output" (Peischl 1995). Most current LIS articles addressing benchmarking are specific to health science librarianship. Johnson (2019, 96) states that "health sciences librarians have long been involved in systematic reviews and are now involved in scoping reviews." It is critical to keep in mind, however, that whatever technique(s) is used to assess performance, it should be related to the organization's goals and objectives.

Other relatively recent attempts to evaluate the effectiveness of libraries have focused on their *outcomes* or actual *impact*. In other words, rather than stop with the measurement of output or performance, an increasing number of researchers are attempting to determine how the lives of individuals are actually affected by their use of libraries and other information resources and services. This is referred to as "user-centered assessment." For example, an impact assessment of a university library would go beyond measures of reference activity and circulation statistics and attempt to determine how the borrowing of books and procurement of answers to reference questions ultimately affect a student's test scores, papers, course grades, and so forth, that is, student success. Impact or effect may well be the most important indicator of a library's effectiveness and represents its most meaningful approach to accountability, but unfortunately, impact is elusive and no doubt more difficult to measure than input and performance. Steffen, Lance, and Logan (2002) measured the impact of public library services on the lives of library users, and Bogel (2012) reported that public library summer reading programs contribute to reading progress and proficiency in students entering the fourth grade. Closter (2015) provides a historical overview of how public libraries developed indicators for evaluating their services and programs. Lance (2002) also has completed studies for individual states to measure the impact of school libraries on student achievement. Lance and Kachel (2018) provide an overview of the school library impact studies that began in 1992 and that have been conducted in twenty-six states. The Association of College and Research Libraries (ACRL), a division of the American Library Association (ALA), has been at the forefront of articulating the value of academic libraries in the higher education community. It has published several reports (Connaway et al. 2017), white papers and reports ("White Papers and Reports" 2011), and presentations ("Presentations | ACRL Value of Academic Libraries" n.d.) and advocating the demonstration of the value of academic libraries through assessment. Several books have been published in the past few years outlining the trends in outcomes assessment for higher education and identifying the library's role in higher education (Matthews 2015).

The Performance Measurement Task Force of the Public Library Association (PLA) completed a three-year project to document best practices for assessment of public libraries called Project Outcome ("PLA | Project Outcome" 2019). There is a free toolkit ("PLA | Project Outcome" 2019) available with resources, training, and assessment tools, including surveys and other measurement and analysis tools to help public librarians assess and evaluate their programs and services. Linda Holfschire discusses public library assessment and evaluation in text box 14.1.

Text Box 14.1: Assessment Evaluations in Public Libraries

Linda Hofschire

Over the past decade, it has become increasingly critical for public libraries to provide data-based evidence to demonstrate their value to stakeholders to secure sufficient funding, as well as to inform decision making about programs and services when resources are limited. In response to this need, a variety of tools (e.g., Impact Survey, Project Outcome) and training opportunities (e.g., Research Institute for Public Libraries, Embedding Evaluation in Libraries) have been developed to equip public librarians to conduct assessment research.

I have been excited to observe and participate in these efforts because of the potential of assessment research to provide significant value to public libraries. By engaging in assessment, public libraries can serve their communities more effectively, as this work enables librarians to plan more strategically, determine how to improve programs and services, and provide evidence of their impact.

Here are a few tips for public librarians who are getting started with assessment:

- Be mindful of the importance of buy-in from internal stakeholders. To implement assessment successfully within your library, you need your administration and staff involved in the project to prioritize this work and to consider it worthy of their effort. Often this begins with starting small (e.g., conducting an assessment that requires minimal resources but produces useful results) so that internal stakeholders can experience the value that assessment brings to their work.
- Develop carefully crafted research questions. Research questions should be specific, relevant, and answerable via empirical research methods.
- Remain focused on your research questions. When developing data collection instruments, it is tempting to add items about a variety of topics as you consider the many things that would be *nice* to know. Instead, limit yourself to items that will provide the information you *need* to know in order to answer your research questions. This approach minimizes burden for study participants and keeps your work strategic and efficient.
- Develop a peer network for feedback and support. Learning to conduct assessment is a journey, and one that is most successful when there are peers by your side.

For examples of assessment research about public library programs and services, please see the following studies that assessed the effects of early literacy programs and services on children and caregivers. Both studies found positive outcomes, including that children participating in storytimes demonstrated early literacy skills (Campana et al. 2016), and that caregivers participating in early literacy programs reported increased knowledge of how children learn to read and confidence that they could prepare their children to be ready to learn to read in kindergarten (Crist et al. 2020).

References

Campana, Kathleen, J. Elizabeth Mills, Janet L. Capps, Eliza T. Dresang, Allyson Carlyle, Cheryl A. Metoyer, Ivette Bayo Urban, et al. 2016. "Early Literacy in Library Storytimes: A

Study of Measures of Effectiveness." *The Library Quarterly* 86(4): 369–88. https://doi.org /10.1086/688028.

Crist, Beth, Courtney Vidacovich Donovan, Miranda Doran-Myers, and Linda Hofschire. 2020. "Supporting Parents in Early Literacy through Libraries (SPELL): An Evaluation of a Multi-Site Library Project." *Public Library Quarterly* 39(2): 89–101. https://doi.org/10.1080 /01616846.2019.1622070.

"Embedded Evaluation in Libraries." 2020. https://www.libraryeval.org.

"Impact Survey." 2019. Text. Public Library Association (PLA). http://www.ala.org/pla /initiatives/impactsurvey.

"PLA | Project Outcome." 2019. https://www.projectoutcome.org.

"Research Institute for Public Libraries." 2020. https://ripl.lrs.org.

A Project Outcome toolkit (https://acrl.projectoutcome.org) also is available for academic libraries. It provides resources for academic librarians to assess and evaluate their programs and services. Case study reports are available as examples of how the toolkit can be used by academic librarians. See text box 14.2, Assessment Evaluations in Academic Libraries, by Lisa Janicke Hinchliffe.

Text Box 14.2: Assessment Evaluations in Academic Libraries

Lisa Janicke Hinchliffe

For me, the value of assessment is that it prompts reflecting on why we are doing the things we are doing. By articulating what we are seeking to achieve, we are positioned to evaluate if we are achieving our goals and if we are investing resources to maximum benefit. Attending to effectiveness and efficiency, we can identify where we are succeeding and where there is opportunity to improve.

I believe librarians develop programs that they believe will have the greatest impact based on the information they have at the time. Assessment adds to what is known and, if something does not work as anticipated, that is useful. Keeping a learning mind-set is important for library assessment. Specific methods and tools should be chosen based on context; however, a learning mind-set applies in all settings at all times.

I've had the opportunity to be involved with a wide range of assessment projects ranging from quick polling on customer service satisfaction to formal program evaluation for accreditation review. One project, done almost two decades ago, influenced me greatly—a comprehensive assessment of the basic communication course at Illinois State University—where I had a chance to learn from two outstanding program coordinators, Cheri Simonds and Stephen Hunt (Hinchliffe et al. 2003; Hunt, Simonds, and Hinchliffe 2001).

The lessons I learned from that project include the value of having assessment mentors. I've had the honor of that role as the curriculum lead for *CARLI Counts*, a leadership program preparing Illinois librarians to make use of the data on the impact of academic libraries on student success for service development and library advocacy. *CARLI Counts* builds on ACRL's Value of Academic Libraries Initiative (2011) and particularly *Assessment in*

Action, a national professional development program for which I served as colead facilitator. The participant project reports from these programs illustrate the power of library assessment ("Assessment in Action: Academic Libraries and Student Success" 2012; "CARLI Counts | CARLI" 2020).

References

"Assessment in Action: Academic Libraries and Student Success." 2012. Text. Association of College & Research Libraries (ACRL). October 9. http://www.ala.org/acrl/AiA.

"CARLI Counts | CARLI." 2020. https://www.carli.illinois.edu/products-services/prof-devel/carli-counts.

Hinchliffe, Lisa, C. Kubiak, S. Hunt, and C. Simonds. 2003. "What Students Really Cite: Findings from a Content Analysis of First-Year Student Bibliographies." In *Proceedings of the 30th Annual National LOEX Library Instruction Conference*, 69–74. Ann Arbor, MI.

Hunt, S., C. Simonds, and L. Hinchliffe. 2001. "Using Student Portfolios as Authentic Assessment." *Journal of Excellence in College Teaching* 11(1): 57–77.

"Value of Academic and Research Libraries." 2011. Text. Association of College & Research Libraries (ACRL). September 13. http://www.ala.org/acrl/issues/value.

OCLC Research through WebJunction developed a three-webinar series for librarians of all types of libraries titled "Evaluating and Sharing Your Library's Impact" ("Webinar Series: Evaluating and Sharing Your Library's Impact" 2020). The recordings and learner guide are available on the series web page ("Webinar Series: Evaluating and Sharing Your Library's Impact" 2020). There also are several blog posts (Connaway 2018a, 2018b) that highlight the takeaways from the webinars and other library evaluation and assessment sources.

Much discussion of assessing library *service quality* is based on customer feedback (Hernon and Altman 1998; Hernon and Whitman 2001). Hernon and Dugan (2002) argued that outcomes assessment must be linked to accountability, which can be measured by user satisfaction and service quality. The economic environment, the convenience of the internet, and the phenomenon of mega-book stores, both online and physical, have encouraged librarians to view library users as customers and to develop library services accordingly. This approach, derived from the business world, "cannot adequately be conveyed by output and performance measures" (Hernon and Altman 1998). In an attempt to assess users' perceptions of library services, the Association of Research Libraries (ARL) offers LibQUAL+ to all types of libraries. It is "a web-based survey that helps libraries assess and improve library services, change organizational culture, and market the library. [The] instrument enables systematic assessment and measurement of library service quality, over time and across institutions" ("LibQUAL+®" n.d.).

With regard to *methods and techniques*, evaluative research is much like basic research. Verification of the explicit or implicit hypothesis requires a design that will show that the desired effect was more likely to occur in the presence of the program than in its absence. Evaluative researchers must be concerned with threats to validity, such as intervening variables, measurement techniques, and faulty operational definitions. Evaluation research conceivably can employ most of the same methods that are used in basic research. Such methods are often labeled according to their primary design (survey, experiment, and the like). Another approach to categorizing evaluation methods used in library and information science is according to the program, service, or resource to be evaluated. A book by Wallace and Van Fleet (2001) has chapters devoted to the evaluation of reference and information services and to library collections, and Connaway and Radford have evaluated virtual reference services (VRS) from a user-centered perspective (Connaway and Radford 2010, 2011; Radford and Connaway 2010, 2012, 2013; Radford, Connaway, et al. 2011; Radford, Radford, et al. 2011). Radford, Costello, and Montague (2020) reported on changes and evaluations of VRS in academic libraries during the COVID-19 pandemic. Other researchers have also evaluated VRS (e.g., see Hunter et al. 2019; Keyes and Dworak 2017). An issue of *Library Trends* has chapters on the evaluation of administrative services, collections, processing services, adult reference service, public services for adults, public library services for children, and school library media services. Lancaster's text includes the evaluation of collections, collection use, in-house library use, periodicals, library space, catalog use, document delivery, reference services, and resource sharing. Matthews' (2017) book *The Evaluation and Measurement of Library Services* "is a comprehensive guide to library assessment and communicating library value" and is a great resource for learning about and "implementing library evaluation and measurement programs" (Hinchliffe 2017).

Much of the assessment literature on academic libraries focuses on student achievement and retention. As previously mentioned in this chapter, the ACRL AiA program has an online collection of individual AiA project reports (Malenfant 2012), and the *Academic Library Impact: Improving Practice and Essential Areas to Research* (Connaway et al. 2017) report also highlights studies on the impact of the academic library on student learning and success and the data collection and analysis methods used as well as how to communicate the academic library's value to higher education stakeholders.

As demonstrated by the studies discussed above, the researcher must collect data or measure what needs to be measured in order to conduct an evaluative study. *Measurement* by itself is not true evaluation, but it is one of the building blocks for quantitative evaluation. Common types of measures for library evaluation studies include number and types of users, number and duration of transactions, user and staff activities, user satisfaction levels, and costs of resources and services. They can be related to input, output, effectiveness, costs, and so forth.

It is critical that the measurement process and the measures be reasonably high in reliability and validity. The validity and/or reliability of measures can be affected by such factors as inconsistent data collection techniques, biases of the observer, the data collection setting, instrumentation, behavior of human subjects, and sampling. The use of multiple measures can help to increase the validity and reliability of the data. They are also worth using because no single technique is up to measuring a complex concept, multiple measures tend to complement one another, and separate measures can be combined to create one or more composite measures (Weiss 1998). (See chapter 4 for further consideration of validity and reliability.)

Many measures are in the form of *statistics*, which in some cases can be drawn from already existing sources of data. Types of statistics include administrative data, financial statistics, collections and other resources or inputs, use and other output/performance measures, outcomes, and staff and salary information. Sources of statistics include governmental agencies, professional associations, and other organizations such as state library agencies. Among the noteworthy sources of library-related statistics are the National Center for Education Statistics (NCES) ("Library Statistics Program" n.d.), the ACRL's Trends and Statistics series ("Academic Library Statistics" 2006), ARL ("ARL Statistics® Survey" n.d.), and federal programs such as the Federal State Cooperative System ("Public Libraries Survey" 2015) and the Integrated Postsecondary Education Data System (IPEDS) ("Integrated Postsecondary Education Data System (IPEDS) | Office of Decision Support | University of South Florida" n.d.). Crawford (2015) used the NCES IPEDS and Academic Library Surveys from 1,328 institutions to determine if there was a relationship between institutional and library expenses, library use, and graduation and retention rates. (See chapter 10 for additional information about sources of statistical data.) The collection of data, must, of course, be followed by an *analysis* of data, as is the case for any other kind of research.

There are many studies addressing evaluation and assessment research that can be consulted for those who wish to know more about this topic (e.g., see Ackermann and Kremer 2015; Admin. 2006; Britto and Kinsley 2018; Dobbs 2017; Forbes and Bowers 2014; Harker and Klein 2016; Hoffman 2016; Mallon et al. 2019; Marquez and Downey 2016; McCartin and Dineen 2018; Montgomery 2017; Oakleaf 2010, 2018). The book titled *The Evaluation and Measurement of Library Services* (Matthews 2017) devotes considerable attention to evaluation process and models, methodological concerns, issues related to the evaluation of specific types of libraries and library services, and how to communicate the results of an evaluative study.

ACTION RESEARCH

A major type of applied research, and one sometimes treated interchangeably with applied research, is action research. However, action research differs from applied research in that "it has direct application to the immediate workplace of the researcher, whereas applied research may have the broader purpose of improving the profession at large" (Togia and Malliari 2017). Togia and Malliari (2017, 48) state that action research "aims at solving problems and bringing about change in organizations." Isaac and Michael (1995) assert that the purpose of action research is "to develop new skills or new approaches and to solve problems with direct application to the classroom or working world setting." They characterize action research as practical, orderly, flexible and adaptive, and empirical to a degree, but weak in internal and external validity.

Isaac and Michael identified the following basic steps in action research:

1. Defining the problem or setting the goal.
2. Reviewing the literature.
3. Formulating testable hypotheses.
4. Arranging the research setting.
5. Establishing measurement techniques and evaluation criteria.
6. Analyzing the data and evaluating the results. (Isaac and Michael 1995, 59)

Sagor identified four sequential stages in the action research process:

1. Clarifying vision and targets;
2. Articulating theory;
3. Implementing action and collecting data; and
4. Reflecting on the data and planning informed action. (Sagor 2005, 6–7, 10)

It is important to remember that the process is cyclical, which means it is continuous. It shifts from action and critical reflection, with continuous refinement and interpretation based on what is learned in the earlier cycles.

As can be seen, these steps do not differ significantly from those typically followed in a basic research study. Sometimes these steps may be carried out somewhat less rigorously than for basic research, and hypotheses, if any, may be treated in a more flexible manner, but this is not the intent of action research. Typically, the data are provided to library decision makers, who in turn take some action; for example, they may improve a service, develop a new one, or discontinue a service.

Kristiansson (2007) made a case for the use of scenario planning as "an accompanying tool in the context of action research." The purpose for building scenarios is to address critical events and uncertain conditions and to create action plans. The technique provides opportunities for generating new ideas, which can be used for library strategic planning.

As an action research technique, scenario planning involves workshops or dialogue sessions "where participants discuss library development with focus on strategies, practices and knowledge about the library's surroundings" (Kristiansson 2007). Scenario planning provides an opportunity for library staff to gather information in a structured environment to create plans of action.

Innovation Research

Innovation research also can be used for library strategic planning. It is a type of action research since it is centered on identifying solutions where there are gaps within an organization or market. It is used for introducing or significantly improving a product, service, practice, and technology.

Studies suggest that innovations in public libraries include technology, access to information, and better services for patrons and diverse communities (Gorham and Bertot 2018). Innovations can increase the value of public libraries in their communities (Skinner 2017). Potnis, Winberry, Finn, and Hunt (2019, 30) reported 80 innovations in 108 award-winning public libraries in the United States. The authors concluded that some of the identified innovations are "commonly implemented initiatives."

Innovation can be disruptive, which is exactly what Mathews (2012) believes is needed in libraries. Although the white paper was published quite a while ago, the message still resonates although some of the examples are dated. Mathews encourages librarians to strive for entrepreneurialism. "Don't think about better vacuum cleaners, think about cleaner floors," is Mathews' (2012, 1) advice. He believes in libraries there is "too much assessment, not enough innovation" (Mathews 2012). However, as previously discussed in this chapter, librarians spend much time on assessment, which is rooted in providing evidence to make policy and procedural decisions.

Evidence-Based Research

Evidence-based research for decision making could be considered a type of applied or action research and has become very popular in the LIS domain. This interest may have been spurred by the twentieth-century movement in health care and policy that calls for health care professionals to make decisions for medical practice based on the current best evidence provided by medical research and data. In an economic environment of decreasing library budgets for staff, materials, and services and increasing library usage, there is a demand for library and information professionals to make decisions based on current valid data.

The quarterly open-access journal *Evidence Based Library and Information Practice* was first published in 2006 "to provide a forum for librarians and other information professionals to discover research that may contribute to decision making in professional practice" ("Evidence Based Library and Information Practice" n.d.) Evidence-based research "reflects both the efforts of practitioners, who 'consume' the results of research in making those decisions, and the efforts of applied researchers, who strive to 'produce' the research evidence intended for use by practitioners" (Eldredge 2006). Recent articles published in the journal emphasize assessment, especially user-centered assessment (Connaway 2014), as a major part of the decision-making process. Evidence-based research has been addressed by professional organizations, practitioners, and researchers.

Evidence-based practice is quite prevalent in the LIS literature and as conference themes. The 10th International Evidence Based Library and Information Practice Conference was held at the University of Strathclyde in Glasgow, Scotland, in June 2019. Todd (2008) makes the case for school librarians to provide evidence to ensure their existence ("10th International Evidence

Based Library and Information Practice Conference" 2019). This interest in evidence-based school librarianship continues. Hughes (2014) reviews international and Australian research addressing the impacts of school libraries and teacher librarians. She makes recommendations for evidence-based research to "advance school libraries and teacher-librarians and enhance student learning" (Hughes 2014). Richey and Cahill (2014) surveyed public school librarians in Texas to identify if and how they applied evidence-based practice. The findings indicated that a large number of the respondents read professional journals and applied what they learned to actual practice. The researchers also reported that they collected informal evidence within their school communities. The findings also indicated that 54.9 percent of the school librarians who responded to the survey reported they collected either quantitative or qualitative data to evaluate the extent to which they met their library program goals.

OCLC has a data science research area to enhance, mine, and expose traditional library data to provide intelligence to librarians to make informed decisions ("Data Science" n.d.). OCLC research scientists also have published numerous papers and presentations using library-generated data, including WorldCat data (Lavoie 2020a, 2020b; Lavoie and Dempsey 2020; Lavoie, Dempsey, and Malpas 2020; Lavoie and Malpas 2015; Lavoie et al. 2015; Malpas and Lavoie 2020) to make collection decisions for preservation, digitization, sharing, storing, and deaccessioning; to compare collections; to identify the characteristics of collections; and to determine whether to provide resources in electronic or paper format. The prevalence of the literature addressing evidence-based research exemplifies the interest and importance this method has continued to gain in the library and information professions in the past several years.

Community-Based and Participatory Research

Community-based research (CBR) is a type of action research that is used to understand the problems associated with social systems and to change them (Troppe 1994). Often referred to as community-based participatory research (CBPR) "originally developed in public health research . . . to address the complex social, economic, and physical factors—such as poverty, air pollution, racism, inadequate housing, and income inequalities that play a role in determining health status" (libparlorcontributor 2019). CBPR not only is conducted in community settings, but also involves community members in the research design and dissemination and implementation of the findings. The influence, control, and participation of nonacademics in the entire research process is critical (Israel et al. 2001).

CBPR also is being used in LIS and computer science research. Senteio (2019) designed a study for an intervention for health information and technology education to older adult African Americans with diabetes and young adults, who are connected to them. Unertl et al. ("Differences between Community-Based Research, Community-Based Participatory Research, and Action Research | Institute for Civic and Community Engagement" n.d.)

compared five health informatics research projects that used CBPR. The authors reported that using CBPR for health informatics research provided more relevant research with a greater impact, a higher degree of engagement with diverse populations, improved internal validity, the opportunity for the development of individuals, and a faster transition from research to action. However, they also identified some challenges of applying CBPR to health informatics research, such as the need to develop requirements for creating sustainable academic-community partnerships and ownership of technology outputs, and to build technical capacity with community partners, also emerged from our analysis. "CBR has as its goal: to achieve social justice through social action and social change" (Institute for Civic and Community Engagement n.d.), which is the focus of much LIS research in the current socioeconomic environment.

SOCIAL JUSTICE RESEARCH

Social justice research is based on the premise that everyone should have equal access to health care, information, justice, and economic opportunity. Librarianship is built on the principles of intellectual freedom and access to information for all regardless of race, economic and educational levels, gender identity, ideas, or religious and political beliefs. Hence research in social justice is of great importance to LIS.

There are five goals of social justice: access to resources, equity (provision of equitable resources that focus on the needs of communities and their members), diversity, participation in policy making by diverse groups, and human rights regardless of socioeconomic status (freedom of speech, voting rights, and other basic rights) ("The Five Principles of Social Justice" n.d.).

There is much literature representing the multiple dimensions of social justice research in LIS. In 2015 Jaeger, Shilton, and Koepfler (2015) identify the growing attention to social justice research in the professional and scholarly communications of libraries, archives, and museums. The heightened interest in social justice research not only directly aligns with the principles of librarianship, but also with the current global environment. In an opinion piece Xie et al. (2020) made a case that global health crises, such as the COVID-19 pandemic, also are information crises. They recommended needed changes in information science in order to take a lead role in responding to health crises and proposed actions that can be taken for research, education, and practice in information science.

Social justice research also has addressed the biases being identified in library practices and procedures, such as classification systems, vocabularies, knowledge management (Adler 2016; Adler and Harper 2018; Drabinski 2013; Howard and Knowlton 2018; *Made Here | Change the Subject | Season 9 | Episode 22* n.d.), and algorithms developed for discovery and access (Bogost 2015; Reidsma 2019). Access to information and the technology that often is needed to get to that information, often referred to as the digital divide (Aqili and Isfandyari-Moghaddam 2008; Pun 2020; Thompson and Paul 2015; Webber 2020; Willcox 2020), is prevalent in the LIS literature. Dadlani and

Todd (2016) examined high school students' perceptions of social justice while working on a group project and provide an example of how social justice principles can be used in libraries and information organizations. Chu promotes the need to adopt a framework for the scholarship of dialogue in LIS research, which is described in text box 14.3.

Text Box 14.3: Scholarship of Dialogue

Clara M. Chu

Bias, privilege, and exclusion have historically riddled social research, contributing to racism, sexism, classism, and other forms of implicit or explicit oppression. Researchers from the Global North or majority communities have privileged and applied Western methods of research, often as "drive-by" researchers, in their efforts to learn about or support marginalized or developing communities. Considered authorities and advocating objectivity, social researchers have treated these communities as objects rather than subjects. This was obvious at the 2004 IADIS International Conference on Web Based Communities (WBC) in Lisbon, which led to my critical examination of the conference, exposing the need to identify underrepresented voices in cybercommunities, their participation or nonparticipation in research and their nonrepresentation at the conference (Chu 2005). At the WBC conference, researchers expressed interest in the success/welfare of the researched communities, with emphasis on "helping" rather than empowering such communities, on providing solutions rather than creating local sustainable practices, and on speaking of and obtaining recognition for their research rather than enabling researched communities to speak in their own voices. Consequently, I promulgated a scholarship of dialogue to enhance the coverage and process of future WBC conferences and research, and here it is promoted for library and information science (LIS) research.

A scholarship of dialogue is a framework for rethinking and reformulating who conducts research, how it will be conducted, what the focus of the research will be, how it will be disseminated, who provides the leadership, and who speaks for the diverse and marginalized constituencies that are the focus of research. Multiple new and indigenous voices and forms of research will join the established and privileged.

A scholarship of dialogue is my interpretation of Paulo Freire's (Freire and Bergman Ramos 1970) pedagogical practice of dialogue, which involves respect, critical thinking, praxis, and conscientization, and interpreting it to provide a framework for conducting, discussing, examining, and disseminating research. Respect involves active inclusion and an egalitarian and cooperative approach in the development, study, and knowledge dissemination of researched communities. Respect emphasizes agency, acting for oneself in the research process, including its dissemination. Critical thinking is concerned with challenging normativity, naming privileges or top-down power relationships to redraw them, and identifying differences for what they are rather than casting judgments about whether they are better or worse than something. Critical thinking allows the naming of exclusionary practices or scholarship to change them. Praxis, or informed action, enables reciprocal learning, whereby each person is willing to both share knowledge (communities about their structure and values, developers their technical know-how, and researchers their methodology) and learn from the perspectives and questions of others. Each person's experiences, knowledge, and perspectives are valued for themselves, and not determined to be richer or poorer than another's, instituted as high or low culture, or qualified as folk versus modern practice. Conscientization is an awareness of the social world and the development of consciousness to the level where one wants to transform reality in order to create social change. Thus, a scholarship of dialogue fosters reciprocity, equity, diversity, and inclusion in community-engaged research in a proactive struggle against bias, privilege, and exclusion.

References

Chu, Clara M. 2005. "Web-Based Communities Scholarship: From Silence to Dialogue." *International Journal of Web Based Communities* 1(4): 423. https://doi.org/10.1504/IJWBC .2005.008108.

Freire, Paulo, and Myra Bergman Ramos. 1970. *Pedagogy of the Oppressed*. A Continuum Book. New York: Herder and Herder.

There is a body of literature that addresses the inequities of the library profession. These range from LGQBT and other gender inequities; to acism (Brook, Ellenwood, and Lazzaro 2015; Chancellor 2019; Cooke 2016, 2019a, 2019b; Cooke and Sánchez 2019; Gibson 2019; Gibson et al. 2017; Gibson and Hughes-Hassell 2017; Hill 2019; Hudson 2017; Kendrick and Damasco 2019), whether unconscious or conscious; to marginalized populations (Caidi 2021a, 2021b; Caidi, McDonald, and Chien 2012; Dowdell and Liew 2019; Fisher 2018, 2019a, 2019b; Fisher and The Zaatari Camp Librarians 2020; Fisher et al. 2019; Talhouk et al. 2019; Tewell 2018, 2019; Walsh 2018), such as homeless individuals, migrants, and those diagnosed with mental illness or substance abuse.

A recent research project, funded by the Institute for Museum and Library Services (IMLS), *Public Libraries Respond to the Opioid Crisis with Their Communities* (2020), was conducted by OCLC and the PLA, a division of ALA, to study how public libraries in the United States have responded to the opioid crisis by partnering with other community agencies. Eight public libraries in different regions of the United States and in communities that differed in size and based on community demographics and uninsured rate, unemployment data, opioid prescribing rates, and opioid overdoes rates were selected for the case studies. The research team spent several days on-site at each of the eight public libraries to review policy and procedure documentation and to conduct interviews with library staff, library board members, staff at community partner organizations, and community members, who had been affected by the opioid crisis. There are many outputs from the research—journal articles (Allen et al. 2019; Coleman and Connaway 2019; Coleman, Connaway, and Morgan 2020), a call to action (Allen et al. 2020a), case study reports (Allen et al. 2020b), and a summary report (Allen et al. 2019) as well as webinars ("Public Libraries Respond to the Opioid Crisis with Their Communities: Webinars" 2019).

Librarians and library associations have been addressing how they can impact the United Nations 2030 Agenda for Sustainable Development ("Transforming Our World: The 2030 Agenda for Sustainable Development" n.d.). The agenda includes seventeen Sustainable Development Goals (SDGs) ("United Nations Sustainable Development Goals" n.d.) that include targets and indicators. The International Federation of Library Associations and Institutions (IFLA) International Advocacy Program ("Libraries, Development and the United

Nations 2030 Agenda" n.d.) supports libraries in planning and implementing the UN 2030 Agenda and the SDGs. In March 2020 the ALA created the Task Force on United Nations 2030 Sustainable Development Goals to develop a strategic plan "to increase participation by libraries in efforts to achieve the Goals" (Dguerra 2020). The 2020 Annual Meeting of the Association for Information Science and Technology (ASIS&T) selected as its theme Information for a Sustainable World: Addressing Society's Grand Challenges, which included research and sessions addressing the SDGs. The OCLC Global Council also selected the SDGs as its 2020 area of focus, with webinar offerings ("OCLC Global Council: Webinars" 2020) and the dissemination of a survey to identify the impact that libraries can have on the SDGs ("Sustainable Development and Libraries" 2020). Excerpts of the survey were included in chapter 5 as examples. For a discussion of how libraries are making an impact on the SDGs, see text box 14.4, Impact of Libraries on the Sustainable Development Goals, by Christopher Cyr.

Text Box 14.4: Impact of Libraries on the Sustainable Development Goals

Christopher Cyr

In recent years, librarians and information scientists have taken an interest in the United Nations (UN) Sustainable Development Goals (SDGs). "Information for a Sustainable World" was the theme for the Association for Information Science and Technology 2020 annual meeting (Association for Information Science and Technology (ASIST) 2015), the OCLC Global Council selected the SDGs as its Area of Focus for 2021, and the American Library Association created an SDG task force "to develop a multi-year strategic plan in the coming year to increase participation by libraries in efforts to achieve the Goals" (ALA 2020). What are the SDGs, and how can you incorporate them into your research?

Adopted by the UN, in 2015, the SDGs are a list of seventeen goals for global development by the year 2030 (Martin 2015). These goals are broad in nature and cover topics such as poverty, education, infrastructure, climate change, and peace. They are an expansion of a previous effort, carried out by the UN from 2000 to 2015, which included eight Millennium Development Goals.

Librarians played an important role both in shaping and implementing the SDGs. They were most directly involved in Goal 16 (Peace, Justice, and Strong Institutions), where they successfully lobbied for access to information to be included as subgoal 16.10. The Lyon Declaration, drafted by the International Federation of Library Associations (IFLA) and signed by more than 600 libraries, advocated for access to information to be included in order to "ensure that everyone has access to, and is able to understand, use and share the information that is necessary to promote sustainable development and democratic societies" ("About I The Lyon Declaration" n.d.).

Just as librarians have incorporated the SDGs into their activities, you can incorporate them into your research. One way to do this is to use them as a framework for understanding the impact of your research. For example, the Researching Students' Information Choices project (University of Florida, https://guides.uflib.ufl.edu/c.php?g=147840&p=966402), which examines the ways that students evaluate scientific information on the internet, directly is related to Goal 4 (Quality Education), with indirect connections to Goal 9 (Industry,

Innovation, and Infrastructure) and Goal 16 (Peace, Justice, and Strong Institutions). Thinking about the project in this context can give guidance for specific recommendations based on your research. A recent report endeavored to do this at a broad level, placing more than 500,000 publications in the context of the seventeen SDGs ("New Digital Science Report Analyses State of the World's Research on the UN's Sustainable Development Goals" 2020).

While the SDGs provide a useful framework for thinking about research, it is important to maintain focus when thinking about the broader impact of a project. Because the seventeen SDGs are interconnected, most projects conceivably can have implications for all of them, so it is important to think about which goals your research could have the greatest impact on and focus on those. Maintaining this focus can allow you to think about your research in the global context without making it overly broad.

References

"About | The Lyon Declaration." n.d. Accessed October 16, 2020. https://www.lyondeclaration.org/about.

"ALA Task Force on United Nations 2030 Sustainable Development Goals." Text. About ALA. April 20, 2020. http://www.ala.org/aboutala/ala-task-force-united-nations-2030-sustainable-development-goals.

Association for Information Science and Technology (ASIST). 2015. "Detailed Conference Program." https://www.asis.org/asist2014/program.html.

Martin. 2015. "Sustainable Development Goals Kick Off with Start of New Year." *United Nations Sustainable Development* (blog). https://www.un.org/sustainabledevelopment/blog/2015/12/sustainable-development-goals-kick-off-with-start-of-new-year.

"New Digital Science Report Analyses State of the World's Research on the UN's Sustainable Development Goals." 2020. *Digital Science.* May 7. https://www.digital-science.com/blog/news/new-digital-science-report-analyses-state-of-the-worlds-research-on-the-uns-sustainable-development-goals.

UF, Tara Cataldo. n.d. "Guides @ UF: Researching Students' Information Choices: Home." Accessed October 16, 2020. https://guides.uflib.ufl.edu/RSIC/home.

There has been much written in the LIS education literature about the integration of social justice into the curriculum (Cooke 2019a; Dali and Caidi 2020; Fritch 2018; Gibson and Hughes-Hassell 2017; Gibson, Hughes-Hassell, and Threats 2018; Hudson 2017; Irvin 2019; Kumasi and Manlove 2015; Mehra 2019; Noble and Sullivan 2014). This may help in addressing some of the current challenges of first recruiting diverse individuals into librarianship and then welcoming and retaining them.

DECOLONIZING METHODOLOGIES

"A decolonising research methodology is an approach that is used to challenge the Eurocentric research methods that undermine the local knowledge and experiences of the marginalised population groups" (Keikelame and Swartz 2019, 1). It is important to use a lens that reflects the groups that are being studied. In this way the researcher and those who are being researched (the participants) share equal power. The researcher does not have power over those being researched. When working with indigenous people, it is critical to be respectful of their traditions and culture in order to build relationships (Dankowski 2020). It also is crucial to share the findings of the research "in culturally appropriate ways and in language that can be understood" (Smith and Books 2012). Tolia-Kelly and Raymond (2020) explore the effects of imperialism of other cultures through practices and representations at museums. See text box 14.5 for Lilley's discussion of indigenous research methodologies.

Text Box 14.5: Indigenous Research Methodologies

Spencer Lilley

A rewarding aspect of conducting research in an indigenous environment is the opportunity to develop strong relationships with the community you work with. Past approaches to research with indigenous peoples focused mostly on observations and understanding of the researcher, who "owned" the project and its outcomes. In contrast, indigenous approaches focus on creation of an environment where the researcher becomes part of the community; the research is collaborative. As a researcher, it is imperative to locate oneself and be open about your background; who you are; where you are from (including any indigenous affiliations); what has influenced your life; and how this has impacted on your development as a person and researcher.

Researchers also need to be conscious that indigenous peoples should determine what research they wish to engage with, which might require negotiation with elders/advisers within the community. Indigenous research usually involves the use of qualitative data-gathering techniques which are respectful of that communities' values and beliefs. Critical to the analysis of data collected is an understanding of the communities' worldview, requiring an indigenous lens to be used. This understanding can be very challenging for a non-indigenous researcher and might require further collaboration with indigenous researchers or an advisory board, to ensure codes and themes used during qualitative data analysis reflect the values, customs, and beliefs of the community. Researchers also need to understand that indigenous peoples are socially and culturally diverse; what works with one community will not necessarily apply elsewhere. Consult Lilley (2018) for a stronger insight into indigenous research methods and their application, and Smith (2012) for an understanding of the relationship between indigenous peoples and research.

References

Lilley, Spencer. 2018. "Methodologies for Conducting Research in an Indigenous Context." *Library and Information Research* 42(126): 72–94. https://doi.org/10.29173/lirg751.
Smith, Linda Tuhiwai. 2012. *Decolonizing Methodologies: Research and Indigenous Peoples.* 2nd ed. London: Zed Books.

POLICY RESEARCH

The ALA supports advocacy and public policy in the areas of "library funding, broadband equity, e-rate, fair use and balanced copyright, and equitable access to digital content" ("Advocacy and Public Policy" 2020). Dick Kawooya, in text box 14.6, provides more information on the importance of public policy research.

Text Box 14.6: What Is Policy Research and Why Is It Important?

Dick Kawooya

Policy research or policy studies, whether public or information policy, takes on different forms that reflect the purpose of the research. Policy research can be studies of policy content; studies of policy process; studies of policy outputs; evaluation studies (evaluating policy implementation); information for policy making; process advocacy; policy advocacy, and analysis of analysis (Browne 1997). My policy research, in the areas of copyrights and access to information, and intellectual property and innovation, encompasses a combination of the above approaches (Armstrong and De Beer 2010; Kawooya 2008).

I am interested in understanding the intersection between policy content, processes, policy making, and advocacy. I study people's interpretation of laws and policies, and how that translates into practice at individual and institutional levels. I often start off with doctrinal review of the law, copyright in this case, to gain a deep understanding of the legal traditions, statutory provisions, case law where applicable, and administrative and regulatory aspects of the law. The doctrinal review is followed by the analysis of practices, which encompasses everything from individual understanding of the law to how institutions interpret and implement laws and policies through institutional policies and procedures. I recognize that laws do not exist in a vacuum. Policy research is most complete when people and an institutional interpretation of laws are analyzed alongside the doctrinal analysis of the law. Finally, I do advocacy because policy is about people and their ability to access and use information. The goal is for the policy research to influence public policy (Jaeger, Taylor, and Inouye 2019).

References

Armstrong, Chris, and Jeremy De Beer. 2010. *Access to Knowledge in Africa: The Role of Copyright.* Cape Town, South Africa: UCT Press. https://library.oapen.org/handle/20.500 .12657/25283.

Browne, Mairéad. 1997. "The Field of Information Policy: 2. Redefining the Boundaries and Methodologies." *Journal of Information Science* 23(5): 339–51. https://doi.org/10.1177 /016555159702300501.

Jaeger, Paul T., Natalie Greene Taylor, and Alan Inouye. 2019. *Foundations of Information Policy.* Chicago: ALA Neal-Schuman.

Kawooya, Dick. 2008. "An Examination of Institutional Policy on Copyright and Access to Research Resources in Uganda***." *International Information & Library Review* 40(4): 226–35. https://doi.org/10.1080/10572317.2008.10762787.

INTERNATIONAL AND COMPARATIVE LIBRARIANSHIP

Parker's definition of international librarianship still is relevant today and continues to be used by the scholars studying in this area:

International librarianship consists of activities carried out among or between governmental or non-governmental institutions, organizations, groups or individuals of two or more nations, to promote, establish, develop, maintain and evaluate library, documentation and allied services, and librarianship and the library profession generally, in any part of the world. (Parker 1974)

Lor, one of the premiere scholars in international and comparative librarianship and whose discussion of doing research in international comparative LIS follows, states, "international librarianship is a field of activity, rather than a scientific discipline" (2010a). This does not mean that international librarianship should not be studied scientifically. As previously discussed with social justice research, international librarianship continues to be of great importance to scholarship and practice. See Lor's text box 14.7 for additional thoughts on international and comparative research in LIS.

Constantinou, Miller, and Schlesinger (2017) provide case studies of American librarians who traveled to other countries to participate in sponsored programs to address issues associated with the provisions of information sharing and equitable access of information and technology in different socioeconomic environments. Bordonaro (2017) calls for reframing the attitudes and practice of international librarianship through inclusivity and positivity and transitioning from international librarianship to global librarianship:

Often international and comparative librarianship are discussed together as demonstrated in this chapter. There is a long-standing debate over whether comparative librarianship is a research method or a subject matter. As a subject, it deals with phenomena in librarianship that can be compared. As a research method, it provides the framework for conducting an appropriate comparative analysis. In either case, comparative librarianship often has an international element.

"It is commonly stressed in defining the term that (1) comparative librarianship involves two or more national, cultural, or societal environments; (2) the study includes a comparable comparison; and (3) it induces philosophical or theoretical concepts of librarianship through the analysis of similarities and differences of phenomena in various environments" (Wang 1985, 109). Danton (1973) and others have argued that the scientific method of inquiry is the most satisfactory method for comparative studies in librarianship, while recognizing that history and comparison are essential elements of this process. Lor (2010b, 2850) stated that if the analysis does not involve the formal testing of patterns of similarities and differences, "the study is not truly comparative." The four basic steps for research in comparative librarianship have been identified as description, interpretation, juxtaposition, and comparison. Specific data collection techniques have included case histories, personal interviews, surveys, observation, and documentary analysis.

For a more detailed analysis of international and comparative librarianship, refer to Lor's (2019a, 2019b) books and bibliography of journals and articles ("Top Journals Cited in International and Comparative Librarianship" 2019) that address these topics. IFLA (n.d.) was founded on the core values of international librarianship and provides a publication series ("Global Studies in Libraries and Information" 2014–.) and events on the subject.

Text Box 14.7: Doing Research in International and Comparative LIS

Peter Johan Lor

Much involvement in international resource sharing and collaborative projects and participation in the work of UNESCO and international professional bodies such as the International Federation of Library Associations (IFLA)—and maybe also growing up as a first-generation immigrant, speaking three languages—all led to my interest in international and comparative research in LIS, as does my belief that the exchange of good-quality information among nations can foster international understanding, tolerance, and peace.

The methods and tools of research in international and comparative librarianship do not differ much from those in LIS generally, although research design in international comparative studies requires careful thought, for example in respect to the choice of entities to be compared. Here LIS researchers can learn much from comparative researchers in education and political science. Throughout, the influence of language and cultural differences must be taken into account. LIS phenomena cannot be fully understood outside the context of their national cultural, socioeconomic, and political situations.

A fair knowledge of at least one other language helps, as does the experience of living abroad—preferably long enough for the novelty and subsequent irritation to be replaced by a sympathetic understanding, humility, and empathy. Linguistic "false friends" can trip up the unwary Anglophone, even within the international varieties of English. In France, a *librairie*, is a bookstore, not a library. There it is a *bibliothèque*, and that is not an exact equivalent of an American or British library. Similarly, concepts like community, democracy, and freedom of expression seldom translate directly (Bertrand 2009). The seductive availability of web-based questionnaires is a trap for the unwary beginner. "Garbage in, garbage out" applies here. Good-quality data require painstaking conceptualization, and concepts should be refined in collaboration with local colleagues who speak the languages to be used in your instruments (Vakkari et al. 2016). In the social sciences the days of the "transatlantic questionnaire" are past. Would it were so in LIS!

The two articles cited are good examples of qualitative and quantitative approaches, respectively. Many examples are discussed in Lor (2019).

References

Bertrand, Anne-Marie. 2009. "Inventing a Model Library 'à La Française.'" *Libraries & the Cultural Record* 44(4): 471–79. https://doi.org/10.5555/lcr.2009.44.4.471.

Lor, Peter Johan. 2019. *International and Comparative Librarianship: Concepts and Methods for Global Studies*. Berlin: Walter de Gruyter.

Vakkari, Pertti, Svanhild Aabø, Ragnar Audunson, Frank Huysmans, Nahyun Kwon, Marjolein Oomes, and Sei-Ching Joanna Sin. 2016. "Patterns of Perceived Public Library Outcomes in Five Countries." *Journal of Documentation* 72(2): 342–61. https://doi.org/10.1108/JD-08-2015-0103.

DELPHI STUDY

The Delphi study or technique was developed by RAND in the 1950s ("Delphi Method" n.d.) to identify national security threats impacted by the use of technology during the Cold War and was accepted as an academic research method in the 1970s (Lund 2020). The method involves soliciting anonymous responses from a group of experts to sequential questionnaires to arrive at expert consensus on a specific topic or issue. Lund (2020, 929) states that "variants of the e-Delphi (online survey/email method) are increasingly common, particularly in LIS Delphi studies that focus on general information science." It can be employed for issues that are quantitative and nonquantitative in nature and helps to support informed decision making. The Delphi study is designed to generate consensus by systematically refining prior responses of study participants. "This form of data gathering is effective when policy level decision making is necessary" (Losee and Worley 1993). For example, a library administrator might need to develop a data management plan and policy for the development of metadata, discovery, preservation, and reuse of research data. After reviewing the professional literature, networking with colleagues at conferences, and talking to researchers about their data reuse needs and expectations, the administrator would develop a list of experts on data management policies and a list of relevant issues. The latter list would then be distributed to the experts for their reactions, which could be suggestions for revision of the list and/or possible resolutions of the issues. The administrator would revise the list based on the responses. The list would be sent back to the experts for further suggestions, if any. This process would continue for more rounds of polling until a consensus among the experts had been reached. This methodology also is useful when the participants are hostile toward one another, argumentative, or unable to meet easily in person (Miller and Salkind 2002).

Lund (2020) provides an informative review of the uses of the Delphi method in LIS research. He concludes that although the Delphi method is not heavily used in LIS research, studies using this method are consistently published in some prestigious LIS journals.

SUMMARY

A number of specific research methods are introduced in this chapter. Applied research and action research methods, including evaluative research and assessment, innovation research, evidence-based research, and community-based and participatory research are described. Evidence-based and evaluative research methods can be used by librarians to articulate the value of libraries to stakeholders and for strategic planning. Innovation research has the potential to have a transformative impact on library policies, procedures, and offerings. Community-based participatory research originated with public health research and emphasizes the equal involvement of nonacademic researchers in all phases of the project—planning, design, dissemination, and implementation.

Social justice research in LIS is a growing area of scholarship and includes reviewing library practices and procedures using a more inclusive and diverse lens. Librarians also are rethinking the provision of services to accommodate the needs of marginalized populations, and the UN SDGs have become more broadly addressed in LIS. There also is much discussion within the profession on the recruitment, retention, and advancement of librarians who represent a more diverse population. Although some progress has been made, there is evidence in the literature that there is a long road ahead of us as a profession. However, the focus on educating the next generation of LIS professionals is encouraging.

The continued interest in international and comparative librarianship indicates the importance of this research in the current political and socioeconomic environment. The Delphi study, although not widely used, consistently has been used in LIS research to arrive at consensus on a specific topic or issue and often is used for policy making and decision making. The discussion of various methods and their uses in LIS in this chapter is not, however, exhaustive. Nor are the descriptions detailed enough to provide adequate instruction in how to use the methods. Those wishing to employ one or more of these methods or who are interested in learning more about them should refer to the numerous references to other standard texts on research methods, and appropriate readings included in this chapter.

REFERENCES

"Academic Library Statistics." 2006. Text. Association of College & Research Libraries (ACRL). September 1. http://www.ala.org/acrl/publications/trends.

Ackermann, Eric, and Jacalyn A. Kremer. 2015. "Putting Assessment into Action: Selected Projects from the First Cohort of the Assessment in Action Grant." *Association of College and Research Libraries.*

"ACRL Project Outcome." 2019. https://acrl.projectoutcome.org.

Adler, Melissa. 2016. "The Case for Taxonomic Reparations." *Knowledge Organization* 43(8): 630–40. https://doi.org/10.5771/0943-7444-2016-8-630.

Adler, Melissa, and Lindsey M. Harper. 2018. "Race and Ethnicity in Classification Systems: Teaching Knowledge Organization from a Social Justice Perspective." *Library Trends* 67(1): 52–73. https://doi.org/10.1353/lib.2018.0025.

Admin. 2006. "Standards for Libraries in Higher Education." Text. Association of College & Research Libraries (ACRL). August 29. http://www.ala.org/acrl/standards/standardslibraries.

"Advocacy and Public Policy." 2020. Text. American Library Association. http://www.ala.org/advocacy/advocacy-public-policy.

"ALA Task Force on United Nations 2030 Sustainable Development Goals." Text. About ALA. April 20, 2020. http://www.ala.org/news/press-releases/2020/03/ala-creates-task-force-united-nations-2030-sustainable-development-goals#:~:text=CHICAGO%20%E2%80%94The%20American%20Library%20Association,efforts%20to%20achieve%20the%20Goals.

Allen, Scott G., Larra Clark, Michele Coleman, Lynn Silipigni Connaway, Chris Cyr, Kendra Morgan, and Mercy Procaccini. 2019. "Public Libraries Respond to the Opioid Crisis with Their Communities: Summary Report." Dublin, OH: OCLC.

Allen, Scott G., Larra Clark, Michele Coleman, Lynn Silipigni Connaway, Chris Cyr, Kendra Morgan, and Mercy Procaccini. 2020a. "Call to Action: Public Libraries and the Opioid Crisis." OCLC. May 12. https://www.oclc.org/research/publications/2020/oclcresearch-call-to-action-public-libraries-and-the-opioid-crisis.html.

Allen, Scott G., Larra Clark, Michele Coleman, Lynn Silipigni Connaway, Chris Cyr, Kendra Morgan, and Mercy Procaccini. 2020b. "Public Libraries Respond to the Opioid Crisis with Their Communities: Case Studies." OCLC. May 12. https://www.oclc.org/research/publications/2019/oclcresearch-public -libraries-respond-to-opioid-crisis/supplemental.html.

Applegate, Rachel. 2013. *Practical Evaluation Techniques for Librarians*. Santa Barbara, CA: Libraries Unlimited, an imprint of ABC-CLIO.

Aqili, Seyed, and Alireza Isfandyari-Moghaddam. 2008. "Bridging the Digital Divide—The Role of Librarians and Information Professionals in the Third Millennium." *The Electronic Library* 26 (April): 226–37. https://doi.org/10 .1108/02640470810864118.

"ARL Statistics® Survey." n.d. Association of Research Libraries. Accessed July 5, 2020. https://www.arl.org/arl-statistics-salary-survey.

Baker, Sharon L., and Wilfrid Lancaster. 1991. *The Measurement and Evaluation of Library Services*. Arlington, VA: Information Resources Press.

Barclay, Donald A. 2017. "Space and the Social Worth of Public Libraries." *Public Library Quarterly* 36(4): 267–73. https://doi.org/10.1080/01616846.2017 .1327767.

Barnes, Ilana. 2013. "Geospatial Services in Special Libraries: A Needs Assessment Perspective." *Public Services Quarterly* 9(2): 180–84. https://doi.org/10 .1080/15228959.2013.785904.

Bertot, John Carlo, Charles R. McClure, and Joe Ryan. 2001. *Statistics and Performance Measures for Public Library Networked Services*. Chicago: American Library Association.

Bishop, Wade, and Lauren H. Mandel. 2010. "Utilizing Geographic Information Systems (GIS) in Library Research." *Library Hi Tech* 28(4): 536–47. https:// doi.org/10.1108/07378831011096213.

Bogel, Gayle. 2012. "Public Library Summer Reading Programs Contribute to Reading Progress and Proficiency." *Evidence Based Library and Information Practice* 7(1): 102–4. https://digitalcommons.fairfield.edu/education-facultypubs/25.

Bogost, Ian. 2015. "The Cathedral of Computation." *The Atlantic*. January 15. https://www.theatlantic.com/technology/archive/2015/01/the-cathedral -of-computation/384300.

Bordonaro, Karen. 2017. *International Librarianship at Home and Abroad*. Kent: Elsevier Science. http://www.myilibrary.com?id=1010357.

Bowlby, Raynna. 2011. "Living the Future: Organizational Performance Assessment." *Journal of Library Administration* 51(7–8): 618–44. https://doi.org/10 .1080/01930826.2011.601267.

Britto, M., and K. Kinsley. 2018. "Academic Libraries and the Academy: Strategies and Approaches to Demonstrate Your Value, Impact, and Return on Investment." *Association of College and Research Libraries*, January. https:// digitalcommons.fairfield.edu/library-books/11.

Brook, Freeda, Dave Ellenwood, and Althea Eannace Lazzaro. 2015. "In Pursuit of Antiracist Social Justice: Denaturalizing Whiteness in the Academic Library." *Library Trends* 64(2): 246–84. https://doi.org/10.1353/lib.2015.0048.

Brown, Karen, and Kara J. Malenfant. 2016. *Documented Library Contributions to Student Learning and Success: Building Evidence with Team-Based Assessment in Action Campus Projects*. Chicago: Association of College and Research Libraries. http://www.ala.org/acrl/sites/ala.org.acrl/files/content/issues /value/contributions_y2.pdf.

Brožová, Helena, and Dana Klimešová. 2011. "Knowledge and Group Decision-Making Using Knowledge Maps in GIS." In *Proceedings of the European*

Conference on Knowledge Management, edited by Franz Lehner and Klaus Bredl, 166–75. Conference held September 1–2, 2011, Passau, Germany. Reading, UK: Academic Conferences.

Caidi, N. 2021a. "Curating Post-Hajj Experiences: Information Practices as Community-Building Rituals." In *Narrating the Hajj,* edited by M. W. Buitelaar and R. L. vanLeeuwen.

Caidi, N. 2021b. "Mediated Spaces of Collective Rituals: Sacred Selfies at the Hajj." In *Oxford Handbook of Religious Space,* edited by Jeanne Halgren Klide. Oxford, UK: Oxford University Press.

Caidi, N., S. McDonald, and E. Chien. 2012. "Community Networks and Local Libraries: Strenghtening Ties with Communities." In *Connecting Canadians: Investigations in Community Informatics,* 341–66. Athabasca, AB: University of Athabasca Press.

Chancellor, Renate L. 2019. "Racial Battle Fatigue: The Unspoken Burden of Black Women Faculty in LIS." *Journal of Education for Library and Information Science* 60(3): 182–89. https://doi.org/10.3138/jelis.2019-0007.

Closter, Matthew. 2015. "Public Library Evaluation: A Retrospective on the Evolution of Measurement Systems." *Public Library Quarterly* 34(2): 107–23. https://doi.org/10.1080/01616846.2015.1036705.

Coleman, Michele, and Lynn Connaway. 2019. "Public Libraries Respond to the Opioid Crisis in Collaboration with Their Communities: An Introduction." *Collaborative Librarianship* 11(1): Article 8. https://digitalcommons.du.edu /collaborativelibrarianship/vol11/iss1/8.

Coleman, Michele, Lynn Connaway, and Kendra Morgan. 2020. "Public Libraries Respond to the Opioid Crisis with Their Communities: Research Findings." *Collaborative Librarianship* 12(1): Article 6. https://digitalcommons.du.edu /collaborativelibrarianship/vol12/iss1/6.

Connaway, Lynn Silipigni. 2014. "Why Libraries? A Call for Use-Centered Assessment." *Textos Universitaris de Biblioteconomia | Documentacio* 32: 1.

Connaway, Lynn Silipigni. 2018a. "Rust Never Sleeps—Not for Rockers, Not for Libraries." *OCLC Next* (blog). August 1. https://blog.oclc.org/next/rust -never-sleeps-not-for-rockers-not-for-libraries.

Connaway, Lynn Silipigni. 2018b. "Advice from the Trenches: You're Not Alone." *Hanging Together* (blog). August 10. https://hangingtogether.org/ ?p=6790.

Connaway, Lynn Silipigni, William Harvey, Vanessa Kitzie, and Stephanie Mikitish. 2017. *Academic Library Impact: Improving Practice and Essential Areas to Research.* Chicago: Association of College & Research Libraries. http://www .ala.org/acrl/sites/ala.org.acrl/files/content/publications/whitepapers /academiclib.pdf.

Connaway, Lynn Silipigni, and Marie L. Radford. 2010. "Virtual Reference Service Quality: Critical Components for Adults and the Net-Generation." *Libri* 60(2): 165–80. https://doi.org/10.1515/libr.2010.015.

Connaway, Lynn Silipigni, and Marie L. Radford. 2011. "Seeking Synchronicity: Revelations and Recommendations for Virtual Reference." OCLC. https:// www.oclc.org/content/research/publications/2011/synchronicity.html.

Constantinou, Constantia, Michael J. Miller, and Kenneth Schlesinger. 2017. *International Librarianship: Developing Professional, Intercultural, and Educational Leadership.* Albany: State University of New York Press.

Cooke, Nicole A. 2016. *Information Services to Diverse Populations: Developing Culturally Competent Library Professionals.* Santa Barbara, CA: Libraries Unlimited.

Cooke, Nicole A. 2019a. "Leading with Love and Hospitality: Applying a Radical Pedagogy to LIS." *Information and Learning Sciences* 120(1/2):119–32. https://www.emeraldinsight.com/doi/10.1108/ILS-06-2018-0054.

Cooke, Nicole A. 2019b. "Impolite Hostilities and Vague Sympathies: Academia as a Site of Cyclical Abuse." *Journal of Education for Library and Information Science* 60(3): 223–30. https://utpjournals.press/doi/10.3138/jelis.2019-0005.

Cooke, Nicole A., and Joe O. Sánchez. 2019. "Getting It on the Record: Faculty of Color in Library and Information Science." *Journal of Education for Library and Information Science* 60(3): 169–81. https://doi.org/10.3138/jelis.60.3.01.

Cox, Allan B., and Fred Gifford. 1997. "An Overview to Geographic Information Systems." *The Journal of Academic Librarianship* 23(6): 449–61. https://doi.org/10.1016/S0099-1333(97)90169-5.

Crawford, Gregory A. 2015. "The Academic Library and Student Retention and Graduation: An Exploratory Study." *Portal: Libraries and the Academy* 15(1): 41–57. https://doi.org/10.1353/pla.2015.0003.

Dadlani, Punit, and Ross J. Todd. 2016. "Social Justice as Strategy: Connecting School Libraries, Collaboration, and IT." *The Library Quarterly* 86(1): 43–75. https://doi.org/10.1086/684143.

Dali, Keren, and Nadia Caidi. 2020. *Humanizing LIS Education and Practice: Diversity by Design.* Abingdon, Oxon, UK, New York: Routledge.

Dankowski, Terra. 2020. "Decolonizing Knowledge: Libraries Can Aid Truth and Reconciliation by Restoring Indigenous Cultural Memory." *American Libraries Magazine* (blog). https://americanlibrariesmagazine.org/blogs/the-scoop/decolonizing-knowledge.

Danton, J. Periam. 1973. "The Dimensions of Comparative Librarianship." *American Library Association.* https://search.proquest.com/docview/1290675917/citation/EB786C6C591842BAPQ/1.

"Data Science." n.d. OCLC Research. Accessed July 4, 2020. https://www.oclc.org/research/areas/data-science.html.

Davis, Charles H., and James E. Rush. 1980. *Guide to Information Science.* Westport, CT: Greenwood Press.

"Delphi Method." n.d. Accessed November 15, 2020. https://www.rand.org/topics/delphi-method.html.

"Differences between Community-Based Research, Community-Based Participatory Research, and Action Research | Institute for Civic and Community Engagement." n.d. Accessed November 14, 2020. https://icce.sfsu.edu/content/differences-between-community-based-research-community-based-particpatory-research-and.

Dobbs, Aaron W. 2017. *The Library Assessment Cookbook.* Chicago: Association of College and Research Libraries. https://cds.cern.ch/record/2295946.

Dowdell, Louise, and Chern Li Liew. 2019. "More than a Shelter: Public Libraries and the Information Needs of People Experiencing Homelessness." *Library & Information Science Research* 41(4): 100984. https://doi.org/10.1016/j.lisr.2019.100984.

Drabinski, Emily. 2013. "Queering the Catalog: Queer Theory and the Politics of Correction." *The Library Quarterly* 83(2): 94–111. https://doi.org/10.1086/669547.

Eldredge, Jonathan. 2006. "Evidence-Based Librarianship: The EBL Process." *Library Hi Tech* 24(3): 341–54. https://doi.org/10.1108/07378830610692118.

Elliott, Rory. 2014. "Geographic Information Systems (GIS) and Libraries: Concepts, Services and Resources." *Library Hi Tech News* 31(8): 8–11. https://doi.org/10.1108/LHTN-07-2014-0054.

"Evidence Based Library and Information Practice." n.d. Accessed November 15, 2020. https://journals.library.ualberta.ca/eblip/index.php/EBLIP/about.

Fisher, Karen E. 2018. "Information Worlds of Refugees." In *Digital Lifeline? ICTs for Refugees and Displaced Persons*, edited by Carleen F. Maitland, 79–112. Cambridge, MA: MIT Press.

Fisher, Karen E. 2019a. "Refugee Women Forging Resilience." In *Empowering Women through Painting—Jordan*, Seven Circles, 226–27. Amman, Jordan: Jabal Amman.

Fisher, Karen E. 2019b. "UNHCR Za'atari Camp Libraries: Building Futures for Syrian Women and Girls." Presented at the IFLA August 26, 2019, in Athens, Greece, at Session 144, Women, Information and Libraries SIG with Libraries without Borders: Ethics, Perspective, and Voice: Building Best Practices to Serve Women and Girls. https://www.ifla.org/node/92390.

Fisher, Karen E., and The Zaatari Camp Librarians. 2020. "Bringing Books to the Desert." *American Libraries Magazine.* https://americanlibrariesmagazine .org/2020/07/01/bringing-books-desert-zaatari-refugee-library.

Fisher, Karen E., Eiad Yafi, Carleen Maitland, and Ying Xu. 2019. "Al Osool: Understanding Information Behavior for Community Development at Za'atari Syrian Refugee Camp." In *Proceedings of ACM 9th International Conference on Communities and Technologies,* 273–82. Conference held in Vienna, Austria, June 2019. New York: Association for Computing Machinery. https://dl .acm.org/doi/10.1145/3328320.3328395.

"The Five Principles of Social Justice." n.d. Accessed November 14, 2020. https:// onlinedegrees.kent.edu/political-science/master-of-public-administration /political-science/master-of-public-administration/community/five-principles -of-social-justice.

Forbes, Carrie, and Jennifer Bowers. 2014. *Rethinking Reference for Academic Libraries: Innovative Developments and Future Trends*. New York: Rowman & Littlefield.

Fritch, Melia Erin. 2018. "Teaching as a Political Act: Critical Pedagogy in Library Instruction." *Educational Considerations* 44(1). https://doi.org/10.4148 /0146-9282.1868.

Gibson, Amelia, Sandra Hughes-Hassell, and Megan Threats. 2018. "Critical Race Theory in the LIS Curriculum." In *Re-Envisioning the MLS: Perspectives on the Future of Library and Information Science Education*, edited by Johnna Percell, Lindsay C. Sarin, Paul T. Jaeger, and John Carlo Bertot, 44B: 49–70. Advances in Librarianship. Bingley, UK: Emerald. https://doi.org/10.1108 /S0065-28302018000044B005.

Gibson, Amelia N. 2019. "Civility and Structural Precarity for Faculty of Color in LIS." *Journal of Education for Library and Information Science* 60(3): 215–22. https://doi.org/10.3138/jelis.2019-0006.

Gibson, Amelia N., Renate L. Chancellor, Nicole A. Cooke, Dahlen Sarah Park, Shari A. Lee, and Yasmeen L. Shorish. 2017. "Libraries on the Frontlines: Neutrality and Social Justice." *Equality, Diversity and Inclusion: An International Journal* 36(8): 751–66. https://doi.org/10.1108/EDI-11-2016-0100.

Gibson, Amelia N., and Sandra Hughes-Hassell. 2017. "We Will Not Be Silent: Amplifying Marginalized Voices in LIS Education and Research." *The Library Quarterly* 87(4): 317–29. https://doi.org/10.1086/693488.

Given, Lisa M., and Heather Archibald. 2015. "Visual Traffic Sweeps (VTS): A Research Method for Mapping User Activities in the Library Space." *Library & Information Science Research* 37(2): 100–108. https://doi.org/10.1016/j.lisr .2015.02.005.

"Global Studies in Libraries and Information." 2014. IFLA. Accessed November 15, 2020. Berlin, Munich, and Boston: De Gruyter Saur. https://www.ifla.org /publications/global-studies-in-libraries-and-information.

"Global Studies in Libraries and Information." 2014. *Global Studies in Libraries and Information.* Series Editor, Janine Scmidt. Berlin, Munich, and Boston: De Gruyter Saur.

Gorham, Ursula, and John Carlo Bertot. 2018. "Social Innovation in Public Libraries: Solving Community Challenges." *The Library Quarterly* 88(3): 203–7. https://doi.org/10.1086/697701.

Halpin, Eddie, Carolynn Rankin, Elizabeth L. Chapman, and Christopher Walker. 2015. "Measuring the Value of Public Libraries in the Digital Age: What the Power People Need to Know." *Journal of Librarianship and Information Science* 47(1): 30–42.

Harker, Karen R., and Janette Klein. 2016. "Collection Assessment, SPEC Kit 352." Washington, DC: Association of Research Libraries. https://publicat ions.arl.org/Collection-Assessment-SPEC-Kit-352.

Hernon, Peter, and Ellen Altman. 1998. *Assessing Service Quality: Satisfying the Expectations of Library Customers.* Chicago: American Library Association.

Hernon, Peter, and Robert E. Dugan. 2002. *An Action Plan for Outcomes Assessment in Your Library.* Chicago: American Library Association.

Hernon, Peter, and John R. Whitman. 2001. *Delivering Satisfaction and Service Quality: A Customer-Based Approach for Librarians.* Chicago: American Library Association.

Hill, Renee F. 2019. "The Danger of an Untold Story: Excerpts from My Life as a Black Academic." *Journal of Education for Library and Information Science* 60(3): 208–14. https://doi.org/10.3138/jelis.2019-0008.

Hinchliffe, Lisa Janicke. 2017. "Foreword." In *The Evaluation and Measurement of Library Services,* 2nd ed., by Joseph R. Matthews, xvii–xviii. Santa Barbara, CA: ABC-CLIO.

Hoffman, Starr. 2016. *Dynamic Research Support in Academic Libraries.* Chicago: Association of College and Research Libraries.

Howard, Sara A., and Steven A. Knowlton. 2018. "Browsing through Bias: The Library of Congress Classification and Subject Headings for African American Studies and LGBTQIA Studies." *Library Trends* 67(1): 74–88. https://doi .org/10.1353/lib.2018.0026.

Hudson, David James. 2017. "On 'Diversity' as Anti-Racism in Library and Information Studies: A Critique." *Journal of Critical Library and Information Studies* 1(1). http://dx.doi.org/10.24242/jclis.v1i1.6.

Hughes, Hilary. 2014. "School Libraries, Teacher-Librarians and Student Outcomes: Presenting and Using the Evidence." *School Libraries Worldwide* 20(1): 29–50.

Hunter, Julie, Samantha Kannegiser, Jessica Kiebler, and Dina Meky. 2019. "Chat Reference: Evaluating Customer Service and IL Instruction." *Reference Services Review* 47(2): 134–50. https://doi.org/10.1108/RSR-02-2019-0006.

"Integrated Postsecondary Education Data System (IPEDS) | Office of Decision Support | University of South Florida." n.d. Accessed November 14, 2020. https://www.usf.edu/ods/data-and-reports/ipeds.aspx.

"International Federation of Library Associations and Institutions (IFLA)." n.d. Accessed November 15, 2020. https://www.ifla.org.

Irvin, Vanessa. 2019. "'I Have Two Legs, Not Four': Navigating the -Isms of the LIS Minefield." *Journal of Education for Library and Information Science* 60(3): 231–38. https://doi.org/10.3138/jelis.2018-0061.

Isaac, Stephen, and William B. Michael. 1995. *Handbook in Research and Evaluation: A Collection of Principles, Methods and Strategies Useful in the Planning, Design, and Evaluation of Studies in Education and Behavioral Sciences.* 3rd ed. San Diego: EdITS.

Israel, B. A., A. J. Schulz, E. P. Parker, and A. B. Becker. 2001. "Community-Based Participatory Research: Policy Recommendations for Promoting a Partnership Approach in Health Research." *Education for Health: Change in Learning & Practice* 14(2): 182–97.

Jaeger, Paul T., and Gary Burnett. 2010. *Information Worlds: Social Context, Technology, and Information Behavior in the Age of the Internet.* New York: Routledge.

Jaeger, Paul T., Katie Shilton, and Jes Koepfler. 2015. "The Rise of Social Justice as a Guiding Principle in Library and Information Science Research." *The Library Quarterly* 86(1): 1–9. https://doi.org/10.1086/684142.

Janes, Joseph. 2013. "Making Friends with Research: Collaborating Can Yield Better Results Than Working Alone." *American Libraries* 45(3/4). https://americanlibrariesmagazine.org/2012/12/19/making-friends-with-research.

Johnson, Anna Marie. 2019. "Connections, Conversations, and Visibility: How the Work of Academic Reference and Liaison Librarians Is Evolving." *Reference & User Services Quarterly* 58(2): 91–102. https://doi.org/10.5860/rusq.58.2.6929.

Johnston, Melissa P, and Bradley Wade Bishop. 2011. "The Potential and Possibilities for Utilizing Geographic Information Systems to Inform School Library as Place." *School Libraries Worldwide* 17(1): 1–12.

Jurow, Susan R. 1993. "Tools for Measuring and Improving Performance." In *Integrating Total Quality Management in a Library Setting*, edited by Susan B. Bernard, 120. New York: Haworth.

Keikelame, Mpoe Johannah, and Leslie Swartz. 2019. "Decolonising Research Methodologies: Lessons from a Qualitative Research Project, Cape Town, South Africa." *Global Health Action* 12(1). https://doi.org/10.1080/16549716.2018.1561175.

Kendrick, Kaetrena Davis, and Ione T. Damasco. 2019. "Low Morale in Ethnic and Racial Minority Academic Librarians: An Experiential Study." *Library Trends* 68(2): 174–212. https://doi.org/10.1353/lib.2019.0036.

Keyes, Kelsey, and Ellie Dworak. 2017. "Staffing Chat Reference with Undergraduate Student Assistants at an Academic Library: A Standards-Based Assessment." *The Journal of Academic Librarianship* 43(6): 469–78. https://doi.org/10.1016/j.acalib.2017.09.001.

Klarman, Herbert E. 1982. "The Road to Cost-Effectiveness Analysis." *The Milbank Memorial Fund Quarterly. Health and Society* 60(4): 585–603. https://doi.org/10.2307/3349692.

Koury, Regina, Beth Downing, and Jenny Lynne Semenza. 2012. "GIS: An Annotated Guide to Selected Resources." *Collection Building* 31(3): 98–102. https://doi.org/10.1108/01604951211243489.

Kristiansson, Michael René. 2007. "Strategic Reflexive Conversation—A New Theoretical-Practice Field within LIS." *Information Research* 12(4). http://informationr.net/ir/12-4/colis/colis18.html.

Kumasi, Kafi D., and Nichole L. Manlove. 2015. "Finding 'Diversity Levers' in the Core Library and Information Science Curriculum: A Social Justice Imperative." *Library Trends* 64(2): 415–43. https://doi.org/10.1353/lib.2015.0047.

Lancaster, Wilfrid. 1993. *If You Want to Evaluate Your Library . . .* 2nd ed. Champaign: University of Illinois, Graduate School of Library Science.

Lance, Keith Curry. 2002. "What Research Tells Us about the Importance of School Libraries." *Knowledge Quest* 31 (Supplement): 17–22.

Lance, Keith Curry, and Debra E. Kachel. 2018. "Why School Librarians Matter: What Years of Research Tell Us." *Kappan Online* (blog). https://kappanonline .org/lance-kachel-school-librarians-matter-years-research.

Lavoie, Brian. 2020a. "Maple Leaves: Discovering Canada through the Published Record." OCLC. May 4. https://www.oclc.org/research/publications/2019 /oclcresearch-maple-leaves-discovering-canada-through-published-record .html.

Lavoie, Brian. 2020b. "The US and Canadian Collective Print Book Collection: A 2019 Snapshot." OCLC. May 4. https://www.oclc.org/research/publications /2019/oclcresearch-us-and-canadian-collective-print-book-collection-2019 .html.

Lavoie, Brian, Eric R. Childress, Ricky Erway, Ixchel M. Faniel, Constance Malpas, Jennifer Schaffner, and Titia van der Werf. 2015. *The Evolving Scholarly Record.* Dublin, OH: OCLC Research. https://www.oclc.org/research/publications /2014/oclcresearch-evolving-scholarly-record-2014-overview.html.

Lavoie, Brian, and Lorcan Dempsey. 2020. "An Exploration of the Irish Presence in the Published Record." OCLC. August 26. https://www.oclc.org/research /publications/2018/oclcresearch-irish-published-record.html.

Lavoie, Brian, Lorcan Dempsey, and Constance Malpas. 2020. "Reflections on Collective Collections." *College & Research Libraries.* https://doi.org/10.5860 /crl.81.6.981.

Lavoie, Brian, and Constance Malpas. 2015. *Stewardship of the Evolving Scholarly Record: From the Invisible Hand to Conscious Coordination.* Dublin, OH: OCLC Research. https://www.oclc.org/research/publications/2015/oclcresearch -esr-stewardship-2015.html.

Lewis, Vivian, Steve Hiller, Elizabeth Mengel, and Donna Tolson. 2013. "Building Scorecards in Academic Research Libraries: Performance Measurement and Organizational Issues." *Evidence Based Library and Information Practice* 8(2): 183–99. https://doi.org/10.18438/B8T02Z.

libparlorcontributor. 2019. "Community-Based Participatory Research in Libraries: Reevaluating the Researcher's Role in Research." *The Librarian Parlor* (blog). April 9. https://libparlor.com/2019/04/09/community-based-partici patory-research.

"LibQUAL+®." n.d. *Association of Research Libraries* (blog). Accessed November 14, 2020. https://www.arl.org/libqual.

"Libraries, Development and the United Nations 2030 Agenda." n.d. International Federation of Library Associations and Institutions. Accessed November 15, 2020. https://www.ifla.org/libraries-development.

"Library Statistics Program." n.d. National Center for Education Statistics. Accessed November 14, 2020. https://nces.ed.gov/surveys/libraries.

Lor, Peter Johan. 2010a. "International and Comparative Librarianship." *Peter Johan Lor* (blog). 2010. https://peterlor.com/international-comparative-librarianship.

Lor, Peter Johan. 2010b. "International and Comparative Librarianship." In *Encyclopedia of Library and Information Science,* 3rd ed., Marcia J. Bates and Mary Niles Maack. Boca Raton: CRC Press, Vol. IV, 2847–55.

Lor, Peter Johan. 2019a. *International and Comparative Librarianship: A Thematic Approach.* Berlin/Boston: Walter de Gruyter GmbH. https://public.ebook central.proquest.com/choice/publicfullrecord.aspx?p=5157523.

Lor, Peter Johan. 2019b. *International and Comparative Librarianship: Concepts and Methods for Global Studies.* Berlin: Walter de Gruyter & Co.

Losee, Robert M., and Karen A. Worley. 1993. *Research and Evaluation for Information Professionals*. 2nd ed. San Diego: Academic Press.

Lund, Brady D. 2020. "Review of the Delphi Method in Library and Information Science Research." *Journal of Documentation* 76(4): 929–60. https://doi.org/10.1108/JD-09-2019-0178.

Made Here | Change the Subject | Season 9 | Episode 22. n.d. Accessed November 14, 2020. https://video.vermontpbs.org/video/change-the-subject-23nbpj.

Malenfant, Kara J. 2012. "Assessment in Action: Academic Libraries and Student Success." Text. Association of College & Research Libraries (ACRL). October 9. http://www.ala.org/acrl/AiA.

Malenfant, Kara J., and Karen Brown. 2017. "Creating Sustainable Assessment through Collaboration: A National Program Reveals Effective Practices." Occasional Paper #31. University of Illinois and Indiana University, National Institute for Learning Outcomes Assessment.

Mallon, M. N., L. Hays, C. Bradley, R. Huisman, and J. Belanger. 2019. "Reviews and Remarks. The Grounded Instruction Librarian: Participating in the Scholarship of Teaching and Learning." *Association of College and Research Libraries* 17: 99–100. https://doi.org/10.1080/15367967.2019.1701481.

Malpas, Constance, and Brian Lavoie. 2020. "Strength in Numbers: The Research Libraries UK (RLUK) Collective Collection." OCLC. May 4. https://www.oclc.org/research/publications/2016/oclcresearch-strength-in-numbers-rluk-2016.html.

Mandel, Lauren H. 2010. "Geographic Information Systems: Tools for Displaying In-Library Use Data." *Information Technology and Libraries* 29(1): 47–52. https://doi.org/10.6017/ital.v29i1.3158.

March, Gregory H. 2011. "Surveying Campus GIS and GPS Users to Determine Role and Level of Library Services." *Journal of Map & Geography Libraries* 7(2): 154–83. https://doi.org/10.1080/15420353.2011.566838.

Marquez, Joe J., and Annie Downey. 2016. *Library Service Design: A LITA Guide to Holistic Assessment, Insight, and Improvement*. Lanham, MD: Rowman & Littlefield.

Mathews, Brian. 2012. "Think Like a Start Up: A White Paper to Inspire Library Entrepreneurialism." https://vtechworks.lib.vt.edu/handle/10919/18649.

Matthews, Joseph R. 2004. *Measuring for Results: The Dimensions of Public Library Effectiveness*. Westport, CT: Libraries Unlimited.

Matthews, Joseph R. 2015. *Library Assessment in Higher Education*. 2nd ed. Santa Barbara, CA: Libraries Unlimited.

Matthews, Joseph R. 2017. *The Evaluation and Measurement of Library Services*. 2nd ed. Santa Barbara: ABC-CLIO. https://public.ebookcentral.proquest.com/choice/publicfullrecord.aspx?p=5105809.

McCartin, Lyda Fontes, and Rachel Dineen. 2018. *Toward a Critical-Inclusive Assessment Practice for Library Instruction*. Sacramento, CA: Library Juice Press.

McClure, Charles R. 1989. "Increasing the Usefulness of Research for Library Managers: Propositions, Issues, and Strategies." *Library Trends* 38 (Fall): 282.

Mehra, Bharat. 2019. "The Non-White Man's Burden in LIS Education: Critical Constructive Nudges." *Journal of Education for Library and Information Science* 60(3): 198–207. https://doi.org/10.3138/jelis.2019-0012.

Meuth, Nancy, and Mia Costa. 2011. "GIS Trends in Libraries." *Information Bulletin* 42(3): 86–91.

Miller, Delbert C., and Neil J. Salkind, eds. 2002. *Handbook of Research Design and Social Measurement*. 6th ed. Thousand Oaks, CA: Sage.

Montgomery, Susan E. 2017. *Assessing Library Space for Learning*. Lanham, MD: Rowman & Littlefield.

Nazari, Maryam, and Sheila Webber. 2011. "What Do the Conceptions of Geo/Spatial Information Tell Us about Information Literacy?" *Journal of Documentation* 67(2): 334–54. https://doi.org/10.1108/00220411111109502.

Noble, Safiya U., and Elizabeth Sullivan. 2014. "Changing Course: Collaborative Reflections of Teaching/Taking 'Race, Gender, and Sexuality in the Information Professions.'" *Journal of Education for Library and Information Science* 55(3): 212–22.

Oakleaf, Megan J. 2010. *The Value of Academic Libraries: A Comprehensive Research Review and Report*. Chicago: Association of College and Research Libraries, American Library Association.

Oakleaf, Megan J. 2018. *Academic Library Value: The Impact Starter Kit*. Chicago: ALA Editions. https://www.alastore.ala.org/content/academic-library-value-impact-starter-kit.

"OCLC Global Council: Webinars." 2020. OCLC. November 3. https://www.oclc.org/go/en/sustainable-development-goals/webinars.html.

Ottensmann, John R. 1997. "Using Geographic Information Systems to Analyze Library Utilization." *The Library Quarterly* 67(1): 24–49. https://doi.org/10.1086/629909.

Parker, Stephen J. 1974. "International Librarianship—A Reconnaissance." *Journal of Librarianship and Information Science* 6(4): 219–32. https://journals.sagepub.com/doi/abs/10.1177/096100067400600401?casa_token=XyX55JMEYvwAAAAA:No9tGy4JpNl0EZHkrItLCj54Jm3Rg7yelbZrXnCX1qi1vbuVrWbvDcOhOc6gKf1K—BfiZ0aq9DUng.

Peischl, Thomas M. 1995. "Benchmarking: A Process for Improvement." *Library Administration & Management* 9(2): 100.

"PLA | Project Outcome." 2019. https://www.projectoutcome.org.

Potnis, Devendra, Joseph Winberry, Bonnie Finn, and Courtney Hunt. 2019. "What Is Innovative to Public Libraries in the United States? A Perspective of Library Administrators for Classifying Innovations." *Trace: Tennessee Research and Creative Exchange*. https://trace.tennessee.edu/utk_infosci/epubs/61. doi:10.1177/0961000619871991.

"Presentations | ACRL Value of Academic Libraries." n.d. Accessed November 14, 2020. https://acrl.ala.org/value/?page_id=39.

"Public Libraries Respond to the Opioid Crisis with Their Communities." 2020. WebJunction. February 26. https://www.webjunction.org/explore-topics/opioid-crisis.html.

"Public Libraries Respond to the Opioid Crisis with Their Communities: Webinars." 2019. WebJunction. https://www.webjunction.org/explore-topics/opioid-crisis/webinars.html.

"Public Libraries Survey." 2015. Institute of Museum and Library Services. June 3. https://www.imls.gov/research-evaluation/data-collection/public-libraries-survey.

Pun, Raymond. 2020. "Bridging the Digital Divide: Strategies Employed by Libraries." https://www.infobase.com/blog/featured/mitigating-the-digital-divide-strategies-employed-by-libraries.

Radford, Marie L., and Lynn Silipigni Connaway. 2010. "Getting Better All the Time: Improving Communication and Accuracy in Virtual Reference." In *Reference Renaissance: Current & Future Trends*, edited by Marie L. Radford and R. D. Lankes, 39–54. New York: Neal-Schuman.

Radford, Marie L., and Lynn Silipigni Connaway. 2012. "Chattin' 'Bout My Generation: Comparing Virtual Reference Use of Millennials to Older Adults." In *Leading the Reference Renaissance: Today's Ideas for Tomorrow's Cutting Edge Services*, edited by Marie L. Radford, 35–46. New York: Neal-Schuman.

Radford, Marie L., and Lynn Silipigni Connaway. 2013. "Not Dead yet! A Longitudinal Study of Query Type and Ready Reference Accuracy in Live Chat and IM Reference." *Library & Information Science Research* 35(1): 2–13. https://doi.org/10.1016/j.lisr.2012.08.001.

Radford, Marie L., Lynn Silipigni Connaway, Patrick A. Confer, Susanna Sabolcsi-Boros, and Hannah Kwon. 2011. "'Are We Getting Warmer?' Query Clarification in Live Chat Virtual Reference." *Reference & User Services Quarterly* 50(3): 259–79.

Radford, Marie L., Laura Costello, and Kaitlin Montague E. 2020. "Chat Reference in the Time of COVID-19: Transforming Essential User Services." Presented at the ALISE Annual Conference.

Radford, Marie L., Gary P. Radford, Lynn Silipigni Connaway, and Jocelyn A. DeAngelis. 2011. "On Virtual Face-Work: An Ethnography of Communication Approach to a Live Chat Reference Interaction." *The Library Quarterly* 81(4): 431–53. https://doi.org/10.1086/661654.

Reidsma, Matthew. 2019. *Masked by Trust: Bias in Library Discovery*. Sacramento, CA: Library Juice Press. https://works.bepress.com/mreidsma/5.

Richey, Jennifer, and Maria Cahill. 2014. "School Librarians' Experiences with Evidence-Based Library and Information Practice." *School Library Research* 17: 25.

Sagor, Richard. 2005. *The Action Research Guidebook: A Four-Stage Process for Educators and School Teams*. Thousand Oaks, CA: Corwin, a Sage company.

Senteio, Charles. 2019. "Promoting Access to Health Information: A Method to Support Older African Americans with Diabetes." *Aslib Journal of Information Management* 71(6): 806–20. https://doi.org/10.1108/AJIM-02-2019-0043.

Sheridan, Judson D. 1988. "Perspectives from 202 Jesse Hall: The Research Continuum." *Graduate School and Research Notes* 14(6): 1.

Sin, Sei-Ching Joanna. 2011. "Neighborhood Disparities in Access to Information Resources: Measuring and Mapping U.S. Public Libraries' Funding and Service Landscapes." *Library & Information Science Research* 33(1): 41–53. https://doi.org/10.1016/j.lisr.2010.06.002.

Skinner, Julia. 2017. "Innovation in Harlem: Using the Change in Historic Institutions Model to Study a Public Library's Development." *The Library Quarterly* 87(2): 136–49. https://doi.org/10.1086/690738.

Smith, Linda Tuhiwai, and Dawson Books. 2012. *Decolonizing Methodologies: Research and Indigenous Peoples*. 2nd ed. London: Zed Books.

Steffen, Nicolle O., Keith Curry Lance, and Rochelle Logan. 2002. "Time to Tell the Who Story: Outcome-Based Evaluation and the Counting on Results Project." *Public Libraries* 41 (July–August): 222–28.

"Sustainable Development and Libraries." 2020. OCLC. November 5. https://www.oclc.org/go/en/sustainable-development-goals.html.

Talhouk, Reem, Aal Konstantin, Anne Weibert. Mike Krieger, Volker Wulf, Karen Fisher, Franziska Tachtler, Suleman Shahid, Syed Ishtiaque Ahmed, and Ana Maria Bustamante Duarte. 2019. "Refugees & HCI: Situating HCI within Humanitarian Research." In *Proceedings of ACM 9th International Conference on Communities and Technologies,* 1–4. Conference held in Vienna, Austria. New York: Association for Computing Machinery. https://doi.org/10.1145/3290607.3311754.

Tenopir, Carol. 2013. "Building Evidence of the Value and Impact of Library and Information Services: Methods, Metrics, and ROI." *Evidence Based Library and Information Practice* 8(2): 270–74.

"10th International Evidence Based Library and Information Practice Conference." 2019. https://www.eblip10.org.

Tewell, Eamon C. 2018. "The Practice and Promise of Critical Information Literacy: Academic Librarians' Involvement in Critical Library Instruction." *College & Research Libraries* 79(1): 10–34. https://doi.org/10.5860/crl.79.1.10.

Tewell, Eamon. 2019. "Reframing Reference for Marginalized Students: A Participatory Visual Study." *Reference & User Services Quarterly* 58(3): 162. https://doi.org/10.5860/rusq.58.3.7044.

Thompson, Kim M., and Anindita Paul. 2015. "'I Am Not Sure How Much It Will Be Helpful for Me': Factors for Digital Inclusion among Middle-Class Women in India." *The Library Quarterly* 86(1): 93–106. https://doi.org/10.1086/684144.

Todd, Ross. 2008. "The Evidence-Based Manifesto for School Librarians." *School Library Journal* 4. https://www.slj.com/?detailStory=the-evidence-based-manifesto-for-school-librarians.

Togia, Aspasia, and Afrodite Malliari. 2017. "Research Methods in Library and Information Science." In *Qualitative versus Quantitative Research,* edited by Sonyel Oflazoglu, Vol. Chapter 3, 43–64. Rijeka, Croatia: InTech. http://dx.doi.org/10.5772/intechopen.68749.

Tolia-Kelly, Divya P., and Rosanna Raymond. 2020. "Decolonising Museum Cultures: An Artist and a Geographer in Collaboration." *Transactions of the Institute of British Geographers* 45(1): 2–17. https://doi.org/10.1111/tran.12339.

"Top Journals Cited in International and Comparative Librarianship." 2019. Based on the bibliography of: Peter Johan Lor (2019) International and comparative librarianship: Concepts and methods for global studies. Berlin and Boston: De Gruyter Saur. https://pjlor.files.wordpress.com/2019/05/journals-most-cited-in-the-bibliography-1.pdf.

"Transforming Our World: The 2030 Agenda for Sustainable Development." n.d. Accessed November 15, 2020. https://sustainabledevelopment.un.org/post2015/transformingourworld.

Troppe, Marie. 1994. *Participatory Action Research: Merging the Community and Scholarly Agendas.* Providence, RI: Campus Compact.

Unertl, Kim M., Chris L. Schaefbauer, Terrance R. Campbell, Charles Senteio, Katie A. Siek, Suzanne Bakken, and Tiffany C. Veinot. 2016. "Integrating Community-Based Participatory Research and Informatics Approaches to Improve the Engagement and Health of Underserved Populations." *Journal of the American Medical Informatics Association* 23(1): 60–73. https://doi.org/10.1093/jamia/ocv094.

"United Nations Sustainable Development Goals." n.d. United Nations. Accessed November 9, 2020. https://sdgs.un.org/goals.

The Value and Impact of Australian Public Libraries: A Summary of Studies and Reports since 2010. 2017. Australian Public Library Alliance and Australian Library and Information Association. https://www.alia.org.au/sites/default/files/The%20value%20and%20impact%20of%20Australian%20public%20libraries%202010-2017_1.pdf.

Wallace, Danny P., and Connie Jean Van Fleet. 2001. *Library Evaluation: A Casebook and Can-Do Guide.* Englewood, CO: Libraries Unlimited.

Walsh, Benjamin. 2018. "Public Library and Private Space: Homeless Queer Youth Navigating Information Access and Identity in Toronto." In *IFLA WLIC.* Kuala Lumpar, Malaysia. http://library.ifla.org/2144/1/114-walsh-en.pdf.

Wang, Chih. 1985. "A Brief Introduction to Comparative Librarianship." *International Library Review* 17(2): 107–15.

Webber, Sarah Chase. 2020. "The Library's Role in Bridging the Digital Divide." Urban Libraries Council. https://www.urbanlibraries.org/blog/the-librarys -role-in-bridging-the-digital-divide.

"Webinar Series: Evaluating and Sharing Your Library's Impact." 2020. WebJunction. September 20. https://www.webjunction.org/news/webjunction/webinar -series-research-assessment.html.

Weiss, Carol H. 1998. *Evaluation Methods for Studying Programs and Policies.* 2nd ed. Upper Saddle River, NJ: Prentice Hall.

"White Papers and Reports." 2011. Text. Association of College & Research Libraries (ACRL). September 11. http://www.ala.org/acrl/issues/whitepapers.

Willcox, James K. 2020. "Libraries and Schools Are Bridging the Digital Divide during the Coronavirus Pandemic." *Consumer Reports.* https://www.consumer reports.org/technology-telecommunications/libraries-and-schools-bridging -the-digital-divide-during-the-coronavirus-pandemic.

Xie, Bo, Daqing He, Tim Mercer, Youfa Wang, Dan Wu, Kenneth R. Fleischmann, Yan Zhang, Linda H. Yoder, Keri K. Stephens, Michael Mackert, and Min Kyung Lee. 2020. "Global Health Crises Are Also Information Crises: A Call to Action." *Journal of the Association for Information Science and Technology* 71(12): 1419–23. https://doi.org/10.1002/asi.24357.

15

Presentation and Dissemination of the Research Project

Regardless of how well a research project is conceived and conducted, if its findings are not disseminated in some fashion, its value will be negligible. The research report, whether it is an unpublished document or a journal article, in either electronic or print format, remains an important vehicle for the dissemination of results. Researchers should not consider their task complete until the research findings have been made available to the appropriate audience and in the most effective form possible. Lindlof and Taylor (2019, 370) urge researchers to "go public" with their findings, by "writing, authoring, and publishing some kind of final report." Newman (1998, 19) went so far as to say that "original scholarship and the publication that emerges from it are the moral obligations of those who accept public money to perform as intellectuals." Bachman and Schutt (2014, 442) assert that "the goal of research is not just to discover something but to communicate that discovery to a larger audience—other social scientists, government officials, your teachers, the general public—perhaps several of these audiences." Wildemuth (2017, 414) advises that "improvements in our professional practice should be based on a strong foundation of evidence about the effectiveness of different approaches." It is obvious, but worth stating, that it is impossible to make evidence-based decisions unless LIS research is published and accessible to the broad academic community through publications and presentations, as well as web-based archives of research findings (Connaway, Radford, and OCLC Research 2011; Radford, Connaway, and Shah 2011).

GENERAL OBJECTIVES OF THE RESEARCH REPORT

The general objectives of the research report are to acquaint the reader with the problem that has been investigated, to present the results of the study,

465

and to explain its implications or importance. The report should present the data fully and adequately; the data should support the report's interpretations and conclusions. The report should interpret the data for the reader and demonstrate how the data help to resolve or understand the problem or the research questions.

In meeting these objectives, the research report should be as well-structured and logical as possible. It should be a straightforward document that sets forth clearly and precisely what the researcher has done to solve, or at least to investigate, the research problem. It need not be a literary masterpiece, but it should be well-organized, readable, and clearly written. Failing to clearly describe the problem, method, findings, and implications of the results severely limits the impact of all the hard work that's been done.

GENERAL OUTLINE OF THE RESEARCH REPORT

In "Guest Editorial" in *College & Research Libraries*, Connell provided tips for authors for planning and writing a research paper (Connell 2010; Holloway and Brown 2016). She includes a succinct explanation of components that should be included in a typical, thorough research paper. Her suggestions are similar to the more detailed outline that follows. Not all reports will present these items in exactly this order, or even include all of them. Others may include additional points. Most of these items have been discussed in some detail elsewhere in this book and therefore are listed briefly here.

The Preliminaries/Front Matter

The preliminaries or front matter consist of the following parts:

- Abstract: a brief summary that restates the problem, the procedures, the main findings, and the major conclusions. It usually is about two hundred words or less in length. It is considered optional unless the report or journal format specifically calls for it.
- Title: in effect, part of the abstract and should, within a reasonable length, be descriptive of the study.
- Copyright notice: US copyright protection is effective for the life of the author plus seventy years. All US publications automatically receive US copyright protection, but there are possible advantages to be gained from actually registering a publication with the US Copyright Office.
- Acknowledgments (optional).
- Table of contents: important if the report is relatively long.
- List of tables (where applicable).
- List of figures (where applicable; graphic illustrations other than tables).

The Text

Following the preliminaries, the text incorporates the body of the report and consists of the following sections:

- Introduction and problem.
- Brief introduction. This section may not be considered desirable in every case, as it usually summarizes the report and therefore becomes somewhat redundant. It can help to express the purpose of the study at an early point in the report.
- Statement of the problem. This section typically includes a brief review of research relevant to the problem.
- Identification of subproblems, if any.
- Delimitations of the study.
- Conceptual definitions of key terms.
- Abbreviations, if needed.
- Statement of the need or justification for the study.
- A note on the organization of the remainder of the report.
- Review of related literature. This section will build on the briefer literature review provided for the problem statement. It should provide the conceptual basis for the hypothesis or research questions, which will follow. It also may draw on related subject fields. If individuals are cited, their authority should be indicated.
- Conceptual framework of the study. As is true for the proposal, many researchers prefer that this section precede the literature review, and they often include it in the introductory or problem section.
- Hypothesis(es) and/or research questions.
- Assumptions. These basic assumptions help to support the logic of the hypothesis or the development of the research questions.
- Operational definitions of important concepts.
- Design of the study. This is broader than the basic research method (e.g., survey), which should already be apparent at this point. The description of the design should be clear and precise about what was done and how it was done.
- The population and sampling procedures, if any. This section should include a description of the research locale or setting, if important.
- Sources of relevant data, including criteria for admissibility.
- Data collection techniques and instruments.
- Data analysis techniques.
- Results.
- Descriptive statistics, if utilized.
- Inferential statistics. This is the section in which hypotheses, if any, are tested.
- Themes, patterns, and relationships that emerged from the coding of the data, if qualitative methods are used.
- Other findings. This is an optional section of miscellaneous findings or results not directly related to the hypothesis.

- Summary of results.
- Summary and conclusions.
- Summary of the study.
- Interpretations and conclusions.
- Limitations of the results.
- Recommendations, if any, for future research and for practice.

The Back Matter

Following the body of the text, the back matter generally consists of the following:

- References: the list of citations or footnotes, if not provided at the appropriate locations in the text.
- Bibliography: a list of other "classic" studies and highly relevant items; it also will include the references, if not listed separately.
- Appendices: supplementary material not essential to an understanding of the text.

GUIDELINES FOR ORGANIZING AND PRESENTING THE RESEARCH REPORT

Organization of the Report

In organizing a research report of any length, it is always a good idea to develop and follow a detailed outline. When writing the report, it helps to organize the information by employing appropriate headings. Various manuals of style can be used for guidance in selecting headings (*Publication Manual of the American Psychological Association* 2019). One common approach is to use centered headings for the major divisions (all uppercase letters), followed in a logical, hierarchical order by free-standing second-level headings (capitals and lowercase); paragraph sideheads (i.e., third-level headings that run into the paragraphs; underscored, first word only capitalized, followed by a period); and fourth-level headings (capitals and lowercase, underscored).

Footnotes and Documentation. In citing information and ideas borrowed from other works, it is important to use accepted guidelines or manuals of style. The specific style to be employed may be left up to the author, though many journals and book publishers do prescribe a certain format. Regardless of who determines the style to be used, it is important to be consistent throughout the report. Wrangling citations has become easier with the advent of citation managers such as RefWorks, Zotero, and Mandalay along with the affordances of LIS indexes and databases that provide citation formatting for all indexed articles in the major citation styles (including APA, Chicago/Turabian, MLA, etc.). Additionally, university writing centers and libraries have added guides to citation styles that are extremely helpful, such as the Purdue Online Writing Lab (https://owl.purdue.edu/owl/purdue_owl.html), which provides an introduction to general writing, academic writing, sample papers, bibliographies, and citation formats. There really is no excuse for sloppy, inaccurate, or incomplete citations these days.

To avoid plagiarism, another general guideline is that if material is borrowed from any source, whether it be a direct quotation or a paraphrase, then both the author and the work should be cited. If the quotation, or borrowed information, is extensive, beyond the concept of "sampling" a small amount of text, and the report may be published or copyrighted, the writer should secure in writing from the holder of the copyright (usually the publisher) permission to reprint the material. In addition to the footnote or reference, the words "Reprinted by permission of the publisher (or author)" should be placed in an appropriate location or added to the footnote. Plagiarism is unethical and must not be done. It is considered a serious offense and may result in consequences (including dismissal from academic programs for student researchers). Care must be taken when cutting and pasting from electronic documents to ensure that these excerpts are tracked and properly cited. Losing track of what was easily "cut and pasted" can happen if the researcher is not vigilant and careful.

Prose Style of the Report. It generally is recommended that a research report be written in the past tense, as it is a report of events that already have occurred. It usually is suggested that the writer employ the passive voice, which means that no identifiable subject is performing an act, and avoid the first person (see Creswell (2008, 86, 193–94) for a differing opinion as well as some other suggestions for writing and presenting the results of research).

The prose itself should be clear, exact, and efficient and should use simple English. Regarding efficiency, Creswell and Poth (2016) recommend being concise and Hillway (1964, 265) argued that every statement that the writer makes should fall into one of the following four categories: (a) a direct statement of fact, (b) a basic assumption, (c) an expression of expert opinion, or (d) the author's personal opinion. It may be advisable to consider eliminating any other type of statement (Hofschire 2020, 19).

Text Preparation. In preparing the text for the research report, it is advisable to adhere to standard guidelines. Needless to say, general standards for neatness, accuracy, punctuation, and so forth should be met. Aesthetics also are worth considering; for example, ample space should be left for margins and between the headings and text. Word processing and electronic publishing software facilitate the revision process. Electronic dictionaries and spell checkers are useful—but not foolproof—to identify misspellings, and electronic thesauri are helpful in selecting alternative words.

Graphic Presentation, Visualization, and Display of Data. As discussed in chapters 8 and 10, data visualization and graphics can in some cases present information more clearly and succinctly than can prose. At the very least, visual presentations can help to supplement explanations and data presented in the text. There is a host of types of graphic presentation software available, including statistical tables, line graphs, bar charts, pie charts, flowcharts, pictographs (simple pictures or cartoons), and maps. In using graphic representations, it is important to remember, however, that they only should be used to facilitate the understanding of data. They are not intended to entertain and must not distract from the purpose of the text. Data displays and representations should be kept as simple as possible, and they should be clear and accurate.

When designing data visualizations, the writer is obligated to see that each one is referred to in the text. It also is important that they be self-contained. In other words, each graphic should contain a title, an explanation of any symbols used, instructions on how to read or use the graphic, a brief description of what it is intended to show, and an indication of the sources of the data. Place visualizations as close as possible to the points in the text where they are first discussed.

Tufte is one of the most well-known writers on the topics of information design and data visualization. He is an American statistician and professor emeritus of political science, statistics, and computer science at Yale University. His books were published between 1997 and 2006, and they contain great ideas on how to visualize data (Tufte 1997a, 1997b, 2001, 2006a, 2006b). To learn more about data visualization, see text box 15.1.

Text Box 15.1: Data Visualization

Margaret Zimmerman

In the past two years, I've begun to use an increasing number of data visualizations. For me personally, adding data visualizations to my work meant embarking into territory that was outside of my comfort zone. Data visualizations, even as a term, sound like something difficult to conceptualize and create. However, once they are understood, an intricate visualization can be easily created using simple software and can add tremendous depth to academic writing. After all, the highest calling of our field is to make information accessible. Displaying complex data as a visualization may provide lucidity that makes it comprehensible in a way that text or a table of numbers cannot.

Table 15.1 and figure 15.1 display the same data in different ways. Table 15.1 presents a set of numbers that shows numerical correlation coefficients increasing as measures of societal progress increase. The streamgraph (figure 15.1) does the same with the width of the lines. While it can be argued that the table provides more exact information, the purpose of the study was to show that in countries with higher societal rankings there are stronger relationships between literacy rates and library usage. The first visualization displays this but takes effort to understand. The streamgraph shows this in a glance and is accessible to readers who may be intimidated by the numeracy of the table.

It is important to use data visualizations as a tool that add clarity to presenting research results and not simply as a means to make your work look more sophisticated. Figure 15.2 provides another example of a visualization to consider. It is best to think of them as a tool to streamline your findings to make them as straightforward as possible.

Further Reading

Zimmerman, Margaret. 2020. "Information Literacy as a Social Justice Issue: Where's the Research?" *Journal of Information Ethics* 29(1): 45–64.

Table 15.1. Correlation Coefficient of Library Statistics Compared to Literacy Rates in Each Grouping

Library statistics per 1 million people	Lowest HDI	Medium HDI	Highest HDI	Lowest Literacy	Medium Literacy	Highest Literacy	Lowest Progress	Medium Progress	Highest Progress
Libraries	0.409	0.341	0.640	0.077	0.018	0.654	0.358	0.575	0.373
Full time staff	0.243	0.674	0.577	0.344	0.185	0.673	0.065	0.474	0.493
Registered users	0.134	0.070	0.512	0.073	0.061	0.485	0.032	0.344	0.449
Physical visits	0.382	0.418	0.430	0.327	0.250	0.494	0.238	0.384	0.501

Library statistics per 1 million people	Low Income	Low Middle Income	Upper Middle Income	High Income		Lowest GII	Medium GII	Highest GII
Libraries	0.131	0.270	0.389	0.562		0.172	0.219	0.666
Full time staff	-0.323	0.485	0.498	0.482		0.105	0.403	0.637
Registered users	0.833	0.281	0.132	0.460		0.005	0.009	0.349
Physical visits	0.111	0.452	0.287	0.508		0.049	0.273	0.426

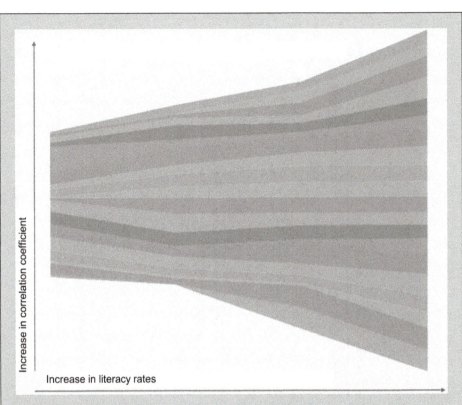

Figure 15.1. Relationship of Library Usage Statistics and Literacy Rates

Countries with the highest measure of HDI

Higher Education 47	Health Literacy 28	E-Learning 24	Priority Journal 22

Psychology 19 / Child 18 / Controlled Study 18

Information Seeking 26 / Assessment 23 / Curricula 21

Surveys 18 / Major Clinical Study 16 / Practice 16

Australia 30 / Questionnaire 25 / Norway 22 / Social Media 20

Information Dissemination 16

Countries with the lowest measure of HDI

Pakistan 29

Postgraduate Students 9 / Adolescent 6

Ethiopia 5 / Librarian 5

University Libraries 9 / Developing Countries 6

Malaria 5 / Risk Factor 5

Nigeria 21

Information Literacy Skills 7 / Health 6

Medical 5

Figure 15.2. Comparison of Words from Countries with High and Low Measures of HDI

Dissemination of the Research

Presentations: In Person and Virtual. Researchers often are invited or required to present their research to others in an oral form. One way to get feedback on research in progress is to submit it to a professional conference for presentation. Good national venues for submitting and presenting your research include the American Library Association's Library Research Round Table ("LRRT" 2020), Library History Round Table ("LHRT" 2017), Association of College and Research Libraries ("ACRL" n.d.), and the Reference and User Services Association Reference Research Forum ("RUSA" n.d.). Additionally, work can be submitted and presented at international organizations and conferences such as Association for Library Science and Technology ("ASIS&T" n.d.), International Federation of Library Associations and Institutions ("IFLA" n.d.), Research Libraries UK ("RLUK" n.d.), California Academic & Research Libraries ("CARL" n.d.), Association of European Research Libraries ("LIBER" n.d.), and Libraries in the Digital Age ("LIDA" n.d.). For presentation tips, *Organizing and Managing Your Research: A Practical Guide for Postgraduates,* Phelps, Fisher, and Ellis (2007), provide a step-by-step guide to planning, managing, organizing, writing, presenting, and publishing research. This book is targeted to students, as well as new and career researchers. Their tips and strategies for presenting research include the following:

Preparing the Speech

- Take as many opportunities as possible to speak in public.
- Know your audience.
- Plan the structure.
- Practice your speech as many times as possible.
- Have everything you need for your presentation ready well beforehand.
- Get to know the room (or virtual platform) you will be in for your presentation.
- Greet a few people as they arrive.

Delivering the Speech

- Control your nerves before you start.
- Have a glass of water at hand.
- Know the *exact* words you are going to start with in the introduction.
- Make an initial impact.
- Acknowledge your audience.
- Be confident.
- Keep your talk at a high level, with a few main points.
- Do not read your paper or your ppt slides.
- Speak slowly and clearly.
- Use pauses to good effect.
- Avoid padding your content.
- Avoid filler words such as like, um, ah, okay, sort of, or you know.
- Establish eye contact and rapport with your audience.

- Incorporate some humor or narrative.
- Manage your time well.
- Be prepared to be flexible.

Concluding Your Speech

- Acknowledge people who helped you along the way.
- Remember to conclude, rather than just trail off. Signpost with "in conclusion," or words to that effect.
- Use questions and discussion well.
- Above all, enjoy yourself. (Phelps, Fisher, and Ellis 2007, 260–62)

Additionally, it is highly recommended that you practice your speech in front of a friendly audience and time it. Sometimes you are allowed only a short amount of time, and you do not want to be given the "stop" signal when you are only halfway through your results. If this does happen, say "in conclusion" and take one more sentence or two to conclude (no more). You always can say more in the question-and-answer period if there is one. Best to be graceful in these situations. Shore's *Grad School Essentials: A Crash Course in Scholarly Skills* is witty, practical, and easy. It provides examples of how to read, write, speak, act, and research in a more professional and scholarly manner (Shore 2016).

There are numerous presentation software packages available. Some of the more popular are PowerPoint, Prezi, and Haiku Deck. For a list of alternative presentation software, see Croxton's ("40 Presentation Software & Powerpoint Alternatives for 2017" 2019) post.

Virtual Presentations. During times of travel restrictions due to safety concerns, most presentations of research are given virtually, via platforms such as Zoom, WebEx, Microsoft Teams, and Skype. These platforms have many affordances that allow for quality audio and video, but they are not without technical difficulties and cause fatigue ("Johnson: What's That Again?" 2020, 75). During the pandemic, Zoom quickly became the most downloaded app, surpassing TikTok with approximately 94 million downloads from April to June of 2020 (Naqvi 2020). Post-COVID-19, Zoom and other video conferencing software will no doubt continue to be popular options for research dissemination. The above recommendations for preparing, delivering, and concluding your presentation still apply, although there are differences. When delivering a virtual presentation, it is important to get to know the platform and its affordances, how to display and advance slides, how to manage chat questions, etc. Austin gives these tips for looking and sounding "as good as possible": (1) "Perfect your lighting": sit with a window to your side, or try an LED "fill light" to dampen harsh indoor lights; (2) "Upgrade your webcam": adding an external webcam will upgrade the poor quality of laptop webcams, or use your smart phone; and (3) "Don't forget a mic": recommending a dedicated microphone that can dramatically improve your audio ("7 Quick Tips to Up Your Video Calling Game" 2020). Anticipate that there may be technical difficulties with your presentation, or that of others, so be prepared to cut your presentation time if necessary. Even though most people are now familiar with common platforms, there may be speakers or moderators who have less familiarity or encounter unusual issues (such as low bandwidth or faulty hardware). It is also imperative that at all times when you are not speaking to be sure to mute yourself and be careful when your video is on not to forget that you are on camera at all times. Some recommend turning off mic and video unless you are actively presenting to avoid embarrassing results, such as a dog barking, a child crying, random appearances of your family, or worse calamities. The key is to present yourself and your research in a professional manner to enhance your credibility and authority. See text box 15.2 for strategies for managing your social media presence and for online networking.

Text Box 15.2: Strategies for Managing Your Scholarly Identity on Social Media and Developing Scholarly Networks

Strategies for Scholarly Identity Management

- Update as you go, as you do with your résumé or curriculum vita (CV). Once you've created your profiles and added existing publications, update every time you publish to avoid a time-consuming backlog.
- Keep track of numbers and analytics. Find your ORCID ID and SCOPUS ID and check/ update them periodically using the general strategies listed above. Put them on your CV for easy reference.
- Choose consistent identifying information. Use the same name, email address, and picture across platforms to collocate your online scholarly identity presence.
- Check email regularly. Many platforms will send updates via email that may facilitate scholarly identity maintenance or help you control your online presence.
- Keep track of publications. Find a strategy that works best for you, such as use of an online citation manager like Zotero (www. zotero.com) or a spreadsheet that you maintain, to keep track of your publications and various ways your name may appear (e.g., middle initial or not). Have PDFs of your publications for your own reference and/or to share if open access.
- Create a checklist. Have a checklist of the order in which you update SI platforms to ensure new publications will appear across the board (Radford, Chayko, and Ammari 2020).

Strategies for Scholarly Identity/Social Media Networking

- Shape and periodically reshape your social media bios and profiles. Remember: If you do not control your brand and identity, the internet (Google) will do it for you. Keep your photos and bios up to date and eye-catching. Be interesting, be positive, be you!
- Systematically curate and build a list of appropriate contacts to follow. Include professionals you admire in your field or a related field plus friends who also want to use social media professionally.
- Increase your list of meaningful contacts by following the people whom your contacts follow.
- Use social media to get a sense of the key issues and debates among those in your field(s) and the tone and frequency with which others post. Eavesdrop on interesting

conversations (this is allowed since it is public), use hashtags, retweet or repost interesting ideas, adding your own commentary.

- Begin to jump in on others' conversations carefully and strategically when you have something to add (or a question). Do not do this too often with people you don't know, especially the same people over and over whom you don't know (or it looks like stalking). Some face-to-face conversational norms apply here. Engage others by saying something smart or flattering, adding something meaningful to a conversation, being sincere or funny, etc.
- Keep these conversations going, and begin to do this with some regularity and consistency. The others in the convo may start to follow you, and you may even really get to know one another and become part of one another's professional networks. Do not overdo this, especially all at once, but it is a good way to initiate or solidify collegial relationships. Becoming friendly online tends to prompt individuals' desire to meet face-to-face in the future, gives them a means to do so, and lends familiarity and comfort when face-to-face meetings do occur.
- Think about how you can add value to those you follow. Find and post great links, share information in an interesting and perhaps witty way, make them smile, make them think. Be yourself: authentic, human, simultaneously professional and personal.
- Take part in social media chats, events, webinars, and the like. Mostly observe the chat, especially at first, and then jump in when you really have something to say. You can make lots of connections and relationships this way.
- Do not hesitate to take your digital relationships offline. Use social media to drive face-to-face (FtF) interactions: suggest coffee at conferences or meet-ups when you are traveling in contacts' area. Suggest group meet-ups at conferences and events.

Once developed, keep your connections alive and strong (and keep yourself in their networks) with occasional "likes," retweets, short notes or affirmations, introductions to others, sending links to relevant info, etc.

EVALUATING THE RESEARCH REPORT

When reading a report of research, the informed, critical reader will generally look for the following: (a) adequacy of documentation, (b) accuracy of sources, (c) correctness of interpretation of sources, (d) appropriateness of data analysis, (e) basis for conclusions, (f) format and style, and (g) evidence of creativity. But there are many specific criteria worth considering, and they may be categorized according to the major sections of a typical research report. A checklist of such criteria, many of which were taken from Wynar (1962, 129–130), follows.

Suggested Criteria for Judging a Research Report

Background

- Is the title descriptive, accurate, and of a reasonable length?
- Does the introduction give a clear indication of the general scope of the research?
- Is the reason or purpose for the research sufficiently indicated?

- Is the problem clearly stated and analyzed into definite subordinate questions or issues where appropriate?
- Is the logic of the analysis of the problem sound? In other words, have the critical factors been identified, relationships properly identified, and so forth?
- What is the hypothesis or research question?
- Is the hypothesis of social or theoretical significance, and is it stated so that it can be resolved or tested?
- Are the variables clear? Have they been designated as independent and dependent variables where appropriate? Are there any logical consequences or implications?
- Are the basic assumptions needed to support the hypothesis made clear?
- Are adequate operational or working definitions provided?
- Is the coverage of previous, related research adequate? Is the report related to the earlier studies?

Design of the Study

- Does the research design seem adequate and logical for the solution of the problem?
- Are the reasons for its choice adequately explained?
- Was the methodology explained in an understandable way so that it can be replicated?
- If important terms are used in an unusual sense, are they defined?
- Are the data collected adequate for the solution of the problem? In other words, do we have satisfactory measurements of the relevant variables?
- Are the data sufficiently quantitative (when appropriate) for the solution of the problem?
- Are the instruments used by the investigator adequate reflections of the conceptual variables of the study (i.e., do they measure the variables in a reliable and valid manner)?
- If sampling procedures were used, were they adequately explained?
- If the sample was supposedly random, was it in fact chosen so that each member of the population had an equal chance of being selected?
- If the researcher used the sample for generalizing, was it adequate for doing so?
- How reliable and valid is the design overall?

Treatment of the Data

- Are the data presented as an integral part of the logical solution of the problem?
- What techniques were used to analyze the quantitative (and/or qualitative) data? Do they seem to be appropriate and effective?
- Were graphical and/or tabular formats appropriately used to display pertinent data?
- Is there evidence of care and accuracy in the collection and treatment of the data?
- Is irrelevant material or information excluded?
- Do the inferences based on the data seem to be sound?

Summary and Conclusions

- Do the conclusions actually serve to answer questions or issues raised in the study?
- Are all conclusions based essentially on data made known to the reader?
- Are conclusions free from mere unsupported opinions?
- Are the limitations or qualifications of the conclusions clearly and concisely expressed?
- Are applications and recommendations, when included, judiciously made?
- Can the conclusions be generalized to a larger population?
- Did the researcher appear to be aware of the theoretical implications, if any, of the research?
- Did the researcher make recommendations for future research?

Appendices

- If there is an appendix, is it supplementary in nature, rather than essential to an understanding of the text?
- Does it include all original data?

Bibliography

- Does it appear that one style manual was followed (i.e., is the bibliographic style consistent)?

Entire books devoted to the evaluation of research articles include those written by Pyrczak (2014) and Girden (2010). Paul and Elder (2007) developed a template that can be used to assess the quality of any research paper or project. They assert that all research:

- Has a fundamental PURPOSE and goal.
- Addresses a fundamental QUESTION, problem, or issue.
- Identifies data, INFORMATION, and evidence relevant to its fundamental question and purpose.
- Contains INFERENCES or interpretation by which conclusions are drawn.
- Is conducted from some POINT OF VIEW or frame of reference.
- Is based on ASSUMPTIONS.
- Is expressed through and shaped by CONCEPTS and ideas.
- Leads somewhere (i.e., has IMPLICATIONS and consequences). (Paul and Elder 2007, 20)

Those reading and evaluating research reports should be particularly watchful for certain common faults. Among these weaknesses are the following:

- Broad, sweeping statements without sufficient evidence or documentation to support them.
- A lack of precision in statements, or a tendency to state ideas vaguely.

- A weak organization and arrangement.
- A failure to describe fully and clearly the method by which the hypothesis was tested, or even a failure to test the hypothesis. Similarly, if there are research questions, the ways in which these were addressed and answered should be explained in full.
- A lack of direct linking of the problem to the hypothesis. As previously discussed, the hypothesis should represent at least a partial solution to the problem, and therefore must be related to it.
- A failure to distinguish adequately between the problem and the purpose of the study. In essence, the problem represents what was studied, and the purpose indicates why it was studied.
- Incorporating information or materials from some source without clearly indicating how they were derived from that source.
- Bringing new elements, concepts, or ideas into the summary and/or conclusions without having introduced them earlier in the study.
- Writing the final report as originally conceived rather than as the findings dictate. The researcher must be sensitive to the results of the research and not be hesitant to reflect them in the conclusions, even when they are contrary to expectations. (Hillway 1964, 274–75)

Text Box 15.3: Editor's Advice

John Budd, Co-Editor, Journal of Education for Library and Information Science (JELIS)

1. What is the worst mistake or one of the worst mistakes prospective authors make?

   - The worst mistake a novice author can make is to submit a paper to more than one journal at the same time. This tends to waste the time of editors and reviewers. More journals are now asking authors to affirm that a manuscript is not under review anywhere else. Authors do need to be aware that they should submit to one journal at a time and to wait for a decision from the editor before submitting the paper to another journal.
   - Authors *must* pay attention to the style requirements of the journal to which they are submitting. An author who does not follow stylistic requirements—perhaps especially bibliographic style—may well have the paper returned unread.
   - In addition to style, authors *must* examine the scope of the journal. Many papers are returned to authors because they are out of scope; that is, the content of the paper is not in concert with that of the journal.

2. What best practices are you able to offer prospective authors?

   - Read articles from journals that appear to fit the topic about which one is writing. This will give authors ideas about the content of the journals, as well as the styles of the journals. This information is invaluable to authors and it is a practice that should inform *prior* to composition of a paper, as well as during and after the process. Not only does the practice help authors learn from what has been written, but it can sensitize authors to the styles of journals.

- Authors will almost always benefit by giving what they write to someone else to read before they submit it to a journal. Some would go so far as to say that one should not give the paper to a friend, because a friend may not be sufficiently critical of the paper. What authors need is constructive criticism in order to present the best-developed paper possible.

3. What do you look for in a submission?

- As is hinted at previously, probably the first thing an editor looks for is consistency of style and fit with scope. When those are not present, the paper is likely to be returned to the author unread. This is a technical matter, but it is essential.
- When a paper does appear to fit the journal, the first thing that is probably sought is a cogent, cohesive, and articulate problem statement. There may be a need for a set of research questions, but even a conceptual piece needs a sound problem statement. The paper must be addressing something, and the articulation of what is addressed must be clearly stated.
- Related to the above item, the problem statement must be sufficiently important that readers will find it interesting and something from which they will learn. It is problematic to say that the statement should be unique (almost nothing is entirely unique), but it should present a new and/or creative perspective so that there can be something new learned from the work.
- It may seem a simple thing, but the literature review should be up-to-date and complete. Reviewers of the manuscript will also want to see a complete literature review. Missing one or two key items is not likely to result in rejection of the manuscript, but it will probably signal that revisions need to be made.
- If statistical methods are used, the sampling and data collection must be conducted according to the conventions of effective statistical analysis. Too often sampling is one area where authors do not follow conventions and employ sampling techniques that are not amenable to inferential analysis. Consulting with a statistician is not only okay, but it may be a necessary operation to ensure that the power of the test is adequate and that sampling is efficacious.
- Ultimately, the conclusion of the paper should bring everything together, not merely to summarize what has gone before, but to present the meaning of the paper. The significance of the problem, the completeness of the method, the extent of the findings, and the significance of the paper should be clearly stated. In short, the lessons to be learned by the work should be explicit.

Text Box 15.4: Editor's Advice

June Abbas, Editor-in-Chief, Library & Information Science Research

1. What is the worst mistake or one of the worst mistakes prospective authors make?

One of the worst mistakes an author can make is failing to review the scope statement for the journal to which they are submitting. Scope statements provide useful information about the focus of the journal, topics typically published by the journal, as well as topics the journal may not publish. Reviewing the scope statement will help the prospective author determine if the journal is the appropriate venue for their article. Doing so can also avoid disappointing desk rejection decisions.

2. What best practices are you able to offer prospective authors?

Journals include "author instructions" that guide the author through the development and submission process. Instructions about length, formatting, structure, headings, and components to include in the submission are usually provided in author instructions. A prospective author should read and adhere to author instructions closely. Failing to do so may result in prereview revisions, a delayed review period, and a longer proofing and publication process.

3. What do you look for in a submission?

The first thing I look for in a submission is "fit." Does the topic of the manuscript fit the scope of the journal? If the topic is novel and innovative, but it doesn't quite fit the scope, I consider whether it is possible to work with the author to revise the manuscript to fit the scope. The second most important aspect I look for in a submission is the quality of the research design, choice of appropriate methods for the study, and novelty of the research method, or if not novel, application of a known method to a new context. A submission must be within the scope of the journal, but also be of interest to journal readers. If the fit and quality are not present, then it is likely the submission will receive a desk reject decision and not be sent out for review.

PUBLISHING RESEARCH RESULTS

It is never too soon to start thinking about publishing venues for your current research project. Text boxes 15.3, 15.4, 15.5, and 15.6 are included to give you some sage advice along with an idea of how LIS journal editors evaluate submitted works. Hahn and Jaeger (2013) assert that deciding "where to publish should not be left until you are done writing, as the intended outlet will shape the tone, length, audience, formatting, and focus of the piece." They believe that the most important consideration about where to publish is the type of audience that one desires to reach, be it professionals, researchers, or a broader readership. If you are targeting scholarly journals in LIS, they recommend: *Library Quarterly, Journal of Academic Librarianship, portal,* and *College & Research Libraries(C&RL)*. Practitioner-oriented journals include *Library Hi Tech, Information Technology and Libraries*, and *Journal of Library Administration*. Professional magazines include *American Libraries, Library Journal,* and *College & Research Libraries News* (Hahn and Jaeger 2013). Hahn and Jaeger (2013) also provide a useful table of categories of publications, presentations, and service that build a publication record, which includes highly competitive and less competitive publications, unpublished presentations (such as conference papers and keynote addresses) and support/service/recognition (such as journal editing, editorial board membership, and book reviewing). It is worth mentioning here that considering highly competitive out-lets for publishing usually involves a potentially long review cycle of blind peer review, which could involve rounds of revision on the author's part. The result, however, is of higher quality and will be likely to have greater impact. For these journals, one worthwhile recommended first step is to take a look at the jour-nal's website to get an idea of the scope of articles they publish and guidelines for authors. One effective strategy is to email the editor before submission, to start a conversation about the work and to test the water to see if the piece to be submitted fits within the desired content. Perusing several issues of target journals or their table of contents also is important to get a sense of topics, length, tone, and type and frequency of citations.

For relative beginners, one pathway might be to start with a submission to a conference. Calls for papers come out months ahead of the event, and only may request an abstract, not a completed study. In this case, it is possible to project what can be accomplished by the conference date and write this up. The Librarian and Research Knowledge Space (LARKS) website includes a list of links to which to submit a research proposal for ALA conferences and meet-ings (http://www.ala.org/research/larks/present-publish). This page also has aggregated information and links to publication opportunities in the top library journals.

Several publications provide advice on getting published for librarians (Hahn and Jaeger 2013; McKnight 2009; Wildemuth 2017). It may be daunt-ing to submit your first manuscript for publication, but it is reassuring to know that journal editors are always looking for high-quality work. LIS profes-sionals already have an understanding of indexing and abstracting services, how journals are ranked in prestige, how to gage the time required for the evaluation and publication process, and how peer-review operates (McKnight 2009). McKnight recommends having multiple projects in the pipeline at once: "If you want to be prolific, use the convoy approach. At any given time have different projects at different stages. If one project has a breakdown that requires repairs or gets bumped back a few months, the others keep moving on. While you are always browsing and musing about professional issues, you can also be proposing a new piece of research, doing the research for some-thing you have proposed, writing the draft about something else and respond-ing to reviewers' suggestions in the revision of a manuscript from an even earlier project. There will always be delays and wrong turns, but with several projects in process, they won't be complete roadblocks to your productivity" (McKnight 2009, 116). Another important way to increase productivity is through collaboration, which is explored below.

Collaboration

Working collaboratively with others can enable one researcher to draw on the strengths of others who may have complementary skills. Piracha and Ameen (2016) analyzed five leading LIS research journals, finding that the majority were single authored and contributed by LIS faculty members. Nall and Gustavson (2010), as well as Lamothe (2012), recommend collaboration to increase output quantity and quality. It is vitally important to choose collaborators wisely, since not everyone has similar ideas about expected norms for shared work. Often successful collaborations can result in multiple projects, presentations, and publications. Recognizing when collaboration is unsuccessful is best done at the beginning of a project, before both people have invested significant time and energy. It is highly recommended that an open and frank discussion about authorship and expectations (who will be lead author, who will do what and when) be held as soon as possible, and that there be clear understandings of roles, responsibilities, and deadlines. Once these target dates have been set, one advantage that collaboration offers is that these agreed on deadlines with others become imperatives that hold one accountable. Disappointing or letting down others is a formidable reason to keep to deadlines. Janes asserts that collaboration yields better results than working as a single author and recommends increasing the amount of collaboration with teams that include academics and practicing librarians: "When our professional and scholarly communities come together and understand each other and each other's perspectives, the results of that research can be even more powerful in both venues" (Janes 2013, 19).

As noted above, publishing results is a professional responsibility as "librarians have a fundamental responsibility to contribute to professional communication" (Neal 1995, 199). As discussed throughout this book, and especially in chapters 1 and 12, assessment efforts and community-based research are essential for informing evidence-based practice, and need to be made public to be useful to the broad profession.

Using the same sampling frame for journals as Nisonger and Davis (2005), discussed below, Finlay and colleagues examined "4,827 peer-reviewed articles from twenty Library and Information Science (LIS) journals published between 1956 and 2011" to identify those written by practitioners. Unfortunately, the authors reported a decrease in practitioner-authored articles between 2006 and 2011 of a total of 31 percent (Finlay et al. 2013).

Early in the process of "getting published," the would-be author must decide on the format to be employed, the report vehicle, and the likely audience. Among the most common formats are monographs; scholarly articles in journals; papers delivered at professional meetings (often appearing in conference proceedings); unpublished reports such as dissertations and those indexed by Education Resources Information Center (ERIC); and grey literature, which includes documents in both electronic and print formats produced and "not controlled by commercial publishing, i.e., where publishing is not the primary activity of the producing body" (Howard 2020). Grey literature has become more easily accessible through grey literature databases and content producers' ability to make documents available on the web and through social media. Reports and some grey literature may not be considered publications in the conventional sense, but some unpublished reports and most dissertations represent original research.

Researchers who have decided to publish their research results in the journal article format must know the journals (vehicles) in which they might publish; select a subject for a manuscript (essentially done when the research was initiated); determine the methodology and style of writing to employ; write the manuscript; carefully prepare the manuscript for submission (as dictated by the journal's instructions to authors); work with the editor in the review of the manuscript; and, if the article is accepted for publication, tend to the final editing and proofreading of the manuscript and galley proofs (Johnson 1985).

Busha and Harter (1980, 374) noted that "the selection of a publication vehicle in which to communicate a research report should depend upon the topic of the study, the nature of the material presented, and the desired audience." In 2005, Nisonger and Davis (2005) published an analysis and ranking of LIS journals based on the perceptions of LIS education program deans and directors of large research libraries.

Manzari (2013) published a study in 2013 that uses the same list of seventy-one journals used in the Nisonger and Davis (2005) study discussed above but sent it to full-time faculty of American Library Association (ALA) accredited programs in LIS. The faculty were asked to rank the journals from one to five, with one being the lowest and five being the highest, based on the "journal's importance to their research and teaching" (Manzari 2013, 44). Three journals were in the top five for the rankings by both mean and mode. The highest five LIS journals ranked by mode by deans in the Nisonger and Davis (2005) study also were listed by faculty as the five most prestigious LIS journals: *Information Processing and Management, Journal of Documentation, JASIST, Library & Information Science Research*, and *Library Quarterly* (Manzari 2013).

Wusu and Lazarus (2018) provided a list of the twenty-five top most popular publishing journals in LIS research in an analysis of 6,498 records from 1980 through 2017. Their top ten journals with fifty or more citations include:

- *Cochrane Database of Systematic Review*
- *Journal of Documentation*
- *Library & Information Science Research*
- *Library Trends*
- *Journal of the Medical Library Association*
- *Journal of the American Society for Information Science and Technology*
- *Library Quarterly*
- *Information Research*
- *Journal of Education for Library and Information Science*
- *Scientometrics* (Wusu and Lazarus 2018, 15)

It is recommended that you decide early which journal you want to submit your work to, so that you can tailor your writing to that journal. One worthwhile practice is to send an email to the journal editor describing your article and asking if this seems to be a good fit. This practice opens a dialog with the editor, who is usually delighted to receive these types of queries in their never-ending quest for quality manuscripts to publish. Additionally, read several issues of a target journal to get a feel for the writing style and the topics that are within the journal's scope.

When journal referees evaluate manuscripts, they generally address criteria similar to those used to evaluate research reports (see the criteria previously provided in this chapter). In the Author Guidelines published by C&RL, the main considerations for reviewers are the following ("Submissions" n.d.):

Does the manuscript make a new contribution to the literature?

Is the method used appropriate to the subject?

Does the evidence presented support the hypothesis?

Does the author communicate clearly with an educated, yet not necessarily specialized, audience?

Does the literature review place the research or opinions in perspective?

Text Box 15.5: Editor's Advice

Paul T. Jaeger, Co-Editor, Library Quarterly, and Editor, Advance in Librarianship

After earning your MLIS degree, you probably would not think that you should apply for jobs as a veterinarian. However, far too often, authors make a similar mistake when submitting papers for publication. You may want to publish in a certain journal or conference because of its reputation or prominence or audience, but that desire alone will not make your paper appropriate for a certain venue.

Before submission, authors should do research to ensure that their paper fits within the scope of the venue; at a minimum, read the venue's statements about the scope of what it publishes and review the titles in the tables of contents for recent issues or proceedings, as the case may be. Better yet, read an assortment of sample papers from the venue to ascertain a clear sense of what it covers. Unfortunately, this practice is not followed by many authors, leaving editors to "desk reject"—that is, reject it without sending it for review—many papers that should never have been submitted to the venue in the first place.

Identifying an appropriate venue for your paper is a good start, but hardly the only place that authors regularly make missteps. In most cases, your work will be contributing to an already ongoing discourse, and even if it is an undiscovered area of research, it will be building on previous work in related areas. For example, you may have great new ideas related to information literacy, but that does not mean that you can ignore the preceding discourse about literacy. Situating a new idea in context helps readers understand what is new and why it is important. Frequently, though, papers are submitted in which the author seems unaware or disinterested in the rest of the discourse about their topic.

And the notion of newness is equally important as well—your paper should be making a contribution. Many submissions that editors receive come perilously close to fitting the James Brown song "Talking Loud and Saying Nothing." The contribution of your paper can be in theory, research questions, methods, analysis, or a combination thereof. You can take existing data and analyze it in a new way, explore a piece of hidden history, or bridge two lines of discussion for the first time. Even in a heavily studied area, there will still be much that is new to uncover. When you submit your paper, it should be clear to the reader wherein the contributions can be found.

If you take the basic steps detailed above, you will have made it possible for editors to work with your submission. While you are at it, you will also facilitate the path of your paper through the publication process if you are attentive to practical requirements as well. Follow the venue's citation style and other stylistic guidelines, stay within the word or page count, meet the deadlines provided by the venue, carefully edit your paper for grammar, and address the comments that you receive from editors and reviewers. Simply submitting the final paper of a course that is still in the format of a course paper is not likely to lead to much publication success.

Authors often get so focused on the difficulty and scariness of the publication process that they forget that venues need good papers. Editors hope that every new paper that they receive will be publishable; they root for submissions that will make readers think, challenge assumptions, or extend the discourse in an area of research. Editors of journals and conferences have chosen to devote a portion of each workday, perhaps a significant portion of their entire careers, to unpaid work focused on finding, nurturing, improving, and bringing attention to the writings of other authors. If you work to ensure that your paper meets the expectations of the venue at the time of submission, you will be greatly increasing the likelihood that your paper will ultimately be published.

Text Box 15.6: Editor's Advice

Xiuzhen (Jenny) Zhang, Associate Editor, Information Processing & Management

1. What is the worst mistake or one of the worst mistakes prospective authors make?

   One of the worst mistakes that authors can make is mixing up the different sections of the paper. Research papers are well structured documents and typically comprise sections such as Introduction, Related Work, Methodology, Experiments, Results and Discussions, and Conclusion. Readers expect to see the description of the research problem and the background for the research in the Introduction section. If research questions are presented much later in a paper, authors are relying on readers to read very carefully to find them, and they may easily lose interest. It is therefore crucial that authors set up the structure for a paper and adhere to it.

2. What best practices are you able to offer prospective authors?

   - Write abstracts that highlight your research findings. The abstract of a paper provides the first impression on readers and therefore is critically important. Describing findings in the abstract will create a strong opening and attract readers.
   - Use appropriate tables and figures. A paper that only has text is boring. Tables and figures will highlight important information and explain data more effectively, especially for summarizing results.
   - Include current references for your research area. Old references cannot represent the state of the art. Discussing the most recent references will set up a strong background for your research, and the results and findings established in this context are therefore more convincing.

3. What do you look for in a submission?

   - Clear introduction of research questions or challenges worthy of investigation.
   - Comprehensive literature review that clearly identifies the gap in the current literature.
   - Coherent presentation of the proposed methodology or study design that addresses the research questions.
   - Thorough description of experiments and deep analysis of results.
   - Objective discussions of research findings in the context of the current literature.

LIS journals that are peer-reviewed will send your manuscript to several experts for feedback. The editor will then summarize their reviews and give you the verdict, publish as is (possible but extremely rare), resubmit with minor revision (also rather rare), resubmit with medium to major revision, or reject. The goal generally is to get an "R&R" (revise and resubmit), as this means that the editor wants to publish your piece as long as you do the suggested revisions faithfully. If you have any questions at this point, be sure to ask the editor. When you are lucky enough to get an "R&R," be sure to carefully compose and also submit a letter to the editor that describes your revisions, addressing each point that the editor/reviewers suggested.

If you receive a reject, consider rewriting the piece and submitting to another journal. Sometimes articles are rejected because they are "out of scope" of the journal, although if you had already opened an email conversation with the editor prior to submission, this time-wasting step can be averted.

Would-be authors wishing to report their research results in book format must follow a procedure not much different from that for publishing a journal article. An author will need to identify a publisher that focuses on the discipline and content area of the manuscript, submit a book proposal or sample chapter, if requested, negotiate the terms of the contract, write the manuscript, and submit it to the publisher in the agreed-on format and time frame. Just as one should take care to select the most appropriate journal, one should shop around for a book publisher. Factors to consider in selecting a publisher include pricing, design, marketing, editorial assistance, production schedule, review process, and royalty arrangements. *Times Higher Education* (Murray 2014) published straightforward advice from academic book authors that could prove to be quite helpful.

The University Library at the University of Illinois at Urbana-Champaign has a LibGuide on publishing in LIS that is useful ("Publishing in IS" n.d.). A blog, Academic Writing Librarians ("Academic Writing Librarians" n.d.; "Academic Writing Librarians: Top Tips from Journal Editors" n.d.; "Academic Writing Librarians: Top Tips from Published Authors" n.d.), maintained by the library at Maynooth University, offers many helpful hints for those interested in writing for LIS journals, such as tips from published authors and journal editors and resources for academic writing. Another helpful source for identifying LIS publishing venues is the LIS Publications Wiki provided by the School of Information at San Jose State University, which features a list of LIS scholarly journals, professional and trade publications, with links to the publication sources. The wiki also profiles ("About | LIS Publications Wiki" n.d.; Gordon 2004) LIS book publishers including: ALA Editions, Association of College & Research Libraries (ACRL), Libraries Unlimited, Library Juice Press, Routledge, Rowman & Littlefield, Society of American Archivists (SAA), the University of Chicago Press, and more ("Book Publishers | LIS Publications Wiki" n.d.). The New Members Round Table (NMRT) of ALA hosts a discussion group, NMRTWriter (nmrtwriter@lists.ala.org), dedicated to supporting librarians wishing to write and publish articles and books. See text boxes 15.7 and 15.8, below, for more tips on ways to increase productivity.

Graduates of doctoral programs are encouraged to publish their dissertations as books and/or to summarize them for publication in a journal, as one or more articles. In doing so, they should remove much of the redundancy typical of dissertations, decrease some of the details regarding previous research and methodology, and relate the work to the concrete world as much as possible. The *Publication Manual of the American Psychological Association* addresses converting a dissertation into an article (*Publication Manual of the American Psychological Association* 2019).

Other ways to disseminate and publish research results are through blogs and social media. These venues do not replace the more traditional forms of dissemination, such as publishing in journals or books, but provide new opportunities to promote research to audiences who may not seek out traditional publishing outlets. Blog posts give researchers opportunities to test theories, hypotheses, and ideas, as well as provide a venue for discussion and to share highlights or unexpected results in a more informal and concise (and usually quicker) way. Twitter, Facebook posts, and YouTube videos provide venues for researchers to share short teasers, with references or links to blogs, presentations, abstracts, articles, and reports. Uploading presentations to SlideShare and citations and papers to ResearchGate and LinkedIn are other ways to amplify interest in one's research. Carrigan's (2020) book, *Social Media for Academics* includes several chapters on the possibilities of promoting and sharing research through social media, and also a chapter on the dark side of social media. See also Radford et al. 2020.

Text Box 15.7: Publish or Perish: How to Boost Productivity

What do experts recommend as practical suggestions for how to boost your research productivity? (By the way, these tips work for writing research papers while you are in a graduate program too!) Research and writing can be enjoyable but also can be challenging. There are a multitude of responsibilities, ever-present and demanding deadlines, nonstop email, and numerous distractions that can keep us from writing.

A book by Boice (2000) is highly recommended as one of the most useful resources on this topic. He offered ten suggestions for increasing research and writing productivity based on long years of research on publication productivity. Although this work is geared toward new academic faculty members, its content is highly relevant for library researchers. Here are Boice's ten rules:

Wait (for inspiration, for the eureka moment, and curb impatience). "Waiting requires patience at holding back from impulsivity, rushing, and busyness" (Boice 2000, 273).

Begin early (before you are ready). This can "foster early, informal beginnings at tasks we might rather avoid now and do under deadlines" (Boice 2000, 273).

Work in short regular sessions (do not wait until you have an entire day to write, a consistent schedule of writing 1 hour per day will bring surprising results). Those who write in "brief, daily sessions write with less pain, with more productivity and quality, and with higher likelihood of acceptance in prestigious outlets" (Boice 2000, 274).

Stop (pause). Boice recommends pausing at times for contemplation and reflection. Some people use a timer to interrupt for a 5-minute stretch every hour, if needed. Online tools, such as Workrave (http://www.workrave.org) or Rescue Time (www.rescuetime.com) give frequent alerts to take breaks and has a restriction on daily time to help prevent repetitive strain injury. Frequent breaks also prevent eyestrain.

Balance preliminaries with formal work. Boice recommends spending about the same amount of time on creating quick drafts and outlines as on actual writing.

Moderate overattachment and overreaction. Share drafts early and often. Seek and welcome editing suggestions.

Moderate negative thoughts (e.g., "This project is too big"; "I'm behind deadline"; "I will never get this done!"). Negative thinking is depressing and discouraging (Boice 2000, 276).

Moderate emotions. Those who "work with constancy and moderation: Evidence unmistakable superiority in producing manuscript pages . . . [and] report more ease, satisfaction, and joyfulness" (Boice 2000, 276).

Let others do some of the work. Boice (2000) argues that productivity is boosted for those who are not afraid to ask for help. He says pride usually stops us from asking for help and/or collaboration.

Limit wasted effort. Boice (2000) asserts that failure can come when one is on the brink of success, so take care that you pay attention to the follow-through and finishing of projects.

Reference

Boice, Robert. 2000. *Advice for New Faculty Members*. Boston: Pearson.

Text Box 15.8: Publish More! Advice for Increasing Productivity

Here are additional recommendations for students, librarians, and researchers wishing to boost productivity:

Be open to ideas (read publications and regularly attend research presentations). One question that aspiring researchers often ask is: "How do I find a topic for my research?" If you are fortunate, you may have a "burning question" that you want to answer/explore, but you also may struggle to figure out a research focus. Research ideas can be found by reading professional journals; by attending virtual or in-person talks, conferences, and symposia that feature research; and in discussions with colleagues and friends. Ameen, Batool, and Naveed conducted focus groups with students in LIS graduate programs in Pakistan. They found three major difficulties that hampered formulation of research topics: (1) conceptual clarity, (2) poor time management, and (3) lack of research culture. Participants experienced anxiety in identifying a research topic, especially when they encountered duplication—when someone else had already covered the ground they were planning to investigate. They were found to rely primarily on "previously produced theses, research articles and their supervisors' help" for developing their own work (Ameen, Batool, and Naveed, 2019, 596–600).

Review articles also can be helpful, such as one by Hodoun-Wusu and Lazarus (Wusu and Lazarus, 2018, 1873), who conducted a bibliometric analysis of major trends in LIS research. They compiled a list of the twenty-five most frequently found keywords. Published research agendas also offer topics as well as suggested research questions. These are published on a wide range of LIS topics, such as the one by Kankanhalli, Charalabidis, and Melloui (2019, 304–309) on the internet of things (IoT) and artificial intelligence (AI) for smart government; or by Shorish and Hall (2019) on the ACRL research agenda for scholarly communication; or by Young Adult Library Services Association (YALSA) on the national research agenda ("What Does YALSA's National Research Agenda Have to Offer

You?" 2017). Another approach is to browse online conference programs and/or online proceedings from related organizations, such as ACRL (*ACRL 2019 Proceedings*, 2019), the Association for Library and Information Science Education (ALISE) (*Proceedings of the Association for Library and Information Science Education Annual Conference* n.d.), the Association for Information Science and Technology (ASIS&T) (*Proceedings of the Association for Information Science and Technology*, n.d.), the Library Research Seminar (LRS) (2014) and the ALA (Schedule-at-a-glance | ALA Annual 2019), and the iConference (*iSchools, Inc.—iConference 2020 Summary* n.d.) to see what topics of interest are popular.

Here are some additional suggestions.

- Streamline and aggregate your citation process (use an online tool for citation/bibliographic data management). The sooner you invest the time to download and start using one of these software tools (such as Zotero, Mendeley, Endnote, or RefWorks) the better. These save time and allow you to curate the resources you need for assignments or writing projects all in one place. Choosing which one to use is personal, or the library or organization where you work may have a subscription that you can use. Wikipedia has an excellent article that compares a long list of reference management software ("Comparison of Reference Management Software" 2020).
- Put first things first (prioritize). Time management wizard Stephen Covey (2004) suggested that we need to know what our priorities are. Once we have decided our top priorities, he argued that we schedule and commit our time for tasks like research and writing, which are not urgent but are important. Otherwise they become lost in the daily grind.
- Find your rhythm (what works for you?). If you are to schedule and commit time for writing, when and where does this work for you? Only you know if you are most productive in the morning, afternoon, or evening. Can you commit to writing for short periods of time every day? Or longer stretches twice a week? Are you able to work at home, or is a cybercafe or coffeehouse more conducive to your writing? Finding what works for you is essential to writing success. For a great read on this topic, see Daniel Pink's (2018) book *When: The Scientific Secrets of Perfect Timing*. Pink also is a big advocate of taking breaks during writing sessions, which can have an impact. He advocates regular micro breaks (20-20-20 rule that every 20 minutes look at something 20 feet away, for 20 seconds) or taking a 5-minute break every hour, or taking a walk at lunch, preferably outdoors if possible (Pink 2018).
- Synergize (work-research connection, multipurposing your reports, newsletter articles, etc.). You may already have worked on several reports, projects, or class assignments that could be written up for publication. Ivins (2014) provided tips in her article "Upcycling Masters of Science in Library and Information Science (MSLS) Coursework into Publishable Content." She noted that "new librarians can more rapidly generate publishable material by exploiting a rich mine of their own high-quality writing: their MSLS coursework" (Ivins 2014, 1). Your existing papers can be important starting points for research projects or can perhaps be inspirations for topics you want to pursue in more depth. Synergizing also takes the form of having one thing work for more than one purpose. For example, an assessment report of an information literacy pilot project (or program) at your library can be worked into a conference presentation and then into a paper for publication.
- Work to your strengths and interest (focus and enjoyment). Since you are going to be making an effort across a span of time to conduct research and write it up for presentation or publication, it makes sense that your topic should enable you to work to your strengths and both capture and sustain your interest. From our personal experience, if a

topic for a writing project is not engaging, the time spent on it can be excruciatingly painful. If, on the other hand, the project is one that catches and holds attention, the piece can feel like it is writing itself. Knowing and playing to your strengths is equally important (e.g., you are gregarious and like to engage with people, individual interviews and focus group interviews would be enjoyable; or you prefer to work in solitary, perhaps surveys or work with big data sets would be more conducive to your style).

- Break the task into incremental steps (baby steps). Writing a master's thesis, journal article, research report, book, or dissertation can seem daunting, but any large project can be broken down into small steps. Sometimes getting started is the most difficult part, so starting with an outline is one way to work. Then you can select one part of the outline to work on. Suppose you decide to start by doing a literature review. This could be done in three steps: finding, reading plus note taking, and writing. First, devote several hours to searching the databases for pertinent articles and downloading these. The next day a goal could be to sort and read the ones that looked most interesting, taking notes as you go along, adding them to your reference software manager (see first bullet). When all the articles have been read, you can draft a few paragraphs summarizing this work that will go into the literature review. Cited references from these articles may lead to more reading.
- Set target dates (your personal deadlines). Setting target dates goes along with breaking the work into steps. If you have a firm deadline (e.g., for a course assignment or conference paper submission), you can work backward from that date to set incremental targets for yourself. The tighter the deadline, the more important it is to have incremental target dates. In addition, if you are working collaboratively, you will have to have your assigned work done in ample time for your collaborator to read and revise it before submission.
- Create a plan (get specific). Covey recommended "beginning with the end in mind" (Covey 2004). Thinking through an entire research project is a way to get a good handle on your ultimate goal. The plan should have an overview of the timeline for the project, with specific steps and target dates. If you are working with a collaborator(s), tracking who will be responsible for what is important. Applications for grant projects can require a detailed timeline of activities tied to budget (Radford and Connaway, 2005; Radford, Connaway, and Shah, 2011).
- Capture ideas (keep a writing notebook or online document, such as Google doc). One important way to bolster productivity is to keep track of your ideas. Many researchers keep a writing or research notebook or electronic document in which they record incremental steps and target dates and due dates from calls for papers. This notebook/document also could be used to jot down ideas for your current project, or for future projects, so you do not lose them.
- Find time! Sharpen your time management skills. Text box 1.3 in chapter 1 provides advice on this topic.
- Consider collaborative writing sessions in which you meet either in person at a coffee shop or other location, or virtually on Zoom or another platform, to write together on different projects in silence. This can be done in pairs or in larger groups. Usually, these sessions start with brief goal setting for each person, and then individuals write in silence for a set time (usually 45 minutes to an hour). At the end of the session, there is a quick check in on accomplishing goals. If there is agreement to continue, another round can take place. Collaborative writing of this type can heighten productivity and afford mutual support, as writing can be a solitary or isolating experience for some, especially during extended writing experiences, such as a master's thesis or dissertation.

References

ACRL 2019 Proceedings. 2019. Association of College and Research Libraries.

Ameen, K., S. H. Batool, and M. A. Naveed. 2019. "Difficulties Novice LIS Researchers Face While Formulating a Research Topic." *Information Development* 35(4): 592–600. https://doi.org/10.1177/0266666918774875.

"Comparison of Reference Management Software." 2020. In *Wikipedia.* https://en.wikipedia.org/w/index.php?title=Comparison_of_reference_management_software&oldid=985412208.

Covey, S. R. 2004. *The 7 Habits of Highly Effective People: Powerful Lessons in Personal Change.* Rev. ed. Free Press.

iSchools, Inc.—iConference 2020 Summary. n.d. Accessed November 6, 2020. https://ischools.org/iConference-2020-Summary/#quick_links.

Ivins, T. 2014. "Upcycling MSLS Coursework into Publishable Content." *Endnotes: The Journal of the New Members Round Table* 5(1): 1–16.

Kankanhalli, A., Y. Charalabidis, and S. Mellouli. 2019. "IoT and AI for Smart Government: A Research Agenda." *Government Information Quarterly* 36(2): 304–309. https://doi.org/10.1016/j.giq.2019.02.003

Library Research Seminar (LRS). 2014. *Schedule.* http://www.library.illinois.edu/lrs6/schedule.html.

Pink, D. 2018. *When: The Scientific Secrets of Perfect Timing.* Riverhead Books.

Proceedings of the Association for Information Science and Technology. n.d. Association for Information Science and Technology.

Proceedings of the Association for Library and Information Science Education Annual Conference. n.d. Association for Library and Information Science Education Annual Conference.

Radford, M. L., and L. S. Connaway. 2005, 2008. *Seeking Synchronicity: Evaluating Virtual Reference Services.* OCLC. https://www.oclc.org/content/research/areas/user-studies/synchronicity.html.

Radford, M. L., L. S. Connaway, and C. Shah. 2011. *Cyber Synergy: Seeking Sustainability through Collaboration between Virtual Reference and Social Q&A Sites* [Grant Proposal]. Rutgers University and OCLC. http://citeseerx.ist.psu.edu/viewdoc/download?doi=10.1.1.434.1004&rep=rep1&type=pdf.

Schedule-at-a-glance | ALA Annual 2019. 2019, May 1. https://2019.alaannual.org/whats-happening/schedule-glance.

Shorish, Y., and N. Hall. 2019. "Creating the ACRL Research Agenda for Scholarly Communication: A Move towards More Equitable, Open Systems." *College & Research Libraries News.* https://doi.org/10.5860/crln.80.8.430.

"What Does YALSA's National Research Agenda Have to Offer You? Discover How YALSA's National Research Agenda Can Impact Your Practice." 2017. *Young Adult Library Services* 15(4): 4–6.

Wusu, O. H., and N. G. Lazarus. 2018. "Major Trends in LIS Research: A Bibliometric Analysis." *Library Philosophy and Practice* 22: 1–21.

SUMMARY

Unless the results of research are properly communicated, all of the efforts that went into the research are of local value (say for an in-house user survey for assessment purposes), but of no value to the broader library profession. The first basic step required for disseminating the results of research is the writing of a report. This report should be a straightforward document that clearly, precisely, and efficiently describes what the researcher has done to investigate a problem.

The research report should be well organized and generally follow a standard, recommended format. The researcher should exercise care in the documentation and writing of the report. It should be clean and error free. Graphic displays should be used where appropriate to visualize data that may be difficult to understand. The writer should be aware of what the informed reader would be looking for and be careful to avoid the common faults of research reports.

In writing the report and looking ahead to its publication, the researcher should keep in mind the audience that it should reach and the method of publication or dissemination likely to be used. It is important to be aware of the review mechanisms of journals and professional conferences/proceedings and to tailor manuscripts to their criteria and interests.

Researchers should not underestimate the value of disseminating and promoting research in face-to-face and virtual presentations and through multiple social media outlets, which may reach different audiences. In conclusion, the importance of reporting research results should not be underestimated. The research report, regardless of format, is what communicates specific information to an audience, adds to the general body of knowledge, and hopefully stimulates further research.

REFERENCES

"About | LIS Publications Wiki." n.d. Accessed November 5, 2020. https://ischoolwikis.sjsu.edu/lispublications/about.

"Academic Writing Librarians." n.d. *Academic Writing Librarians* (blog). Accessed November 5, 2020. http://academicwritinglibrarian.blogspot.com/.

"Academic Writing Librarians: Top Tips from Journal Editors." n.d. *Academic Writing Librarians* (blog). Accessed November 5, 2020. http://academicwritinglibrarian.blogspot.com/p/top-tips-from-journal-editors.html.

"Academic Writing Librarians: Top Tips from Published Authors." n.d. *Academic Writing Librarians* (blog). Accessed November 5, 2020. http://academicwritinglibrarian.blogspot.com/p/blog-page_22.html.

"ACRL." n.d. Text. Association of College & Research Libraries. Accessed November 4, 2020. http://www.ala.org/acrl.

"ASIS&T." n.d. Association for Information Science and Technology. Accessed November 4, 2020. https://www.asist.org.

Bachman, Ronet D., and Russell K. Schutt. 2014. *The Practice of Research in Criminology and Criminal Justice.* 5th ed. Los Angeles: Sage.

"Book Publishers | LIS Publications Wiki." n.d. Accessed November 5, 2020. https://ischoolwikis.sjsu.edu/lispublications/wiki/book-publishers.

Busha, Charles H., and Stephen P. Harter. 1980. *Research Methods in Librarianship: Techniques and Interpretation.* Cambridge, MA: Academic Press.

"CARL." n.d. California Academic & Research Libraries Association. Accessed November 4, 2020. http://www.carl-acrl.org.

Carrigan, Mark. 2020. *Social Media for Academics.* 2nd ed. Thousand Oaks, CA: Sage.

Connaway, Lynn Silipigni, Marie L Radford, and OCLC Research. 2011. *Seeking Synchronicity: Revelations and Recommendations for Virtual Reference.* Dublin, OH: OCLC Research.

Connell, Tschera Harkness. 2010. "Writing the Research Paper: A Review." *College & Research Libraries* 71(1): 6–7.

Creswell, John W. 2008. *Research Design: Qualitative, Quantitative, and Mixed Methods Approaches.* 3rd ed. Thousand Oaks, CA: Sage.

Creswell, John W., and Cheryl N. Poth. 2016. *Qualitative Inquiry and Research Design: Choosing among Five Approaches.* Thousand Oaks, CA: Sage.

Finlay, S. Craig, Chaoqun Ni, Andrew Tsou, and Cassidy R. Sugimoto. 2013. "Publish or Practice? An Examination of Librarians' Contributions to Research." *Portal: Libraries and the Academy* 13(4): 403–21. https://doi.org/10.1353/pla.2013.0038.

"40 Presentation Software & Powerpoint Alternatives for 2017." 2019. CustomShow. https://www.customshow.com/best-powerpoint-alternatives-presentation-programs.

Girden, Ellen R. 2010. *Evaluating Research Articles from Start to Finish.* 3rd ed. Thousand Oaks, CA: Sage.

Gordon, Rachel Singer. 2004. "Getting Started in Library Publication." *American Libraries* 35(1): 66–69.

Hahn, Trudi Bellardo, and Paul T. Jaeger. 2013. "From Practice to Publication: A Path for Academic Library Professionals." *College & Research Libraries News* 74(5): 238–42. https://doi.org/10.5860/crln.74.5.8944.

Hillway, Tyrus. 1964. *Introduction to Research.* 2nd ed. Boston: Houghton Mifflin.

Hofschire, Linda. 2020. "Data Visualization on a Budget: Simple Tips, Techniques, and Low-Cost Tools." *Computers in Libraries* 40(5). https://www.infotoday.com/cilmag/jul20/Hofcshire--Data-Visualization-on-a-Budget.shtml.

Holloway, Immy, and Lorraine Brown. 2016. *Essentials of a Qualitative Doctorate.* Abingdon, Oxfordshire, UK: Routledge.

Howard, Allison. 2020. "LibGuides: Grey Literature." https://guides.lib.usf.edu/grey_literature/start_here.

"IFLA." n.d. International Federation of Library Associations and Institutions. Accessed November 4, 2020. https://www.ifla.org.

Janes, Joseph. 2013. "Making Friends with Research: Collaborating Can Yield Better Results Than Working Alone." *American Libraries* 45(3/4). https://americanlibrariesmagazine.org/2012/12/19/making-friends-with-research/

Johnson, Richard D. 1985. "The Journal Article." In *Librarian/Author: A Practical Guide on How to Get Published,* edited by Betty-Carol Sellen, 21–35. New York: Neal-Schuman.

"Johnson: What's That Again?" 2020. *The Economist.*

Lamothe, Alain R. 2012. "The Importance of Encouraging Librarians to Publish in Peer-Reviewed Publications." *Journal of Scholarly Publishing* 43(2): 156–67. https://doi.org/10.1353/scp.2012.0004.

"LHRT." 2017. Text. Library History Round Table. October 8. http://www.ala.org/rt/library-history-round-table/lhrt-journal.

"LIBER." n.d. Association of European Research Libraries. Accessed November 4, 2020. https://libereurope.eu.

"LIDA." n.d. Libraries in the Digital Age. Accessed November 4, 2020. http://lida.ffos.hr.

Lindlof, Thomas R., and Bryan C. Taylor. 2019. *Qualitative Communication Research Methods.* 4th ed. Los Angeles: Sage.

"LRRT." 2020. Text. Library Research Round Table. April 22. http://www.ala.org/rt/lrrt.

Manzari, Laura. 2013. "Library and Information Science Journal Prestige as Assessed by Library and Information Science Faculty." *The Library Quarterly* 83(1): 42–60. https://doi.org/10.1086/668574.

McKnight, Michelynn. 2009. "Professional Publication: Yes, You Can!" *The Journal of Academic Librarianship* 35(2): 115–16. https://doi.org/10.1016/j.acalib .2009.01.001.

Murray, Dale E. 2014. "10 Point Guide to Dodging Publishing Pitfalls." Times Higher Education World University Rankings. March 6. https://www .timeshighereducation.com/features/10-point-guide-to-dodging-publishing -pitfalls/2011808.article.

Nall, Clark, and Amy Gustavson. 2010. "Surviving the Tenure Process: A Model for Collaborative Research." *Endnotes* 1(1): 1–8.

Naqvi, Kaleem. 2020. "Zoom Becomes Most Downloaded App, Overtakes TikTok." *Technology Times.* July 21. https://www.technologytimes.pk/2020/07/21 /zoom-becomes-most-downloaded-app-overtakes-tiktok.

Neal, James G. 1995. "Editorial: The Librarian Research and Publication Imperative." *Library & Information Science Research* 3(17): 199–200.

Newman, John. 1998. "Academic Librarians as Scholars." *College & Research Libraries News* 59(1): 19.

Nisonger, Thomas E., and Charles H. Davis. 2005. "The Perception of Library and Information Science Journals by LIS Education Deans and ARL Library Directors: A Replication of the Kohl-Davis Study." *College & Research Libraries* 66(4): 341–77.

Paul, Richard, and Linda Elder. 2007. *The Miniature Guide to Critical Thinking: Concepts and Tools.* 4th ed. Dillon Beach, CA: Critical Thinking Press.

Phelps, Renata, Kath Fisher, and Allan Ellis. 2007. *Organizing and Managing Your Research: A Practical Guide for Postgraduates.* Los Angeles, CA: Sage.

Piracha, Hasaeeb Ahmad, and Kanwal Ameen. 2016. "Emerging Research Trends in Library and Information Science: A Content Analysis of Core LIS Journals." *Pakistan Library and Information Science Journal* 47(4): 56–68.

Publication Manual of the American Psychological Association. 2019. 7th ed. Washington, DC: American Psychological Association.

"Publishing in IS." n.d. University Library, University of Illinois at Urbana-Champaign. https://www.library.illinois.edu/infosci/profession/publishing.

Pyrczak, Fred. 2014. *Evaluating Research in Academic Journals: A Practical Guide to Realistic Evaluation.* Glendale, CA: Pyrczak.

Radford, Marie L., Mary Chayko, and Tawfiq Ammari. 2020. "Developing Your Mediated Scholarly Identity." Doctoral Colloquium, Rutgers University, November 4.

Radford, Marie L., Lynn Silipigni Connaway, and Chirag Shah. 2011. "Cyber Synergy: Seeking Sustainability through Collaboration between Virtual Reference and Social Q&A Sites." Grant Proposal. Institute of Museum and Library Services (IMLS): Rutgers University and OCLC. http://citeseerx.ist.psu.edu /viewdoc/download?doi=10.1.1.434.1004&rep=rep1&type=pdf.

Radford, Marie L., Vanessa Kitzie, Stephanie Mikitish, Diana Floegel, Gary P. Radford, and Lynn Silipigni Connaway. 2020. "'People Are Reading Your Work,' Scholarly Identity and Social Networking Sites." *Journal of Documentation* (ahead-of-print). https://doi.org/10.1108/JD-04-2019-0074.

"RLUK." n.d. Research Libraries UK. Accessed November 4, 2020. https://www .rluk.ac.uk.

"RUSA." n.d. Text. Reference & User Services Association. Accessed November 4, 2020. http://www.ala.org/rusa.

"7 Quick Tips to Up Your Video Calling Game." 2020. *Time.* https://time.com /5861183/video-calling-tips.

Shore, Zachary. 2016. *Grad School Essentials: A Crash Course in Scholarly Skills.* Oakland: University of California Press.

"Submissions." n.d. College & Research Libraries. Accessed July 6, 2020. https:// crl.acrl.org/index.php/crl/about/submissions#authorGuidelines.

Tufte, Edward R. 1997a. *Visual Explanations: Images and Quantities, Evidence and Narrative*. Cheshire, CT: Graphics Press.

Tufte, Edward R. 1997b. *Visual and Statistical Thinking: Displays of Evidence for Making Decisions*. Cheshire, CT: Graphics Press.

Tufte, Edward R. 2001. *The Visual Display of Quantitative Information*. 2nd ed. Cheshire, CT: Graphics Press.

Tufte, Edward R. 2006a. *Envisioning Information*. Cheshire, CT: Graphics Press.

Tufte, Edward R. 2006b. *Beautiful Evidence*. Cheshire, CT: Graphics Press.

Wildemuth, Barbara M. 2017. *Applications of Social Research Methods to Questions in Information and Library Science*. 2nd ed. Santa Barbara, CA: ABC-CLIO.

Wusu, Oluwaseyi H., and Nneka G. Lazarus. 2018. "Major Trends in LIS Research: A Bibliometric Analysis." *Library Philosophy and Practice* 22: 1–21.

Wynar, Dan. 1962. *Syllabus for Research Methods in Librarianship*. Denver: Graduate School of Librarianship.

Author Index

Subject Index

About the Authors

LYNN SILIPIGNI CONNAWAY is director of library trends and user research at OCLC Research. She is past president of ASIS&T, the recipient of the 2016 Association for Library and Information Science Educators Service Award (ALISE), the 2019 ALISE/ProQuest Methodology Paper Competition, the 2020 ALISE Connie Van Fleet Award for Research Excellence in Public Library Services to Adults, the Association for Information Science and Technology (ASIS&T) 2019 Watson Davis Award, and the 2020 Distinguished Alumna Award at the University of Wisconsin–Madison Information School. With Marie L. Radford, she was a recipient of the 2012 Reference and User Services Association (RUSA) Reference Service Press Award and the 2013 ALISE Bohdan S. Wynar Research Paper Competition. Connaway is past chair of the ACRL Value of Academic Libraries Committee. She held the Chair of Excellence at the Universidad Carlos III de Madrid. She is coauthor of the fourth and fifth editions of *Basic Research Methods for Librarians* with Ronald R. Powell and of the sixth edition of *Research Methods in Library and Information Science* with Marie L. Radford. Connaway is a frequent international speaker and author.

MARIE L. RADFORD is chair and professor in the Department of Library and Information Science at Rutgers, The State University of New Jersey's School of Communication and Information. Her latest books are *Conducting the Reference Interview,* 3rd ed., with Catherine Sheldrick Ross and Kirsti Nilsen (2019), *Library Conversations: Reclaiming Interpersonal Communication Theory for Understanding Professional Encounters* with Gary Radford (2017), and *Research Methods in Library and Information Science,* 6th ed., with Lynn Silipigni Connaway (2017). With Lynn Silipigni Connaway, she was co-PI of the "Seeking Synchronicity" and "Cyber Synergy" grant projects funded by IMLS,

527

Rutgers, and OCLC. With Lynn Silipigni Connaway, she was a recipient of the 2012 Reference and User Services Association (RUSA) Reference Service Press Award and the 2013 ALISE Bohdan S. Wynar Research Paper Competition. Her research focuses on qualitative approaches, interpersonal communication within virtual and traditional reference service, and postmodern approaches to library problematics. She gives frequent keynotes and presentations at national and international library conferences and publishes extensively in LIS journals. She received the 2010 ALA/RUSA Mudge Award for distinguished contributions to reference.